Frommer's
England & Scotland
1st Edition

By Stephen Brewer, Jason Cochran,
Joe Fullman, Lucy Gillmore & Donald Strachan

Published by
FROMMER MEDIA LLC

ISBN 978-1-62887-206-4 (paper), 978-1-62887-207-1 (e-book)

Editorial Director: Pauline Frommer
Editor: Elizabeth Heath
Production Editor: Donna Wright
Photo Editor: Helen Stallion
Cartographer: Andrew Murphy

For information on our other products or services, see www.frommers.com. Frommer Media LLC also publishes its books in a variety of electronic formats.

Manufactured in China   5   4   3   2   1

HOW TO CONTACT US

In researching this book, we discovered many wonderful places—hotels, restaurants, shops, and more. We're sure you'll find others. Please tell us about them, so we can share the information with your fellow travelers in upcoming editions. If you were disappointed with a recommendation, we'd love to know that, too. Please write to: Support@FrommerMedia.com

FROMMER'S STAR RATINGS SYSTEM

Every hotel, restaurant and attraction listed in this guide has been ranked for quality and value. Here's what the stars mean:

★   Recommended
★★   Highly Recommended
★★★   A must! Don't miss!

AN IMPORTANT NOTE

The world is a dynamic place. Hotels change ownership, restaurants hike their prices, museums alter their opening hours, and busses and trains change their routings. And all of this can occur in the several months after our authors have visited, inspected, and written about these hotels, restaurants, museums and transportation services. Though we have made valiant efforts to keep all our information fresh and up-to-date, some few changes can inevitably occur in the periods before a revised edition of this guidebook is published. So please bear with us if a tiny number of the details in this book have changed. Please also note that we have no responsibility or liability for any inaccuracy or errors or omissions, or for inconvenience, loss, damage, or expenses suffered by anyone as a result of assertions in this guide.

CONTENTS

LIST OF MAPS v

1 THE BEST OF ENGLAND & SCOTLAND 1

2 ENGLAND & SCOTLAND IN CONTEXT 16

3 SUGGESTED ITINERARIES IN ENGLAND & SCOTLAND 38

Regions in Brief 39

England in 1 Week 41

The Best of Scotland in 1 Week 45

England & Scotland in 2 Weeks 47

The History, Castles & Gardens of Southern England in 9 Days 48

4 LONDON 54

Exploring London 63

Where to Stay 115

Where to Eat 132

Shopping 143

Entertainment & Nightlife 145

5 THE THAMES VALLEY & ST ALBANS 147

Windsor & Eton 148

Oxford 157

St Albans 172

6 KENT & SUSSEX 179

Canterbury 180

Whitstable & the North Kent Coast 188

Kent's Castles & Gardens 192

Rye, Hastings & Battle 197

Brighton 201

Chichester & Arundel 211

7 OLD WESSEX: THE BEST OF HAMPSHIRE, WILTSHIRE, DORSET & SOMERSET 217

Winchester 218

Salisbury & Stonehenge 227

Sherborne & North Dorset 234

Dorchester 237

Bath 240

8 DEVON & CORNWALL 253

Exeter 254

Dartmoor National Park 261

Fowey 266

Penzance & the Penwith Peninsula 269

St Ives 274

9 THE COTSWOLDS 279

Burford 282

Bibury 284

Painswick 287

Bourton-on-the-Water 289

Stow-on-the-Wold 293

Broadway 297

Chipping Campden 301

10 THE HEART OF ENGLAND 305

Stratford-upon-Avon 306

Birmingham 319

The Welsh Marches 332

Ironbridge 340

11 CAMBRIDGE & EAST ANGLIA 343

Cambridge 344

Dedham & Constable Country 360

Lavenham 361

The Suffolk Coast: Southwold to Aldeburgh 364

Norwich 369

12 NORTHWEST ENGLAND 381

Manchester 382

Chester 398

Liverpool 404

13 THE LAKE DISTRICT 414

Windermere & Bowness 422

Grasmere 425

Coniston 427

Hawkshead 429

Keswick 431

14 YORKSHIRE & THE NORTHEAST 437

York 438

Harrogate & Around 446

Whitby & Around 449

Durham 453

Newcastle & Gateshead 459

15 EDINBURGH, THE LOTHIANS & ST ANDREWS 471

Exploring Edinburgh 478

Side Trips from Edinburgh 508

St Andrews 514

16 THE SCOTTISH BORDERS 519

Jedburgh 521

Kelso 524

Melrose 528

Selkirk 532

Peebles 533

17 GLASGOW, THE WEST COAST & THE SOUTHERN HEBRIDES 538

Exploring Glasgow 543

Where to Stay 557

Where to Eat 559

Shopping 561

Entertainment & Nightlife 563

Side Trips from Glasgow 566

The West Coast & the Southern Hebrides 573

Inveraray 573

The Isle of Arran 578

The Kintyre Peninsula 583

The Isle of Gigha 586

The Isle of Islay 587

The Isle of Jura 591

Mull 592

18 THE HIGHLANDS & THE ISLE OF SKYE 599

Inverness 600

Along Loch Ness 609

Aviemore 611

Nairn & Cawdor Castle 614

The Black Isle Peninsula 617

Sutherland & the Far North 620

Caithness 626

Wester Ross 630

The West Highlands 633

Kyle of Lochalsh 639

The Isle of Skye 642

19 PLANNING YOUR TRIP TO ENGLAND & SCOTLAND 656

Getting There 657

Getting Around 658

Tips on Accommodations 663

Fast Facts England & Scotland 667

Index 675

LIST OF MAPS

England in 1 Week 43

Scotland in 1 Week 47

England & Scotland in 2 weeks 49

Southern England in 9 days 51

London Attractions 64

Southbank & The City 91

Greenwich 99

London Hotels 116

London Restaurants 134

Thames Valley 149

Oxford 159

Kent & Sussex 181

Canterbury 183

Kent Castles & Gardens 193

Brighton 203

Old Wessex 219

Winchester 221

Salisbury 229

Bath 241

Devon & Cornwall 255

Dartmoor National Park 263

The Cotswolds 281

The Heart of England 307

Stratford-upon-Avon 309

Birmingham 321

East Anglia 345

Cambridge 347

Norwich 371

Northwest England 383

Manchester 385

Chester 399

Liverpool 405

The Lake District 417

Yorkshire & Northeast England 439

York 441

Newcastle & Gateshead 461

Edinburgh & Environs 475

Edinburgh Attractions 480

Edinburgh Hotels & Restaurants 494

The Scottish Borders 521

Glasgow & Side Trips 541

Glasgow 544

Argyll & the Islands 575

The Isle of Arran & the Kintyre Peninsula 579

The Isle of Islay 589

The Scottish Highlands 602

The Isle of Skye 643

ABOUT THE AUTHORS

Stephen Brewer has been writing travel articles and guides for almost three decades. He frequently writes about England, Germany, and Italy for Frommer's.

Jason Cochran is a two-time winner of Guide Book of the Year by the Society of American Travel Writers' Lowell Thomas Travel Journalism Competition. He is the author of *Frommer's EasyGuide to London and Frommer's EasyGuide to Disney World, Universal, and Orlando*. His writing appears in publications including *Travel + Leisure*, the *New York Post*, *USA Today*, *Entertainment Weekly*, and *Budget Travel*, and he has been a regular commentator on, among others, *CBS This Morning*, *The Early Show* (CBS), *BBC World*, *Good Morning America*, and *CNN*. He is the former Executive Editor of AOL Travel and the current editor-in-chief of Frommers.com.

Joe Fullman has been a travel writer for more than 15 years, during which time he has written for most of the major guidebook publishers, including Rough Guides, Lonely Planet, Cadogan, AA and, of course, Frommer's. He is the author of guides to London, England, Berlin, Venice, Las Vegas, Costa Rica, Belize and Seville and has contributed to guides to Paris, Italy, Turkey, Central America, and the Caribbean.

Lucy Gillmore was the deputy travel editor at The Independent newspaper but after eight years on the travel desk, left London to move to Scotland. She specializes in travel and food and writes for newspapers such as The Guardian, *The Independent* and *The Times* and magazines including *Food and Travel*, *Olive*, *House & Garden* and *Conde Nast Traveller*. After a couple of years in Edinburgh she headed even further north and now lives in the hills above Loch Ness in the Highlands.

Donald Strachan is a Scottish travel writer and journalist who has lived most of his life "down south" in England. He has written about the country, and wider European travel, for publications all over the world including the Guardian, CNN.com, *National Geographic Traveller*, and *Sydney Morning Herald*. Over the last decade, he has authored or co-authored several guides for Frommer's, including *Great Britain Day by Day* and *Frommer's Italy*.

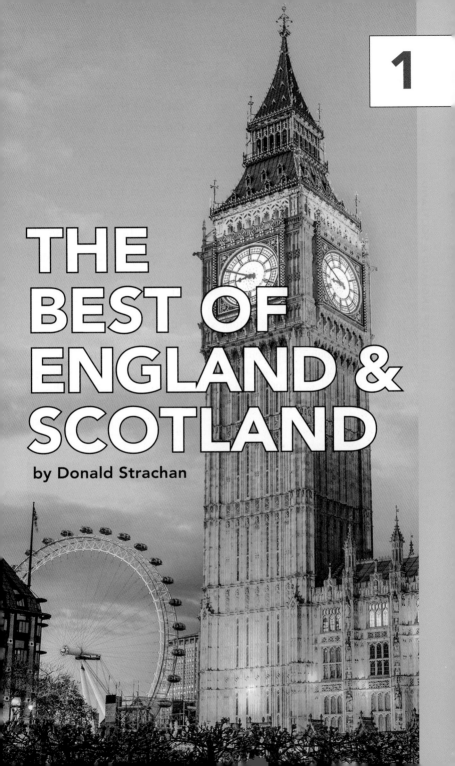

THE BEST OF ENGLAND & SCOTLAND

by Donald Strachan

Where to begin your journey through the two major countries of the United Kingdom? In these pages, we share the best of the best: the things we love, and that we think you will, too. From the teeming streets of cosmopolitan London to a far-flung, unspoiled green and pleasant land that hasn't changed for centuries, England and Scotland are greater than the sum of their parts. A respect for the past rubs along with a vibrant and innovative outlook, evident in places like the Eden Project and Tate Modern. In Manchester, Edinburgh, and Brighton you'll find tremendous diversity and a dynamic cultural life.

Start with **London** and its historic sights (the Tower, St Paul's), plus its British Museum (free, like most museums here), expansive parks, and even more expansive shopping. For an insider take on urban England, move on to Manchester, a cradle of industry now reborn; **Liverpool,** with its Beatles history; and small, esoteric cities with sublime

PREVIOUS PAGE: **The Elizabeth Tower of the Palace of Westminster (Big Ben), with the London Eye.** ABOVE: Derwenter, the Lake District.

architecture, such as Georgian **Bath** and studious **Oxford.** Each will inspire you in a different way. Scotland's cities certainly aren't left behind: **Edinburgh** never fails to dazzle with its contrasting Old and New Towns. **Glasgow** claims Scotland's top art galleries, best nightlife, and unbeatable shopping.

Beyond the city limits, England and Scotland have still more to offer, from the brooding glens and mountains of the **Highlands** to the pancake-flat fenlands of **Norfolk** and **Suffolk,** and the scenery of the **Lake District** that so inspired the Romantic poets. Amid it all are 13 National Parks, taking in the majestic bleakness of **Dartmoor** and the **North York Moors** and rolling hills of the Sussex **South Downs.** And the backdrop changes quickly; a day's journey can take you across several different landscapes. Outdoor enthusiasts can choose mountain ranges, river valleys, or rugged moorland. You'll find top golf courses, first-class fishing, limitless hiking, and a variety of wildlife. There's dramatic coastline, too, from **Cornwall** in the southwest to **Whitby,** whose ruined abbey inspired Bram Stoker's "Dracula."

THE best AUTHENTIC EXPERIENCES

- **Having a pint:** It could be at a centuries-old pub on the Yorkshire Moors or a little place in the backstreets of London; it might be a famous inn or somewhere unassuming in any town. There's nothing that helps you appreciate the scenery quite like a pint glass filled with good British beer.

- **The view over London from the top of St Paul's:** You really can climb up to that glorious cathedral dome, which has 360-degree views over the capital. It gives the feeling that you're at the heart of where modern London began. If that's uplifting, the view down is deliciously dizzying. See p. 92.

- **Uncovering a bargain at a London street market:** A jumble of open-air stalls and warrens of indoor arcades combine to make **Portobello Road** the quintessential West London market. Haggle hard and you'll likely get 15% off the asking price. Saturday is the best day, when even the crowds can't ruin the fun.

- **Whisky tasting on the Isle of Islay, Scotland:** Check your spelling—it's whisky, never whiskey—then debate with locals over the peat-and-seaweed scented merits of Bowmore, Lagavulin, Laphroaig, Bunnahabhain, and others. See p. 589.

- **Reveling on London's South Bank:** England's arts quarter takes in both the 1950s' beauty of the Royal Festival Hall (RFH) and the brutal modernism of the National Theatre. Street theatre rubs shoulders with classic productions, and there's usually something for free in the grand foyer of the RFH. See chapter 4.

o **Having a bath in Bath:** The stunning, steaming **Roman Baths** (p. 244) are there to visit, with lunch at the **Pump Room;** then you can sample the waters at the modern **Thermae Bath Spa** (p. 245) with its open-air pool and views across the UNESCO World Heritage rooftops.

o **Edinburgh at Festival time:** Every August Edinburgh erupts in a spectacular celebration of culture, art, dance, politics, music, and street performance as a clutch of festivals—headed by the Edinburgh International

City Hall and the Shard, on London's South Bank.

Festival, the unstoppable Fringe, and the Military Tattoo—sweep across every venue in the city. See p. 488.

o **Shopping in the grandest department stores of them all:** And, no, we don't mean Harrods. Liberty of London, founded in 1875 and moved to its current half-timbered, mock-Tudor home in 1924, and Selfridges, both designed and built by Americans, redefined sales methods and played crucial roles in world history. See "Shopping" in chapter 4.

THE best HOTELS

o **The Witchery, Edinburgh:** It's like bedding down in a historical movie set. Theatrical rooms drip in luxurious fabrics, with thick velvet drapes, chunky four-posters, antique furniture, and roll-top baths. The Witchery is the perfect antidote for travellers who are bored with bland beige minimalism. See p. 498.

o **The Feathered Nest, Nether Westcote, Cotswolds:** A lovely stone house in a picturesque village nicely mixes country antiques, sophisticated-yet-casual décor, open hearths, and sublime views of pastures and woodlands. It is the ideal Cotswolds retreat. See p. 295.

o **Lion and Pheasant, Shrewsbury:** The lower floors of two 16th-century townhouses are a delightful warren of nooks and crannies which open into cozy hearth-warmed dining rooms. Guest rooms are done in soothing neutrals and non-obtrusive Scandinavian

The Feathered Nest Country Inn, Nether Westcote, The Cotswolds.

furnishings that let the old beams, dormers, and fireplaces work their charms. See p. 338.

o **Gray's Court, York:** A 21st-century boutique hotel that's also steeped in royal heritage and history—and complete with Georgian dining room and oak-paneled Jacobean Long Gallery, alongside rooms you quickly sink into. It's the perfect base for exploring a small city that played a pivotal role in British history for almost two millennia. See p. 443.

THE best RESTAURANTS

o **The Fat Duck, Berkshire:** Nothing shows England's role as a culinary innovator more than this multi-awarded restaurant, a window into the singularly creative mind of Heston Blumenthal. The earthy porridge (snails, oats, ham, almonds) is genius, and dishes such as salmon poached in licorice gel are a whimsical treat. See p. 155.

o **Wheeler's Oyster Bar, Whitstable, Kent:** This old fishing port has transformed itself into the home of the oyster, and its quayside is lined with stalls. But Wheeler's is a little bit special. Founded in 1856, its tiny back-room restaurant is quaint enough, and the seafood cooking dishes out real fireworks. If they're fully booked—and they nearly always are—the streetside counter does takeout. See p. 190.

o **Mr. Thomas's Chop House, Manchester:** It's easy to imagine yourself among mustachioed 19th-century burghers as you settle into this Victorian pub whose traditional British food throws caloric caution to the winds. Corned beef hash simmered for 10 days, or homemade steak and kidney pie, might cause your waistcoat buttons to pop. See p. 393.

o **Brewery Tap, Chester:** Beers from Chester's Splitting Feathers brewery accompanies sausages and other hearty fare. Ingredients come from within a few miles of town—some from pigs fed on left-over grains from the brewing process. See p. 403.

o **Rules, London:** It might even be the oldest restaurant in London, but what's certain is that Rules was established as an oyster bar in 1798. Long a venue for the theatrical elite and literary beau monde, it still serves the same traditional dishes that delighted Edward VII and his mistress, Lillie Langtry, who began their meals with champagne and oysters upstairs. The food's good; the atmosphere is great. See p. 133.

THE best FAMILY EXPERIENCES

o **Chowing down at Cadbury World, Birmingham:** It's not the magical world of Willy Wonka . . . but it's as close as you'll get in England. Kids and parents will come away with a new appreciation for chocolate as big business. And how many tours end in the world's largest candy store? See p. 324.

o **Discovering the Glasgow Science Centre:** Housed in a titanium-clad pod on the south bank of the River Clyde, this family-focused attraction inspires and informs all ages on the concepts behind science and technology. Learning is fun and interactive, and an IMAX cinema provides some wow-factor. See p. 554.

o **Kicking back on the sands of Southwold beach, Suffolk:** This is old-school seaside in a genteel way, with ice creams, gentle waves, and an Edwardian pier. And for grown-ups, there's the Lord Nelson pub to slip off to at the top of the steps. See p. 365.

Southwold beach, Suffolk.

- **Exploring underground Edinburgh:** Journey deep into Edinburgh's dark side via a tour through its spooky underground vaults and long-buried city streets. Listen to tales of grim goings-on as you travel through this subterranean realm, home to many of the city's ghosts. See p. 491.

- **Losing your way in the world's most famous hedge maze:** The green labyrinth at Hampton Court twists and turns for almost half a mile. When you extricate yourselves, stroll through centuries of architectural styles at this stunning palace, home of many an English monarch. Don't forget to pick up a kids' activity trail. See p. 104.

- **Boat tripping from Mull:** Take your family on a sea safari aboard one of several boats that depart Tobermory's harbor. Tours range from 2-hour jaunts to the local seal colony, to all-day whale-watching adventures. See p. 592.

- **Ships ahoy at the Historic Dockyard, Portsmouth:** Still a major naval berth, Portsmouth's Historic Dockyard is also the final resting place of English maritime icons. HMS *Victory* helped beat the French at the 1805 Battle of Trafalgar—and carried the body of its dead commander, Admiral Lord Nelson home in a brandy barrel. Three centuries earlier, the *Mary Rose* sank as King Henry VIII watched in horror. They're both preserved and on show here—you can even explore below-decks on the *Victory.* See p. 225.

- **Walking down Diagon Alley, near St Albans:** A vast sound stage just outside London preserves several sets, endless props and gadgets, and original costumes from eight successful "Harry Potter" movies. This is no theme park: It gives visitors a genuine insight into movie-making. The newest 2015 arrival is the original Hogwart's Express. See p. 178.

THE best MUSEUMS

- **British Museum, London:** When Sir Hans Sloane died in 1753, he bequeathed to England his collection of art and antiquities. This formed the nucleus of a huge collection that grew with the acquisitions of Empire, and now includes such remarkable objects as the Rosetta Stone and the Parthenon Marbles (which Greece still want back). See p. 66.

- **National Gallery, London:** A "who's who" of Western painting—from da Vinci to Velázquez to Rembrandt to Cézanne—fills this astounding art museum. The Sainsbury Wing has one of the world's great Renaissance art collections. See p. 69.

- **Tate Britain, London:** Sir Henry Tate, a sugar producer, started it all with 70 or so paintings, and the original Tate site now concentrates on British art dating back to 1500. The collection grew considerably when artist J. M. W. Turner bequeathed some 300 paintings and 19,000 watercolors. It's the best place in the country to view Pre-Raphaelite works, too. See p. 79.

The Sainsbury Wing at The National Gallery, London.

o **Sainsbury Centre for the Visual Arts, Norwich:** Grocery store heirs Sir Robert and Lady Sainsbury collected these paintings, sculptures, and *objets d'art* over 40 years—Pacific Island fly swatters, Olmec figures, portraits by Modigliani and Francis Bacon—all creatively displayed in one of Sir Norman Foster's first buildings. See p. 373.

o **Ashmolean, Oxford:** The collection is well stocked with ancient archaeological wonders. The building oozes mid-19th century neoclassical grandeur. The displays and layout are pure 21st century. It's a winning combination. See p. 160.

o **Sir John Soane's Museum, London:** The former home of the architect that built the Bank of England is stuffed with curios, sculpture, and serious art—just as he left it on his death in 1837. It's London's most intriguing small museum. See p. 71.

o **Victoria & Albert Museum, London:** This is the greatest decorative arts museum in the world and has the largest collection of Renaissance sculpture outside Italy. It is also strong on medieval English treasures and has the best collection of Indian art outside India. See p. 88.

THE best CASTLES & PALACES

o **Holyroodhouse, Edinburgh:** Sealing the foot of Edinburgh's Royal Mile, the Palace of Holyroodhouse remains the Queen's official residence in Scotland (she still hosts garden parties when she's in town). Dripping with tales of murder, pomp, fine art, and antique furniture, palaces don't come much finer. See p. 482.

o **Tintagel Castle, Devon:** Whether or not King Arthur really lived here atop steep cliffs above the churning sea is beside the point. It's making the precarious climb just for the views, which take in the most dramatic coastal scenery in the southwest. See p. 260.

o **Alnwick Castle, Northumberland:** Kids will recognize this towered and turreted castle as "Hogwarts" in the first two Harry Potter movies.

Alnwick Castle, Northumberland.

Alnwick is the second largest inhabited castle in England, and its renowned grounds contain the world's largest treehouse and a Poison Garden, planted with species known for their ability to kill. See p. 465.

o **Leeds Castle, Kent:** Britain's most genteel castle sits in the middle of a lake surrounded by landscaped parkland. Pack a picnic, walk, and marvel at a serene sight that has survived for centuries. See p. 195.

o **Edinburgh Castle:** The ancient volcanic plug it crowns has been occupied since at least 900 B.C., and over its 3,000 years has witnessed some of the bloodiest events in Scottish history. See p. 478.

o **Blenheim Palace, near Oxford:** One of England's largest houses was built in the early 18th century for war hero, the Duke of Marlborough. Its architect John Vanbrugh—one of the most celebrated of the age—fell out with the duke's wife and never saw the building completed. But he left a masterpiece of the English Baroque, later the birthplace of Winston Churchill and the only private address in England which is still known as a "palace." See p. 171.

THE best OF THE OUTDOORS

o **Taking the Ullswater Steamer, Cumbria:** There's nothing like being huddled up against the mist as the little Victorian boat sails the length of the Lake District's pristine showpiece. Stand on deck, taking photos as the scenery changes around every bend, and hop off halfway back for a hike. See p. 419.

o **Teeing off on the St Andrews links:** Known as the "home of golf," St Andrews claims a collection of prime links courses, including the iconic **Old Course.** Book a tee time well in advance to enjoy a round at this golf shrine, where the courses are shaped by nature and undiminished by time. See p. 515.

o **Wildlife watching at Blakeney National Nature Reserve, Norfolk:** A 4-mile sand spit, backed by dunes, mud flats, and marshes, hosts England's largest colonies of breeding seals. The adjoining **Cley Marshes** is one of the first stops in England for geese, ducks, and wading birds as they head south from the Arctic. See p. 379.

o **Going wild on Dartmoor:** Ominous and brooding, this sprawling moorland park undulates for miles, rising to steep hills, then plunging into deep gorges. Walking or driving across this landscape is an adventure, all the more so when a herd of wild ponies runs by, a storm hard on their heels. Little wonder this wildness inspired Arthur Conan Doyle's spookiest tale, "The Hound of the Baskervilles." See p. 261.

o **Standing on Hadrian's Wall, Northumberland:** It leaves you speechless, the breathtaking scale of this Roman monument, which weaves off in either direction, across hill and dale, coast to coast. Walking all 73 miles is the ultimate achievement, but pop into the remains of its forts if you can't. See p. 463.

o **Photographing Glencoe:** A trek through Glencoe, on foot or by car, is one of the most dramatic journeys in Scotland. The whole place has a brooding, almost claustrophobic grandeur, peppered (or is that your imagination?) with memories of the most notorious massacre in Scots

Glencoe, in the Scottish Highlands.

history. You'll feel as if the bare, bleak mountains are hemming you in: Capture it on camera, if you can. See p. 637.

THE best FREE THINGS TO DO

o **Visiting the great (state) museums:** Britain's state museums and galleries—including most of the big names—show off their permanent collections for free. In London alone, this includes the **British Museum, National Gallery, National Portrait Gallery, Tate Britain, Tate Modern, Natural History Museum, Science Museum, V&A,** and more. See "Exploring London," p. 63. Outside the capital, add Liverpool's **Walker Gallery** (p. 410), the **National Museum of Scotland** (p. 483), and York's **National Railway Museum** (p. 442) to your to-do list.

o **Bagging a Munro, the Highlands:** A "Munro" is any Scottish mountain over 3,000-feet high. The original list was compiled by Hugh Munro in 1891, and the current count stands at 283. You have to start somewhere, so why not on Britain's highest mountain, which looms 3¾ miles southeast of Fort William? At 1,342m (4,403 ft.), the snow-capped granite mass of **Ben Nevis** dominates this part of Scotland. A trip to its summit can be done in a day, but you must come properly prepared. See p. 633.

o **Roaming the Canals, Birmingham:** These urban waterways were the highways of the Industrial Revolution. Following their quays and towpaths shows off the city's past, as much as the many lofts and restaurants signal Birmingham's rebirth. See p. 322.

o **Walking the Roman Walls, Chester:** A walk along Britain's largest remaining circuit of Roman walls evokes the days when the legions defended the empire, Saxons warded off raiding Vikings, and Normans did battle with Welsh warriors. Views over the countryside and the city of Roman, medieval, and Georgian monuments are lovely. See p. 401.

o **Watching the sunset from Waterloo Bridge:** This famous river crossing is perfectly positioned to watch the embers of the day dissipate behind the Houses of Parliament. The view is so memorable that it moved the Kinks to produce a chart-topping song in 1967, "Waterloo Sunset," with the lines, "As long as I gaze on / Waterloo sunset / I am in paradise." Look east to catch the last rays as they bounce off the dome of St Paul's Cathedral, the ancient spires of Wren's City churches, and the towering glass skyscrapers of 21st-century "New London." See chapter 4.

o **Browsing the stalls at London's Borough Market:** The sight and smell of fresh produce (and grilling meat) are heaven at this focal point for London foodies. Tucked under the railway near London

Bridge Station, there's a feel of the past, combined with the eco-friendly ethics that are so very now. See p. 140.

THE most OVERRATED

- **Punting on the Cam, Cambridge:** Okay, lying in a boat and gliding past some of the most storied colleges in the world can be romantic. But it's so much more satisfying to soak in Cambridge's atmosphere from its medieval lanes, sweeping lawns, and elsewhere on terra firma—minus the risk of dunking yourself in front of onlookers.

- **Walking down the main street of Clovelly, Devon:** We agree—Clovelly is just lovely. But you have to pay to enter the village, just for the pleasure of climbing down its precipitous cobblestoned High Street. The tiny cottages with flowery terraces are picturesque, but England has plenty of similar scenes that are free of charge and easier to navigate.

- **Visiting Stonehenge, Wiltshire:** There's no denying the historical importance of these ancient standing stones. With rocks that weigh in at 50 tons a piece—and each several millennia old—the windswept spot really does give you a creepy feeling. It's just that there's not too much to see. Visit, sure; but allow less itinerary time than you'd think. The lack of cheap public transport to the site is another gripe. We've always found **Avebury** (p. 233) a more enchanting Neolithic site.

THE best NEIGHBORHOODS

- **Castlefield and the Quays, Manchester:** Cobbled canalside paths, massive brick coal warehouses, and a network of railways, are preserved in the 17-acre **Castlefield Urban Heritage Park.** Much of Britain's industrial might centered on the nearby Quays, docklands that flourished with the opening of the Manchester Ship Canal in the 1890s, to connect the city with Liverpool and the sea. More than 5,000 ships a year sailed in and out. The area's **Museum of Science of Industry** (p. 389) and **Imperial War Museum** (p. 386) are essential stops. See chapter 4.

- **London's East End:** The capital's fashionable folk haunt the streets and alleyways of "new" East London. Shop the niche designer boutiques and vintage stores of Shoreditch, Brick Lane, and Columbia Road, then dine out on pho, Indian street food, or Turkish BBQ, washed down with a craft beer from one of east London's microbreweries. If you still have the energy Shoreditch, Hoxton, and Dalston are jumping well into the small hours. See chapter 4.

- **Stockbridge, Edinburgh:** It's like a village within the city limits. Lying north of the New Town, Stockbridge is a pretty neighborhood with a smattering of delis, gastropubs, and designer boutiques. There's

Inverleith Park, the Botanic Gardens, and you can head down to the Water of Leith, a river that winds through the city to the historic docklands at Leith. See chapter 15.

THE best ARCHITECTURE

- **Salisbury Cathedral, Wiltshire:** The most architecturally unified of England's many great Gothic cathedrals owes its harmony to the speed at which it was built. It took under 40 years from 1220. It's been painted by Constable and repaired by Sir Christopher Wren, and still stands proud over this quaint city's water meadows. See p. 228.

- **The Royal Mile, Edinburgh:** Stunning views, narrow closes, and dark *wynds* (alleys) spread out in all directions along this historic street, which forms the backbone of Edinburgh's medieval Old Town. Take in the many free museums, and enjoy the seething sea of life as you roam. See chapter 15.

- **Gateshead Millennium Footbridge, Newcastle:** This curving, modernistic bridge looks like a blinking eye when it tilts to let boats past along the River Tyne. At other times it's a graceful, rainbow-like presence between the quays of Newcastle and the art quarters of Gateshead. See p. 459.

- **The Borders Abbeys, Scotland:** Four great ruined abbeys—Kelso, Dryburgh, Jedburgh, and Melrose—cluster around the heart of the Scottish Borders. Brought to their knees by the English and then the Reformation, these former ecclesiastical power-houses remain magnificent even in ruins. See chapter 16.

- **Oxford:** The city of dreaming spires and cobbled lanes is like a "best of" compilation covering a thousand years of English architecture. See p. 157.

- **Tate Modern, London:** Enter this former power station beside the River Thames and your jaw drops at the size of its cathedral-like piston hall, which usually houses outrageous art installations, from twisting metal slides to monstrous spiders. Delve deeper

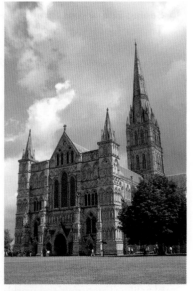
Salisbury Cathedral.

into the museum to find Dalis, Warhols, Picassos, and a restaurant with one of London's best views. See p. 93.

o **Sherborne Abbey, Dorset:** As a way for Gothic-era builders to spread the weight of a roof, fan vaulting developed in England's West Country in the 14th century. The nave of Sherborne's abbey church has one of the country's most impressive examples. See p. 236. **King's College Chapel,** Cambridge (p. 346) has another fine fan vault.

undiscovered ENGLAND

o **Enjoying winter in the garden, Cambridge:** The University Botanic Garden is lovely year-round, but few visitors explore during the winter, when intelligent planting reveals a wealth of multihued stems and bark, plus winter-flowing plants, giving way to Lenten roses and early wild daffodils. See p. 350.

o **Visiting "Another Place" on the Lancashire coast:** A hundred figures cast in iron rise from the sand for 2 miles along the coast at Crosby, north of Liverpool. As they gaze out to sea, you can do the same. See p. 413.

o **Walking in King Harold's final footsteps, East Sussex:** There's something eerie but exciting about walking on the grassy spot where English history changed forever. The site of the Battle of Hastings— the beginning of the Norman Conquest—is quietly impressive, with an excellent visitor center. See p. 197.

o **Seeing England as Turner saw it, Kent:** The simplistic but stunning **Turner Contemporary** gallery sits on the seafront in Margate. It was built on the very spot where J. M. W. Turner stayed to paint Kent seascapes. The light here, on England's eastern tip, is sensational, and illuminates the building at sunset. See p. 189.

secret SCOTLAND

o **The Trossachs:** Ruled for generations by the MacGregor clan, the Trossachs combine mist-shrouded lochs with legends of Rob Roy. Spend half a day following the A821 from Callander to Aberfoyle as it threads through dramatic terrain, and detour to Loch Katrine. See chapter 17.

o **Haunting the Castles:** Scotland is littered with ancient castles. Many—such as **Urquhart** (p. 609) on Loch Ness and cliff-top **Tantallon** (p. 513)—stand in ruined splendor. Others such as Macbeth's very own **Cawdor** (p. 614) are luxurious, legendary family homes.

o **The Falkirk Wheel:** A triumph of Scottish engineering, this gleaming clawlike structure is the world's first (and only) rotating boatlift. The

Cawdor Castle, Nairn, Scotland.

Wheel effortlessly swings boats the 35m (115 ft.) between the Union and Forth and Clyde canals, using only a tiny amount of power and Archimedes' Principle. See p. 508.

o **Sir Walter Scott's home, Abbotsford:** Burns is Scotland's most famous bard, but it was Sir Walter Scott who was responsible for challenging preconceptions about the Scottish Highlands—changing it in the public mind from a wild, inhospitable place to a land of soaring mountains, majestic stags, and rushing rivers. Visit his Borders home and its visitor center to find out more about his life and works, which included "Rob Roy" and "The Heart of Midlothian." See p. 528.

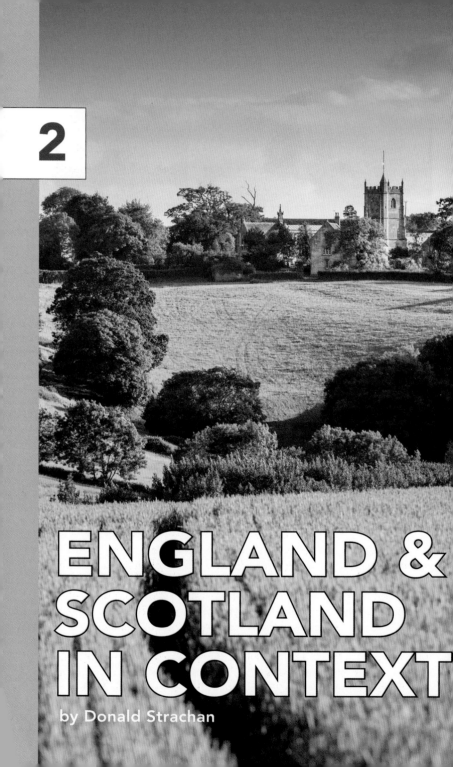

2

ENGLAND & SCOTLAND IN CONTEXT

by Donald Strachan

Exploring England and Scotland is like climbing a mountain range—you always want to carry on to see what's over the next peak or around the next corner. It's addictive, and there's no shame in carrying around a sightseeing wish list—as long as you take your time ticking things off. England and Scotland may not be big countries but they're crammed full of incredible sights—and not just historic sights, either. Sport, music, theatre, fashion, and even food here are among the best in the world. You might be visiting a region for the first time but be warned: Once you've seen one part of England and Scotland you'll want to see more.

ENGLAND & SCOTLAND TODAY

England and Scotland made world news in late 2014, as a referendum gave Scots the right to choose to remain within the Union or to become an independent nation. At times the race seemed very close, but in the end the people voted to retain the marriage with England, thanks in part to a late offer of increased powers for their domestic legislature, the Scottish Parliament. The final scores for independence were 55% No to 45% Yes. However, Scottish Nationalists remain in power in Scotland, and it seems likely that independence will return to the national agenda again. For now at least, you won't need to show your passport to cross the border between the two countries in this guide—but at sporting events, Scots will still be heard singing "Flower of Scotland" instead of "God Save the Queen."

Fraternal feuds aside, Britain never stands still, and the most obvious recent sign of its futuristic ambitions is **The Shard,** the shimmering, glassy tower near London Bridge that is now Europe's tallest building. It soars 337m (1,107 ft.) above the city and provides a fitting backdrop for both the medieval Tower of London and the Victorian masterpiece of Tower Bridge. By architect **Renzo Piano,** it is the pinnacle, literally, of the postmodern architecture that has swept urban Britain. Other examples in London include the **Lloyd's building** by **Richard Rogers** and 30 St Mary Axe, dubbed the **"Gherkin"** by Sir Norman Foster.

Back at ground level, a few years of economic downturn have seriously affected employment, lifestyle, and attitudes across the U.K. The 2010–15 government, a coalition between the right-wing Conservatives and more centrist Liberal Democrats, cut services, from health to

PREVIOUS PAGE: **A village and farmlands in The Cotswolds.**

road-mending, while increasing taxes. Britain's vibrant cultural life is still being pressurized as, for example, the arts, humanities, and education struggle for funding. The cuts have bitten, and public frustration has manifested itself in significant support for separatist political parties, including the Scottish National Party (who want to separate from England) and UKIP (who want Britain out of the EU). The 2015 re-election of Conservative David Cameron as Prime Minister may ultimately increase the centrifugal forces affecting political Britain.

But life goes on, and there also continues to be a lot to shout about, as a dynamic cultural milieu of independent thinking, eccentricity and verve mean talent is often appreciated. From the Academy-award winning "The King's

The Shard, London, Europe's tallest building.

Speech," Adele's "21," and One Direction, to Carol Ann Duffy becoming the first woman Poet Laureate and Hillary Mantel's critically acclaimed historic novel and TV series "Wolf Hall," these are lands that revel in diversity. Plus—of course—there's still "Downton Abbey." Newcastle, Liverpool, and Manchester have all benefitted from major urban overhauls: There's more to urban Britain than just London.

CLANS & KILTS

To the outsider, Scotland's deepest traditions appear to be based on the clan system of old, with all its paraphernalia of tartans and bagpipes. But this is a romantic illusion. In fact, a good part of the Scots—the 75% of the population who live in the central Lowlands, for example—have little or no connection with the clansmen of earlier times.

The clan tradition dates from the tribal units of the country's earliest Celtic history. Power was organized around chieftains, who commanded loyalty from the inhabitants of a region in exchange for protection against invasion. The position of chieftain wasn't hereditary, and land was owned by the clan. Rigidly militaristic and paternalistic—the stuff with which Scottish legend is imbued— the clan tradition is still emphasized today, albeit in a friendlier fashion than the bloody clan days.

THE MAKING OF ENGLAND & SCOTLAND

Prehistory & the Romans
(3600 B.C.–ca. A.D. 400)

England and Scotland have several prehistoric sites, among which the most famous is **Stonehenge** near Salisbury (p. 230), which experts believe was a temple, possibly started in 3600 B.C. and added to over subsequent centuries. **Hadrian's Wall** (p. 463) is the most dramatic piece of architecture to survive from the Roman era, although there are also **Roman baths** at Bath (p. 244) and remains of Roman walls, villas, temples, and forts elsewhere, including a Roman Theatre at St Albans (p. 174).

Little is known about the early tribes and invaders of Scotland. By the time the Romans tried to invade in A.D. 82, the land was occupied by a people known as the Picts (or "Painted Ones"). Despite spectacular bloodletting, the Romans failed to conquer the country, and so the building of Hadrian's Wall marked the northern limits of Rome's influence. Today, however, the remains of the great wall lie firmly in England, with the Scottish border farther north.

To the south in England, there were constant clashes between the tribes over territory, which is why they failed to unite to prevent the first Roman invasion by Julius Caesar, the Roman governor of Gaul (France and Belgium), in 55 B.C., and later in A.D. 43–44, when Emperor Claudius invaded, capturing present-day Colchester. Although Colchester remained the capital for a while, by A.D. 47 the Romans had founded

Hadrian's Wall at Walltown Crags.

Londinium as a garrison and trading settlement. Remains of Roman London are still being discovered as new developments are built, and you can see part of London's original Roman wall near the **Tower of London** (p. 94).

There was little effective resistance to the Roman fighting machine, although there was one well-known uprising, led by Queen Boudicca of the Iceni tribe who ruled parts of East Anglia. The Romans had tried to force their will on Boudicca by publicly whipping her, and she subsequently led a rebellion that razed Colchester. Then she marched on London (there's a statue of Boudicca in **Parliament Square;** p. 76) and rampaged through St Albans, then known as Verulamium—70,000 people were supposedly killed. She was eventually defeated in the so-called "Battle of Watling Street" at an unknown location around A.D. 60.

After 350 years of rule, the Romans went home, abandoning the Romano-Britons. By 410, the Germanic Saxons, Jutes, and Angles had carved out settlements in southern and eastern England, and the Saxons went on to dominate all but the far north, where the Romano-Britons were forced to flee. The Saxon kings reigned supreme until the Vikings started taking an interest in England and Scotland. They were eventually driven from southern England by King Alfred the Great of Wessex, whose headquarters were at **Winchester** (p. 218). The Vikings were strong in the Northeast, as the **Jorvik Viking Centre** in York (p. 442) illustrates.

The Saxons maintained control of some southern regions, and Saxon king Edward the Confessor assumed the throne in 1042. Childless, he promised the crown to William, Duke of Normandy. Later his adviser, Harold Godwinson, swore to support William's claim to the throne. When Edward died in 1066 and Harold succeeded him, he surely knew

A statue of ancient Queen Boudicca, Parliament Square, London.

trouble lay ahead. After fighting a Viking invasion in the northeast, Harold had to march south to meet the Normans at **Battle** (p. 197), near **Hastings,** in Sussex. Harold lost and died—the end of the Saxon era.

The Middle Ages (1066–1599)

The Normans quickly colonized England—William's suc-

cess came partly from his building impregnable castles wherever they were needed. In 1078, for example, he built the original castle at **Windsor** (p. 151). He was crowned King William I at **Westminster Abbey** (p. 80) in 1067, and his supporters went on to build simple motte and bailey castles on the lands William gave them. The mottes—mounds of earth—still survive in many places; some were incorporated into the stone castles that replaced the original wooden baileys, or keeps.

The Normans are also renowned for their religious architecture, with **Ely Cathedral** in Cambridgeshire (p. 356) among the most glorious examples of their work.

The French Gothic style of architecture invaded in the late 12th century, trading rounded arches for pointy ones—an engineering discovery that freed churches from the heavy Norman walls and allowed ceilings to soar. The style is divided into three overlapping periods: Early English (1150–1300), Decorated (1250–1370), and Perpendicular (1350–1550). The best example of Early English is **Salisbury Cathedral** (p. 228). The first to use pointy arches was **Wells Cathedral** (p. 251).

In Scotland, cultural assimilation with England gained pace under David I (1081–1153), who made land grants to many Anglo-Norman families, providing Scotland with a feudal aristocracy and bringing in ancient names such as Bruce, Fraser, and Lindsay. He also embarked on a lavish building spree. The now-ruined **abbeys of Jedburgh, Kelso, Melrose,** and **Dryburgh** are his legacy.

England's next significant king after William was Henry II, the first of the Plantagenet dynasty, who came to the throne in 1154. This French nobleman had made strategic marriages and, when he married Eleanor of Aquitaine, he owned more of France than the French king. They had eight children, among them Richard "the Lionheart," who came to the throne as Richard I in 1189 and became an English folk hero—ironic because he didn't like cold, wet England and preferred to fight for

Dryburgh Abbey in The Scottish Borders, burial place of Sir Walter Scott.

Christianity in the Crusades. His brother and successor, King John was so unpopular that the Norman barons, whose families had been given their land by William I after the conquest, forced him to sign the **Magna Carta** in 1215 to limit his power. The Magna Carta gave all freemen (barons) rights and liberties, but more importantly, meant English monarchs were no longer above the law. This became the basis of the American Bill of Rights.

The Plantagenets ruled for the next 200 years. The most significant for the Scots was Edward I, who yearned to conquer the entire island. Many of Scotland's legendary heroes lived during this period: Sir William Wallace (1270–1305), who drove the English out of Perth and Stirling; Sir James Douglas, the "Black Douglas" (1286–1330), who terrorized the English borders; and Robert the Bruce (1274–1329), who finally succeeded in freeing Scotland from England. Scotland's independence was formally recognized in the 1328 Treaty of Edinburgh–Northampton.

Meanwhile, ordinary folk were having a hard time. The **Black Death,** or plague, which had ravaged Europe reached England in 1348. It killed one-third of the European population and half of England and Scotland, and returned in 1361, 1374, and regularly thereafter until about 1670.

Among the Plantagenet courtiers was **Geoffrey Chaucer,** who wrote "The Canterbury Tales"—stories told by a group of pilgrims as they journeyed from London to Canterbury where Thomas Becket, Henry II's Archbishop, had been murdered by Henry's knights. The "Tales" were written in English in the late 1300s, unusual at the time because Latin and French dominated the written word.

The Tudors (1485–1603)

The reign of Henry Tudor—as Henry VII of England—is considered to be the close of the Middle Ages. He ended rivalry and war between the Houses of Lancaster and York by marrying Elizabeth of York, the eldest child of former King Edward IV. Henry was a clever king: Avoiding costly wars, forging trade alliances to create more wealth, setting up councils in the north, and reforming the judicial system. Next in line, flamboyant Henry VIII inherited a fortune from his father in 1509, and a wife from his elder brother Arthur. Arthur had married the King of Spain's eldest daughter, Catherine of Aragon, in 1501, but the sickly heir to the throne died 5 months later. Catherine came with a huge dowry so Henry VII petitioned the Pope to have the marriage annulled so that his new heir, Henry, could marry her and keep the cash.

The marriage went forth and Catherine gave birth to several children, but only daughter Mary survived—and Henry wanted a son. By now he also wanted Anne Boleyn, born at **Blickling Estate** in Norfolk (p. 379) and a member of his wife's court. Henry now petitioned the Pope in 1530 for an annulment to his marriage with Catherine, but the Pope didn't want to upset the Spanish king. A few years later, Anne became pregnant, and Henry secretly married her in 1533. When the Pope declared the marriage invalid, Henry announced himself Head of the Church of England, confirmed by an Act of Parliament in 1534. The **Reformation** had begun. In 1538 Henry was excommunicated from the Catholic Church and eventually closed all monasteries and nunneries and sold off their land (the "Dissolution of the Monasteries"). Four more wives were to follow, before Henry was buried in St George's Chapel at **Windsor Castle** (p. 151).

If Henry's life was dramatic, what happened next was extraordinary. His sickly son succeeded him as Edward VI, aged 10. During Edward's 5-year reign, the Church of England finally became Protestant and adopted an English Book of Common Prayer. Although Edward was devout, he obviously couldn't have made those decisions himself, and that atmosphere of religious fervor intensified when Edward was succeeded by his Catholic elder sister in 1553. Mary reintroduced Catholic bishops, revived heresy laws, and pronounced Protestantism a treasonable offense punishable by death. She had 300 Protestants burned at the stake during her 4-year reign. It's no wonder she was called Bloody Mary.

Her sister Elizabeth was under house arrest at **Hatfield House** (p. 177) when the news of Mary's death arrived. She was crowned Queen in 1559 at Westminster Abbey. The Virgin Queen had many suitors but managed to play one against another so she could retain her own power. Elizabeth reversed Mary's Catholic laws and worked with Parliament to create an Anglican form of Protestantism that tolerated Catholicism, but she was often the target of Catholic plots, many involving her cousin, Mary Queen of Scots (see below).

Mary Queen of Scots

When Mary Stuart, Queen of Scots (1542–87), took up her rule, she was a Roman Catholic of French upbringing trying to govern an unruly land to which she was a relative newcomer. Daughter of Scotland's James V and France's Mary of Guise, she became queen at only 6 days of age. At the age of 15, she married the heir to the French throne, but returned to Scotland after his death. Mary then set out on two roads that were anathema to the Scots: to make herself absolute monarch in the French style and to impose Roman Catholicism. The first alienated the Scottish nobles, and the second made her the enemy of John Knox and the Calvinists. After a series of disastrous political and romantic alliances, her life was ended by the executioner's axe in England. The execution order was reluctantly issued by her cousin Elizabeth I, who considered Mary's presence a threat to the stability of the English throne. You can follow the dramatic story of her life at the string of palaces where she once lived. In the Borders there's **Mary Queen of Scots' Visitor Centre** (p. 523), while in Edinburgh, at **Holyroodhouse** (p. 482), you can see where her Italian secretary, David Rizzio, was stabbed 56 times in front of her. The Queen also used to stay at **Falkland Palace** for hunting and hawking.

The Tudor Age was a time of some of England's finest literature. Shakespeare (1564–1616) was creating his vast body of work, with his plays being performed in London at the Globe Theatre, which opened on the south bank of the Thames in 1599. A re-creation today sits just along the river (p. 78). A contemporary was Ben Jonson (1572–1637), a playwright, poet, and actor, best known for his satirical plays.

Union Between Scotland & England, then Civil War

Mary's son (see "Mary Queen of Scots," above) succeeded where his unfortunate mother had failed. In 1603, James VI of Scotland also assumed the throne of England as James I, Elizabeth's heir and the first Stuart monarch. His coronation united England and Scotland and finally broke the power of the Scottish lords.

Despite hopes for peace, religion again became the source of discontent. James—and his heir, Charles I—attempted to promote a Church of Scotland governed by bishops, in opposition to the Presbyterian Church's self-ruling organization. So incensed were the Scots that in 1638 they signed the **National Covenant,** which not only reasserted the Reformation's principles but also questioned the King's right to make laws, a role the Covenanters believed should be filled by Parliament.

Yet Charles I believed strongly in the divine right of kings. When the English Parliament stripped away much of his authority in 1642, Charles went north to organize an army against the Parliamentary forces centered in London. A civil war ensued, with the forces of Parliament led to victory by Oliver Cromwell (1599–1658). Charles fled to Scotland, but the Scots turned him over to Parliament, and in 1649 he was convicted of treason and beheaded. Under the ensuing Commonwealth, Cromwell assumed a dominant political role and became Lord Protector in 1653. King in all but name, he ruled England until his death.

The Restoration (1660–89)

Among the legacies of Cromwell's Commonwealth are a deep-seated unease about military rule and a religious tolerance colored by a suspicion of extremism. But the Restoration—when King Charles II returned—was notable primarily for its revelry, and at times shocking, licentiousness.

Sports and theatres were high on Charles's agenda. He was patron of the theatre, and "Restoration comedy" was known for its bawdy plots and satire, poking fun at political figures and topical events. William Wycherley's 1675 play "The Country Wife" is still performed today.

This was also a period of scientific expansion. Mathematician Isaac Newton studied the composition of light, invented a reflecting telescope, and, most famously of all, set out his theory of gravity and the laws of motion in 1687—2 years after Charles II's death.

Architect Christopher Wren was also a mathematician, and in 1661 was made Professor of Astronomy at Oxford University. His knowledge of physics and engineering led to his being commissioned to design the **Sheldonian Theatre** in Oxford (p. 164) in 1664. But it was the **Great Fire of London** in 1666, which really gave him the opportunity to shine.

London at the time was still a medieval city of half-timbered buildings. Buildings were very close together in a maze of alleys and narrow streets. The city was filthy, with open sewers and little access to clean water, and plague was a recurring problem. It peaked in 1665 during a hot summer, with more than 1,000 Londoners dying every week. The plague continued to pick off victims, but in September 1666, a fire started at the king's baker's shop in Pudding Lane, in the old city. The ovens had not been put out properly overnight,

The Monument to commemorate the Great Fire of London in 1666.

sparks escaped, and fire spread through the wooden buildings. It was so intense that the lead roof of the old St Paul's Cathedral melted before the building burned down, along with 84 other churches.

The fire is commemorated by the **Monument** (p. 90), a 61.5m (202-ft.) tower topped by an urn of golden flames. It was designed by Sir Christopher Wren, and if you climb the 311 spiral steps you can see many of the other buildings Wren built after the fire, when modern London was created. Wren's greatest triumph was the new **St Paul's Cathedral** (p. 92). But Wren also designed 51 other new churches, as well as the **Royal Observatory** at Greenwich (p. 102), through which the Prime Meridian line runs. Wren also designed **Trinity College Library** in Cambridge (p. 349).

Charles II was succeeded by his brother James II in 1685, an unpopular heir because he was openly Catholic. He appointed Catholics to key posts and dismissed Parliament so he could rule without interference. In 1688 his wife gave birth to a son, which was the last straw for England's Protestant nobility. They invited James's Protestant daughter from his first marriage and her Dutch husband William of Orange to take the throne.

Glorious Revolution & Jacobite Rising

William of Orange arrived with a small army and was supported by the English military chiefs whom James had alienated, marching on London in what became known as the Glorious Revolution. James fled, and a new Parliament declared his abdication in 1689, leaving the throne free for the joint monarchs William III and Mary II. Their reign brought the end of a monarch's divine right to rule England and Wales. Parliament passed the Bill of Rights, preventing the throne from passing laws or raising taxes without Parliament's consent, so a monarch could never dismiss Parliament. The Bill also prevented Catholics from taking the throne.

Mary died of smallpox in 1694 and William died in 1702. They had no surviving children so Mary's sister, Anne, succeeded William. It was during her reign that England and Wales became politically united with Scotland to create the United Kingdom of Great Britain with the **1706 Act of Union.**

When the English Parliament stripped Catholic James II of his crown and imported Protestant monarchs William and Mary from Holland, the exiled ex-king and then his son James Edward (the Old Pretender), became focal points for Scottish unrest. The Jacobites—the name comes from Jacobus, the Latin form of James—attempted unsuccessfully in 1715 to place the Old Pretender on the English throne and restore the Stuart line. Although James died in exile, his son Charles Edward (the Young Pretender), better known as Bonnie Prince Charlie, carried on his father's dream. Charismatic but with an alcohol-induced instability, he was the central figure of the 1745 Jacobite uprising. The **Glenfinnan Monument** at the head of Loch Shiel (west of Fort William; p. 636) marks the spot where he raised his standard.

Although the revolt was initially promising, the Jacobite forces were eventually crushed at the **Battle of Culloden.** You can still walk this battlefield near Inverness today (p. 600). Fearing a rebirth of similar types of Scottish nationalism, the clan system was rigorously suppressed; clans that supported the Jacobite cause lost their lands, and until 1782, the wearing of Highland dress was illegal.

One of the greatest legacies of Anne's reign was architecture. Queen Anne buildings are particularly notable, and among the best known is **Blenheim Palace** (p. 171) in Woodstock, Oxfordshire. It was built for the Churchill family to reward the first Duke of Marlborough (John Churchill) for leading British troops to victory over the French in the 1704 Battle of Blenheim, part of the complex and bloody Wars of the Spanish Succession. Sir Winston Churchill was born there in 1874.

Anne had 17 children but only one survived birth—and he died at age 11. Parliament had already passed the Act of Succession to ensure the Protestant heirs of Sophia of Hanover (James I's granddaughter) could claim the throne, rather than James II's Catholic heirs, so Anne was succeeded by George of Hanover in 1714.

The Georgians (1714–1830)

Neither George I, nor his son George II, learned to speak English, sticking to their native German. Unsurprisingly they were disliked by the people. George III was the first English-born king in the Hanover line, and although he is chiefly remembered for losing the American colonies and going mad (as portrayed in Alan Bennett's 1991 play and the subsequent film "The Madness of King George"), at least he could speak English.

Georgian England was a cruel and lawless period. This was the era of Dick Turpin, the highway robber who brought terror to Essex until his death in 1739. It was also a time of piracy: Blackbeard was born in Bristol in 1718 and looted ships off North Carolina. There were at least 200 hanging offenses—from murder to stealing fish—while bear-baiting, badger-baiting, and cock fights were regarded as entertainment.

The Georgians had a keen eye for design, though, as evident from the period's architecture. In London, architect John Nash was responsible for **Regent Street** and remodeled **Buckingham Palace** (p. 73), while architect John Soane designed the Bank of England in the City.

In the 18th century **Scottish literature** really started to blossom, with a spate of lucid and powerful prose written in English:

Buckingham Palace.

novelist Tobias Smollett ("Roderick Random"), economist Adam Smith ("The Wealth of Nations"), philosopher David Hume ("A Treatise of Human Nature"), and James Boswell, friend and biographer of Dr. Samuel Johnson. It was also in the 18th century that Robert Burns (1759–96) produced his famous verses combining the humor and vigor of Scottish speech with the lilt of Scottish songs. Burns, known especially for love lyrics and satires, is Scotland's national bard, and revered throughout the world.

The infamous **Clearances** between 1750 and 1850 changed Scotland's demographics forever. Small farmers, or crofters, were expelled from ancestral lands to make way for sheep grazing. Increased industrialization, continued civil unrest, migration to urban centers, and a massive wave of immigration to the United States, Canada, Australia, South Africa, and New Zealand all contributed to depopulation of the countryside and a dispersal of the Scottish ethic throughout the world. You can still see the ruins of deserted crofts, farmsteads, and villages all over the Highlands.

The **Regency architectural style** covers the years 1811 to 1820, the period before the Prince Regent became king. It is best illustrated in Brighton's **Royal Pavilion** (p. 204), the Prince's India-inspired summerhouse on England's South Coast. Many of Bath's beautiful Georgian buildings were also Regency haunts.

Bath became the most fashionable city outside London during the Regency period thanks to its ancient spa. Novelist Jane Austen included the city's **Assembly Rooms** (p. 243) in two of her novels—"Persuasion"

THE GEORGIAN arts SCENE

The arts flourished during the Georgian era: "Robinson Crusoe" author Daniel Defoe visited the east of England and wrote about East Anglia (see chapter 11) in "Tour Through the Eastern Counties of England 1722." In 1726 "Gulliver's Travels" was published by Jonathan Swift, an Anglo-Irish clergyman, and artist William Hogarth created satirical illustrations of the country's low morals. Among his most famous work was "A Rake's Progress," a series of prints based on paintings now at **Sir John Soane's Museum** in London (p. 71). His work was in sharp contrast to the genteel portraits by Joshua Reynolds and Thomas Gainsborough, which are in London's **Tate Britain** (p. 79).

William Blake, born in 1757, brought a vision of heaven and hell with his illustrations and engravings for books and poetry, and his epic "Jerusalem." John Constable, born in the Suffolk countryside in 1776, was starting to make waves with his landscapes, which he produced until his death in 1837. J. M. W. Turner was a landscape painter whose work flourished well into the Victorian era. His depictions of light are remarkable; the **Turner Contemporary** museum is at Margate in Kent, where he spent time. His life was the subject of Oscar-nominated 2014 biopic "Mr. Turner."

The mid-18th century to the early 19th century was also the era of the Romantic Poets, including Percy Bysshe Shelley, Lord Byron, Samuel Taylor Coleridge, and William Wordsworth, whose "Daffodils" is perhaps the most oft-quoted for its simple sentiments, but much of the group's work combined a romantic view of England with a social conscience.

The towering Scottish writer of the era was Sir Walter Scott (1771–1832), novelist and poet, known for Medieval Romanticism ("Ivanhoe") and perceptive description of character and locales ("The Heart of Midlothian").

and "Northanger Abbey." There's a Jane Austin Centre at the handsome **Royal Crescent** (p. 247), built between 1767 and 1774 and regarded as the pinnacle of Palladian architecture in Britain.

With the British defeat of Napoleon at Waterloo in 1815, Britain was emerging as the most powerful country in Europe. The Industrial Revolution had started around the town of Ironbridge in Staffordshire, where the **Ironbridge Gorge Museums** can be found (p. 341), and the world's first steam-driven passenger railway was opened between Stockton and Darlington in 1825. The **National Railway Museum** in York has possibly the world's greatest rail-related collection (p. 442).

The Victorians (1837–1901)

England and Scotland are still often defined by the Victorian Age. Britain became the most industrialized country in the world, fueled mainly by coal. Urban development boomed. But Victorian Britain was a hard place. The most influential Victorian writer was Charles Dickens, who knew from first-hand experience the misery of poverty: His father's financial problems landed them in a debtor's prison in 1824. By

Victoria's time he had established himself as a journalist and wrote "Oliver Twist" (1837–39), "David Copperfield" (1849–50), and "Great Expectations" (1860–61).

Born in Edinburgh, Robert Louis Stevenson (1850–94) penned such classics as "Treasure Island" and "The Strange Case of Dr. Jekyll and Mr. Hyde," as well as poems, especially for children.

The Pre-Raphaelite movement transformed painting in the Victorian era. There are fabulous collections at **Tate Britain** in London (p. 79) and the **Birmingham Museums & Art Gallery** (p. 323). Art critic John Ruskin greatly promoted the work of the Pre-Raphaelite Brotherhood (notably its founder William Holman Hunt, John Everett Millais, and Dante Gabriel Rossetti), but he was also a poet, conservationist, and social revolutionary—campaigning for free schools and libraries. His home, **Brantwood,** in the Lake District (p. 428) was visited by luminaries like Charles Darwin.

The fairytale version of the Middle Ages portrayed by the Pre-Raphaelite painters influenced Gothic Revival architecture. "Revival" is a bit misleading, as its practitioners usually applied Gothic features at random. The best example is the **Houses of Parliament** in London (1835–52). **Charles Barry** designed it and his clock tower, usually called **Big Ben** after its biggest bell, has become an icon.

The queen that gave her name to the age, Victoria, was only 18 when she took the throne in 1837, and married her cousin Prince Albert of Saxe-Coburg-Gotha 3 years later. Contrary to Victoria's image as a gloomy killjoy, she was lively and independent when young, and very much in love with Albert. The couple was not popular, though, until Prince Albert began to win public recognition for his work on behalf of Britain.

His most impressive triumph was the Great Exhibition of 1851 in the huge glass-built Crystal Palace in London's **Hyde Park** (p. 110). This showcased Britain's industrial and technological achievements, as well as exhibits from colonized countries. The exhibition's profits funded the construction of the **Natural History Museum** (p. 86), **Science Museum** (p. 88), and **Victoria & Albert Museum** (p. 88) in London. Tragically, 4 years later Albert was dead from typhoid.

Victoria never recovered from his death and retired to their favorite family home, Osbourne House on the Isle of Wight. She wore black for the rest of her life, and withdrew from public life. But by her death at the beginning of the 20th century, Britain had the world's largest Empire, a booming economy, and a growing middle class.

World Wars I & II (1914–45)

After the prosperity of the brief Edwardian era (1901–10), Britain joined World War I in August 1914, when Germany refused to withdraw from Belgium. Among the soldiers who chronicled the horror of trench warfare was Rupert Brooke, a Cambridge graduate who wrote the 1912 war poem "The Old Vicarage, Grantchester." You can visit **Grantchester** (p. 355) to see the village church mentioned in his poem, where the clock has been stopped at "ten to three"—and where there's honey still for tea.

The wartime prime minister was Liberal Party leader Lloyd George, who was put in charge of the war effort and given much of the credit for the Allies' military success. Lloyd George said he wanted to create "a land fit for heroes," but recession following the war delivered only unemployment—particularly in the industrial heartlands.

By September 1939, Britain was at war again, and Oscar-winning film "The King's Speech" tells the story of how George VI announced the outbreak of World War II. However, the emerging national hero was Winston Churchill (knighted by the present Queen Elizabeth in 1953). As prime minister, Churchill became the symbol of Britain's fighting spirit during World War II. The **Churchill War Rooms** (p. 73) in London's King Charles Street brings the conflict to life for visitors of all ages.

In June 1940 Churchill announced: ". . . the Battle of France is over. I expect that the Battle of Britain is about to begin." France surrendered 4 days later and by July, German fighter planes were attacking shipping in the English Channel and coastal towns. By August, RAF airfields were under attack and in September, London and other important cities were targeted. There are several Battle of Britain museums in England, but by far the most important is the **Imperial War Museum Duxford** (p. 359) near Cambridge. The fight for air supremacy was over by fall 1940 with the RAF on top. "Never in the field of human conflict, was so much owed by so many to so few," was Churchill's famous tribute.

Post-War England & Scotland (1945–Present Day)

The war ended in Europe in May 1945, with Britain heavily in debt and the economy ruined. Towns and cities needed to be rebuilt. Strict rationing, introduced in 1940, wasn't completely lifted until 1954.

The postwar break-up of the British Empire was reflected in major domestic social reforms. Free secondary school education had only been introduced in 1944, and after the war the Labour Party won the 1945 General Election by a landslide. It nationalized the coal industry in 1947, and in 1948 the National Health Service (NHS) was established to provide free hospital and medical provision. The 1948 Olympic Games were held in London, symbolically the first since the Berlin Games of 1936.

George Orwell's novel "Nineteen Eighty-Four" was published in 1949, warning about the perils of totalitarian government and coining the phrase "Big Brother," but the 1950s also brought optimism.

King George VI died unexpectedly of lung cancer in 1952 and Queen Elizabeth came to the throne. Novels of the period focus on the new social mobility. John Braine's 1957, "Room at the Top," about a young man's attempt to escape the working class, became the first of Britain's "New Wave" films in 1959. Braine was among the writers labeled "Angry Young Men" after the 1956 John Osborne play "Look Back in Anger."

A General Election put Margaret Thatcher and the Conservatives into power in 1979, and her economic policies divided the nation as unemployment dramatically increased. Her popularity was only secured by the 1982 Falklands "War" (officially only a "conflict") and victory, when Britain defended its South Atlantic islands against Argentina. Thatcher's political success was cemented by free-market agreements with the United States, and her domestic success was underlined by the growing prosperity of Britain's new homeowners and shareholders after council houses were sold off and nationalized industries were privatized.

EATING & drinking

Britain is a foodie island. There are more than 100 restaurants with one Michelin star in England alone. There are another 20-plus with two stars, and four with that ultimate accolade of three stars. One of them belongs to Gordon Ramsay, who seems to be on American TV more than the President; another, the **Fat Duck** at Bray (p. 155), is the masterwork of another TV star, Heston Blumenthal and his molecular cooking style. Several restaurants in Scotland also have stars.

It says a lot about British cuisine, once so derided, where an emphasis on locally sourced produce is now king. Even high-street chain restaurants are largely of a decent standard (you rarely go wrong at a Pizza Express), and you'd have to be extremely unlucky not to stumble on a good Indian restaurant (or "curry house"). Add to that Chinese, Thai, and Italian places, plus Spanish tapas restaurants, as well as all those fish-and-chips shops and coffee shops, and you'll never want for food.

You will find increasingly good pub food, with gastropubs offering fare that outstrips that of many restaurants. There are seafood delights (Morecambe Bay prawns, Whitstable oysters, Loch Etive mussels, Cromer crabs, jellied eels in London's East End, kippers and other smoked fish around the land). Local

lamb, estate-raised beef and venison, gourmet sausages and pies are all likely on the menu.

The country is undergoing a craft-beer revolution. Look out for breweries like Kernel and Beavertown (London), Thornbridge (the Midlands), and Siren (Berkshire), among many, many others. England has wine, too, with several vineyards in southern England making excellent examples, including award-winning, Champagne-style Nyetimber. In Scotland, the national drink is whisky (note the spelling). An important distinction among whiskies is whether they're blends or **single malt.** Many connoisseurs prefer single malts, whose tastes depend on their points of origin. These are usually seen as sipping whiskies, and not to be served with ice.

"New Labour" took power in 1997, under the leadership of the youngest prime minister in over 180 years, Tony Blair (43 years old). This was an age of optimism and Blair became Labour's longest-serving prime minister, but his tenure in the U.K. became increasingly shrouded in his support for actions in Iraq. Gordon Brown succeeded his long-term sparring partner Blair in 2007 but by 2010 had resigned as prime minister and Leader of the Labour Party. The 2010 election saw Conservative David Cameron elected, as head of a center-right coalition. Cameron was re-elected in 2015, this time with a slender majority of Conservative MPs.

In 1999, Scotland was allowed to elect its own Parliament for the first time since its 1707 union with England. Based at Edinburgh, the Parliament has the power to tax and make laws, as well as to legislate on such matters as healthcare, education, public transport, and public housing. Scotland is still represented in the main British Parliament in London, and must bow to the greater will of London in matters of foreign policy.

Literature in Britain has never been stronger. Erudite fantasy has become big-selling reality for Philip ("The Golden Compass") Pullman and J.K. (Harry Potter) Rowling, but there are far more esoteric novels that have become bestsellers. Read almost anything by A. S. Byatt, Hillary Mantel, Ian McEwan, Jeanette Winterson, Zadie Smith, and Will Self and it is possible to see the introspection and inventiveness of modern Britain.

WHEN TO GO
Climate

Don't come to England and Scotland for the weather, though it's nowhere near as bad as many visitors expect. You can't be an island on the edge of the Atlantic Ocean without experiencing some rain brought over by westerly winds; the west coast of Scotland and England get the worst of this, but you'll enjoy plenty of warm, sunny, summer days all over.

Like all countries, mountainous areas can have local cloud and drizzle so the Highlands, Lake District, and other rugged areas in the north have their own weather trends. Particularly enjoyable are the light summer evenings, when daytime stretches until at least 10pm at the summer solstice in June (although in winter it can be dark before 4pm). Rain is most likely in the latter part of the year, but there's no "dry season" here, hence Wimbledon tennis in late June being regularly disrupted.

Daytime temperatures can range from 30° to 95°F (−1° to 35°C), but they rarely stay below 36°F (2°C) or above 79°F (26°C) for too long. Evenings are usually cool, even in summer, but hot July and August days can be muggy—particularly on London's Tube network (also known as

London's Average Daytime Temperatures & Rainfall

	JAN	FEB	MAR	APR	MAY	JUNE	JULY	AUG	SEPT	OCT	NOV	DEC
TEMP. °F	39	39	45	48	55	61	61	64	59	52	46	43
TEMP. °C	4	4	7	9	13	16	16	18	15	11	8	6
RAINFALL (IN)	2.1	1.6	1.5	1.5	1.8	1.8	2.2	2.3	1.9	2.2	2.5	1.9

Edinburgh's Average Temperature & Rainfall

	JAN	FEB	MAR	APR	MAY	JUNE	JULY	AUG	SEPT	OCT	NOV	DEC
TEMP. °F	38	39	42	45	50	55	59	58	54	49	42	40
TEMP. °C	3	3	5	7	10	12	15	14	12	9	5	4
RAINFALL (IN)	2.2	1.6	1.9	1.5	2.0	2.0	2.5	2.7	2.5	2.4	2.5	2.4

the Underground), which is not air-conditioned. Note that the British like to keep hotel thermostats about 10°F (6°C) below the American comfort level.

WHEN YOU'LL FIND BARGAINS   Summer's warmer weather gives rise to many outdoor music and theatre festivals. But winter offers savings pretty much across the board. The cheapest time to fly to England or Scotland is usually during the off season: from late October to mid-December and from January to mid-March. In the last few years, the long-haul airlines in particular have offered some irresistible fares during these periods. Remember that weekdays are often cheaper than weekends.

You can also avoid crowds, to some extent, by planning trips for November or January through March. Sure, it may be rainy and cold—but the country doesn't shut down when the tourists thin out, although many rural attractions such as National Trust properties close for the winter. By arriving after the winter holidays, you can also take advantage of post-Christmas sales, which these days start on December 26 or 27. There's usually another major sales period in stores in mid-summer.

Calendar of Events

JANUARY

As Big Ben strikes midnight, London rings in the **New Year with fireworks** over the Thames and the Eye. It's so crowded that in 2015, the city began limiting attendance to 100,000 and requiring tickets. They cost £10 and can be booked via www.london.gov.uk/nye starting in late September.

London's **New Year's Day Parade** crowns the capital's festive season with pomp and frivolity. More than 10,000 dancers, acrobats, musicians, and performers assemble in the heart of the city every year for a "celebration of nations." Over 400,000 people regularly descend on central London to admire the revelry—be sure to arrive early to secure a good space. www.londonparade.co.uk.

London's large Chinese community welcomes the **Chinese New Year** with a colorful bang. Discover cultural events throughout the city center and catch lion dances and performances in Trafalgar Square and Leicester Square. The New Year celebrations are one of the biggest in the world outside of China. www.china townlondon.org.

For fans of Robert Burns, Ayr (near his birthplace) and Dumfries are the best places to celebrate **Burns Night** on January 25. Naturally, during the celebrations, there's much toasting with Scotch and eating of haggis. www.burns museum.org.uk.

FEBRUARY

As a preview to its annual **Food and Drink Festival,** Chester hosts its famous **Cheese Rolling Championships.** Locals cheer on the Cheshire team as they take on their Lancashire and Stilton rivals over a creative obstacle course, in a charmingly curious celebration of Chester's cheese-making tradition. www.visit chester.com.

MARCH

St Patrick's Day may have started in Ireland but nowadays it's celebrated throughout the world, not least in Manchester, which hosts one of Europe's biggest celebrations. Lasting roughly 2 weeks, the **Manchester Irish Festival** pays tribute to the Emerald Isle with parties, music, comedy, theater, sport, and dance, culminating with the St Patrick's Day parade, which regularly attracts up to 150,000 people. www.irishfestival. co.uk.

APRIL

The **Grand National** at Aintree Racecourse in Liverpool is widely regarded as the greatest steeplechase in the world. The atmosphere is compelling, with racegoers exchanging tips and debating the relative merits of the contending horses and jockeys. www.aintree.co.uk.

Although it draws some 35,000 runners, the **London Marathon** is also a kick for spectators, so hotels tend to fill up ahead of it. The starter pistol fires in Greenwich, and the home stretch is along Birdcage

Walk near Buckingham Palace. www.virginmoneylondonmarathon.com.

The **Oxford and Cambridge University Boat Race,** in London in early April, is another great tradition. Rowers battle it out on the Thames between Putney and Chiswick bridges, with the riverbanks taking on a festival atmosphere. www.theboatraces.org.

MAY

Bohemian, beachfront Brighton comes into its own each summer. In May, the city's **Brighton Festival** returns with 3 weeks of energetic arts-themed performances, heavily influenced by whichever illustrious creative is that year's Artistic Director. www.brightonfestival.org.

London's **Chelsea Flower Show** is Europe's premier gardening event, with imaginative garden designs creating a floral wonderland over an 11-acre site at the Royal Hospital in Chelsea. www.rhs. org.uk/chelsea.

JUNE

Trooping the Colour is a quintessentially English experience of pomp and ceremony that celebrates Queen Elizabeth II's birthday and sees central London bedecked in flags and regaled by pageantry. Troops form a procession along St James's Park and the Queen herself can be glimpsed enjoying the spectacle at the head of the parade. www.royal.gov.uk.

Whether Londoners are right to claim it as the world's greatest tennis tournament is one thing, but the top-seed players, strawberries and cream, and the infamous rain delays distinguish **Wimbledon** from other Grand Slams. www.wimbledon.org.

JULY

The Proms concerts at London's Royal Albert Hall take over the capital's classical musical calendar every summer and, with some justification, can claim to be the greatest classical music festival in the world. Over 8 weeks, the Royal Albert Hall resounds with dozens of experimental concerts, all amid a staple diet of symphony orchestra performances. www. bbc.co.uk/proms.

AUGUST

The **Edinburgh International Festival** is Scotland's best-known festival, held for 3 weeks each August. More than 1,000 shows are hosted and 1,000,000 tickets sold. Numerous other festivals are also held in Edinburgh at this time, celebrating everything from books to jazz. www. eif.co.uk.

Around a million people throng the streets of west London for the **Notting Hill Carnival,** Europe's biggest Caribbean festival. Floats make a circuit of the area and sound systems blast out music all day. Sample jerk chicken as you savor a soundtrack of calypso, soul, funk, and reggae. www.thenottinghillcarnival.com.

Manchester stages one of the biggest **Pride** events in Europe, offering a host of parties, parades, and LGBT celebrations as the city sways in a fiesta of fun. www.manchesterpride.com.

SEPTEMBER

In conjunction with the Great River Race in September, nearly half a million souls attend **Totally Thames,** London's largest free open-air arts festival, which includes more than 250 stalls selling food and crafts (Southwark Bridge is closed for a giant feast), a flotilla of working river boats, circus performers, and antique fireboats, tugs, and sailboats. The Night Carnival is a lavish procession of thousands of lantern-bearing musicians and dancers crawling along the water. Everything is topped off with barge-launched fireworks. www.totallythames.org.

Peek inside some 700 of the English capital's most famous buildings and best-kept architectural secrets at the **London Open House Weekend.** Explore the Foreign Office, the Bank of England, and other landmark buildings that are normally obscured from public view. www.londonopenhouse.org.

OCTOBER

Exemplifying just how provocative the British art world can be, the **Turner Prize**

A street dancer at the Notting Hill Carnival, London.

is awarded to a Brit under 50 and can be relied upon to court controversy year after year. Nominees' works are displayed at London's Tate Britain. www.tate.org.uk.

NOVEMBER

Foiled in his attempt to blow up London's Houses of Parliament and murder King James I on November 5, 1605, Guy Fawkes was executed and the safety of the king celebrated with the lighting of bonfires throughout the country. The tradition continues with towns throughout the country celebrating **Bonfire Night** around November 5. Children are distracted from its more macabre connotations by sugary candyfloss (cotton candy) and toffee apples, and the huge fireworks display.

DECEMBER

Hogmanay in Edinburgh begins on New Year's Eve and merges into New Year's Day festivities. Events include a torchlight procession, a fire festival along Princes Street, a carnival, and street theater. www.edinburghshogmanay.com.

Public Holidays

England has **eight public holidays:** New Year's Day (Jan 1); Good Friday and Easter Monday (usually Apr); May Bank Holiday (first Mon in May); Spring Bank Holiday (last Mon in May, or first in June); August Bank Holiday (last Mon in Aug); Christmas Day (Dec 25); Boxing Day (Dec 26). If a date such as Christmas Day falls on a Saturday or Sunday, the public holiday rolls over to Monday. **Scotland's public holidays** are slightly different: January 2 replaces Easter Monday; the August holiday is at the beginning rather than end of the month; and there's an additional holiday for St Andrew's Day (Nov 30).

3

SUGGESTED ITINERARIES IN ENGLAND & SCOTLAND

by Donald Strachan

Y ou want to get the most out of your trip in the short time that you have available, right? This short chapter has some suggestions for several ways to use your miles wisely. The first itineraries are general highlights tours covering the very best that England and Scotland have to offer for those with limited time. Following those are a couple of itineraries for travellers with special interests, or who wish to explore a smaller part of this island in more depth.

REGIONS IN BRIEF

England and Scotland are part of the United Kingdom, which comprises England, Wales, Scotland, and Northern Ireland. Only 50,327 sq. miles—about the size of New York State—England has an amazing amount of countryside and wilderness and an astonishing regional, physical, and cultural diversity. Scotland is geologically older, less populated, with equally historic cities and low-rise mountain ranges that have taken on almost mythical status: the Highlands.

England

LONDON   Around 7 million Brits live here, although "London" nowadays extends more than 609 sq. miles. The "City of London" is rather different, just 1 sq. mile inside what is left of the old Roman walls, and now Europe's financial hub. The rest of the city (as opposed to the City) gives way to suburbs, urban "villages" and local boroughs.

THE THAMES VALLEY   England's most famous river continues westward from London toward its source in the Cotswolds. A land of meadows, woodlands, attractive villages, market towns, and rolling hillsides, this is one of England's most scenic areas. Highlights include **Windsor Castle** (Elizabeth II's residence) and the university city of **Oxford.**

KENT & SUSSEX   This is the land of Admiral Nelson and Virginia Woolf, Sir Winston Churchill and Turner. It's where you'll find the boisterous seaside city of **Brighton;** and **Canterbury,** famed for its pilgrimages and cathedral. Kent and Sussex are blessed with countless castles and stately homes, including **Leeds Castle** and **Chartwell,** where Churchill lived.

OLD WESSEX: HAMPSHIRE, WILTSHIRE, DORSET & SOMERSET   Southwest of London lies the heart of the old kingdom of Wessex, the historic precursor to a united England. These four largely rural counties possess three of England's great **cathedrals**—Winchester, Wells, and

PREVIOUS PAGE: **An open-top tour bus on Tower Bridge, London.**

Salisbury—and Europe's most significant prehistoric monument, **Stonehenge.** Also here is **Bath,** with its Roman baths and Georgian architecture, and plenty of literary heritage, including Thomas Hardy and Jane Austen.

DEVON & CORNWALL   Devon has **Dartmoor National Park**, and its northern and southern coastlines are peppered with resorts and villages such as Clovelly. In Cornwall, you're never more than 20 miles from a beautiful, rugged coastline, which terminates at **Land's End.**

THE COTSWOLDS   This is a pastoral land of honey-hued limestone villages where rural England unfolds before you like a storybook. Start at Burford, the traditional gateway to the area, continuing on to Bourton-on-the-Water, Lower and Upper Slaughter, and Stow-on-the-Wold.

THE HEART OF ENGLAND   This region encompasses both Shakespeare country and the Midlands, with its rejuvenated capital at **Birmingham.** The Midlands was the birthplace of the Industrial Revolution, but its foremost tourist town looks a little farther back to the time of Tudor England's Bard: **Stratford-upon-Avon.**

CAMBRIDGE & EAST ANGLIA   East Anglia is a geographic bulge northeast of London, comprising four flat counties. Go there to see **Ely Cathedral** and the university city of **Cambridge**. The jewel of the trendy Suffolk coast is the genteel seaside resort of **Southwold.**

THE NORTHWEST   Here you'll find the magnificent port city of **Liverpool,** once a major gateway to the U.S., and childhood home to the most famous pop group of all, the Beatles. There's also **Manchester,** Britain's one-time industrial heart, and now a hip, happening place. Along with those you've got the charming walled city of **Chester.**

THE LAKE DISTRICT   Here is some of England's most dramatic scenery: A lake around every bend, hemmed in by ominous peaks (snow-tipped until late spring), with tiny roads and little towns. It's a place of poetry and literature, home to, among others, Wordsworth, Samuel Taylor Coleridge, John Ruskin, and Beatrix Potter. **Windermere** is perhaps the best location for touring the area, but there are many other charming spots, including **Grasmere** and **Ambleside.**

YORKSHIRE & THE NORTHEAST   **York,** with its immense minster and medieval streets, has the history (though **Hadrian's Wall,** built by the Romans, has an equal historical claim). **Newcastle** is now a throbbing arts and culture hub. **Durham** has one of Britain's finest Norman churches, and **Fountains Abbey** is among the country's great ecclesiastical ruins.

Scotland

EDINBURGH & THE LOTHIANS   Half medieval and half Georgian, Edinburgh is at its liveliest every August during its Festival, but you can visit **Edinburgh Castle** and Holyroodhouse and walk the **Royal Mile** year-round. Opening on to the North Sea, the university town of **St Andrews** is the capital of golf and boasts many great courses.

THE BORDERS   Witness to a turbulent history, the Borders between England and Scotland are rich in castle ruins and Gothic abbeys, and also proved a rich mine for the fiction of Sir Walter Scott. Highlights are **Kelso,** which Scott found "the most beautiful," and **Melrose,** site of the ruined Melrose Abbey and Scott's former home of Abbotsford.

GLASGOW, THE WEST COAST & THE SOUTHERN HEBRIDES   A renaissance has come to the once-grimy, Victorian industrial city of **Glasgow.** As well as the lively nightlife, there are several museums, notably the Burrell Collection, Hunterian Art Gallery, and Kelvingrove Art Gallery and Museum. The **Argyll Peninsula** is centered at **Oban,** a bustling resort and port. **Loch Lomond** and the **Trossachs** form a National Park containing a breathtaking combination of moors, mountains, and lakes. This stretch of west-facing coast also provides access to many Hebridean Islands, including the whisky isle of **Islay.**

THE HIGHLANDS & THE ISLE OF SKYE   The Highlands' capital is **Inverness,** one of the oldest inhabited areas in Scotland. Top attractions nearby are **Loch Ness,** home of the legendary "monster," and **Cawdor Castle,** famously linked with Macbeth. The **Isle of Skye** is a mystical island, and the only one connected to the mainland by a toll-free bridge.

ENGLAND IN 1 WEEK

If you're coming to England for a short time, you want to make the most of it. Our week-long tour does just that. It might seem packed, but limiting much of the travel to short bursts helps you see more sights. The tour gives you a good dip into London (the **Tower of London, British Museum**), and then takes you on a highlights trip of places you could name almost without thinking (**Windsor Castle, Stratford-upon-Avon, Oxford**).

DAYS 1 & 2: London Calling

On **DAY 1** start on the banks of the Thames, the mighty river that flows through London. A ride on the **London Eye** observation wheel (p. 77) near Westminster Bridge, is one way to get your city bearings. Afterwards, cross Westminster Bridge with its wonderful view of the **Houses of Parliament** to the clock tower **Big Ben** (p. 76). Walk past them and you're at **Westminster Abbey** (p. 80), where most of England's queens and kings have been crowned and where many lie at rest. There's time for the **National Gallery** (p. 69), where you can take in the gallery's must-see paintings, which include Van Gogh's sunflowers and works by

Constable, Monet, and da Vinci. Dip next door to the **National Portrait Gallery** (p. 70), too. Dine around **Covent Garden** (p. 132), the former fruit and vegetable market, now full of shops, bars, street artists, and restaurants.

On **DAY 2**, start at the world's most impressive city castle, the **Tower of London** (p. 94). Afterward, walk out onto **Tower Bridge** and marvel at the Victorian engineering feat. Take a river bus for the short ride past the Tower, South Bank, and Savoy Hotel to Embankment Pier, then walk to the **British Museum** (p. 66). This is one of the world's greatest treasure-troves—much of it plundered from other parts of the globe when Britannia ruled the waves.

You have time for **St Paul's,** masterpiece of architect Sir Christopher Wren. Cross the **Millennium Bridge** to **Tate Modern** (p. 93), a vast power station now one of the world's most exciting art museums. There's dining, culture, and nightlife along the **South Bank.**

DAY 3: Royal Windsor & its Castle

This is a perfect daytrip, and calmer than the previous 2 days: Windsor and **Windsor Castle** (p. 151) are just a half-hour train ride from London. Wander through **St George's Chapel,** where monarchs are entombed; and stroll the **Jubilee Gardens.** You'll need at least 2 hours, and maybe a bit more for a riverside stroll, too.

Head back to London, and you might want to have a quiet walk in **Hyde Park** (p. 110) and **Kensington Gardens** (basically the

The view from The London Eye.

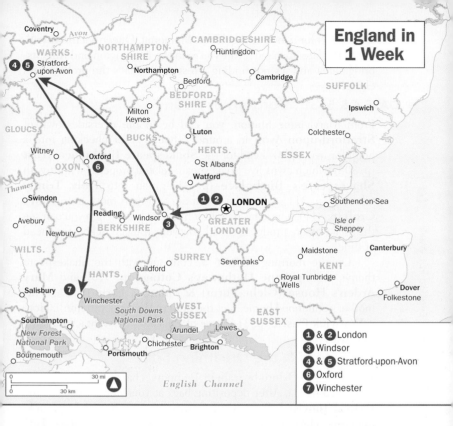

England in 1 Week

- **1** & **2** London
- **3** Windsor
- **4** & **5** Stratford-upon-Avon
- **6** Oxford
- **7** Winchester

The Albert Memorial at Kensington Gardens, London.

same park) for a look at the Albert Memorial, Queen Victoria's tribute to her late husband. Now you're in the Kensington and Knightsbridge area and it's not finding a restaurant that's the problem, it's choosing.

DAYS 4 & 5: Stratford-upon-Avon

From Marylebone Station, you can be in the riverside town of **Stratford-upon-Avon** in around 2 hours. After checking into a hotel for two nights, head for the **Shakespeare Birthplace Trust** (p. 308), which owns five Shakespeare-related properties. Start with **Shakespeare's Birthplace** (p. 312); pop into **Holy Trinity Church** (p. 311), where he is buried; and then move onto **Hall's Croft** (p. 311), where his daughter Susanna lived. Then you can see the Shakespeare production we know you arranged tickets for ahead of time . . . .

On the morning of **DAY 5**, continue with the Shakespeare theme, visiting **Anne Hathaway's Cottage** (p. 310), and **Mary Arden's House (Glebe Farm) & Palmer's Farm** (p. 311), his mother's childhood home. Get the train to Warwick (30 min.). Here is **Warwick Castle** (p. 314), one of England's most intact standing fortresses.

DAY 6: Oxford & the Dreaming Spires

You can get to Oxford by train in 1½ hours, changing at Banbury or Leamington Spa. After depositing bags at your hotel, head for the **Oxford Tourist Information Centre** (p. 158) for a 2-hour walking tours. Have a late lunch and a pint at the 17th-century **Turf Tavern** (p. 170); it's where Bill Clinton used to drink while at university.

Make for the **Ashmolean** (p. 160), which rivals the British Museum's ancient hoard. Around the corner is the quirky **Pitt-Rivers Museum** (p. 163), the collection of early anthropologist General Pitt-Rivers.

DAY 7: Winchester, Wessex's Ancient Capital

It takes just over an hour to get to Winchester on the train. This 9th-century stronghold of King Alfred the Great, has one of England's great **cathedrals** (p. 222)—also the burial place of novelist Jane Austen. Stroll along the banks of the River Itchen to the **Hospital of St Cross** (p. 221), almshouses run by a charitable institution founded in the 1100s. Winchester has a thriving **dining scene,** too (p. 224). Reserve your favorite ahead of arrival. You can return to your Oxford hotel for the night, stay overnight in Winchester, or make tracks for London on the quick Winchester–London Waterloo train (1 hr.).

THE BEST OF SCOTLAND IN 1 WEEK

Although it's impossible to see all of Scotland in 1 week, it should be enough time to see the major sights of Edinburgh and Glasgow, with time to take in Loch Lomond and the Highlands beyond.

DAYS 1 & 2: Edinburgh

After checking into your hotel, head straight out to the Old Town's **Royal Mile** (p. 478), which runs between two of the city's main attractions, **Edinburgh Castle** (p. 478) and the **Palace of Holyroodhouse** (p. 482). Visit one before lunch, the other in the afternoon. If you save Holyroodhouse, you should also have time to visit to the **Scottish Parliament** (p. 484). Late in the afternoon, walk down into the New Town for some shopping along **Princes Street.**

On **DAY 2**, spend the morning admiring masterpieces in the **National Gallery of Scotland** (p. 485) and the historic treasures of the **National Museum of Scotland** (p. 483). In the afternoon, visit the Greek-inspired **Calton Hill** (p. 487) in the east of Edinburgh and the **Royal Botanic Garden** (p. 488), one of Britain's finest.

DAY 3: Glasgow, Scotland's Largest City

On **DAY 3**, get an early start, pick up a rental car, and drive to Glasgow, which is only 40 miles west of Edinburgh. (Or take the train—around 1 hr.—and defer collecting your rental car until tomorrow.) You can probably arrive in time to check into a hotel and

Autumn color in the Royal Botanic Garden, Edinburgh.

see the **Burrell Collection** (p. 555) before lunch. In the afternoon, either visit the **Kelvingrove Art Gallery and Museum** (p. 552) or the **Hunterian Art Gallery** (p. 551). If you have kids in tow, a better bet may be the **Glasgow Science Centre** (p. 554), on the banks of the River Clyde.

DAY 4: Loch Lomond's "Bonnie Banks"

From Glasgow, on **DAY 4**, take a drive 20 miles northwest to **Balloch** (p. 570), a good center for exploring the area around Loch Lomond. Take to the water on one of **Sweeney's Cruises** (p. 570). If you return in time, you can also explore **Balloch Castle Country Park** (p. 571).

DAY 5: Fort William, Gateway to the Highlands

From Glasgow (or Balloch, if you spend the night there), strike out for **Fort William,** 104 miles north of Glasgow. On the shores of Loch Linnhe, Fort William is the best stopover between Glasgow and Inverness, capital of the Highlands. Arrive in time for lunch, taking in views of **Ben Nevis,** the highest mountain in Scotland. In the afternoon, visit the ruins of **Old Inverlochy Castle** (p. 635) and **Neptune's Staircase** (p. 635). Spend the night in Fort William.

DAYS 6 & 7: Inverness & Some Highland Highlights

Fort William to Inverness is a drive of a mere 68 miles—but you'll want to take it slowly. Drive along the western bank of

Fort William on the shores of Loch Linnhe, with Ben Nevis in the background.

1 & **2** Edinburgh
3 Glasgow
4 Loch Lomond
5 Fort William
6 & **7** Inverness

Loch Ness (p. 609), keeping your eye out for the elusive monster. Close to Drumnadrochit you can also explore the ruins of **Urquhart Castle** (p. 609). Spend what's left of your day exploring historic Inverness. Stay overnight in Inverness, and then set out to see the **Culloden Battlefield** (p. 604), with its Graves of the Clans, romantic **Cawdor Castle** (p. 615), and **Fort George** (p. 604). Either overnight again in Inverness or head towards your departure airport. It's a drive of around 160 miles back to Edinburgh.

ENGLAND & SCOTLAND IN 2 WEEKS

This itinerary combines the best weeks in England and Scotland to build an all-Britain itinerary that should take 2 weeks to complete—though of course, if you can linger longer, traveling "slow" or taking side trips, you should. One easy break would be to pause on the line between London and Edinburgh in historic **York** (p. 438). There's no need to arrange a rental car for the English portion or for seeing Edinburgh, but you will need one when you head out into the wilds of Scotland.

DAYS 1–6: London, Windsor, Stratford-upon-Avon & Oxford

See "England in 1 Week," above, but travel back to London directly from Oxford at the end of **DAY 6**.

DAY 7: En Route to Edinburgh

This is a travel day. Your best options for London–Edinburgh transit are to **fly** (1 hr., plus airport transfers at each end) or the hassle-free **train** journey, arriving at historic Edinburgh Waverley Station in approximately 5½ hours. Spend a low-key evening soaking up the atmosphere of one of Europe's prettiest capitals.

DAYS 8–14: Edinburgh, Glasgow, Loch Lomond & the Highlands

Follow the itinerary laid out in "The Best of Scotland in 1 Week," above.

THE HISTORY, CASTLES & GARDENS OF SOUTHERN ENGLAND IN 9 DAYS

This tour of Southern England requires a car, for a relaxing swing through the byways and along the coast. It also makes a perfect add-on to England's iconic highlights (see "England in 1 Week," above). England's gardens are integral to the rural experience, and in some cases they have been growing for centuries. This tour takes you to those that are at the very pinnacle of horticulture and beauty. Naturally they are at their best from June to September, but these are also designed to be year-round spectacles, with winter foliage, spring bulbs, and rich late-season hues.

DAY 1: Kew's Royal Botanic Gardens

London's great garden, **Kew** (p. 105) is a fantastic world tucked away behind high walls on the city's southwestern fringe—one that lays claim to containing more than one in eight of all known plant species. You can generally find parking, but there is also a Kew Gardens stop on the Tube's District Line. This is a full day out at any time of year as there are 121 hectares (300 acres), which vary from clipped formal gardens to wild woodland areas.

DAY 2: Runnymede, Stonehenge & Old Sarum

You're heading for the ancient standing stones at Stonehenge, but first an added attraction: Drive out of London heading west onto the M3, turn on the M25, then come off at junction 13 onto the A308. On the rural banks of the Thames is **Runnymede** (p. 150). It was here in 1215 that King John sealed the Magna Carta, the document that first made monarchs subject to the law like everyone else. You can walk through the meadows, and even go on a boat ride.

0 50 mi
0 50 km

C. Wrath
Wick
Stornoway
Ullapool
Outer
Hebrides
St Kilda
N. Uist
Inverness
Loch
Ness
13 14
S. Uist
Skye
Cairngorms
National Park
Aberdeen
Fort William
12
SCOTLAND
Oban
Mull
Loch Lomond &
The Trossachs
National Park
11
Dundee
Islay
Stirling
Edinburgh
7-9
NORTH
SEA
Glasgow
10
ATLANTIC
OCEAN
North Channel
Ayr
Northumberland
National Park
Newcastle
upon Tyne
Londonderry
(Derry)
NORTHERN
IRELAND
Carlisle
L. Neagh
Belfast
Lake District
National Park
North York Moors
National Park
Galway
REPUBLIC
OF IRELAND
Dublin
Isle of
Man
Yorkshire Dales
National Park
York
Leeds
IRISH SEA
Manchester
Anglesey
Liverpool
Peak District
National Park
Lincoln
The Wash
Chester
Snowdonia
National Park
Birmingham
Norwich
The Broads
National Park
WALES
Stratford-upon-Avon
ENGLAND
Brecon Beacons
National Park
4 5
6
Cambridge
Pembrokeshire
Coast Nat'l Park
Cardiff
Bristol
Oxford
LONDON
1 2
Bath
Windsor
3
Exmoor
National Park
Salisbury
South Downs
National Park
Dover
Str. of Dover
New Forest
National Park
Southampton
Isle of
Wight
FRANCE
Land's
End
Plymouth
Dartmoor
National Park
English Channel

1 & 2 London
3 Windsor
4 & 5 Stratford-upon-Avon
6 Oxford
7-9 Edinburgh
10 Glasgow
11 Loch Lomond
12 Fort William
13 & 14 Inverness

Get back onto the M3 and head southwest, turning onto the A303. If you're lucky with the traffic you may get to **Stonehenge** (p. 230) in 90 minutes. The monumental stone circle in the middle of Salisbury Plain is a must-see site, even though, with main roads running past, it can be a disappointment for some. You walk around the circle at a distance, so while you'll be glad to have done it, you won't spend as long here as you likely anticipated. Return to spend a couple of nights in Salisbury via **Old Sarum** (p. 229), the ancient fortified town that pre-dated Salisbury but was dismantled in the 1200s.

The Mary Rose Museum at Portsmouth Historic Dockyard.

DAY 3: Stourhead & Salisbury

The great 18th-century garden at **Stourhead** (p. 234) is 26 miles west of Salisbury in the serene Wiltshire countryside. The huge lake, which reflects the temples, grottos, and trees lining its banks, leaves you breathless, but it is only part of the 1,072-hectare (2,650-acre) estate. This landscaped garden is much the same as when it was created in 1740; flowering shrubs are everywhere and rare trees thrive. There are endless walks to enjoy. Return to Salisbury for the night, perhaps in time for evensong at **Salisbury Cathedral** (p. 228).

DAY 4: Portsmouth & Arundel

Southeast of Salisbury, Portsmouth is dripping in naval history, and its **Historic Dockyard** (p. 225) is a fantastic place for youngsters. It's home to Admiral Nelson's flagship, **HMS *Victory,*** and a new museum dedicated to the *Mary Rose.* The **HMS Warrior** is an 1860 iron-hulled, steam-powered warship, with ladders, hatches, and other gymnastics. There are docks to run around, boat rides, and exhibitions.

It's a short hop from here (28 miles to be exact) to **Arundel** (p. 211), an ancient Sussex town on the River Arun. Have a wander and do some window browsing along pretty Tarrant Street, but concentrate on **Arundel Castle** (p. 212). Take an hour or so to explore its Old Masters paintings, the walled gardens and grounds. You don't want to be too late leaving if you're staying or dining at **Amberley Castle** (p. 215), a real castle several miles away that is now a luxury

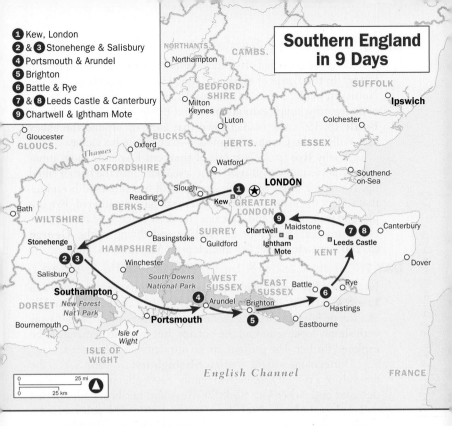

1 Kew, London
2 & 3 Stonehenge & Salisbury
4 Portsmouth & Arundel
5 Brighton
6 Battle & Rye
7 & 8 Leeds Castle & Canterbury
9 Chartwell & Ightham Mote

Southern England in 9 Days

hotel worth busting the budget for. Try to book a table at its **Queen's Room Restaurant** (p. 216) for a memorable meal in 12th-century surrounds.

DAY 5: Brighton, City by the Sea

You probably won't want to leave Amberley, but less than half an hour away is Brighton, the fun capital of the south coast. At beach level there are pubs, seafood bars, shops, cafes, and other seaside fun. Close together are the **Fishing Museum** (p. 202) and **Jack and Linda's Brighton Smokehouse** (p. 208), where you can line up for a hot mackerel sandwich. Head onto the pier for views back onto the seafront. A few minutes' walk away is the **Royal Pavilion** (p. 204), a royal holiday home from the Regency era, and a must-see extravagance of Oriental design. On the grounds is **Brighton Museum** (p. 203), a fine collection of furniture, art, and local history.

The rest of the day you can wander the backstreets: **The Lanes** and (especially) **North Laine** are filled with quirky designer shops. If you still have the energy, Brighton's **nightlife** (p. 209) is legendary.

DAY 6: Sussex Past: Battle & Rye

Just along the coast is a place that was at the turning point of British history. In the Battle of Hastings, King Harold was defeated by the Normans, marking the end of Saxon rule. The battlefield is the site of an award-winning exhibition. Spend the morning here, and visit **Battle** (p. 197), the market town that grew up around the abbey that William the Conqueror founded to celebrate his victory.

Nearby **Rye** (p. 197) is one of southern England's most atmospheric ancient towns. It used to be a sea port until the harbor silted up. It's now 2 miles from the sea but still has timbered hostelries that reflect its history as a place where smugglers gathered. Rye is a place to walk around and soak up; you don't come here for any specific attraction. End your day staying and dining at the **George** (p. 200), or eating fresh fish and chips at **Marino's** (p. 200).

DAY 7: Leeds Castle & Sissinghurst Castle Garden

From your Rye hotel, you've got less than an hour's drive to get to **Leeds Castle** (p. 195), England's most perfect castle, in the middle of a serene lake amid rolling grounds. Some castles you can get away with simply looking around the outside, but this one demands to be explored further. The gardens are an attraction in themselves.

Thirteen miles to the south is **Sissinghurst** (p. 196). Set on the grounds of a ruined Elizabethan manor, Sissinghurst was created by designer and writer Vita Sackville-West and her husband, novelist and diplomat Harold Nicholson, in the 1930s. The pair created a year-round delight; the dreamlike **White Garden** is a highlight, but there's also a spring garden full of daffodils and a vegetable garden that shows how it should be done, in style and execution, all with the surviving tower looming over them. Press onward to Canterbury for the evening, 29 miles northeast, and check in for 2 nights.

DAY 8: Canterbury

Canterbury (p. 180) is the ecclesiastical capital of England, and home base of the Anglican Church. It's been a place of pilgrimage for centuries, and the start of the Via Francigena, the pilgrims' path from Canterbury to Rome. Start at the **Cathedral; St Augustine's Abbey** is next door. Canterbury is also well stocked with good places to eat. We especially love **The Goods Shed** (p. 186), a permanent farmers' market, tapas bar, and restaurant inside an old warehouse.

If you see the sights quickly and fancy a side trip, it's only a 45-minute train journey to the pretty seaside resort of **Whitstable** (p. 188), famed for its quaint streets and fine local oysters. An alternate afternoon trip could take you to **Margate** (30 min. by train; p. 188), a classic English seaside town that fell into disrepair, but which is now getting back on its feet. Explore the seafront and jolly beach, but you're here for the **Turner Contemporary** (p. 189) a stark, white building on the seafront which celebrates J. M. W. Turner, whose iconic seascapes were painted at this very spot when there was a lodging house here.

DAY 9: Back to London via Ightham Mote & Chartwell

En route back to London, just off the M25, are two of southern England's finest National Trust properties. **Chartwell** (p. 192) was the long-time home of Winston Churchill. Not only do you get to see his papers, you also see the gardening work he did in his spare time and can tour his painting studio, still hung with many of his accomplished works. It's only a few miles from here to **Ightham Mote** (p. 194), a moated Tudor manor house and gardens. From there, allow at least 1½ hours to get back to central London.

3

SUGGESTED ITINERARIES IN ENGLAND & SCOTLAND

History, Castles & Gardens in 9 Days

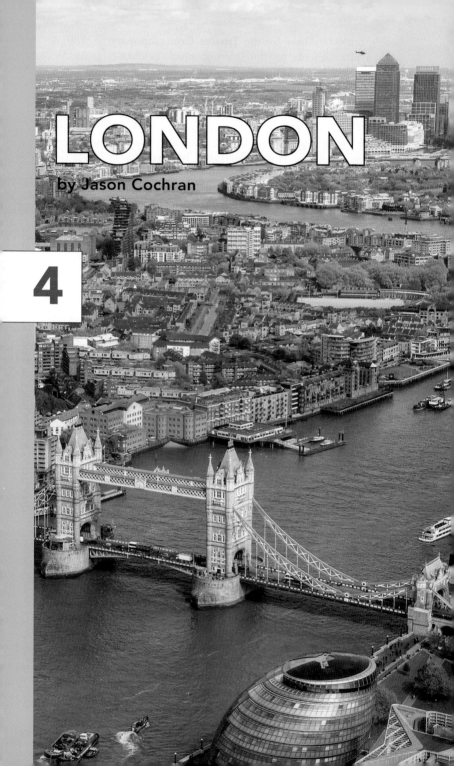

LONDON

by Jason Cochran

4

W hether you realize it or not, London shaped your destiny. There's hardly a quarter of the globe that it hasn't changed. The United States was founded in reaction to London's edicts. Australia was first colonized with London's criminals. Modern Canada, South Africa, and New Zealand were cultivated from London. India's course was irrevocably changed by the aspirations of London businessmen, as were the lives of millions of Africans who were shipped around the world while Londoners lined their pockets with profits. You're holding proof in your hands of London's pull: that you bought this book, written in English somewhere other than in England, is evidence of London's reach across time and distance. And its dominion continues to this day: London is the world's most popular destination for foreign tourists.

London is inexhaustible. You could tour it for months and barely get to know it. Few cities support such a variety of people living in remarkable harmony. That diversity makes London like a cut diamond; approach it from a different angle each day, and it presents an entirely fresh shape and color—London is many things in every moment.

Essentials

ARRIVING Transatlantic flights almost always land at Heathrow, Europe's busiest international airport (LHR; 17 miles west), or Gatwick (LGW) 31 miles south. With a few minor exceptions, the other four airports, Stansted (STN; 37 miles northeast), Luton (LTN; 34 miles northwest), London City (LCY; in London's Docklands area), and Southend (SEN; 42 miles easy) serve flights from Europe, and they're where cut-rate flyers and executive jets tend to go. Every airport offers some kind of rail connection to the central city, and that's the smart way to go. Tickets can be bought at windows in the arrivals halls, at machines, or online, where you get a discount. You'll rarely have to wait more than 20 minutes for the next train.

National Express (www.nationalexpress.com; © **08717/818-8178**) buses will also take you from all airports (except Southend) for

PREVIOUS PAGE: **View of Tower Bridge and London from The Shard, Europe's tallest building.**

AIRPORT	COST/AVG. TIME USING NATIONAL RAIL	HOURS OF RAIL SERVICE
Heathrow (LHR), HeathrowAirport.com	Heathrow Express (www.heathrow express.com): £21.50 single, £35 return, kids 5 to 15 £10.70/£17.50*/15 minutes OR Heathrow Connect: £10.10 single/30–45 minutes	Four times hourly 5:07am to 11:55pm
Gatwick (LGW), GatwickAirport.com	Gatwick Express (www.gatwick express.com): £20 single, £35 return (in person) £18/£31 (online), kids £10/£17.50 and £9/£15.55/30 minutes *or* Thameslink & Great Northern: £11 single/30 to 50 minutes	Four times hourly 3:30am to 12:30am
Luton (LTN), www.London-Luton.co.uk	Thameslink & Great Northern: £14 single including 5-min. shuttle bus, 45 minutes	Six times hourly 5am to midnight
Stansted (STN), StanstedAirport.com	From £19 single, £32 return/47 minutes	Four times hourly 5:30am to 12:30am
London City (LCY), LondonCityAirport.com	N/A	DLR: 5:30am to midnight
London Southend (SEN), www.southendairport.com	Greater Anglia: £17 single/53 minutes	4am to 11pm

*Online fare. Tickets £5 more if you wait to pay on board.

** As if you'd be daft enough to want a taxi after seeing those prices and times, you're more likely to find one by booking ahead. Check www.london-luton.co.uk, www.stansted airport.com, and www.southendairport.com for list of the latest approved companies. Addison Lee (www.addisonlee.com) is an established minicab company, and Heathrow has a partnership with Green Tomato Cars (www.greentomatocars.com). All services offer discounted prices for children.

less than £10 each way, although given traffic we don't recommend it. It's also the least expensive way to get from city to city in Britain (but not the fastest—that's usually the train), and because the country's not very big, it rarely takes more than a few hours to reach anyplace. Even Scotland is only 5 hours away. **Megabus** (www.megabus.com; ✆ **090/0160-0900** or +44-141-352-4444), which serves more than 100 cities across Europe, charges as little as £1.50 for early bookings, although £19 to £45 for Edinburgh is a more typical rate. It accepts bookings 2 months ahead; book online to avoid phone fees. Both coach services depart from the miserable Victoria Coach Station, located behind Victoria railway station.

RAIL SERVICE TO	COST/TIME USING TUBE OR DLR	COST/AVG. TIME FOR NATIONAL EXPRESS SHUTTLE SERVICE TO CENTRAL LONDON	COST/AVG. TIME TO AIRPORT BY TAXI
Paddington	£5.70 cash or £5.10 Oyster/75 minutes on Piccadilly Line	£6 single, kids 11 to 16 £3, under 11 free, from £5.50 each way (www.national express.com)/50–70 minutes	£65–£85/70 minutes
Gatwick Express: Victoria; T&GN: St Pancras, Farringdon, Blackfriars, or London Bridge	N/A	£8 each way (www.national express.com)/90 minutes	£100/70 minutes
St Pancras, Blackfriars, or London Bridge	N/A	From £9 (www.nationalex press.com)/90 minutes (runs 24 hr.)	£100/80 minutes**
Liverpool Street	N/A	From £12 single (www. nationalexpress.com)/ 60–100 minutes	£99/80 minutes**
N/A	£4.80 cash, £3.30 Oyster/25 minutes on Docklands Light Railway	N/A	£25–£40/20 to 40 minutes
Liverpool Street	N/A	N/A	£80–£100/60 to 80 minutes

Driving in London?

Don't do it! In bad traffic, a trip from Heathrow to the western fringe of London can take 2 hours. And once you're in the city, just about every technology is deployed against you. There's a hefty fee just to drive to the city center. Roads are confusingly one-way. Cameras catch and ticket your honest driving errors. Parking is a fantasy. Many North Americans think of cars as the default transportation mode, but in London, trains are the thing. The only time to *maybe* drive a car is if you're on a cross-country tour—but in cities, it won't be easy for you.

What's the best place to hear about inexpensive ground tours? Hostels. Drop into one; most of their lobbies are papered with brochures. Don't neglect their bulletin boards, either, since you may catch wind of a shared-ride situation that'll often cost you no more than your share of the gasoline (in Britain, *petrol*).

A few coach companies also travel to Europe, usually crossing the Channel with a ferry. Because of the pressure put on the market by mushrooming no-frills airlines, rates are extremely low. You'll pay as little as £21 one-way to Paris via **Eurolines** (www.eurolines.co.uk; ☎ **08717/ 81-81-78;** 8–10 hr. each way). Brussels or Amsterdam are £25 with a 7-day advance purchase. The trade-off: It can take all day, sunrise to sunset, to reach Paris by this method.

The original railway builders plowed their stations to every town of size, making it easy to see the highlights of the United Kingdom without getting near a car. The British whine about the declining quality of the service, but Americans, Canadians, and Australians will be blown away by the speed (and the cost, if they don't book ahead) of the system. Find tickets to all destinations through **National Rail** (www.national rail.co.uk/cheapestfare; ☎ **08457/48-49-50**) or the indispensable **TheTrainLine.com**. Seats are sold 12 weeks ahead, and early-bird bookings can yield some marvelous deals, such as £26 for a 4-hour trip to Scotland (£125 last-minute is common). When hunting for tickets, always search for "off-peak" (non-rush hour) trips going or coming from London in general, not a specific London station, because each London terminal serves various cities. Unfortunately, not every train company website accepts international credit cards; TheTrainLine does.

Tickets bought reasonably in advance will still be cheaper than what you'd pay for the same trips on a **BritRail pass** (www.britrail.com; must purchase outside the U.K.), good on long-distance train but on local London transport, and few tourists ride rails with the near-daily regularity that would make a timed pass pay for itself. Check prices against the U.S. seller **Rail Europe** (www.raileurope.com; ☎ **800/622-8600**).

New Year's Eve fireworks over Big Ben.

We're living in marvelous times: The **Channel Tunnel** opened two decades ago (although they *still* seem to be working out the kinks), so you can reach London's St Pancras from Paris in an incredible 2 hours and 15 minutes. Book via **Eurostar** (www.eurostar.co.uk; ✆ **08432/186-186** in the U.K. or +44 1233/61-75-75; phone bookings are US$7 more) itself or the U.S.-based **Rail Europe** (www.raileurope.com; ✆ **800/361-7245** in North America), which also sells European rail passes. Check both sites, since prices can differ, but do it early, because rates boom as availability decreases. Pay attention to the special offers on Eurostar's site; deals go as low as £69 round-trip in summer.

GETTING AROUND   Londoners call their 402km (249-mile) metro system the Underground, its official name, or just as commonly, "the Tube." Its distinctive logo—a red "roundel" bisected by a blue bar—debuted in 1913 as one of the world's first corporate symbols and is one of the city's most ubiquitous sights. It's the oldest subway system on earth—the first section opened in 1863 while America was fighting its Civil War—and it often acts its age, with frequent delays and shutdowns.

There are 13 named lines, plus the Docklands Light Railway (DLR) serving East London and a tram line in South London, which together serve nearly 300 stations. Lines are color-coded: the Piccadilly is peacock purple, the Bakerloo could be considered Sherlock Holmes brown, and so on. Navigating is mostly foolproof. Look for signs pointing to the color and name of the line you want. Pretty soon, more signs separate you according to the direction you want to go in, based on the Tube map. If you know the name/color of the line you want, as well as the direction of your destination, the signs will march you to the platform you need. Nearly every station is combed with staircases. You'll shuffle through warrens of cylindrical tunnels, many of them faced in custard-yellow tiles and overly full of commuters, and you'll scale alpine escalators lined with ads. Stand to the right so "climbers" can pass you.

The Tube shuts down nightly from Sunday to Thursday. Exact times for first and final trains are posted in each station (using the 24-hr. clock), but the Tube generally operates from 5:30am (0530) to just after midnight (0000), and Sundays 7am (0700) to 11:30pm (2330). On Friday and Saturday nights, many lines in Central London run all night long: "Night Tube" trains are the Piccadilly, Victoria, Central, and Jubilee lines, plus the Charing Cross branch of the Northern line. Still, if you plan to take the train after midnight, always check the Night Tube map beforehand.

One of the groovier things about the Underground is the electronic displays on platforms that tell you how long it'll be until the next train. A 24-hour information service is also available at ✆ **0343/222-1234.** The best resource is the TFL Journey Planner, online at **www.tfl.gov.uk/journeyplanner**. The best resource is the free app **Citymapper,** which tells you which Tube, bus, or train to use, how long it takes, and includes mapped walking directions to the nearest stop.

Options for purchasing Tube travel are as follows:

1. **In cash, per ride.** Only fools buy at vending machines per ride. Why? The math. To travel a mile in zone 1 on the Underground, the cash fare is £4.80 ($7.40).

2. **Via Travelcard.** Aimed at tourists, it's an unlimited pass for 1 or 7 days on the Tube, rail, and bus. "Day Anytime" Travelcards for zones 1 through 3 with no timing restrictions are £12. If you find you have to pop into a zone that isn't covered by your card, buy an extension from the ticket window before starting your journey; it's usually £1.50 to £2 more. 7-Day Travelcards cost adults £32.10 for travel anytime in zones 1 and 2. For Travelcard prices that include more zones, visit **www.tfl. gov.uk/tickets**.

3. **Via Oyster Pay As You Go (PAYG).** This is the best option, and it's what locals use. Rub this credit card–size pass on yellow dots at the turnstiles and you get the lowest fares. You load it with cash and it debits as you go, no tickets required, on all forms of in-city public transit. No matter how many times you ride the Tube (debited at £2.30 in zone 1—that's a lot better than the £4.80 cash fare!) and bus (debited as £1.50—you can't pay cash on a bus), the maximum taken off your card in a single day will **always be less** than what an equivalent Day Travelcard would cost. Getting an Oyster usually requires a £5 deposit, but you can get that back before you skip town at any Tube ticket office (there's also a desk at Heathrow; ID may be requested). It won't get erased if you keep it beside your mobile phone. And if you don't use up all the money you put on it, you can get a refund as long as there's less than £10 value left on your card. (Travelcards offer no refunds for unused monies.)

It's most economical to get an Oyster PAYG and then do everything you can to plan days during which you don't take transport at all. A significant aspect of that strategy is choosing a hotel that's within walking distance of lots of the things you want to do. Trains go shockingly slowly (34kmph/21 mph is the *average* and has been for over 100 years); and in the center of town, stops are remarkably close together and the stairs can wear you out. In fact, if your journey is only two or three stations, you'll often find it less strenuous to simply walk.

CITY LAYOUT London's neighborhoods were laid out during a period of wagon and foot traffic, when districts were defined in narrower terms than we define them today; indeed, for centuries people often lived complete lives without seeing the other side of town. As a vestige of the old times, when the southern banks of the River Thames were swampy and undesirable, most of the major attractions in the city center lie on the north side of the water and are within a short walk of it, but today, more than 8 million people reside within a few miles of it.

The Neighborhoods in Brief

SOHO, COVENT GARDEN & CENTRAL WEST END   London's undisputed center of nightlife, restaurants, and theatre, the West End seethes with tourists and merry-makers. Oxford Street is the city's premier shopping corridor; the western half between Oxford Circus and Marble Arch is the classier end, with marquee department stores such as Selfridges and Marks & Spencer. Prim Trafalgar Square, dominated by the peerless National Gallery, has often been called London's focal point.

THE CITY   The City is where most of London's history happened. It's where Romans cheered gladiators. It's where the Great Fire raged. And, more recently, it's where the Deutsche Luftwaffe focused many of its nocturnal bombing raids, which is why you'll find so little evidence of the aforementioned events. Outside of working hours, the main thing you'll see in The City is your own reflection in the facade of corporate fortresses. Although this is where you'll find such priceless relics as the Tower of London, St Paul's Cathedral, the Tower Bridge, the Bank of England, and the Monument, many remnants are underfoot, since much of the spider web of lanes and streets dates back to the Roman period.

WESTMINSTER, INCLUDING ST JAMES'S   It's a district tourists mostly see by day. South of Trafalgar Square, you'll find regiments of robust government buildings but little in the way of hotels or food. Just a block east,

Covent Garden Market main entrance.

the area gives way to the proud riverside promenade of Victoria Embankment, overlooking the London Eye, and just a block west, to the greenery of St James's Park, in effect, Buckingham Palace's front yard. North of the park, the staid streets of St James's are even more exclusive than Mayfair's.

SOUTH BANK & SOUTHWARK   During Southwark's recent rehabilitation from a crumbling industrial district, a blighted power station became one of the world's greatest museums (the Tate Modern), The Bard's theatre was recreated (the Globe), and a sublime riverfront path replaced the coal lightermen's rotting piers. A dramatic showpiece (the National Theatre) anchors them. Now, the South Bank, which stretches from the London Eye east to Tower Bridge, has reclaimed its status as a pleasure garden, and its once-dank railway viaducts are filled with cafes, reasonable restaurants, and foodie heaven Borough Market.

KENSINGTON, KNIGHTSBRIDGE & EARL'S COURT   Here, one expensive neighborhood bleeds into another. South Kensington draws the most visitors to its grand museums, the V&A, the Natural History Museum, and the Science Museum; and Knightsbridge is where moneyed foreigners spend and brag—London now has the most billionaires in the world, nearly twice as many as New York or Moscow. Kensington Palace, at the Gardens' western end, is where Diana lived and it's the official London home of Prince William and Kate and their royal offspring.

[Fast FACTS] LONDON

Doctors   Ask your hotel first. Then try the G.P. (General Practitioner) finder at **www.nhs.uk**. North American members of the **International Association for Medical Assistance to Travelers** (IAMAT; www.iamat.org; © **716/754-4883,** or 416/652-0137 in Canada) can consult that organization for lists of local approved doctors. **Note:** U.S. and Canadian visitors who become ill while they're in London are eligible only for free *emergency* care. For other treatment, including follow-up care, you'll pay £60 to £150 just to see a physician.

Electricity   The current in Britain is 240 volts AC. Plugs have three squared pins.

Emergencies   The one-stop number for Britain is © **999**—that's for fire, police, and ambulances. It's free from any phone. Less urgent? Call 111.

Internet   Wi-Fi flows freely at pubs, cafes, museums, and nearly all hotels. Virgin Media (www.virginmedia.com/wifi) provides Wi-Fi in many Tube stations but not between them. Visitors can buy passes for £2 (1 day), £5 (1 week), or £15 (1 month).

Post Office   One of the most central locations is 1 block east of Trafalgar Square at 24/28 William IV St., WC2. It is generally open from 9am to 6pm and it is closed on Sundays.

Pharmacies   Every police station keeps a list of pharmacies (chemists) that are open 24 hours. Also try **Zafash,** a rare chemist that is open 24 hours, 233-235 Old Brompton Rd., SW5 (© **020/7373- 2798;** Tube: Earl's Court); and **Bliss,** open daily 9am to midnight, 5-6 Marble Arch, W1 (© **020/7723-6116;** Tube: Marble Arch).

About British Money

The British pound (£1), a small, chunky, gold-colored coin, is usually accepted in vending machines, so you can never have too many in your pocket. It's commonly called a "quid." Like money in America, Canada, and Australia, it's divided into 100 pennies (p)—the plural, "pence," is used to modify amounts over 1p. Pence come in 1p, 2p, 5p, 10p, 20p, and 50p coins. You'll see large £2 coins, too. Bills come in £5, £10, £20, and £50. Now and then, you'll receive notes printed by the Bank of Scotland; they're perfectly valid, but an increase in forgeries means some shops refuse them. Banks will exchange them.

Be quick when using ATMs. Retrieve your card immediately from ATM slots; many machines suck them in within 10 to 15 seconds, for security. Should that happen, you'll have to petition the bank to have it returned to you.

Tipping **Waiters** should receive 10% to 15% of the bill unless service is already included—*always* check the bill to see if service was already added, because traditions are changing. At pubs, tipping isn't customary unless you receive table service. Fine hotels may levy a service charge, but at the finest ones, grease the staff with a pound here and there. Staff at B&Bs and family-run hotels don't expect tips. Bartenders and chambermaids need not be tipped. There's no need to tip **taxicab drivers** but most people round up to the next £1, although a 10% to 15% tip is becoming increasingly standard.

EXPLORING LONDON

England has been a top dog for 500 years, and London is where it keeps its bark. Many of the world's finest treasures came here during the Empire and never left. In London, riches hide everywhere. The major attractions could occupy months of contemplation. But the sheer abundance of history and wealth—layer upon layer of it—means that London boasts dozens of exciting smaller sights, too. You could spend a lifetime seeing it all, so you'd better get started.

Pass on the London Pass

The heavily promoted **London Pass** (www.londonpass.com) gets you into a bevy of attractions for a fixed price (such as £52 a day or £71 for 2 days), but is unlikely to pay off in the small amount of time you're given to use it. Only the version that lasts 6 days (£116 adult, £80 child) would potentially pay off, but still only marginally and only if you don't take much time for meals.

Soho, Covent Garden & Nearby

The British Library ★★★ MUSEUM   One of the planet's most precious collections of books, maps, and manuscripts, the **Treasures of the British Library** are displayed in a climate-controlled suite of black cases and rich purple carpeting. The display changes, but it has included:

o Two of the four known copies of the **Magna Carta,** 800 years old in 2015.

London Attractions

0   1/2 mi
0   1/2 km

See "Southbank & The City" map, p. 91

London Navigation

THE CITY	Neighborhood
EC4	Post Code
CITY	Borough

London street signs usually list the post code and borough name. In general, "West End" destinations have a post code beginning with a W and "East End" destinations have a post code beginning with an E.

London Transportation

Bank ⊖	Underground Station
Camden Rd. ▣	British Rail Station
DLR	Docklands Light Rail

UNDERGROUND LINES

- Bakerloo
- Central
- Circle
- District
- East London
- Hammersmith & City
- Jubilee
- Metropolitan
- Northern
- Piccadilly
- Victoria
- Waterloo & City

Albert Memorial **2**	Liberty **16**
Apsley House **17**	London Zoo **8**
BBC Broadcasting House Tour **12**	Madame Tussauds **10**
	Museum of Childhood **32**
The British Library **27**	Natural History Museum **5**
Buckingham Palace (State Room Tour) **24**	Queen's Gallery **25**
Changing the Guard **23**	Ripley's Believe it or Not! **19**
The Charles Dickens Museum **30**	Royal Academy of Arts **18**
Churchill War Rooms **28**	Royal Albert Hall **3**
Clarence House **22**	Royal Mews **26**
"Eros" Statue **20**	Science Museum **4**
Fortnum & Mason **21**	Selfridges **14**
Geffrye Museum **31**	Sherlock Holmes Museum **9**
Handel House Museum **15**	Speakers' Corner **13**
Harrods **7**	V&A **6**
Kensington Palace **1**	Wallace Collection **11**
	Westminster Abbey **29**

- The Beatles' first lyric doodles: "A Hard Day's Night" on Julian Lennon's first birthday card (with a choo-choo on it) and "Strawberry Fields Forever," scratched on Lufthansa airline notepaper.

- The **Diamond Sutra,** the oldest known printed book, which was found in a Chinese cave in 1907 and was probably made by woodblock nearly 600 years before Europeans developed similar technology.

- Michelangelo's letter to his dad telling him he had finished the Sistine Chapel and pages from **Leonardo da Vinci's notebook,** in mirror writing.

- Music in the hand of Mozart, Handel, Beethoven, and Mendelssohn (*The Wedding March*)—you can listen to the final works on headphones.

The King's Library, some 85,000 tomes assembled by King George III, floats in a glassed-in central tower and forms the core of the collection. The hall contains the **Philatelic Exhibition,** 500 vertical drawers containing thousands of rare stamps.

96 Euston Rd. NW1. www.bl.uk. ✆ **01937/546-060.** Free. Mon and Wed–Fri 9:30am–6pm, Tues to 8pm, Sat 9:30am–5pm, Sun 11am–5pm. Tube: King's Cross St Pancras.

The British Museum ★★★ MUSEUM   Founded in 1753 and first opened in 1759 in a converted mansion, the British Museum is as much a monument to great craftsmanship as it is to the piracy carried out by 18th- and 19th-century Englishmen, who, on their trips abroad, plundered whatever goodies they could find and then told the bereft that the thievery was for their own good. Yet the exquisite taste of these English patriarchs is unquestionable, and now the British Museum may be the museum to beat all the rest. In fact, it's the top attraction in the country.

Holdings are grouped in numbered rooms by geography, with an emphasis on the Greek and Roman Empires, Europe, and Britain. Dominating the center of the glass-roofed **Great Court,** the round, cream-and-gold **Reading Room,** completed in 1857, was once part of the British Library. Patrons had to apply for tickets, and they included Lenin and Karl Marx, who developed their political theories here; other habitués included Bram Stoker, Sir Arthur Conan Doyle, and Virginia Woolf, who wrote upon entering "one stood under the vast dome, as if one were a thought in the huge bald forehead which is so splendidly encircled by a band of famous names." The Reading Room still houses some 25,000 books, but is usually closed to the public.

Consider renting a hand-held audio/video tablet (£5, both adult and kids' versions) that spotlights 200 of the best objects. From 10:30am to 3pm on weekends, the museum lends free kids' backpacks including

Interior, The British Museum.

discovery maps. The website also has free themed tour plans—useful because maps range £2 to £6 depending on the level of information you want. But don't miss:

- The museum's most famous, and most controversial, possessions are the so-called **Elgin Marbles,** gingerly referred to as **The Sculptures of the Parthenon** (rooms 18 and 19) to disguise imperialist provenance. These slab sculptures (called friezes and metopes), plus some life-size weathered statuary, once lined the pediment of the famous Parthenon atop Athens' Acropolis. They're laid out in the gallery in the approximate position in which they appeared on the Parthenon.

- Fragments of **sculptures from The Mausoleum at Halikarnassos,** one of the lost Seven Wonders of the Ancient World, loom in room 21.

- The pivotal **Rosetta Stone** (196 B.C.), in room 4, is what helped linguists crack hieroglyphics, and its importance to anthropology can't be exaggerated. Napoleon's soldiers found it in Egypt in 1799, but the British nabbed it in 1801.

- The eerie array of **Egyptian Mummies** in rooms 62, 63, and 64 petrify living children and on your visit, they'll probably be thronged as usual. In addition to the wizened, raisin-like corpses, there are painted coffins; and the hair and lung of the scribe Sutimose, dating to 1100 B.C.

- Kids also stare moon-eyed at crumpled, leather-faced **Lindow Man** in room 50; he was discovered, throat slit, in a Cheshire bog nearly 2,000 years after his brutal demise.

There's the **Great Court Restaurant** above the Reading Room that serves a full afternoon tea from 3pm for just £20—a bargain (© **020/7323-8990**).

Great Russell St., WC1. www.thebritishmuseum.org. ℭ **020/7323-8299.** Free. Sat–Thurs 10am–5:30pm and Fri 10am–8:30pm, closed New Year's Day, Good Friday, and Dec 24–26. Tube: Tottenham Court Road or Holborn or Russell Square.

The Charles Dickens Museum ★ MUSEUM   Although Dickens moved around a lot, his last remaining London home, which he rented for £80 a year when he was 30, is now his testament. A museum since 1925, and restored to a period look, these four floors don't exude many vibes from the old guy; after all, he departed in 1839 after staying less than 2 years. Still, his celebrity got a kick-start while he lived here: *Oliver Twist* and *Nicholas Nickleby,* arguably his biggest hits, were written while he was in residence, a short stroll from the Foundling Hospital for orphans. As you inspect his desk, his razor, bars from a prison where his spendthrift dad was locked up, an unpleasant realization sets in: Charles Dickens was a compelling character, but also a jerk—tough on his kids and unfaithfully cruel to his wife. The museum doesn't sugarcoat a complicated life.

48 Doughty St., WC1. www.dickensmuseum.com. ℭ **020/7405-2127.** £8 adults, £4 kids 6–16, £6 seniors/students. Daily 10am–5pm. Tube: Chancery Lane or Russell Square.

The Courtauld Institute of Art Gallery ★★★ MUSEUM   Art historians consider the Courtauld one of the most prestigious collections on earth. Its two-level selection is small but supreme, with several masterpieces you will instantly recognize. Among the winners are an early version of Manet's scandalous *Le Déjeuner sur l'herbe,* depicting a naked

Edouard Manet's "A Bar at the Folies-Bergère," The Courtauld Gallery.

woman picnicking with two clothed men, and the artist's *A Bar at the Folies-Bergère,* showing a melancholy barmaid standing in front of her disproportionate reflection. There are multiple Cézannes, Toulouse-Lautrecs, and Gauguins. Degas' *Two Dancers on a Stage* is popular, as is Van Gogh's *Self-Portrait with Bandaged Ear.* Especially rare is a completed Seurat, *Young Woman Powdering Herself,* which depicts his mistress in the act of dressing and initially included his own face in the frame on the wall—he painted over it with a vase of flowers to avoid ridicule. **Somerset House,** the museum's home, was once a naval center. The central courtyard has a grove of 55 ground-level fountains that delight small children, and it's the scene of both popular summer concerts and a winter ice rink, plus a cafe by the popular charcuterie-bakery Fernandez & Wells. The terrace overlooking the Thames can be enjoyed for free.

Somerset House, Strand, WC2. www.courtauld.ac.uk. ✆ **020/7848-2526.** Daily 10am–6pm, until 9pm one Thurs/month. £6 adults, £5 children/seniors/students; posted prices are higher and include a "voluntary donation." Tube: Temple.

London Transport Museum ★★ MUSEUM   It's hard to imagine London without its wheeled icons: the red double-decker bus, the black taxi, and the Tube are the best of their kind in the world and a draw for visitors. In this soaring Victorian-era hall, which takes about 2 hours to tour, their development and evolution are traced with impeccable technology and detail. Besides landmark vehicles, such as Number 23, a steam locomotive that powered the Underground in its most unpleasant days, there's also plenty of the system's famous Edwardian and Art Deco posters, many of which are so stunning they're art unto themselves—because of them, the gift shop, which doesn't require a ticket, is worth attention. Designers will appreciate the background on Johnston, the distinctive typeface created by Frank Pick in 1916 for the Underground, now considered London's unofficial font. You'll learn a great deal about the shifts in London life, and you'll likely feel a twinge of embarrassment about the state of your own town's public transportation. Kids run wild here, so adults who come to learn history will need a little patience.

Covent Garden, WC2. www.ltmuseum.co.uk. ✆ **020/7565-7298.** £16 adults, free for kids under 18. Sat–Thurs 10am–6pm, Fri 11am–6pm, last admission 45 min. before closing. Tube: Covent Garden.

National Gallery ★★★ MUSEUM   Few museums can compete with the strongest, widest collection of paintings in the world—one of every important style is on display, and it's almost always the best in that genre. There are 2,300 Western European works, which is plenty to divert you for as long as you can manage. As you enter via the main Portico Entrance, galleries imperceptibly surge through time in a clockwise arrangement. The best course is to start in the Sainsbury Wing (through room 9 or from Pall Mall East) and backtrack, which will order viewings more or less chronologically. At the basement Espresso Bar, use the

ArtStart computers to locate up to 6 works and to print out a free map to them. Among the many noteworthy holdings:

- Sandro Botticelli fell under the spell of the reformer Savonarola. He burned many of his finest paintings in the Bonfire of the Vanities and changed to an inferior style, so his best works are rare; **Venus and Mars** (1485, room 58), depicting the lovers reclining, is one of them.

- Michelangelo's **The Entombment** (around 1500, room C) is unfinished but powerful. The feminine figure in the red gown is now thought to be St John, but it's hard to know, since the artist favored masculine traits.

- Kids love Holbein's **The Ambassadors** (1533, room 4), full of symbolic riddles that refer to the guy on the left, and famous for a stretched image of a skull that can only be viewed in proper perspective from the side.

- Kids also love Quinten Massys' grotesque, porcine **An Old Woman** ("*The Ugly Duchess*"; 1513, room 65), thought to be a satire on ladies who try to look younger than they are, but possibly a woman suffering from a disease. Not so funny if it's the latter, hilarious if it's the former.

- George Stubbs' life-size portrait of rearing stallion **Whistlejacket** (room 34) stops everyone in their tracks; it was painted for its proud owner.

There's much more: George Seurat's almost-pointillist **Bathers at Asnieres** (1884, room 44), Van Gogh's **Sunflowers** (room 45, another in 46), Jan van Eyck's **The Arnolfini Portrait** (Sainsbury Wing, room 56), a mysterious but fabulously skillful depiction of light that dates to 1434, years ahead of its time. **Brueghels. Cézannes. Uccellos.** There's so much art here that you may want to go twice during your visit. Trafalgar Sq., WC2. www.nationalgallery.org.uk. ℂ **020/7747-2885.** Free. Sat–Thurs 10am–6pm and Fri 10am–9pm. Tube: Charing Cross or Leicester Square.

The National Portrait Gallery ★★★ MUSEUM Here, the names from your high school history textbook flower into flesh-and-blood people, and the accompanying biographies are so sublimely evocative (Samuel Johnson is described as "massive, ungainly, plagued with nervous tics") that subjects come alive. Take the escalator to the top and work your way down over about 2 hours. The oldest works (Tudors, Jacobeans, Elizabethans) come

It's Free!

The following attractions named in this guide charge no admission fees for their permanent collections. Not a shabby lineup!

The British Library; The British Museum; Museum of London; Museum of London Docklands; The National Gallery; National Maritime Museum; The National Portrait Gallery; The Natural History Museum; The Royal Observatory; The Science Museum; The Tate Britain; The Tate Modern; The V&A.

first, and you'll progress forward in time—adding photography when canvas fatigue sets in. One of the most instantly recognizable paintings is the **Ditchley portrait of Elizabeth I** (room 2), in which the queen's jeweled gown spreads like wings and Her Majesty firmly glares at the viewer under stormy skies. Right away, it becomes clear that many artists are slyly commenting on the disposition of their sitters. The troublesome **Henry VIII** is shown in several likenesses. One is a delicate 1537 paper cartoon by Hans Holbein

The National Portrait Gallery.

the Younger (for a mural at Whitehall—a rare survivor from that palace), in which the king suspiciously peers with flinty grey eyes—hinting at a shiftiness that all who knew him feared (room 1). One painting of **King Edward VI,** painted when he was 9, is executed in a distorted manner that requires it to be viewed from a hole on the right side of its case (room 1). You'll also find **George Washington** (he was born an Englishman, after all, room 14). In room 18, look for the sketch of **Jane Austen** by her sister Cassandra—friends said it stank. The **Brontë Sisters** appear together in an 1834 portrait found folded atop a cupboard in 1914; their brother Patrick, the artist, was painted out but his ghostly image is eerily reappearing (room 24).

Fortunately, the portraits don't stop when cameras were invented. The image of **Margaret Thatcher,** demure in a chair, makes the Iron Lady look sweet as your granny (room 32); she is faced down by Paul Emsley's warm oil-on-canvas of **Catherine, HRH The Duchess of Cambridge** (2012). The rooftop Portrait Restaurant has a breathtaking view taking in Nelson's Column and Big Ben's tower (✆ **020/7312-2490**).

St Martin's Place, WC2. www.npg.org.uk. ✆ **020/7312-2463.** Free. Sat–Wed 10am–6pm, Thurs–Fri 10am–9pm, last admission 45 min. before closing. Tube: Leicester Square.

Sir John Soane's Museum ★★ MUSEUM   These two town houses on the north side of Lincoln's Inn Fields are so overloaded with furniture, paintings, architectural decoration, and sculpture, that navigation is a

When he finished his legendary fountain in the middle of Piccadilly Circus in 1893, sculptor Alfred Gilbert thought the playful maritime-themed sculptures on its base would be celebrated. Audiences have minds of their own. They responded to the archer god on top. But they even got that bit of admiration wrong—they thought he represented Eros, god of erotic love, when Gilbert had actually intended Anteros, god of requited love. Today, even Piccadilly Circus isn't a circus (roundabout) anymore—it's an interchange—but the ceaseless tourist crowd photographing Gilbert's misunderstood masterpiece at least puts the circus back into Piccadilly. Gilbert's fabulous fountain is now dry and full of McDonald's wrappers, but his misidentified god, ironically the one who punishes mortals for failing to return love, nevertheless blesses the city as an icon.

challenge. The Georgian architect, noted for his egotistic neoclassicism (the Bank of England) as much as for his aesthetic materialism, bequeathed his home and its contents as a museum for "amateurs and students." His oddball abode, which his will decreed must be left precisely as it was on the day he died, is a melee of art history in which precious paintings and sculpture jostle for space like baubles in a junk shop. Ask to join a tour of the **Picture Room,** built in an 1823 expansion, so you can watch its hidden recesses be opened, revealing layer upon buried layer of works (such as William Hogarth's 8-painting *The Rake's Progress,* a documentary of dissolution), filed inside false walls. Look sharp for Canalettos (which often fetch £9 million at auction) and a J. M. W. Turner (ditto). You have to wonder how Soane could legally acquire antiquities such as the sarcophagus of Seti I, carved from translucent limestone, and you won't know because almost nothing is marked. Download one of three free MP3 tours to make sense of the untidiness. Or take a 1-hour tour (£10): Tues and Fri at 11:30am, Wed and Thurs at 3:30pm. Mostly, a visit reminds you of the unseemly way in which privileged Englishmen used to stuff their homes with classical art as a way of stocking up on a sense of righteousness—but that doesn't mean it's not wondrous.

12 Lincoln's Inn Fields, WC2. www.soane.org. © **020/7405-2107.** Free. Tues–Sat 10am–5pm, candlelit nights the first Tues of the month 6–9pm. Tube: Holborn.

Westminster & Nearby

The Banqueting House ★ HISTORIC SITE   The glorious palace of Whitehall was home to some of England's flashiest characters, including Henry VIII. In a wrenching loss for art and architecture—it burned down in 1698. But if you had to pick just one room to survive, it would have been the one that did, designed with Italianate Renaissance assurance by Inigo Jones. Completed in 1622, Henry never set foot in it; but another fateful king set his *last* foot in it: In 1649, Charles I walked onto the scaffold from a window that stood in the present-day staircase, and met his doom under an axe wielded by Cromwell's republicans. The reason to come here is to gape at the nine grandiose ceiling murals by Peter Paul Rubens in which the king is portrayed as a god. They give you a bold clue as to why the rabble would want to see His Highness brought low. Whitehall at Horseguards Ave., SW1. www.hrp.org.uk. ℭ **084/4482-7777.** £6 adults, children under 16 free, £5 seniors/students, including audio tour. Posted rates are higher and include a "voluntary donation." Daily 10am–5pm. Tube: Charing Cross or Westminster.

Buckingham Palace ★★ HISTORIC SITE   If you were to fall asleep tonight and wake up inside one of the **State Rooms,** you'd never guess where you were. Is it opulent? No question. But if ever gilding, teardrop chandeliers, 18th-century portraits, and ceremonial halls could be considered standard-issue, Buckingham Palace is your basic palace. Queen Elizabeth's mild tastes—call it "respectable decadence" of yellows and creams and pleasant floral arrangements, thank you very much—is partly the reason. Remember, too, that much of this palace was built or remodeled in the 1800s—not so long ago in the scheme of things—and that the Queen considers Windsor to be her real home. All tickets are timed and include an audio tour that rushes you around too quickly. The route threads through the public and ceremonial rooms at the back of the palace. If you want to see highlights of the formal gardens, that's another £8. Highlights include the 50m-long (164-ft.) **Picture Gallery** filled mostly with works amassed by George IV, an obsessive collector; the 14m-tall (46-ft.) **Ballroom,** where the Queen confers knighthoods; the parquet-floored **Music Room,** unaltered since John Nash decorated it in 1831, where the Queen's three eldest children were baptized in water brought from the River Jordan; and a stroll through the thick **Garden** in the back yard. It's definitely worth seeing—how often can you toodle around the spare rooms in a Queen's house, inspecting artwork given as gifts by some of history's most prominent names? But it's no Versailles. If you're in London and spot her standard of red, gold, and blue flying above, you'll at least know the Queen is home. (If it's the Union Jack, she's gone.) So near, yet so far. Buckingham Palace Rd., SW1. www.royalcollection.org.uk. ℭ **020/7766-7300.** £21 adults, £12 children 5–16, £19 seniors/students. Apr, late July to late Aug daily 9:30am–7:30pm, Sept 9:30am–6:30pm, last admission 2 hr. 15 min. before closing. Tube: Victoria or Green Park.

Churchill War Rooms ★★★ MUSEUM/HISTORIC SITE   One of London's most fascinating museums is the secret command center used by Winston Churchill and his staff during the most harrowing moments of World War II, when it looked like England might become German. Here, in the cellar of the Treasury building, practically next door to 10 Downing Street, the core of the British government hunkered down where one errant bomb could have incinerated the lot of them. When the War ended, the bunker was abandoned, but everything was left just as it was in August 1945, and when it was time to make it a museum, everything was intact—from pushpins tracing convoy movements on yellowed world maps to rationed sugar cubes hidden in the back of a desk drawer. Midway through, you disappear into the **Churchill Museum,** the most cutting-edge biographical museum open at this moment. Exhaustively displaying every conceivable facet of his life (his bowtie, his bowler hat, and even the original front door to 10 Downing Street), it covers the exalted statesman's life from entitled birth through his antics as a journalist in South Africa (where he escaped a kidnapping and became a national hero), to, of course, his years as prime minister. You even learn his favorite cigar (Romeo y Julieta) and brandy (Hine). The entire museum is atwitter with multimedia displays, but the centerpiece will blow you away: a 15m-long (50-ft.) Lifeline Interactive table, that looks like a long file cabinet and covers every month of Churchill's life. Touch a date, and a projected file "opens" with rare documents, photos, or, for critical dates in history, animated Easter eggs that temporarily consume the entire table (select the original Armistice Day or the *Titanic* sinking to see what we mean).

Clive Steps, King Charles St., SW1. www.iwm.org.uk. © **020/7930-6961.** £16 adults, £9 kids 5–15, £13 seniors/students; posted prices are higher and include a "voluntary donation." Daily 9:30am–6pm, last admission 5pm. Tube: Westminster.

Clarence House ★ HISTORIC SITE   The Queen dictates who lives at which palace, and she herself lived at this four-story mansion, a part of St James's Palace, before she took the throne. Her mother dwelled here

Interior, Churchill War Rooms.

for nearly half a century until her 2002 death at age 101, and now it's chez Charles and Camilla. Charles, having a keener sense of public relations than any royal before him, decided to open the house, where royals have lived since 1827, during the summer months when the family is away. You won't get to poke around the Prince's medicine cabinet since you can only see the ground floor, which still feels like an old lady's parlor. Clarence is more like a grand townhouse than a mansion fit for a king and that reflects the Windsors' homey, cluttered style, heavy on paintings of horses and light on gilding and glitter.

Stableyard Rd., SW1. www.royalcollection.org.uk. © **020/7766-7303.** £10 adults/ seniors/students, £6 children 5–16. Daily, Aug Mon–Fri 10am–4pm, Sat–Sun 10am– 5pm, last admission 4:30pm. Tube: Green Park.

Hayward Gallery ★ MUSEUM   The principal exhibition space of the Southbank Centre, a vital non-profit arts center, hosts terrific blockbuster shows, usually about £11, which have included Ansel Adams, Roy Lichtenstein, 1920s Surrealism, and modern African art. Some smaller exhibits are free, as are frequent music events at its cafe/bar, Concrete. There are major plans to overhaul the space—but no one can agree into just what. For now, don't miss the Undercroft, a neglected concrete space under the building along the Thames, which, for years, skateboarders have commanded as a landmark in their sport.

South Bank Centre, Belvedere Rd., SE1. www.southbankcentre.org.uk. © **087/1663-2501.** Mon noon–6pm, Tues–Wed and Sat–Sun 10am–6pm, Thurs–Fri 10am–8pm. Tube: Waterloo.

HMS *Belfast* ★ MUSEUM   You'll feel as if the powerful 1938 warship, upon being retired from service in 1965, was simply motored to the dock wearing its grey patchwork camouflage livery and instantly opened as an attraction. Nearly everything, down to the checked flooring and decaying cables, is exactly as it was, making the boat a fascinating snapshot of mid-century maritime technology. Authenticity also makes it a devil to navigate, especially if you have any bags with you—sorry, no cloakrooms, sailor. Getting around her various decks, engine rooms, and hatches requires dexterity and a well-calibrated inner compass. You can roam as you wish, visiting every cubby of the ship from kitchen to bridge, all the while being thankful that it wasn't you who was chasing German cruisers (the *Belfast* sank the *Scharnhorst*) and backing up the D-Day invasion in this tough tin can. The price is too high for those with a lukewarm interest, but the new Upper Deck bar, atop the visitor center, has stellar views of the Tower of London and Tower Bridge—and an afternoon champagne cream tea that costs just £14. Thanks, World War II!

Morgan's Lane, Tooley St., SE1. www.iwm.org.uk. © **020/7940-6300.** £14 adults, free for children under 16, £11 seniors/students; posted prices are higher and include a "voluntary donation." Mar–Oct daily 10am–6pm, Nov–Feb daily 10am– 5pm, last admission 1 hr. before closing. Tube: London Bridge.

Houses of Parliament ★★ LANDMARK   Luckily, the nation allows you to tour a dozen stately halls and even to wander through its vaunted House of Lords and House of Commons when they're not in session. Choose a 100-minute guided group, and that presents the usual issues of audibility and pace, or take it easy with the new 2-hour audio guide (and eavesdrop on groups whenever you want). Massive Westminster Hall, one of the world's most precious spaces and a UNESCO World Heritage Site, was built in 1097 by William Rufus, son of William the Conqueror. Richard II commissioned its oak hammer-beam ceiling before he was deposed in the 1390s. Charles I, William Wallace, Sir Thomas More, and Guy Fawkes were all condemned in it, monarchs lie in state in it—and your role in it is to pick up your audio tour.

The rest of the Palace is roughly divided into three areas: those for the House of Lords (whose members inherit seats, done in rose with an unbelievable gilt sitting area where Queen Victoria would preside on designated occasions); the House of Commons (by far the most powerful, elected by the people, but plainer, with seats of blue-green under a hanging forest of microphones); and some flabbergasting lobbies, sitting rooms, and the "Robing Room" (golds, browns, burgundies), which the Sovereign flits through when she shows up once a year to kick off sessions. You walk right onto the floor of both Houses. Many delicious details are elucidated, from the knock-marks on the Commons door made by the Crown's emissary, the Black Rod, to the line in the carpet members may not cross when in the throes of vigorous debates. Frustratingly, the Elizabeth Tower (1859) beside the Houses—better known as

The River Thames flows past Big Ben and the Houses of Parliament.

Ritual Abuse

I'm only telling you this because I love you: **Changing the Guard** (Buckingham Palace; www.royal.gov.uk; free; 11:30am daily in May–July, and every other day in other months, cancelled in heavy rain; Tube: St James's Park, Victoria, or Green Park), sometimes called Guard Mounting, is an underwhelming use of 40 minutes of your time. Arrive at Buckingham Palace at least 45 minutes ahead if you don't want to face the backs of other tourists. A marching band advances from Birdcage Walk (often, playing themes from *Star Wars, West Side Story,* or ABBA—so much for traditional English customs!), then members of the Queen's Life Guard—two if the Queen's away, three or four if she's in—do a change around their sentry boxes. And that's it, give or take additional prancing.

Guards patrol all day, without crowds, at both Buckingham Palace and at Horse Guards Arch on Whitehall (which does its own, un-crowded change at 11am, 10am Sun). Or park yourself at **Wellington Barracks,** just east of the Palace along Birdcage Walk, by 11am, and catch the Inspection of the Guard that happens before the same guards march over to the Palace for the main event. Then use the day's golden hours for something less touristy.

Big Ben—is only open to U.K. residents. Booking House tours ahead is advisable, but you can try your luck at the ticket office next to the Jewel Tower, across the street.

Bridge St. and Parliament Sq., SW1. www.parliament.uk/visiting. ☎ **020/7219-4114.** Most Saturdays and Mon–Sat in Aug: 9am–4:15pm, but always check ahead. £25 adults, £20 seniors/students, £10 children 5–15, children under 5 free. Reservations recommended. Tube: Westminster.

Imperial War Museum London ★★ MUSEUM   One of London's unexpectedly gripping museums has a deceptive name. It's not just for military buffs, and it's no gun-fondling armory. Instead of merely showcasing implements of death, the latest tenant of the commodious former mental hospital known as Bedlam takes great care to share the sensations, feelings, and moods of soldiers and civilians caught in past conflicts. In addition to easy-to-grasp background on major wars, the museum balances tanks and planes with intimate storytelling that unravels propaganda and connects you to the human experience. In 2014, in time for the centenary of World War I, the IWM was expensively renovated into a remarkably modern facility, making it even more worth a trip.

Lambeth Rd., SE1. www.iwm.org.uk. ☎ **020/7416-5000.** Free. Daily 10am–6pm. Tube: Lambeth North or Elephant & Castle.

London Eye ★★★ OBSERVATIONAL WHEEL   Erected in 1999 as the Millennium Wheel, it rises above everything in this part of the city—at 135m (443 ft.), it's 1½ times taller than the Statue of Liberty. The 30-minute ride above the Thames affords an unmatched and unobstructed perspective on the prime tourist territory. On a clear day, you can see to Windsor, but even on an average day, the entire West End bows down before you. The whirl is adulterated by a lame "4D Experience" movie (the camera moves through London while a fan blows in your face) but that's included in the price. Each of the 32 enclosed capsules, which accommodate up to 28 people at once, is climate-controlled and rotates so gradually that it's easy to forget you're moving—which means it will upset only the desperately height-averse. By the time you reach the top, you'll have true 360-degree views unobstructed by the support frame. The ticket queue often looks positively wicked, but it moves quickly, chewing through 15,000 riders a day, 800 per revolution. *Tip:* Booking on the Web saves waiting in the ticketing queues, and it gives other advantages: You can pick your time ahead and you'll save 10% off the price listed below. There's a host of

The London Eye.

ticket options—you can pay more to go anytime you want rather than stick to a reservation, but a standard ticket satisfies most needs.

Riverside Building, County Hall, SE1. www.londoneye.com. ✆ **0871/781-3000.** £22 adults, £16 children 4–15, free under 4, £19 seniors. Jan–Mar and Sept–Dec 10am–8:30pm, Apr–Jun to 9pm, Jul–Aug to 9:30pm. Tube: Waterloo or Westminster.

Shakespeare's Globe ★ MUSEUM/LANDMARK A painstaking recreation of an outdoor Elizabethan theatre, it tends to bewitch fans of history and theatre, but it can put all others to sleep. Arrive early since the timed 40-minute tours fill up. Get a bad time, and you'll be stuck waiting for far too long in the UnderGlobe, the well-crafted but exhaustible exhibition about Elizabethan theatre. Also avoid matinee days, since tours don't run during performances. The open-air theatre was made using only Elizabethan technology such as saws, oak framing, pegs, and plaster panels mixed with goat's hair (the original recipe called for cow's hair, but the breed they needed is now extinct). The first Globe burned down when a cannon fired during a performance caused its thatched roof to catch fire. It took a special act of Parliament, plus plenty of hidden sprinkler systems, to permit the construction of the first thatched roof in London since the Great Fire. The original theatre was the same size (and stood just to the southeast), but it crammed 3,000 luckless souls. Today, just 1,600 are admitted for performances. If you'd like to see the location of the **Rose Theatre,** a true Shakespeare original, go around the corner to 56 Park St., where its foundations, discovered in 1989 and now squatted over by a modern office building, are open for visitors on Saturdays from 10am to 5pm (www.rosetheatre.org.uk; ℂ 020/7261-9565; free).

21 New Globe Walk, SE1. www.shakespearesglobe.com. ℂ **020/7401-9919.** £14 adults, £8 children 5–15, £12 seniors, £11 students. Daily early Oct to early Apr 9:30am–5pm, late Apr to early Oct 9am–5pm. Tube: London Bridge.

Tate Britain ★ MUSEUM   Tourists often wonder about the difference between the Tate Modern and this, its sister upstream on the Thames. Well, the Modern is for contemporary art of any origin, and the Britain, besides its calmer and more civilized affect, is mostly for British-made art made after 1500. Shifting objectives consistently rotate beloved paintings into storage, a frustrating habit with Tate, but some masterpieces can be relied upon. J. M. W. Turner's trenchant *The Field of Waterloo* (room 1810) was painted in 1818, 3 years after the battle; its shadowy piles of corpses, and of bereaved family members searching them, made viewers question his patriotism. The oil-on-canvas *Carnation, Lily, Lily, Rose* (1840) is by another American who settled in London, John Singer Sargent, and it depicts children holding paper lanterns so luminous that when it was first exhibited in 1887, its worth was instantly recognized and it was purchased for the nation. John Everett

Museums: After Hours

Many attractions offer extended opening times for evening viewing. Often, extra inducements are tossed in, such as wine and sketch classes at the National Portrait Gallery and DJs at the V&A. These are the major "Lates" events that can really free up your daytime touring to include more sights:

Attraction Late Opening	
British Museum (p. 66)	Friday to 8:30pm
Courtauld Gallery (p. 68)	Thursday to 9pm (once a month)
Handel House Museum (p. 83)	Thursday to 8pm
Hayward Gallery (p. 75)	Thursday and Friday to 8pm
London Zoo (p. 108)	Friday to 10pm (selected nights)
National Gallery (p. 69)	Friday to 9pm
National Portrait Gallery (p. 70)	Thursday and Friday to 9pm
Natural History Museum (p. 86)	Friday to 10:30pm (last of month)
Royal Academy (p. 83)	Friday to 10pm
Science Museum (p. 88)	Wednesday to 10pm (last of month)
Sir John Soane's Museum (p. 71)	Tuesday to 9pm (first of month)
Tate Britain (see above)	Friday to 10pm (once bi-monthly)
Tate Modern (p. 93)	Friday and Saturday to 10pm
Victoria & Albert Museum (p. 88)	Friday to 10pm (last of month)

Millais' depiction of a drowning **Ophelia** (1840) is also considered a treasure; the artist painted the plants in the summer so he'd get them right and waited until winter to paint his model, a hat-shop girl, in a tub of water. Naturally, she caught a severe cold (he paid for her doctor's bill after her father threatened to sue). Check out the sculptures, too, including forms by **Henry Moore** and Barbara Hepworth. But the crowning attraction here is the **Turner Galleries,** with their expansive collection. J. M. W. Turner (1775–1851), the son of a Covent Garden barber, was a master of landscapes lit by misty, perpetual sunrise, and his paintings testify to both his undying popularity and his British tendency to convey information purely by implication.

Millbank, SW1. www.tate.org.uk/britain. © **020/7887-8888.** Free. Daily 10am–6pm. Tube: Pimlico.

View from the Shard ★ OBSERVATION DECK   The Shard, the tallest building in Europe (but not even in the top 50 worldwide), has an extremely expensive observation deck with timed tickets. The jagged 306m-tall (1,016-ft.) tower doesn't exactly fit in with its neighbors. Signs work hard to incessantly remind you how big it is. Even its prices are bigger: souvenir photos cost £25. After two ear-popping fast elevator rides, you emerge 244m (800 ft.) up to some weird angel-like synth music and vertiginous floor-to-ceiling windows far, far over the city—so far that after the initial impression, casual visitors aren't likely to discern most of what they're seeing. A few levels up, there's a second, half-outdoor level, shielded at body-level from the elements. There's no seating (although staff will fetch a folding chair if you need one), no restaurant, and no washrooms, but you can spend as much time up here as you want. There is one novel addition: Point a "digital telescope" in the distance, and the attached screen reveals the same view at different times of day. The unblinking truth? The London Eye is more memorable.

Joiner St., SE1. www.theviewfromtheshard.com. © **0844/499-7111.** £30 adults, £24 kids 4–15, £5 discount booked 24 hr. ahead. Summer: daily 10am–10pm; Winter: Sun–Wed 10am–7pm, Thurs–Sat 10am–10pm. Tube: London Bridge.

Westminster Abbey ★★★ HISTORIC SITE   If you have to pick just one church to see in London—nay, one church in the entire *world*—this is the one. The echoes of history are mind-blowing: The current building dates from the 1200s, but it was part of a monastery dating to at least 960. Every English monarch since 1066 has been crowned here (with three minor exceptions: Edward V, Edward VIII, and possibly Mary I). Seventeen monarchs are interred here (their deaths date from 1066–1760), as are dozens of great writers and artists. Kate and William married here, and he will be crowned here. A visit should take about 3 hours and should begin early, since entry

The High Altar at Westminster Abbey.

lines are excruciating. Unlike St Paul's Cathedral, which has an airy, stately beauty, the much smaller Westminster is more like time's attic, packed with artifacts, memorials, tombs and shrines. Take your time and don't get swept along in the current of visitors; there are stories to be told in every square meter of this place.

Inside the sanctuary, tourists are corralled clockwise from the North Transept. The royal tombs are clustered in the first half of the route, in the region of the High Altar, where coronations and funerals are conducted. The most famous rulers of all time are truly *here*—not in story, but in body, a few inches away behind marble slabs. Some are stashed in cozy side chapels (which once held medieval shrines before Cromwellians bashed them to pieces during the Reformation), but the oldest are on the sanctuary side of the ambulatory (aisle). The executed **Mary Queen of Scots** was belatedly given a crypt equal to that of her rival, **Elizabeth I,** by Mary's son **James I,** who gave himself only a marker for his own tomb beneath **Henry VII**'s elaborate resting place. James I's daughter Sophia, who died aged 3 days, has a creepy bassinet sarcophagus in the Lady Chapel.

The South Transept is **Poet's Corner,** where Britain's great writers are honored. You'll see many plaques, but most (Shakespeare, Austen, Wilde, the Brontës) are merely memorials. The biggest names who truly lie underfoot are Robert Browning, Geoffrey Chaucer (he was placed here first, starting the trend), Charles Dickens, Thomas Hardy (buried without his heart), John Gay, Rudyard Kipling, Dr. Samuel Johnson, Laurence Olivier, and Alfred Lord Tennyson. Ben

Jonson is commemorated here, but is buried in the Nave near Isaac Newton and Charles Darwin.

Now for a few Abbey secrets:

- That oak seat between the Sanctuary and the Confessors' Chapel, near the tomb of Henry V, is the **Coronation Chair.** Unbelievably, every English monarch since 1308 has been crowned on this excruciating-looking throne. The slot under the seat is for the 152kg (336-lb.) Stone of Scone, a central part of Irish, Scottish, and English coronations since at least 700 B.C. After spending 7 centuries in the Abbey (except for when Scottish nationalists stole it for 4 months in late 1950), the Stone was returned to Scotland in 1996, where it's on view at Edinburgh Castle. It will return for every future coronation.

- **Oliver Cromwell,** who overthrew the monarchy and ran England as a republic, was buried with honors behind the High Altar in 1658. Three years later, after the monarchy was restored, his corpse was dug up, hanged, decapitated, the body tossed into a common grave, and its head put on display outside the Abbey. Cromwell's daughter, who died young, was mercifully allowed to remain buried in the Abbey.

- The **Quire** is where the choir sings; it comprises about 12 men and 30 or so boys who are educated at the adjoining Westminster Choir School, the last of its type in the world. The wooden stalls are so delicate they're dusted using vacuum cleaners.

The door to the **Chapter House** was made between 924 and 1030 and is Britain's oldest-known door. The Abbey's oft-overlooked **Museum,** in a vaulted undercroft, contains some astounding treasures, including **Edward III's death mask** (thought to be the oldest of its kind in Europe; it's made of walnut and doesn't ignore his facial droop, which resulted from a stroke), **ancient jewelry** "found in graves" (translation: pried from skeletons), the **fake Crown Jewels** used for coronation rehearsals, 14th-century leather shoes and Roman tiles unearthed on the grounds, and the fateful **Essex Ring,** which Elizabeth I gave to her confidant Robert Devereux, telling him to send it if he needed her. He tried to, but his enemies intercepted it, and he was beheaded at the Tower in 1601. Oops.

Next door, pop into **St Margaret's Chapel** (free), which the monks built in 1523 so they'd be left alone in peace. The Germans didn't comply: Some southern windows were destroyed by a bomb and were replaced by plain glass, and in addition to damage to the north wall, Pew 3 remains charred.

Broad Sanctuary, SW1. www.westminster-abbey.org. ✆ **020/7222-5152.** £18 adults, £8 children 11–18, £15 seniors/students, free for children under 11. Generally open Mon–Tues and Thurs–Fri 9:30am–4:30pm, Wed 9:30am–7pm, Sat 9:30am–2:30pm, last admission 1 hr. before closing, closed Sun. for worship. Check ahead for closures. Tube: Westminster.

Marylebone & Mayfair

BBC Broadcasting House Tour ★★ MUSEUM In 2014, the Beeb began admitting tourists to its lavish, newly renovated nerve center for news and radio. You may not recognize many of the references to the programs that emanate from here, but the scope of the 8-story-high active newsroom (some 6,000 people work in the building, many in 12-hour shifts) and the histories of the older studios such as Radio Theatre are transfixing. A highlight is the old Broadcasting House, from which Winston Churchill made his "we shall fight on the beaches" speech and de Gaulle broadcast his resistance movement. You can also apply for tickets to tapings on the BBC website. There's a small kiosk for BBC-themed trinkets, and *Dr. Who* fans, rejoice: You can take pictures beside a Tardis at the tour's starting point. At night, look up at the illuminated column on the roof—it shoots a beam into the sky at 10pm, during the nightly news, to commemorate slain journalists.

Portland Place, W1. www.bbc.co.uk/tours. ℗ **0370/901-1227.** £14 adult, £12 seniors, £11 students, £9 kids aged 9–15, no kids under 9, no same-day bookings. Daily 10am–6pm. Tube: Oxford Circus.

The Handel House Museum ★ MUSEUM/HISTORIC SITE Here's a pleasant *Messiah* complex. This Mayfair building, the German-born composer's home from 1723 to his death in 1759, has lived many lives—before the museum's 2001 opening, conservators chipped 28 layers of paint off the interior walls to uncover the original grey color. You'll see a 15-minute video on Handel's life, and then move on, often attended by old dears serving as volunteers, to see the few humble rooms. You're best off coming during one of the house's many concerts, held every week or so in a plain recital room (£7–£10). Handel fans should also investigate the composer's collection at the Foundling Museum, where he was a crucial patron.

25 Brook St., W1. www.handelhouse.org. ℗ **020/7495-1685.** £7 adults, £2 kids ages 5–16 except Sat–Sun (free), £6 seniors/students. Tues–Wed and Fri–Sat 10am–6pm, Thurs 10am–8pm, Sun noon–6pm. Tube: Bond Street.

Royal Academy of Arts ★★ MUSEUM Britain's first art school was founded in 1768 and relocated here to Burlington House, a Palladian-style mansion that now has a splendid courtyard in which to enjoy a coffee and an exclusive new restaurant, the Keeper's House. A few of its 18th-century state rooms, the six John Madejski Fine Rooms, can be seen on tours. (Charles Darwin's *Origin of the Species* papers were delivered for the first time in the Reynolds Room on July 1, 1858.) The meat, really, is on the third floor. First, that's where to find Michelangelo's only marble sculpture in Britain, an unfinished circular relief of Mary with the babies Jesus and John. The biggest event is the annual **Summer Exhibition,** which since the late 1700s has displayed the best works, submitted anonymously; careers have been made by it. Don't miss the wooden red

"Phone Box No. 1" tucked behind the front gate—it was the 1924 proto-type for what we now recognize as an international icon.

Burlington House, Piccadilly, W1. www.royalacademy.org.uk. ℰ **020/7300-8000.** Free. Sat–Thurs 10am–6pm, Fri 10am–10pm, last admission 30 min. before closing. John Madejski Fine Rooms by free tour only: Tues–Fri 1pm, Wed–Fri also at 3pm, Sat 11:30am. Tube: Piccadilly Circus or Green Park.

Speakers' Corner ★ LANDMARK   Near the northeast corner of Hyde Park, where Edgware Road meets Bayswater Road, Londoners of yore congregated for public executions. By the early 1800s, the gathered crowds were jeering at hangings instead of cheering them, and the locale's reputation for public outcry became entrenched. Laborers and suffragettes once fomented social change here, but these days, you're more likely to encounter a rogues' gallery of kooks and idealists. Anyone can show up, always on Sunday mornings after 7am, with a soapbox (or, these days, a stepladder), plus an axe to grind, and orate about anything from Muslim relations to the superiority of 1970s disco. In true British style, most speakers refrain from profanity. Even the heckling is usually polite. "Communists, violent racists, vegetarians," reported Arthur Frommer in 1957. "They undergo the finest heckling in the world, a vicious repartee . . . ." The blather continues until late afternoon.

Sundays starting at 7am. Tube: Marble Arch, exits 4, 5, 8, or 9.

The Wallace Collection ★★★ MUSEUM   A little bit V&A (decorative arts and furniture), a little bit National Gallery (paintings and portraits), but with a boutique French flair, the Wallace celebrates fine living in an extravagant 19th-century city mansion, the former Hertford House. Rooms drip with chandeliers, clocks, suits of armor, and furniture, usually of royal provenance, and there's not a clunker among the paintings. While other museums were stocking up on Renaissance works, the Wallaces, visionaries of sorts, were buying 17th-century and 18th-century artists for cheap. You might recognize Jean-Honoré Fragonard's *The Swing* (Oval Drawing Room), showing a maiden kicking her slipper to her suitor below. Peter Paul Rubens' *The Rainbow Landscape* is also here, as is the world's most complete room of furniture belonging to Marie-Antoinette. Thomas Gainsborough's *Mrs. Robinson 'Perdita'* (West Room) depicts the sloe-eyed actress in mid-affair with the Prince of Wales; she holds a token of his love, a miniature portrait, in her right hand. Be in the Ground Floor State Rooms at the top of the hour, when a chorus of golden musical clocks announce midday direct from the 1700s. Kids should grab a free trail map, which leads them to the most attention-holding works. Though the lovely Wallace Restaurant, in the covered courtyard, has stupidly high prices, its afternoon tea is a reasonable £15.

Hertford House, Manchester Sq., W1. www.wallacecollection.org. ℰ **020/7563-9500.** Free. Daily 10am–5pm. Tube: Bond Street.

Kensington

Albert Memorial ★ LANDMARK   Albert, Queen Victoria's German-born husband (and, um, first cousin), was a passionate supporter of the arts who piloted Britain from one dazzling creative triumph to another. But when he died suddenly of typhoid (some say Crohn's disease) in 1861 at age 42, the devastated Queen abruptly withdrew from the gaiety and remained in mourning until her death in 1901, shaping the Victorian mentality. She arranged for this astounding spire—part bombast, part elegy—to be erected in 1872 opposite the concert hall he spearheaded. Some of its nearly 200 figures represent the continents and the sciences, and some, higher up, represent angels and virtues. It's Victorian high-mindedness in stone. At the center, as if on an altar, is Albert himself, gleaming in gold. Tours go at 2 and 3pm on the first Sunday of each month, March to December (© **020/7936-2568,** no reservations required; £7).

Kensington Gardens. Tube: South Kensington.

Apsley House ★★ MUSEUM   This is how you'd be rewarded if you became a national war hero: You got Hyde Park as a backyard. In 1815, Arthur Wellesley defeated Napoleon and became the Duke of Wellington and later, prime minister. The mansion, still in the family (they maintain private rooms), is filled with splendid thank-you gifts showered upon him by grateful nations, including a thousand-piece silver set from the Portuguese court, but he never seemed to get his nemesis off his mind. Under the grand staircase stands a colossal nude statue of Napoleon that the little emperor despised; the Duke cherished it as a token of victory. Apsley's supreme art stash, which was largely looted by the French from the Spanish royal family and never went home, includes a few Jan Brueghel the Elders, Diego Velázquez's virtuosic *The Waterseller of Seville*, and Correggio's *The Agony in the Garden*. The Duke and his best friend lived here together after their wives died, and the whiff of faded masculine glory pervades like cigar smoke. In other circumstances, the Duke and Napoleon, who both liked fancy finery and fancier egos, would have been buddies. If you're also visiting Wellington Arch (see below), a joint ticket will save about £3.

149 Piccadilly. www.english-heritage.org.uk. © **0870/333-1181.** £7 adults, £4 children, £6 seniors/students, including an audio tour. Apr–Oct Wed–Sun 11am–5pm, Nov–Mar Wed–Sun 11am–4pm. Tube: Hyde Park Corner.

Kensington Palace ★ HISTORIC SITE   Most people know it as the place where Lady Diana raised Princes William and Harry with Prince Charles from 1984 to 1996, but now it's where Prince William, Kate, George and infant Charlotte live when in London. It has been a royal domicile since 1689, when William and Mary took control of an existing home (then in the country, far from town, which inflamed William's asthma) and made it theirs. Handsome and haughty, with none of the symmetry that defined later English tastes, it's not as ostentatious as you might expect. The venerable palace was stripped of a sense of import by a recent renovation and now it's a spook house for art snobs.

The King's Apartments, pegged to King George III and Queen Caroline, is explained to visitors not with a detailed historical dossier but with a scratch-and-sniff guide to odors that might have filled the palace once—kids love such sensationalism, and the costumed characters wandering about, but anyone who can reach the pedals knows it's all style over substance. Queen Victoria has her own section, but rather than teaching visitors what enabled a girl of 18 to rise to successfully control the most powerful empire in the world, she is shown in terms of gender roles: as a good girl, a loving wife, and a grieving widow. One room draped in black leads you to believe Prince Albert died in it, but no, he died at Windsor. Thankfully, the walk-through still includes the magnificent King's Staircase, lined with delicate canvas panels; the staircase is considered so precious that it was only opened to the public in 2004, 105 years after the rest of the palace first accepted sightseers. Also, in the Gallery there's a working Anemoscope, which has told the outside wind direction since 1694, and a map of the world as known in that year. You'll also see gowns worn by HM the Queen, Diana, and Princess Margaret, who also lived here. If you're short on time, the Palace is no longer a must-see.

Kensington Gardens, W8. www.hrp.org.uk. ✆ **084/4482-7777.** £15 adults, children under 16 free, £12 seniors/students including audio tour; posted prices are higher and include "voluntary donation." Mar–Oct daily 10am–6pm, Nov–Feb daily 10am–5pm, last admission 1 hr. before closing. Tube: High Street Kensington or Queensway.

Natural History Museum ★★ MUSEUM The commodious NHM, which attracts 5.3 million visitors a year, is a true blockbuster museum and it's good for several hours' wander, but you'll have plenty of company. In all ways, it's a zoo. You get a hall of dinosaur bones, a taxidermist's menagerie, and case after case of stuffed goners. Mostly, you'll encounter the wildest creatures of all: lurching, wailing, scampering children in all their varieties. On weekends and school holidays the outdoor queue can be an hour long, so go at opening and enter through Exhibition Road for lighter crowds. The trove is rich: At the top of the stairs, the **Treasures** gallery holds such historically meaningful stuff as a dodo skeleton and Britain's only moon rock. The pretend kitchen full of hiding places for insects and **Creepy Crawlies** (the **Green Zone**) is a longtime visitor favorite, as is the **Red Zone** (the Earth Galleries), anchored by a toned-down, ride-along mock-up of a Japanese supermarket jolted by the 1995 Kobe earthquake. Even the dinosaurs (in the Blue Zone) are supplemented by scary robotic estimations of how they sounded and moved. The **Darwin Centre's** Cocoon looks like a seven-story egg laid in the back atrium; hidden inside are some 20 million bottled specimens

The Natural History Museum.

(including those that came back on the *Beagle*) on 27km (17 miles) of shelves. The cathedral-like 1880 Victorian building is an unforgettable landmark. Its columns crawl with carved monkeys clinging, and plants creep across ceiling panels. All that and the requisite ceiling whale.

Cromwell Rd., SW7. www.nhm.ac.uk. © **020/7942-5000.** Free. Daily 10am–5:50pm. Tube: South Kensington.

Royal Albert Hall ★★ LANDMARK

In addition to being a great concert venue, the Royal Albert is also one of London's great landmarks, and you don't need a seat to enjoy it. The hall was conceived by Queen Victoria's husband Albert and opened in 1871, a decade after his death. The hall contains such oddities as Britain's longest single-weave carpet (in the corridors), the Queen's Box (still leased to the monarchy), and a spectacular glass dome (41m/135 ft. high and supported only at its rim). Be warned: You don't go backstage (that's for groups only). Some 320 performances a year are presented, many with less than 24 hours' set-up time, and a flow of sightseers would be in the way.

Kensington Gore, SW7. www.royalalberthall.com. © **0845/401-5045.** Lobby free, tours £12 adults, £10 seniors/students. Tours available most days, times vary; generally 9:30am–4:30pm. Tube: South Kensington.

Saatchi Gallery ★★★ MUSEUM

In Chelsea, the most celebrated collection of contemporary art, ranging from shockingly revealing sculpture to exhibitions of bright new talent from China or Africa, came from adman Charles Saatchi, a gossip column denizen with a knack for selecting trenchant pieces that make you think. The impressive collection is the resident in the three-story, 6,500-sq.-m (70,000-sq.-ft.) former Royal Military Asylum building (1801) in Chelsea, complete with a cafe and bookshop. The socially risky, eye-bending experiments—one 2014 show covered the wall of a gallery with swarms of papier-mâché ants—make the Tate Modern's choices look conservative. It's not a good place for kids, though, since the philosophy is to present art without rope barriers.

Duke of York Square, SW3. www.saatchi-gallery.co.uk. © **020/7811-3070.** Free. Daily 10am–5pm. Tube: Sloane Square.

4

LONDON | Exploring London

Science Museum ★★ MUSEUM   It's really two museums, one classic and one far-out, that have been grafted together, but both are about the triumph of man over his environment. The old-school section, which began collecting in 1857 and is split over six levels, is an embarrassment of riches from the artifact archives of science and technology: 1969's *Apollo 10* command module; "Puffing Billy," the world's oldest surviving steam engine; and the first Daguerreotype camera from 1839. The upper floors are full of model ships and 1950s computers, veterinary medicine, and in the hangarlike third floor, aviation. Highlights there: a complete De Havilland Comet, which was the first jetliner (1952), and a modified Vickers Vimy bomber, the first plane to cross the Atlantic without stopping. The high-concept wing buried in the back of the ground floor is easy to miss, but seek it out. A cobalt-blue cavern for interactive games and displays, it bears little relation to the mothballed museum you just crossed through. The Antenna exhibition (ground floor) is exceptionally cutting-edge, and updated regularly with the latest breakthroughs; past topics have included biodegradable cell phones implanted with seeds and building bricks grown from bacteria. The interactive exhibits of Launchpad (heat-seeking cameras, dry ice, and the like) enchant kids. Information Age, an advanced, £16.5 million wing delving into the progression of communication, opened in 2014.

Exhibition Rd., SW7. www.sciencemuseum.org.uk. ✆ **087/0870-4868.** Free. Daily 10am–6pm. Tube: South Kensington.

V&A ★★★ MUSEUM   As a decorative arts repository, the Victoria & Albert, occupying a haughty High Victorian edifice, is all about the eye candy of everyday objects and if you're paying attention, it tells the story of mankind through the development of style and technique. As for how to tour it, the ground floor, a jumbled grid of rooms, has lots of good stuff, but lots more bric-a-brac (Korean pots, 1,000-year-old rock crystal jugs from Egypt) that you'll probably walk past with polite but hasty appreciation. The second, third, and fourth levels have less space and therefore are more manageable. Rooms are arranged by country of origin or by medium (ironwork, tapestries, and the like). Not to miss:

o The seven **Raphael Cartoons** (room 48a), 500 years old in 2015, are probably the most priceless items. These giant paper paintings—yes, paper—were created by the hand of Raphael as templates for the weavers of his ten tapestries for the Sistine Chapel. The colors are fugitive, meaning they're fading: Christ's red robe, painted with plant-based madder lake, has turned white—his reflection in the water, painted with a different pigment, is still red.

o In the just-renovated, sky-lit **Cast Court** (rooms 46 and 46a), find casts of the greatest hits in Renaissance art. They were jumbled here

The V&A's Medieval and Renaissance room.

like a yard sale of antiquity in 1873 for the poor, who could never hope to see the real articles for themselves. Find Ghiberti's doors to the baptistery at Florence's San Giovanni, whose design kicked off the artistic frenzy of the Renaissance. Michelangelo's *David*, floppy puppy feet and all; he was fitted with a fig leaf for royal visits.

- Tipu Sultan of India hated imperialists. So, in the 1790s he commissioned an automaton of a tiger devouring one. A crank on **Tippoo's Tiger** (room 41) activates a clockwork that makes an Englishman's hand flail and an organ makes his gaping mouth moan. In the end, Tipu was killed by Europeans and the English got his Tiger after all. It has been a crowd favorite since 1808, when it was part of the East India Company's trophy museum.

- The **Hereford Screen** (1862, Ironworks balcony) is a liturgical riot by Gilbert Scott, the architect of the "Eros" (p. 72). It took 38 conservators 13 months to restore the 8-ton choir screen to its full golden, brassy, painted, Gothic glory.

- The **Gilbert Collection** (rooms 70–73) of impossibly fine jewel boxes, cameos, silver, and mosaics amassed by a rich enthusiast is so impressive it once had its own museum at Somerset House.

Also visit the V&A's western exterior. Scarred during the Blitz, the stonework was left unrepaired as a memorial.

Cromwell Rd., SW7. www.vam.ac.uk. ℂ **020/7942-2000.** Free. Daily 10am–5:45pm, Fri until 10pm. Tube: South Kensington.

The City & South Bank

The Monument ★ LANDMARK   Back in 1677, it was the tallest thing (61m/200 ft.) in town and it made people gasp. Today, it's easy to miss. The Monument was erected to commemorate the destruction of the city by the Great Fire in 1666. Its 61m (202 ft.) height is also the distance from its base to the site of Thomas Farynor's bakery in Pudding Lane to the east, where the conflagration began. There's only one thing to do in this fluted column of Portland stone: Climb it. The spiral staircase of 15cm (6-in.) steps, which has no landings, gradually narrows as it ascends to the outdoor observation platform—a popular suicide spot until 1842, when a cage was installed. Go on a pleasant day unless you'd like a good wind whipping. Check out the metal band snaking down the north side; it's a lightning rod, and it crosses along an inscription, in Latin, that blamed Catholics for starting the fire (the insult was chiseled off in 1831). It discounts tickets in combo deals with the Tower Bridge Exhibition (for both: £11 adults, £5 kids 5–15, £7 seniors/students).

Monument St. at Fish St. Hill, WC4. www.themonument.info. © **020/3627-2552.** £4 adults, £3 seniors/students, £2 kids under 16. April–Sept daily 9:30am–6pm, Oct–Mar to 5:30pm, last admission 30 min. before closing. Tube: Monument or Bank.

Museum of London ★★★ MUSEUM   The tale of London is the tale of the Western world, so this repository's miraculous cache of rarities from everyday life wouldn't be out of place in the greatest national museums of any land. This huge storehouse contains so many forehead-smackingly rare items that by the time you're two-thirds through it, you'll start to lose track of all the goodies you've seen. When it comes to the history of this patch we call London, no stone has been left unturned—literally—because exhibits start with archaeological finds (including ele-phant vertebrae and a lion skull) before continuing to 3,500-year-old spearheads and swords found in the muck of the Thames.

Voices from the past come alive again in chronological order: There's a 1st-century oak ladder that was discovered preserved in a well, Norman chain mail, loaded gambling dice made of bone in the 1400s, a leather bucket used in vain to fight the Great Fire of 1666, a wooden prison cell from 1750, Selfridge's original bronze Art Deco elevators, and far, far more. The biggest drawback is that you need to budget a few hours, otherwise you'll end up in a mad rush through the entire lower floor covering the Great Fire to now. You also don't want to miss the Victorian Walk, a kid-friendly recreation of city streets, shops. You also can't miss the Lord Mayor's state coach, carved in 1757, which garages here all year awaiting its annual airing at the Lord Mayor's Show in November. The museum, which overlooks a Roman wall fragment out-side, is easy to combine with a visit to St Paul's, and it sells one of the best selections of books on city history. It also runs an excellent second

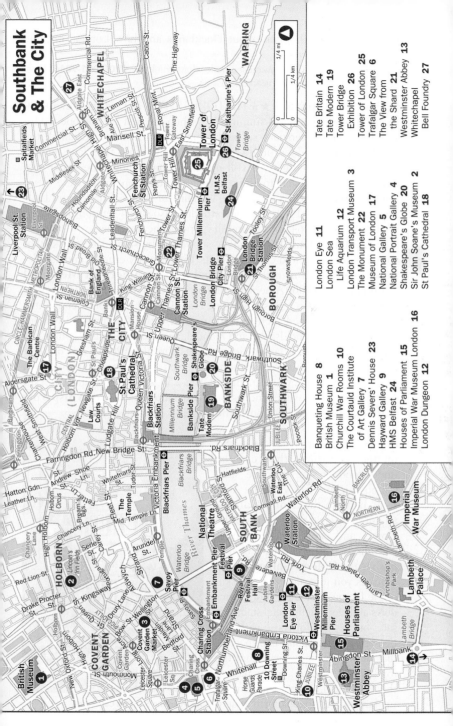

Southbank & The City

WAPPING

WHITECHAPEL

Spitalfields Market

Liverpool St. Station

THE CITY (LONDON)

St Paul's Cathedral

The Barbican Centre

Law Courts

HOLBORN

COVENT GARDEN

Covent Garden Market

British Museum

Charing Cross Station

Whitehall

10 Downing Street

Horse Guards Parade

Westminster Abbey

Houses of Parliament

Westminster Millennium Pier

London Eye Pier

SOUTH BANK

National Theatre

BANKSIDE

Shakespeare's Globe

Tate Modern

BOROUGH

SOUTHWARK

London Bridge Station

H.M.S. Belfast

Tower of London

Tower Bridge

St Katharine's Pier

Lambeth Palace

Imperial War Museum

River Thames

Banqueting House **8**
British Museum **1**
Churchill War Rooms **10**
The Courtauld Institute of Art Gallery **7**
Dennis Severs' House **23**
Hayward Gallery **9**
HMS Belfast **24**
Houses of Parliament **15**
Imperial War Museum London **16**
London Dungeon **12**

London Eye **11**
London Sea Life Aquarium **12**
London Transport Museum **3**
The Monument **22**
Museum of London **17**
National Gallery **5**
National Portrait Gallery **4**
Shakespeare's Globe **20**
Sir John Soane's Museum **2**
St Paul's Cathedral **18**

Tate Britain **14**
Tate Modern **19**
Tower Bridge Exhibition **26**
Tower of London **25**
Trafalgar Square **6**
The View from the Shard **21**
Westminster Abbey **13**
Whitechapel Bell Foundry **27**

1/4 mi

1/4 km

museum in East London about Docklands and how London became such a trading power.

150 London Wall, EC2. www.museumoflondon.org.uk. ✆ **020/7001-9844.** Free. Daily 10am–6pm. Tube: Barbican or St Paul's.

St Paul's Cathedral ★★★ HISTORIC SITE   St Paul's cost £750,000 to build, an astronomical sum in 1697 when the first section opened for worship. Wren overspent so badly that decoration was curtailed; the mosaics weren't added until Queen Victoria thought the place needed spiffing up. Stained glass is still missing, which allows the sweep and arch of Wren's design to shine through. Many foreigners were introduced to the sanctuary during the wedding of Prince Charles and Lady Diana Spencer in 1981, but the cathedral also saw a sermon by Martin Luther King in 1964 and Churchill's funeral the next year.

The **High Altar** has a canopy supported by single tree trunks that were hollowed out and carved, and its 15th-century crucifix and candlesticks require two men to lift. Behind it is the **American Memorial Chapel** to the 28,000 American soldiers who died while based in England in World War II. In a glass case, one leaf of a 500-page book containing their names is turned each day. The **organ,** with 7,000 pipes, was regularly played by Mendelssohn and Handel, and the lectern is original. The **Great West Doors,** largely unused, are 27m high (90 ft.) and on their original hinges; they're so well-hung that even a weakling can swing them open. If you're fit, you can mount the 259 steps (each an awkward 13cm tall (5 in.), with benches on many landings) to the **Whispering Gallery,** 30m (98 ft.) above the floor. Famously, its acoustics are so fine you can turn your head and mutter something that can be understood on the opposite side. Climb higher (you've gone 378 steps now) to the **Stone Gallery,** an outdoor terrace just beneath the Dome, and catch your breath, if you choose, for the final 152-step push to the **Golden Gallery,** which requires you to scale the inner skin of the Dome, past ancient oriel windows and along tight metal stairs. It's safe, but it's not for those with vertigo or claustrophobia. The spectacular 360-degree city view from the top (85m/279 ft. up), at the base of the Ball and Lantern (you can't go up farther), is so beautiful that it

Approaching St Paul's Cathedral.

defies full appreciation. For more than 250 years, this was the tallest structure in London, and therefore the top of the world.

If you miss the **Crypt,** you'll have missed a lot. In addition to memorials to the famous dead (such as Florence Nightingale) and plenty of obscure war heroes, you'll find the tombs of two of Britain's greatest military demigods: **Admiral Horatio Nelson** (whose body was preserved for the trip from the battlefield by soaking in brandy and wine), and **Arthur Duke of Wellington** (flanked by flags captured on the field of battle; they will hang there until they disintegrate). To the right of the OBE Chapel, in **Artists Corner,** there's a monument to poet **John Donne** that still bears the scorch marks it suffered in Old St Paul's during the Great Fire (they're on its urn, and it was the only thing that survived), and you'll find the graves of the artists **J. M. W. Turner** and **Henry Moore,** plus **Christopher Wren** himself, who rests beneath his masterpiece. "I build for eternity," he once said, and so far, so good.

St Paul's Churchyard, EC4. www.stpauls.co.uk. (C) **020/7246-8357.** £17 adults, £8 children 7–16, free children under 6, £15 seniors/students, including guided tour, up to £2 cheaper online. Mon–Sat 8:30am–4:30pm, open for worship only on Sun, Whispering Gallery and Dome open at 9:30am and are cleared at 4pm. Tube: St Paul's.

Tate Modern ★★★ MUSEUM   In 2000, Bankside's chief eyesore, a goliath power station—was ingeniously converted into the national contemporary art collection and is now as integral to London as the Quire of Westminster Abbey or the Dome of St Paul's, with 5.3 million annual visitors, making it Britain's number-two attraction. The mammoth Turbine Hall, cleared of machinery to form a meadowlike expanse of concrete, hosts works created by major-league artists. Holdings focus on art made since 1900 and are divided into four loose areas of thought: On Level 2, there's Poetry and Dream (about surrealism) plus a changing exhibition (usually £10); on Level 3, you'll see Transformed Visions (post-war works) and another paid exhibition; on Level 4, Structure and Clarity (abstract art) and Energy and Process (arte povera, a radical movement). The Tate website is updated with what's on display either here or in the Tate Britain (p. 79), which is helpful considering the facilities will be in continuous upheaval until 2016, when a 10-story southern expansion is completed. The Tate Modern Restaurant on Level 6 can be inhospitable due to crowds—but there are 30 first-come bar seats facing floor-to-ceiling glass and the indelible panorama of St Paul's and the Thames. Afternoon tea is just £15, and the fish and chips platter with mushy peas has our approval for flavor if not price (£17). You can get the same dish for £6 less in the cafe on the second floor, but without that stirring view. At lunch, kids under 12 eat free if a grown-up buys a main course.

Bankside, SE1. www.tate.org.uk/modern. (C) **020/7887-8888.** Free. Sun–Thurs 10am–6pm, Fri–Sat 10am–10pm. Tube: Southwark.

Tower Bridge Exhibition ★★ LANDMARK   In the late 1800s, there was no bolder display of a country's technological prowess than a spectacular bridge. This celebrates one such triumph. The museum is like two attractions in one. The first satisfies sightseers who have dreamed of going up in the famous neo-Gothic towers and crossing the high-level observation walkways. For them, it's a close encounter with a world icon. The second aspect delves into the steam-driven machinery that so impressed the world in 1894, and that will hook the mechanically inclined. The original bascule-raising equipment, representing the largest use of hydraulic power at the time, remains in fine condition despite being retired in favor of electricity in 1976. The raising of the spans is now controlled by joystick from a cabin across the road from the entrance (check "Bridge Lift Times" on the website). How did it survive the Blitz when everything around it got flattened? The Luftwaffe needed it as a visual landmark.

Tower Bridge, on the Tower of London side, SE1. www.towerbridge.org.uk. ☏ **020/7403-3761.** £9 adults, £4 children 5–15, £6 seniors/students. Apr–Sept daily 10am–6pm, Oct–Mar daily 9:30am–5:30pm, last admission 30 min. before closing. Tube: Tower Hill or Tower Gateway DLR.

The Tower of London ★★★ MUSEUM/HISTORIC SITE   It's the most famous castle in the world, a UNESCO World Heritage Site, and a symbol of not just London, but also of a millennium of English history. Less a tower than a fortified minitown of stone and timber, its history could fill this book. Suffice it to say that its oldest building, the four-cornered White Tower, went up in 1078 and the compound that grew around it has served as a palace, prison, treasury, mint, armory, zoo, and now, a lovingly maintained tourist attraction that no visitor should neglect. It's at the very heart of English history, and exploring its sprawl should take between 3 and 5 hours. Grab a copy of the free "Daily Programme," which runs down the times and places of all the free talks, temporary exhibitions, and mini performances. The prime excursion is the **Yeoman Warder's Tour,** led with theatrical aplomb by one of the Beefeaters who live in the Tower (there are about 100 residents, including families, but only one Beefeater, Moira Cameron, is female) and preserve it. Those leave every 30 minutes from just inside the portcullis in the Middle Tower.

The key to touring the Tower is to arrive close to opening. As you enter the **Crown Jewels** exhibition (see it first), you'll glide via people-movers past cases of glittering, downlit crowns, scepters, and orbs worn (awkwardly—they're 2.3kg/5 lb. each) by generations of British monarchs. Check out the legendary 105-carat Koh-I-Noor diamond, once the largest in the world, which is fixed to the temple of the **Queen Mother's Crown** (1937), along with 2,000 other diamonds; the Indian government has been begging to get the stone back. The 530-carat Cullinan I, the world's largest cut diamond, tops the Sovereign's **Sceptre**

A Beefeater holds a resident raven at the Tower of London.

with the Cross (1661). The **Imperial State Crown,** ringed with emeralds, sapphires, and diamonds aplenty, is the one used in the annual State Opening of Parliament. After those come candlesticks that could support the roof of your house, trumpets, swords, and the inevitable traffic jam around the **Grand Punch Bowl** (1829), an elaborate riot of lions, cherubs, and unicorns that shows what it would look like if punch bowls could go insane. Because Oliver Cromwell liquidated every royal artifact he could get his hands on, everything dates to after the Restoration (the 1660s or later). Clearly, the monarchy has more than made up for the loss. Touring the four levels of the cavernous **White Tower** takes in a wide span of history, including a fine stone chapel, Norman-era fireplaces and toilets, and the gleaming **Line of Kings** collection of the Royal Armoury.

After you're finished in here, you'll have an excellent overview of how the whole complex worked. Once you've got those two areas under your belt, take your time exploring the rest. On Tower Green is the circular glass memorial designating the **Scaffold Site,** where the unlucky few (including sitting queens Anne Boleyn and Lady Jane Grey) are said to have lost their heads. In reality, we don't know exactly where they were

The Ravens, Forevermore

Ravens probably first visited the Tower in the 1200s to feast on the dripping corpses of the executed, who were taken from Tower Hill (the public execution ground, near the present-day Tube stop) and affixed to the battlements as a warning. You've probably heard the legend that if the ravens ever leave the Tower, England will fall—so seven of the carnivorous birds are kept in cages north of Wakefield Tower, where they are fed raw meat, blood-soaked cookies, and the occasional finger from a tourist dumb enough to stick one between the bars.

killed, but Queen Victoria wanted a commemorative site set, and this spot was chosen.

Tower Hill, EC3. www.hrp.org.uk. ✆ **084/4482-7777.** £22 adults, £10 children 5–15, £17 students/seniors, £55 families, posted prices are higher and include a "voluntary donation." Nov–Feb Tues–Sat 9am–4:30pm and Sun–Mon 10am–4:30pm, Mar–Oct Tues–Sat 9am–5:30pm and Sun–Mon 10am–5:30pm, last admission 30 min. before closing. Tube: Tower Hill or Tower Gateway DLR.

East London

Dennis Severs' House ★★★ MUSEUM   This 1724 town house was dragged down by a declining neighborhood until the 1970s, when eccentric Californian Dennis Severs purchased it for a pittance, dressed it with antiques, and delighted the intelligentsia with this amusingly pretentious imagination odyssey—he called it "Still Life Drama." Other museums are unrealistically neat and cordoned off, but his house looks lived-in so the past feels as real as it truly was. As Severs, who died in 1999, put it, "In this house it is not what you *see,* but what you have only just *missed* and are being asked to imagine." You could go during the day, but go on Monday or Wednesday after dark for "Silent Night." As you approach, the shutters are closed and a gas lamp burns. You're admitted by a manservant who speaks very little; he motions you to explore the premises, room by room, silently and at your own pace. Suddenly, you're in the parlor of a reasonably prosperous merchant in the 1700s, and the owners seem to be home. Candles burn, a fire pops in the hearth, the smell of food wafts in the air, and a black cat dozes in the corner. Out on the street, you hear footsteps and hooves. Room by dusky room, you

A room at Dennis Severs' House.

silently explore corners overflowing with the implements of everyday life of past ages. It's as if the residents were just in the room, leaving toys on the stairs, beds rumpled, mulled wine freshly spilled, and tea growing cold. By the time you reach the last of ten rooms, the attic, you'll have accompanied the house and its occupants through its decay into a collapsing slum. "Silent Night" is one of London's most invigorating diversions.

18 Folgate St., E1. www.dennissevershouse.co.uk. © **020/7247-4013.** Day visits: Sun noon–4pm, selected Mondays noon–2pm, Silent Night: Mon 6–9pm, also Wed 6–9pm from Oct–May. Reservations required only for evenings. Monday day visits £7, Sunday visits £10, Silent Night visits £14. Tube: Liverpool Street.

Geffrye Museum ★★ MUSEUM The complex, a U-shaped line of dignified brick houses built in 1714 feels removed from the rush of the East End. Inside is a walk through the history of the home: recreations of typical middle-class London abodes from the 1600s to the late 20th century, artfully arranged to appear lived-in, and complete with explanations of each item on display. To some, they're rooms full of furniture. To others, the Geffrye is a chance to understand how people of the past lived. You know which person you are. One building here is a restored almshouse for the poor; book timed tours to see how charity cases lived back in the day (check the website for the schedule; £3 adults, free for children under 16). On weekends, there are discussions, lectures, and kid-oriented crafts workshops, which gives the place much more energy than you'd expect from a design-based attraction. Especially on fine days from April to October, the grounds are an exceptional place to relax. The walled herb garden encourages touch, and its period plots are cultivated with plants used in several eras, including Elizabethan and Victorian times.

136 Kingsland Rd., Shoreditch, E2. www.geffrye-museum.org.uk. © **020/7739-9893.** Free, including audio tour. Tues–Sun 10am–5pm. Tube: Hoxton.

Museum of Childhood ★★ MUSEUM The awesome V&A Museum chronicles kid-dom through the ages in this location, pulling from a considerable collection of toys, clothing, dollhouses, books, teddy bears, and games. Objects are placed at kids' eye level with simplified descriptions. Child-rearing history is also addressed; look for the "Princess Bottle" of 1871, which had a reservoir shape that allowed for quick milk dispensing but also incubated bacteria, a fact that wasn't realized until countless babies died. The MoC's glass-and-steel building began its life in South Kensington as the home of the nascent V&A collection but was re-erected here in the 1860s—the fish-scale mosaic floor was made by female prisoners, many of whom were separated from their own kids.

Cambridge Heath Rd., E2. www.museumofchildhood.org.uk. © **020/8983-5200.** Free. Daily 10am–5:45pm. Tube: Bethnal Green.

Museum of London Docklands ★★★ MUSEUM   If you dig the head-spinning Museum of London (p. 90), here's a similarly lush, ultimately redeeming treatment to life in London's East End. This place tells the real story of the working men who sweat to put the teacups into more privileged hands, and the labor that circulated profits from the slave trade into City banks. Housed in a brick warehouse from 1804, the three-floor museum traces the history of working on the Thames, starting with Anglo-Saxon times. You can inspect an intricate model of the medieval London Bridge, which was stacked with homes and businesses but clogged the river's flow so drastically that it was a threat to life. You'll also roam "Sailortown," a creepy warren of quayside alleys, all shanties and low doorways, meant to evoke the area's early 19th-century underworld. Finally, the spotlight shifts to the harrowing Blitz, when the whole area was obliterated by fire from the sky and forced to reinvent itself as a corporate citadel. There's also an interactive, river-themed play area for kids, Mudlarks.

No. 1 Warehouse, West India Quay, E14. www.museumoflondon.org.uk/docklands. © 020/7001-9844. Free. Daily 10am–6pm. Tube: West India Quay DLR or Canary Wharf.

Whitechapel Bell Foundry ★ MUSEUM/HISTORIC SITE   America's Liberty Bell. Montreal Cathedral's Great Bell. Big Ben himself. Name an important chimer from Western history, and chances are Whitechapel Bell Foundry cast it. Sure, the Liberty Bell cracked, by which time it was too late to exchange it, but the foundry's craftsmanship is not in question—Guinness verified it as Britain's oldest manufacturing company, established in 1570, with lineage traceable to 1420. Back then, fulsome industries such as metalworking were found in the East End, where the prevailing winds would carry the grime out of town. This foundry, still operating in a brick-front building from the late 1600s, conducts tours of its cramped, messy workshops on some Saturdays—always when workers are off duty, because flying sparks and molten metal sting a little. A visit isn't plastic in any way; tours (book weeks or months ahead) dodge piles of metal dust, sand, shavings, and aged workbenches. Every aspect of the craft, from casting to buffing, is given its due. There's also a small museum and shop (teeny bells, musical scores for handbells), open weekdays, which don't require tickets.

32-34 Whitechapel Rd., E1. www.whitechapelbellfoundry.co.uk. © 020/7247-2599. Shop open Mon–Fri 9am–4:15pm; tours 2 Saturdays monthly at 10am, 1:15, and 4pm. £12, no one under 14 admitted. Tube: Aldgate East.

Greenwich

As soon as you step off the ferry 30 minutes east of Central London, you're in a UNESCO World Heritage Site. If you don't have time to go into the countryside, Greenwich will give you that small-town English feel.

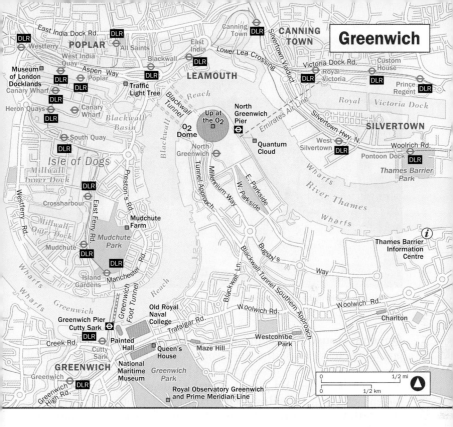

Cutty Sark ★★ HISTORIC SITE   This handsome wooden ship, launched in 1869 when it was expected to last only 30 years, is today the only tea clipper left in the world and a symbol of English economic muscle. Against the odds, she still has nearly all of her fabric and riggings—a 2007 fire didn't consume them because they were in storage for a restoration that was already underway. Now she floats over a dry dock that's skirted by a glass canopy so visitors can go inside, topside under tarps, and peep beneath her brassed keel. It's a slight cheat, because she originally had a hull coated with Muntz metal, bitumen, and felt, but hey, she looks incredible. She'll never be speedy again, but she'll always look hot. King William Walk, SE10. www.rmg.co.uk/cuttysark. ℂ **020/8312-6608.** £12 adults, £6 kids 5–15, £10 seniors/students, posted prices are higher and include a "voluntary donation." Mid-Sept to July 10am–5pm, late July to mid-Sept, 10am–6pm, last admission 1 hr. before closing. Tube: Cutty Sark DLR, Greenwich river ferry, or Greenwich National Rail.

Maritime Greenwich ★★★ HISTORIC SITE/LANDMARK   Situated on a picturesque slope of the south bank of the Thames, Greenwich once was home to Greenwich Palace, where both Henry VIII and Elizabeth I were born. The last part of the palace to be constructed, **The**

The National Maritime Museum, Greenwich.

Queen's House (1616, Inigo Jones), still stands, but most of the grounds were rebuilt in the late Georgian period as the equally palatial Royal Hospital, a convalescence haven for disabled and veteran sailors now known as the **Old Royal Naval College.** High on the hill, in Greenwich Park, is the **Royal Observatory,** and between them stands the **National Maritime Museum.** So many of these treasures are owned by the state that many entrance fees are waived; you can play the whole day without paying more than a few pounds. Stop by the visitor center, alongside the *Cutty Sark,* for background information.

Old Royal Naval College, SE10. www.ornc.org. © **020/8269-4747.** Free. Grounds open 8am–6pm. Tube: Cutty Sark DLR or Greenwich National Rail.

The National Maritime Museum ★★ MUSEUM   Don't be put off by the topic. The world's largest maritime museum is extraordinarily kid-friendly, brimming with toys such as steering simulators and a giant playground that looks like a world map. Because so much of Britain's history from the 17th to 20th centuries was transacted via the high seas, this place isn't just about boats and knots. The facility has an endless supply of artifacts that would do any museum proud. Highlights include a musical stuffed pig clutched in a lifeboat by a *Titanic* passenger; and, most ghoulishly, the bloodstained breeches and bullet-punctured topcoat that Admiral Lord Nelson wore on the day he took his fatal shot. Get the creeps from relics from Sir John Franklin's ill-fated 1848 Arctic expedition, including lead-lined food tins that likely caused the explorers to go mad and probably eat each other. Also excellent is the Atlantic Worlds display, which plumbs the British role in the slave trade, something few London museums touch upon. The museum is not too flashy to present the viewpoint that through the East India Company, England looted India—in fact, the word *looted* has Hindi origins. There are also big set pieces such as figureheads, models, antique instruments, and entire wooden vessels. Weekends are full of free kids' events that bring out London families, and the fun Greenwich Market is running nearby then, too. Romney Rd., Greenwich, SE10. www.nmm.ac.uk. © **020/8858-4422.** Free. Daily 10am–5pm. Tube: Cutty Sark DLR, Greenwich river ferry, or Greenwich National Rail.

Old Royal Naval College ★ HISTORIC SITE/LANDMARK This 1696 neoclassical complex, primarily the work of Wren, is mostly used by a university but offers two main sights: the Painted Hall and the Chapel. The **Painted Hall** has incredible paintings by Sir James Thornhill that took nearly 2 decades to complete. It was the setting for the funeral of Admiral Nelson, but it may never have looked more glorious than today, because a 2013 restoration removed years of candle grime. **The Chapel,** in the Greek Revival style, is the work of James Stuart. If the ORNC's stately symmetry rings a bell, that's because it was used as a stand-in for Paris in the movie musical *Les Misérables.* It's also where

Old Royal Naval College, Greenwich.

you'll find **Meantime Brewing Company** (www.meantimebrewing. com), one of the city's hottest microbrewers. It has plenty of garden space where you can kick back with very stiff pints.

Greenwich, SE10. www.ornc.org. ☎ **020/8269-4747.** Free. Grounds daily 8am–6pm, buildings daily 10am–5pm, Royal Chapel opens Sun at 11am for worship. Tour reservations ☎ **020/8269-4799,** 90 min., £5 adults, free for children under 16. Tube: Cutty Sark DLR, Greenwich river ferry, or Greenwich National Rail.

The Queen's House ★ MUSEUM/HISTORIC SITE   Viewed from the river and framed by the newer Old Royal Naval College, the Queen's House enjoys as elegant a setting as a building could wish for. Inigo Jones took 22 years to come up with a then-revolutionary, Palladian-style summer retreat for Charles I's wife, Henrietta Maria, but it was completed only in 1638, just before the Civil Wars cut both Charles and his building schemes off at the head. Henrietta scurried off to France. The house has a few ho-hum galleries and displays (lots of paintings of ships and battles), but its nautilus-shaped Tulip staircase, plus other rooms, are considered to be haunted by an unknown specter, so have a camera ready.

Romney Rd., SE10. www.rmg.co.uk. ☎ **020/8312-6565.** Free. Daily 10am–5pm. Tube: Cutty Sark DLR, Greenwich river ferry, or Greenwich National Rail.

The Royal Observatory ★★ HISTORIC SITE/MUSEUM   Commanding a terrific view from the hill in Greenwich Park, with the towers of Canary Wharf spread out in its lap, the Observatory is yet another creation of Christopher Wren (from 1675), and the place from which time zones emanate. Historically the Empire's most important house for celestial observation, it houses significant relics of star-peeping, but sadly, the paid areas are a tourist trap. Most of the good stuff—marked on the map in red—is free, including a small Astronomy Centre and an exhibition on time. The only things admission get you is an unremarkable ceiling-projection planetarium and the bulk of the Flamsteed House by Wren, which includes a collection of clocks that cracked the mystery of measuring longitude, ushering the English Empire to worldwide dominance. Most people plunk down admission not because they care about those but to get access to the Meridian Courtyard. The Prime Meridian, located at precisely 0° longitude (the equator is 0° latitude), crosses through the grounds and tourists pay at least £7 to wait an hour for a silly Instagram moment of straddling the line with a foot in two hemispheres at once—but they don't have to. The line continues north of the courtyard, where it's free, and there's never a wait.

Greenwich Park, Greenwich, SE10. www.rmg.co.uk. ☎ **020/8312-6565.** Free for most of grounds. Flamsteed House and Meridian Courtyard £6 adults, £5 seniors/students, £2 kids under 16; planetarium £7 adults, £5 kids 5–15, £6 seniors/students; combination ticket £12 adults, £6 kids under 16, £10 seniors/students. Daily 10am–6pm, last admission 5:30pm. Tube: Cutty Sark DLR, Greenwich river ferry, or Greenwich National Rail.

Up at the O2 ★★ TOUR Climbers, about 10 at a time, hook into a safety rigging system and follow a guide over a tensile fabric catwalk laid a few feet over the O2 Dome's roof, from south to north, to an observation platform at the zenith of the structure. There they pause for 15 minutes of photos of East London (the City is mostly hidden behind Canary Wharf's towers). Beneath them, humming like a ship at sea, is a Dome conquered. The excursion isn't for the height-averse—at your highest, you're 52m (171 ft.) above the ground (the weight cutoff is 130kg/286 lbs., and you have to be at least 10 years old), but it's also not scary since you're tethered, the shoes they lend you grip well, and if the weather's bad, you get matching jumpsuits like Ooompa-Loompas. The climb, which is more like a stroll up a steep hill, takes 45 minutes, and the rest of a 90-minute experience consists of getting harnessed and psyched up. Peninsula Sq., SE10. www.theo2.co.uk/upattheO2. © **020/8463-2000.** Climbs from £26 for adults and children. Climbs begin at 10am and end at 6pm to 10pm, depending on the season. Tube: North Greenwich or North Greenwich ferry.

Attractions Outside Central London

Two blockbuster attractions just outside London are **Windsor Castle** ★★★ (p. 151) and **Warner Bros. Studio Tour London—The Making of Harry Potter** ★★★ (p. 178), both discussed at length in the next chapter.

Dulwich Picture Gallery ★★ MUSEUM A 15-minute train ride from Victoria and an 8-minute walk lands you in a pretty village-like enclave of South London. In just a few rooms, the Gallery keeps one of the world's most vital collections of Old Master paintings of the 1600s and 1700s. A visit is almost indescribably serene, the better to stare into the face of one of its star masterpieces, Rembrandt's *A Girl at a Window*—how did he capture her bemusedly frank expression? A handheld video tour offers backstories of 10 works, such as the portrait of young Venetia Stanley, painted when she was discovered dead in bed and her distraught husband summoned Van Dyck to capture her beautiful corpse. Twist ending: Her beloved might have poisoned her. At the airy cafe, grab tea with Devon clotted cream for £6. Gallery Rd., Dulwich Village, SE21. www.dulwichpicturegallery.org.uk. © **020/8693-5254.** £6 adults, free for children under 18, £5 seniors/students, special exhibitions cost more. Tues–Fri 10am–5pm, Sat–Sun 11am–5pm. National Rail: West Dulwich Station.

Hampton Court Palace ★★★ MUSEUM/HISTORIC SITE If you have to pick just one palace to visit in London, select this one because there's so much more to do than look at golden furniture. A 35-minute commuter train ride from London Waterloo (they go every half-hour), Hampton Court looks like the ideal palace because it defined the ideal: The redbrick mansion was a center for royal life from 1525 to

Hampton Court Palace, Surrey.

1737, and its forest of chimneys stands regally in 24 hectares (59 acres) of achingly pretty riverside gardens, painstakingly restored to their 1702 appearance. Guides pander to Tudor scandals to make history more interesting, and days are full of events, which may include re-enactments of gossipy events by costumed actors, Tudor-style cook-offs in the old kitchens, Shakespeare plays in the hammer-beamed Great Hall, or ghost tours. Whatever you do, don't neglect the 24-hectare (59-acre) **gardens** and make time to lose yourself in the Northern Gardens' shrubbery **Maze,** installed by William III; kids giggle their way through to the middle of this leafy labyrinth.

East Molesey, Surrey. www.hrp.org.uk. © **084/4482-7777.** £18 adults, £8 children 5–15, £15 seniors/students, posted prices are higher and include a "voluntary donation." March to late Oct daily 10am–6pm and late Oct to Mar daily 10am–4:30pm, last admission 1 hr. before closing. National Rail: Hampton Court from Waterloo Station.

Highclere Castle ★★★   The 8th Earl and Countess of Carnarvon still dwell under the sandstone turrets that are known to TV viewers as the idyllic and stately *Downton Abbey.* Time and spendthrift earls took their toll on this historic home, and as recently as 2009, more than 50 rooms were uninhabitable due to mold and leaks. The current Earl faced repair bills of around £12 million, so he welcomes visitors to admire his home and spend the day exploring the 1,000 acres of private countryside. At Highclere, the basement is full not of servants but mummy stuff. The 5th Earl is the guy who bankrolled Howard Carter's 1923 discovery and emptying of King Tut's tomb in Luxor, so unseen beneath Lord Grantham's feet lay items taken from the tombs of Egypt. Highclere is only open for 60 to 70 days a year but they're scattered all over the calendar. The castle is typically open Easter Week, bank holiday weekends, and from mid-August to mid-September. Taking a group tour guarantees you a ticket, but those sell out months ahead and herd you along. If you show up independently at either 10am or 2:30pm, you can get a walk-up ticket even though advance tickets are sold out, but that involves taking a 52-minute train from Paddington or a National Express bus to the adorable town of Newbury and then a 15 taxi from there.

Highclere Park, Newbury. www.highclerecastle.co.uk. *©* **01635/253-204.** £20 adults, £18 students/seniors, £13 children 4–16.

Home of Charles Darwin (Down House) ★★ HISTORIC HOUSE

Charles Darwin made one of history's most important voyages, but once back in England, he barely left his home here in the idyllic parish village of Downe. You'll find out about the man and his life (did you know the father of evolution married his own first cousin?) and, guided by an audio tour narrated by Sir David Attenborough, you'll explore his study, his greenhouse, and his enchanting garden of lawns and breezy fields. There are two charming country pubs to enjoy while you wait for the bus back; your Oyster card will get you here.

Luxted Rd., Downe, Kent. www.english-heritage.org.uk. *©* **01689/859-119.** £10 adults, £9 seniors/students, £6 kids 5–15. April–Sept daily 10am–6pm, Oct–Nov daily 10am–5pm, Nov–Mar Sat–Sun 10am–4pm. National Rail: Bromley South and then bus 122 and a 7-min. walk.

Kenwood ★★ HISTORIC HOUSE

Get that country house high without leaving the city. Just restored, Kenwood is a sublime 18th-century job by Robert Adam with a sigh-inducing southern view across Hampstead Heath. Inside, the walls are hung with paintings that would be the envy of the National Gallery, including Vermeer's *The Guitar Player,* a John Singer Sargent, and a Rembrandt self-portrait. There's no better place to enjoy an English summer than its lawns or alongside its ornamental pond.

Hampstead Lane, NW3. www.english-heritage.org.uk. *©* **020/8348-1286.** Free. House: daily 10am–5pm; grounds: 8am–dusk. Tube: Archway or Golders Green, then bus 210.

Royal Botanic Gardens, Kew ★★ PARK/GARDEN

The 121-hectare (300-acre) gardens, with many expansive lawns, is a UNESCO World Heritage Site. As you'd expect, the glasshouses are world-class—there are 2,000 varieties of plants, many descended from specimens collected in the earliest days of international sea trade. Of the seven conservatories, the domed **Palm House,** built from 1844 to 1848 and jungle-warm, is probably the world's most recognizable greenhouse,

The Palm House at Royal Botanic Gardens, Kew.

while the **Temperate House** contains the world's largest indoor plant (the 17.7m/58-ft.-tall Chilean wine-palm, planted in 1843—not a typo). It's undergoing a £34 million restoration until 2018 but they've relocated most of its plants (except the *Encephalartos woodii* cycad, extinct in the wild and too fragile to move). Other attractions include a bamboo garden, a water lily pond, **Treehouse Towers** (a play area for children aged 3–11), and, it must be said, a heartwarmingly charming village outside the gates. Kew's storied contributions to botanical science are not mired in the past; it provides a free app that lets you scan labels to learn more and find blooms. Be aware that many of the goodies clamp down in winter (including Kew Palace, included in the price), so this is best in the summer.

Kew, Richmond, Surrey. www.kew.org. ✆ **020/8332-5655.** £15 adults, £14 seniors/students, free for kids 16 and under. Daily 9:30am–4:15pm in winter, to 6pm in fall, and 6:30pm in spring and summer. Tube: Kew Gardens.

Wimbledon Lawn Tennis Museum ★ MUSEUM   For those of us who can't get to the tournament (see below), there's still something to see the rest of the year. It's sort of like a Hall of Fame on Wimbledon, with artifacts going back to 1555, although the British have never been prouder than they are now that Scotsman Andy Murray brought home the trophy after 77 years. There is no other museum in the world where a ghostly video apparition of John McEnroe appears in a locker room to vent about opponents. He comes in peace. No need to duck.

Church Rd., SW19. www.wimbledon.com/museum. ✆ **020/8946-6131.** Daily 10am–5pm. £12 adults, £7 children, £10 seniors/students. Tube: Southfields or Tooting Broadway, then bus 493; or National Rail to Wimbledon Station, then bus 493.

It's easy watching the Wimbledon Championships on TV for 2 weeks in late June and early July, but seeing it in person is a trickier matter. Because tickets for the final matches go to VIPs, you're more likely to catch famous players during the early rounds, when the club's 19 grass courts are all in use. Roaming access to all but three of those (surcharges of £37–£101 are levied for Centre, No. 1, and No. 2 courts), and tickets (distributed by lottery the previous summer) can be had for the price of a "ground pass" (which cost, at most, £20). Around 6,000 ground passes are distributed each morning starting at 9:30am, so arrive before that (the local council gets angry if it's before 8am), and if you snag one, you'll probably be inside by noon, when matches begin. Another clever way to get in is to bum tickets off people as they get tired and leave for the day (just don't offer money—the organizers hate that because they sell unused tickets, too, for charity). A few more ground passes are resold after 3pm for £5 to benefit charity. On weekdays and rainy days, your chances of getting unfilled seats for the best courts are better, since people are working or huddling indoors. And after 5pm, ground-pass rates dip to, at most, £14, which isn't such a bad deal since matches continue until 9pm. It's all ridiculously complicated, so check ahead (www.wimbledon.com/en_GB/tickets) to make sure the rules are the same.

Overrated Attractions

In every city, you find attractions that are heavily publicized but, once seen, are revealed to be time poorly spent. London provides a variety of such overpriced pursuits. Still, parents of bored children might discover these inauthentic sights are just the tonic to placate the kids.

ArcelorMittal Orbit OBSERVATION TOWER   The 114.5m-tall (376-ft.) vertical scribble has observation decks at 76m (249 ft.) and 80m (262 ft.), but it barely matters when there's not much to look at. It originally overlooked the Olympics but the torch and the games are gone, so it peers into a stadium many miles from town. Wear a jacket because it gets windy in the exposed areas, and take your vitamins because a lift takes you up, but you have to use 455 steps down. And no, it doesn't orbit.
Queen Elizabeth Olympic Park. arcelormittalorbit.com. © **0333/800-8099.** £15 adult, £7 children 3–6, £12 seniors/students. Daily 10am–6pm, last admission 5pm. Tube: Stratford.

Emirates Air Line OBSERVATION GONDOLA   Opened in time for the Olympics as a Thames crossing between the ExCeL convention center and the O2 dome, it's simply an enclosed, 10-person gondola that shuttles between two places most tourists never go, and it's too far from the City to be of much panoramic use. Oyster cards work on it.
www.emiratesairline.co.uk. © **0843/222-1234.** £4 adult, £2 child (without Oyster card); or £3 adult, £2 child (with Oyster). Mon–Fri 7am–9pm, Sat 8am–9pm, Sun 9am–9pm. Tube: North Greenwich or Royal Victoria DLR.

The London Dungeon HAUNTED HOUSE Avoid it like the plague. It's a sophomoric gross-out with locations in 9 cities that sops up overflow from the London Eye. Costumed actors bray at you as you're led through darkness from set to set, each representing a period of English history as a 13-year-old boy might define them. Plague-ridden rubber corpses "sneeze" on passersby, a prostitute exposes one of Jack the Ripper's mutilated victims, and Sweeney Todd commands you to sit in his chair. The climax is a pair of indoor carnival rides. If you dread being picked on by bad stand-up comics, you're going to hate this place. If you can't resist, at least bundle it with the London Eye for a discount.
County Hall, Westminster Bridge Rd., SE1. www.thedungeons.com. ☎ **0871/243-2240.** £25 adults, £20 kids 5–15, £23 students, £7–£8. Times shift constantly but are roughly daily 10am–5pm. Tube: Westminster or Waterloo.

London Sea Life Aquarium AQUARIUM Sure, it's fun to see sharks under your feet and penguins on a faux floe. But sorry Charlie, the truth is there is nothing here you can't see at other fish zoos, there are more than three dozen other locations by Sea Life, the McDonald's of fish tanks, and this one feels as cramped as a 16th-century galleon.
County Hall, Westminster Bridge Rd., SE1. www.sealifelondon.co.uk. ☎ **0871/663-1678.** £22 adults, £16 kids 3–15, free kids under 3. Mon-Thurs 10am–6pm, Fri–Sun 10am–7pm, last admission 1 hr. before closing. Tube: Waterloo or Westminster.

The London Zoo ZOO It's not about the pedigree. No, it has an esteemed history going back to 1828 as a menagerie for members of the Zoological Society of London. It's just that it's ultimately just a zoo, and a smallish one at that, with few large animals. A pair of Sumatran tigers are not enough to justify the high-ticket price, especially for a first-time London visitor who could be learning about the city instead.
Outer Circle Rd., Regent's Park, NW1. www.zsl.org. ☎ **020/7722-333.** £24 adults, £18 children 3–15. Daily 10am–6pm. Tube: Camden Town, then bus no. 274.

Madame Tussauds TOURIST MUSEUM Have you ever heard of Shah Rukh Khan? Cheryl Cole? Olly Murs? If that might as well be in Swedish, you're not going to get much joy out of this ferociously priced, miserably crowded wax trap. The execution of its doppelgangers, which you can usually touch is generally superb. That's not the issue. The focus of this world-famous waxworks is on British celebrities. A 5-minute, Disney-esque ride, "The Spirit of London," invokes every conceivable London stereotype, from the Artful Dodger to plague victims. As you glide through, you'll suddenly wonder if you're the real dummy here.
Marylebone Rd., W1. www.madame-tussauds.com/london. ☎ **0871/894-3000.** Pricing varies, but peaks at £30 adults, £26 children, £19 seniors, £15 for entries after 5pm; daily 9:30am–5:30pm, longer on weekends and holidays. Tube: Baker Street.

The Queen's Gallery MUSEUM The Queen inherited the mother of all art collections—7,000 paintings, 30,000 watercolors, and half a million prints, to say nothing of sculpture, furniture, and jewelry—but she shows only a tiny fraction. The few works (budget 1 hr.) are undoubt-edly exceptional (one of the world's few Vermeers, a Rubens' self-portrait given to Charles I, glittering ephemera by Fabergé), but they're not the cream of what she owns. There's more exciting stuff to be had for free at the National Gallery. The Gallery and the Royal Mews can be seen on a joint ticket (£16 adults, £9 children 5–16, £15 seniors/students).

Buckingham Palace Rd., SW1. www.royalcollection.org.uk. ✆ **020/7766-7301.** £10 adults, £5 children 5–16, £9 seniors/students. Daily 10am–5:30pm, last admission 4:30pm. Tube: Victoria.

Ripley's Believe It or Not! TOURIST MUSEUM   Like foot fun-gus, the worthless rip-off has spread wherever tourists tread. Now it's in London. Its halls of oddities (like a portrait of Diana made from lint) are not worthwhile even for kitsch value. It's the definition of a tourist trap, and it costs more than Westminster Abbey! Opt for the "or Not" option.

1 Piccadilly Circus, W1. www.ripleyslondon.com. ✆ **020/3238-0022.** £27 adults, £25 seniors/students, £20 kids 5–15. Daily 10am–midnight. Tube: Piccadilly Circus.

The Royal Mews MUSEUM   Most visitors pop in to what amounts to the Queen's garage in about 15 minutes. You'll see stables fit for a you-know-who and Her Majesty's Rolls-Royces (many of which, at Prince Charles' behest, run on green fuels). You'll also overdose on learning about regulations for when this set of harnesses may be used and when that leather must be polished. The Queen's Gallery and the Mews can be seen on a joint ticket (£16 adults, £9 children 5–16, £15 seniors/students).

Buckingham Palace Rd., SW1. www.royalcollection.org.uk. ✆ **020/7766-7302.** £9 adults, £5 children 5–17, £8 seniors/students. Apr–Oct 11am–5pm, Nov–Mar 10am–4pm, last admission 45 min. before closing. Tube: Victoria.

The Sherlock Holmes Museum TOURIST MUSEUM   Set up a house as if it were really the home of a fictional character, prop up some shabby mannequins, and then charge tourists to see it. That's the scheme and it has worked for years, so much so that there's often a line.

221b Baker St., NW1. www.sherlock-holmes.co.uk. ✆ **020/7224-3688.** £10 adults, £8 children under 16. Daily 9:30am–6pm. Tube: Baker Street.

Outdoor London

Epping Forest ★★★ PARK/GARDEN   Mostly because its soil is unsuitable for farming, for a millennium it remained a semi-virgin woodland, so it's the best place to get a feel for what Britain felt like before humans denuded its land. It's the largest open space in Lon-don, 6,000 acres, 12 miles long by 2½ miles wide, and containing a universe of diversions—650 plant species, 80 ponds where waterfowl splash, and even some 1,500 species of fungi. Getting lost in the wood is feasible, but not likely, since it stretches in a single direction. Henry VIII built a timber-framed hunting lodge in 1542 that was inherited by his daughter Elizabeth and, astoundingly, still stands: **Queen Elizabeth's Hunting Lodge.**

Rangers Rd., Chingford, E4. www.cityoflondon.gov.uk. ✆ **020/8529-6681.** Free. Daily 6am–dusk, Lodge: daily 10am–5pm. Tube: Snaresbrook or Wood Street.

The Green Park ★★ PARK/GARDEN   The area south of Mayfair between Hyde Park and St James's Park was once a burial ground for lepers, but now is a simple expanse of meadows and light copses of trees. It doesn't have much to offer except pastoral views, and most visitors find themselves crossing it instead of dawdling in it, although its springtime flower beds (brightest in Mar and Apr) are marvelous. Don't sit in one of those striped deck chairs unless you've got a few bob to pay as rent.

Piccadilly, SW1. ✆ **030/0061-2350.** Free. Open 24 hr. Tube: Green Park.

Greenwich Park ★★ PARK/GARDEN   Decently sized (183 acres), it was once a deer preserve maintained for royal amusement; a herd of them still have 13 acres at their disposal. It's been a Royal Park since the 15th century, although the boundary wasn't formally defined until James I erected a brick wall around it in the early 1600s, much of which still survives. From the top of its clean-swept main hill are marvelous views of the Canary Wharf district, and the world-famous **Royal Greenwich Observatory** (p. 102), commissioned in 1675 by Charles II.

Greenwich Park, SE10. www.royalparks.gov.uk. ✆ **030/0061-2380.** Free. Daily 6am–dusk. National Rail: Greenwich or Maze Hill, or Cutty Sark. DLR or Greenwich ferry.

Hampstead Heath ★★★ PARK/GARDEN   Some 7 million visitors a year come to the 320-hectare (791-acre) Heath, in northwest London, to walk on the grass, get enveloped by thick woods, and take in the view from the magnificent Pergola, a beguiling, overgrown Edwardian garden, and a true London secret. The Heath is a perennial locale for aimless strolls and furtive trysts. The Heath has several sublime places to rest, including the just-restored **Kenwood House** (p. 105), a neoclassical home from 1640 adorned with miles of gold leaf and important paintings by Reynolds, Turner, and Vermeer; and the inviting and woody **Spaniards Inn** (www.thespaniardshampstead.co.uk; ✆ **020/8731-8406;** Tube: Hampstead). The Heath's hilltop is another favored lookout point.

www.cityoflondon.gov.uk/hampsteadheath. ✆ **020/7606-3030.** Free. 7:30am–dusk. Tube: Hampstead or Hampstead Heath Overground.

Hyde Park & Kensington Gardens ★★★ PARK/GARDEN   Bordered by Mayfair, Bayswater, and Kensington, together the two conjoined are the largest park in the middle of the city. Hyde Park is home to the famous **Speakers' Corner** (Tube: Marble Arch, p. 84), a meandering lake called the Serpentine, and the Diana, Princess of Wales Memorial Fountain (Tube: South Kensington). The most famous promenade is Rotten Row, probably a corruption of "Route de Roi," or King's Way, which was laid out by William III as his private road to town; it runs along the southern edge from Hyde Park Corner. Kensington Gardens, which flows seamlessly from Hyde Park, only opened to plebes like us in 1851, and retains its country-manor quality. You'll also find the **Serpentine Gallery** (west of West Carriage Dr. and north of Alexandra Gate; www.serpentinegallery.org; *Ⓒ* **020/7402-6075;** Tues–Sun 10am–6pm; free; Tube: South Kensington), a popular venue for its modern art exhibitions and an art bookshop. Volunteers sometimes run guided tours of the park's quirks; check the bulletin boards at each park entrance to see if one's upcoming. Borrow a Boris Bike and cruise around this giant green playground, and don't forget to look for Sir George Frampton's marvelous bronze statue of Peter Pan (1912) near the west shore of the Long Water. Hyde Park, W2. www.royalparks.org.uk. *Ⓒ* **030/0061-2100.** Free. Hyde Park open daily 5am–midnight, Kensington Gardens open daily 6am–dusk. Tube: Hyde Park Corner, Marble Arch, or Lancaster Gate.

Queen Elizabeth Olympic Park ★ PARK/GARDEN A bracing dearth of trees, paired with a layout that herds crowds, make the park feel a lot like a theme park in which all of the attractions up and left. Most of the amenities are things that only excite locals who remember when it was recently a wasteland. The Pringle-shaped Aquatics Centre and Velopark are striking, but this park is only of interest if you want to see the stadium you saw on TV; even the torch is gone, and the ArcelorMittal Orbit tower is ultimately not as exciting as you think it will be. Stratford, E20. www.QueenElizabethOlympicPark.co.uk. *Ⓒ* **020/3288-1800.** Free. Daily 6am–dusk. Tube: Stratford.

Regent's Park ★★★ PARK/GARDEN It's the people's park (195 hectares/487 acres), best for sunning, strolling long expanses and darting

A summer performance at Regent's Park.

into the bohemian neighborhoods that fringe it. Once a hunting ground, it was very nearly turned into a development for the buddies of Prince Regent (later King George IV), but only a few of the private homes were built; Winfield House, near the western border of the park, has the largest garden in London after the Queen. The American ambassador lives there—surprised? The most breathtaking entrance is through John Nash's elegant Park Crescent development, by the Regent's Park and Great Portland Street Tube stations. North of the park, just over the Regent's Canal and Prince Albert Road, **Primrose Hill Park** (Tube: Chalk Farm or Camden Town) affords a panorama of the city from 62m (203-ft.) high.

Regent's Park, NW1. www.royalparks.gov.uk. ℂ **030/0061-2300.** Free. Daily 5am–dusk. Tube: Baker St., Great Portland St., or Regent's Park.

St James's Park ★★ PARK/GARDEN   The easternmost segment of the contiguous quartet of parks that runs east from Kensington Gardens is bounded by Whitehall to the east and Piccadilly to the north. James I laid it out in 1603 and Buckingham Palace redeveloped it a century later. Its little pond, St James's Park Lake, hosts ducks and other waterfowl. The Russian ambassador made a gift of pelicans to the park in 1667, and six still call it home; they're fed their 13kg (28 lb.) of whiting daily at 2:30pm at the Duck Island Cottage. The park has a fine view of Buckingham Palace's front facade, where royal couples smooch on balconies. The real draw is people-watching, since a cross-section of all London passes through here. Not a place for

Buckingham Palace and St James's Park Lake.

The Hidden Park

Sure, everybody knows about London's famous green spaces, but there's one recreation area, which stretches from London's northwest to its east through gentrified lanes and industrial wasteland alike, that few tourists are told about. It's the **Regent's Canal,** which threads from Paddington through Camden, Islington, and East London before joining with the Thames (86 ft. lower) just before Canary Wharf. It was completed in 1820 to link with canals all the way to Birmingham and feed the city's massive seagoing trade. In those days, barges were animal-drawn and the districts along the waterway were rat-infested and perilous, but today, it's one of the frontiers for development; many of the horse tracks are leafy promenades and shadowy warehouses have become affluent loft condos. Along the shore, you'll pass docks where houseboat barges tie up; their owners can be found topside, making conversation with passersby. The most popular segment is probably the crescent just north of Regent's Park. **London Waterbus** (www.londonwaterbus.com; ☏ **020/7482-2550**) ferries riders in longboats for £8.

picnics or ball throwing, there's little in the way of amenities or activities, unless you count voyeurism.
The Mall, SW1. www.royalparks.org.uk. ☏ **020/7930-1793.** Free. Open 5am–midnight. Tube: St James's Park.

Trafalgar Square ★★ PARK   Once a stable, Trafalgar Square has evolved to become the setting for demonstrations, such as infamous riots over poll taxes and unemployment. The English gather here for happy things, too, as they did for the announcement of V-E Day (May 8, 1945), and as for free summer performances. The statue of Lord Nelson (1843), who sacrificed his life in 1805 to defeat Napoleon Bonaparte, looks down Whitehall from 167 feet up; climb the portico of the National Gallery (p. 69), and you'll see a heart-stirring view of Big Ben's tower. The northwestern plinth of Trafalgar Square was designed for an equestrian statue of its own, but money ran out and it stood empty from 1841. And what of Trafalgar's Square's famous pigeons? Until the early 1990s, the square swarmed with them—the fluttering flock was estimated to peak at 35,000. But with the help of captive hawks, they were banished for overactive excretion.
Free. Open 24 hr. Tube: Charing Cross or Leicester Square.

Victoria Park ★★ PARK/GARDEN   The largest and finest open space in East London, this was the capital's first public park. Bordered by canals and divided in two by Grove Road, it covers just under 87 hectares (220 acres) and contains two lakes, formal gardens, and a bandstand. Notable features include an 1862 drinking fountain and two arches from the pre-1831 London Bridge—now turned into benches. In summer, big music events come here. The park also forms the central section of the **Jubilee Greenway Walk,** a route marked out in 2009 in honor of the Queen's Diamond Jubilee, and stretching for exactly 60km (37 miles)—1 km for each year of her reign—from Buckingham Palace to the Olympic Park.

Grove Rd., E3. www.towerhamlets.gov.uk/victoriapark. ✆ **020/7364-2494.** Free. Daily 6am–dusk. Tube: Mile End/Overground, Hackney Wick or Homerton.

Organized Tours & Excursions

There are so many guides to choose from—the best ones are led by government-accredited "Blue Badge" professionals, so always look for the Blue Badge—that you could fill a week with walking tours alone. Plenty of qualified operators cater to groups, but many others will let you join individually: **City of London Guided Walks** (www.city oflondonguides.com; £7), run by the government—so its facts are unimpeachable—and light on theatrics; **Eating London Tours** (www.eatinglondontours.co.uk; £65), a 3¹/₂-hour, stuff-yourself-silly walking romp though some of the greatest victuals in the East End; **Greenwich Guided Walks** (www.greenwichtours.co.uk; ✆ **020/ 8858-6169,** £8) run by the local council in Greenwich; **Muggle Tours** (www.muggletours.co.uk; ✆ **07917/411-374;** £12 adults, £10 children 11 and under) for Harry Potter fans; and the indomitable **London Walks** (www.walks.com; ✆ **020/7624-3978** most tours £9), which is both reliable and entertaining.

Narrated bus tours often make you wait 15 to 30 minutes for the next bus each time you get off, which can add up to hours wasted, and although your ticket will be good for 24 hours, don't expect to catch anything between 6pm or so until after 9am the next morning. Day tickets may come with a free walking tour (Changing the Guard, Jack the Ripper) and a hop-on, hop-off pass for the river shuttle boat. Both of those perks must often be used during the same 24 hours as the bus ticket's validity. The three major players in town, which cost £25 to £33 for adults, are **Big Bus Tours** (www.bigbustours.com; ✆ **020/7808-6753**), **Golden Tours Open Top Bus Tours** (www. goldentours.com; ✆ **020/7630-2028** (U.K.) and **800/509-2507** (North America), and **The Original Tour London Sightseeing** (www.theoriginaltour.com; ✆ **020/8877-1722**). You might have a more enjoyable time seeing the city's waterfront landmarks and Green-wich from the Thames using **City Cruises** (www.citycruises.com; ✆ **020/774-0400;** £8 single, £12 return). The most economical way to see the town if you have limited time is from the top of a red double-decker city bus: The **15 bus,** which crosses the city northwest to southeast, takes in Paddington, Oxford Street, Piccadilly Circus, Trafalgar Square, Fleet Street, St Paul's, and the Tower of London.

Especially for Kids

On paper, some of London's museums sound as if they'd be too dry, but in reality, they bend over backward to cater to children—sometimes even at the expense of adult minds. Every major museum, no exceptions, has an on-site cafe for lunch, and nearly all of them offer activity packs to helps kids engage with the exhibitions. Make your way to Covent Garden's **London Transport Museum** (p. 69), where kids can pretend to drive a bus and explore other eye-level exhibits. Then bring your brood a 15-minute walk north to the **British Museum** (p. 66) and hook them up with crayons and pads, exploration backpacks, and the special 12-object collections tour geared to young minds. Just east you'll find a city park just for children: The 7-acre **Coram's Fields ★** (www.corams fields.org) was set aside in 1739 for an orphanage at a time when 75% of London kids died before the age of 5. Its southern stone gate is where mothers once abandoned their babies in desperation. Today, no adult may enter without a child, and it's the scene of daily joy between parents and children; there's a petting zoo, two playgrounds for all ages, sand pits, and a paddling pool. Take the Piccadilly Line to South Kensington, where the **V&A** (p. 88) has hundreds of hands-on exhibits for kids (look for the hand symbol on the maps), such as trying on Victorian costumes to trying on armor gauntlets. The plain-speaking signs and robotic dinosaurs of the **Natural History Museum** (p. 86) impress kids as much as the airplanes and space capsules over their heads at the world-class **Science Museum** (p. 88)—both institutions furnish even more kids' trails and activities for free.

WHERE TO STAY

Accommodations are subject to a Value Added Tax (VAT) of 20%. Happily, almost all small B&Bs include taxes in their rates, although you may be charged 3% to 5% to use a credit card. More expensive hotels (those around £150 or more) tend to leave taxes off their tariffs, which can result in a nasty surprise at checkout.

Soho, Covent Garden & Nearby
EXPENSIVE

Hazlitt's ★★★   A stay is like a slumber in a time machine. Each room is its own individual historic universe, the centerpiece of which is a deep oak or carved four-poster bed. Around you is a bathroom with antique fixtures and heavy silk curtains that, when pulled closed after a long day, make you feel as if you are the master of your own Georgian town house—plus, of course, modern expectations such as AC, flat-screen TV, and safes. Breakfast including fresh-baked croissants arrives on a tray every morning, delivered by discreet staff. When you step out your front

London Hotels

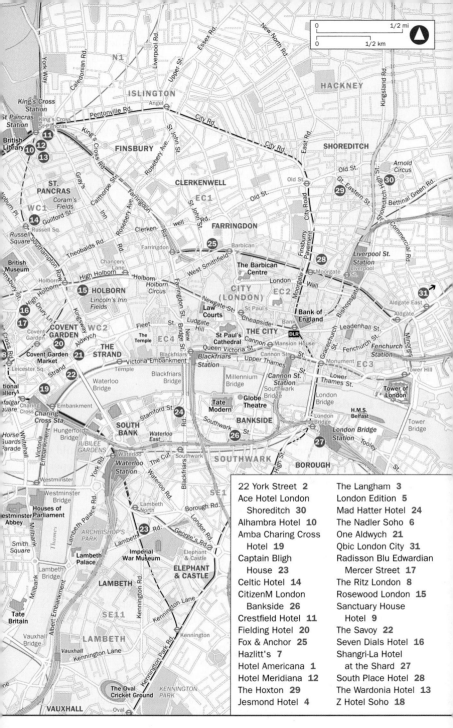

22 York Street **2**	The Langham **3**
Ace Hotel London Shoreditch **30**	London Edition **5**
	Mad Hatter Hotel **24**
Alhambra Hotel **10**	The Nadler Soho **6**
Amba Charing Cross Hotel **19**	One Aldwych **21**
	Qbic London City **31**
Captain Bligh House **23**	Radisson Blu Edwardian Mercer Street **17**
Celtic Hotel **14**	The Ritz London **8**
CitizenM London Bankside **26**	Rosewood London **15**
	Sanctuary House Hotel **9**
Crestfield Hotel **11**	The Savoy **22**
Fielding Hotel **20**	Seven Dials Hotel **16**
Fox & Anchor **25**	Shangri-La Hotel at the Shard **27**
Hazlitt's **7**	
Hotel Americana **1**	South Place Hotel **28**
Hotel Meridiana **12**	The Wardonia Hotel **13**
The Hoxton **29**	Z Hotel Soho **18**
Jesmond Hotel **4**	

door, you can retreat to the Library or step into the thick of Soho, completing the opulent fantasy. "Dandyism is a variety of genius," wrote William Hazlitt, a great writer of his age. That statement may not be true, but it sounds good. He died here when it was a rooming house, in 1830 at age 52.

6 Frith St., W1. www.hazlittshotel.com. © **020/7434-1771.** 30 units. Rooms £215–£354. Tube: Tottenham Court Rd. **Amenities:** Room service; free Wi-Fi.

The Langham ★★   In 1863, while Americans were shooting each other in farmyards, London was assembling the first and most celebrated grande dame hotel in Europe. The polished lobby is perfumed, the lifts swathed in leather, the rooms are private cocoons of ordered wainscoting, enveloping beds, and bathrooms with toiletries in pink paper cartons kept in a box by the sink. Its Palm Court has been serving high tea (£40) since 1865. For its brag-worthy reputation, the Langham is favored by moneyed tourists from the Far East, and for service and discretion, along with that long history, there are few peers. The tariff is also something for the record books, but that's the price you pay to be in the company of Lady Di, Wallis Simpson, and Winston Churchill, who rightly favored it, and Arthur Conan Doyle, who sent Sherlock Holmes here in several stories.

1c Portland Place, Regent St., W1. www.langhamhotels.com. © **020/7636-1000.** 380 units. £312–£444. Tube: Oxford Circus. **Amenities:** 2 restaurants; 2 bars; spa; business center; swimming pool; free Wi-Fi.

The London Edition ★★   Style superstar Ian Schrager turned his attention to a worn-out century-old hotel on the tatty Tottenham Court Road end of Oxford Street in Fitzrovia—convenient to nearly everything by foot—and opened an instant hotspot. On the surface, it would seem to be a calculated mix of classy and irreverent—but look deeper and you'll find a carefully run hotel where staff is more friendly than their current cool status might dictate. Rooms don't slouch a bit—although the dark wood panel decor may remind you of a 1970s basement rumpus room. Beds are piled with softness and bathrooms stocked with every convenience from robes to cotton swabs. It's also—this must be said—the place to stay if you love hot guys, since the porters and desk staff seem to have been hired as much for the cornflower blue of their eyes as for their service credentials. Chef Jason Atherton's bistro-inflected Berners Tavern, and the adjoining lobby bar (get the Elderflower Power Sour cocktail) are favorites among moneyed hipsters. All is run by Marriott.

10 Berners St., W1. www.editionhotels.com/london. © **020/7781-0000.** 173 rooms. Rooms £285–£415. Tube: Tottenham Court Rd. **Amenities:** Room service; 24-hr. fitness center; free bottled water; loaner laptops; free Wi-Fi.

One Aldwych ★★★   The pie-shaped, onetime headquarters of the *Morning Post,* built in 1907, contains a consistently high-quality boutique with two restaurants, a sculpture-filled lobby lounge, and a

A studio suite at One Aldwych.

theatrically lit, chlorine-free underground swimming pool where the printing presses used to be. Rooms are contemporary and designed with environmentalism in mind, have beds to sink into, and some even sneak a view of the Thames. The staff is truly five-star in that it tries to meet needs without being asked, and its location feels impossibly considerate, too: steps from Covent Garden and Trafalgar, a walk down Strand to St Paul's, and a quick and gorgeous stroll over the Waterloo Bridge to the glories of Southbank.

1 Aldwych, WC2. www.onealdwych.com. ⓒ **020/7300-1000.** 105 units. Doubles from £264–£312. Tube: Covent Garden or Temple. **Amenities:** 2 restaurants; cocktail bar; pool; gym; free Wi-Fi.

Rosewood London ★★★ This stylish hotel is entered through a stone courtyard arch of a gloriously elaborate edifice (constructed as the Pearl Assurance citadel). It's the *ne plus ultra* of London's modern luxury properties. A foyer sheathed entirely in brass! Songbirds by the lifts! Toilet paper as indulgently soft as puppies' ears! Rooms so quiet you could hear a champagne bubble pop. They're also lush: giant 46" LCD TVs are standard, as is Italian bedding you sink into like a swimming pool. If it weren't for the hard reality of the tariff, it'd be enough to sour you that the rest of the planet can't be executed with such theatricality. The pleasures of the British Museum and Covent Garden are both 5 minutes away.

252 High Holborn, WC1. www.rosewoodhotels.com/london. ⓒ **020/7781-8888.** 262 units. £320–£510. Tube: Holborn. **Amenities:** Restaurant; bar; lounge; fitness center; spa; free Wi-Fi.

A suite at Rosewood London.

The Ritz London ★ There are few five-star hotels as otherworldly as The Ritz, which opened in 1906 at the height of the Belle Époque. Long the haunt of wealth and power—the Ritz's chief amenity is obsequiousness, and its talent for that makes it one of the most sought-after temporary addresses on Earth. The rooms, while fine and embarrassingly spacious, are reassuringly dowdy in the way that a wealthy philanthropist aunt might prefer—lots of lemons, greens, and fussy furniture. Beds are enormous, furnishings and paintings are well-maintained throwbacks to the turn of the last century, flowers are fresh. But the Ritz's real magic is the scene. Each afternoon the lobby, which runs the Piccadilly length of this palatial building, becomes a de facto runway for visitors who have dressed up for its famous High Tea at the Palm Court, its lush Lalique-encrusted Rivoli Bar, or its showplace restaurant. No one can linger for more than a few seconds in one spot before a suited staff member materializes to ask what you need, implying you look out of place; the Ritz has perfected the fickle art of hostile hospitality. By the same token, one gets the distinct impression that should a staff member fail to meet your own demands or place a fork at an improper angle, they would be whisked through backstage doors for flagellation, possibly by their own remorseful hand. And that's the Ritz—although it styles itself as a paragon of service, not everyone belongs there, and if you happen to wonder if you're the type who does, it might not be the place for you.

Piccadilly, W1. www.theritzlondon.com. ℂ **020/7493-8181.** 134 units. Rooms from £414. Tube: Green Park. **Amenities:** Restaurant; tea room; bar; fitness room; room service; free Wi-Fi.

The Savoy ★ Few cities can claim hotels as iconic as The Savoy, which merits a visit even if you, like most people, cannot afford to stay there. From the shimmering gleam of its Art Deco porte cochere to the palatial receiving rooms off the lobby, the Savoy has vibrated with high history, half Edwardian and half Jazz Age, since 1889. The American Bar

WHAT TO EXPECT AT town house hotels

Unfortunately, the famous English B&B is an endangered species, at least in central London. There's a drastic housing crunch—since 2009, 80% of private sector jobs created in all of the U.K. were created in London, and as a result, house prices shot up. Neighborhoods that were once dependable for cut-price lodging (Gloucester Place in Marylebone, Ebury Street in Victoria, Gower Street in Bloomsbury) are being gentrified, and B&Bs that don't convert to luxury apartments must either jack up rates or sell out to company-managed hotels that hire foreign-born desk staff who barely know London better than you do. B&Bs aren't the value they were even 5 years ago.

The ones that survive usually occupy "listed" buildings. What does that mean? It means that it has historical or architectural importance—for example, it's an example of a fine Georgian town house or an original stately Victorian terrace home. To keep developers from knocking down a gem, "listed" buildings are protected. Changing anything down to the color of the paint requires permission, and that is tough to come by. American tourists who are unused to London's listed buildings often post huffy online reviews about the very things that define town house hotels. That hotel is not a dump! It's carrying the torch of English hospitality.

Rooms are small by American standards. Interior walls were added to subdivide the original rooms; most subdivision was done in the mid–20th century to fill a housing gap after many of the city's big hotels were destroyed in the war. You are unlikely to have a closet and in some rooms suitcases can be hard to open without using the bed. The largest rooms in such B&Bs usually face the front.

Bathrooms are even smaller. In the old days, guests shared bathrooms. Now, to suit changing tastes, landlords wedged booths containing the staples (toilet, shower, sink) into rooms that weren't designed to have them.

Don't expect an elevator, or "lift." It takes years of begging and a small fortune to convince the council to permit the installation of an elevator, so few hotels have one. Assume you'll have to use the stairs. They may be narrower than you're used to, but on the bright side, the banisters are pretty. Rooms on higher floors require climbing, but they also receive more light, less noise, and often cost less.

Ceilings get lower as you go higher. Until the 20th century, the floors of fashionable town houses served distinct functions. The cellar was for kitchens and coal storage. The ground floor was usually used for living rooms. The first and second floors were reserved for bedrooms, and the top floor was for servants and for the children's nursery, which accounts for the slightly lower ceilings there.

Not all windows are double glazed. You think you hear traffic now? Imagine when horses and carriages clattered up the cobbles at all hours. If you're a light sleeper and your chosen B&B doesn't have double glazing, simply ask for a room at the back.

has been a hushed laboratory for upscale cocktails for a century. A small museum about the Savoy's history, open to anyone, reminds you how much happened here: Churchill puffing, Chaplin mugging, Gilbert and Sullivan pattering in its theatre, Monet and Whistler painting the Thames from its windows. Your every need, from floral to gourmet, will be addressed with abject elegance and for a dear price, but would you be surprised to learn that the hotel, run by Fairmont and owned by the nephew of the King of Saudi Arabia, now tackily exploits its Hollywood past by hanging paintings of movie stars in its Thames Foyer and placing photos of them on nightstands? Good night, Burt Lancaster.

Strand, WC2. www.fairmont.com/savoy-london. ✆ **800/257-7544** (U.S.) or 020/ 7836-4343 (London). 268 units. Rooms from £390. Tube: Embankment or Temple. **Amenities:** 3 restaurants; 2 bars; swimming pool; gym; spa; business center.

MODERATE

Amba Hotel Charing Cross ★★
The railway terminal hotel above Charing Cross Station was opened in 1865 and underwent many lives (and Blitz damage). Now the Amba is a well-run, upper-moderate hotel that dips its toes into luxury trimmings (heated bathroom floors, illuminated wardrobes, walk-in showers) without going over-the-top on price. The location is spectacular and could command higher rates: steps from Trafalgar Square and morning strolls on the Thames. Breakfast is taken with a view toward St Martin-in-the-Fields, and at night, some 350 candles are placed throughout the hallways and up the sweeping grand.

The Strand, WC2. www.amba-hotel.com/hotels/united_kingdom/london/charing-cross. ✆ **0871/376-9012.** 200 units. Rooms £169–£322. Tube: Charing Cross or Embankment. **Amenities:** Restaurant; bar; business center; free Wi-Fi.

The Fielding Hotel ★★
It's nearly impossible to beat the location, just steps from Covent Garden food and shopping. In this early 19th-century warren of tight staircases and fire doors, appealingly cramped, attractively decorated, and sometimes slightly airless tiny rooms snuggle you with a certain throwaway charisma. Room 10 has a sitting area that catches lots of afternoon light thanks to its corner position and copious windows. Everything's en suite. Trivia: Oscar Wilde was convicted of gross indecency in the Bow Street Magistrates' Court next door.

4 Broad Court, Bow St., WC2. www.thefieldinghotel.co.uk. ✆ **020/7836-8305.** 24 units. Doubles £140–£180. Tube: Covent Garden or Holborn. **Amenities:** Pass to nearby fitness center; free Wi-Fi.

The Nadler Soho ★★★
This custom build, announced by an Art Nouveau sculpture of the Greek goddess of the moon, gets moderate lodging right by providing style without pretension or hidden extra fees. Quiet, high-design rooms are compact but nonetheless kitted out with wide beds, mini-kitchens, a microwave, big glassy bathrooms with rain showers, plenty of power points, a half-hour of free national calls a day, and HDTVs that double as music players. Deluxe rooms, at the top of the middle-rate scale, sleep up to four. There's no restaurant, but all of Soho is heaving right outside your door—reason alone to book here.

10 Carlisle St., W1. www.thenadler.com. ✆ **020/3697-3697.** 78 units. Rooms £135–£255. Tube: Tottenham Court Road or Piccadilly Circus. **Amenities:** Free Wi-Fi.

Radisson Blu Edwardian Mercer Street ★★   This funky luxury hotel is packed into one of the oddly shaped points on the Seven Dials intersection, and the resulting jigsaw leads to some fun and surprising room configurations. It also means you're close to the city's best shopping, dining, and entertainment. There's a real boutique hotel feel, from the sassy art and velvety soft goods to the fact your HD screen runs off Apple TV technology. Deluxe rooms come with free movies and a daily cocktail, but often the Standard rooms are priced incredibly well for the area.

20 Mercer St., WC2. www.radissonblu-edwardian.com. ℂ **020/7836-4300.** 137 units. Rooms £149–£263. Tube: Covent Garden. **Amenities:** Bar/restaurant; fitness center; free Wi-Fi.

INEXPENSIVE

Alhambra Hotel ★★★   A well-kept, family-run spot, the comforting Alhambra is an inn with heart, and a top value. Its proprietors, have owned the land for decades and aren't at risk of being elbowed out, take pride in the family business, and they keep the prices low. Picture simple but dignified rooms (LCD TVs but no phones, always spotless) squeezed into old spaces and freshened up with bright bedspreads; cream pinstripe wallpaper; inviting royal blue carpeting; and built-in desks. Frank Valoti, the patriarch, does the cooking, and he dabbles in art, too; in the basement breakfast area, check out the pastel still life he drew to show Europeans what's included in his generous full English breakfast. If you share a bathroom, there are plenty to go around. The same family runs an annex across the street that has the same high standards.

17-19 Argyle St., WC1. www.alhambrahotel.com. ℂ **020/7837-9575.** 52 units. Doubles £80–£111, includes breakfast. Tube: King's Cross St Pancras. **Amenities:** Lobby computer; free Wi-Fi.

Celtic Hotel ★★   Few other budget hoteliers put as much heart their work as the Marozi family; making sure guests are acclimated to London by answering questions, obliging dietary requests, and filling bellies with a cooked breakfast that's so enormous (try the banana yogurt) that lunch might be optional. Its quirkiness is what longtime regulars love about the place—rooms do not have TVs or phones, furniture is endearingly mismatched, and the lounge is a hub for socializing with fellow guests. Add £6 to £22 if you don't want to share shower or toilet.

61-63 Guilford St., WC1. www.celtichotel.com. ℂ **020/7837-6737.** 30 units. Doubles from £82, includes breakfast. Tube: Russell Square. **Amenities:** 2 lounges; free Wi-Fi.

Crestfield Hotel ★★   Every city needs a few unabashedly basic, secure choices that aren't grim. Rooms here are tiny, freshly painted and done up with lace curtains, but there's no lift. Bathrooms (most rooms have their own, with toilet) are essentially tiled cubicles with drains in the floor, but the £100 family room for four is a true steal. Room 9, a

4

LONDON | Where to Stay

double, is located on a landing facing the back, so it's even quieter than most. If you're only staying on weekdays, ask for a special deal, because the hotel sees a lot of weekend trade. Private bathrooms cost £10 to £15 more. Seriously, what more do you require?

2-4 Crestfield St., WC1. www.crestfieldhotel.com. © **020/7837-0500.** 52 units. Doubles £60, includes breakfast. Tube: King's Cross St Pancras. **Amenities:** Bar; free Wi-Fi.

Hotel Meridiana ★   This is what a value hotel should be: not lavish, but you happily get what you pay for. Walls can be thin, rooms truly teeny, many rooms share bathrooms, but everything is spotless and breakfast (served in a room so small that sometimes you have to wait your turn) is a proper cooked one. Heating and hot water are reliable, too, which isn't always the case in buildings of this age. If you just want a place to sleep where you'll have no regrets about hygiene or price, this no-frills B&B is a decent choice. You're unlikely to get as much value.

43-44 Argyle Sq., WC1. www.hotelmeridiana.co.uk. © **020/7713-0144.** 27 units. Doubles from £88, includes breakfast. Tube: King's Cross St Pancras. **Amenities:** Free Wi-Fi.

Jesmond Hotel ★★★   Glyn Beynon does a solid job of running the family B&B where he grew up, in a historic Georgian town house (ask to read the history he wrote of it). The Jesmond is far beyond the expectations of its tariff range. Bathrooms have larger-than-average showers, windows are soundproofed to keep out the roar of Gower Street's bus traffic, and the house's 18th-century coal chute is a kitchen where full English breakfasts are served in a cellar breakfast room that doubles as a day lounge. The back garden is cultivated with flowers and wooden chairs. It's simple, it's friendly, and it's still one of London's last "they're charging *how* much?" values. Pay for 6 nights from October to March, and you can stay for 7. Don't confuse this place with the Jesmond Dene, a B&B on Argyle Square in King's Cross—it's very good, too, but not as central as the Jesmond.

63 Gower St., WC1. www.jesmondhotel.org.uk. © **020/7636-3199.** 15 units. Doubles £85–£110, includes breakfast. Tube: Goodge Street. **Amenities:** Free Wi-Fi.

Seven Dials Hotel ★   There are nearly no budget hotels near Covent Garden. If you're this central, you can charge more. Here, though, everything is little: the stairway, the rooms—and correspondingly, the rates. Furniture and bathroom doors wrestle for supremacy, still, there's usually enough storage space, a TV mounted on an armature, a basic writing desk, teeny clean bathrooms, and firm beds. Forget the lack of a lift and all the ways it's average. Its situation on Monmouth Street, steps from pubs, shops, and bars around Covent Garden, is without compare. Dump your bags and go play, because the price is right.

7 Monmouth St., WC2. www.sevendialshotel.com. © **020/7681-0791.** 18 units. Doubles £110–£120, includes breakfast. Tube: Covent Garden. **Amenities:** Free Wi-Fi.

HOW TO HACK high rates

To save money on lodging, remember five simple rules:

1. **Off-season is cheaper.** Many big hotels have two seasons: April through September and October through March (excluding holidays). Prices will be 10% to 25% cheaper in winter. Interestingly, very few family-owned B&Bs and inns bother with this system, pricing uniformly.

2. **To save, stay longer.** I haven't found a family-run hotel that wasn't willing to lower prices for anyone staying more than 5 or 6 nights.

3. **Mind the crowds.** Soho, a party zone, is cheaper on weekdays; The City, a business enclave, is cheaper on weekends.

4. **Go mom-and-pop.** Their rates usually include taxes, but big hotels' don't.

5. **Last-minute deals are rare, but do exist.** Routes for looking into deals are Hotwire.com, Priceline.com, and the same-day booking app Hotel Tonight.

The Wardonia Hotel ★   The Wardonia has a fresher look than many of its neighbors, but spoiler alert: rooms are wee—like *sooooo* tiny. But so is the price. The style is the usual—very simple in blue and white fabrics and plain brown wainscoting, bathrooms with showers but not tubs—although the crazy low rates, which haven't gone up in half a decade, are something to astound and make pricey London possible for some budgets. Everything's en suite, but there's no breakfast. The Wardonia is plainly a value contender.
46-54 Argyle St., WC1. www.wardoniahotel.co.uk. ✆ **020/7837-3944.** 65 units. Doubles £55. Tube: King's Cross St Pancras. **Amenities:** Free Wi-Fi.

The Z Hotel Soho ★★★   Here's the formula: extremely compact rooms, glassy sleek style, thrilling location, and since extras such as breakfast are pre-paid when you book, there's a skeleton staff, keeping costs down. The formula works because it's done with design smarts: quality bedding and the 40-inch TVs but no closets and drawers. Quarters are close (around 9 sq. m/90 sq. ft.), but quirky, with a zig-zaggy courtyard and a roof deck with a nifty view of the Palace Theatre. If you share a room with a platonic friend, note bathrooms, though stocked with Thierry Mugler toiletries, are enclosed by panels of fogged glass. Just be sure to pronounce it "zed." Rhymes with bed—what it's good for. There is a second location in much less desirable Victoria, a block west of the station (5 Lower Belgrave St., SW1; ✆ **020/3589-3990;** 106 units, 60% windowless) and another just south of Piccadilly Circus.
17 Moor St., W1. www.thezhotels.com. ✆ **020/3551-3701.** 85 units. Rooms usually £145–£195. Tube: Leicester Square. **Amenities:** Cafe; free Wi-Fi.

Southwark & Westminster

EXPENSIVE

Shangri-La Hotel at the Shard ★★   Be warned that if you decide to book at the Shangri-La, you must be prepared to never leave it. Staying here, on the 36th to 52nd floors of this glass-sheathed skyscraper, means that your room will be encased with floor-to-ceiling windows overlooking the entire city. No structure in London will be higher than you. When you take a bath (in your marble-clad washroom), you may feel as if you're flying over the Thames and the Tower of London, and when you swim in the horizon pool in the sky above St Paul's, the vista is so surreal you may wonder if it's all dream. Such glassy heaven comes with décor and amenities that are inflected by the Asian culture from which the Shangri-La brand hails. The Thames and the famous Borough Market are right at its base. Rates are higher than other luxury hotels in town but, so are the rooms, and that seems to justify it to nearly everyone's satisfaction.

31 St Thomas St., SE1, www.shangri-la.com/london/shangrila. ⓒ **020/7234-8000.** 202 units. King rooms from £375. Tube: London Bridge. **Amenities:** Restaurant; bar; fitness center; pool; in-room Nespresso coffee and tea; free Wi-Fi.

MODERATE

CitizenM London Bankside ★★★   This affordable Dutch hotel chain is blossoming, deservedly so, and its welcome concept of smart-and-stylish quarters without added fees makes it the best casual choice in Southwark. The glassy open-plan lobby seems to hum day and night with people sipping coffees and telecommuting. Check-in is self-guided

The lobby at CitizenM London Bankside.

by kiosk, and rooms are compact—almost podlike—but arranged with genius. Platform beds are massive and piled with pillows, curvy bathrooms slotted into the space with calculated aplomb, and you control everything from motorized blinds to the color of the room's mood lighting with a bedside tablet. There's even a library of free movies (including porn of all persuasions—it's a Dutch company, and it's sassy). New properties offering the identical concept in Holborn, Tower Hill, and Shoreditch have been announced for 2015.

20 Lavington St., SE1. www.citizenm.com/london-bankside. © **020/3519-1680.** 192 units. Doubles £109–£189. Tube: Southwark or London Bridge. **Amenities:** Free movies; free Wi-Fi.

The Mad Hatter Hotel ★★   Decent pub hotels, which are hotels above pubs, are a dying breed in London. Here, sizable, good-value rooms feel like they were lifted from a business hotel. Think decent-size bathrooms with tub/showers, rose-colored bedspreads, and a lift. The modest prices are a big deal for someplace so central: 5 minutes from the Tate Modern and just over Blackfriars Bridge from the City.

3-7 Stamford St., SE1. www.madhatterhotel.co.uk. © **020/7401-9222.** 30 units. Doubles from £140, includes breakfast. Tube: Southwark or Blackfriars. **Amenities:** Free Wi-Fi.

Sanctuary House Hotel ★   Once, many pubs ran nondescript inns as sidelines. The pub here is just a so-so Fuller's location (it owns hundreds of them), but the hotel upstairs is a creaking, well-tended reward unto itself for value and charm, and the staff is unusually responsive for such a small property. The look plays up its Victorian origins with plenty of handsome wood trim, but with the modernized bathrooms and soft beds. Even more miraculously, it's so near Big Ben that you can hear the bell peal. Across the street, the InterContinental charges twice as much.

33 Tothill St., SW1. www.sanctuaryhousehotel.co.uk. © **020/7799-4044.** 34 units. Doubles £150–£270. Tube: St James's Park or Westminster. **Amenities:** Free Wi-Fi.

INEXPENSIVE

Captain Bligh House ★★★   For a delicious taste of local London life without venturing far from the center of town, the Bligh, where Captain William Bligh lived after that sordid mutiny, is a transporting choice. Artists Gayna and Simon approach their wee guesthouse, built in the 1780s, as a quiet home from home: Units have little kitchens, and you get a starter pack of breakfast supplies. Although the excellent Imperial War Museum is across the street, it's not a neighborhood crawling with tourists, so you'll kick back at the local pub and jump the many bus lines that go past. The value is over-the-top.

100 Lambeth Rd., SE1. www.captainblighhouse.co.uk. © **020/7928-2735.** 5 units. Doubles from £88–£114. Tube: Lambeth North. **Amenities:** In-room kitchen; free Wi-Fi.

Other Top Hotels

EXPENSIVE

South Place Hotel ★★★ Plugged-in, stylish, and sexy: That's the crowd this hotel goes for, and you'll feel that way, too. The first hotel to be built from the ground up in The City for a century, every inch was run through the design filter, and much of the art was commissioned by celebrated contemporary artists. Rooms, charcoal-grey with wool carpets, are large, hushed and fully up-to-date with luxury expectations, so you'll find plenty of outlets, AV connections, blackout blinds closed from a bedside panel, and a big bed you can flop around in. The two restaurants, Angler and a 3 South Place Bar & Grill, have lured both named chefs and some of the liveliest professionals from the City for dinner before they head east to the party grounds at Spitalfields. Despite the hot scene, it never ignores the relaxation of its guests. On weekends, rates can dip to £170.

3 South Place, EC2. www.southplacehotel.com. ✆ **020/3503-0000.** 80 units. Doubles from £213. Tube: Moorgate or Liverpool Street. **Amenities:** 2 restaurants; 3 bars; guests' lounge; gym; spa; business center; free Wi-Fi.

MODERATE

22 York Street ★★ You might wonder at first if you have knocked on the door of a private Marylebone home of some bohemian doctor or lawyer. Inside, Michael and Liz Callis go for a farmhouse feel, with warm wooden floorboards, plenty of antiques and oriental rugs, and large bathrooms, almost all of which have tub/shower combinations. Guests get their own keys and are let loose to treat the five-level premises as their own, which includes plenty of tea, coffee, and biscuits for munching. Adding to the home-away-from-home feel, breakfasts are served in the kitchen at a communal country table where you meet your fellow guests. The food includes some fantastic pain au chocolate. Although they're not explicitly banned, kids may not feel comfortable.

22 York St., W1. www.22yorkstreet.co.uk. ✆ **020/7224-2990.** 10 units. Doubles from £150, includes breakfast. Tube: Baker Street. **Amenities:** Free Wi-Fi.

Ace Hotel London Shoreditch ★★ A stay at this epicenter of Shoreditch Cool isn't about service but about style, since the Ace's agreeable pretentions have become a "lifestyle brand" for the fashionably impressionable. Pretty people tap away on laptops all day at the lobby workbenches, pretty people dine at its restaurant (Hoi Polloi), which publishes its menu on newsprint just 'cause, and well-dressed drunk people thump away in its basement club until all hours. Accommodation is cushy where it counts (huge beds and bathrooms, built-in window sofas) and styled with self-knowing false irreverence when it won't affect your comfort (instead of drawers you use plastic crates, your bedspread is denim, and there's a guitar—an Ace signature). It's inauthentic, but fun, and the rates aren't crazy. If you've grown up enough to have some money but haven't left the all-night partying behind, the Ace wins.

100 Shoreditch High St., E1. www.acehotel.com/london. ℂ **020/7613-9800.** 97 units. Doubles £135–£279. Tube: Shoreditch High Street or Liverpool Street. **Amenities:** Restaurant; rooftop bar; basement club; gym; free Wi-Fi.

The Fox & Anchor ★   We all claim to want an old-fashioned English inn, but do you really want the chintz, the lace curtains, and the blank walls? In the thick of Smithfield's nightlife (so bring earplugs if you require them), this fun little find took a tiny old-fashioned pub hotel and upgraded it so it only *looks* old—brass sinks, mullioned windows, wood floors, yet they're also current with sound systems and flat-screen TVs. Downstairs, of course, there's a Victorian-era pub of mahogany, brass, and etched glass. It was also upgraded from the authentic original.

115 Charterhouse St., London EC1. www.foxandanchor.com. ℂ **020/7550-1000.** 6 units. Doubles from £120–£222, includes breakfast. Tube: Barbican or Farringdon. **Amenities:** Restaurant; bar; free Wi-Fi.

INEXPENSIVE

Hotel Americana ★   Beige-simple, without unnecessary flourish, but extremely well-maintained, the Americana is a strong value in a neighborhood besieged by rising rates. Robert, the chatty and opinionated longtime manager, is exactly the kind of authority on London (and on everything, really) that you wish to encounter behind a B&B desk. All rooms have showers, tiny TVs, a safe, and plenty of light. Although it's comprised of two conjoined town houses, there's a wee lift, and it's also very near Regent's Park and steps away from a launderette.

172 Gloucester Place, NW1. www.americanahotel.co.uk. ℂ **020/7723-1452.** 29 units. Doubles £99–£156, includes breakfast. Tube: Baker Street or Marylebone. **Amenities:** Free Wi-Fi.

The Hoxton ★   Self-consciously quirky rooms brag exposed brick walls, rain showers, and industrial-chic set pieces like dim lighting, metal, and stained wood. Continental breakfast is delivered each morning via a bag you hang on the door, which can make you feel like a monkey at the world's hippest zoo, and there's free water and milk for your little fridge. The public spaces, including a grill styled after an American diner, are hangouts in their own right. Rates average £179 and up, though weekends can be dramatically cheaper; as little as £99. A second, 174-room Hox recently opened at 199-206 High Holborn, near Covent Garden.

81 Great Eastern St., EC3. www.hoxtonhotels.com. ℂ **020/7550-1000.** 208 units. Rooms £99–£269, includes breakfast. Tube: Aldgate or Tower Hill. **Amenities:** Restaurant, 1 hr. free local calls; free Wi-Fi.

Qbic London City ★★   From an affordable design hotel chain in Holland, Qbic is a wacky antidote to the formula budget hotels.

Everything you need—bed, outlets, bathroom with a rain shower, TV—is part of a prefabricated unit that dominates the middle of the room. It's not a capsule hotel, just a hotel that figured out a way to build everything into a single multi-purpose unit, with plenty of room to walk around it and stash your suitcase. Your lamp is made out of a coiled and immobilized garden hose, your clothing rack a strange ladder/planter of some sort—it's just fun. There are free coffee and tea machines on every floor, and a preposterously funky lobby where organic continental breakfast is served daily (extra). You'll be within walking distance to Brick Lane, the Tower of London and the scene of Spitalfields. It's a kick, the managers are sensitive to local culture, and it's worth every penny.

42 Adler St. E1. london.qbichotels.com. © **020/3021-3300.** 171 units. Windowless rooms from £69, windowed doubles from £79. Tube: Aldgate East. **Amenities:** Free coffee; lounge; free Wi-Fi.

The Moderate Hotel Chains

A few reliable hotel chains specialize in moderately priced rooms and have locations across the city, including in prime locations no family-owned B&B can afford. Be warned—so many Europeans habitually turn to these that their prices frequently rise past the point of value, so these are best when booked far in advance. In addition to these names, look into **Motel One** (www.motel-one.com), a stylish German newcomer, which has rates from £89 at a Tower Hill property.

easyHotel ★   This is how you do London super-cheaply while avoiding hostels. Reservations typically cost £25 for double rooms if you book 6 months ahead, and £35 to £90 if you procrastinate. Its revelation is, to others, a curse: prefabricated room units that differ only in how little floor space you're given (the smallest are 6 sq. m./65 sq. ft.). Beds are double-size with white duvets, with rarely an inch of space between mattress and wall. No phone, no hair dryer, no frills at all. You may find a long ledge on which to pop a travel alarm clock, but bathrooms aren't more than plastic cubicles combining a shower, toilet, and sink in one water-splashed closet. The cheapest rooms don't even have windows. Want to watch TV? You'll pay £5 for 24 hours. Want housekeeping? £10. Wi-Fi is pay-as-you-use. This is no-nonsense sleep.

www.easyhotel.com. No phone reservations. 5 locations in central London. Rooms from £25–£90.

Ibis Hotels ★★   This 600-strong French chain is distinguished by its trademark 3-foot-square windows, its just-off-the-margins locations, and its simple but cheerful decor. You'll get a double bed, bathroom with shower, climate control, a 24-hour kitchen, TV, phone, at least one outlet, and a built-in desk. Breakfast (extra) is usually served from 4am, making this a smart choice if you need to catch an early flight or train. But let's be frank: You'd have to be mad to think these rooms are worth the price once they go above £170, so book as far ahead as possible. There's also **Ibis Styles,** the "all-inclusive" brand that is slightly more upscale and includes breakfast and Wi-Fi, and **Ibis Budget,** a bare-bones crash pad once known as Etap or Formule 1; rooms sleep up to three people, and have free Wi-Fi and TV, but few other frills.

Ibishotel.com. No English-reservations hotline. 6 locations around the city. Rooms £60–£209, varying by season and location. **Amenities:** Free Wi-Fi.

Premier Inn ★★★ This is many British travelers' favorite hotel brand. At 50,000 bedrooms and growing, it's the largest hotel chain in the United Kingdom, and rooms (maximum of two adults) offer a king-size bed, bathtub and shower, tea- and coffee-making facilities, TV, phone, iron, AC (sometimes), at least three outlets, and a desk. Increasingly, it requires you to check in at a kiosk, eliminating local interaction, but that tells you about the tourist churn that this company is going for. Many locations include a mass-appeal bar/cafe, Thyme. Prices start at £19 nearly a year ahead, but final prices can rival a much nicer hotel's. Like airline tickets, prices rise as availability dwindles, and in busy times, soar far higher than where they should be, so book ahead or look elsewhere. The brand runs a cheaper and tinier concept, **Hub by Premier Inn** (www.hubhotels.co.uk); locations are near Covent Garden, King's Cross, Spitalfields, and the Tower of London. Hub rooms are just 11.4 sq. m. (123 sq. ft.), and functions such as AC and TV are controlled by app.

10 locations around the city. www.premierinn.com. ✆ **0845/099-0095.** Rooms from £80–£126. **Amenities:** Bar/cafe; 30 min. free Wi-Fi daily, then £3 for 24 hr.

Travelodge ★ Rates start at a head-slapping £19 for a non-flexible reservation if you book 11 months ahead. That more than makes up for the thinnest amenities of the economy brands. With more than two dozen locations in greater London, it's nicer than the American Travelodge brand, which isn't related to it. Expect king-size beds, bathtub and shower, TV (but no phone, hair dryer, or toiletries), paid in-room movies, a wardrobe, at least one power point, and a desk. Breakfast, if offered, is about £8 more. "Family rooms" have a pullout couch but cost the same as a double. Search its site for a grid of available London hotels.

www.travelodge.co.uk. ✆ **08719/848484.** Rooms £65–£116. **Amenities:** Bar/cafe (often); Wi-Fi £3 a day.

Tune Hotels ★★ This Malaysian import provides everything you need in a modern crash pad but nothing else: en-suite power shower, round-the-clock reception, air conditioning, but not even a closet—you get hangers. If you want more, you pay a few pounds more at a time: towel rental, TV, Wi-Fi, safe, hair dryer, and even windows come at a price. The a la carte model keeps costs down but isn't a path to luxury, yet the facilities are clean and designed with minimalist zip. Don't write off a windowless room's power to mediate jet lag. Prices are as low as £35 months in advance and go to £125 or so last-minute.

www.tunehotels.com/london. No phone. 5 locations in the city. Rates can range from £35–£125.

WHERE TO EAT

The English palate has finally caught up with the rest of the world. Cabbage is no longer the national affliction. If London's stomachs suffer from anything today, it's from a trend toward overpriced places that appeal more to vanity and conspicuous consumption than value and authentic hospitality.

Soho, Covent Garden & Nearby

EXPENSIVE

Arbutus ★★★ CONTEMPORARY EUROPEAN   A pair of celebrated city chefs, Anthony Demetre and Will Smith, opened an exquisite restaurant with the intention of serving magnificent modern food at reasonable prices, and they have triumphed, winning a Michelin star for their efforts. The changing menu might include Welsh Elwy Valley lamb, English pea soup, Dorset crab, Scottish organic salmon, or braised pig's head. Some of these may sound dauntingly adventurous, but deliciousness is assured. Service is also impeccable, and wines are available in carafes equal to a third of a bottle. Between 5 and 6:30pm, you'll find great deals such as £10 for the plat du jour plus a carafe of wine.

63-64 Frith St., W1. www.arbutusrestaurant.co.uk. ℂ **020/7734-4545.** Mains £16–£21; £19 2-course/£21 3-course pre-theatre set menu 5–6:30pm. Mon–Thurs noon–2:30pm and 5–11pm, Fri–Sat noon–2:30pm and 5–11:30pm, Sun noon–3pm and 5:30–10:30pm. Reservations recommended. Tube: Tottenham Court Road.

J. Sheekey ★★ SEAFOOD   Smartly turned out waiters prep you with so many strange fish-eating implements that your place setting starts to look like a workstation at Santa's workshop. Such presentational flourishes are appropriate to theatreland, where this has been a bistro-style classic for years. The least expensive main dish option, fish pie, is fortunately its trademark, but there are plenty of other choices, from shrimp-and-scallop burgers to a delectable lemon sole, plus a changing slate of game and meats. Children are welcomed. The adjoining horseshoe-shaped Oyster Bar (same hours without a mid-afternoon break) does a limited menu that includes a velvety rich crab bisque with cognac (£9).

28-32 St Martin's Court, WC2. www.j-sheekey.co.uk. ℂ **020/7240-2565.** Main courses £16–£42; weekend set-lunch menu, 3 courses £27. Mon–Fri noon–3pm and 5:30pm–midnight, Sat noon–3:30pm and 5:30pm–midnight, Sun noon–3:30pm and 5:30–11pm. Reservations recommended. Tube: Leicester Square.

Rules ★★ TRADITIONAL BRITISH   For a high-end kitchen that takes British cuisine seriously, go with an icon. In fact, Rules is London's oldest restaurant, cooking since 1798, and its patrons have included Graham Greene, Charles Dickens, Evelyn Waugh, and Edward VII. Its view of a dining experience is steeped in its own hype; beer comes in a "silver tankard," for example, and the landmarked dining rooms are an overdressed mélange of yellowing etchings, antlers, and rich red fabrics. But what's on the table is indisputably high-class London: English-reared meat like roast loin of roe deer, whole roast squab or grouse (it serves 18,000 game birds annually), and cocktails like that famous one made of tonic, juniper, and quinine. Its nearest rival, Simpsons-in-the-Strand at the Savoy hotel, has been going since 1828, but that has become overly touristy. This is the heartier choice.

35 Maiden Lane, WC1. www.rules.co.uk. 🕾 **020/7836-5314.** Mains £18–£29. Mon–Sat noon–11:45pm, Sun noon–10:45pm. Tube: Covent Garden.

The Wolseley ★★★ CONTEMPORARY EUROPEAN   "No Flash or Intrusive Photography please," chastises a footnote on the menu. That's because this opulent bistro in the Grand European style, is home base for celebrities and power lunchers. Built as a luxury car dealership for a doomed manufacturer, then used as a bank, a decade ago it became the caviar-scooping, oyster-shucking, tea-pouring. Waiters are unattainably attractive and look down their noses as they gingerly place salad Niçoise and Swiss souffle, enacting the calculated Continental crispness we crave.

160 Piccadilly, W1. www.thewolseley.com. 🕾 **020/7499-6996.** Mains £15–£20. Mon–Fri 7am–midnight, Sat 8am–midnight, Sun 8am–11pm. Tube: Green Park.

MODERATE

Bill's ★★ INTERNATIONAL   A 5-minute walk from the British Museum and handy for many uses—big breakfasts, lunches, dinner, afternoon tea, feeding kids, or downing cheap cocktails—this casual and affordable small group of restaurants started as a green grocer and is rigorous about quality ingredients. In few other London establishments will you find mac and cheese, burgers, pecan pie, and Caesar salad together on the same menu. It's a lifesaver when you're indecisive or in need of drama-free grub served briskly, which is why you'll be glad to hear there are also locations near Piccadilly Circus (36-44 Brewer St., W1), the Long Acre shopping street (St Martin's Courtyard, WC2; Tube: Covent Garden), and off Strand (21 Wellington St., WC2; Tube: Temple).

41 Kingsway, WC2. www.bills-website.co.uk. 🕾 **020/7836-8368.** Mains £9–£13. Mon–Fri 7am–11pm, Sat 8am–11pm, Sun 8am–10:30pm. Tube: Holborn.

Blanchette ★ FRENCH   Divinely assembled tasting plates focus on ingredients: grilled hanger steak with snails, grilled asparagus with aged

London Restaurants

Arbutus 3	J. Sheekey 8
Bar Italia 5	Poppies 27
Beigel Bake 25	The Princess
Bill's 13	Louise 15
The Black Friar 20	Punjab Restaurant 14
Blanchette 2	Regency Café 7
Borough Market 21	Restaurant Story 23
Browns 9	Rochelle Canteen 24
Café in the Crypt 10	Rules 12
Ceviche 4	St John Bread
E. Pellicci 26	and Wine 28
The Fryer's Delight 17	The Stockpot 6
The George Inn 22	The Wolseley 1
Gordon's Wine Bar 11	Ye Olde Cheshire
Great Queen	Cheese 19
Street 16	Ye Olde Mitre 18

Comté cheese, hot bread delivered in a brown paper bag and soft butter spread with a wooden paddle. The look is much like a casually urbanized French farmhouse of rough wood, exposed brick, and a long bar ideal for tasting charcuterie and sipping wine. And Blanchette wants you to love wine like the French: There's only one beer on the menu.

9 D'Arblay St., W1. www.blanchettesoho.co.uk. ☎ **020/7439-8100.** Small plates £3–£8. Mon–Sat noon–11pm, Sun noon–5pm. Tube: Oxford Circus.

Browns ★ TRADITIONAL BRITISH   In London, there's a Browns for fashion, and a Brown's Hotel, but Browns the spacious brasserie is the Browns you can afford. Installed in the former Westminster County Courts, this high-quality, Brighton-based English chain serves updated English food and imported beer. Expect lots of indulgently hearty dishes such as fish pie in cream and white wine sauce; steak, mushroom and Guinness pie; a house salad with beets, quinoa, pumpkin seeds, artichoke hearts and more; or a nice fat wild boar and chorizo burger. British tradition—starchy but welcoming to casual tourists—is the main product here: There's another Browns at 47 Maddox St. in Mayfair (Tube: Oxford Circus), a riverside one near Tower Bridge (Butlers Wharf; Tube: London Bridge or Tower Hill), and one at 2 Cardinal Walk (Tube: Victoria).

82-84 St Martins Lane, WC2. www.browns-restaurants.com. ☎ **020/7497-5050.** Mains £9–£15, Sunday roast £11–£15. Mon–Thurs 8am–10:30pm, Fri 8am–11pm, Sat 10am–11pm, Sun 10am–10:30pm. Tube: Leicester Square.

Ceviche ★★★ PERUVIAN   This relative newcomer is my firm favorite in Soho. Owner Martin Morales quit his job at Disney's European music division to pursue his true passion: food. Now he has a cookbook and runs this hopping, no-attitude Peruvian hangout that pours the best pisco sour in town. Favorite small plates include Amor Amar scallops dish with lúcuma fruit puree, the don ceviche made with Amarillo chili tiger's milk, and the succulent corazón mío of beef skewers marinated in panca chili anticuchera. Once your tongue tastes its first citrusy zip, you'll feel compelled to come back. If you want to understand the vibrancy of London's newfound passion for cuisine exploration, this is the place.

17 Frith St., W1. www.cevicheuk.com. ☎ **020/7292-2040.** Small plates £7–£12. Mon–Sat noon–11:30pm, Sun noon–10:15pm. Reservations suggested. Tube: Piccadilly Circus or Tottenham Court Road.

Great Queen Street ★★★ TRADITIONAL BRITISH   Here, the essence of gastropub cuisine in the convenient environs of Covent Garden. There's a pub feel—scuffed wood floors, burgundy walls, sconces capped with fringed mini-shades. The slow-cooked dishes are clean and reassuringly ingredient-proud. Samples include Old Spot (a breed of pig) pork chops with sticky shallots, griddled quail with celery salt; and lamb's

shoulder cooked for 7 hours and accompanied by gratin dauphinoise—
that one feeds four, which hints at the social atmosphere encouraged
here. The Cellar Bar, open until midnight, serves cold dishes from the
same menu.

32 Great Queen St., WC2. www.greatqueenstreetrestaurant.co.uk. ℂ **020/7242-
0622.** Mains £12–£25. Lunch Mon–Sat noon–2:30pm and Sun 1–4pm, dinner Mon–
Sat 6–10:30pm. Tube: Covent Garden or Holborn.

INEXPENSIVE

Bar Italia ★★ COFFEE/ITALIAN   Italians settled Soho in the 1940s,
and before they decamped for the suburbs, they installed a set of mod,
gleaming coffee bars and cafes. This straggler from 1949 is a haunt of
slumming celebrities and artists, yet modest enough for the rest of us.
While this institution is busy all day—making simple sandwiches and
delivering pastries—it swells with revelers after midnight. Even Rome
doesn't have bars that steam, press, and shuffle coffee across such defi-
antly worn '50s linoleum with such gusto. "Like everything in this city
that Londoners really enjoy, it reminds us of being abroad," quipped the
Guardian. Whatever; it practically oozes hipness.

22 Frith St., W1. www.baritaliasoho.co.uk. ℂ **020/7437-4520.** Coffee £3–£4, pizza
£10–£11, panini £7. Mon–Sat 6:30am–4:30am, Sun 6:30am–2am. Tube: Leicester
Square.

Café in the Crypt ★ INTERNATIONAL   This is the most delicious
graveyard in town, and a perennial savior of budget travelers. Under the
sanctuary of the historic St Martin-in-the-Fields church at Trafalgar
Square, atop the gravestones of 18th-century Londoners, one of the
West End's sharpest bargains is served. The menu at this dependable
cafeteria changes daily, but satisfying options always include a few hot
meat mains, a vegetarian choice, soups, salads, and a traditional English
dessert such as plum fruit cobbler with custard poured warm from a jug,
all homemade. The soup-and-pudding deal is £7 and afternoon tea is but
£6. April to September, it also serves al fresco on the plaza at street level.

Trafalgar Sq., WC2. www.stmartin-in-the-fields.org. ℂ **020/7766-1158.** Mains
£6–£8. Mon–Tues 8am–8pm, Wed 8am–10:30pm, Thurs–Sat 8am–9pm, Sun 11am–
6:30pm. Tube: Charing Cross.

Gordon's Wine Bar ★ INTERNATIONAL   The atmosphere is
matchless at London's most vaunted wine bar. It was established in
1890 (when Rudyard Kipling lived upstairs) and, thank goodness, hasn't
been refurbished since. These tight, craggy cellars beneath Villiers
Street are wallpapered with important newspaper front pages from the
20th century—Thatcher's resignation, the death of King George VI—
while ceiling fans threaten to come loose from their screws. Dozens of
wines and sherries by the glass are around £5; you can select from a
marble display of English and French cheeses or a steam table of hot

4

food, and in good weather, the event expands along Embankment Gardens with casual al fresco meals such as stuffed peppers and marinated pork loin. Come down well before offices let out to secure seating; it won't accept bookings.

47 Villiers St., WC2. www.gordonswinebar.com. ℂ **020/7930-1408.** Meals £7–£10. Mon–Sat 11am–11pm, Sun noon–10pm. Tube: Charing Cross or Embankment.

Punjab Restaurant ★★★ INDIAN   Ignore that it looks like every other hack kitchen sponging off the Covent Garden tourist trade—this place predates the recent curry trend, which is why it survived the crest of the popularity wave. Punjab has been cooking since 1947—it proclaims itself the oldest North Indian restaurant in the U.K. Cooking is light on the oil and *ghee* (clarified butter). Meats and tandoori are well marinated, and so they arrive tender. Flavors dovetail gorgeously with every bite, winding up with a slight spicy twang. The menu is cheeky, too: "If you have any erotic activities planned for after you leave us, perhaps you should resist this sensational garlic naan." Reserve ahead or face the queue.

80 Neal St., WC2. www.punjab.co.uk. ℂ **020/7836-9787.** Mains £8–£10. Mon–Sat noon–11:30pm, Sun noon–10:30pm. Tube: Covent Garden.

Regency Café ★★★ TRADITIONAL BRITISH   The "caff" diner, once a staple of London life, is rapidly being swept into Formica heaven by trendy bistros. Among the few holdouts still feeding Westminster's cops, security guards, and bureaucrats, is the 1940s Regency, an elegy to another age in yellowed white tiles and bolted-down plastic chairs. This isn't a gastronomic treasure (the fryer is in heavy use, white bread heaped high, and sausage a food group); it's an anthropological one. Big-value food including homemade meat pie is prepared with lightning speed and your order is jarringly bellowed so that you can come fetch it.

17-19 Regency St., SW1. ℂ **020/7821-6596.** Mains £3–£8. Mon–Fri 7am–2:30pm and 4–7:30pm, Sat 7am–noon. Tube: Pimlico or Westminster.

The Stockpot ★ INTERNATIONAL   High on function and low on glitz, it has been serving scrimping visitors and families for years. It got me through many a lean day of backpacking. No dish, be it spaghetti Bolognese, pork steak, or coq au vin, will set you back more than £7. Everything's good and all portions overflow their plates. Staff waits around with dishrags on their shoulders, and the wall is hung with old drawings of gentlemen, just to class things up. On one memorable visit, a brief power outage interrupted dinner. "Just like the food," my neighbor inveighed, "it has a certain Eastern Bloc flavor." For those who can barely afford to visit London, the Stockpot is salvation. Forget the ravens at the Tower. When the Stockpot goes, London is over.

18 Old Compton St., W1. ℂ **020/7287-1066.** Mains £6–£7. Mon–Tues 11:30am–11:30pm, Wed–Sat 11:30am–midnight, Sun noon–11:30pm. Tube: Leicester Square or Tottenham Court Road.

LONDON food chains WE RECOMMEND:

London, like so many other cities, is experiencing an economic shift that is squeezing out mom-and-pop establishments in favor of better-heeled chains, so you'll often see these mid-priced, kid-friendly names cropping up on storefronts wherever you go. They're reliable and taste good, so consider them, too:

- **Busaba Eathai:** Peppy noodles and Asian dishes at communal tables.

- **Carluccio's:** New York–style Italian. Tile walls, pasta, fish, meats, coffees.

- **Giraffe:** Every kind of comfort food, extremely family-friendly.

- **Ping Pong:** Chinese dim sum in a vibrant, hip environment, plus cocktails.

- **Pizza Express:** Artisan-style pie. No one pays full price; see

  www.pizza-express.com/latest-offers for consistent discounts such as 25% off.

- **Simply Food:** Marks & Spencer's standalone shops for sandwiches, truly delicious ready-made dishes, and well-selected, inexpensive wines.

- **Wagamama:** Hearty noodle bowls eaten at shared long tables.

- **Wahaca:** Substantial Mexican done well with British-grown ingredients.

The City & Southwark
EXPENSIVE
Restaurant Story ★★★ MODERN BRITISH   The moment you sit, your server lights a white taper and you slide your menu from the leafs of *Sketches by Boz* by Dickens, who started his life penniless nearby. By the time about six *amuse bouche* "snacks" hits you (cod skin studded with emulsified cod roe, a sweet black eel mousse "Storeo"), your candle has melted, you're told that the wax was actually edible beef fat, and you're handed a pouch of fresh-baked bread to sop up the drippings. And there are 10 more frivolously surprising small-plate courses to go. The dramatic and whimsical delights are by hot young talent Tom Sellers, and his prix-fixe menu, which never stops dazzling with flavor duets, speaks of London cooking both old and new: scallop Carpaccio with cucumber balls rolled in dill ash; Jensen's gin (Sellers loves gin) and apple consommé topped with garlic blossoms; and "Three Bears" porridge—one sweet, one salty, one just right. It's food you'll be talking about. Reserve ahead.
201 Tooley St., SE1. www.restaurantstory.co.uk. ✆ **020/7183-2117.** Six courses £60, ten courses £80. Tues–Sat noon–2:30pm, 6:30–9:30pm. Reservations essential. Tube: London Bridge or Bermondsey.

MODERATE
Rochelle Canteen ★★ BRITISH   A sublime secret is hidden away, discovered only if you ring a doorbell beside a green door in a brick wall. You'll pass through the grassy yard of an 1880s school, and in the old bike

139

shed, join a daytime garden party. The changing menu is rigorously British, without flourish, of high-quality, and fresh: green pea soup, roast sirloin, cuttlefish ink stew, fish and chips, loose-leaf tea. Your companions will be artists, designers, and professionals, many of whom now lease space in the former school, plus the occasional kid, if they behave as well as a Victorian child. In fine weather, it's easier to find a seat because dining spills outdoors, the better to enjoy jugs of rhubarb and ginger fizz.

Rochelle School, Arnold Circus, E2. www.rochelleschool.org. ℂ **020/7729-5677.** Mains £13–£15. Mon–Fri 9am–2:30pm. Reservations suggested. Tube: Shoreditch High Street.

INEXPENSIVE

Beigel Bake ★★ BAKERY   The city's most famous bakery, Jewish or otherwise, never closes but there's often a line. The queue moves quickly, and the patronage is a microcosm of London, ranging from bikers to hipsters to arrogant yuppies to the homeless. Its beigels ("BI-gulls") are not as puffy or as salty as the New York "bagel" variety, but they even come filled for under £2. Its pastries are gorgeous, too: The chocolate fudge brownie, less than £1, could be nursed for hours. Watching the clerks slice juicy chunks of pink salt beef in the window, then slather it onto a beigel with nostril-clearing mustard from a crusty jar, is an attraction unto itself. Londoners complain it's touristy, but if it's a tourist trap, why does it still serve coffee for only 60p?

159 Brick Lane, E1. ℂ **020/7729-0616.** Daily 24 hr. Tube: Shoreditch High Street.

Borough Market ★★★   INTERNATIONAL/TAKE-AWAY   A chronicle of overstimulation, it combines Victorian commercial hubbub with glorious, farm-fresh flavors, rendered as finger food for visitors. About a dozen vendors sell their countryside meats, cheeses, and vegetables all week long, but the market blooms beneath its metal-and-glass canopy Thursdays through Saturdays, when more than 100 additional vendors unpack and the awe-inspiring, touristy scene hits overcrowded swing. The least crowded time is Thursdays between 11am and noon; Saturdays are plain nuts. If there's any country that has farming down, it's England, and this market is its showplace. Follow the crowd to the west end of the fence by the cathedral to **Kappacasein** dairy (www.kappacasein.com), which places great wheels of cheese under burners and sloughs bubbling swaths of it onto plates of boiled new potatoes (it's called *raclette*, £6). **Roast Hog** (www.roasthog.com) slices pig off a turning spit. You can't export either melt-in-your-mouth **Bath soft cheese** (www.parkfarm.co.uk) or aromatic unpasteurized **Gorwydd Caerphilly** cheese (www.trethowansdairy.co.uk). The **Brindisa** booth (www.brindisa.com) facing Stone Street, feeds a steady line its grilled chorizo sandwich with oil-drizzled pequillo peppers from Spain (£4); and

Buying bread at Borough Market.

Shellseekers, the fishmonger in the center, is known for hand-dived Devon scallop, served in its shell and topped with a bacon and sprout stir-fry (£6). **Roast** (www.roast-restaurant.com) has a stall for rich meats such as roast pork belly with crackling and Bramley apple sauce and beef with horseradish cream (both £7). Outside on Stone Street, opposite the well-stocked **Market Porter** pub, three more finds: **Monmouth Coffee** (www.monmmouthcoffee.com) is one of London's most revered roasters; **Gelateria 3bis** has an ultra-creamy *fior di latte* flavor made from rich English milk plus a warm chocolate fountain for pre-filling cones; and **Neal's Yard Dairy** (www.nealsyarddairy.co.uk), stacked high and tended by clerks in caps and aprons, is the gold standard for English cheese.

8 Southwark St., SE1. www.boroughmarket.org.uk. ✆ **020/7407-1002.** Mon–Wed 10am–3pm, Thurs 11am–5pm, Fri noon–6pm, Sat 8am–5pm. Tube: London Bridge.

The Fryer's Delight ★★ TRADITIONAL BRITISH/TAKE-AWAY In this age, no one would dare name their joint something as hydrogenated as The Fryer's Delight. Fortunately, this joint is not of this age. It's a true old-world chippy, where the fry fat is from beef drippings, chips come in paper wrappings, the wooden booths and checkered floor date to the lean postwar years, and the men behind the counter gruffly demand to have your order. Seamy? Not at all—it's just a last hanger-on from the dying fish-and-chips tradition, so get a taste while you still can.

19 Theobald's Rd., WC1. ✆ **020/7405-4114.** Meals £5–£6. Mon–Sat noon–10:30pm. Tube: Holborn or Chancery Lane.

Spitalfields & Shoreditch

EXPENSIVE

St John Bread & Wine ★★ TRADITIONAL BRITISH Hand-in-hand with the gastropub trend is "nose-to-tail" eating. That's when your chef doesn't waste a single part of the animal, resulting in tastes that were commonplace to his agrarian English forefathers (heart, cockscomb, marrow) but are new to most North American tongues. Most places charge, um, an arm and leg for it, but you can sample it at this lower-priced offshoot of the influential St John restaurant. Walls are simple white, chairs are plain wood, and the kitchen staff is serious about good food. Try dishes like cold lamb with chicory and anchovy, smoked sprat (sardines) with horseradish, and laver bread (made with seaweed) with oats and bacon. A meal here can be an adventure (ever eaten dandelion?). Don't skimp on dessert: Brown bread ice cream is one such staple.

94-96 Commercial St., E1. www.stjohnbreadandwine.com. ℂ **020/7251-0848.** Mains £7–£9 before 6pm, around £15 after 6pm. Mon–Sat 9am–11pm, Sun 9am–9pm. Reservations recommended. Tube: Aldgate East or Shoreditch High Street.

MODERATE

E. Pellicci ★★★ TRADITIONAL BRITISH London's tradition of mid-century diners, or "caffs," is quickly being gentrified into nostalgia, but this fry-up on deeply authentic and unflashy Bethnal Green Road has been run by the affable Nevio family since 1900. The Deco interior, a fantasia of sunburst icons, chrome, and primrose, was carved by a regular in 1946 and is now protected by law. You'll be boisterously welcomed with open arms—Mama, cooking her Italian specialties like cannelloni, may wave to you from the kitchen—and you'll spend a happy meal sharing a table with strangers. As proof of your acceptance by the regulars, after you're done you may be sent out with a parting gift of homemade cake. There's no more iconic caff in town; certainly none happier.

332 Bethnal Green Rd., E2. ℂ **020/7739-4873.** Mains £2–£8. Mon–Sat 7am–4pm. Tube: Shoreditch High Street or Bethnal Green.

Poppies ★★ SEAFOOD Big crispy portions flopping on big oval plates eaten with a big knife and fork to big 1950s sock-hop music: The franchise-ready Poppies does for British fish and chips what jukebox diners have done for mid-century American food. For all its theatricality, it hews to authenticity: The chief dish, cooked to order, is sustainably caught and sourced from third-generation fishmonger T. Bush at Billingsgate Market, and even the uniforms worn by the "Poppetes" waitresses—a red sailor frock with a jaunty, bellhoppy cap—come from Collectif in Camden's Stables Market. There's also chicken, jellied eels, and lush green salads. There's a second location in Camden Town (30 Hawley Crescent., NW1; ℂ **020/7267-0440**).

FIVE pubs YOU'LL LOVE

Be they truly ancient, stunningly beautiful, happily situated, or simply charming, the following pubs are all unlikely to let you down. All of them serve food of some kind (burgers, meat pies, and the like) for at least part of the day.

The Black Friar ★★ Deservedly protected by landmark status, this 1904 Art Nouveau masterpiece, a short walk from St Paul's near the Thames, is as jolly as the fat friars that bedeck it in bronze, wood, and glass. 174 Queen Victoria St., EC4. www.nicholsonspubs.co.uk. ✆ **020/7236-5474.** Mon–Sat 10am–11pm, Sun noon–10:30pm. Tube: Blackfriars.

The George Inn ★★★ Unquestionably one of the most important ancient pubs still standing, this one-time coaching inn traces its lineage to at least 1542. Shakespeare knew it, and now it's protected by the government. 77 Borough High St., SE1. www.nationaltrust.org.uk/george-inn. ✆ **020/7407-2056.** Mon–Sat 11am–11pm, Sun noon–10:30pm. Tube: London Bridge.

The Princess Louise ★ A fantasy of elaborate Victorian-era decor near the British Museum. Etched glass, bar lamps, marble urinals—even the beers are authentically old-school. 208 High Holborn, WC1. www.princesslouisepub.co.uk.

✆ **020/7405-8816.** Mon–Fri 11am–11pm, Sat noon–11pm, Sun noon–6:45pm. Tube: London Bridge.

Ye Olde Cheshire Cheese ★★★ It played host to Dr. Samuel Johnson, Charles Dickens, Yeats, Wilde, and Thackeray. There are six drinking rooms, but the front bar—of pallid light, antique paintings of fish, and the stuffed carcass of Polly the Parrot—is the most magical. Wine Office Court, off 145 Fleet St. ✆ **020/7353-6170.** Mon–Sat 11am–11pm. Tube: Blackfriars, Temple, or Chancery Lane.

Ye Olde Mitre ★★ Suspended in a hidden courtyard and between centuries, this extremely tiny enchanter was once part of a great palace. The entrance on the left grants you access to "the Closet," a fine example of a semi-private sitting area called a "snug." 1 Ely Court, off Ely Place, EC1. www.yeoldemitre holborn.co.uk. ✆ **020/7405-4751.** Mon–Fri 11am–11pm, closed weekends. Tube: Farringdon or Chancery Lane.

6-8 Hanbury St., E1. www.poppiesfishandchips.co.uk. ✆ **020/7247-0892.** Mains £10–£12. Mon–Thurs 11am–11pm, Fri–Sat 11am–11:30pm, Sun 11am–10:30pm. Tube: Shoreditch High Street or Liverpool Street.

SHOPPING

Appropriately for a city obsessed with class, London's prime shopping streets aren't usually defined so much by what they sell as by how much you'll spend to bring home their booty. **Oxford Street** (www.oxford street.co.uk), the king of London shopping streets supports the biggest mass-appeal names, including Topshop, H&M, Primark, and a few lollapalooza department stores like John Lewis, and Marks & Spencer. Boy, are weekends crowded!

The ultimate high-end purchasing pantheon is **New Bond Street,** which runs from Oxford Street to Piccadilly, partly as Old Bond Street.

best SHOPPING PALACES

Fortnum & Mason (181 Piccadilly, W1; www.fortnumandmason.london; ℰ **020/7734-8040;** Tube: Green Park or Piccadilly Circus)   So venerable is this vendor, which began life in 1707 as the candle maker to Queen Anne, that in 1922 archaeologist Howard Carter used empty F&M boxes to tote home the treasures of King Tut's tomb. The veddy British department store has a focus on gourmet delectable; its glorious Food Hall is where dreams are made and fortunes spent.

Harrods (87-135 Brompton Rd., SW1; www.harrods.com; ℰ **020/7730-1234;** Tube: Knightsbridge)   Now owned by the Qatari Investment Authority, a miraculous holdover from the golden age of shopping has been retooled into a bombastic mall appealing largely to moneyed foreigners who want to show off. Tourists beeline for the souvenir "emporium" on the 2nd floor (bags, mugs and teddy bears aplenty).

Liberty (210-220 Regent St., W1; www.liberty.co.uk; ℰ **020/7734-1234;** Tube: Oxford Circus)   Founded in 1875, it made its name as an importer of Asian art and as a proponent of Art Nouveau style. Now its focus is distinctly British. The store's stationery and scarf selections are celebrated, and the beauty hall is one of the best.

Selfridges (400 Oxford St., W1; www.selfridges.com; ℰ **0800/123-400** [U.K.] or 113/369-8040 [from overseas]; Tube: Bond Street or Marble Arch)   Selfridges fills the real-life role in London that many tourists think Harrods does, and aside from Harrods' olive drab sacks, no shopping bag speaks louder than a canary yellow screamer from Selfridges. Since its 1909 opening by Harry Gordon Selfridge, an American marketing genius from Marshall Field's in Chicago, Selfridges pioneered many department store practices; and sees some 17 million visitors each year.

Every account-draining trinket maker us here, including Van Cleef & Arpels, Harry Winston, Chopard, and Boucheron. Asprey's, at 165-169, sells adornments few can afford, but its Victorian facade is a visual treat for all.

Jermyn Street, the quintessential street for the natty man, is home to several haberdashers that have been in business for more than a century (Harvie & Hudson, Hilditch & Key, Hawes & Curtis, and Turnbull & Asser—dresser of Chaplin, Churchill, Prince Charles, and James Bond) as well as specialists such as Tyrwhitt for shirts, Daks, and T. M. Lewin. It connects to Piccadilly by **Princes Arcade,** strong on shoes.

Every lane around the north side of Covent Garden is full of the usual brands but also some one-off names. A half century ago, Soho's **Carnaby Street** was for the mod crowd, but today, expect mainstream sporty choices such as North Face and Vans. Better for browsing is **Kingly Court,** a former warehouse converted into a mini-mall for up and coming designers (carnaby.co.uk). **Redchurch Street,** once a down-at-heel lane in Shoreditch, is now at the forefront for hipsters and stylists.

ENTERTAINMENT & NIGHTLIFE

With hundreds of theatres, nightclubs, and music halls, London has more to offer on a single night than many cities muster in an entire year, and its output influences the whole world. Here are some after-dark stalwarts.

If you are desperate to see a specific theatre piece, book tickets before you leave home. Check **The Society of London Theatre** (www.officiallondontheatre.co.uk) for a rundown of what's playing and soon to play, as well as discounts. Given a lead-time of a few weeks, the established **LastMinute.com** sells tickets for half price, as does **Love-Theatre.com** (click "Special Offers"). The website **www.theatre.co.uk** posts discount codes for West End shows. Unless you buy discounted seats directly from the box office of the theatre, there's only one intelligent place to get same-day tickets: **TKTS** (south side of Leicester Square; tkts.co.uk; Mon–Sat 10am–7pm, Sun noon–3pm; Tube: Leicester Square), operated by the Society of London Theatre. It sells same-day seats for as much as half off—the best stuff is sold in the first hour of opening.

The **English National Opera** (www.eno.org) and **Royal Opera House** (www.roh.org.uk), both in Covent Garden, are world-famous, and the latter is also home to the **Royal Ballet.** You'll find eclectic musical performances at the famous **Royal Albert Hall** (www.royalalberthall.com), the progressively programmed King's Place (www.kingsplace.co.uk), and the more traditional **St Martin-in-the-Fields** church on Trafalgar Square (www.stmartin-in-the-fields.org) and the home of the Royal Philharmonic Orchestra, **Cadogan Hall** (www.cadoganhall.com).

Bars and pubs are a huge part of London's cultural identity, and the thickest choice of those lie in Soho and around Shoreditch, Hoxton, and Dalston, all the East End, where the venues can afford to be more cutting-edge. The king of dance clubs remains **Fabric**

GLBT London

London has the most varied and vibrant gay and lesbian scene in the world. The city claims more than 100 pubs, clubs, and club nights, and a dozen saunas—beat that, San Francisco or New York! The music seems to crank a few notches louder when the jolly and outrageous Pride London (www.pridelondon.ca) season rolls along, in late June or early July. Daily gay-oriented pursuits have traditionally been centered around Soho, where the bars take on a festive, anyone-is-welcome flair; after work, guys spill into the streets. But as a mark of an integrated city, nearly every neighborhood now has its own gay pubs or gay nights. **Boyz** (www.boyz.co.uk) and **QX Magazine** (www.qxmagazine.com) post schedules that favor club events. The Sapphically inclined should turn to **Gingerbeer** (www.gingerbeer.co.uk) and www.planet-london.com for listings.

GETTING THE scoop ON NIGHTLIFE

Complete listings for entertainment are published Saturdays in the London papers, but you don't have to wait until you arrive. Excellent online sources for things to do include **Londonist.com**, **LondonCalling.com**, **TimeOut.com/London**, **Townfish.com**, and the Twitter accounts Everything London (**@LDN**), **@LeCool_London** (nightlife), and **@SkintLondon** (for cheap or free activities). These are good, too:

○ **Visit London:** The "Tickets and Offers" section of its website is assiduously updated and, even better, it's free. (www.visitlondon.com)

○ **Metro:** Free in racks at Tube stations, most copies are gone by mid-morning, but commuters leave copies behind on the trains; it's considered green to recycle a pre-read newspaper. (www.metro.co.uk)

○ **The Evening Standard:** Free at Tube stop entrances in mid-afternoon—some days, there's an accompanying lifestyle magazine in a nearby stack. ES is also available online for free. (www.standard.london)

(77a Charterhouse St., EC1; www.fabriclondon.com; ℂ **020/7336-8898;** Tube: Farringdon or Barbican), a former butchery that for more than a decade has had lines around the block. The **Ministry of Sound** (103 Gaunt St., SE1; www.ministryofsound.com; ℂ **020/7740-8600;** Tube: Elephant & Castle) is known for its top-notch sound system and upper-crust DJs.

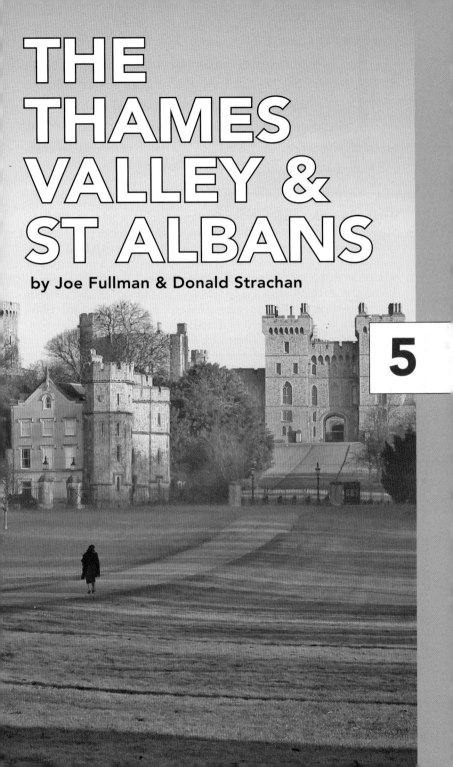

THE THAMES VALLEY & ST ALBANS

by Joe Fullman & Donald Strachan

5

The misty, rolling landscapes of the Chilterns and Thames Valley are rooted in 1,000 years of English history. Much of the tourist buzz comes from the region's connections with English high society: Royal castles, racecourses, rowing galas, and Britain's poshest university town. Yet it's also the home of innovative chefs and a dynamic local theatre scene.

Windsor Castle is still home to the Royal Family, a place to enjoy the pageantry of the daily Guard Mounting ceremony (or to even see the Queen herself). Upriver, the ancient university town of **Oxford** is dripping with history, elaborate medieval architecture, and a lively student population that gives it a cosmopolitan atmosphere. It is also the cultural capital of the region, with a range of plays, performances, and concerts almost every night. Take in some Shakespeare at the **Oxford Playhouse,** or a high-quality classical recital at the **Sheldonian,** before wandering over to the **Jericho Tavern** for a late-night folk concert.

Travel back to Roman times at **St Albans,** or take a peek into the lives of the English nobility at **Blenheim Palace.** You can meditate on the roots of freedom at **Runnymede,** where King John signed Magna Carta, and wander the corridors of **Eton,** England's oldest school.

In a region with such a storied past, ancient pubs and English ales take center stage. Grab a pint at Oxford's **White Horse,** or sample craft beers in St Albans, home of the Campaign for Real Ale. The region's creative, contemporary side is on show in a host of innovative institutions: Dine on snail porridge at Heston Blumenthal's **Fat Duck,** or some of Britain's best modern French cuisine at **Raymond Blanc's** exalted restaurant.

WINDSOR ★ & ETON

23 miles W of London

Windsor is a charming, largely Victorian town, with a few remnants of Georgian architecture. All this is completely overshadowed of course by its great castle, which dominates the area like a giant crown of stone. **Windsor Castle** has been the home of the royal family since the reign of Henry I some 900 years ago, and despite the inevitable crowds, this is a sight you should not miss; the **State Apartments** are especially lavish, adorned with paintings from the royal collection.

PREVIOUS PAGE: **The Long Walk, Windsor Great Park, with Windsor Castle in the distance.**

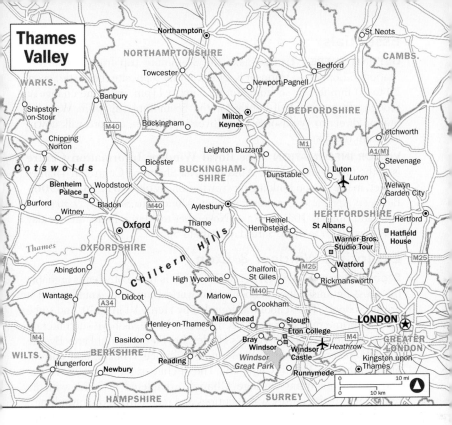

Trips Along the Thames

Stretching for 184 miles, the **Thames Path ★** is a walking trail that follows the river from its source, in the Cotswolds, through Oxford, Henley, and Windsor all the way to London's Docklands. It usually takes a minimum of 10 days (with plenty of pubs and B&Bs along the way), but you can also tackle smaller sections; see

www.nationaltrail.co.uk/thames-path. For the less energetic, boats glide along the river, offering a languid alternative to the road. **Salter's Steamers** (www.salters steamers.co.uk; ✆ **01865/243421**) runs segments between Windsor and Oxford from late May to mid-September. Most cost around £5 to £8.

Just across the Thames via the pedestrian Windsor Bridge, **Eton** is smaller, essentially one narrow High Street of mostly Georgian structures, shops, and pubs leading to Britain's poshest private school.

A word of warning: Given its fame, Windsor is not abundantly supplied with enticing places to stay or eat. Consider seeing it on a day-trip from London or Oxford.

Essentials

GETTING THERE **Trains** make the 35-minute trip from Paddington Station in London to Windsor & Eton Central (opposite the castle) every 20 to 30 minutes or so from around 5am to 11pm, with one change at Slough. Trains run half-hourly for the 55-minute trip from Waterloo Station direct to Windsor & Eton Riverside Station, a short walk downhill from the castle.

VISITOR INFORMATION The **Royal Windsor Information Centre** is at the Old Booking Hall, Windsor Royal Shopping Centre on Thames Street, in the station building (www.windsor.gov.uk; ✆ **01753/743900**). Between April and October it is open Monday to Saturday 9:30am to 5pm and Sunday 10am to 4pm; November to March hours are Sunday to Friday 10am to 4pm, Saturday 10am to 5pm.

Exploring Windsor & Eton

Eton College ★ HISTORIC SITE   Eton is home of what is arguably the most famous public school in the world (non-Brits would call it a private school). The school was founded by Henry VI in 1440, and since then 20 prime ministers have been educated here, as have such literary figures as George Orwell, Aldous Huxley, Ian Fleming, and Percy Bysshe Shelley. Recent notable students include Prince William, and current prime minister David Cameron. The architectural highlight is the Perpendicular Gothic **College Chapel,** completed in 1482, with its remarkable 15th-century wall paintings and reconstructed fan vaulting.

The history of Eton College is depicted in the **Museum of Eton Life,** located in vaulted wine cellars under College Hall (originally used as a storehouse by the college's masters). The displays include a turn-of-the-20th-century boy's room, schoolbooks, and canes used by senior boys to apply punishment. Note that admission to the school and museum is by **guided tour only.** Tours were suspended during building work from 2014 through early 2016. Call ahead to check timetables.
Keate's Lane, Eton. www.etoncollege.com. ✆ **01753/671000.** Call for pricing; reservations required. Exit the M4 at exit 6 to Windsor; park here, walk past Windsor Castle, cross the Thames footbridge and follow Eton High Street to the college.

Runnymede ★ HISTORIC SITE   Three miles southeast of Windsor lies Runnymede, a 188-acre water meadow ("mead") on the south side of the Thames. This is where it's believed that King John put his seal on Magna Carta ("the Great Charter") in June 1215, after intense pressure from his feudal barons and lords. The charter forced the king to accept a long list of individual liberties and is regarded as the founding document of English constitutional law, as well as inspiration for the U.S. Constitution (a copy is displayed in D.C.'s National Archives).

A short hike up 50 granite steps is the poignant **John F. Kennedy Memorial,** an acre of ground given to the United States by the people

The Magna Carta Memorial at Runnymede.

of Britain in 1965. The memorial itself is a 7-ton block of Portland stone, engraved with lines from President Kennedy's inauguration speech in 1961. Further along is the **Magna Carta Memorial,** a large pillar of granite under a domed classical pavilion. A longer walk takes in the huge **Commonwealth Air Forces Memorial,** dedicated to over 20,000 Allied airmen and -women who died in World War II and have no grave. Runnymede. www.nationaltrust.org.uk/runnymede. ✆ **01784/432891.** Free; parking £2/hr. (max. £7/day). Daily dawn to dusk.

Windsor Castle ★★★ CASTLE Looming high above the town, Windsor Castle is an awe-inspiring site, an enormous hulk of stone dating back to the days of William the Conqueror. The castle was originally constructed in wood in the 1080s; Henry II started to rebuild it in stone in the 12th century and was the first monarch to live at Windsor. The history and art are undeniably impressive, but what really draws the crowds is the royal family; this is one of the three homes of Queen Elizabeth II. Windsor is the world's largest inhabited castle and the Queen is often in residence, especially on weekends (when the Royal Standard flies). Getting a glimpse is not that hard; the town's hoteliers often have advance notice of when Her Majesty comes and goes.

You should definitely grab one of the free **audioguides** at the entrance, as not much is labeled inside the castle. Allow 2 hours or so for a full visit. The tour route leads along the battlements, past the iconic **Round Tower ★** and to **Queen Mary's Dolls' House ★**. A palace in perfect miniature, the Dolls' House was given to Queen Mary in 1924. Each room is exquisitely furnished, and every item is made exactly to scale. Working elevators stop on every floor, and there is running water in all five bathrooms.

The **State Apartments** ★★★ (closed second half of Jan) are a series of lavish rooms still used for ceremonial and state functions, and dripping with artwork. The route takes in the aptly named Grand Staircase and Grand Vestibule, smothered with swords and suits of armor. Art takes center stage, with several works by Rubens and William Dobson—"the lost genius of British art"—adorning the King's Drawing Room. In the relatively modest King's Dressing Room is Rembrandt's self-portrait, as well as Breughel's "Massacre of the Innocents." The Queen's Dressing Room has Van Dyck's triple portrait of Charles I. The King's Dining Room, with its Gobelin tapestries, is the most spectacular space, while more Van Dyck portraits of Charles I adorn the Queen's Ballroom.

The elegant **Semi-State Rooms** ★★ (usually open Oct–Mar only) were created by George IV in the 1820s for his personal use. Seriously damaged by a fire in 1992, they returned to their former glory 5 years later, with **St George's Hall** once again the setting for formal

Changing of the Guard, Windsor Style

Even if you don't see the Queen in Windsor, the **Changing of the Guard** ★ (or "Guard Mount") here offers more pageantry than the London version. The guard marches through the town, stopping traffic as it wheels into the castle to the tunes of a full regimental band. From April to July, the ceremony takes place Monday to Saturday at 11am. The rest of the year, the guard is changed at 11am on alternate days (except Sun). Call ℂ **020/7321-2233** for a schedule.

Changing of the Guard, Windsor Castle.

St George's Chapel, on the grounds of Windsor Castle.

banquets. The **Crimson Drawing Room** evokes George IV's flamboyant taste, with its silk damask and sumptuous art, while a suit of armor belonging to Henry VIII stands in the **Lantern Lobby** (where the 1992 fire started).

Architecturally the most rewarding part is **St George's Chapel** ★★★ (closed Sun, except for worship, and for official ceremonies), a perfect expression of the Medieval Perpendicular style and containing the tombs of 10 sovereigns. The present St George's was founded in 1475 by Edward IV, on the site of the original Chapel of the Order of the Garter. The nave contains the tomb of George V (1936) and Queen Mary (1953). Just off the nave in the Urswick Chapel is the Princess Charlotte memorial; if she had survived childbirth in 1817, she, and not her cousin Victoria, would have ruled the British Empire. In the north nave aisle is the tomb of George VI (1952), the speech-impaired monarch featured in the Oscar-winning movie "The King's Speech," joined by Queen Elizabeth the Queen Mother and Princess Margaret in 2002. The nearby altar contains the remains of Edward IV (1483), while the Edward IV Quire, with its carved 15th-century choir stalls, evokes the pomp and pageantry of medieval days. Look up to admire Henry VIII's lavish Tudor wooden oriel window. The vault beneath the choir contains the Charles I (1649), along with Henry VIII (1547) and his third wife, Jane Seymour (1537; the only one who bore him a son). On the way out you'll pass the tombs of Henry VI and Edward VII (1910), Victoria's son. Castle Hill, Windsor. www.royalcollection.org.uk. ✆ **020/7766-7304.** £19 adults, £17 students and seniors, £11 children 5–17, £48 families; when State Apartments are closed: £10 adults, £9 students and seniors, £7 children 5–17, £27 family. Mar–Oct daily 9:45am–5:15pm; Nov–Feb daily 9:45am–4:15pm.

Windsor Great Park ★ PARK   Just to the south of Windsor sprawls this 5,000-acre park, once a private royal hunting ground but mostly open to the public today. You can pick up **Long Walk** just south of the castle on Park Street, then stroll 2½ miles to the statue of King George III on Snow Hill for the best views of the area. The hill lies in the enclosed **Deer Park,** where red deer are often grazing in open view; look out also for several hundred green parakeets fluttering around, descendants of escaped pets living in the park since the late 1990s.

From Snow Hill you should also see **Frogmore House ★**, built in the 1680s and purchased by King George III as a country retreat for Queen Charlotte in 1792. On the grounds lies the **Royal Mausoleum,** the burial place of Queen Victoria and Prince Albert. The house is usually open to the public 5 or 6 days each year; see www.royalcollection.org.uk/visit/frogmorehouse for details. The Mausoleum is currently closed to the public.

Just 30 minutes' walk southeast of Snow Hill (1¼ hr. from Windsor on foot), the **Savill Garden ★** forms part of the Royal Landscape section at the southern end of the park. Created in the 1930s, these 35 acres form one of the finest ornamental gardens in England. The display starts in spring with rhododendrons, camellias, and daffodils beneath the trees; then, throughout the summer, spectacular displays of flowers and shrubs are presented in a natural and wild state. If driving, the garden is 5 miles from Windsor, signposted off the A308.

Adjoining Savill Garden are the **Valley Gardens,** full of shrubs and trees in a series of wooded natural valleys running to **Virginia Water,** an ornamental lake created in 1753. Both are open daily year-round. The Valley Gardens are free, but it's £7 to park at Virginia Water.

Windsor Great Park. www.thecrownestate.co.uk/windsor. ✆ **01784/435544.** Park free; admission to Savill Garden (www.theroyallandscape.co.uk). £10 adults, £9 seniors, £4 children 6–16, £26 families. Daily 10am–6pm (Nov–Feb 4:30pm).

Organized Tours

Between Easter and September, walking tours of Royal Windsor usually depart every Saturday at 11:30am and Sunday at 2:30pm. The cost is usually £8 per person. Advance booking is essential via the Royal

Windsor Information Centre (p. 150), from where the walks depart. **City Sightseeing Open Top Bus Tours** (www.city-sightseeing.com) make 50-minute loops of Windsor and Eton with 11 hop-on, hop-off stops (Apr–Nov daily 10am–4pm, every 30 min.). Tickets, valid for 24 hours, are £13 for adults, £6 for children 5 to 15.

Where to Stay

A room at bay-fronted B&B **Alma House** ★, 56 Alma Road (www.alma house.co.uk; ✆ **01753/862983**), offers an affordable alternative to pricey Windsor hotel rates. It's in a residential neighborhood, but still just a 10-minute walk from the castle gates. Rooms are all en suite with free Wi-Fi, and cost between £75 and £85 for a double.

EXPENSIVE

Macdonald Windsor ★★ A gentle aroma of scented candles welcomes you into Windsor's best hotel. This Georgian building was transformed in 2010—with warm purple and taupe, and a keen eye for design—into an elegant hotel. Rooms reach a high standard of décor, with walk-in showers and soft mattresses. A suite at the front looks out over Windsor's High Street; some smaller rooms have almost no view at all. The restaurant has a rep for its Scottish-sourced steaks.

23 High St., Windsor. www.macdonaldhotels.co.uk/windsor. ✆ **01753/483100.** 120 units. Doubles £125–£300. **Amenities:** Restaurant; bar; room service; free Wi-Fi.

Where to Eat

Cornucopia Bistro ★ FRENCH There's a hokey feel to the vaguely Parisian décor, with framed playbills from the Folies-Bergère, and a chanteuse soundtrack. But this central bistro offers the most dependable dining in Windsor, especially with a 2- or 3-course lunch at £10 or £13. The menu is mostly straight-down-the-line French, with sole meunière, pan-fried escalope of veal, and a cassoulet with confit duck, Toulouse sausage, and white beans. Cooking is good and reliable, rather than

---

Bray: Fat Ducks & Fine Dining

Just a couple of miles upstream from Windsor, **Bray**—population less than 5,000—is the unlikely home of two of only four U.K. restaurants to have been awarded three Michelin stars. The hype really is justified at **The Fat Duck** ★★★, High Street, Bray (www. thefatduck.co.uk; ✆ **01628/580333**)—home of culinary sorcerer Heston Blumenthal. Who said that ice cream can't be made with crab, or that porridge can't

be made with snails? Reservations months in advance are essential. Blumenthal also owns the **Hind's Head** pub ★★ (www. hindsheadbray.com; ✆ **01628/626151**) across the road; mains generally cost £18 to £25. The **Waterside Inn** ★★★ (www.waterside-inn.co.uk; ✆ **01628/ 620691**) on nearby Ferry Road is helmed by Alain Roux, where the equally beautiful French cuisine will blow you away. Mains range £37 to £55.

Hind's Head gastropub, Bray.

spectacular, but this is the best sensibly priced restaurant in town. Reservations are advisable for evenings and weekends.

6 High St., Windsor. www.cornucopia-bistro.co.uk. ☎ **01753/833009.** Mains £12–£22. Mon–Thurs noon–2:30pm and 6–9:30pm; Fri–Sat noon–2:30pm and 6–10pm; Sun noon–2:30pm.

Two Brewers ★ PUB FARE   Established in 1792, this small pub shows its age in a very satisfying way. Think old plank floors, wood-clad walls, roaring fireplaces, and locals who know all the staff by name (and vice versa). A short dining menu features mostly pub classics—honey-roasted ham with fried eggs and home-cooked chips; liver and bacon with onion gravy—alongside the occasional Mediterranean flourish, such as crispy lamb salad with feta cheese and olives. You can also just stop by for a pint of beer or a glass of wine. No children.

34 Park St., Windsor. www.twobrewerswindsor.co.uk. ☎ **01753/855426.** Mains £12–£16. Mon–Thurs noon–2:30pm and 6:30–10pm, Fri noon–2:30pm, Sat noon–5pm, Sun noon–8:30pm.

Shopping

What Windsor lacks in compelling hotels, it makes up for with high-quality shopping. At **Billings & Edmonds** ★ (132 High St., Eton; www.billingsandedmonds.co.uk; ☎ **01753/861348**), you may just think you've wandered into a time warp: This distinctive clothing store supplies school wear, suits made to order, and a complete line in cufflinks, shirts, ties, and accessories. **Royal Farms Windsor Farm Shop** ★ (Datchet Rd., Old Windsor; www.windsorfarmshop.co.uk; ☎ **01753/623800**) sells produce from the Queen's estates, including pheasants and partridges bagged at royal shoots. The meat counter is especially awesome, with its cooked hams and massive ribs of beef. There's also a café. **Woods. of Windsor ★** (50 High St., Windsor; www.woodsof windsor.co.uk; ✆ **01753/868125**), a colorful English perfumery sibce 1770 sells soaps, shampoos, and hand and body lotions, all prettily packaged in pastel-floral and bright old-fashioned wraps.

Windsor's best shopping precinct is **Windsor Royal Shopping ★** (Thames St., Windsor; www.windsorroyalshopping.co.uk; ✆ **01753/ 797070**), inside the atmospheric old railway station. Tenants are mostly high-quality chains—fashion and cosmetics—but there are a few more alluring merchants, including cigar specialist **Havana House** (www. havanahouse.co.uk; ✆ **01753/833334**) and **Hardy's Original Sweet Shop** (www.hardyssweets.co.uk; ✆ **01753/854242**), a Victorian-style confectioner, chockablock with traditional British sweets.

Entertainment & Nightlife

Windsor is fairly quiet at night: The most atmospheric place for a pint is **Two Brewers** (see "Where to Eat," above). The **Carpenters Arms,** 4 Market St. (✆ **01753/863739**), is another traditional pub in the center of town, dating back to the 1800s. The town's major cultural venue is the **Theatre Royal,** Thames Street (www.theatreroyalwindsor.co.uk; ✆ **01753/853888**), with a tradition of putting on plays that goes back two centuries. This is one of the best regional theatres in England, often drawing first-rate actors from London's West End. Performances are usually Monday to Saturday at 8pm, with weekday matinees. Most tickets cost £13 and £35.

OXFORD ★★★

54 miles NW of London

Dominated by the grand colleges of **Britain's oldest university,** Oxford offers as picturesque an urban environment as England can muster. This is no museum city, however. The hallowed halls and gardens of ancient colleges may be architectural gems, but students live and work in them year-round. And away from the scenic assortment of spires, quads, and chapels, there are modern shopping areas that are as functional—and utilitarian—as any in the land. Nonetheless, Oxford retains a special sort of magic. The High Street hasn't changed much since Oscar Wilde strolled it, and the water meadows and spires that inspired John Donne, Christopher Wren, C. S. Lewis, and J. R. R. Tolkien are still there.

The city's museums are, as you might expect of such a renowned center of learning, among the country's best, packed with wonders accumulated throughout the ages. But to really immerse yourself in Oxford's rich heritage, try exploring its pubs, where you'll be drinking in oak-paneled rooms once frequented by Samuel Johnson, Lawrence of Arabia,

Graham Greene, Bill Clinton, Margaret Thatcher, and other luminaries too numerous to mention.

Essentials

GETTING THERE **Trains** from London's Paddington Station reach Oxford in around 1 hour; direct trains depart every 30 minutes.

If you're **driving,** take the M40 northwest from London and follow the signs. **Parking** is a nightmare in Oxford; it will cost you around £30 per day in town (and cars are banned from much of the center anyway). If you can find a spot, metered parking in St Giles is £4 for a maximum of 2 hours. There are five large **park-and-ride** lots (www.parkandride. net) around the city's beltway, all well signposted. After 9:30am Monday to Friday, and all day Saturday and Sunday, you pay £2.25 for a round-trip bus ride into the city center. The buses run every 10 to 12 minutes until 7:30pm, then every half hour until 11:30pm Monday to Saturday, and between 11am and 5pm on Sundays.

VISITOR INFORMATION The **Oxford Tourist Information Centre** is at 15-16 Broad St. (www.visitoxfordandoxfordshire.com; ✆ **01865/ 252200**). It sells a comprehensive range of maps, brochures, and

---

Guided Tours: Ghosts, "Morse" & Picnics on the River

For an easy orientation, take a 1-hour, open-top bus tour with **City Sightseeing Oxford** (www.citysightseeingoxford.com; ✆ **01865/790522**). Tours start from the railway station; other pickup points are Gloucester Green Bus Station, Christ Church, Queen's College, and Trinity College. Buses leave daily at 9:30am and then every 10 to 15 minutes in the summer and every 30 minutes in winter. The last bus departs at 4pm November to February, at 5pm March and October, and at 6pm April to September. The cost is £13 for adults, £11 for students, £10 for seniors, and £7 children 5 to 14 years old; a family ticket costs £36. Tickets can be purchased from the driver and are valid for 24 hours.

If you have more energy, take the entertaining 2-hour **walking tour** of the city and the major colleges from the Oxford Tourist Information Centre (see above), daily at 11am and 1pm, and also at 2pm on Saturdays. These cost £9 for adults and £6 for children 16 and under,

but only include entry to colleges that don't charge admission fees. The Tourist Information Centre also offers a long list of excellent **theme tours,** including everything from "Magic, Murder & Mayhem" and "Pottering in Harry's Footsteps" to "Medieval Oxford," and a 2-hour "Inspector Morse Tour" (Mar–Sept Sat, Mon, and Fri 11:15am and 1:30pm; £10).

For something spookier, try **Bill Spectre's Oxford Ghost Trails** (www. ghosttrail.org; ✆ **07941/041811**), on Friday and Saturday at 6:30pm from the Tourist Information Centre. Dressed as a Victorian undertaker, Bill regales his charges with the most famous and gruesome Oxford ghost stories. He charges £8 for adults and £6 for children.

Finally, **Oxford River Cruises** (www.oxfordrivercruises.com; ✆ **0845/ 2269396**) runs boat tours along the River Thames, including a tranquil 50-minute "Oxford Experience" (Apr–Oct; £12 adults, £6 children 15 and under).

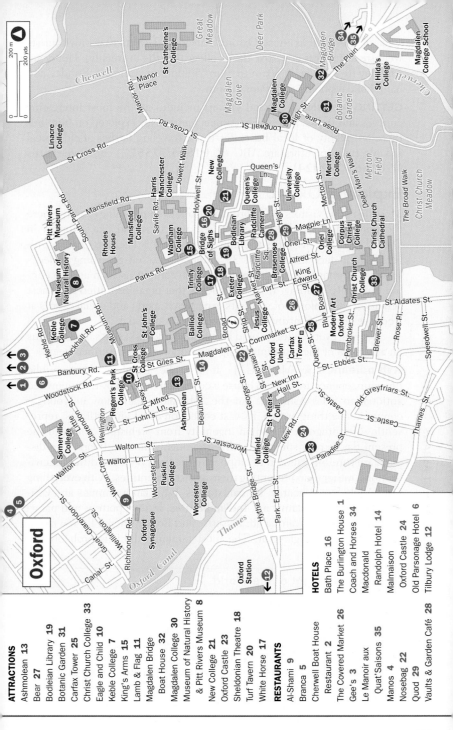

Oxford

ATTRACTIONS

Ashmolean **13**
Bear **27**
Bodleian Library **19**
Botanic Garden **31**
Carfax Tower **25**
Christ Church College **33**
Eagle and Child **10**
Keble College **7**
King's Arms **15**
Lamb & Flag **11**
Magdalen Bridge
Boat House **32**
Magdalen College **30**
Museum of Natural History
& Pitt Rivers Museum **8**
New College **21**
Oxford Castle **23**
Sheldonian Theatre **18**
Turf Tavern **20**
White Horse **17**

RESTAURANTS

Al-Shami **9**
Branca **5**
Cherwell Boat House
Restaurant **2**
The Covered Market **26**
Gee's **3**
Le Manoir aux
Quat'Saisons **35**
Manos **4**
Nosebag **22**
Quod **29**
Vaults & Garden Café **28**

HOTELS

Bath Place **16**
The Burlington House **1**
Coach and Horses **34**
Macdonald
Randolph Hotel **14**
Malmaison
Oxford Castle **24**
Old Parsonage Hotel **6**
Tilbury Lodge **12**

souvenirs, as well as those Oxford University T-shirts that only tourists wear (real students advertise their college, not the university). Hours are Monday to Saturday 9:30am to 5pm (5:30pm in summer); Sunday and bank holidays hours are 10am to 3pm.

GETTING AROUND   Central Oxford includes all the most interesting colleges and sights, and is very compact and easily explored on foot, but there are plenty of local buses for those traveling farther afield. Local reliable **taxi** operators are ABC (*© **01865/775577**) and Radio Taxis (*© **01865/242424**).

Exploring Oxford

Most first-time visitors to Oxford have trouble determining exactly where the university is. Indeed, the quickest way to sound like a tourist in Oxford is to ask, "Where's the university?" This is because Oxford University is in fact made up of 39 autonomous, self-governing colleges sprinkled throughout the town; there is no campus as such and no central university building. It is the colleges that organize tuition and most activities; the majority of students experience sports and social events at a college level and mixing between colleges is unusual.

Touring every college would be a formidable task, so it's best to focus on a handful of the most intriguing and famous ones described below.

Ashmolean ★★ MUSEUM   It may be Britain's oldest public museum, opened in 1683 to house a collection built up by the renowned antiquarian Elias Ashmole, but the Ashmolean can show its younger competitors a thing or two. Its vast collection of art and artifacts, representing the progress of human ingenuity from prehistoric times to the present day, is now spread over five thoroughly modern floors. The displays are carefully curated to emphasize the links between different civilizations, rather than presenting them as distinct entities. With everything from Anglo Saxon hoards, Roman statues, Egyptian mummies and Chinese paintings to Islamic art, Indian bronzes, Iranian pottery, and paintings by the likes of Van Gogh, Pissarro, and Renoir, there's far too much to take in on a single visit. The most famous exhibit is probably the

---

Oxford's Light of the World

The reproduction in St Paul's Cathedral, London, is seen by more people, but William Holman Hunt's original masterpiece, **"The Light of the World" ★★** has been on display at red-brick **Keble College,** Parks Road (www.keble.ox.ac.uk; *© **01865/272727**), since 1872. The Pre-Raphaelite painting, depicting Jesus preparing to knock on an overgrown and long-unopened door, hangs in the college chapel. Keble College is open to the public during vacations (July, Aug–Sept; Christmas: mid-Dec to mid-Jan; and Easter: mid-Mar to mid-Apr) between 2 and 5pm. Admission is free.

Alfred Jewel ★ (floor 2), a gold, enamel and quartz creation believed to have been made for King Alfred the Great in the ninth century. The terrace of the restaurant is a great spot for a summer bite to eat.

Beaumont St. at St Giles. www.ash molean.org. ✆ **01865/278000.** Free. Tues–Sun 10am–5pm.

Bodleian Library ★★ LIBRARY This famed university library was established in 1602 in the heart of Oxford. Over the years, it has expanded from the **Old Library** on Catte Street, and now includes the iconic **Radcliffe Camera** ★, a nearby

The Bodleian Library at Oxford, established in 1602.

domed 18th-century building. The Bodleian is home to an astonishing 50,000 manuscripts (including Mendelssohn's autographed "Hebrides Overture" and Jane Austen's unfinished novel, "The Watsons"), and more than 11 million books—like the British Library in London, it is entitled to a copy of every book published in the U.K. You can enter the **Exhibition Room** and wander the quadrangles of these handsome structures for free, but to get a better understanding of their history take a guided **tour** of the interior; buy tickets at the lodge to the right of the Great Gate on Catte Street.

Catte St. www.bodleian.ox.ac.uk. ✆ **01865/277162.** £1 Divinity School only (children 4 and under free); £7 for standard tour, £5 minitour (30 min.), £13 extended tour. Exhibition Room Mon–Fri 9am–5pm; Sat 9am–4:30pm; Sun 11am–5pm. Closed Dec 24–Jan 3. Call ahead to confirm specific tour times.

Carfax Tower ★ CHURCH For a bird's-eye view of the city, climb the 99 steps up this 75-ft. Gothic church tower in the center of town. Carfax Tower is all that remains of St Martin's Church, which stood on this site from 1032 until 1896, when most of it was demolished to accommodate a wider road. Look for the church clock on the facade, adorned by two "quarter boys" who hit the bells every quarter-hour.

Carfax, Queen St. (at the end of High St.). ✆ **01865/790522.** £2 adults, £1 children 15 and under. Children 4 and under not admitted. Daily 10am–5:30pm (Nov–Mar closes 3:30pm). Closed Dec 24–Jan 1.

Christ Church ★★ CHURCH Nothing quite matches the beauty and grandeur of Christ Church, the largest of the Oxford colleges.

A Secret Home for Old Masters

Often overlooked by the average visitor is an unheralded little gem known as **Christ Church Picture Gallery ★** (✆ **01865/276172**), entered through the Canterbury Quad of Christ Church. (To visit the gallery without paying for entrance to the college, enter through Canterbury Gate off Oriel Square, from King Edward Street.) Here you'll come across a stunning collection of Old Masters, mainly from the Dutch, Flemish, and especially the Italian schools, including works by Botticelli, Michelangelo, and da Vinci. The gallery is open July through September, Monday to Saturday from 10:30am to 5pm, Sunday 2 to 5pm; October through May, Monday and Wednesday to Saturday from 10:30am to 1pm and daily 2 to 4:30pm; and June on Monday and Wednesday through Saturday from 10:30am to 5pm and Sunday 2 to 5pm. Admission is £4 for adults, £2 for students and seniors. If you've already paid to visit the college, you get a 50% discount.

Established by Cardinal Wolsey in 1525, the college has a well-deserved reputation for exclusivity, wealth, and power: It has produced 13 British prime ministers, with other alumni including John Locke, John Wesley, William Penn, W. H. Auden, and Lewis Carroll. More recently, many scenes from the "Harry Potter" films were shot here.

Self-guided tours begin in the **cloister** and continue into the 1529 **Great Hall ★★**, the official college dining room, with portraits by Gainsborough and Reynolds. From here the route goes through the **Tom Quad,** the largest quadrangle of any Oxford college, and on to the most distinctive main entrance in Oxford, Christopher Wren's **Tom Tower ★** completed in 1682. The tower houses Great Tom, an 18,000-lb. bell. It rings at 9:05pm nightly, which used to be closing time for all colleges. (Students now have keys.) From the quad the tour continues to the 12th-century **Christ Church Cathedral,** once part of a medieval monastery and containing the shrine of St Frideswide, patron saint of Oxford.

St Aldates. www.chch.ox.ac.uk. ✆ **01865/276150.** £8 adults, £7 students, seniors and children 17 and under, free for children 5 and under. Mon–Sat 9am–5:30pm, Sun 2–5:30pm. Last admission 4:30pm.

Magdalen College ★★ HISTORIC SITE   Pronounced *Maud*-lin, this is arguably the most beautiful college in Oxford, thanks to its bucolic location on the banks of the River Cherwell and some dazzling Gothic architecture, notably the elegant Magdalen Tower. There's even a deer park in its grounds. The college was founded in 1458 by William of Waynflete, bishop of Winchester and later chancellor of England. It's influential alumni range from Thomas Wolsey to Oscar Wilde.

Soaring above the High Street, Magdalen Tower is the tallest building in Oxford (144 ft.), completed in 1509 and where the choristers sing in Latin at dawn on May Day. You can also visit the 15th-century chapel, where the same choir sings Evensong Tuesday to Sunday at 6pm.

High St. www.magd.ox.ac.uk. ℂ **01865/ 276000.** £5 adults, £4 children, seniors and students. June–Sept daily noon–7pm; Oct–May daily 1–6pm or dusk (whichever is earlier). Closed Dec 23–Jan 3.

Museum of Natural History & Pitt Rivers Museum ★★

MUSEUM These conjoined collections can easily provide a whole day's worth of fascinated browsing. You enter the **Natural History Museum** first, which occupies a large Victorian hall with a cast iron and glass roof that makes it look a bit like a railway station. All the most eye-catching exhibits are placed front and center, regardless of thematic cohesion. You'll find displays dedicated to biodiversity, the animals of "Alice in Wonderland," insects, the megalosaurus (the first named dinosaur, discovered nearby), minerals, and the last dodo (the dried head and foot held by the museum represent some of the last surviving remains of this archetypally doomed bird), as well as a sperm whale skull and fossil casts of a T-Rex and an iguanodon. From here, you can wander up and down the rows, uncovering a treasure trove of zoological, entomological, and geological specimens.

A Quiet Oasis

The oldest in Great Britain, the **Botanic Garden,** opposite Magdalen (www. botanic-garden.ox.ac.uk; ℂ **01865/ 286690**), was planted in 1621 on the site of a Jewish graveyard from the early Middle Ages. Bounded by a curve of the Cherwell, it is the best place in Oxford to escape the hordes. The garden is open March to October, daily 9am to 5pm (until 6pm May–Aug); November to February, daily 9am to 4pm (last admission 45 min. before closing). Admission is £5 for adults, £3 for seniors and students, and free for children aged 15 and under.

The Pitt Rivers Museum, Oxford.

Head through a doorway at the far end into the gloomy, bafflingly arranged world of the **Pitt Rivers Museum.** Augustus Pitt Rivers was one of Victorian Britain's foremost archaeologists and the collection reflects his eclectic interests with more than 500,000 ethnographic objects from all over the world—from North American totem poles to Japanese Noh masks; from South American shrunken heads to Benin court art. These are displayed largely according to themes rather than by culture, resulting in a fascinating mish-mash of different objects and styles.

Parks Rd. and S. Parks Rd. **Museum of Natural History:** www.oum.ox.ac.uk. *℗* **01865/272950.** Free. Daily 10am–5pm. **Pitt Rivers Museum:** www.prm.ox.ac.uk. *℗* **01865/270927.** Free. Mon noon–4:30pm, Tues–Sun 10am–4:30pm.

New College ★★ HISTORIC SITE   New College is another must-see, for its exceptional architecture and spacious grounds. It's also a favorite "Harry Potter" location and has seen Kate Beckinsale, Hugh Grant, Naomi Wolf, and Louisiana Governor Bobby Jindal pass through its pristine grounds. The college was founded in 1379 by William of Wykeham, Bishop of Winchester, and the real masterpiece here is its **Chapel ★★**. It contains stained glass by Joshua Reynolds, Jacob Epstein's expressive sculpture of Lazarus, and El Greco's masterful painting, "St James." In the beautiful gardens, stroll past the remains of the old city wall that now runs through the college grounds.

Holywell St. www.new.ox.ac.uk. *℗* **01865/279500.** Easter–Oct £4 adults, £3 seniors and students, free for children 16 and under; Nov–Easter free. Easter–Oct daily 11am–5pm; Nov–Easter daily 2–4pm.

Oxford Castle ★ CASTLE   The Oxford Castle Quarter is a shopping and heritage complex developed on the ruins of a fortress built by the Normans around 1071. Most of the castle was destroyed during the English Civil Wars, and the site served as a prison until 1996, when part of it became the Malmaison hotel. Other than perusing the restaurants and shops, the highlight here is **Oxford Castle—Unlocked,** a guided tour taking to the most historic parts of the site: St George's Tower, a 900-year old crypt, the 11th-century motte and bailey castle mound, and the old prison cells. Costumed guides play characters such as Civil War radical John Lilburne, and "sneaky thief" Elizabeth Boswell.

11 New Rd. (at Castle St.). www.oxfordcastleunlocked.co.uk. *℗* **01865/201657** or 01865/260666. Guided tour £10 adults, £9 seniors and students, £7 children 5–15, free for children 4 and under. Daily 10am–5pm, last tour 4:20pm.

Sheldonian Theatre ★ THEATRE   This exceptional piece of Palladian architecture stands next to the Bodleian, and was completed in 1668 according to a design by Sir Christopher Wren. As well as admiring the immaculate interior and ceiling frescos, you can climb to the cupola

Punting the River Cherwell

Punting on the River Cherwell is an essential, if slightly eccentric, Oxford pastime. At the **Cherwell Boathouse,** Bardwell Road (www.cherwellboathouse.co.uk; ✆ **01865/515978**), you can rent a punt—a flat-bottomed boat that seats up to five people and is maneuvered by a long pole and a small oar—for the hourly rate of £15 (weekdays) or £18 (weekends), plus a £75 to £90 deposit. **Magdalen Bridge Boathouse,** Old Horse Ford, High Street (www.oxfordpunting.co.uk; ✆ **01865/202643**), has an hourly charge of £20. Punts are available from mid-March to mid-October, daily from 9:30am to 9pm.

and enjoy fine views over Oxford. University ceremonies are regularly held here, but it also hosts a varied program of classical recitals and concerts; contact the **Oxford Playhouse** (p. 169) for tickets.

Broad St. www.ox.ac.uk/sheldonian. ✆ **01865/277299.** £4 adults, £3 seniors, students, and children aged 15 and under. Mar–Oct Mon–Sat 10am–12:30pm and 2–4:30pm; Nov–Feb Mon–Sat 10am–12:30pm and 2–3:30pm. Closed during events.

Where to Stay

EXPENSIVE

Macdonald Randolph ★   Opposite the Ashmolean, the Randolph is a microcosm of Oxford itself: venerable, staunchly English, steeped in tradition (it opened back in 1864), but still willing to put on a bit of a show for the tourists. The rooms, as is typical of hotels of this era, are of varying sizes (some of the bathrooms are quite small), while the lounges are cavernous, but everything is lavishly fitted out. The Randolph makes great play of its associations with "Inspector Morse," various scenes from which were filmed in its bar, now named the Morse Bar.

Beaumont St. www.macdonaldhotels.co.uk/our-hotels/macdonald-randolph-hotel. ✆ **01865/256400.** 151 units. Doubles £180–£300. **Amenities:** Restaurant; 2 bars; babysitting; concierge; room service; spa; free Wi-Fi.

Old Parsonage ★★   This restored 17th-century building is still one of Oxford's most charming choices, and seems to occupy a world all its own—where the clocks stopped decades ago. There are many delightful old quirks—low ceilings, heavy oak doors—with décor that is best described as a modern take on the traditional English country house. All facilities are state of the art, though some rooms are on the small side.

1 Banbury Rd. www.oldparsonage-hotel.co.uk. ✆ **01865/310210.** 30 units. Doubles £195–£330. **Amenities:** Restaurant; bar; room service; free Wi-Fi.

MODERATE

Bath Place ★   Oxford's hotels don't come much more central than this, right in the historic heart of the city. Don't go expecting five star luxury, however. Reached down a cobbled alleyway, this is made up of a gnarly network of converted 17th-century cottages next to the Turf Tavern (p. 170) with all the benefits (heaps of charm, antique styling, canopied beds, bathtubs) and problems (steep winding stairs, slightly cramped, creaky rooms) that this entails.

4-5 Bath Place. www.bathplace.co.uk. ✆ **01865/791812.** 15 units. Doubles £125–£195, includes breakfast. **Amenities:** Free Wi-Fi.

Burlington House ★ If you don't fancy staying in the busy city center, then this superior, reasonably priced B&B about 15 minutes' walk (or a quick bus ride) north may be just the ticket. Inside everything is spic and span, the place is run with what seems like almost military efficiency. The rooms are comfortable and modern with large beds and power showers. Excellent, hearty breakfasts—featuring homemade granola, free-range eggs and bacon—will prepare you for the walk back.

374 Banbury Rd. www.burlington-hotel-oxford.co.uk. ✆ **01865/513513.** 12 units. Doubles £97–£160, includes breakfast. Bus: 2 or 7. **Amenities:** Free Wi-Fi.

Coach & Horses ★★ A 10-minute walk east from the action, this B&B is run by a very friendly, super helpful couple who serve up some of the best breakfasts in town. The eight rooms spread over two floors are large, with stripped wood floors, comfy modern furniture, bathrooms with power showers and tubs, and a sparkly, fresh feel. A real find.

62 St Clement's St. www.oxfordcoachandhorses.co.uk. ✆ **01865/200017.** 8 units. Doubles £135–£145, includes breakfast. **Amenities:** Free Wi-Fi.

INEXPENSIVE

Tilbury Lodge ★★ Presided over by supremely friendly hosts, who are liable to foist a cuppa on you as soon as you arrive, this makes up in comfort what it (only slightly) lacks in character. In a modern house in a quiet western suburb, Tilbury offers well appointed, spacious rooms, modern bathrooms and plenty of little extras—bathrobes, foot-massage machines, lots of sweet treats—to make your stay just that little bit special. Generous English and Mediterranean breakfasts are included.

5 Tilbury Lane. www.tilburylodge.com. ✆ **01865/862138.** 9 units. Doubles £90–£130, includes breakfast. Bus: 4C, S1. Closed Dec–Jan. **Amenities:** Free Wi-Fi.

Where to Eat

EXPENSIVE

Le Manoir aux Quat' Saisons ★★★ CONTEMPORARY FRENCH The area's most lionized restaurant is around 12 miles southeast of the city center. Opened by the acclaimed chef, and more lately TV personality, Raymond Blanc in 1984, the hotel restaurant's elegant, French-inspired, locally sourced creations have received rave reviews for more than three decades. With dishes that include roasted venison loin with celeriac and truffles, and veal kidneys with alliums and red wine jus, this is as exquisite (and expensive) as you could hope for. The £82 lunch menu offers the best value. Reservations required.

Church Rd., Great Milton. www.belmond.com/le-manoir-aux-quat-saisons-oxfordshire. ☎ **800/237-1236** in the U.S., or 01844/278881. Mains £48–£54 lunch or dinner; set lunch £82 (5 courses); set dinner £138 (5 courses), £159 (7 courses). Daily 7–10am, noon–2:30pm, and 7–10pm.

MODERATE

Branca ★ ITALIAN This longstanding local favorite serves traditional Italian

Dessert at Le Manoir aux Quat' Saisons, Great Milton.

cuisine with a modern slant in the trendy suburb of Jericho, where there are lots of other decent bars and restaurants. The risottos—including a seafood and saffron version and one with butternut squash and taleggio cheese—are practically fabled, and prices are reasonable, particularly if you stick to the *cicheti* (tapas-like small plates) and house chianti. If the recipes inspire, you can pick up the ingredients in the restaurant's deli next door.

111 Walton St. www.branca.co.uk. ☎ **01865/556111.** Mains £12–£18; pasta and risotto from £8; pizza from £10. Daily noon–11pm.

Cherwell Boathouse ★ FRENCH/CONTEMPORARY ENGLISH It's a bit of a walk from the center, but this is the sort of place where you can easily while away an afternoon. It boasts a grand, rustic interior, but the real draw is the outdoor terrace where you can watch boats on the River Cherwell—you can even hire one of your own at the adjacent punt station (p. 165). Fortify yourself with something from the changing menu, which makes the most of seasonal produce.

Bardwell Rd. www.cherwellboathouse.co.uk. ☎ **01865/552746.** Fixed-price dinner £22–£28; Mon–Fri set lunch £14–£18. Daily noon–2:30pm and 6–9:30pm. Bus: Banbury Rd.

Gee's ★ CONTEMPORARY ENGLISH Housed in a striking, late 19th-century conservatory and adorned with flowers, this is one of the city's finest settings—and in Oxford, that's saying something. The menu is a international mish-mash, featuring dishes from England (venison shank), Italy (wild mushroom cannelloni) and the U.S. (burgers), but they're all expertly prepared. Live jazz is staged on Sunday evenings.

61 Banbury Rd. www.gees-restaurant.co.uk. ☎ **01865/553540.** Reservations recommended. Mains £14–£20; set lunch and pre-theatre menu £13–£17. Mon–Sat noon–2:30pm, Sun noon–3:30pm; daily 6–10:30pm.

Undercover Cheap Eats

Prices tend to be high at Oxford restaurants, but there are bargains to be had in the **Covered Market ★** (between the High Street and Cornmarket; www.oxford-coveredmarket. co.uk). Most places take cash only. The excellent little Thai place, **Sasi's** (10am–5pm daily; ℂ **01865/247434**) offers two selections on rice for just £6. The original **Ben's Cookies** (Mon–Sat 8am–5:30pm, Sun 10am–4pm; www.bens cookies.com; ℂ **01865/247407**) bakes up delicious cookies for around £2. You can get fine British and European cheeses at the **Oxford Cheese Company** (www.oxfordfinefood.com; ℂ **01865/721420**) or home-baked breads and cakes from **Nash's Oxford Bakery** (www.nashsbakery.co.uk; ℂ **01865/242695**). And there's always **Brown's** (Mon–Sat 8:30am–5pm; ℂ **01865/243436**), a no frills café that does a mean fry-up. The "full English" (2 bacon, 2 sausage, fried egg, baked beans or tomatoes, and toast) is just £6.

INEXPENSIVE

Al-Shami ★ LEBANESE   At the end of a residential street, this is an excellent value Lebanese restaurant with set menus from £15 that comprise a seemingly endless procession of dishes—making it well suited to large groups or families. The menu is huge, featuring some 40 cold and hot mezze—everything from stuffed vine leaves to chicken wings. Mains from the grill include various assortments of kebabs, shawarma, and baked fish. There are plenty of vegetarian options.

25 Walton Crescent, Jericho (at Richmond St.). www.al-shami.co.uk. ℂ **01865/ 310066.** Mains £7–£12; mezze £3–£5. Cover charge £1 per person, plus 10% service charge. Daily noon–midnight.

Manos ★★ GREEK   This small corner café has steadily built up a reputation as one of the city's most convivial eateries—it's particularly popular in the Christmas party season. There's nothing fancy about it; the food is traditional Greek fare—dolmathes, Greek salads with lots of feta, mezze plates, chicken souvlaki, moussaka—served in generous portions while piped folk music jangles away in the background. In summer, go for the charming outdoor area with vines growing in pots.

105 Walton St. www.manosfoodbar.com. ℂ **01865/311782.** Mains £7–£9. Mon–Wed 10:30am–9pm; Thurs–Fri 10:30am–10pm; Sat 9:30am–10pm; Sun 11:30am–8pm.

Nosebag ★ CAFE/HEALTH FOOD   Just off the main drag above a Malaysian restaurant, this decades-old establishment has become a local byword for simple, healthy eating. It offers a menu stuffed with salads, quiches, stir-fries, and the like. The interior is basic, but you come for the food, which isn't exactly bargain priced but comes in good-sized portions. Vegetarians are well catered for with curry and pasta choices.

6-8 St Michael's St. www.nosebagoxford.co.uk. ℂ **01865/721033.** Mains £9–£13. Mon–Thurs 9:30am–10pm; Fri–Sat 9:30am–10:30pm; Sun 9:30am–9pm.

Vaults & Garden Café ★ CAFE/HEALTH FOOD   On a busy Saturday, this place can be heaving with people, but it's worthwhile hanging around to try and get a seat. Occupying the wonderfully atmospheric setting provided by a dimly lit, 14th-century hall, the café works in a canteen style with a counter of prepared food and long communal tables (plus extra seating in a pretty outdoor garden). Turnover is quick. The changing menu is fairly small but genuinely tasty, featuring the likes of free range chicken fricassee, organic beef bourguignon, and garbanzo bean tagine. Breakfasts and afternoon teas are also served.

University Church of St Mary the Virgin, Radcliffe Sq. ✆ **01865/279112.** www. vaultsandgarden.com. Mains £6–£9. Mon–Thurs 9:30am–9:30pm; Fri–Sat 9:30am–10pm; Sun 9:30am–8:30pm.

Shopping

Alice's Shop, 83 St Aldates (www.aliceinwonderlandshop.com; ✆ **01865/723793**), housed in a 15th-century building is filled with "Alice in Wonderland" themed memorabilia; apparently Alice Liddell, the model for Alice, used to buy sweets here when it was a general store. **Castell & Son (The Varsity Shop),** 13 Broad St. (www.varsityshop. co.uk; ✆ **01865/244000** or 113 High St. (✆ **01865/249491**), is the best outlet for clothing and souvenirs with Oxford logos. For books, the venerable **Blackwell's,** 48-51 Broad St. (bookshop.blackwell.co.uk; ✆ **01865/333536**) is the most comprehensive source of all things academic. **Albion Beatnik,** 34 Walton St. (✆ **07737/876312**) is a quirky alternative that also operates as a tearoom and hosts poetry readings and live music. It's open until 8pm (11pm Wed–Sat).

Entertainment & Nightlife

Students tend to "unwind" in pubs, private college bars (which have "bops" or discos), and student apartments in Oxford, so the nightlife can seem relatively tame. There is, however, a steady supply of high-quality classical and choir music on offer, and a few places offer more energetic live music. In any case, the pubs are some of the most historic and atmospheric in the country.

Acclaimed orchestras playing in truly lovely settings mark the **Music at Oxford** series (www.musicatoxford.com), based at the **Oxford Playhouse Theatre,** Beaumont Street (www.oxfordplayhouse. com; ✆ 01865/244806). Tickets range £10 to £42. Many performances are held in the Sheldonian Theatre (p. 164) and Christ Church Cathedral (p. 162). The box office is open Monday to Saturday from 9:30am to 6pm (or until half an hour after the start of an evening performance) and on Sunday starting at least 2 hours before a performance.

New Theatre, George Street (www.newtheatreoxford.org.uk or www.ticketmaster.co.uk for tickets; ✆ **01865/320760**), is Oxford's primary theatre. Tickets range from £10 to £50. Comedy, ballet, drama,

PUBS WITH A pedigree

Pubs lie at the heart of Oxford social life. Almost every pub in the center has a long (and sometimes notorious) history. Real ales are a staple, and plenty of places serve aromatic mulled wine in the winter.

The congenial **King's Arms,** 40 Holywell Street ((✆ **01865/242369**), comprises a warren of rooms where a mix of students, tourists, and professors gather to sample the assortment of ales and lagers. The **Lamb & Flag** at 12 St Giles (✆ **01865/ 515787**) has been around since 1695 and is owned by St John's College. Thomas Hardy used the pub as a setting in his novel "Jude the Obscure."

A short block from the High, over-looking the north side of Christ Church, the **Bear ★**, 6 Alfred Street (www.bear oxford.co.uk; ✆ **01865/728164**), is an Oxford institution dating back to 1242 (the current building was built in the early 17th century), and mentioned time and again in English literature.

At the 17th-century **Eagle and Child,** 49 St Giles St. (✆ **01865/302925**), literary history suffuses the dim, paneled alcoves. In the 1930s and 1940s it was frequented by the Inklings, a writer's group that included the likes of C. S. Lewis and J. R. R. Tolkien. In fact, "The Chronicles of Narnia" and "The Hobbit" were first read aloud at this pub. It's a must-visit for Tolkien fans; the Rabbit Room is adorned with extracts from his work (some original).

Another pub with roots in the 13th century, the **Turf Tavern ★★**, 7 Bath Place (off Holywell St.; www.theturf tavern.co.uk; ✆ **01865/243235**), is reached via narrow St Helen's Passage, which branches off from New College Lane or from Bath Place. It was "the local" of future U.S. president Bill Clinton during his days at Oxford and has a chalkboard listing many of the famous visitors over the years (including Liz Taylor and Richard Burton). It's unapologetically touristy but in warm weather, it's pleasant to sit in one of the adjoining gardens.

The tiny **White Horse ★**, 52 Broad St. (www.whitehorseoxford.co.uk; ✆ **01865/204801**), squeezed between Blackwell's bookstores, is always a good place to soak up the collegiate atmosphere. It's one of Oxford's oldest pubs, dating from the 16th century, a popular feature in the "Inspector Morse" series and renowned for its real ales and fish and chips (£9).

Most Oxford pubs open from around 11am to midnight Monday to Saturday, and 11am to 10:30pm on Sunday. Pints of beer range £3 to £4.

opera, and even rock contributes to the variety. We recommend you purchase tickets in advance. The box office is open Monday to Saturday from 10am to 8pm (to 6pm if there is no evening performance).

Freud Café, 119 Walton St. (www.freud.eu; ✆ **01865/311171**) is an 18th-century Greek Revival church—columned facade, stained-glass windows and all—turned bar, jazz and folk venue with an expansive array of cocktail choices (the food is rather mediocre). There is no cover. Hours are Monday to Thursday 5pm to 11pm, Friday 5pm to 2am, Saturday 10am to 2am, and Sun 10am to 11pm.

O2 Academy Oxford, 190 Cowley Rd. (www.o2academyoxford. co.uk; ✆ **0844/4772000**), is the best indie-music venue in the city;

tickets £11 to £25. Shows usually start at 6pm Tuesday to Saturday, and also at 2:30pm on Saturday.

The **Jericho Tavern,** 56 Walton St. (www.thejerichooxford.co.uk; © **01865/311775**) has a beer garden and live music (mostly alt-rock or folk) is featured Friday and Saturday (Radiohead played their first gig here in 1986), when a £5 to £9 cover is charged. It's open Monday to Friday noon to midnight, Saturday and Sunday 10am to midnight.

Thirst, 7-8 Park End St. (www.thirstbar.com; © **01865/ 242044**), is a popular student hangout with a cocktail bar and a small garden. Resident DJs rule the night. It's open Sunday to Wednesday 7:30pm to 2am, Thursday to Saturday 7:30pm to 3:30am.

A Side Trip to Woodstock & Blenheim Palace

The small country town of **Woodstock,** 8 miles northwest of Oxford, was the birthplace in 1330 of the Black Prince, ill-fated son of King Edward III. Today it's a picturesque collection of 18th-century stone houses and the gateway to **Blenheim Palace.** There's little of interest in the town itself, though the **Oxfordshire Museum ★**, Fletcher's House, Park St. (© **01993/811456**), is worth a look; it chronicles the history, culture, and crafts of Oxfordshire and has a Dinosaur Garden with "Jurassic" plants and a full-size replica of a megalosaurus. The museum is free, open Tuesday to Saturday 10am to 5pm and Sunday 2 to 5pm.

Bus S3, operated by **Stagecoach** (www.stagecoachbus.com; © **01865/772250**), leaves Oxford about every 20 minutes during the day. The trip to Woodstock takes a little more than 30 minutes. If you're driving, take the A44 from Oxford.

Blenheim Palace ★★★ PALACE   The extravagantly baroque Blenheim Palace is England's answer to Versailles. Blenheim is still the home of the Dukes of Marlborough, descendants of the first duke John Churchill, victor of the Battle of Blenheim (1704), a crushing defeat of Britain's archenemy Louis XIV. Blenheim was built for him as a gift from Queen Anne in the 1720s. The family, virtually bankrupt, hung on to the palace thanks to the brutally commercial marriage of Charles, 9th Duke of Marlborough (1871–1934), to Consuelo Vanderbilt, heiress to the wealthy American railroad dynasty. Blenheim was also the birthplace of the 9th duke's first cousin, Sir Winston Churchill. The room in which he was born in 1874 is included in the palace **tour,** as is the Churchill exhibition: four rooms of letters, books, photographs, and other relics.

The palace was designed by Sir John Vanbrugh, who was also the architect of Castle Howard (p. 451); the landscaping was created by Capability Brown. The interior is loaded with riches: antiques, porcelain, oil paintings, and tapestries. The present owner is the 12th Duke of Marlborough (b. 1955). The duke's colorful early life, which saw him imprisoned on three occasions for drugs and driving offences, led to his father, the 11th duke, dubbing him the "black sheep" of the family and

The Churchill Exhibition at Blenheim Palace, Woodstock.

taking legal measures to prevent him inheriting the estate. However, they patched up their differences before the 11th duke's death, in 2014.

Insider tip: **Marlborough Maze ★**, 1,800 ft. from the palace, is the largest symbolic hedge maze on earth, with an herb and lavender garden, a butterfly house, and inflatable castles for children. Be sure to look for the gift shop, tucked away in an old dairy. Here you can purchase a wide range of souvenirs, handicrafts, and even locally made preserves.

Churchill's Final Resting Place

The small village of Bladon, about 6½ miles northwest of Oxford and a short drive from Blenheim Palace, is the final resting place of Sir Winston Churchill. Following his state funeral in St Paul's Cathedral, Churchill was buried in Bladon in January 1965. His relatively modest grave lies at the **Church of St Martin** (📞 **01993/880546**), a simple Gothic structure rebuilt in the 1890s. Churchill's white tomb also contains the remains of his wife, Clementine, who was buried here in 1977. To reach St Martin's Church from Oxford, take the A44 toward Woodstock, and then go on the A4095 toward Whitney.

Brighton Rd., Woodstock. www.blenheimpalace.com. 📞 **08700/602080.** £23 adults (parks and gardens £14), £18 students/seniors (parks and gardens £10), £12 children 5–15 (parks and gardens £7), and £59 families (parks and gardens £30); free for children 4 and under. Daily 10:30am–5:30pm. Last admission 4:45pm. Closed mid-Dec to mid-Feb (except for park).

ST ALBANS ★

27 miles NW of London; 45 miles SW of Cambridge

Across the Chiltern Hills from the Thames Valley—and founded as the Roman town of Verulamium in the 1st century A.D.—is **St Albans.**

The small modern city grew up on the hill above the Roman site 500 years later, and it's still home to some of the best **Roman ruins** in the country, as well as a vast and venerable **Cathedral.** The city was named after a Roman soldier who became the first Christian martyr in England, in the late 3rd or early 4th century. A great **Abbey** grew up to protect his shrine, becoming a major pilgrimage site in the Middle Ages—a role it has started to regain in recent decades. St Albans flourished in later years as the first major stop on the coaching route north from London, which explains the large number of **historic pubs** in the center today.

St Albans was also the hometown of **Samuel Ryder** (1858–1936), a successful seed merchant and later city mayor, who took up golf late in life after a period of poor health. He went on to inaugurate the Ryder Cup matches between pro golfers from the United States and Britain, now one of professional sport's most anticipated events.

Essentials

GETTING THERE   Thameslink **trains** (www.thameslinkrailway.com) whisk you from London's St Pancras Station to St Albans City in 20 to 35 minutes. If you're **driving,** take the M25 junction 21A or 22; M1 junctions 6, 7, or 9; and finally the A1(M) junction 3. **Parking** at several garages is signposted in the center of town.

VISITOR INFORMATION   The **Tourist Information Centre** is at the Old Town Hall, Market Place (www.enjoystalbans.com; ✆ **01727/ 864511**). Hours are Monday to Saturday 10am to 4:30pm. For events and local info, it's also worth consulting **www.allaboutstalbans.com**.

Exploring St Albans

The heart of St Albans is a thriving shopping area of Victorian, Georgian, and modern buildings, but there are plenty of medieval remnants around the cathedral, especially along George Street and Market Place. Climb the 93 steps to the top of the **Clock Tower ★** on the High Street for a birds-eye view of the town and cathedral (✆ **01727/751815;** Easter–Sept Sat–Sun 10:30am–5pm). The tower itself was completed in 1412, and houses a curfew bell that dates to 1335.

St Albans' quirkiest attraction is the **St Albans South Signal Box ★**, Ridgmont Road (www.sigbox.co.uk), a disused railway signal box dating to the 1890s. The Victorian signaling station has been restored by volunteers and is open for the public to see—and play with its now-working signals—one or two Sundays each month. Admission is free.

The history-focused **Museum of St Albans** closed in 2015 to prepare for its relocation to a new civic museum planned to open during 2017.

Cathedral & Abbey Church of St Alban ★ CATHEDRAL   This majestic cathedral is the oldest site of continuous Christian worship in

Britain. It's been in use for at least 1,300 years. It houses the **Shrine of St Alban,** the first British Christian martyr, who was buried here after being executed by the Roman authorities between A.D. 250 and 304. Construction of the cathedral dedicated to him began in 1077. It is one of England's earliest Norman churches, but also exhibits a patchwork of architectural styles, from Romanesque to Gothic. The flint and red-brick walls are especially unusual; many of the bricks, especially the flattened ones visible in the Norman tower, were scavenged from Verulamium, the old Roman city at the foot of the hill.

Inside the nave, exposed 13th-century frescoes hint at the color and imagery that would have daubed the walls before the Dissolution of the Monasteries. Behind the altar—adorned by an elaborate altarpiece known as the **Wallingford Screen** (1480s), destroyed in the time of Henry VIII and restored in the 1880s—lies the Shrine of St Alban itself, reconstructed in the 1890s (the original was also destroyed during the reign of Henry VIII). Free guided tours run daily.

The modern **Chapter House** contains an information desk, gift shop, and the Abbot's Kitchen restaurant. In addition to church services, organ recitals and orchestral performances are often open to the public. Sumpter Yard, Holywell Hill (on the High St.). www.stalbanscathedral.org. © **01727/860780.** Free (donations welcomed). Daily 8:30am–5:45pm.

Roman Theatre ★ HISTORIC SITE   Built around A.D. 140, this is the most intact example of a Roman theatre (as opposed to amphitheatre) in Britain, an evocative sight just a short distance from the remains of Verulamium. Not much remains, of course, but the stage and banked seating are clearly visible, and a stage column has been re-erected to give some sense of its former grandeur. In its time, the theatre would have hosted everything from bear baiting to classical plays. Hemel Hempstead Rd., Bluehouse Hill. www.romantheatre.co.uk. © **01727/835035.** £3 adults, £2 students and seniors, £2 children 5–16, free for children 4 and under. Daily 10am–5pm (until 4pm in winter).

Verulamium Museum ★★ MUSEUM   Set on the edge of a vast, delightful park—which houses most of St Albans' Roman remains—this museum traces the history of Roman Verulamium from its pre-invasion status as Verlamion, a stronghold of the Catuvellauni tribe, to the departure of Britain's

A Roman mosaic at the Verulamium Museum, St Alban's.

Roman occupiers around A.D. 410. The town had a varied history, with plenty of mishaps along the way, notably when it was destroyed entirely during the revolt led by Boudicca, queen of the native Iceni tribe. The collection is stuffed with the remnants of everyday life in the Roman period, from stone coffins to coins to religious artifacts.

Verulamium has also been the source of some of Britain's best-preserved Roman mosaics—displayed here, as well as in the remains of a townhouse mosaic floor left *in situ* close by. Below the floor is an intact **Hypocaust,** an heating system dating back around 1,800 years.

The museum is laid out in an appealing way for kids, too.

St Michael's St. www.stalbansmuseums.org.uk. © **01727/751810.** £5 adults, £4 seniors and children 5–16, free for children 4 and under, £12 families. Mon–Sat 10am–5:30pm, Sun 2–5:30pm. Hypocaust closes 4:30pm (Oct–Mar 3:45pm).

Organized Tours

The Tourist Information Centre (p. 173) provides entertaining themed **guided walks** (www.stalbanstourguides.co.uk) that generally cost £4 for adults and £2 for children 5 to 15 (children 4 and under are free). These include "Ghosts and Ghouls," "There's More to the Tudors than Henry VIII," "A Roman City Revealed," and "Crime and Punishment."

Where to Stay

St Albans is such an easy daytrip from nearby London—especially by rail—that staying in town is not a necessity, unless you feel the desire to escape the big city.

St Michael's Manor ★★   The location of this independent, family-run hotel is a delight—on one of St Albans' prettiest historic streets, over-looking manicured lawns and its own lake. Rooms inside the manor house (which dates to 1585) are decorated with a mix of strong contemporary tones and classical elements, and each has a mattress you just sink into. It's well worth springing a little extra (£10–£20 per night) for a "Premier" unit, which are significantly larger and have bigger beds than the basic "Deluxe" rooms. Three Premier rooms also have a garden view, which you need to request (and you should). Even if you are not staying, the hotel's orangery is also a good spot for afternoon tea (from £10), and reserving ahead on weekends is essential. No elevator.

Fishpool St. www.stmichaelsmanor.com. © **01727/864444.** 30 units. Doubles £135–£240, includes breakfast. **Amenities:** Restaurant; bar; room service; free Wi-Fi.

Where to Eat

Foragers @ the Verulam Arms ★ WILD FOOD   This informal pub-restaurant in a Victorian inn a few minutes' walk from the cathedral specializes in wild food: As much of the menu as possible is shot, foraged, grown or reared in the St Albans area. The rustic menu is short (4 starters, 4 mains) and, of course, seasonally dependent. Expect the likes of smoked wood pigeon served on a Waldorf salad with anise aioli followed by rump of lamb with champ mash and watermint crumble. Follow their suggested beer and wine pairings or go with a "wild" cocktail or a fine house brew made out back in a tiny microbrewery. At £17/£20, the 2- and 3-course menu available Monday to Thursday evening and Monday to Saturday at lunch is an excellent value.

41 Lower Dagnall St. www.the-foragers.com. ℭ **01727/836004.** Mains £14–£18. Mon–Sat noon–2pm and 6:30–10pm; Sun noon–6pm.

Freddie's ★ MODERN EUROPEAN   This modern stalwart of the local dining scene is a dependable choice for a taste of the Mediterranean in the city center. Flavors are generally big, and combinations fun: Think salmon and pea soufflé with paprika cream sauce followed by cod loin wrapped in Parma ham served with potato galette. There's a good choice for vegetarians, too, as well as a kids' menu. Staff is ultra-friendly.

52-56 Adelaide St. www.freddies.org.uk. ℭ **01727/811889.** Mains £13–£23. Daily noon–2:30pm and 6–10pm.

Shopping

The twice-weekly **charter market** has been held every Wednesday and Saturday since at least 1287. It takes place along St Peter's Street and features over 170 stalls, a mixture of discounted factory merchandise, fruit and vegetable sellers, and upscale purveyors of everything from merino-wool blankets to artisan cheese. A **Farmers' Market** runs on the second Sunday of each month, from 8am to 2pm. See www.stalbans farmersmarket.co.uk for details.

You'll find a selection of intriguing shops amid the quieter streets and lanes clustered around the cathedral. For antiques and local crafts, visit **By George Arts and Crafts** ★, 23 George St. (ℭ **01727/853032**), St Albans's venerable antiques and craft center. Fans of the graphic novel should check out **Chaos City Comics** (ℭ **01727/838719**), at 20 Heritage Close, High Street. It's open Monday to Friday 11am to 5:30pm, Saturday 10am to 5:30pm and Sunday noon to 4pm. Check out www.shopstalbans.co.uk for extra retail inspiration.

Entertainment & Nightlife

St Albans' nightlife centers on a thriving **pub scene** and a small but healthy roster of provincial **theatre.** The Company of Ten, with its base at the **Abbey Theatre** ★, Westminster Lodge, Holywell Hill (www.abbeytheatre.org.uk; ℭ **01727/857861**), is one of the leading amateur companies in Britain, and presents 10 productions each season in the main auditorium or a smaller studio. Tickets usually cost £10 to £12. Touring shows, comedy, and concerts use the **Alban Arena,** Civic Centre (www.alban-arena.co.uk; ℭ **01727/844488**).

The **Odyssey ★**, 166 London Rd. (www.odysseypictures.co.uk; ✆ **01727/453088**) is an original Art Deco cinema that now seats 500 every evening for first-run movies in relaxed, regal surrounds. Book comfortable seats with tables downstairs to see movies in grand comfort.

As befits an ancient town (and the home of the Campaign for Real Ale, or CAMRA), St Albans boasts some classic old pubs, notably **Ye Olde Fighting Cocks,** 16 Abbey Mill Lane (www.yeoldefighting cocks.co.uk; ✆ **01727/869152**), one of the oldest watering holes in England (it's in between the cathedral and Roman site). Named after the cockfights that once took place here, the pub allegedly dates back to A.D. 793, though the current site probably dates to the 11th century. The dark, timber-smothered interior is the perfect place to enjoy traditional cask ales.

Another atmospheric spot for a pint is **The Goat,** 37 Sopwell Lane (www.goatinn.co.uk; ✆ **01727/833934**); there are usually 4 real ales on tap. This Tudor inn has been serving drinks since the 1580s. **The Boot,** centrally located at 4 Market Place (www.thebootstalbans.com; ✆ **01727/857533**), rounds out a history-laden bar hop; this alehouse has been open since at least 1719 in a creaky medieval building. It's a decent venue for live bands (usually Sundays), as is the **Farmer's Boy,** 134 London Road (www.farmersboy.co.uk; ✆ **01727/860535;** music usually Thurs), which serves beers from its own microbrewery, Verulam. The **Verulam Arms** (see "Where to Eat," above) is an original Victorian pub run by wild-food specialists The Foragers.

Side Trips from St Albans

Hatfield House ★ HISTORIC HOME   This stately Jacobean mansion and its beautifully manicured gardens make for an alluring daytrip from London or St Albans. Built in 1611 for Robert Cecil, 1st Earl of Salisbury and Chief Minister to King James I, it has been the home of the Cecil family ever since (the current owner is the 7th Marquess of Salisbury). Yet Hatfield is even more famous for the royal palace that previously occupied this spot, the childhood home of Elizabeth I. In 1558, Elizabeth learned of her succession to the throne of England while at Hatfield; the site of this famous moment is marked by the **Queen Elizabeth Oak.**

Indeed, though only the **Banqueting Hall** of the first palace remains, it is the Elizabeth association that gives the house much of its appeal. The **Marble Hall** contains the celebrated "Rainbow Portrait" of Elizabeth. The **State Rooms** contain the most important paintings, furniture, and tapestries. More recently, the house served as Lara Croft's stately home in the "Tomb Raider" movies, starring Angelina Jolie.

6 miles east of St Albans by the A414. www.hatfield-house.co.uk. ✆ **01707/287010.** House and gardens £16 adults, £15 seniors, £8 children 5–15, £44 families; gardens only £10 adults, £9 seniors, £6 children 5–15. House Easter–Oct Tues–Sun 11am–4:30pm; gardens 11am–5:30pm.

Dumbledore's office at Warner Bros. Studio Tour London—The Making of Harry Potter, Leavesden.

Warner Bros. Studio Tour London—The Making of Harry Potter ★★★ MUSEUM   London's most popular new family outing is like a DVD of extra features come to life, and it's as gripping as the fine museums can be. On the very lot where history's most successful film franchise were shot, it seems that every set, prop, prosthetic, wig, and wand was lovingly saved for this exhaustive walk-though feast. You could spend hours grazing the bounty, from the students' Great Hall to Dumbledore's roost to Dolores Umbridge's den to the actual Diagon Alley and Hogwarts Express steam engine. Book your entry time for early in the day so you'll have time to wander. An astounding 1:24 scale model of Hogwarts Castle embedded with 2,500 fiber optic lights, is 50 feet across and takes up an arena-size room lit to simulate day and night. And you won't *believe* the gift shop. Easy 15-minute trains go three times an hour from Euston Station—not, fans sigh, from Platform 9¾ at King's Cross. Warner Bros. Studios Leavesden, Aerodrome Way, Leavesden, Hertfordshire. www.wbstudiotour.co.uk. ✆ **08450/840-900.** £33 adults, £26 children 5–15, under 5 free, £101 family of 4. Reservations required. First tours 9–10am, last tours 4–6:30pm, closes 3 hr. after last tour time. National Rail: Watford Junction, then a £2 shuttle bus that meets trains.

KENT & SUSSEX

by Donald Strachan

The Southeast might at first seem like "England Lite"—perfectly pleasant but lacking the mountains, might, and grandeur of other regions. But look a bit deeper, and you find a world within a world, a place offering extraordinary experiences and serene beauty. And from London, it's a lot easier to get here than to those distant English and Scottish peaks and lakes.

This is not a region for big cities. **Canterbury,** in Kent, with its glorious cathedral is the seat of England's traditional religion. **Brighton,** the Sussex resort, is an unlikely city; a vibrant mix of arts and bawdy seaside fun. Little **Chichester** has the air of a country town. In **Rye** and **Arundel** you can connect with the past—and even stay in a medieval castle.

The county of Kent is nicknamed the **Garden of England,** a lush place dotted with stately homes and gardens (such as Winston Churchill's former home, **Chartwell**). Move west into Sussex to find the **South Downs,** a chain of hills—the heart of Britain's newest National Park—that stretch for 100 miles and provide walks with views of country and coast. It is an ancient landscape, where forests mix with wild heathland.

The bounty of the sea is everywhere. Sample the oysters of **Whitstable** from quayside stalls, or fresh and smoked fish along Brighton's unpretentious seafront. The produce from Kent's market gardens provides the garnish, and the county also grows copious amounts of hops that are turned into real ales by small local brewers. There is an increasing number of vineyards, too, in both Kent and Sussex.

This is the land that sent Nelson off to sea (from Chatham dockyards); where Turner painted his evocative seascapes (on the site of Margate's **Turner Contemporary** museum); and where the mighty **White Cliffs** delineate Dover and the beyond. And it's all easily accessible on a daytrip or weekend away from London.

CANTERBURY ★★

60 miles SE of London

This medieval city appeared in "The Canterbury Tales," Chaucer's 14th-century story of pilgrims telling fables as they journey from London to the shrine of St Thomas Becket, Archbishop of Canterbury, who was murdered by four knights of Henry II just after Christmas 1170. His shrine was torn down in 1538 on orders of Henry VIII, but Canterbury was already drawing visitors from all over Christendom. The city also

PREVIOUS PAGE: **Dover's famous white cliffs, with Coast Guard Cottages in the foreground.**

marked the starting point of the Via Francigena, Europe's most important pilgrimage route that linked Canterbury with Rome.

Today it is the **ecclesiastical capital of England** and still houses the Archbishop of Canterbury, leader of the Church of England. The slaying of Thomas Becket was its most famous historical incident, but it has witnessed other major events, too. Richard the Lionheart popped in on his way back from the Crusades; Henry VIII's Catholic daughter "Bloody" Mary ordered 41 Protestants to be burned at the stake here between 1555 and 1558; and Charles II passed through on the way to claim his crown in 1642. There remain traces of the old city walls, but Canterbury suffered under the bombs of the Blitz in 1941. Today it's a busy mix of daytrippers and students from the University of Kent, with (seemingly) a busker on every corner. There's still plenty to see, not least the **cathedral,** one of Britain's great religious monuments. The city also makes a strategic base for exploring the Kent coast and countryside.

Essentials

GETTING THERE Canterbury is well connected by **rail.** For example, there are trains to Canterbury from London's Victoria (1½ hr.), St Pancras (around 1 hr. on the high-speed line), and Charing Cross (1¾ hr.) stations. A cheaper public transit option is the National Express **bus** (www.nationalexpress.com) from Victoria Coach Station. It takes 1¾ to 2 hours and leaves hourly, costing from £7 each way.

If you're **driving** from London, take the A2, and then the M2. Canterbury is signposted all the way. The heart of the city is traffic free, but it's only a short walk from several parking areas to the cathedral (see www.canterbury.gov.uk/parking).

VISITOR INFORMATION The **Canterbury Visitor Centre,** 18 High St. (www.canterbury.co.uk; ℰ **01227/862162**), is generally open Monday to Saturday 9:30am to 5pm (until 7pm Thursday), Sunday 10am to 5pm.

Exploring Canterbury

Beaney House of Art & Knowledge ★★ MUSEUM Inside a Victorian building, this unusual museum displays an amalgam of local art, private collections, and amateur anthropological finds collected by missionaries during the days of Empire. Each room has an individual identity; one minute you're considering the military odds-and-ends of the Royal East Kent Regiment, the next sublime Flemish stained glass, paintings by Van Dyck and Walter Sickert (who lived in Canterbury between 1934 and 1938), and plenty more. There's also an onsite cafe.

18 High St. www.canterbury-museums.co.uk. ℰ **01227/862162.** Free. Mon–Wed and Fri–Sat 9am–5pm, Thurs 9am–7pm, Sun 10am–5pm.

Canterbury Cathedral ★★★ CATHEDRAL This is one of the most visited sites in Britain, and still one of the holiest places of pilgrimage in Europe. St Augustine, sent by Pope Gregory the Great,

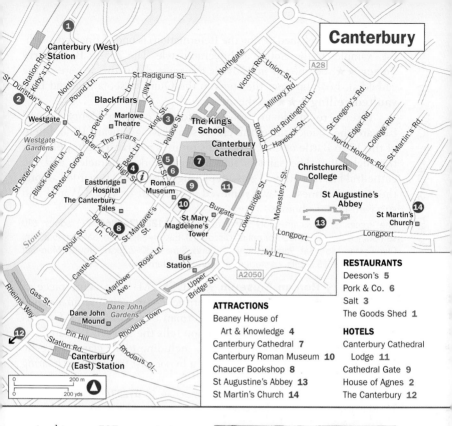

RESTAURANTS

Deeson's **5**
Pork & Co. **6**
Salt **3**
The Goods Shed **1**

HOTELS

Canterbury Cathedral
  Lodge **11**
Cathedral Gate **9**
House of Agnes **2**
The Canterbury **12**

ATTRACTIONS

Beaney House of
  Art & Knowledge **4**
Canterbury Cathedral **7**
Canterbury Roman Museum **10**
Chaucer Bookshop **8**
St Augustine's Abbey **13**
St Martin's Church **14**

arrived in A.D. 597 as a missionary and became Canterbury's first archbishop, establishing his seat ("Cathedra"). It was here too, in 1170 that Thomas Becket was murdered in the northwest transept, next to what is now the **Chapel of Our Lady Martyrdom.**

The cathedral, along with St Augustine's Abbey and St Martin's Church (see below), form a World Heritage Site. Foundations date from the time of Augustine, but the earliest part of the building is the great Norman-Romanesque **Crypt ★** from around A.D. 1100, which contains traces of 12th-century wall painting, in **St Gabriel's Chapel.** The **Quire ★★★** (which housed Becket's shrine

Interior, Canterbury Cathedral.

until it was demolished during the Reformation) is one of England's earliest examples of the Gothic architectural style. The 235-ft. **Bell Harry Tower ★★**, completed in 1505, is the most distinctive feature of the cathedral. Look up from the steps to the Quire to see a splendid **fan-vaulted ceiling ★★★** overhead.

Elsewhere inside are medieval tombs of King Henry IV and Edward the Black Prince, the eldest son of King Edward III and hero of the 1346 Battle of Crecy. Becket's tomb is in **Trinity Chapel,** near the high altar. The saint is said to have worked miracles, and the cathedral has rare stained glass depicting those feats. Regarded among the country's finest, it was removed at the start of World War II and survived Hitler's bombs.

The Precincts. www.canterbury-cathedral.org. ✆ **01227/762862.** £11 adults, £10 seniors, £7 children (check for online discounts). Easter–Sept Mon–Sat 9am–5:30pm; Oct–Easter Mon–Sat 9am–5pm; year-round Sun 12:30–2:30pm. Tours (Mon–Sat 10:30am–2pm) £5 adults, £4 students/children, £10 family.

Canterbury Roman Museum ★ MUSEUM   The centerpiece of this refreshing—though slightly overpriced—museum is an original Roman mosaic unearthed when a German bomb hit central Canterbury in 1942. The rest of the collection tells the story of Roman Canterbury through archaeological finds, including tools, glass, domestic items, and the impressive remains of a hypocaust (under-floor heating system).

11A Butchery Lane. www.canterbury-museums.co.uk. ✆ **01227/785575.** £8 adults, £6 students and seniors; up to 2 children free per paying adult. Daily 10am–5pm.

St Augustine's Abbey ★★ RUINS   Founded sometime after A.D. 597, this is where Canterbury cathedral's founder, St Augustine, was buried; only ruins remain, but it is still a major religious site. After Augustine was sent by Pope Gregory to convert the Saxons, Ethelbert, the Saxon king, allowed Augustine and his followers to build a church outside the city walls, and it endured until Henry VIII tore it down. It rivaled the cathedral in size, and the ruins are still cathedral-like in their proportions. Nearby are abbey buildings that were converted into a royal palace by Henry VIII and by several monarchs, including Elizabeth I and Charles I. Entry includes an audio tour and the small museum.

Corner of Lower Chantry Lane and Longport. www.english-heritage.org.uk. ✆ **01227/767345.** £5 adults, £5 students and seniors, £3 children 5–15. Apr–Sept daily 10am–6pm; Oct Wed–Sun 10am–5pm; Nov–Mar Sat–Sun 10am–4pm.

St Martin's Church ★ CHURCH   The oldest church in the English-speaking world still used for worship, this was Augustine's first project when he arrived in A.D. 597. It was built on the site of an existing Roman building. The nave is mostly masonry but with occasional Roman brick; the chancel is similar, but its east wall is flint, although parts of it are wholly of Roman brick. The atmospheric graveyard surrounding it feels straight from a horror B-movie.

Church St. www.martinpaul.org. © **01227/768072.** Free. Daily, daylight hours.

ORGANIZED TOURS

Canterbury Historic River Tours ★ (www.canterburyrivertours. co.uk; © **07790/534744**) operates 40-minute rowboat trips along the River Stour (with commentary) that lets you see Canterbury from a different angle. Prices are £9 for adults, £8 for seniors and students, £6 for children 12 to 16, £5 for children 11 and under, and £23 for a 4-person family ticket. March through October, tours leave daily every 15 to 20 minutes between 10am and 5pm from King's Bridge.

Where to Stay

MODERATE

Canterbury Cathedral Lodge ★ The shell is modern brick, but hotel's design evokes a medieval monastery cloister, with low-rise buildings around a leafy garden. The U-shape means every bedroom in the main hotel has a cathedral view. Rooms are simple and modern, decked out in light wood. If you request a twin made up as a double, you'll get a little more space; regular doubles are small by American standards. Breakfast is Kentish—the hotel is part of a scheme that guarantees at least 60% of produce on your table is local. Free cathedral access is included for all guests, who also have exclusive access to the cathedral Precincts after visitor gates close at 9pm.

The Precincts. www.canterburycathedrallodge.org. © **01227/865350.** 35 units. Doubles £89–£135, includes breakfast. **Amenities:** Bar; free Wi-Fi.

House of Agnes ★★ This B&B is a lot more rock'n'roll than you're expecting when you walk through an old wooden door close to Canterbury West Station. The Tudor building has the timber-framed rooms, but each one in the main house is also decked out in the theme of world cities. Individual décor evokes Tokyo, Paris, Marrakesh, Mumbai, or Venice. Eight "Stables rooms" out back are more contemporary and open out to the large walled garden. And the quirky name? It comes from Charles Dickens' "David Copperfield"; this very house is mentioned as the fictional home of Agnes Whitfield. No children 5 and under.

71 St Dunstan's St. www.houseofagnes.co.uk. © **01227/472185.** 16 units. Doubles £80–£135, includes breakfast. **Amenities:** Bar; bike rental (prebook); free Wi-Fi.

INEXPENSIVE

The Canterbury ★ This roadside hotel is all about its value and amenities. Rooms in the main building are midsized, with some quaint, old-fashioned character; it's well worth the little extra to upgrade to a four-poster bed for all but the lightest sleepers, as those rooms are on the front side but well soundproofed. The rear annexe rooms, with an unfussy modern style, and are even quieter and cheaper, but less characterful. The amenities in this price range are outstanding: Free parking, a courtyard garden, indoor pool and sauna, and guest discounts at the small spa. Central Canterbury is a 10-minute walk away.

140 Wincheap. www.thecanterburyhotel.co.uk. ℂ **01227/453227.** 11 units. Doubles £75–£125, includes breakfast. **Amenities:** Bar; pool; sauna; spa; free Wi-Fi.

Cathedral Gate ★ It's impossible to fault the location, overlooking a medieval square right next to Canterbury Cathedral's Christchurch Gate—some rooms at the back look right at the cathedral itself. The slightly yesteryear feel to the place is very much part of the charm. Rooms are a mix of ensuite and with shared facilities. And it all fits, labyrinth style, into a rowhouse that dates to the 1400s, complete with exposed beams and floors that slope every which way but level.

36 Burgate. www.cathgate.co.uk. ℂ **01227/464381.** 24 units. Doubles £82 without bathroom; £113 with bathroom, includes breakfast. **Amenities:** Free Wi-Fi.

Where to Eat

For a filling lunch on the go, **Pork & Co. ★**, 18 Sun Street (www.pork andco.co.uk; ℂ **01227/450398**), does one thing and does it very well. Pulled pork is slow cooked for 14 hours and served in a handcooked brioche roll with a choice of sauces and toppings, including red slaw and apple sauce. A pork roll to go costs £5.

Deeson's ★ BRITISH   The look of this place, on a cobbled street right in the center, is informal—upcycled furniture and chunky wooden pub tables—but the menu offers a serious take on Kent cooking. Dishes are firmly British, but switch comfortably between the traditional—say, roast loin of saltmarsh lamb—and modern dishes such as pan roasted duck with a duck leg cottage pie and damson puree.

25-27 Sun St. www.deesonsrestaurant.co.uk. ℂ **01227/767854.** Mains £11–£24. Mon–Sat noon–3pm and 5–10pm, Sun noon–10pm.

The Goods Shed ★★ MODERN EUROPEAN   Food at this lively place defines the term "market fresh." An old storehouse next to Canterbury West Station has been converted into a farmers' market and food hall, with a restaurant, **Rafael's ★★**, totally focused on market produce. The menu gets chalked up just before service; perhaps Indian spiced leek chowder with scallops and chorizo followed by roast duck breast with red cabbage and prunes. Under the same roof, **Wild Goose ★★** (www.wildgoosefood.com) serves English tapas such as potted pheasant with gooseberry chutney.

Station Rd., West. www.thegoodsshed.co.uk. ℂ **01227/459153.** Mains £12–£19. Tues–Fri 8–10:30am, noon–2:30pm, and 6–9:30pm; Sat 8–10:30am, noon–3pm, and 6–9:30pm; Sun 9–10:30am, noon–3pm.

Salt ★★ ENGLISH   Tapas, English style: This place reimagines the Catalan cava bar with a Kentish accent. It looks with part, with Tudor beamed ceilings, farmhouse tables, and slate slab floor. Dishes are seasonal and local, and each of around 15 small plate dishes typically makes use of bold, upfront flavors. Depending on when you arrive, expect to find the likes of pig cheek with piccalilli (a sour pickle of chopped vegetables, mustard, and turmeric), wood pigeon with elderberry sauce, or wild mushrooms with poached duck egg and celeriac.

13 Palace St. www.saltcanterbury.co.uk. ✆ **01227/788595.** Tapas £3–£7. Daily noon–3pm; Mon–Sat 6–9:30pm.

Shopping

The Goods Shed ★★ (see above) is a large, ethically sound food market, and while you might not be able to take home the fresh produce, you'll find small souvenirs such as chutneys and mustards. The **Chaucer Bookshop ★**, 6 Beer Cart Lane (www.chaucer-bookshop.co.uk; ✆ **01227/453912**), sells first editions (both old and modern), out-of-print books, leather-bound editions, and a large selection of local history titles.

Entertainment & Nightlife

The Foundry ★★, White Horse Lane (www.thefoundrycanterbury. co.uk; ✆ **01227/455899**), is the brewpub for Canterbury Brewers, with a shifting range of local real ales, as well as Belgian and American inspired craft beers, on around 10 pumps. It's all brewed next to the bar on a very small scale. They also do takeout if you're looking for a drinkable souvenir. For something a little more subdued, sink into a leather sofa at the **Champagne Bar at the County Hotel ★**, High Street (www.abode canterbury.co.uk; ✆ **01227/766266**). Inside The Goods Shed (see "Where to Eat," above), **Wild Goose ★★** is a fine place to linger over a glass of wine or local craft beer and a plate of English-style tapas. It's right next to Canterbury West Station.

Canterbury also has a lively arts scene. The **Gulbenkian Theatre ★**, University of Kent, Giles Lane (www.thegulbenkian.co.uk; ✆ **01227/ 769075**), features touring drama, comedy, and live music, as well as regular movies. It's on the edge of town, so you'll need to drive or get a taxi. Named after Elizabethan dramatist Christopher Marlowe, the **Marlowe Theatre ★**, The Friars (www.marlowetheatre.com; ✆ **01227/ 787787**), was totally rebuilt in daring modernist style. The program features drama, jazz, and classical concerts, along with dance, comedy, opera, and ballet. Tickets generally cost £10 to £40.

A Side Trip to Dover

It's a 30-minute train ride from Canterbury East Station to the Kent seaport of Dover. The best view of Dover's famous **white cliffs ★** is from aboard a ferry to or from France. Otherwise, walk to the end of the Prince of Wales pier. From here, the cliffs loom above.

Dover Castle ★★ CASTLE   Rising nearly 400 ft. above the port is one of the oldest, strongest, and best-known castles in England. Its keep was built at the command of Henry II, around 1180, but the castle saw active duty as recently as World War II. The **Great Tower** ★★ interior offers a multimedia experience of the court of Henry II—an ambitious attempt to recreate a medieval palace, with hangings, furnishings, and other objects created by craftsmen. You can walk the battlements and laze on the lawns. The castle also houses the **Secret Wartime Tunnels** ★★, 200 ft. below ground, which actually date back to medieval times. They were first adapted during the Napoleonic Wars to house cannons in case the French invaded. They were turned into a secret World War II headquarters of Operation Dynamo, when 300,000 troops were evacuated from Dunkirk. Touring them (including an operating theatre and hospital), you can feel the weight of the white cliffs above you, and can hardly imagine what it must have been like during the war's darkest days. Don't miss the hidden cliff-top balcony, where Churchill stood during the Battle of Britain. The castle can make a full day out for the family.

Castle Hill. www.english-heritage.co.uk. © **01304/211067.** £18 adults, £16 students/seniors, £11 children, includes Secret Wartime Tunnels. Apr–Sept daily 10am–6pm (Aug from 9:30am); Oct daily 10am–5pm, Nov–Mar Sat–Sun 10am–4pm.

WHITSTABLE & THE NORTH KENT COAST ★

Whitstable: 50 miles SE of London; xx miles NW of Canterbury

This is one of England's few areas of north-facing coast, and has a very different light than other regions—which is why the painter J. M. W. Turner was drawn to it. It is an area that has long relied on the sea, whether for its shellfish bounty (**Whitstable**), the fun of the seaside (**Margate**), or the history of one of England's most important naval dockyards (**Chatham**).

Essentials

GETTING THERE   **Trains** run from London's St Pancras Station twice an hour (70 min.) and hourly from Victoria (90 min.). It's around 20 minutes farther along the same line to Margate. There are two trains an hour from Canterbury West to Margate (30 min.), and four trains an hour from Canterbury East to Whitstable, but the route takes up to 1 hour. A better bet from Canterbury is the **bus** (35 min.): Take bus no. 4 from Canterbury Bus Station (return from Whitstable High Street on the no. 6). Two trains per hour connect Whitstable and Margate in 20 minutes.

By **car** from London head south on the M25 east, then the M20. At junction 7 head east on the A249 and then join the M2, also east. When the motorway ends, take the A299.

Perhaps the best way to get there is by **bike.** The 7-mile **Crab and Winkle Way ★** follows one of England's pioneering railway lines, which linked Whitstable with Canterbury, and is easy riding all the way.

VISITOR INFORMATION & SPECIAL EVENTS   Whitstable's tourist office is based inside the **Whitstable Shop,** 34 Harbour St. (*©* **01227/ 770060**). Alternatively check online at **www.canterbury.co.uk/ tourist-information**. Whitstable has a busy schedule of weekend and summer events, including **Whitlit,** an annual literary festival held each May. See **www.whitlit.co.uk**. A popular **Oyster Festival** (www.whit stableoysterfestival.co.uk) is held every July.

Exploring Whitstable

It's hard to put your finger on the precise ingredients of Whitstable's appeal. But it has plenty: The little seaport is a magnet for weekenders and vacationers from London and all over southeast England. It's pretty, certainly, but not quaint or museumlike in its perfection. The small **harbor** is still a place of work, not just for shellfish boats but for an unsightly

Turner's Margate

Margate was one of England's earliest seaside resorts, where 18th-century tourists came to enjoy the newly fashionable, health-giving properties of sea bathing. **Margate Main Sands** has a long stretch of golden sand that still has charms from past times, such as donkey rides and deckchairs.

Like many British resorts, it has been through hard times. Its rebirth has been led by **Turner Contemporary ★**,

Beachgoers at Margate Main Sands.

Rendezvous (www.turnercontemporary. org; *©* **01843/233000**), a gallery and exhibition space opened in 2011 to celebrate the painter J. M. W. Turner (1775–1851). He first came here to go to school at age 11, he returned to sketch here at age 21, and from the 1820s until his death in 1851, he was a regular visitor—more than 100 of his works were inspired by this coast.

The modernist building is on the site of the Cold Harbour guesthouse, where Turner often stayed, and it recreates the sea and quayside views that he saw. It's the biggest exhibition space in the Southeast outside London, and stages contemporary shows, as well as exhibitions themed around Turner. It's open Tuesday to Sunday 10am to 6pm. Admission is free.

While you're here, dip into Margate's **Old Town ★** where you'll find a number of independent shops, vintage boutiques, and art galleries with works by local painters who, like Turner, are drawn to the unique light of the Kentish coast.

aggregates factory, too. In short, Whitstable doesn't try too hard—and is all the better for it. For **food,** bracing beachfront strolls, and jovial, self-assured atmosphere, it can't be beat.

Whitstable is primarily known for its oysters—these spiny saltwater mollusks have led the town's renaissance. Its quayside is awash with stalls selling oysters, crab, whelks, cooked fish, and lots of chips. At the daily **Fish Market,** stalls sell the catch and you can buy traditional fish and chips, or whitebait and chips to eat on paper plates.

On weekends between March and Christmas, the **Whitstable Harbour Village** (www.whitstableharbourvillage.co.uk) is a collection of local food and craft vendors. Any day of the week, window browsers will love **Harbour Street ★**, with art galleries, clothes boutiques, craft stores, and shops selling vintage fashions and artisan cheese. Between High Street and the sea, a network of narrow alleys—evocatively named **Squeeze Gut Alley**—were used as escape routes by smugglers in the 1700s.

Whitstable also makes an excellent base for exploring **Canterbury** (p. 180) and many of Kent's best **castles and gardens** (p. 192).

Where to Stay

For something more surprising than a hotel, you can stay in a **wooden fisherman's hut ★★** right on Whitstable beach. The huts have been there for over a century, and have been converted into snug, modern 2-story mini-apartments. Huts sleeping up to 5 cost £75 to £225 per night, depending on season. Weeknights are significantly cheaper, and there's a 2-night minimum for Friday and Saturday. Book online at www.whitstablefishermanshuts.com or call ℰ **01227/280280.**

The Marine ★   There's a fresh, seaside feel to the earth-tone rooms here. It is well worth paying around £20 extra to secure a Superior unit, each of which has a traditional wooden balcony facing the sea. Standard rooms on the floor above are similar in size and décor, but have no balcony and smaller windows. Staff is very friendly; book well ahead for a weekend stay. From the hotel, it's a pleasant 15-minute walk past colorful beach huts to the center of Whitstable.

Marine Parade, Tankerton, Whitstable. www.marinewhitstable.co.uk. ℰ **01227/ 272672.** 30 units. Doubles £75–£150, includes breakfast. **Amenities:** Restaurant; bar; free Wi-Fi.

Where to Eat

There's a lot of fine food sloshing about Whitstable. For a salt-beef sandwich washed down with a local craft beer (or decent cup of coffee), stop in at **Waltshaw's ★**, 19 Harbour St. (www.waltshaws.co.uk; ℰ **01227/771917**).

Wheeler's Oyster Company ★★★ SEAFOOD   Forget fine dining: This is a place to get your fingers dirty at a shrine to sublime seafood.

Everything is prepped, cooked, or smoked in-house, even the occasional item (such as king shrimp) that must be flown in. There's a counter with a few stools and a tiny room in the back with informal restaurant tables, where you're accommodated in 2-hour sittings. Food is often catch dependent, but there are always oysters—intensely flavored wild Whitstable natives from September and April, locally farmed rock oysters all year—as well as food from the smoker, including salmon, eel, and hake. There are entrees too, often their lasagne of local lobster. Even if you can't get a seat, order from the takeout counter (open until 9pm) and choose from the likes of oysters shucked to go, or a smoked mackerel sandwich. Booking ahead is essential; bring your own beer or wine.

8 High St., Whitstable. www.wheelersoysterbar.com. © **01227/273311.** Mains £20–£24; small plates £8–£9. Seatings Thurs–Tues at 1, 3, 5, and 7:30pm (Sun 7pm). Counter: Mon–Tues and Thurs–Fri 10:15am–9pm, Sat 10am–10pm, Sun 11:30am–9pm.

Entertainment & Nightlife

This is not a town for nightclubbers, but does have plenty of traditional **pubs** that can stay lively til late. The **Ship Centurion ★**, 111 High St. (© **01227/264740**), is a super-friendly seaside pub serving filling food such as smoked haddock pie (£4) and English ale on tap, including a "mild." This almost forgotten traditional dark beer is almost stoutlike in color, but smoother and with lower alcohol levels. Nearby "micropub" the **Black Dog ★**, 66 High St. (no phone), looks like a movie set from a Victorian smugglers' tale. The **Old Neptune,** Marine Terrace (© **01227/272262**), has outdoor seating right on the beach.

A Side Trip to Chatham

It's around 35 minutes by train (alight at Chatham or Gillingham) or 45 minutes by car from Whitstable to Chatham's Historic Dockyard.

Historic Dockyard Chatham
★★ HISTORIC SITE From the Spanish Armada to the Falklands Crisis, ships were built and repaired here. By the mid-18th century it was the largest industrial area in the world, employing thousands of skilled workers. Records

The Victorian-era HMS *Gannet* at Historic Dockyard Chatham.

date back to 1547 and most of the English fleet wintered here. Nelson's flagship, HMS *Victory*, was built here and launched in 1765. Today the dockyard exudes history, and has featured in movies such as "Sherlock Holmes," with Robert Downey, Jr., and "The Golden Compass."

In addition to beautifully preserved buildings, you can visit the Victorian Navy sloop HMS *Gannet*, the submarine HMS *Ocelot*, and the World War II destroyer HMS *Cavalier*. There's also a huge covered slipway from 1838 with a display of a Midget sub, tank, and other vehicles; an exhibition about Nelson and the Battle of Trafalgar (1805); a Victorian covered ropery (still in use); the Royal Navy Lifeboat Institute's national lifeboat collection, and more. Kids love the place, too.

The Historic Dockyard, Chatham. www.thedockyard.co.uk. ℂ **01634/823800.** £19 adults, £17 seniors, students, and veterans, £12 children 5–15, £50 families. Apr–Oct daily 10am–6pm; Nov and mid-Feb to Mar 10am–4pm.

KENT'S CASTLES & GARDENS ★★

Kent is home to a wealth of country houses, castles, and gardens, many of them among the finest in England. **Leeds Castle** is perhaps the most romantic castle anywhere, but there's so much more to see around the county. Names like Anne Boleyn, Winston Churchill, Charles Darwin, and William Waldorf Astor crop up as you tour. You'll need a **car** to get around. If you're starting from London, it's an easy drive (many routes head southeast; all reach the M25 ring road, Kent's unofficial northern boundary) with most of our favorite places doable as a daytrip. You can also base yourself in **Canterbury** (p. 180) or **Rye** (p. 197).

Exploring Kent's Castles & Gardens

Chartwell ★★ HISTORIC HOME   This was the home of Sir Winston Churchill from 1922 until his death in 1965. It's not as grand as his birthplace (**Blenheim Palace;** p. 171), but has wonderful views over the Weald of Kent from the terrace. Rooms are as if the politician had just stepped out into the garden: maps, documents, photographs, pictures, mementos, and so forth. There are displays of his trademark suits and hats, as well as gifts from people around the world in thanks for leading the Allies to wartime victory. Churchill was an accomplished artist—it proved useful therapy in a lifelong battle against depression— and many of his paintings are displayed in a garden studio. *Insider tip:* The house can get busy, and entry is on a timed ticket so it pays to get there early.

Mapleton Rd., Westerham. www.nationaltrust.org.uk/chartwell. ℂ **01732/868381.** House, garden, and studio £13 adults, £7 children 5–16, £33 families (garden only £6/£3/£16). House: Mar–Oct 11am–5pm. Garden and studio: daily 10am–5pm (or dusk if earlier).

Down House ★ HISTORIC HOME   Charles Darwin lived here for 40 years until his death in 1882. When he moved in he wrote: "House

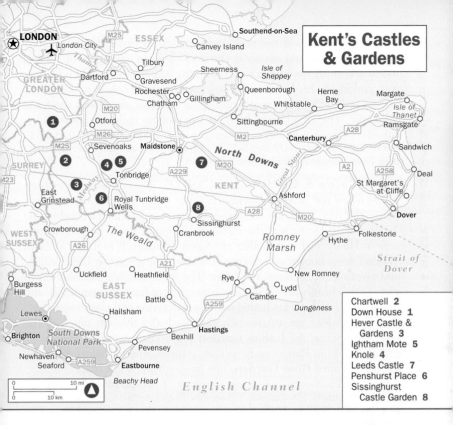

Kent's Castles & Gardens

Chartwell	**2**
Down House	**1**
Hever Castle & Gardens	**3**
Ightham Mote	**5**
Knole	**4**
Leeds Castle	**7**
Penshurst Place	**6**
Sissinghurst Castle Garden	**8**

Chartwell, Winston Churchill's home at Westerham.

ugly, looks neither old nor new." Nevertheless, he lived there "in happy contentment" for four decades. The drawing room, dining room, billiard room, and study have been restored to the way they were when Darwin was working on his famous, and still controversial book, "On the Origin of Species" (1859). Original landscaping remains, along with the Sand Walk, the "Thinking Path" where Darwin took his daily solitary walk.

Luxted Rd., Downe. www.english-heritage.org.uk. © **01689/859119.** £10 adults, £9 students and seniors, £6 children 5–16, £27 families. Apr–Sept daily 10am–6pm; Oct daily 10am–5pm; Nov–Mar Sat–Sun 10am–4pm.

Hever Castle & Gardens ★★ CASTLE   Hever Castle dates from 1271, when the massive gatehouse, outer walls, and moat were built. Some 200 years later, the Bullen (or Boleyn) family added a comfortable Tudor house. Hever was the childhood home of Anne Boleyn, second wife of Henry VIII and mother of Queen Elizabeth I. In 1903, William Waldorf Astor bought and restored the castle, building the Tudor Village and creating the gardens and lakes. The Astor family's contribution to Hever's rich history are seen in the collections of furniture, paintings, and art, as well as the workmanship in the woodcarving and plasterwork.

The gardens are ablaze with vibrant shades through much of the year. The spectacular **Italian Garden** ★★ contains statuary and sculpture dating from Roman to Renaissance times. The formal gardens also include a walled **Rose Garden,** fine topiary work, and a maze.

Hever, near Edenbridge. www.hevercastle.co.uk. © **01732/865224.** Castle and gardens £16 adults, £14 students and seniors, £9 children 5–15, £43 families. Daily mid-Feb–Nov: Gardens 10:30am–6pm; castle noon–6pm (closes at 4:30pm Feb, Mar, Nov); late Feb to Mar and Nov closed Mon–Tues.

Ightham Mote ★★ HISTORIC HOME   Ightham Mote, dating from 1320, is a gorgeous moated manor house with many Tudor holdovers such as the chapel with its painted ceiling, timbered walls, and ornate chimneys. You cross a stone bridge over a moat to its central courtyard, and from the **Great Hall** ★ with its magnificent windows, a Jacobean staircase leads to the old chapel. Other highlights include the crypt and a dog kennel that is a Grade I listed building in itself. Through its long history, the manor passed from one medieval knight to another, to Henry VIII's courtiers. and then to wealthy Victorians. When the last owner died (an American responsible for much of the restoration) he left the house to the National Trust, which chose to keep the Robinson Library laid out as it was in a 1960 edition of "Homes & Gardens."

Mote Rd., Ivy Hatch. www.nationaltrust.org.uk/ightham-mote. © **01732/810378.** £11 adults, £5 children 5–15, £27 families. Mar–Oct daily 11am–5pm (closes dusk if earlier); Nov–Feb 11am–3pm.

Knole ★★ HISTORIC HOME   Begun in the mid-15th century by Thomas Bourchier, Archbishop of Canterbury, and set in a 1,000-acre medieval deer park, Knole is one of the largest private houses in England

and one of the finest examples of pure English Tudor-style architecture. Henry VIII "liberated" the former archbishop's palace from the church in 1537. He spent considerable sums on Knole, but history records only one visit (in 1541) after extracting the place from the reluctant Archbishop Cranmer. It was a royal palace until Queen Elizabeth I granted it to Thomas Sackville, 1st Earl of Dorset, whose descendants still live here. (Virginia Woolf used Knole as the setting for her novel, "Orlando.")

The house covers 7 acres and has 365 rooms, 52 staircases, and 7 courts. Elaborate paneling and plasterwork are the backdrop for 17th- and 18th-century tapestries, rugs, Elizabethan and Jacobean furniture, and art from Gainsborough, Reynolds, and Van Dyck.

Sevenoaks. www.nationaltrust.org.uk/knole. © **01732/462100.** £11 adults, £5 children 5–15, £27 families. House: Mar–Oct Tues–Sun 11am–4pm. Gardens: Mar–Sept Tues 10am–5pm. Parkland: daily dawn to dusk.

Leeds Castle ★★★ CASTLE   Once described by Lord Conway as the loveliest castle in the world, Leeds Castle dates from A.D. 857. First constructed of wood, it was rebuilt in 1119 in stone on two small islands in the lake, making it an almost impregnable fortress. In the 1400s, King Henry VIII took to it and converted it into a lavish royal palace for his first wife, Queen Catherine of Aragon.

The 6th Lord Fairfax, as well as owning the castle, owned 2 million hectares (5 million acres) in Virginia and was a close friend and mentor of the young George Washington. The last private owner, the Hon. Lady Baillie, restored the castle with a superb collection of art, furniture, and

Leeds Castle dates to 857 A.D.

tapestries, and bequeathed it to the Leeds Castle Foundation. Since then the royal apartments, known as **Les Chambres de la Reine** (the Queen's Chambers), in the **Gloriette,** the oldest part of the castle, have been open to the public. The Gloriette, the last stronghold against attack, dates from Norman and Plantagenet times with later additions by Henry VIII.

Within the surrounding parkland, a lovely place to walk, is a wild-wood garden and a collection of rare swans, geese, and ducks, as well as the **Culpepper Garden**, an English country flower garden. The **Dog Collar Museum** speaks for itself, with a collection dating back to the Middle Ages. Beyond are greenhouses, a maze, and an underground grotto.

7 miles east of Maidstone. www.leeds-castle.com. ℰ **01622/765400.** £24 adults, £21 seniors and students, £16 children 4–15 (10% cheaper online). Daily Apr–Sept 10:30am–6pm; Oct–Mar 10:30am–5pm (last admission 2 hr. before closing).

Penshurst Place & Gardens ★★ HISTORIC HOME   Penshurst is one of England's outstanding country houses, as well as one of its great defended manors, standing in a peaceful rural setting that has changed little over the centuries. Between 1338 and 1341, Sir John de Pulteney, four times lord mayor of London, built the manor house whose **Great Hall** still forms the heart of Penshurst. Henry VIII's son, the boy king Edward VI, presented the house to Sir William Sidney and it has remained in the family ever since. The **Nether Gallery** ★★, below the Elizabethan **Long Gallery** ★ with its suite of ebony-and-ivory furniture, houses the Sidney family collection of armor. You can also see the splendid **Baron's Hall** ★★, the oldest part of the building. On the **grounds** are a woodland trail and maze, plus an adventure playground.

7 miles northwest of Royal Tunbridge Wells. www.penshurstplace.com. ℰ **01892/870307.** House and grounds £11 adults, £7 children 5–16, £30 families; grounds only £9 adults, £6 children 5–16, £27 families. Apr–Oct daily: house noon–4pm, grounds 10:30am–6pm. Mid-Feb to Mar Sat–Sun only, same hours.

Sissinghurst Castle Garden ★ GARDEN   In 1930 Bloomsbury set writer and noted gardener Vita Sackville-West and her diplomat husband Harold Nicolson moved into the property. The grounds had fallen into disrepair but Vita turned them around, using the ruins of an Elizabethan manor as a focal point. Today they are truly spectacular. In spring, the gardens are awash with flowering bulbs and daffodils fill the orchard. The white garden reaches its peak in June. The large herb garden, a skillful montage that reflects Sackville-West's profound plant knowledge, has something to show all summer long. The cottage garden, with its flowering bulbs, is at its finest as summer fades.

Biddenden Rd., near Cranbrook. www.nationaltrust.org.uk/sissinghurst. ℰ **01580/710700.** £12 adults, £6 children 5–15, £29 families. Mid-Mar to Oct daily 11am–5:30pm or dusk; by tour only Nov–Dec daily 11am–3pm, Jan–Feb Sat–Sun 11am–3pm.

RYE ★★, HASTINGS & BATTLE ★

Rye: 70 miles SE of London; Hastings: 63 miles SE of London

Rye was once one of England's most important ports—and a notorious smugglers' haunt—until the harbor began silting up in the 1700s and the sea receded. The old "port" of Rye was left high, dry, and 2 miles inland. The town was under the ownership of a French abbey from the 1000s, but reclaimed for England in 1247 by Henry III. It was all but leveled (by the French, again) in 1377, only to be rebuilt in Elizabethan style. Come here to wander narrow, twisting cobblestone streets and admire the ancient buildings, which prop each other up like a house of cards.

Just along the coast is **Hastings,** the site (approximately) of the Battle of Hastings in 1066, where King Harold was defeated by the invading troops of William, Duke of Normandy. From that point England's history became entwined with that of the continent. The fighting actually took place at what is now **Battle Abbey** (6 miles northwest of Hastings), but William used Hastings as his base. The town is a rather faded seaside resort, but has an arts-driven revival in full swing at Hastings Stade.

Essentials

GETTING THERE You will need a **car** to see Rye, Hastings, and Battle efficiently. If you're driving to Rye from London, take the M25 then M20 southeast to Ashford. At Ashford, turn south on the A2070 and A259, following signs. Hastings is a further 12 miles southwest on the A259. To reach Battle and Hastings direct from London, head south from the M25 on the A21, past Sevenoaks and Tonbridge.

From London, there are several **trains** every hour to Hastings, from Victoria (hourly) or Charing Cross (half-hourly) direct, and from St Pancras (hourly, changing at Ashford International). Journey time is between 1½ hours and 2 hours. For Battle, use the Charing Cross service and alight at Battle, 3 stops before Hastings. For Rye, take the hourly train from St Pancras Station, with a change at Ashford International; journey time is 1¼ hours.

VISITOR INFORMATION This corner of East Sussex is promoted as "1066 Country," with a single information website at **www.visit 1066country.com**. There are also walk-in tourist information centers: **Rye Tourist Information Centre** is at 4-5 Lion St. (✆ **01797/22904**), open daily April to September 10am to 5pm, October to March 10am to 4pm. **Hastings Tourist Information Centre,** Aquila House, Breeds Place (✆ **01424/451111**), is open Monday, Tuesday, Thursday, and Friday 9am to 5pm, Wednesday 10am to 5pm, Saturday 10am to 4pm, and Sunday 10:30am to 4pm.

Exploring Rye & Hastings
RYE

Rye's old town's entrance is **Land Gate,** where a single lane of traffic passes between hulking 40-ft. stone towers. The top of the gate has holes through which boiling oil used to be poured on unwelcome visitors—French raiding parties, for example. Beyond it lies the center, a jumble of whitewash, crooked clapboard, and cobblestones; its little streets are full of antiques sellers, tearooms, and bookstores. Genuine "attractions" are limited, but Rye has lovely old inns, a disarming charm, and a good location for exploring East Sussex and western Kent.

Lamb House ★ HISTORIC HOME Author Henry James lived here from 1898 to 1916. Many of his mementos are scattered throughout the big, brick house, which has a large walled garden with mature trees. Its previous owner joined the gold rush in North America but perished in the Klondike, and James bought it for a modest £2,000. Some of his best-known books, including "The Ambassadors," were written here.

West St. (at the top of Mermaid St.), Rye. www.nationaltrust.org.uk/lamb-house. ℂ **01580/762334.** £5 adults, £3 children. Mid-Mar to mid-Oct Tues and Sat 2–6pm.

Rye Castle Museum ★ MUSEUM The town museum is split between two sites, the more engaging being the **Ypres Tower ★**. Built as part of a fortification in 1249, it served served as Rye's prison for 400 years. Views from the tower stretch for miles: Much of what you can see south of the town used to be under water. The nearby small **Museum** has eclectic exhibits from Rye's history.

Elizabethan-era houses in Rye.

St Mary's Church ★ CHURCH   Rye's 12th-century church is an impressive—but eccentric—ensemble of architecture and accessories. It's hard to miss the gilded **16th-century clock,** halfway up the tower, and powered by a pendulum that still swings inside. The giant face is flanked by cherubs, known as Quarter Boys because of their striking of the bells on the quarter-hour. If you're energetic you can climb the wooden stairs and ladders up the bell tower for another impressive view. Church Sq., Rye. www.ryeparishchurch.org.uk. © **01797/224935.** Free (contributions appreciated). Tower £3 adults, £1 children 7–16 (1 free child per adult). June–Sept daily 9:15am–5:15pm; until 4:15pm rest of the year.

HASTINGS & BATTLE

Battle Abbey & Battlefield ★★ BATTLEFIELD/RUINS   It was on Senlac Hill where King Harold, last of England's Saxon kings, fought to the death against Norman invaders on October 14, 1066. Harold was killed by an arrow through the eye—at least, that's what the Bayeux Tapestry appears to show. Whether the tale is true or not, Hastings certainly signaled the end of Anglo-Saxon England. The site's modern visitor center features a sword-rattling film about the battle, while interactive displays portray England at the time of the Norman Conquest. A tour of the battlefield takes you to the very spot where King Harold is said to have died. Battle Abbey itself was founded here by William the Conqueror to celebrate his victory, but most of it is in a state of noble ruin, destroyed on the orders of Henry VIII. This is a great attraction for children, with a play area, activity sheet, and places to run around with a replica sword (available in the gift shop). High St., Battle. www.english-heritage.org.uk. © **01424/775705.** £8 adults, £7 students and seniors, £5 children 5–15, £21 families. Apr–Sept daily 10am–6pm, Oct daily 10am–5pm, Nov–Mar Sat–Sun 10am–4pm.

Hastings Castle ★ CASTLE/RUINS   This was the first Norman castle in England, built immediately after the Norman conquest. Now only ruins remain on the hilltop site overlooking the sea. The fortress was unfortified by King John in 1216, and was later used as a church. There is an audiovisual presentation of the castle's history, as well as the battle of 1066. It's a nice walk, or you can take the West Hill Lift, a funicular connects with George Street, in the town center. Castle Hill Rd., West Hill, Hastings. www.smugglersadventure.co.uk. © **01424/422964.** £5 adults, £4 seniors and students, £4 children, £15 families. Easter–Oct daily 10am–4pm. Feb–Easter Sat–Sun 10am–4pm (weather permitting).

At the eastern end of Hastings' seafront is **Hastings Stade ★**, the shingle beach (or "Stade") where England's largest fleet of beach-landed fishing boats comes ashore—the clapboard fish and net sheds, and market, are very much alive. There's also the charming **Fishermen's Museum** (www.hastingsfish.co.uk; ✆ **01424/461446**), filled with nautical exhibits. Admission is free, and it's open daily. The Stade area is also being redeveloped with an artsy edge, most obviously at the **Jerwood Gallery** ★ (www.jerwoodgallery.org; ✆ **01424/728377**), which opened in 2012 to display the legacy of philanthropist John Jerwood. His painting collection includes several big names in British art, including Lowry, Sickert, and Augustus John. There's also a dedicated space for temporary exhibitions, which are often big draws. The Jerwood is open Tuesday to Sunday 11am to 5pm. Admission costs £8 adults, £3 children 5–16, £20 family of up to 5.

Where to Stay & Eat

Rye makes the best base around here. If you fancy fresh fish and chips eaten straight from a cardboard box, **Marino's** ★, 38 The Mint, Rye (✆ **01797/223268**) is a dependable local choice. Fish and chips to go costs £5 to £8. It is open daily from 11am to 9pm.

George in Rye ★★   A coaching inn dating to 1575, there's a real fresh seaside air about the rooms inside. They are spread mazelike over the 16th-century main building and adjoining structures, and even the smallest is a good size, with quality mattresses and Frette linens. Climb up room grades to add a rolltop bath. You need to book ahead for the restaurant downstairs: It specializes in steak and seafood, and is always packed with diners enjoying the likes of pigeon breast with lardons and quail egg, lemon sole with brown shrimp butter and samphire, or a T-bone cooked in the charcoal oven. Main courses range £10 to £22.

High St., Rye. www.thegeorgeinrye.com. ✆ **01797/222114.** 24 units. Doubles £125–£325, includes breakfast. **Amenities:** Restaurant; bar; room service; free Wi-Fi.

Mermaid Inn ★   As the facade proudly announces, this timbered hotel was built—in fact, "rebuilt"—in 1420. It's been an inn pretty much since, housing everyone from priests fleeing Protestant Europe to the notorious Hawkhurst Gang of 18th-century smugglers to Canadian troops during World War II. There's almost nothing inside to remind you of the 21st century: Public spaces are clad in Tudor-style wood. Rooms are decked out in medieval style, including eight with four-poster beds. The restaurant serves gastropub fare, using local ingredients such as Romney Marsh lamb and South Coast scallops. Lunch main courses range £10 to £14; at dinner it's £30 for two courses, £37 for three courses.

Mermaid St., Rye. www.mermaidinn.com. ✆ **01797/223065.** 31 units. Doubles £150–£220, includes breakfast. **Amenities:** Restaurant; bar; room service; free Wi-Fi.

Shopping

Rye's pottery, white glazed and hand-painted, has been made here for centuries. **Rye Pottery** ★, Wish Ward (www.ryepottery.co.uk; ✆ **01797/ 223038**), keeps the tradition going. Forget mugs and trinkets: Here are statues depicting characters from Chaucer's "The Canterbury Tales" and the Bayeaux Tapestry.

BRIGHTON ★

52 miles S of London

Brighton is a party place. It's where Londoners flee for a day out or a fun weekend. It's packed with bars, restaurants, and weekender-friendly hotels. It was one of England's first seaside resorts, and then went through a bad time when its clientele started holidaying abroad. Now it's back, brighter and brasher than ever, and has taken on the ambience of London—which is only an hour away—with boutique lodgings, hip nightspots, and trendy shops. It's not for everyone, though: Once you're here, you'll find little respite from the crowds, and its beaches are pebble. Yet many visitors can't help falling in love with the place.

It was the fun-loving Prince of Wales (later George IV) who boosted Brighton to its lofty position, when he hit town in 1783. Brighton blossomed, adding rows of attractive townhouses and smart squares. From the Prince Regent's title came the word "Regency," which sums up a period style (but specifically refers to the years between 1811 and 1820). The Regent's extravagant **Royal Pavilion** home is still here.

George IV's successor, Queen Victoria found the place a bit too much. Graham Greene's 1930s thriller "Brighton Rock"—later adapted as 1940s film noir—and The Who's 1979 movie "Quadrophenia" both give a flavor of the 20th-century city. Despite its being surrounded by old-time fun—the beachfront lined with bars, fish-and-chips shops, and cheap souvenir stalls; the pier with its amusements—Brighton is indeed fashionable once again.

Essentials

GETTING THERE   **Trains** depart London Victoria (Southern Rail) or London Blackfriars (Thameslink) approximately every 15 minutes; the journey takes around an hour. Regular National Express **buses** from London's Victoria Coach Station and take around 2½ hours.

By **car**, the M23 (signposted from central London) leads to the A23, which takes you straight into Brighton. However, parking is inconvenient and expensive: Take the train.

VISITOR INFORMATION   Brighton's **Tourist Information Service** (www.visitbrighton.com; ✆ **01273/290337**) is now largely a phone and email service (visitor.info@visitbrighton.com). Lines and inboxes are staffed Monday to Saturday 10am to 4pm (also Sun in summer). There are **Visitor Information Points** with leaflets dotted around the city, including at the station and the **Brighton Centre,** King's Road (corner of West. St.). You can book a free introductory 2-hour walk around the

Victorian-era Brighton Pier.

city led by an enthusiastic local via Visit Brighton's "Greeter" service; check **www.visitbrighton.com/greeters**.

GETTING AROUND   You really don't want to drive around Brighton—parking is a hassle, and the seafront gets clogged with traffic. There are plenty of local **buses** (www.buses.co.uk; © **01273/886200**). You can get a Saver ticket (£5 for adults, £9 for families for up to 5) for unlimited travel on daytime buses. It's available in shops, at newsagents, online, and direct from the bus driver.

SPECIAL EVENTS   There's always something going on, but the big beast is the **Brighton Festival** (www.brightonfestival.org; © **01273/709709**). Staged each May, it is the largest arts festival in England, featuring drama, visual arts, dance, and concerts ranging from classical to rock.

Exploring Brighton

Brighton's **Seafront** ★★ exists on two levels: There's a wide promenade and cycleway that runs along King's Road, above the level of the beach; and there's the beachfront path, down some steps, which is awash in candy sellers and mini-carousels, bars, and shellfish stalls. It runs from **Brighton Pier** (a Victorian structure now featuring a rollercoaster and other hair-raising, rides, plus bars and restaurants) to the entrance of the old **West Pier,** with businesses occupying arches under the road.

Star attractions are **Jack and Linda's Brighton Smokehouse** (see "Where to Eat," below); the free **Brighton Fishing Museum** (www.brightonfishingmuseum.org.uk), complete with fishing boat, memorabilia, and old photos; the **Fortune of War** (© **01273/205065**),

ATTRACTIONS
Brighton Fishing Museum **9**
Brighton Flea Market **14**
Brighton Museum
 & Art Gallery **5**
Fortune of War **4**
Ohso Social **10**
Royal Pavilion **7**
SeaLife Brighton **11**

RESTAURANTS
Chilli Pickle **3**
Food for Friends **6**
Jack & Linda's Brighton
 Smokehouse **8**
Regency **2**
Twenty-Four
 St George's **15**

HOTELS
Nineteen **12**
Paskins **13**
Pelirocco **1**

Brighton

a beachfront pub that has been going since 1882; and the **Ohso Social** (www.ohsobrighton.co.uk; © **01273/46067**), a cafe/bar/restaurant with a terrace with views over the pier (great in the evening as the lights come on). You'll find music pouring out of bars, bands playing on the beach, inline skaters whizzing by, and people out for a stroll.

If you simply want some quiet time on the beach, walk for around 10 minutes west from West Pier toward **Hove,** where crowds thin out.

Brighton Museum & Art Gallery ★★ MUSEUM   This is one of southern England's best provincial collections, especially strong in the decorative arts and design. The surrounds aren't bad, either, inside a grandiose Victorian building on the former site of George IV's stables. In fact, this was one of Britain's first purpose-built museums.

There's plenty you'd expect to find in any civic museum, including fascinating snapshots of Brighton's history: as the darling of Regency society, as the original venue for the "dirty weekend," and as the seafront battleground between rival gangs of "Mods" and "Rockers" in 1964. The real star exhibits are in the furniture and decorative arts gallery, which includes examples from most of the leading 19th- and 20th-century design movements including Arts and Crafts furniture, Art Deco (Lalique glass), Art Nouveau (including Charles Rennie Mackintosh), Aestheticism, Bauhaus, and even a sofa designed by Salvador Dali.

Royal Pavilion Gardens. www.brightonmuseums.org.uk/brighton. © **03000/290900.** Free. Tues–Sun 10am–5pm.

Royal Pavilion ★★ HISTORIC HOME/ARCHITECTURE From the outside, the Pavilion appears a bit seaside-resort garish, painted an unattractive beige. Yet the place is a pleasure palace of another kind. This was the royals' idea of a seaside hideaway. It's a phantasmagoric ensemble of Oriental architecture, furniture, glasswork, and other fittings; a playful place that fitted in with the resort's wild reputation when it was built. Everywhere you look, mythical creatures writhe on ceilings, walls, and artwork. It was created for the Prince Regent, later King George IV, between 1787 and 1823. Queen Victoria later stayed here, but both it and Brighton were a little too much for her prim and proper tastes.

The **Dining Room ★★★** is simply superb, the 24-seat table under a domed roof (painted to resemble a palm canopy) from which hangs the most amazing chandelier you'll ever see: a huge dragon breathing fire over floral lights and shards of mirror. The **Music Room ★** is hardly less breathtaking: big enough to stage a concert, with eight chandeliers and a fireplace from which another dragon emerges.

The Pavilion is also a child of the Industrial Revolution that was starting to sweep Britain; the original wooden farmhouse construction was surrounded by an innovative iron frame on which the rest was built. The Pavilion was a hospital for Indian soldiers during World War I (operations were performed in the **Great Kitchen ★**), and narrowly escaped being demolished after World War II.

Royal Pavilion Gardens. www.bright onmuseums.org.uk/royalpavilion. © **01273/290900.** £11 adults, £9 students/seniors, £6 children, £28 families, free for children 4 and under. Apr–Sept daily 9:30am–5:45pm; Oct– Mar daily 10am–5:15pm.

The Dining Room at the Royal Pavilion.

SeaLife Brighton ★ AQUARIUM   This was the world's first aquarium, opening as the Royal Aquarium in 1872. It retains a "Twenty Thousand Leagues Under the Seas" feel, thanks to its subterranean setting. There is plenty to see here: rays, crabs, and other local sea life as well as exotic fish. That's just the opener before you walk into a **Rainforest Adventure** jungle zone; then a glass tunnel snaking through a massive tank alive with fish, sharks, and a pair of magnificent turtles. (Lulu the Green Turtle is 70-plus years old and weighs 335 lbs.) **Jurassic Seas** focuses on marine dinosaurs like the Plesiosaurus and Megalodon, as well as species that have outlived them and survive to this day.
Marine Parade. www.visitsealife.com/Brighton. ℂ **0871/4232110.** £18, £15 per person for 2 or more people; discounts online. Daily 10am–5pm.

Where to Stay

For a longer stay in Brighton or neighboring Hove, apartment rentals will save you money and give you more space; great if you have kids because the most characterful Brighton hotels tend to have relatively small rooms. You'll find a good range of apartments, townhouses, and cottages via local specialists **Brighton Holiday Homes** ★ (www.brightonholidayhomes. co.uk; ℂ **01273/624459**) and **Best of Brighton** (www.bestofbrighton. co.uk; ℂ **01273/308779**).

MODERATE

Nineteen ★★   This elegant 200-year-old townhouse offers bright-white, ultra-modern rooms with intact period coving, dark oak boards, and original artworks hung on the walls, plus plenty of gadgetry: smart TVs, Bluetooth speakers, and Wi-Fi throughout. Superior units are slightly bigger with much larger bathrooms. The location is right at the heart of Brighton's action; double-glazed windows kill background noise. Noon checkout is another friendly touch.
19 Broad St. www.nineteenbrighton.com. ℂ **01273/675529.** 7 units. Doubles £76–£160, includes breakfast. 2-night minimum Sat–Sun (except Nov–Jan). **Amenities:** Concierge; room service; free Wi-Fi. Closed 2 weeks in Jan.

Paskins ★   It's Art Nouveau all the way at this Regency townhouse hotel, with Tiffany lamps and sinuous lines used liberally throughout. Smallish rooms are decorated in light hues with occasional Art Deco touches—a mirror here, a lampshade there. (Plus one with 4-poster bed and rainfall shower done in an English country-house style.) The promenade is 100 yards from the front door—from your bed you can hear waves lapping at the shore. Don't oversleep, though, because breakfast is a major event, with vegetarian, vegan, fish, New York, and Mediterranean breakfasts offered, alongside a traditional "full English."
18-19 Charlotte St. www.paskins.co.uk. ℂ **01273/601203.** 19 units. Doubles £100–£150, includes breakfast. **Amenities:** Free Wi-Fi.

LITERARY lights: **WOOLF & KIPLING**

Sussex was home to several artistic and literary figures. **Charleston ★★★** (www. charleston.org.uk; ✆ **01323/811265**), on the A27 at Firle, was the country residence of artists Vanessa Bell and Duncan Grant, the glittering faces of the influential Bloomsbury Group early in the 20th century. The house is a work of art in itself, with the pair's decorative style covering walls, doors, and furniture. There are pieces by Picasso, Renoir, Delacroix, and more. Virginia and Leonard Woolf, novelist E. M. Forster, and biographer Lytton Strachey visited often. (Virginia was Vanessa's sister.) The walled garden has a Mediterranean theme, with enigmatic sculptures. It is open April to October, Wednesday to Saturday 1 to 6pm (July–Aug from noon) and Sunday 1 to 5:30pm. Admission is £11 for adults, £10 for students and seniors, £6 for children 6 to 16, and £31 for families. You can see the house only with a 1-hour tour, except Sundays when visits are open access. The annual literary- and arts-focused **Charleston Festival** (late May) is a regular sell-out.

Just east of Brighton, near Lewes, is Rodmell, where Virginia Woolf lived until her death in 1941. **Monk's House ★** (www.nationaltrust.org.uk/monks-house; ✆ **01273/474760**) was bought by Virginia and Leonard Woolf in 1919, and Leonard remained there until his death in 1969. This 17th-century clapboard cottage—where Woolf did much of her writing—is open April to October, Wednesday to Sunday, 1 to 5pm (£5 adults, £3 children 5 to 15, £13 families).

In the village of Burwash, on the A265, 29 miles northeast of Brighton, is **Bateman's ★** (www.nationaltrust. org.uk/batemans; ✆ **01435/882302**), the 17th-century house in which author Rudyard Kipling lived from 1902 until his death in 1936. "Heaven looked after it in the dissolute times of mid-Victorian restoration and caused the

Pelirocco ★★   Outside it's a handsome townhouse hotel on one of Brighton's Regency squares. Inside, rooms are outrageously themed: "Soviet chic" in the Stoli Salon; Sex Pistols memorabilia in "Pretty Vacant"; "couples friendly" fittings and plenty of dark satin in Nookii. You get the idea. And there are no half measures: Schemes are out there and uncompromising, and followed through right down to the pillow slips and desk chairs. Front side rooms have square and oblique sea views. plus a little balcony, for £20–£30 extra. This is a Brighton original, made for adult travelers with a taste for the offbeat.

10 Regency Sq. www.hotelpelirocco.co.uk. ✆ **01273/327055.** 19 units. Doubles £99–£185. **Amenities:** Bar; free Wi-Fi.

Where to Eat

EXPENSIVE

Twenty-Four St George's ★ MODERN EUROPEAN   This elegant restaurant is a short cab ride from the center—or a 20-minute walk along the seafront—but well worth the detour. There's a polite, slightly vicar to send his bailiff to live in it for 40 years, and he lived in peaceful filth and left everything as he found it," wrote the creator of "The Jungle Book" about the place. Bateman's is filled with rugs, bronzes, and other mementos collected in India and elsewhere. The house and gardens are open daily from 10am to 5pm (house opens 11am), but close at dusk if that falls before 5pm. Admission costs £10 for adults, £5 for children 5 to 15, and £24 for families.

The Garden Room at Charleston country house, Firle.

formal feel to the interior, with starched-white tablecloths and neat cutlery. The food is modern and forward-looking, yet with an eye for tradition. Expect the likes of a ballotine of chicken and prunes followed by a trio of Victorian beef cuts (filet, shin, and short rib) then a cinnamon and honey crème brulee. Service is pitch-perfect.

24-25 St George's Rd., Kemp Town. www.24stgeorges.co.uk. ℂ **01273/626060.** Mains £13–£24. Tues–Sat 5:30–10pm; also Sat 12:30–2pm.

MODERATE

Chilli Pickle ★★ MODERN INDIAN   The loud décor and central location appear to scream "chain." But first impressions are deceptive: The food at this Indian street-food inspired canteen is seriously good. Star turns at lunch are the Railway Trays and King Thalis, combi trays with one main such as a Persian white mutton curry, served with pickles, rice, chutney, Indian naan bread, raita and dal. At dinner, try something from the tandoor oven, such as spiced pheasant breast with clove-smoked malai sauce. If you've not tasted the heavily spiced (but rarely fiery-hot) flavours and textures of modern India, Chilli Pickle is a great place to get acquainted. It also does takeout.

17 Jubilee St. www.thechillipickle.com. ℭ **01273/900383.** Mains £11–£17. Daily noon–2:45pm and 6–10:15pm.

Goat cheese souffle at Food for Friends, Brighton.

Food for Friends ★★★ VEGE-TARIAN/VEGAN   This place is a top-rank vegetarian and vegan restaurant; it's also just a great restaurant that happens not to serve meat. Food is a creative mix of local, seasonal, and Mediterranean flavors. A mixed mezze of small plates lets you sample more of the range, which might include beet and parsnip rostis with tamarind and date dip; fig, smoked ricotta, and basil salad with crispy pickled ginger crisps; or shallot dumplings with creamed caraway cabbage. The dining room is bright and modern, with picture windows overlooking the Lanes.

17-18 Prince Albert St. www.foodforfriends.com. ℭ **01273/202310.** Mains £12–£13; small plates £5, or 3 for £12. Daily noon–10pm.

Regency ★ ENGLISH   Like an English seaside take on a Parisian bistro, this place has sea-view windows, wooden furniture, faded elegance, and the buzz of constant chatter. It's also Brighton's best sensibly priced fish restaurant, rightly popular with tourists and locals alike. Concentrate on the fresh fish—there's usually halibut, plaice, skate, and sole alongside fish-and-chip favorites cod and haddock. We recommend you reserve an indoor table, as King's Road gets very busy.

131 King's Rd. www.theregencyrestaurant.co.uk. ℭ **01273/325014.** Mains £9–£13. Daily 8am–10:30pm.

INEXPENSIVE

Jack and Linda's Brighton Smokehouse ★★ SEAFOOD   This place is a Brighton institution. It's built into a little beachfront brick arch under the promenade, so there's no inside seating—perch at an outdoor table or munch your takeout on the beach. The menu is all about the fresh and house-smoked seafood: a grilled mackerel roll with a squeeze of lemon; bread and whitebait; rollmops (pickled herring filets); fresh anchovies. It's all simple, delicious, and prepped while you wait. No credit cards.

197 King's Rd. Arches. No phone. Soups & sandwiches £3–£5. Daily 10am–5pm (approximately); weekends only in winter.

Shopping

Brighton has plenty of fun shopping. **The Lanes ★**, a collection of alleyways and winding, narrow streets between North Street and the sea, is full of boutiques, cafes, and arty stores of all kinds. It's Brighton's traditional antiques and jewelry quarter. If you're thinking of popping the question anytime soon, this is the place to browse for a ring.

North Laine ★★—between North Street and the train station—is the area for new talent, a few blocks of funky, original shops with plenty of one-off and vintage fashions, jewelry, health foods, quirky homewares and accessories. Possibilities are rife along Kensington Gardens, Sydney Street, Gardner Street, and Bond Street. To get the "Brighton look," buy the threads (suits, shirts, and accessories for men) at **Gresham Blake ★★**, 20 Bond St. (www.greshamblake.com; ℂ **01273/609587**).

Bargain hunters head for the indoor **Brighton Flea Market ★**, 31 Upper St James's St. (www.flea-markets.co.uk; ℂ **01273/624006**), open Monday to Friday 10am to 5pm, weekends 10:30am to 5pm.

Entertainment & Nightlife

Offering drama year-round is the **Theatre Royal,** New Road (ℂ **08448/717650**), with pre-London shows, musicals, and family entertainment. There's an edgier feel to the program at the nearby **Brighton Dome ★**, Church Street (www.brightondome.org; ℂ **01273/709709**), where you'll find theatre, opera, ballet, and music in any of 3 separate performance halls. The Dome is also a major venue during the multi-arts **Brighton Festival** (see "Special Events," p. 202). Bigger gigs are held at the **Brighton Centre,** King's Road (www.brightoncentre.co.uk; ℂ **01273/290131**), a 5,000-seat facility featuring mainly mainstream pop music and comedy.

Komedia, 44-47 Gardner St. (www.komedia.co.uk/brighton; ℂ **01273/687171**), is a venue that hosts everything from top indie acts to comedy. **The Latest Music Bar,** 14 Manchester St. (www.the latest.co.uk/musicbar; ℂ **01273/687171**), combines live music with party-style club nights. If niche music is your thing, you'll likely find an exciting schedule at **Concorde 2,** Madeira Shelter Hall, Madeira Drive (www.concorde2.co.uk; ℂ **01273/673311**).

There are plenty of **nightclubs** in Brighton; some have been around for a while, others come and go. Check **www.brightonlife. com** or pick up a copy of free events listing guide "BN1 Magazine" (also online at **www.BN1magazine.co.uk**). There's often free admission early on or midweek rising to £10 or so, but times and prices vary from season to season. **Casablanca,** Middle Street (www. casablancajazzclub.com; ℂ **01273/321817**), offers clubbing with a funk-latin-jazz feel.

brighton's **GAY SCENE**

Brighton has long been regarded as Britain's gay capital. It has the country's biggest gay festival (**Brighton and Hove Pride,** in early Aug; see www.brighton pride.co.uk), and a thriving scene of bars and clubs. Most of the action is in the Gay Quarter in Kemp Town, a compact strip just off the seafront. **Legends** ★, 31 Marine Parade (www.legendsbrighton. com; ✆ **01273/624462**), is one of England's leading gay hotels and also has two venues, **Legends** cafe-bar and **The Basement** nightclub. There's traditionally a lesbian clientele at the **Marlborough,** 4 Princes St. (✆ **01273/570028**), an 18th-century pub opposite the Royal Pavilion which has a cabaret theatre. It's also the home of the **Pink Fringe** LGBT arts group (www.pinkfringe.org.uk; ✆ **01273/273870**), which stages performances year-round. Of the nightclubs, **Revenge,** 32-34 Old Steine (www. revenge.co.uk; ✆ **01273/606064**), is the biggest, with lots of gay-friendly live acts from TV shows such as "X Factor." The **Charles Street Bar & Club** ★, 8 Marine Parade (www.charles-street.com; ✆ **01273/624091**), combines a buzzing downstairs bar with a popular club above. The official tourist office site, **www.visitbrighton.com/gay-brighton**, has a sizable LGBT section. Additional worthy bookmarks are **www.gscene.com** and **www.gaybrighton.com**.

Brighton and Hove Pride Festival.

Pubs are a good place to kick off (or while away) an evening. In the center, the **Colonnade Bar,** New Road (www.thecolonnadebrighton. co.uk; ✆ **01273/328728**), has been serving drinks for over 100 years. If you are serious about beer, there's nowhere better in Brighton than **Craft Beer Co.** ★★, 22-23 Upper North St. (www.craftbeerco.com/pubs/ brighton; ✆ **01273/723736**). There are usually 18 or so keg beers plus six English-style cask ales, as well as more bottles than you could drink in a month. Craft usually has a more sedate feel than many Brighton nightspots. Close to the station, the **Evening Star** ★, 55-56 Surrey St. (✆ **01273/328931**), is the original home of local brewery Dark Star, and another place to dive into the beer scene. **The Cricketers,** Black Lion Street (www.cricketersbrighton.co.uk; ✆ **01273/329472**), is Brighton's oldest pub, parts of which date from 1547.

Bohemia ★, 54-55 Meeting House Lane (www.bohemiabrighton. co.uk; ✆ **07715/905783**), is the hottest bar in town for cocktails. For wine drinkers **Ten Green Bottles,** 9 Jubilee St. (www.ten greenbottles.com; ✆ **01273/567176**), has a central location and a by-the-glass list (from £4). It's also a bottle shop.

CHICHESTER ★ & ARUNDEL ★

Chichester: 31 miles W of Brighton; 69 miles SW of London. Arundel: 21 miles W of Brighton; 61 miles SW of London

Chichester has it all. On one side there's the sea, a natural harbor with 48 miles of coastline, where you'll see plenty of yachts. On the other side is the undulating countryside of the **South Downs,** Britain's newest National Park. And Chichester itself? It has all the charms of a smart market town yet is actually a city, courtesy of its **Cathedral.** It can also boast being the former Roman city of Noviomagus. The streets are neat and historic. It's home to the **Chichester Festival,** one of the country's leading theatrical festivals, which is staged in the 1950s-era **Festival Theatre** in Oaklands Park. This city offers one of the best theatrical escapes from London.

Arundel is a short drive east of Chichester. It is dominated by the might of **Arundel Castle,** yet there is more to it than that: The River Arun crosses it, serene and regal, then meanders, like a scene from the Middle Ages, through water meadows that make for lovely walks.

Essentials

GETTING THERE   Trains depart London's Victoria Station every 30 minutes during the day. The trip takes 1¼ hours to Arundel, another few minutes to Chichester. If you visit Chichester from London for the theatre, you'll be wise to stay over—the last direct train back departs around 9pm. If **driving,** take the A3 from London, turning onto the A283 for Chichester. From Chichester take the A27 10 miles east to Arundel.

VISITOR INFORMATION   Chichester Tourist Information Centre, The Novium, Tower Street (www.visitchichester.org; ✆**01243/775888**), is open October to March, Wednesday to Saturday 10am to 5pm, Sunday 10am to 4pm; April to September hours are Monday to Saturday 10am to 5pm and Sunday 10am to 4pm. **Arundel Visitor Information Point,** inside Arundel Museum, Mill Road (www.sussexbythesea.com; ✆ **01903/882268**), is open daily 10am to 4pm.

Exploring Chichester, Arundel & Around

From Chichester, it's also an easy side trip to the historic naval dockyard and HMS *Victory* at Portsmouth; see "A Side Trip to Portsmouth," p. 225. **West Wittering ★**, 8 miles southwest of Chichester, is one of southern

Arundel Castle and museum.

England's best beaches, a natural, unspoiled sweep of sand a mile or so long and backed by dunes. The sand-dune spit has pleasant coastal walking. See www.westwitteringbeach.co.uk.

In Arundel, shoppers and window browsers should make for Tarrant Street ★, where there's a huddle of stores selling antiques, collectables, and one-off portable homewares.

Arundel Castle ★★ CASTLE   The ancestral home of the dukes of Norfolk, Arundel Castle is a much-restored fortress of considerable importance. Its legend is associated with some of the great families of England, including the Fitzalans and the powerful Howards. This castle received worldwide exposure when it was chosen as the backdrop for "The Madness of King George" (it doubled for Windsor Castle in the movie). Arundel Castle suffered badly during the Civil Wars when it was stormed by Cromwell's troops, in likely retaliation for the sizable contribution to Charles I made by the 14th Earl of Arundel. In the early 18th century the castle had to be rebuilt, and in late Victorian times it was remodeled and extensively restored again. Today it's filled with works by **Old Masters** such as Van Dyck, Canaletto, and Gainsborough.

The castle sits on 16 hectares (40 acres), including a walled kitchen garden and formal gardens reclaimed from car parking several years ago. It is all circled by a 1,100-acre park containing **Swanbourne Lake.**

Mill Rd., Arundel. www.arundelcastle.org. ℂ **01903/882173.** £9–£18 adults, £9–£16 students and seniors, £9 children 5–16, £41–£45 families, free for children 4 and under. April–Oct Tues–Sun, grounds 10am–5pm, castle keep 11am–4:30pm, rooms noon–5pm (last admission 4pm).

Arundel Cathedral ★ CATHEDRAL   Commissioned in 1868, the Roman Catholic Cathedral of Our Lady and St Philip Howard stands at the highest point in Arundel, a fine example of Victorian French Gothic architecture. Joseph A. Hansom, inventor of the Hansom cab—a precursor to the modern taxi, and drawn by a single horse—designed it for the 15th Duke of Norfolk. However, it was not consecrated as a cathedral until 1965. The interior includes the shrine of St Philip Howard, a Catholic convert imprisoned by Elizabeth I.

London Rd., Arundel. www.arundelcathedral.org. Ⓒ **01903/882297.** Free (donations appreciated). Daily 9:30am–dusk.

Chichester Cathedral ★ CATHEDRAL   Completed in 1123, Chichester's cathedral is light and airy and topped by a sharp, narrow spire. This spire was completed in 1867 after an earlier one fell in 1860. As well as being architecturally stunning, the cathedral has an unusual collection of modern art. Look for the stained-glass window by Marc Chagall; the painting, "Noli Me Tangere," of Christ appearing to Mary at Easter by Graham Sutherland; and "The Baptism of Christ" by Hans Feibusch. There is also a 10-ft. high stainless-steel hand of Christ floating in the Nave, the work of internationally renowned sculptor Jaume Plensa.

Cathedral Cloisters, South St., Chichester. www.chichestercathedral.org.uk. Ⓒ **01243/782595.** Free. Daily 7am–6pm (from 7:15am in winter). Guided tours 45 min. Mon–Sat 11:15am and 2:30pm.

Interior, Chichester Cathedral.

South Downs Way

The **South Downs Way** runs for 100 miles, from the promenade at East-bourne, all the way to **Winchester** in Hampshire (p. 218). It climbs the cliffs of **Beachy Head,** passes the giant chalk figure of the Long Man of Wilmington, skirts Charleston (where the Bloomsbury set of artists lived; see p. 206), takes an undulating, breathtaking path to the north of Brighton, and forges onward. It follows chalk ridges, dips into river valleys, crosses bare hillsides, and feels as remote as anything in farther-flung parts of England. It would take an average walker 8 or 9 days to complete (and there are plenty of pubs and hotels on or near the route), but it's as easy to enjoy an afternoon stroll on any of the sections. Stop at one of the parking lots at Beachy Head, for instance, and start walking. Visit **www.nationaltrail.co.uk/south-downs-way** for full information and trail maps.

A view from the South Downs Way footpath.

Fishbourne Roman Palace & Gardens ★ HISTORIC SITE   This is what remains of the largest Roman residence yet discovered in Britain. Built around A.D. 75, it has many mosaic-floored rooms and a surviving under-floor heating system (or "hypocaust"). The manicured gardens have been restored to their extravagant 1st-century plan. Roman artifacts are on display in the Collections Discovery Centre, and there is also a computer graphic reconstruction of the palace.

Roman Way, Fishbourne (2 miles W of Chichester). www.sussexpast.co.uk. ✆ **01243/785859.** £9 adults, £8 students and seniors, £5 children 4–16, £23 families. Mar–Oct daily 10am–5pm; Nov to mid-Dec, Feb daily 10am–4pm.

Pallant House Art Gallery ★ ART MUSEUM   This is a gallery of modern art, with a collection featuring Henry Moore and Graham Sutherland. There's "The Beatles 1962" by Peter Blake, which preceded his design of their "Sgt. Pepper" album cover; the studio and archive of German artist Hans Feibusch (who fled Nazi persecution), plus works by Duncan Grant, Picasso, Lucian Freud, Cézanne, and others.

9 North Pallant, Chichester. www.pallant.org.uk. ✆ **01243/774557.** £9 adults, £4 children 6–16, £20 families (Tues half-price, Thurs free 5–8pm). Tues–Wed and Fri–Sat 10am–5pm; Thurs 10am–8pm; Sun11am–5pm.

Where to Stay

Amberley Castle ★★   The "castle" part of the name is no empty claim: This grand hotel has a portcullis, a fairly intact medieval curtain wall, and 900 years of history—it was first used by the Bishops of Chichester in the 1100s, and some of the oldest parts survive. Rooms are all individual, and have varying amounts of space, though even the smallest are a good size. Décor varies from the baronial style you're expecting—exposed beams, four-poster beds, lancet windows—to more surprising modern splashes and, in some, hydromassage baths. The restaurant—the **Queen's Room** (see "Where to Eat," below)—has some of the best (and best value) fine dining in Sussex.

Amberley, 6 miles north of Arundel. www.amberleycastle.co.uk. ✆ **01798/831992.** 19 units. Doubles £169–£619, includes breakfast. **Amenities:** Restaurant; bar; putting green; room service; tennis court; free Wi-Fi.

Ship ★★   Chichester's best central hotel had a recent refurbishment, and public areas (including a new restaurant, Murray's) evoke the Ritz's Palm Court. Rooms have a flambuoyant feel too, with décor schemes based on six iconic productions at Chichester's Festival Theatre, with original script samples on the walls. If you like to stretch out, upsize to a Superior or Deluxe—the latter also have Nespresso machines and a bit more room space. There's also a fully serviced luxury cottage with private terrace, known as **No. 1 Chichester.** The building itself is a Georgian gem, paid for by Admiral Lord Nelson for his colleague Admiral Sir George Murray.

57 North St., Chichester. www.theshiphotel.net. ✆ **01243/778000.** 36 units. Doubles £125–£189, includes breakfast. **Amenities:** Restaurant; bar; room service; free Wi-Fi.

Where to Eat

On Arundel's prettiest lane, the **Bay Tree** ★, 21 Tarrant Street (www.thebaytreearundel.co.uk; ✆ **01903/883679**), has a menu that evolves as the day goes on. For lunch there are snacks such as Welsh rarebit or omelets, as well as main courses like steak and Guinness pie; in the evening, the emphasis is on more elaborate dishes like slow-roasted pork belly or cod medallions with crayfish risotto. Mains range £11 to £19. It's open daily for lunch and dinner.

Amelie & Friends ★ MODERN EUROPEAN   There's an informal, brasserie-style atmosphere here, but they are deadly serious about their food: It is a great central choice in Chichester for lunch. As you'd expect, the menu is eclectic, mixing English classics such as fish chips and with Mediterranean flavors in such dishes as seared sea bream with sauce vierge or corn-fed chicken breast with Dauphinoise potatoes. There's a courtyard garden out back for alfresco eating.

31 North St., Chichester. www.amelieandfriends.com. ✆ **01243/771444.** Mains £10–£19. Daily noon–2:30pm (Sat until 3pm); Mon–Sat 5:30–11pm.

The Queen's Room at Amberley Castle ★★★ MODERN BRITISH   This is the place to splurge on a meal in Sussex, and offers excellent value at lunch, in particular. There's a delightfully old-fashioned, regal feel to the entire experience, starting with the setting, on an upper floor of Amberley Castle under a 12th-century barrel vault. Start with wood pigeon on a wild garlic risotto, followed by confit shoulder of lamb with pea puree and finishing with a selection of British artisan cheeses. The extensive wine list has labels from all over the world, with particular strengths among European wines. Reservations are essential.

Inside Amberley Castle (see "Where to Stay," above), Amberley, near Arundel. www.amberleycastle.co.uk. ✆ **01798/831992.** Lunch £26 for 2 courses, £31 for 3 courses; dinner £65 for 3 courses; tasting menu £85. Daily noon–2:30pm and 7–9:30pm.

Entertainment & Nightlife

Chichester Festival Theatre ★★   This 1,300-seat theatre on the edge of Oaklands Park opened in 1962 under its first director, Lord Laurence Olivier. The theatre stages plays and musicals—likely to star top names—plus orchestras, jazz, opera, ballet, and a Christmas show. On the same site, the **Minerva Studio Theatre** features more experimental performances. The famed **Chichester Festival** is actually a season of performances that runs from April to September and includes classic and contemporary plays, along with musicals and associated events.

Oaklands Park, Chichester. www.cft.org.uk. ✆ **01243/781312.**

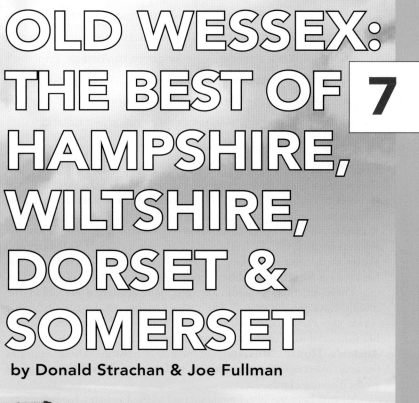

OLD WESSEX: THE BEST OF 7 HAMPSHIRE, WILTSHIRE, DORSET & SOMERSET

by Donald Strachan & Joe Fullman

T he Regency charms of Bath, the prehistoric mysteries of Stonehenge, and the monumental architecture of Salisbury: These are all found in England's oldest counties. The kingdom of Wessex, England's precursor, was ruled from Winchester. A tour of this part of southern England leads you gently from London's coattails to the rural peace of tiny villages and serene, idyllic isolation.

Regal Bath achieved fame and fortune twice in its history, first as a spa in Roman times, then thanks to the Georgian builders of the elegant **Royal Crescent.** That most English of traditions, **afternoon tea** has been big in Bath for centuries, and is paired here with a Sally Lunn or Bath bun. **Avebury** and Stonehenge date back to prehistoric times, long before the Romans invaded Britain. Cathedrals in the small cities of **Salisbury** and **Wells** are as close to the Gothic ideal as you'll find in England, and the fan vaults at **Sherborne Abbey** showcase medieval architectural genius.

There are literary landmarks, too. Jane Austen wrote about the middle-class inhabitants of Hampshire in her six novels, including "Pride and Prejudice" and "Sense and Sensibility." Devotees can visit her memorial in **Winchester Cathedral** and her home, now the **Jane Austen's House Museum,** in nearby Chawton. These counties became "Wessex" once again in the 19th-century **Dorchester** tales of writer Thomas Hardy.

History here has also long been tied to the English Channel. Portsmouth is England's naval capital, and the **Historic Dockyard** is where Nelson's HMS *Victory* and the remains of Henry VIII's flagship, the *Mary Rose,* remain in their final berths.

WINCHESTER ★★

72 miles SW of London; 12 miles N of Southampton

Once one of the big urban beasts of England, Winchester was founded by the Romans in the first century A.D. and grew to prominence in the 9th century, when **Alfred the Great** had it rebuilt according to a street plan that is still followed today. The king is honored by a 20th-century statue on the Broadway. Winchester went on to become England's de facto capital—William the Conqueror was crowned both here and in London—although its influence waned during the medieval period.

Its past glory but a memory, Winchester is now a compact, well-kept market town with almost everything you want to see within easy

PREVIOUS PAGE: **Stonehenge, Britain's most important prehistoric monument.**

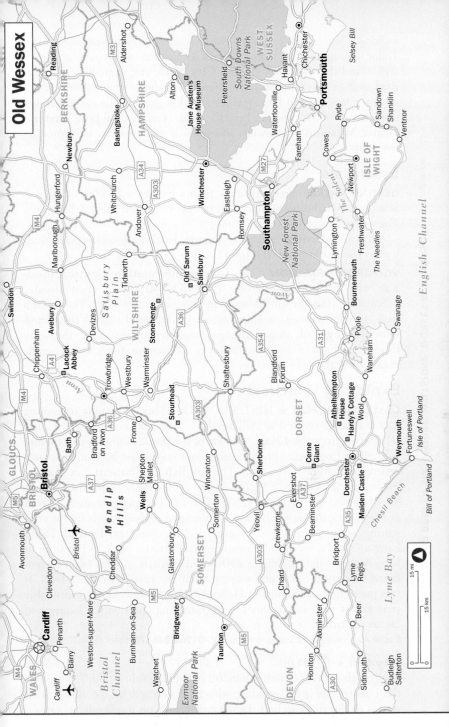

Old Wessex

walking distance. It's packed with historic architecture—Norman, Tudor, Georgian, and more, all mixed together in a typically English style—and there's a well-curated **City Museum,** a medieval **Cathedral,** and an intriguing array of independent shops. Hampshire is also a draw for Jane Austen fans. You can visit her grave in the cathedral, see the (outside of the) house where she died, as well as the **Jane Austen's House Museum** in Chawton, where she lived during her most productive years.

Essentials

GETTING THERE   Frequent daily **trains** run from London's Waterloo Station to Winchester Station, a 10-minute walk northwest of the center. The journey takes just over 1 hour.

If you're **driving** from Southampton, head north on the A335 until it joins the northbound M3; from London, take the M3 southwest.

VISITOR INFORMATION   The **Tourist Information Centre,** Broadway (www.visitwinchester.co.uk; ✆ **01962/840500**), is open Monday to Saturday 10am to 5pm (May–Sept also Sun 11am–4pm). They offer a free "greeter" service to help visitors get oriented: Email **tourism@ winchester.gov.uk** around 10 days ahead of your arrival and they'll try to arrange a local to come and meet you, answer questions, and generally point you in the right direction.

Exploring Winchester

Castle Great Hall ★ HISTORIC SITE   This is the only remaining part of a castle erected by William the Conqueror and rebuilt by Henry III. Dating from the 1200s, it is one of the finest examples of a medieval hall in England, with its timber roof supported by Gothic arches resting on columns of marble. The **English Parliament** met here for the first time in 1246; a Victorian mural lists every Hampshire Member of Parliament between 1283 and 1868. The castle hosted the trial of Sir Walter Raleigh, who was condemned to death in 1603 for conspiring against James I. The giant (18 ft. diameter) **Round Table** hanging on the west wall doesn't in fact stretch back to the time of King Arthur—its 1,220kg (2,690 lb.) of English oak has been carbon dated to around 1280, and was probably the property of Edward I. It was painted at the behest of Henry VIII in the 16th century, probably (and rather typically of this self-aggrandizing king) with a likeness of Henry as Arthur.

Castle Ave. www.hants.gov.uk/greathall. ✆ **01962/846476.** Free. Daily 10am–5pm.

City Mill ★ HISTORIC SITE   Built in 1743 on the site of a medieval original, this is one of only a handful of working urban flour mills left in the country. Its great grinding wheels are turned by the fast-flowing waters of the River Itchen. This happens only on weekends, when you

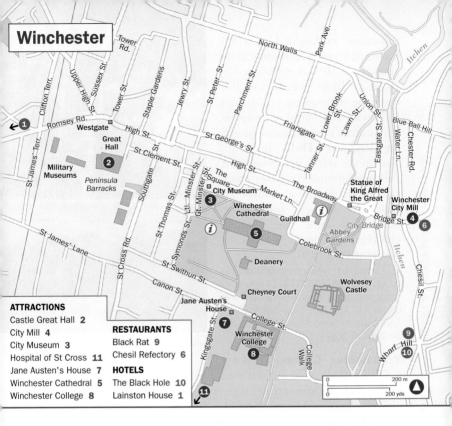

ATTRACTIONS

Castle Great Hall **2**
City Mill **4**
City Museum **3**
Hospital of St Cross **11**
Jane Austen's House **7**
Winchester Cathedral **5**
Winchester College **8**

RESTAURANTS
Black Rat **9**
Chesil Refectory **6**

HOTELS
The Black Hole **10**
Lainston House **1**

can purchase a bag of the resulting flour. The rest of the time, it's not quite as much fun. You can watch videos on the site's history, play with hands-on displays, and spot local wildlife. If you're very (very) lucky you may catch a glimpse of one of the otters living nearby.

Bridge St. www.nationaltrust.org.uk/winchestercitymill. (C) **01962/870057.** £4 adults, £2 children. Mid Feb to Oct daily 10am–5pm; Nov to mid-Feb to 4pm.

City Museum ★★ MUSEUM   One of the better small town museums, this provides a whistle stop tour of 2,000 years of Winchester history. Starting with the city's founding by the Romans as **Venta Bulgarum,** you wind your way through the Anglo-Saxon glory days, the Norman invasion, and the Middle Ages to Winchester's recent incarnation as a low-key center of commerce, as represented by several recreated shop interiors from the 19th and 20th centuries.

The Square. www.winchester.gov.uk/heritage-conservation/museums/city-museum. (C) **01962/863064.** Free. Apr–Oct Mon–Sat 10am–5pm, Sun noon–5pm; Nov–Mar Tues–Sat 10am–4pm, Sun noon–4pm.

Hospital of St Cross ★★ RELIGIOUS SITE   Founded in 1132, the Hospital (for hospitality, not medicine) is the oldest charitable institution in England, and still houses 25 robed Brethren in its almshouses. It was established by Henri de Blois, grandson of William the Conqueror, to sustain local poor and famished travelers. It continues the tradition of providing **Wayfarer's Dole**—bread and ale—to any visitor who requests it. Arranged around the inner courtyard are the Brethren's houses that date from 1450, a 16th-century ambulatory, and the Norman church, begun in 1135 and completed around 1250.

St Cross Rd. www.hospitalofstcross. co.uk. Ⓒ **01962/851375.** £4 adults, £4 students and seniors, £2 children under 13. Apr–Oct Mon–Sat 9:30am–5pm, Sun 1–5pm; Nov–Mar Mon–Sat 10:30am–3:30pm.

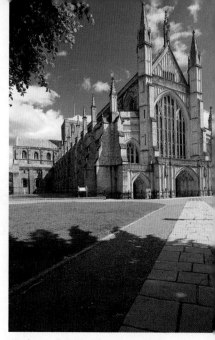

Winchester Cathedral, founded in 1079.

Winchester Cathedral ★★★

CATHEDRAL   The longest medieval cathedral in Britain dates from 1079, and its Norman heritage is still in evidence. When a Saxon church stood on this spot, Swithun, Bishop of Winchester and tutor to young King Alfred, suggested modestly that he be buried outside. Following his subsequent indoor burial, it rained for 40 days. Legends say that if it rains on **St Swithun's Day,** July 15, it'll continue raining for the next 40 days.

The **Perpendicular Gothic nave** is the architectural highlight. The elaborately carved choir stalls from 1308 are England's oldest, as is the retrochoir's medieval tiled floor. The astonishing **Great Screen** was carved between 1470 and 1490, although the original statues fell victim to the Reformation. Those in place today are Victorian replacements.

Jane Austen is buried in the north aisle; her original gravestone makes no mention of her writing (her house on College Street is just south of the cathedral). The son of William the Conqueror, William Rufus (who reigned as William II) is also buried here, as are the bones of Danish King of England, Cnut (985–1035). Guided tours of the cathedral and crypt are free, or you can pay to go up the tower for views over the city.

The Close. www.winchester-cathedral.org.uk. Ⓒ **01962/857200.** £8 adults, £6 seniors, £4 students, free for children under 16. Mon–Sat 9:30am–5pm, Sun 12:30–3pm; free tours hourly 10am–3pm. Tower £6: May–Sept Mon–Fri 2:15pm, Sat 11:30am and 2:15pm; Oct–Nov and Jan–Apr Wed 2:15pm, Sat 11:30am and 2:15pm.

Winchester College ★ CULTURAL INSTITUTION   Winchester College was founded by William of Wykeham, Bishop of Winchester and chancellor to Richard II, who also founded New College, Oxford. Its buildings have been in use since 1393, making it the oldest continuously open school in England. Visits are possible only by an hour-long guided tour, covering the Chamber Court, the 14th-century Gothic chapel, and the College Hall, among other sights. During term time, you can attend Tuesday **Evensong** for free. Arrive at the Porter's Lodge by 5:30pm.

73 Kingsgate St. www.winchestercollege.org/guided-tours. © **01962/621209.** £7 adults, £6 students and seniors. Guided tours Apr–Aug Mon, Wed, Fri, and Sat 10:15am, 11:30am, 2:15pm, and 3:30pm, Tues and Thurs 10:15am and 11:30am, Sun 12:15pm and 3:30pm; Sept–Mar the same except no 3:30pm tour Mon–Sat.

BEYOND THE CITY

Jane Austen's House Museum ★ HISTORIC HOME/MUSEUM The great satirizer of Regency society manners lived in the village of Chawton, just south of Winchester, for 7½ years, during which time four of her six novels were published. Many visitors find the little cottage and gardens surprisingly small, but Austen herself occupied a lower level of the landed gentry than the characters she wrote about. The interiors have been painstakingly recreated with period furniture, and there are a few items of genuine Austen memorabilia, including needlework and jewelry. Children's activities include dressing up and writing with a quill pen. When Austen fell ill in 1816, she moved to College Street in Winchester, where she died in 1817.

Chawton (15 miles east of Winchester). www.jane-austens-house-museum.org.uk. © **01420/83262.** £8 adults, £7 students and seniors, £2 children 6–16. June–Aug daily 10am–5pm; Sept–Dec and Mar–May daily 10:30am–4:30pm; Jan–Feb Sat–Sun 10:30am–4:30pm.

ORGANIZED TOURS

The Tourist Information Centre has a number of helpful free pamphlets, including one that details a self-guided Keats circuit round the environs—Keats' 1819 ode "To Autumn" was inspired by a visit here. Guided **walking tours** depart from the tourist office and last 1½ hours, and cost £5 per adult (children go free). Times vary by season; check at www.winchestertouristguides.com or once you're in town.

Where to Stay

Black Hole ★★   Opened in 2014, this B&B is the latest addition to entrepreneur David Nicholson's "black" empire, which also includes the adjacent pub the Black Boy (see below), restaurant the Black Rat (ditto), and wine bar the Black Bottle. The 10 rooms have been given a loose "prison" theme, with thick wooden and metal doors, 19th-century mug shots adorning the walls, and tin plates in the breakfast room. Although it screams "quirky," it is also extremely comfortable. All rooms have their own style—some with views of the cathedral—but are all the same price.

Wharf Hill, Winchester. www.theblackholebb.co.uk. ✆ **01962/807010.** 10 units. Doubles £100. **Amenities:** Free Wi-Fi.

Lainston House ★★   If even the rather low-key nightlife of Winchester seems a bit much, you're guaranteed a good night's rest at this 17th-century red brick manor a few miles northeast of town. It's set in 63 acres of manicured parkland. Owners have opted for a traditional country house ambience, with antique-filled interiors. Owing to the age of the house, the size of the rooms varies from enormous suites to slightly more cramped double rooms. The restaurant is an attraction in its own right: Cream teas are served every afternoon.

Woodman Lane, Sparsholt, Winchester. www.lainstonhouse.com. ✆ **01962/776088.** 50 units. Doubles £225–£360. **Amenities:** Restaurant; bar; exercise room; room service; 2 tennis courts; free Wi-Fi.

Where to Eat

Black Rat ★★   MODERN ENGLISH   For many, this is the best restaurant in Winchester, a reputation reinforced with the award of a Michelin star. The menu is adventurous but determinedly local—they employ their own forager to track down fresh produce—and may include such delights as rabbit ravioli with burnt hay pasta or pigeon breast with bubble and squeak. Despite its accolades, it has a casual, pub-like vibe.

88 Chesil St. www.theblackrat.co.uk. ✆ **01962/844465.** Mains £18–£22; weekend lunch menu £26 (2 courses), £29 (3 courses). Daily 7–9:15pm; Sat–Sun noon–2:15pm.

Chesil Rectory ★★ MODERN ENGLISH   For diners who like a bit of history with their dinner, step through the low doorway (mind your head) into the city's oldest commercial property, dating to around 1425. It's been a restaurant for a mere 50 years and has become one of Winchester's most feted spots. The interior is reassuringly traditional with exposed wooden beams, while the menu offers a mixture of the resolutely British with the whimsically modern. Expect dishes such as lemon sole with chicory marmalade, blood orange and confit potatoes.

1 Chesil St. www.chesilrectory.co.uk. ✆ **01962/851555.** Mains £14–£21; Mon–Sat lunch and 6–7pm fixed-price 2 courses £16, 3 courses £20. Daily noon–2:20pm; Mon–Thurs 6–9:30pm, Fri–Sat 6–10pm.

Shopping

Winchester is crammed with excellent shops. The **High Street** has all the usual chains, albeit occupying much grander premises than the norm. Along with the adjoining Middle Brook Street, this is the site of the weekly general **market** on Thursday to Saturday from 9am to

6pm, with stalls selling food, flowers, and household goods. An antiques and collectibles market is held on the first Sunday of the month, a farmer's market (**www.hampshirefarmersmarkets.co.uk**) on the second and final Sunday, and an art and design market on the third Sunday.

The various artisan stores along **Parchment Street, Great Minster Street,** and **The Square** provide lots of opportunities for browsing, with plenty of antiques, art, home decor, fashions, and jewelry. The oldest book dealer in town is **P&G Wells,** 11 College Street (www.bookwells.co.uk; ✆ **01962/852016**), offering both new releases and local interest titles.

Entertainment & Nightlife

Your best spots for a decent pint are the tiny, traditional bar at the **Eclipse,** 25 The Square (www.eclipseinnwinchester.co.uk; ✆ **01962/865676**), which was once the rectory of the nearby church of St Lawrence. If you don't mind a gentle 10-minute walk from the center, the **Black Boy ★,** 1 Wharf Hill (www.theblackboypub.com; ✆ **01962/861754**) specializes in local ales. The same owners run the **Black Bottle,** 4 Bridge St. (www.theblackbottle.co.uk; ✆ **01962/621563**), where you can enjoy an interesting range of wines by the glass or bottle.

For a dose of culture, the eclectic program at the **Theatre Royal Winchester,** Jewry Street (www.theatreroyalwinchester.co.uk; ✆ **01962/840440**), might include anything from mainstream comedy to touring opera or a kids' show.

A Side Trip to Portsmouth's Historic Dockyard

You can buy a combination ticket for several attractions on the **Portsmouth Historic Dockyard ★★,** the focal point of the naval city of Portsmouth, 24 miles southeast of Winchester. HMS *Victory,* Victorian fighting ship **HMS *Warrior 1860* ★,** the *Mary Rose,* World War II-era **Boathouse 4,** the **National Museum of the Royal Navy,** and more are linked on a single admission that costs £32 for adults, £29 for students and seniors, £23 for children 5 to 15, and £85 for a family. The ticket also includes a **boat trip** around the working naval harbor (summer only). Stop by the visitor center at Victory Gate (✆ **023/9283-9766**), or buy tickets online at **www.historicdockyard.co.uk**. to save 20%. The site is open daily 10am to 5pm (Apr–Oct until 5:30pm). Last ticket sales are 1 hour before closing. Hourly direct trains from Winchester to Portsmouth Harbour, next to the Dockyard, take 1 hour.

HMS *Victory* ★★★ ICON   The highlight of any visit to the Historic Dockyard is an engaging 50-minute guided tour (free access in summer) of Admiral Lord Nelson's flagship, a 104-gun, first-rate ship that is the oldest surviving commissioned warship in the world, built from over 3,000

Interior of the HMS *Victory*, at Portsmouth Historic Dockyard.

trees and launched May 7, 1765. It earned its at the 1805 Battle of Trafalgar, when the English scored a victory over the combined Spanish and French fleets. The spot on the upper deck where Nelson was shot by a French sniper is marked with a plaque, as is the area below-decks where he lived the final minutes of his illustrious life. His flagship returned to Portsmouth with Nelson's body pickled in one of the ship's brandy barrels. Tall visitors should be prepared for lots of ducking.
www.historicdockyard.co.uk. ✆ **023/9283-9766.** £18 if visited individually; see above for combined Dockyard admission prices. Apr–Oct daily 10am–5:30pm; Nov–Mar daily 10am–5pm.

Mary Rose ★★ HISTORIC SITE/MUSEUM When the *Mary Rose*—Henry VIII's flagship man-of-war—sank during the Battle of the Solent in 1545, it was in full view of the King. When it was raised from the seabed in 1982, it was in full view of the nation, a major TV event. Its state of preservation was remarkable, and has been safe-guarded by this state-of-the-art exhibit. Visitors can view the ancient wooden hull inside its climate-controlled "hot box," as well as some of the 19,000 artifacts recovered with the ship, including weapons, medical instruments, and personal effects belonging to the 350 or so sailors who perished when it sank, many of them barely teenagers. The ship is currently under wraps for conservation work, and will reopen in spring 2016.
www.historicdockyard.co.uk. ✆ **023/9283-9766.** £18 if visited individually; see above for combined Dockyard admission prices. Apr–Oct daily 10am–5:30pm; Nov–Mar daily 10am–4:45pm.

SALISBURY ★★ & STONEHENGE ★★

90 miles SW of London; 42 miles SE of Bath

Long before you enter the city, the spire of **Salisbury Cathedral** comes into view—just as great English landscape painters John Constable and J. M. W. Turner captured it on canvas. The 404-ft. pinnacle of the Early English Gothic cathedral is the tallest in England, but is just one among many historical points of interest in Wiltshire's most visited city.

Once known as "Old Sarum," Salisbury lies in the valley of southern Wiltshire's River Avon. Filled with Tudor inns and tearooms, it is an excellent base for exploring nearby **Stonehenge.** The old market city also has a lively arts scene, and is an interesting destination on its own. If you choose to linger, you find an added bonus: Salisbury's pub-to-citizen ratio is among the highest in England.

Essentials

GETTING THERE   **Trains** for Salisbury depart half-hourly from Waterloo Station in London; the trip takes around 1½ hours. The city also has fast, regular rail connections with Portsmouth (see above). If you're **driving** from London, head southwest on the M3 and then M27 to junction 2, continuing the rest of the way on the A36.

VISITOR INFORMATION   The **Salisbury Information Centre** is on Fish Row (© **01722/342860**), open Monday to Friday 9am and 5pm, Saturday 10am to 4pm, and Sunday 10am to 2pm. Guided history walks (www.salisburycityguides.co.uk) depart from here at 11am, daily April to October, weekends only otherwise. For more information on the city and the rest of Wiltshire, you should consult www.visitwiltshire.co.uk.

SPECIAL EVENTS   During the annual **Salisbury International Arts Festival** (www.salisburyfestival.co.uk) the city drapes itself in banners, and street theater, concerts, children's events, and more are staged everywhere. It takes place from mid-May to the beginning of June.

Exploring Salisbury

Church of St Thomas & St Edmund ★ CHURCH   This medieval church is notable for a 1475 **Doom painting ★★**, above the chancel arch. Once common in English holy buildings, such depictions of the Biblical Last Judgment were largely whitewashed or erased during the Reformation. Salisbury's survived—by chance. Spot the clothed female figure among the naked souls being dispatched to Hell: She was reputedly a local brothel keeper who later repented and gave all her "ill-gotten gains" to charity—still damned, but allowed to retain her modesty.
St. Thomas's Sq. www.stthomassalisbury.co.uk. © **01722/322537.** Free. Daily 8:30am–6pm.

Mompesson House ★ HISTORIC HOME Built in 1701 by Charles Mompesson, while he was a Member of Parliament for Old Sarum (see below), Mompesson House is an archetypal example of the Queen Anne style, and is known for its plasterwork ceilings and paneling. Also used as a location for the 1995 Oscar-winning movie "Sense and Sensibility," it houses an important collection of 18th-century drinking glasses. In summer, there's a garden tearoom.

The Close. www.nationaltrust.org.uk/mompesson-house. © **01722/420980.** £6 adults, £3 children 17 and under, £15 families. Mid-Mar to Oct Sat–Wed 11am–5pm.

Salisbury Cathedral ★★★ CATHEDRAL You'll find no better example of the Early English Gothic architectural style. Construction on the building began in 1220 and took only 38 years to complete. (By contrast, many of Europe's grandest cathedrals took up to 300 years to build.) As a result, Salisbury Cathedral is one of the most homogenous and harmonious of all the great cathedrals—approached in the fading light of a winter's eve, it's an unforgettable sight. The best vantage point for fully appreciating its internal architecture is behind the **choir stalls** (Britain's oldest), looking directly down the nave.

The cathedral's 13th-century octagonal **Chapter House** possesses one of the four surviving original texts of **Magna Carta**—one of the founding documents of democracy and justice, signed by King John at Runnymede (p. 150). Britain's largest cloisters and adjacent Cathedral Close further enhance the cathedral's beauty.

The 404-ft. spire is the tallest in Britain, and was one of the world's tallest structures when completed in 1315. In 1668, architect Sir Christopher Wren expressed alarm at its tilt (notice how internal columns have bowed under the weight), but no further shift has since been measured. If you trust towering 700 year-old architecture, you can explore the heights on a 1½-hour **Tower Tour ★★** costing £9 for adults, £7 for seniors and children 5 to 17, £25 for families. From April to September, there are five tours a day Monday to Saturday (hourly from 11:15am), and two on Sunday (1:15 and 2:15pm). From October to March, there are one or two daily, depending on weather. Children must be 6 or over; acrophobics should consider passing.

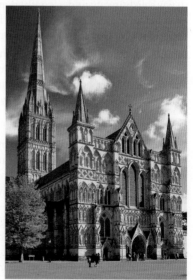

Construction of Salisbury Cathedral began in 1220.

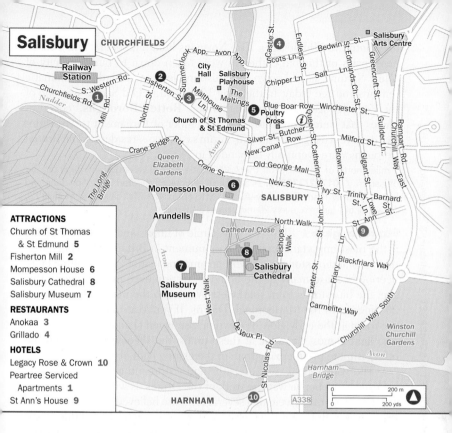

Salisbury

CHURCHFIELDS

ATTRACTIONS
Church of St Thomas
 & St Edmund **5**
Fisherton Mill **2**
Mompesson House **6**
Salisbury Cathedral **8**
Salisbury Museum **7**

RESTAURANTS
Anokaa **3**
Grillado **4**

HOTELS
Legacy Rose & Crown **10**
Peartree Serviced
 Apartments **1**
St Ann's House **9**

The Close. www.salisburycathedral.org.uk. ☏ **01722/555120.** Suggested donation £7 adults, £6 students and seniors, £3 children 5–17, £15 families. Cathedral: Mon–Sat 9am–5pm, Sun noon–4pm; Chapter House: Mon–Sat 9:30am–4:30pm, Sun noon–3:45pm.

Salisbury Museum ★ MUSEUM   This small but intriguing collection houses the **Wessex Gallery ★**, dedicated to the archaeology and heritage of Salisbury from the Palaeolithic era up to the abandonment of Old Sarum (see below) in the 13th century. As well as unearthed finds and historical items, there are a few notable paintings, including a series painted by Rex Whistler in the 1940s and Turner's 1828 panorama of Salisbury painted from the ruins at Old Sarum.

King's House, 65 The Close. www.salisburymuseum.org.uk. ☏ **01722/332151.** £8 adults, £4 children 5–15, £20 families of up to 6. Mon–Sat 10am–5pm (June–Sept also Sun noon–5pm).

Exploring Stonehenge & Old Sarum

Old Sarum ★ RUINS   Believed to have been an Iron Age fortification, Old Sarum was used again by the Saxons and flourished as a walled town into the Middle Ages. The Normans built a cathedral and a castle here; parts of this old cathedral were taken down to build the city of "New Sarum," later known as Salisbury, leaving behind the dramatic remains you see today. In the early 19th century Old Sarum was one of the English Parliament's most notorious "**Rotten Boroughs,**" constituencies that were allowed to send a Member of Parliament to Westminster despite having few—in Old Sarum's case, no—residents. The Rotten Boroughs were eventually disbanded in 1832.

2 miles north of Salisbury (off the A345 Castle Rd.). www.english-heritage.org.uk/oldsarum. ☎ **01722/335398.** £4 adults, £4 seniors, £2 children 5–15. Apr–June and Sept–Oct daily 10am–5pm; July–Aug daily to 6pm; Nov–Mar daily to 4pm. Bus: X5, Activ8, or 501 (approx. every 20 min., takes 8–10 min.).

Stonehenge ★★ RUINS   This circle of lintels and megalithic pillars is the most important prehistoric monument in Britain. The concentric rings of standing stones represent an amazing feat of late Neolithic engineering because many of the boulders were moved many miles to this site: the bluestones from southwest Wales and the massive sarsens just 20 miles from the Marlborough Downs. If you're a romantic, come see the ruins in the early glow of dawn or else when shadows fall at sunset. The light is most dramatic at these times, the shadows longer, and the effect is more mesmerizing than in the glaring light of midday.

The widely held view of 18th- and 19th-century Romantics, who believed Stonehenge was the work of the Druids, is without foundation. The boulders, many weighing several tons, are believed to have pre-dated the arrival in Britain of the Celtic culture, and may be a Neolithic "computer" capable of predicting eclipses. In truth, its ultimate purpose remains a mystery. However, it appears from the beginning to have been a monument to the dead, as revealed by radiocarbon dating from human cremation burials around the brooding stones. The site was used as a cemetery from 3000 B.C. until after the first of the giant stones was erected around 2500 B.C. It was used for about 1,500 years then abandoned.

Getting to Stonehenge

Salisbury Reds (www.salisburyreds.co.uk; ☎ **0845/0727093**) runs three or four buses per hour between Salisbury bus station and Amesbury, a pretty 1 hr. walk away from the stones. Catch buses X5 or Activ8 and get directions ahead of departure from the Salisbury Information Centre (p. 227). Surprisingly, this is as close as you can get by regular public transportation. There is also the **Stonehenge Tour** (www.thestonehengetour.info), which runs hourly (half-hourly in summer) from Salisbury railway and bus stations, returning via Old Sarum, taking 30 to 40 minutes each way. A round-trip ticket costs £14 for adults, £9 for children, £40 for families of up to 5. You can squeeze more value from this jaunt by buying a ticket that includes entrance to Stonehenge and Old Sarum, too. Prices are £26 adults, £16 children, and £75 families.

Archeologists have also uncovered hearths, timbers, and other remains of what was probably the village of workers who erected these monoliths on Salisbury Plain. These ancient ruins appear to form the largest Neolithic village ever found in Britain. The trenches of this discovery, **Durrington Walls,** lie 2 miles northeast of Stonehenge.

Prebooking tickets online is strongly advised, as numbers admitted to the site are controlled with timed admission slots. Also note you'll spend less time here than you'd likely imagine: This is one of Britain's iconic sights, but there's not much to see. Leave time for Salisbury's center, too. A cheaper alternative is to climb **Amesbury Hill,** visible 1½ miles along the A303. From there, you'll get a free panoramic view.

Beside A303 (2 miles west of Amesbury). www.english-heritage.org.uk/stonehenge. ℂ **0870/3331181.** £14 adults, £13 students and seniors, £8 children 5–15, £36 family ticket. June–Aug daily 9am–8pm; Mar 16–May and Sept–Oct 15 daily 9:30am–7pm; Oct 16–Mar 15 daily 9:30am–5pm. Last entry 2 hr. before closing time.

Where to Stay

Peartree Serviced Apartments ★, Mill Road (www.peartreeapart ments.co.uk; ℂ **01722/322055**), are aimed at extended-stay business travelers, but on weekends accept short stays if there's availability. The location beside Salisbury's rail station is convenient rather than romantic, but soundproofing is good, continental breakfast is delivered, parking is free, and apartments are modern, clean, and spacious. Prices for a 1-bedroom unit start cost £80 to £110 per night, an excellent value. For stays under 3 nights, you must call direct.

Legacy Rose & Crown ★   This 13th-century timbered inn stands in a pretty riverside spot just across the water meadow from Salisbury Cathedral (a 10-min. walk away). The key decision is whather to site yourself in the original building—bags of medieval character, but overlooking a (fairly quiet) road—or in the newer Garden Wing, where rooms are modern, slightly larger, but less characterful, and look back across the River Avon to the city (all but 2 have a Cathedral view).

Harnham Rd., Salisbury. www.legacy-hotels.co.uk. ℂ **01722/328615.** 29 units. Doubles £85–£200, includes breakfast. **Amenities:** Restaurant; 2 bars; room service; free Wi-Fi.

St Ann's House ★★   A handsome Georgian row-house turned B&B right in the lively heart of Salisbury. The Premium rooms are the pick of the bunch: four units with en suite bathrooms, antique furniture plucked from a Jane Austen period drama, and preserved Victorian fireplaces. The details scream quality and dedication, from Turkish bed linen to the breakfast, prepared by owner Michael Riley, a former chef. The same husband-and-wife team runs **St Ann's Forge** (www.stannsforge.co.uk), a self-catering rental in a 1500s house.

32-34 St Ann's St., Salisbury. www.stannshouse.co.uk. ℂ **01722/335657.** 9 units. Doubles £74–£110, includes breakfast. **Amenities:** Free Wi-Fi.

Where to Eat

Anokaa ★ MODERN INDIAN   We don't love the neon décor, but this Indian restaurant midway between the center and the station is a bit special. Rich sauces, mildly spiced rather than fiery-hot is the usual style, with a nod to classic Brit ingredients in specialties such as tandoori seared lamb rack with sweet chillies and marjoram or chargrilled guinea hen with tomato and fenugreek. At £9, the lunchtime buffet of Indian salads, three meat and vegetarian mains, plus sides is a good value.
60 Fisherton St., Salisbury. www.anokaa.com. ✆ **01722/414142.** Mains £11–£20. Daily noon–2pm and 5:30–11pm.

Grillado ★ ITALIAN/MEDITERRANEAN   It's a fair way from Salisbury to those azure European seas, but Grillado successfully conjures up the aromas and atmosphere of the Mediterranean. Star of the show is probably the rotisserie chicken, spit-roasted on an open grill. The menu contains a whole lot more, however, cooked with skill and bursting with rustic Italian flavours: Think tuna carpaccio followed by osso buco and saffron risotto. Grillado is another restaurant with an enticing lunchtime deal, just £8 for a simple main with a glass of wine.
68 Castle St., Salisbury. www.grillado.co.uk. ✆ **01722/324350.** Mains £13–£17. Daily noon–2:30pm and 5:30–10:30pm.

Shopping

Salisbury's best indie shopping spot is **Fisherton Mill** ★, 108 Fisherton Street (www.fishertonmill.co.uk; ✆ **01722/500200;** closed Sun–Mon), where a converted Victorian grain mill hosts open artisans' studios selling contemporary crafts, as well as a cafe.

Entertainment & Nightlife

The city's **arts scene** is thriving and varied. The **Salisbury Playhouse** ★, Malthouse Lane (www.salisburyplayhouse.com; ✆ **01722/320333**), is one of the best in southwest England—the program could feature anything from an Austen adaptation to contemporary drama. At the **City Hall,** Malthouse Lane (www.cityhallsalisbury.co.uk; ✆ **01722/434434**), you're more likely to encounter a big-name comedian, a tribute band, or a "Frozen" singalong. The **Salisbury Arts Centre,** Bedwin Street (www.salisburyartscentre.co.uk; ✆ **01722/321744**), within the former St Edmund's Church, offers an occasionally edgy mix of music, contemporary and classic theater, and dance, plus cabaret, comedy, and family shows.

   Salisbury's **pubs** are lively after dark. Standing just outside the center, **Deacons** ★, 118 Fisherton St. (✆ **01722/504723**), has a local rep for serving ale the way it should be. Even in a city full of ancient, half-timbered inns, there's nowhere quite like the **Haunch of Venison** ★, 1 Minster St. (✆ **01722/411313**). The haphazard layout and wood-paneled rooms ooze medieval charm—and are reputedly haunted. **Rai d'Or,** 69 Brown St. (www.raidor.co.uk; ✆ **01722/327137**), may look nondescript, but offers a range of interesting local microbrews.

Side Trips Into Rural Wiltshire

You likely need a **car** to venture into the classic English countryside of northwest Wiltshire. To reach **Stourhead** from Salisbury (40 min.), follow the A36, A303 and B3092 to Stourton, 3 miles northwest of Mere. **Lacock** is beside the A350, 4 miles south of Chippenham. **Avebury** is on the A4361, between Swindon and Devizes, 1 mile off the A4. **Heritage Cycle Tours** (www.heritagecycletours.com; ✆ **01980/862099**) offers a 1-day itinerary that leads you from Marlborough to Avebury and back. The tour costs £45 including cycle rental. You could see all three recommended sites in a single (busy) driving day: Salisbury–Stourhead–Lacock–Avebury–Salisbury is a circular route of about 100 miles.

Avebury ★★ HISTORIC SITE/RUINS   A visit to one of Europe's most expansive prehistoric sites is a more organic experience than a trip to Stonehenge—you can walk right up to and around this "henge" (earthwork and stone circle). Avebury village is spread over a 28-acre site, winding in and out of the circle of more than 100 stones. The stones are made of sarsen, a sandstone local to Wiltshire, and some weigh up to 50 tons. Neolithic tribes are believed to have built the circles as part of a sacred complex that encompasses nearby **Silbury Hill** ★, a 102-ft. mound of chalk and rubble that protrudes from the Wiltshire grassland like an overgrown Egyptian pyramid. It's Europe's tallest manmade mound. Also here is the **Alexander Keiller Museum and Barn,** a collection of archaeological finds dug up during excavations at Avebury. Avebury, Wiltshire. www.nationaltrust.org.uk/avebury. ✆ **01672/539250.** Stone circle: free; museum: £4 adults, £2 children, £11 families. Stone circle: daily dawn to dusk; Museum: Nov–Mar daily 10am–4pm, Apr–Oct daily 10am–6pm.

Lacock & Lacock Abbey ★★ HISTORIC HOME/MUSEUM   If this ancient religious house—founded in 1232—looks more like a country manor, that's because it is. The property was confiscated from the nuns after the Dissolution of the Monasteries in the 1530s and turned into a grand country seat. The first-floor rooms and Great Hall are open to visitors, but more interesting are Lacock's intact Gothic **Cloisters** ★★. The Warming House here is the only room where the nuns were allowed to light a fire, between November 1 and Good Friday only. The Cloisters doubled as Hogwarts in several Harry Potter movies. The Abbey's former barn is home to the **Fox Talbot Museum:** Lacock is where William Henry Fox Talbot carried out his early experiments with photography, making the first negatives in 1833. The galleries tell the story of his discovery and display temporary photography exhibitions. Tiny **Lacock** ★

itself is one of the best-preserved villages in England, with stone cottages, timber-framed houses, and an ancient tithe barn. More Harry Potter scenes were filmed here.

Lacock, Wiltshire. www.nationaltrust.org.uk/lacock. ℂ **01249/730459.** Abbey cloisters, grounds, and museum £9 adults, £5 children, £23 families; admission to whole property £12 adults, £6 children, £29 families. Abbey cloisters, museum, and grounds daily 10:30am–5:30pm (Nov to mid-Feb 11am–4pm); Abbey rooms mid-Feb to Oct Wed–Mon 11am–5pm, Nov to mid-Feb Sat–Sun noon–4pm.

Stourhead ★★ GARDEN/HISTORIC HOME   In a county (and country) of superlative green spaces, Stourhead stands out as the most celebrated example of 18th-century English landscape gardening. More than that, it's a delightful place to wander. Among its trees, flowers, and colorful shrubs are tucked bridges, grottoes, follies, and temples. Here nature is carefully crafted into a work of art.

The **Temple of Flora** was designed by the architect Henry Flitcroft in 1744. The **Grotto,** constructed in 1748, is lined with tufa, a water-worn limestone deposit. The springs of the River Stour flow through the cold bath. The **Pantheon** was built in 1753 to house Rysbrack's statues of Hercules, Flora, and other classical figures. Every corner you roam brings a new angle on this magical creation—take a camera, and you won't need Instagram to make the place sing. Although Stourhead is a garden for all seasons, it is at its most idyllic in summer, when rhododendrons bloom.

The **stately home** at Stourhead is less spectacular. Designed by Colen Campbell, a leader in the Georgian neoclassical revival, it was built for Henry Hoare I between 1721 and 1725.

Stourton, near Mere, Wiltshire. www.nationaltrust.org.uk/stourhead. ℂ **01747/841152.** House and gardens: £14 adults, £7 children 5–16, £34 families; gardens only: £8 adults, £5 children, £20 families. House: mid-Mar to Oct daily 11am–4:30pm; Nov to mid-Mar Sat–Sun 11am–3pm (daily for 3 weeks running up to Christmas). Garden: daily 9am–5pm (Apr–Sept until 7pm).

SHERBORNE ★ & NORTH DORSET

124 miles SW of London; 18 miles N of Dorchester

A little town with preserved medieval, Tudor, Stuart, and Georgian buildings, Sherborne is surrounded by the gentle hills, wooded glades, and chalk downs of rural North Dorset. It was here that Sir Walter Raleigh lived before his fall from fortune, in **Sherborne Castle.** There are also 13 centuries of local Christian history, much of it encapsulated in the stones of Gothic **Sherborne Abbey.** More recently, this was where wartime codebreaker **Alan Turing** (1912–54) was educated, at one of Britain's most prestigious private schools. Turing's life was the subject of Oscar-nominated biopic, "The Imitation Game," partly filmed in town.

Essentials

GETTING THERE   Frequent direct **trains** depart London's Waterloo Station throughout the day, stopping at Salisbury en route. The trip takes 2¼ hours. If you're **driving** from London, take the M3 west, continuing southwest on the A303 and then joining the southbound B3145 beyond Wincanton. Plan for a journey time of around 3 hours.

VISITOR INFORMATION   The **Tourist Information Centre,** Digby Road (www.visit-dorset.com; ℂ **01935/815341**), is open mid-March through August Monday to Saturday 9am to 5pm; September to November Monday to Saturday 9:30am to 4pm; and December through mid-March Monday to Saturday 10am to 3pm.

Exploring Sherborne & North Dorset

Provincial Sherborne's compact center is a delightful place to stroll for an hour, and the cluster of surviving medieval buildings around the abbey is especially atmospheric. **Church Lane,** leading from the Conduit (a Gothic structure where the monks washed their clothes), seems transplanted from another era. **St Johns' Almshouses,** Half Moon Street, were built in 1448, though its cloister is a later neo-Gothic addition. You can see inside from May to September, Tuesday and Thursday to Saturday between 2 and 4pm. A donation is appreciated. Lovers of small, independent stores, especially country fashions and homewares, should

The Cerne Giant at Sherborne.

spend some time window-browsing along **Cheap Street ★**.

Cerne Giant ★ HISTORIC SITE   Nobody is quite sure when a 180-ft., naked—and somewhat explicit—outline of a giant was originally carved into the rolling chalk hills of North Dorset. It may be an ancient fertility symbol. It might be a representation of Hercules. Or it might be a lewd, mocking caricature of Oliver Cromwell, the victorious Parliamentarian leader during the English Civil Wars. You can view and photograph from the roadside, or walk right up to (but not onto) the giant. Cerne Abbas (viewing area by A352, 11 miles south of Sherborne). www.nationaltrust.org.uk/cerne-giant. ℂ **01297/489481.** Free. Daily dawn to dusk.

Sherborne Abbey ★★ CHURCH   This monumental abbey church, founded in A.D. 705 as the Cathedral of the Saxon Bishops of Wessex, dominates the modern town. In the late 10th century, it became a Benedictine monastery, and since the Dissolution it has been Sherborne's rather grand parish church. Look immediately up to see the soaring, intricate **fan-vaulted ceiling ★★★** running the full length of the nave. Fan vaults were a particularly graceful—and peculiarly English—solution to spreading the weight of a large ceiling. They originated here in the West Country in the early 15th century. The ceiling is also notable for the intricate carved bosses and corbels that were so high up that they escaped the destruction of the English Reformation. Pack binoculars to appreciate them fully.

Abbey Close. www.sherborneabbey.com. ☎ **01935/812452.** Free (£2 donation welcomed). Apr–Sept daily 8am–6pm; Oct–Mar daily 8am–4pm.

Sherborne Castle ★ HISTORIC HOME   "Castle" is in fact a misnomer for this Elizabethan residence, built for Sir Walter Raleigh after he decided that it wouldn't be feasible to restore the Old Castle (see below) to suit his stately needs. The original 1594 residence was a square mansion; later owners added four Jacobean wings to make it more palatial. After King James I had Raleigh imprisoned in the Tower of London, the monarch gave the castle to a favorite Scot, Robert Carr. In 1617, it was bought by Sir John Digby, and has been the Digby family home ever since. The mansion was enlarged in 1625, and in the 1750s, the formal Elizabethan gardens and fountains of the Raleighs were altered by **Capability Brown,** who created a serpentine lake between Sherborne's two castles. Highlights of the interior include paintings by Gainsborough, an intact kitchen dating from 1595; and a portrait of Raleigh said to be an accurate likeness.

Off New Rd. (1 mile east of center). www.sherbornecastle.com. ☎ **01935/812072.** Castle and gardens £11 adults, £10 seniors, free for children 15 and under; £6 gardens only. Apr–Oct Tues–Thurs and Sat–Sun 11am–4.30pm.

Sherborne Old Castle ★ RUINS/CASTLE   The town's original castle was built by the powerful Bishop Roger de Caen in the early 12th century, but was seized by the crown at about the time of King Henry I's death in 1135 and Stephen's troubled accession to the throne. The buildings were mostly destroyed in the aftermath of the English Civil Wars, when it was beseiged twice, but three gatehouses, some graceful arcades, and a barrel-vaulted undercroft remain.

Castleton Rd. (½ mile east of center). www.english-heritage.org.uk/sherborne. ☎ **01935/812730.** £4 adults, £3 seniors and students, £2 children 5–15. Apr–Oct daily 10am–5pm (July–Aug until 6pm).

Where to Stay

Local agency **Sherborne Cottages** ★ (www.sherbornecottages.com; ☎ **01935/815335**) has a small, high-quality portfolio of apartments and cottages in and around central Sherborne. All are simply decorated in a modern style, maintained to a high standard, and available for 3 nights and up. Weekly rates range from £350 to £800.

The Eastbury ★ This handsome, flat-fronted Georgian townhouse hotel has the best lodgings in town. Rooms come in four grades, adding space and more contemporary design as you climb. The price/value sweet spot is the Superior units, with extra space, soft furnishings, and 6-foot beds. If you are feeling flush, spring a little more for Luxury unit Cowslip, a large front room tricked out in oriental style complete with a Japanese screen hiding a rolltop bath. From The Eastbury's peaceful courtyard garden to Sherborne Abbey is a mere 3-minute walk.

Long St., Sherborne. www.theeastburyhotel.co.uk. ✆ **01935/813131.** 23 units. Doubles £145–£195, includes breakfast. **Amenities:** Restaurant; bar; access to nearby health club; babysitting (not always available); room service; free Wi-Fi.

Where to Eat

For a late breakfast, light lunch, or the best mug of coffee in town, head to **Oliver's,** 19 Cheap St. (✆ **01935/815005**). The **Digby Tap ★**, Cooks Lane (www.digbytap.co.uk; ✆ **01935/813148**), is a genuinely local pub serving hearty, cheap food (lunch only, Mon–Sat). At The Eastbury (see "Where to Stay," below), **The Conservatory** has a long-standing rep as one of Dorset's best fine dining spots. A 7-course tasting menu costs £55. The Eastbury also serves a refined **afternoon tea.**

The Dining Room ★ When this place opened in central Sherborne in late 2014, it was an instant hit. The food is refreshingly honest, with dishes that are less about culinary fireworks than about simple, classic presentations of Dorset ingredients. Think confit chicken and duck terrine followed by whole roast lemon sole drizzled with a caper-spiked beurre noisette. Except on Sundays, a slightly cheaper lunch menu focuses on bistro food such as slow-braised lamb shoulder, seafood pie, or wild mushroom risotto. Staff is super-friendly, too.

Westbury, Sherborne. www.thediningroomsherborne.com. ✆ **01935/815154.** Mains £12–£19 (lunchtime £8–£10). Wed–Sat noon–2pm and 6:30–9:30pm; Sun noon–3pm and 6:30–8:30pm.

DORCHESTER ★

122 miles SW of London; 40 miles SW of Salisbury

In his 1886 novel, "The Mayor of Casterbridge," Thomas Hardy bestowed upon **Dorchester** literary immortality. Similarities between fictional Casterbridge and 19th-century Dorchester were thinly veiled, and visits to **Hardy's Cottage** are as popular as ever. Dorchester was notable in Roman times, when nearby **Maumbury Rings** filled with the sound of 12,000 spectators screaming for the blood. Get a sense of how wealthy locals lived at England's best-preserved **Roman Townhouse.**

Dorchester remained important enough to warrant a 1669 visit from Cosimo III, Grand Duke of Tuscany, but was later notorious for the Bloody Assizes of "Hanging Judge" Jeffreys: Over 300 local men were executed or transported overseas for involvement in the Duke of Monmouth's unsuccessful 1685 rebellion against King James II. Today Dorchester is a thriving market town with an excellent **County Museum,** but it also seems to go to bed right after dinner. It's a good base for exploring the countryside and coast of southern and western Dorset.

Essentials

GETTING THERE   Direct **trains** run from London's Waterloo Station to Dorchester South at least hourly during the day, stopping en route at Winchester. The trip takes between 2½ and 2¾ hours. If you're **driving** from London, take the M3 then M27 southwest to its end, and continue westward on the A31, following signs to Dorchester. Expect the journey to take around 3 hours, more during peak holiday periods.

VISITOR INFORMATION   The **Tourist Information Centre** is on Antelope Walk (www.visit-dorset.com; ✆ **01305/267992**). It's open April through October, Monday to Saturday 9am to 5pm, and November through March, Monday to Saturday 9am to 4pm.

Exploring Dorchester & Around

About 2 miles southwest of central Dorchester are the remains of the vast Iron Age fort known as **Maiden Castle ★**. The site was occupied for around 4,000 years, and its dramatic hillside concentric fortifications date to the period just before the Romans invaded Britain. The site is well signposted and open to walk round.

Athelhampton House & Gardens ★ HISTORIC HOME   This is one of southern England's great medieval houses, a manor whose earliest rooms date from the reign of King Edward IV, and whose site matches one of King Athelstan's 10th-century palaces. The wood-paneled **Great Hall ★** is resonant of Athelhampton's Tudor roots. The rest is packed with furniture from just about every period since. Thomas Hardy set his short story "The Waiting Supper" here. The **gardens ★** are even more inspiring. Laid out from 1891, their beauty is enhanced by the River Piddle flowing alongside. You'll see tulips and magnolias, roses, and lilies, topiary pyramids, and a 15th-century dovecote.

Athelhampton, near Puddletown. www.athelhampton.co.uk. ✆ **01305/848363.** £13 adults, £3 children 15 and under. Mar–Oct Sun–Thurs 10:30am–5pm; Nov–Feb Sun 10:30am–dusk.

Dorset County Museum ★★ MUSEUM   It's almost impossible to summarize the contents of this small museum. It's dedicated to Dorset's history and heritage, and is stuffed with a varied collection. The

Hardy's Cottage, near Dorchester.

Writers' Gallery ★ revolves around Thomas Hardy (1840–1928), author of "Jude the Obscure" and "Far from the Madding Crowd." There's a recreation of Hardy's study (ca. 1906), where he wrote "The Dynasts" and much of his poetry. It's also fair to say that palaeontology began in Dorset: The first fossils studied by Victorian scientists were scavenged along the nearby "Jurassic Coast" by a local fossil hunter named Mary Anning. The museum has a few worthy specimens, including a giant fossilized pliosaur skull. The original **Victorian Gallery** ★ tells the story of Dorchester's long history as a market town.

High West St. (next to St Peter's Church). www.dorsetcountymuseum.org. ℰ **01305/262735**. £7 adults; free for 2 accompanied children 5–15, additional children £3; free for children 4 and under. Apr–Oct Mon–Sat 10am–5pm (also Sun 10am–4pm in peak season); Nov–Mar Mon–Sat 10am–4pm.

Hardy's Cottage ★ HISTORIC HOME   Thomas Hardy was born in this thatched cottage on the fringe of Thorncombe Wood, Higher Bockhampton, in 1840. The home where he later wrote "Far from the Madding Crowd" (1874), and its lovely cottage garden, are now a National Trust property and open to the public. Unless you're a real Hardy geek, there's not a great deal to see, but the pleasant setting offers a chance to take a stroll and perhaps spot badgers and deer.

Higher Bockhampton (3 miles NE of Dorchester). www.nationaltrust.org.uk/hardys-cottage. ℰ **01305/262366**. £6. Mid-Mar to Oct Wed–Sun 11am–5pm.

Roman Townhouse ★ RUINS   Dorchester's Roman Townhouse is the best preserved of its kind in Britain—though still very much a ruin, dating from the 4th century A.D. Many of the original mosaics from this once grand residence in Roman "Durnovaria" have been left in situ.

Colliton Park (entrance in Northernhay). ℂ **01305/221000.** Free. Open 24 hr.

Where to Stay & Eat

The best spot in town for afternoon tea, a lunchtime light bite, or a selection of daily hot specials is **The Horse with the Red Umbrella ★**, 10 High West St. (ℂ **01305/262019**). Lunch costs £4 to £6; it's closed Sundays. For a good pint of West Country ale, stop in at the **Blue Raddle ★**, 9 Church St. (www.blueraddle.co.uk; ℂ **01305/267762**). Children 13 and under are not admitted. It's closed during the day on Mondays.

Yalbury Cottage ★★　This 300-year-old thatched cottage two miles outside Dorchester is perfect for foodies. Room are sunny and decorated in a "country cottage" style, with occasional modern touches. The real reason to stay here, though, is to eat in the outstanding onsite **restaurant ★★★**, run by chef and co-owner Jamie and open for dinner Tuesday to Saturday and at Sunday lunchtime. Produce—from Tolpuddle lamb to Lyme Regis scallops to New Forest wild mushrooms—is almost all sourced from within a few miles of the front door. Dinner costs £33 to £38 for 2 to 3 courses.

Lower Bockhampton, Dorchester. www.yalburycottage.com. ℂ **01305/262382.** 8 units. Doubles £99–£120, includes breakfast. **Amenities:** Restaurant; bar; free Wi-Fi.

BATH ★★★

115 miles W of London; 13 miles SE of Bristol

Few cities in England are as elegant as Bath. Set in the leafy Avon Valley, the town boomed in the 18th century, when England's high society flocked here to "take the waters." The spa town's ravishing Georgian architecture, Palladian mansions, and aged pubs have been virtually untouched by modern development, making this one of the most enticing destinations in the country; it's also one of the most popular.

Bath's historical roots are commemorated at the **Roman Baths and Pump Room,** sensitively restored and now an illuminating window into the lives of Roman Britons. **Bath Abbey** is the other major historic draw, but the city's **Georgian splendor** is best absorbed by wandering down handsome terraces such as the **Royal Crescent.**

Bath was established by the Romans as a spa in A.D. 43. Today those same waters provide the best cure for a hard day of sightseeing, with **Thermae Bath Spa** providing modern facilities and an open-air pool.

Bath also boasts a surprisingly eclectic dining scene, but afternoon tea is a particular art form here, taken in wonderfully atmospheric venues such as **Sally Lunn's** (home of the famous buns), the Pump Room

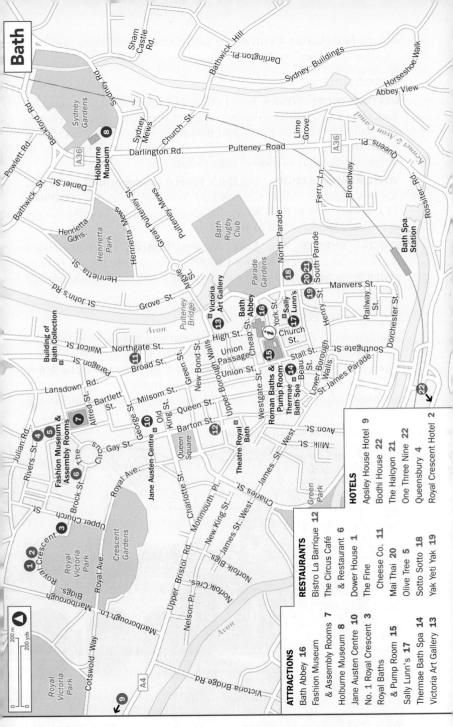

Bath

ATTRACTIONS

Bath Abbey **16**
Fashion Museum
& Assembly Rooms **7**
Holburne Museum **8**
Jane Austen Centre **10**
No. 1 Royal Crescent **3**
Royal Baths
& Pump Room **15**
Sally Lunn's **17**
Thermae Bath Spa **14**
Victoria Art Gallery **13**

RESTAURANTS

Bistro La Barrique **12**
The Circus Café
& Restaurant **6**
Dower House **1**
The Fine
Cheese Co. **11**
Mai Thai **20**
Olive Tree **5**
Sotto Sotto **18**
Yak Yeti Yak **19**

HOTELS

Apsley House Hotel **9**
Bodhi House **22**
The Halcyon **21**
One Three Nine **22**
Queensbury **4**
Royal Crescent Hotel **2**

241

and the **Jane Austen Centre**—the author set much of "Persuasion" and "Northanger Abbey" in the city.

Essentials

GETTING THERE **Trains** leave London's Paddington Station bound for Bath once every half-hour during the day; the trip takes about 1½ hours. The train ride between Bristol and Bath takes 11 to 15 minutes (£7). If you're **driving** from London, head west on the M4 to junctions 17 (A350) or 18 (A46) and follow sings to Bath.

VISITOR INFORMATION The **Bath Tourist Information Centre** is at Abbey Chambers, Abbey Church Yard (www.visitbath.co.uk; ℂ **0906/ 711-2000**), next to Bath Abbey. It's open Monday to Saturday 9:30am to 5:30pm, Sunday 10am to 4:30pm.

SPECIAL EVENTS The **Jane Austen Festival** (www.janeausten festivalbath.co.uk; ℂ **01225/443000**) celebrates the life the famous author every September, with concerts, tours, talks, and dances held all over the city.

Exploring Bath

Bath is easy to explore on foot, with everything a short walk from the Roman Baths and Bath Abbey. John Wood the Elder (1704–54) designed much of the Georgian city; his masterpiece is the elegant **Circus ★★★** of 1768, a series of three Palladian crescents arranged in a circle, at the northern end of Gay Street. Be sure to cross the River Avon via the

The Pulteney Bridge on the River Avon, Bath.

shop-lined **Pulteney Bridge ★,** designed by Robert Adam in 1778 and often compared to the Ponte Vecchio in Florence.

Bath Abbey ★★ CHURCH   Bath Abbey is the last of the great medieval churches of England, a fine example of the late Perpendicular style. The stupendous **West Front** is the sculptural embodiment of a dream that inspired the Abbey's founder, Bishop Oliver King, to pull down an older Norman cathedral in 1499 and build the one you see today. When you go inside and see its ornate windows, you'll understand why the abbey is called the "Lantern of the West." For a bird's-eye view of the city, take the Abbey Tower Tour (45–50 min.), climbing 212 steps to the top of the abbey's vaulted ceiling, the clock face, and belfry.

Abbey Churchyard. www.bathabbey.org. © **01225/422462.** Free (suggested donation £4). Tower tours £6 adults, £3 children 5–15. Abbey: Apr–Oct Mon 9:30am–6pm, Tues–Sat 9am–6pm; Nov–Mar Mon 9:30am–4:30pm, Tues–Sat 9am–4:30pm; yearround Sun 1–2:30pm and 4:30–5:30pm.

Fashion Museum & Assembly Rooms ★ MUSEUM   Once the hub of Georgian society, the Assembly Rooms were where the great and the good of Bath came to dine, dance, socialize, and show of their latest finery. You can take a look at some of this finery, as well as styles of various other eras at the **Fashion Museum,** where a collection of outfits from the 16th to the 21st century is on display. There's even a section where visitors can try on period garments for themselves.

The building itself was the work of by John Wood the Younger in 1771, the man behind the Royal Crescent, and was constructed in the severe neoclassical style of the time. You can visit its main function rooms—the Ball Room, Tea Room, Card Room, and Octagon—and admire interiors once graced by Thomas Gainsborough and Jane Austen.

Bennett St. www.fashionmuseum.co.uk. © **01225/477789.** £8 adults, £7 students and seniors, £6 children 6–16, £24 families, free for children 5 and under. Assembly Rooms free. Nov–Feb daily 10:30am–4pm; Mar–Oct daily to 5pm.

Holburne Museum ★★ MUSEUM   Until recently, this was a staid and rather stuffy local museum. But that all changed following a major revamp. The sturdily tasteful late 18th-century facade has been left almost unchanged, while the back is pure 21st-century, a three-story ceramic and glass extension with bright, stylish galleries that have given the museum new life. Inside you'll find an abundance of decorative arts, ceramics, and silverware from the 17th and 18th centuries, much of it from the collection of the 19th-century local aristocrat Thomas Holborne, and a fine selection of paintings, with works by Gainsborough, Stubbs, and Breughel. The cafe provides access to the **Sydney Gardens,** one of the country's few remaining 18th-century pleasure gardens.

Great Pulteney St. www.holburne.org. © **01225/388569.** Free. Mon–Sat 10am–5pm, Sun 11am–5pm.

Jane Austen Centre ★ MUSEUM   In truth, Jane Austen wasn't all that enamored of Bath despite setting two of her novels ("Northanger Abbey" and "Persuasion") largely in the city. But she is indelibly associated with the place in the public mind. This townhouse, a few doors down from one of the author's actual addresses (no. 25), does a good job of both addressing Austen's indifference and celebrating her life through a mixture of videos, period items, and extracts from her work.

40 Gay St. www.janeausten.co.uk. (*) **01225/443000.** £9 adults, £8 seniors, £7 students, £6 children 6–15, £23 families. Apr–June and Sept–Oct daily 9:45am–5:30pm; July–Aug daily 9:30am–6pm; Nov–Mar Sun–Fri 11am–4:30pm, Sat 9:45am–5:30pm.

No. 1 Royal Crescent ★ MUSEUM   The Royal Crescent is perhaps the city's finest example of **Palladian architecture,** as featured in countless films and TV shows. It was laid out in the 1760s by John Wood the Younger who, with his father (Wood the Elder) did so much to define the look of the 18th-century city. It certainly makes an impressive sight, the great sweeping arc of houses perched imperiously above a neatly tended park. The first house to be erected, No.1, at the eastern end, is now a museum of Georgian life and has been painstakingly restored to its 18th-century heyday with the dining room, drawing room, and "gentleman's retreat" adorned in sumptuous period style.

1 Royal Crescent. www.no1royal crescent.org.uk. (*) **01225/428126.** £9 adults, £7 students and seniors, £4 children 5–16, £22 families. Feb to mid-Dec Tues–Sun 10:30am–5:30pm, Mon noon–5:30pm.

Roman Baths ★★★ & Pump Room ★★ HISTORIC SITE Evidence suggests that Bath's hot springs have been used since prehistoric times, but it was the Romans who first developed the feature, erecting an elaborate bathing complex in the first century. As the empire fell, so the baths went into decline. They were rediscovered and rebuilt by the Georgians whose fondness for "taking the waters" revived Bath's fortunes, turning into one of the 18th century's most fashionable resorts. Today, the **Great Bath** with its steamy green water, surrounded by elaborate

An interior at No. 1 Royal Crescent, Bath

pillars and statues is a wonderfully atmospheric place. Filled with chattering tourists, it gives you a real sense of what the complex must have been like in Roman times, when the baths were the main pivot of social life—even if almost everything above ground level is actually 19th century. Audioguides take you past the remaining ancient Roman structures, including steam rooms, hypocausts, and a plunge pool, and through the **museum** where some of the items discovered during excavation are displayed, including a bust of goddess Sulis Minerva, to whom the baths were dedicated.

The Roman Baths, Bath.

Next to the Roman bath complex stands yet another epicenter of Georgian society, the **Pump Room,** an elegant, late 18th-century restaurant where you can dine while being serenaded by a classical trio. And if that doesn't appeal, you can still admire the interior while popping in for a quick 50p cup of lukewarm—and unpleasant tasting—spa water, pumped from the original spring.

Bath Abbey Church Yard, Stall St. www.romanbaths.co.uk. ✆ **01225/477785.** £14 adults, £13 seniors, £9 children 6–16, £40 families. Jan–Feb daily 9:30am–4:30pm; Mar–June and Sept–Oct daily 9am–5pm; July–Aug daily 9am–9pm; Nov–Dec daily 9:30am–5pm.

Sally Lunn's ★ MUSEUM/CAFE   Sally Lunn's timber-framed medieval tearoom is as much a part of Bath's history as the Roman Baths or the Royal Crescent and—judging by the queues that form outside—just as popular. They come to sample the **Sally Lunn bun,** a sort of giant, bap-shaped brioche created by the eponymous Sally, a French Huguenot who fled here from religious persecution in 1680. Her tiny basement kitchen is preserved as a museum, while upstairs you can enjoy a range of sweet and savory versions of the bun—if you can find a table.

4 North Parade Passage. www.sallylunns.co.uk. ✆ **01225/461634.** Museum 50p adults; children, seniors, and cafe patrons, free. Cafe: Mon–Thurs 10am–9:30pm, Fri–Sat 10am–10pm, Sun 11am–9:30pm. Museum: Mon–Sat 10am–6pm, Sun 11am–6pm.

Thermae Bath Spa ★★ BATHS   The waters at the old Roman baths are unfit for bathing, so if you want to sample the city's celebrated hot

Thermae Bath Spa, overlooking Bath Abbey.

springs make for this plush, modern spa—the water might be 10,000 years old, but the facilities are pure 21st-century. Admission gives you access to the indoor pool, the steam baths, and the Open-Air Rooftop Pool, where you can watch the sun setting over the Abbey while you soak. The historic **Cross Bath** complex, site of a Roman well, is also available for sessions. Aim to visit on a weekday to avoid the busiest times. Queues can stretch round the block on weekends.

Hot Bath St. www.thermaebathspa.com. ℂ **0844/888-0844.** £32 Mon–Fri, £35 Sat–Sun for 2 hr. session. Daily 9am–9:30pm, last entry 7pm; Closed Jan 1–7. Children under 12 not permitted; children 12–16 can use the Cross Bath with an adult.

Victoria Art Gallery ★ GALLERY   Its entrance by the western end of Pulteney Bridge can be difficult to spot, but this gallery is well worth seeking out. It holds a fine collection of British and European decorative arts and paintings. The **Upper Gallery** on the first floor is a fine, high-walled room illuminated by a large skylight that holds selections from the permanent collection, including works by such illustrious locals as Thomas Gainsborough and Walter Sickert. Temporary exhibitions are shown in modern downstairs galleries and cost around £4.

Bridge St. www.victoriagal.org.uk. ℂ **01225/477233.** Free. Tues–Sat 10am–5pm; Sun 1:30–5pm.

ORGANIZED TOURS

To get a unique perspective on Bath, take the **Bizarre Bath Walking Tour** (www.bizarrebath.co.uk; ℂ **01225/335124**), a 1½-hour tour of

Bath's lesser-known sights. It runs nightly at 8pm from Easter to October (no reservations necessary, just show up at the Huntsman Inn, North Parade Passage). Cost is £8 for adults, £5 for students and children. Conventional **open-top bus tours** (50 min.) are operated by **Bath Bus Company** (www.bathbuscompany.com; ☎ **01225/330444**) and cost £14 for adults, £12 for seniors/students, £9 for children 5 to 15. **Free walking tours** are provided by Mayor of Bath Honorary Guides (www.bathguides.org.uk; ☎ **01225/477411;** 2 hr.; Sun–Fri 10:30am and 2pm, Sat 10:30am) from outside the Abbey Churchyard entrance to the Pump Room (May–Sept also Tues and Fri 7pm).

Where to Stay

EXPENSIVE

Apsley House ★★   About a mile west of the center, this house was built for the great military leader, the Duke of Wellington, around 1830, and many of the rooms are named after his famous battles, including Copenhagen, Salamanca, and of course Waterloo. They're all decorated in aristocratic style with swag curtains, dark-wood furniture, gilt-framed oil paintings, and the like. Some have four-poster beds. The result is very charming. Check website for occasional £99 deals.

141 Newbridge Hill. www.apsley-house.co.uk. ☎ **01225/336966.** 13 units. Doubles £140–£270, includes breakfast. **Amenities:** Bar; room service; free Wi-Fi.

Royal Crescent ★   Slap bang in the middle of the city's grandest street, this is as luxuriously appointed as you'd want, albeit with decor that might be a touch more modern than you expect. The bedrooms come with huge beds, elegant decor, fresh flowers . . . the works. There's also a (smallish) spa, a garden and an excellent restaurant, **Dower House.**

16 Royal Crescent. www.royalcrescent.co.uk. ☎ **01225/823333.** 45 units. Doubles £225–£310, includes breakfast. **Amenities:** Restaurant; bar; babysitting; exercise room; indoor heated pool; room service; sauna; free Wi-Fi.

MODERATE

The Halcyon ★   This dashing, youth-oriented hotel occupies a converted 18th-century townhouse. It offers two levels of accommodation: standard rooms, which are comfy if a little small, and studios, which are larger and come with fridges and microwaves. They also have serviced apartments in another property on George Street. The decor is smart—bold color schemes, exposed floorboards, and Philippe Starck bathroom fittings—and there's a popular basement bar/disco.

2-3 South Parade. www.thehalcyon.com. ☎ **01225/444100.** 21 units. Doubles £99–£125. **Amenities:** Bar (Circo; p. 250); free Wi-Fi.

One Three Nine ★   True, it's a good 10-minute—and largely uphill—walk from the action, but this dapper B&B makes a welcome change from the Georgian theme park of central Bath (and there are regular buses to whisk you into town). The exterior is late Victorian, while the interior is scrupulously modern, but also very comfortable.

139 Wells Rd. www.139bath.co.uk. ℂ **01225/314769.** 10 units. Doubles £125–£220, includes breakfast. 2-night min. stay Sat–Sun. **Amenities:** Free Wi-Fi.

Queensbury ★ Here, four Georgian townhouses have been combined to create one of the city's best boutique choices. Rather than pigeonhole itself as one sort of hotel, the Queensbury offers rooms both for guests who want country-house stylings and period features and those who want their facilities a little more up-to-date. The cozy Club rooms are particularly good value and there's an excellent restaurant (p. 248).

Russel St. www.thequeensberry.co.uk. ℂ **01225/447928.** 29 units. Doubles £99–£175. 2-night min. stay Sat–Sun. **Amenities:** Restaurant (Olive Tree; p. 248); free Wi-Fi.

INEXPENSIVE

Bodhi House ★ On the plus side, this family-owned B&B is excellent value, with large, airy rooms. Room 1 is the pick, and has great views over the city from its balcony. On the minus side, it's a 20-minute walk into town—although the generous full English breakfasts should provide you with the necessary energy.

31A Englishcombe Lane. www.bodhihouse.co.uk. ℂ **01225/461990.** 3 units. Doubles £70–£98, includes breakfast. Bus: 17. **Amenities:** Free Wi-Fi.

Where to Eat

EXPENSIVE

Circus Café & Restaurant ★★ ENGLISH This is a great place to drop into at any time of day. It opens for pastries and coffee at 10am, then starts serving lunch at midday, afternoon tea at 3:30pm, before delivering a full dinner service from 5:30pm. The menu proclaims its local produce proudly with "Bath soft cheese," "West Country rabbit," and "rump of Welsh lamb" among others, turned into Elizabeth David-inspired creations by head chef Ali Golden.

34 Brock St. www.thecircuscafeandrestaurant.co.uk. ℂ **01225/466020.** Mains £17–£19. Mon–Sat 10am–midnight.

Olive Tree ★★ MODERN ENGLISH/MEDITERRANEAN A serious contender for local fine-dining, the Olive House is more competitively priced than its rivals. Hearty ingredients dominate the menu in imaginative combinations. Try the starter of quail with watercress purée, potato crisps, marinated raisins, and candied walnuts followed by pan-fried halibut with charred asparagus, parmesan, Jersey Royal potatoes, truffles, and Noilly Prat sauce. Reserve ahead of arrival.

Inside Queensbury Hotel, Russsell St. www.olivetreebath.co.uk. ℂ **01225/447928.** Mains £19–£27; set lunch £21–£26. Mon–Sat noon–2pm and 7–10pm; Sun noon–2pm and 7–9:30pm.

Taking Tea in Bath

Bath is the ideal place to indulge in that quintessentially English tradition of afternoon tea, served with jam, clotted cream, and scones. Try the **Pump Room** ★★ at the Roman Baths (p. 244), which serves a lavish tea for £21 (champagne tea £30). At **Sally Lunn's** ★ (p. 245) you can get Sally Lunn cream tea for £7, which includes a buttered Sally Lunn bun served with strawberry jam and clotted cream. The **Regency Tea Rooms** ★, at the Jane Austen Centre (p. 244), offers "Tea with Mr. Darcy" for £17 to £30 (£27 with champagne), while the **Royal Crescent Hotel** (p. 247) lays on a lavish spread for £32 (£40 with champagne).

Sotto Sotto ★★ ITALIAN Enjoying an atmospheric setting in restored medieval vaults below street level, this is a firm favorite with locals who regularly vote it the city's best Italian restaurant. With an innovative menu—a typical meal could entail a starter of chicken liver pâté on rustic Tuscan bread, followed by sea bass wrapped in smoked Parma ham, topped off with the house tiramisù—it's very reasonably priced and super-friendly. You'll probably need to book ahead.

10 North Parade. www.sottosotto.co.uk. ✆ **01225/330236.** Mains £14–£19. Tues–Sat 6–10pm.

MODERATE

Bistro La Barrique ★★ FRENCH Fancy some French cooking but can't decide what you want? This bistro offers *petits plats*, or French tapas, allowing you to sample a range of small dishes. The portions may be small scale, but the cooking is big on quality. The seafood pancake, filet of sea bass, and baked garlic snails are all good choices. A pre-theater menu of two *plats* and a side for £13 offers the best value.

31 Barton St. www.bistrolabarrique.co.uk. ✆ **01225/463861.** Small plates £7–£9. Mon–Fri noon–2:30pm and 5:30–10:30pm; Sat noon–10:30pm.

Mai Thai ★ THAI With around a half-dozen choices, there's no shortage of places to get Thai food in Bath. This one, near the Parade Gardens, is the pick. In a nicely informal, if slightly cramped setting, wait stuff buzz around taking orders from a menu featuring more than 100 choices covering all the big hitters—including red, green, yellow and massaman curries—as well as lesser known regional specialties. The lunch menu is a real bargain, with a main and steamed rice costing £7.

6 Pierrepoint St. www.maithaibath.com. ✆ **01225/445557.** Mains £8–£14. Daily noon–2pm and 6–10:30pm.

INEXPENSIVE

Fine Cheese Co. ★ DELI/CAFE The shop stocks a bewildering array of artisan cheeses from Britain, France, Italy and beyond, and even offers wedding cake cheeses (tiered towers of cheese) for savory-toothed couples. You can try some sampling platters at the small, and often rather crowded cafe at the back, as well as an array of sandwiches, soups, cakes, and other snacks. Outdoor seating in summer.

29-31 Walcot St. www.finecheese.co.uk. ✆ **01225/483407.** Mains £7, sandwiches £5. Mon–Fri 9:30am–5:30pm; Sat 9am–5:30pm.

Yak Yeti Yak ★ NEPALESE   With around six meat and six vegetarian mains on offer, this basement-set Nepalese eatery has something for everyone. Dishes are delicately, rather than overpoweringly spiced, and include Bakula Banda (spicy stir-fried broad beans and white cabbage) and the highly recommended lamb tamar, slowly cooked with bamboo shoots, black eyed peas and potatoes.

12 Pierrepont St. www.yakyetiyak.co.uk. ✆ **01225/442299.** Mains £6–£9. Mon–Sat noon–2:30pm and 5–10:30pm; Sun noon–2:30pm and 5–10pm.

Shopping

The **SouthGate** outdoor pedestrian mall (www.southgatebath.com) is fast becoming Bath's prime mainstream shopping area. Trendy **Milsom Place** (www.milsomplace.co.uk) has more fashionable designers, while **Walcot Street** is the home of several studios turning out furniture, lighting and, in the case of **Bath Aqua Glass,** 107 Walcot St. (www.bathaquaglass.com; ✆ **01225/428146**), high-quality glass. It's open Monday to Saturday 9:30am to 5pm (demos Mon–Fri 11:15am and 2:15pm, Sat 2:15pm; £5). **St Margaret's Buildings** is lined with independent stores selling vintage clothing, art, antiques, and used books.

Entertainment & Nightlife

As befits one of Britain's oldest cities, there are plenty of characterful pubs in Bath. Look for beers from local microbreweries **Abbey Ales, Bath Ales,** and **Box Steam Brewery.** You'll find them among the cask ales served at the **Bell ★**, 103 Walcot St. (www.walcotstreet.com; ✆ **01225/460426**), which stages live music ranging from jazz and country to reggae and blues on Monday and Wednesday nights and Sundays. The **Raven of Bath,** 6-7 Queen St. (www.theravenofbath.co.uk; ✆ **01225/425045**), advertises its current ales on a chalkboard outside, and is best known for its tasty meat pies.

Vegetarians and students love the **Porter,** 15 George St. (www.the porter.co.uk; ✆ **01225/424104**), a grungier option specializing in vegetarian food (£5–£7) and live music, open-mic nights, DJs, and comedy. Next door at 14 George St. is **Moles** (www.moles.co.uk; ✆ **01225/404445**), Bath's premier dance club and live music venue. For something a bit more sophisticated, the **Circo Bar and Lounge** occupies the cellars below the Halycon hotel (see above), with luxurious Chesterfield sofas and cocktails priced from £8.

Side Trips from Bath

Wells Cathedral ★★★ CATHE-DRAL Begun in the 12th century, this magnificent church is among England's best-preserved examples of early Gothic architecture. The medieval sculpture of its **West Front ★★** is without equal in a country where so much religious statuary was destroyed during the Reformation. This western facade was completed around 1230, the central tower in the 14th century, with the internal fan vaulting erected later still. The most striking interior feature is the **Scissor Arches ★★★**, an amazing feat of engineering; they were built between 1338 and 1348, when the west piers of the crossing tower began to sink. The inverted arches strengthen the top-heavy structure and prevented the tower from collapsing. Master mason William Joy devised this ingenious solution, which has done the job for 6½ centuries.

The Scissor Arches of Wells Cathedral.

Much of the cathedral's stained glass dates from the 14th century, as does the **Lady Chapel ★**, constructed in the Decorated style. Up steps to the north of the crossing is the octagonal, fan-vaulted **Chapter House,** completed in 1306. Young visitors might be more enchanted by the **Wells Clock ★**, which dates from 1390. Every quarter-hour, it chimes, and jousting knights gallop around a platform above its face. Chain Gate, Cathedral Green, Wells. www.wellscathedral.org.uk. ℭ **01749/674483.** Free (donations appreciated). Apr–Sept daily 7am–7pm; Oct–Mar daily 7am–6pm. Guided tours usually Mon–Sat hourly 10am–3pm.

SS Great Britain ★★★ HISTORIC SITE   Bristol's pride and joy, the SS *Great Britain* was the world's first iron steamship when it was launched here in 1843. Two years later it crossed the Atlantic in 14 days—a record at the time. Damaged in a ferocious storm off Cape Horn in 1886, it served out its days as a floating warehouse in the Falkland Islands, and was abandoned in the 1930s. Thanks to a remarkable salvage project in 1970 and subsequent restoration, you can now appreciate the skill and vision of designer Isambard Kingdom Brunel. The revolutionary **Dry Dock** takes you below the water line into a climate-controlled chamber where the awe-inspiring outer hull is preserved, while the adjacent **Dockyard Museum** provides detailed history on the ship. Finally, you get to explore the ship itself, magnificently restored to evoke the 1850s—even smells (coal fires, cooking food) are recreated, and free audioguides add context to the first class and steerage quarters, the engine room, and the bowels of the ship.

When it's in port, a replica of John Cabot's ship, the *Matthew* (see www.matthew.co.uk for cruise times; ✆ **0117/927-6868**), is usually moored just outside the *Great Britain* site. You can usually look around for free during office hours (11am–5pm; donation suggested). Great Western Dockyard, Gas Ferry Rd., Bristol. www.ssgreatbritain.org. ✆ **0117/926-0680.** £14 adults, £13 seniors, £8 children 5–16, £37 families. Apr–Oct daily 10am–5:30pm; Nov–Mar daily 10am–4:30pm. Last admission 1 hr. before closing.

The SS *Great Britain*, **Bristol.**

DEVON & CORNWALL

by Stephen Brewer

You could easily get the impression that the farther west you go in England, the better it gets. The two westernmost counties are places of great beauty and remarkable diversity, with gloomy moors in Dartmouth to golden beaches at St Ives, and a lot in between. Exotic seaside gardens flourish around Fowey, King Arthur's legendary castle clings to a cliff at Tintagel, and pretty storybook villages pop up everywhere, from Clovelly to Mousehole.

Of course, the wild coastlines have been a draw for all sorts of visitors over the centuries, among them writers (Arthur Conan Doyle and Daphne DuMaurier) and artists (Barbara Hepworth and Ben Nicholson), who all of left their legacies. Others come to swim, surf, walk, eat the freshest seafood in the land, and just enjoy this proud and beautiful peninsula.

EXETER ★

201 miles SW of London

The Romans founded the most westerly holding of their empire on the banks of the River Exe in the 1st century A.D. Exeter has been a target of invaders almost ever since—Saxons, Vikings, the Norman armies of William the Conqueror, but none more effective than bombers of the German Luftwaffe, who flattened much of the city between 1940 and 1942. While post war rebuilding has been more practical than artful, the past still pokes through, most spectacularly so in the soaring Norman cathedral but also in a few Roman fragments and some half-timbered Tudor buildings and Georgian crescents from Exeter's 17th and 18th century days as a powerhouse port and center of the wool trade.

Essentials

GETTING THERE   First Great Western **trains** from London's Paddington Station travel to Exeter St David Station every hour; the trip takes 2½ hours. A **National Express bus** (www.nationalexpress.com; ✆ **0871/781-8181**) departs from London's Victoria Coach Station every 2 hours during the day; the trip takes 4½ hours. If you're **driving** from London, take the M4 west, then the M5 south to Exeter.

VISITOR INFORMATION   The **Tourist Information Centre** is at the Civic Centre, Paris Street (✆ **01392/665700**). It's open daily Monday to Saturday 9am to 5pm, and also Sunday 10am to 4pm in July and August.

PREVIOUS PAGE: **A beach near Porthcurno, Penwith Peninsula.**

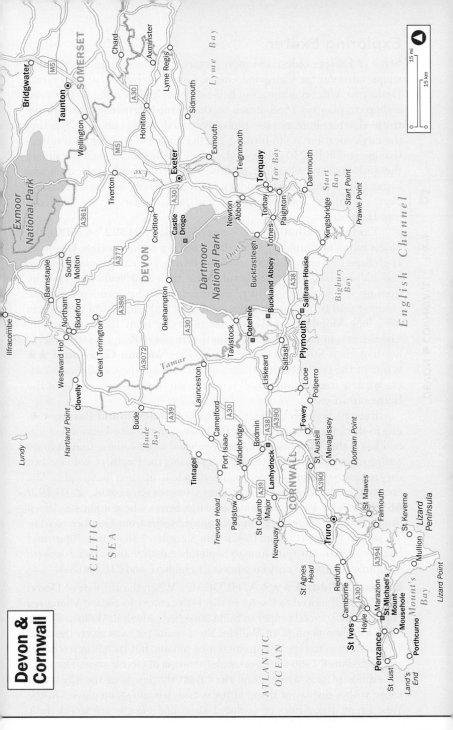

Devon &
Cornwall

Exploring Exeter

Some of Exeter's oldest and most picturesque houses and bow-fronted shops surround the Cathedral Green. Local lore has it that Sir Francis Drake met with his admirals in half-timbered Mol's Coffee House (now a shop) to plan his 1588 attack on the Spanish Armada. Closer to the truth, Exeter bureaucrats probably toiled here cobbling together the city's contribution to funding the fleet, maybe in upper floor offices that are still lit by 230 panes of glass. The "coffee house" status came in the 18th century, when the premises became a gentleman's club and began serving the newly introduced beverage. Drake is also said to have been a regular of the Ship Inn (p. 259), on a medieval lane that leads into High Street.

Exeter Guildhall ★ (www.exeter.gov.uk; ℂ **01392/665500**), the oldest municipal building in England, is the most impressive facade on High Street. Even so, looks can be deceiving: The oak paneled ceremonial hall is delightfully medieval, more than 600 years old, but the frontage is a late-16th-century mishmash of Tudor grandeur that one observer said is "just as picturesque as it is barbarous." You can step in for a look Monday and Wednesday to Friday from 10:30am to 1pm. The oldest remnants of Exeter are at the fringes of Rougemont Gardens, north of High Street off Castle Street. The **Norman Gatehouse** ★★ is one of the few surviving fragments of William the Conqueror's castle, while a fragment of a wall is what's left of the fortifications of the Roman town.

Running beneath Exeter is a network of **Underground Passages** ★, dug in the 14th century to bring fresh water to the city. Unfounded legend has it that the passages have been used as everything from refuges during plague outbreaks to hidey-holes during the English Civil War, but they're quite an impressive engineering feat in their own right. The entrance to the Underground Passages (www.exeter.gov.uk; ℂ **01392/665887**), is on Paris Street, just off High Street where it joins Sidewell Street. They're open for 25-minute guided tours from October to May, Tuesday to Friday, 10:30am to 4:30pm, Saturday 9:30am to 5:30pm, and Sunday 11:30am to 4pm; June to September, daily 9:30am to 5:30pm (to 4:30pm on Sun) and cost £6 adults, £4 children, and £18 families.

Exeter Cathedral ★★ CATHEDRAL When the Bishops of Devon and Cornwall moved to Exeter in the 11th century to escape Viking sea raids, it only seemed proper to build a mighty cathedral. William Warelwast, a bishop-nephew of William the Conqueror, was given the task. Two stout twin towers he commissioned remain, but the church was not completed until 1400 in a spectacular showing of Gothic style. The striking edifice of grey-white stone rises from the lawns of the Cathedral Close with a display of flying buttress and delicate stone glass. On the West Front, three rows of sculpted kings and queens are wonderfully

Exeter Cathedral, completed in 1400.

informal, showing Alfred, Richard II, and others seemingly engaged in conversation for eternity. Just beyond stretches the longest fan-vaulted ceiling in the world, 20m (66 ft.) tall and 90m (300 ft.) high. Artful touches include the minstrel's gallery, carved with instrument-playing angels. It's said that the astronomical clock in the north transept might have inspired the nursery rhyme "Hickory Dickorey Dock." The cathedral's famous choir sings Evensong Monday to Friday at 5:30pm and at 3pm on Saturday and Sunday.

1 The Cloisters. www.exeter-cathedral.org.uk. ✆ **01392/285983.** £6 adults, children 18 and under free. Mon–Sat 9am–5pm, Sun 11am–5pm.

Powderham Castle ★ CASTLE   Dukes and Earls of Devon have called this small fortified manor house just outside Devon home since the late 14th century. The 15th century chapel, with hand-hewn roof timbers and carved pew ends, is one of the few original bits to have weathered turbulent medieval battles and a Civil War siege. Much of the Gothic appearance comes from a 19th-century rebuilding in a "character consistent with an ancient castle" that, in effect, made a castle from the Middle Ages look more like a castle from the Middle Ages. Among the grand rooms hung with tapestries and filled with fine furniture, the most storied might be the Music Room, designed for the colorful and popular William, the 9th Earl of Devon (1768–1835). William was once known as the "most beautiful boy in England" and became infamous for his love affair with William Beckford, an art collector and politician. Beckford was forced to step down from parliament when the affair became public knowledge, and the earl emigrated to America, where he lived in comfortable exile on a Hudson River estate outside New York City. You may recognize the castle from the film *The Remains of the Day*. Powderham, 8 miles south of Exeter in Kenton. www.powderham.co.uk. *☎* **01626/890243.** £12 adults, £10 seniors, £9 children 5–14, £38 families (£1 surcharge mid-July–Aug). Mar–Oct Sun–Fri 11am–4:30pm (until 5:30pm mid-July to late Aug).

Royal Albert Memorial Museum and Art Gallery ★★ MUSEUM A Victorian jewel-box of a building, designed to resemble a Venetian Palace, houses an appealing array of artifacts that includes some stunners like a Greek campaign helmet and the totem poles, colorful moccasins, and other mementoes that Captain Cook brought back from his 18th-century voyages along the Pacific Northwest coast of America. Also intriguing is a showing of medieval cooking pots, combs, and other jetsam of everyday life found in a local rubbish heap.
Queen St. www.rammuseum.org.uk. *☎* **01392/265858.** Free. Tues–Sun 10am–5pm.

Where to Stay

ABode Exeter at the Royal Clarence Hotel ★★★   At this atmospheric 18th-century inn has hosted the likes of Admiral Nelson and is now part of a small luxury chain. The approach is to create a strikingly modern ambiance in traditional settings. The effect is stunning, with a glam bar, handsome pub, and fine restaurant (see below) and understated sophistication in the rooms, which combine snowy white duvets, nice fabrics, and all sorts of high-tech comforts like underfloor heating in the limestone bathrooms. The best feature, though, is centuries-old: face-on views of the cathedral, especially dramatic when it's floodlit at night.
Cathedral Yard. www.abodehotels.co.uk/exeter. *☎* **01392/319955.** 53 units. Doubles from £68. **Amenities:** Restaurant; cafe; 2 bars; babysitting; exercise room; room service; spa; free Wi-Fi.

St Olaves Hotel ★★   A creamy white townhouse just steps from the cathedral has all the trappings of a refined getaway, set within a walled garden and filled with exquisite Georgian woodwork and other period details that, despite the friendly informality, can make you feel you've just stepped into a Jane Austen novel. A spiral staircase floats up to large bedrooms, graciously done with reproduction antiques and old prints and as sedate and refined as the Treasury Restaurant downstairs.
Mary Arches St. (off High St.). www.olaves.co.uk. *☎* **800/544-9993.** 14 units. Doubles from £80. **Amenities:** Restaurant; bar; room service; free Wi-Fi.

Where to Eat

Michael Caines Restaurant at ABode Exeter ★★ FRENCH Michael Caine is one of Britain's most acclaimed chefs, and his ground-floor showplace in the Abode hotel across from the cathedral is one of Britain's culinary temples. Despite the acclaim, meals are like the cream-walled, wood-floored room where they are served, simple yet elegant. The menu changes constantly to reflect what's fresh and in season, but the preparations always show off locally caught fish and shellfish, West Country lamb, and Devon cheeses. Reservations are essential, but well worth the effort to enjoy seemingly modest dishes like sweet potato hash that are in fact complex works of art.

In the ABode Exeter at the Royal Clarence Hotel, Cathedral Yard. www.michael caines.com. ℂ **01392/223638.** Mains £9–£25. Daily noon–2:30pm; Mon–Thurs 6–9:30pm, Fri–Sat 6–10pm, Sun 6–9pm.

Ship Inn ★ ENGLISH   It's said that Sir Francis Drake and Sir Walter Raleigh used to tipple in this 16th-century inn near the cathedral, but even without this somewhat dubious provenance, the beamed and timbered surroundings are an atmospheric place to enjoy a mind-boggling choice of ales and ciders. A paneled upstairs room serves curries and other full meals, while the pub fare downstairs includes a good selection of snacks, fish and chips, and sandwiches.

St Martin's Lane. ℂ **01392/272040.** Main £6–£13. Daily noon–9pm.

Treasury Restaurant ★ CONTINENTAL   The name reflects a mint on the site that once produced coins for Charles I, but this spot is quite a treasure itself. You can dine in an intimate walled garden in good weather, or in a cozy room where a fire burns in the hearth. The menu is influenced by France, but leans towards grilled lamb chops and braised duck leg, pan-fried scallops, and other traditional local fare.

"Down-along" in picturesque Clovelly.

In the St Olaves Hotel, Mary Arches St. www.olaves.co.uk. ℂ **01392/217736.** Mains £16–£25. Daily noon–2pm and 7–9:30pm.

Around Exeter

Exeter is a good base for exploring Dartmoor (see below) as well as the rugged north coast of Devon and Cornwall.

CLOVELLY ★★
55 miles northwest of Exeter

This pretty fishing village on the north coast of Devon is nothing if not unique, as in steep—so steep that residents still haul wares up and down the main street on donkey-pulled sleds. As you make your way past pretty white cottages along the irregular cobbles—you'll have no trouble understanding why this narrow lane has two names: "Down-along" if you're inching your way down the near-vertical incline toward the 14th-century quay, "Up-along" when you're panting your way back up. (Should Down-along appeal more than Up-along, for £2 per person a Land Rover will take you back up via a back road.) Mission accomplished, you've done Clovelly, because there's really not much else to see or do except to make this picturesque trek. When you catch your breath, you can contemplate the still-true words of Victorian author Charles Kingsley (1819–75), who lived here, "It is as if the place had stood still while all the world had been rushing and rumbling past it."

It's not easy to get to Clovelly by public transportation. From Exeter local trains run to Barnstaple (1¼ hr.) and from there frequent buses continue to Clovelly (sometimes you need to change at Bideford). The outing will take all day, most of it spent traveling. If you're driving from Exeter, head west then north on the A30 to the A39; the drive will take about 1½ hours. To gain entry to the village, you're required to buy a ticket from the **Clovelly Visitor Centre** (www.clovelly.co.uk; ✆ **01237/431781**). The cost is £7 for adults, £4 for children 7 to 16, and £18 for families. This fee covers parking for the day; a tour of a fisherman's cottage; and a tiny museum devoted to former resident Charles Kingsley, author of *The Water Babies*. The center is open July to September, daily 10am to 4pm; April to June and October, Monday to Saturday 9am to 5:30pm; and November to March, daily 9am to 4:30pm. To avoid the tourist crowds in the summer, avoid Clovelly from around 11am until 4pm.

From Clovelly, the A39 follows the coast 10 miles northeast to Westward Ho!, where a beach of flat, golden sands stretches for 2 miles.

TINTAGEL ★★
60 miles west of Exeter

The wild, windswept north coast of Cornwall is steeped in legends, and they burst into full flower at the dramatic and romantic ruins of King Arthur's Tintagel Castle. Tintagel is a little more than an hour's drive from Exeter on the A30 and A395.

Tintagel Castle ★★★ CASTLE   The colorful legends about King Arthur come to the fore at this seaside ruin atop a steep. No matter how true or false tales of chivalry and the round table might be, it's known for certain that in the Dark Ages a great warrior had a fortress here—possibly a 6th-century chieftain of mixed Roman and Celtic parentage who led his army in raids against Saxon invaders. Stare at the Atlantic surf crashing against the rocks long enough and it's easy to imagine the fierce fighters preparing for battle on the wind-buffeted cliff. The ruins of the castle that you see today are those of a

The ruins of Tintagel Castle, linked to Arthurian legend.

stronghold built in 1233 for the earls of Cornwall. You'll have to climb 100 rock-cut steps to reach them, and as you huff and puff your way up keep an eye out for sea birds and otters.

Bossiney Rd. (½ mile northwest of Tintagel). www.english-heritage.org.uk. ℗ **01840/770328.** £6 adults, students, and seniors, £4 children 5–15, £16 families. Daily Apr–Sept 10am–6pm, Oct to 5pm, and Nov–Mar to 4pm.

DARTMOOR NATIONAL PARK ★★★
13 miles W of Exeter

Ominous and brooding, this vast, sprawling landscape of heather- and gorse covered moors stretches from Exeter east toward the town of Tavistock, covering 365 square miles in all. The park rises to steep hills as high as 621m (2,037 ft.), and plunges into deep gorges with rushing water. Most of the land is privately owned, and farms and village are scattered throughout the park. More than 500 miles of public footpaths crisscross the moors, where herds of **wild ponies** nibble on the heather and occasionally block traffic on the tiny, winding roads. Dartmoor has its own windswept beauty, though there's a good reason Arthur Conan Doyle set his popular tale, *The Hound of the Baskervilles,* here.

Adding to the otherworldly allure of the region is a mother lode of prehistoric dwellings and monuments. Farmers began clearing the land at Dartmoor 10,000 years ago, and early inhabitants left behind 1,500 burial mounds (cairns), the stone ruins of 5,000 huts and houses, and 70 stone

A footpath and stone bridge in Dartmoor National Park.

rows and 18 stone circles. Long Ash Hill is an especially rich repository of these early stone formations; it's near the eastern boundary of the park, just outside Tavistock near Merivale, about 40 miles southeast of Exeter.

Essentials

GETTING THERE   While it's easiest to get to and around the moors by **car,** you can explore by **bus** and on foot with a little planning. **First Bus** connects Exeter with some villages and towns in the park, where the **Transmoor Link** bus service runs between villages. For timetables, contact **Travel Line** (www.traveline.info; ✆ **0871/200-2233**).

If you're driving from Exeter, head west on the B3212 to such centers as Chagford (see below). Between smaller towns, single-track roads cut across the moors. Prepare to pull over if traffic comes the other way.

VISITOR INFORMATION   The **High Moorland Visitor Centre** (www.visitdartmoor.co.uk; ✆ **01822/890414**) is an essential stop for a thorough exploration of the park. The center is deep within the park in the village of Princetown, about 30 miles southeast of Exeter via A30 and B3212. It's open daily 10am to 5pm. Arthur Conan Doyle stayed in the building that houses the center while researching *The Hound of the Baskervilles.* The views down the windswept hill are the ones that inspired his descriptions of the desolate moors in the novel.

Exploring the Area

Among the towns and villages, lost-in-time **Chagford ★★★**, 20 miles east of Exeter via the A30, is especially charming. It's scenic, too,

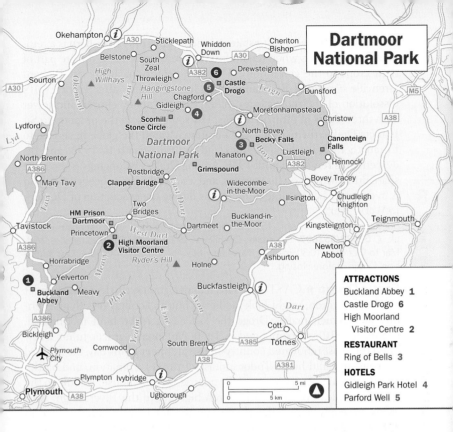

Okehampton ⓘ A30 Sticklepath Whiddon Down Cheriton Bishop

Belstone South Zeal ⓘ A382 6 Drewsteignton

Sourton High Willhays Throwleigh 5 Castle Drogo Dunsford M5

Hangingstone Hill Chagford ○ 4

Gidleigh ○

Lydford Scorhill Stone Circle Moretonhampstead Christow A38

ⓘ North Bovey Becky Falls Canonteign Falls

Dartmoor 3 Lustleigh Hennock

North Brentor National Park Manaton A382 Bovey Tracey

Mary Tavy Postbridge Grimspound Chudleigh Knighton

Clapper Bridge Widecombe-in-the-Moor Ilsington

Two Bridges ⓘ Teignmouth

HM Prison Dartmoor Dartmeet Buckland-in-the-Moor Kingsteignton

Tavistock Princetown A38 Newton Abbot

Horrabridge 2 High Moorland Visitor Centre Ashburton

Yelverton Ryder's Hill Holne

1 Meavy Buckfastleigh ⓘ Dart

Buckland Abbey

Bickleigh Cott Totnes

Plymouth City Cornwood South Brent A385 A38

Plymton Ivybridge ⓘ A381

Plymouth A38 Ugborough 0 ... 5 mi / 0 ... 5 km

ATTRACTIONS
Buckland Abbey **1**
Castle Drogo **6**
High Moorland
  Visitor Centre **2**

RESTAURANT
Ring of Bells **3**

HOTELS
Gidleigh Park Hotel **4**
Parford Well **5**

overlooking the River Teign and surrounded by high granite tors (rocky hilltop outcrops). Plentiful pubs and tea shops make Chagford a good place to stop for lunch and a stroll. The 16th-century **Endecott House** in the town square is named after John Endecott, a Pilgrim and governor of the Massachusetts Bay colony, who lived in Chagford before striking out for America. The 15th-century **Church of St Michael** is entrenched in a tragic back story. According to legend, on October 11, 1641, young Mary Whiddon was married in the church. The new bride and groom had barely made it through the door when a jilted suitor gunned her down. R. D. Blackmore's tells the story in his classic novel *Lorna Doone*, and brides still stop in the churchyard to lay flowers on Mary's grave.

The highest town on the moors is **Princetown,** at 435m (1,427 ft.); it's on the B3212, 30 miles east of Exeter. The High Moorland Visitor Centre is here (see above), and it's a favorite starting point for hill walkers. You probably won't want to linger too long in this gloomy old place, with the early 19th-century, still-operating Dartmoor Prison looming over it.

Buckland Abbey ★★ HISTORIC HOUSE This atmospheric old manor house was built in the 13th century as a monastery for Cistercian monks, who created a vast estate around it. The stone tithe barn is a remnant from the days when tenant farmers were expected to donate part of their crops to the community. The 16th-century navigator Sir Richard Grenville converted Buckland into a fine residence after Henry VIII's dissolution of the monasteries, filling the vast abbey church and tower with three floors of intimate rooms. His son later sold the property to Sir Francis Drake, the mariner who circumnavigated the globe in service to Elizabeth I. Drake lived at Buckland until his death in 1596, and his descendants remained until 1948. Among Drake's belongings is the huge snare drum he took on his voyages, and it's said the drum beats if England is in danger. The last time it did so was during the evacuation of Dunkirk in World War II.

Buckland Abbey, Yelverton, 15 miles southeast of Chagford. www.nationaltrust.org. uk. ✆ **01822/853607.** £10 adults, £5 children 16 and under, £15–£25 families. Mid-Mar to Oct daily 10:30am–5pm; Nov–early Mar Fri–Sun 11am–4:30pm. Last admission 45 min. before closing.

Castle Drogo ★ CASTLE   This massive granite castle, in the hamlet of Drewsteignton, might look medieval, but it's actually less than a century old. Which makes Drogo the last castle to be built in England, begun in 1910 and completed in 1930. Millionaire grocer Julius Drew hired the most renowned country-house architect of his day, Sir Edward Lutyens, to build him a Tudor fantasy of turrets, crenation, and battlements, all built of granite specially quarried for the house. Adding to the effect is a bleak but dramatic perch high above the River Teign, with views sweeping across the gloomy moors. Yet Drew wanted to live in 20th century comfort, as you'll see on a tour of elegant living rooms, an elaborate bathroom, and a kitchen that was thoroughly up to date for the time. The gardens are serene and lovely, designed by noted horticulturalist Gertrude Jekyll. On a circular croquet court you can rent a set and knock some balls through the wickets as if you were a guest at an Edwardian era garden party. For the next couple of years much of the castle will be covered in scaffolding for restoration work.

Drewsteignton, 4 miles northeast of Chagford and 6 miles south of the Exeter-Okehampton Rd. (A30). www.nationaltrust.org.uk. ✆ **01647/433306.** £9 adults, £4 children 16 and under, £13–£22 families. House: Mar–Oct daily 11am–5pm; Nov Sat–Sun 11am–4:30pm; Dec 1–23 daily 11am–4pm. Grounds: Mar–Oct daily 9am–5:30pm; Nov–Dec 23 daily 11am–5pm; Jan–Feb daily 11am–4pm.

ORGANIZED TOURS

An excellent way to explore the park is on one of the guided walks led by rangers of the **Dartmoor National Park Authority (DNPA)**. They vary in difficulty and range from 2 to 6 hours and cost from £3 for a 2-hour walk to £8 for a 6-hour walk. Details are available from the High Moorland Visitor Centre, Tavistock Road, Princetown (www.dartmoor-npa.gov.uk; ✆ **01822/890414**) and also at www.moorland guides.co.uk. The Moorland Visitor Center has put together an audio guide for a 6-mile circular walk that takes in a wide scope of the park's attractions: moorland, a waterfall, and some stone rows. It's available at www.dartmoor.gov.uk.

Where to Eat & Stay

When in Chagford, drop in at Whiddons on High Street (☏ **01647/433-406**) for a cup of tea, and some freshly baked scones and delicate cucumber sandwiches.

Gidleigh Park Hotel ★★★   If there's one spot in England to throw monetary concerns to the winds and savor a country house experience, this gorgeous hotel fashioned out of an Arts and Crafts mansion is it. Huge bedrooms are furnished with hand-crafted pieces and paintings from a noted private collection, and come with perks that include fireplaces, private saunas, and steam rooms. They overlook impeccable gardens and the surrounding hills that might beckon you to follow walking paths across the estate, one way to work up an appetite for a meal in the double-Michelin-starred restaurant by Chef Michael Caines.

Gidleigh Park, 2 miles outside Chagford. www.gidleigh.com. ☏ **01647/432367.** 24 units, 1 cottage. Doubles £305–£530, includes breakfast. **Amenities:** Restaurant; bar; babysitting; lawn bowling; croquet; putting green; spa; tennis; free Wi-Fi.

Parford Well ★★   London's Number 16 set the gold standard for small hotels, and former owner and manager Tim Daniel returned to his native Devon to work the same magic. His stylish and comfortable rooms overlook a well-tended garden, and a wood-burning stove warms a welcoming lounge. A lavish breakfast served in an attractive dining room looking over meadows is a perfect way to ease into a day of walking.

Sandy Park, 1 mile outside Chagford. www.parfordwell.co.uk. ☏ **01647/433353.** 3 units. Doubles £85–£100, includes breakfast. **Amenities:** Lounge; free Wi-Fi.

Ring of Bells Inn ★ PUB FOOD   Country pubs don't get much more authentic than this—there's even a thatched roof, along with a nice terrace and a series of cozy, paneled rooms for a pint and a bite after a bracing walk on the moors. The steak pies are homemade and local ales come right from the barrel. The guestrooms upstairs are cozy and comfortable, and all have private bathrooms and come with breakfast.

North Bovey, Dartmoor. Ringofbells.net. ☏ **01647/440375.** Mains £11–£19. Daily noon–2:30pm and 6–9pm. Rooms from £70 double with breakfast.

> ### Mommie Dearest
>
> In the tiny Dartmoor village of Buckland-in-the-Moor, with its thatched-roof cottages and fluffy Dartmoor ponies, the stone, 13th century **St Peter's Church** has a distinctively modern clock on its tower denotes the hours with letters instead of numbers. Look closely and you'll see they spell out My Dear Mother. A grieving parishioner whose mother had just died donated the clock in 1931.

FOWEY ★★

74 miles SW of Exeter

The Rivers Tamar and Fowey flow through the southeast corner of Cornwall past a clutch of delightful fishing villages. The attractive town of Fowey (pronounced Foy) stretches for a mile or so along the Fowey River to its mouth in Austell Bay. Boats bob in the busy marinas, and the main street, the Esplanade, follows a bluff above the banks of the river. Novelist Daphne du Maurier spent much of her life in Fowey, setting her stories in locales around the town; a nearby country house inspired her most famous novel, *Rebecca*. Two landmarks overlooking Fowey's harbor once provided mariners with protection as well as some spiritual reassurance. **St Catherine's Castle ★** now in ruins, was built here in the 16th century on orders of Henry VIII (you can clamor around the ruins for free). **St Fimbarrus' Church ★** (free admission), down by the quay, was founded in the 7th century by the saint himself, the first bishop of Cork, when he paused in Fowey on the way to Rome. Divine intervention didn't prevent the French from destroying the original church in the 15th century, in retaliation for British raids along the Norman coast.

Essentials

GETTING THERE   The nearest mainline **railway** station is at Liskeard, 19 miles north of Fowey. Liskeard is 3½ hours by **First Great Western** train (www.nationalrail.co.uk; ✆ **08457/000125**) from London's Paddington Station. If you're **driving** take the A38 west, then the A390 southwest to branch off for Fowey.

Fowey, viewed from the Fowey River.

VISITOR INFORMATION Fowey Tourist Information Centre, 5 South St. (www.fowey.co.uk; ℂ **01726/833616;** is open daily 10am to 4:30pm. The **Daphne du Maurier Festival** (www.dumaurier festival.co.uk) held 1 week each May features a mix of talks and readings by authors, as well as musical performances.

Exploring the Area

Aside from yachters, Fowey is especially popular with garden enthusiasts. Some of England's most famous gardens flourish in the lush seaside landscapes around the town.

The Eden Project ★★ GARDEN   Two geodesic domes (biomes) set in a former clay quarry are an environmental showcase that bring exotic climes to the Cornwall coast. The Humid Tropics Biome is a rain forest under glass, while the Warm Temperate Biome is planted with species indigenous to the Mediterranean, South Africa and California, and filled with citrus and olive trees. Aside from being pleasant to wander, the biomes introduce visitors to the importance of plants as medicine, food, and fuel and threats to our fragile ecosystems.

Bodelva, St Austell, 9 miles west of Fowey. www.edenproject.com. ℂ **01726/811911.** £18 adults, £6 children 5–16, free children 4 and under. Mar–late Oct daily 9:30am– 6pm (last admission 4:30pm); Nov–mid Mar daily 9:30am–4:30pm (last entry 3pm). **Note:** Winter hours can vary, so check website before visiting.

Lost Gardens of Heligan ★★★ GARDEN   Visiting this 81-hectare (200-acre) garden is rather like traveling back in time to Queen Victoria's day, the fortunate result of decades of neglect. At the outbreak of World

The Eden Project, near Fowey.

War I, most of the laborers who cared for the Tremayne's family lush gardens were called off to fight and never returned. Brambles and weeds overtook the greenhouses, walls collapsed, vegetable plots and ornamental beds went wild. Beginning in the 1990s, Europe's largest garden restoration project brought Heligan back to its former Victorian glory. Bamboo and palms thrive in the Jungle, planted with specimens that 19th-century botanists carried home from their travels. Heritage fruits and vegetables grow in the Production Gardens. The Wider Estate spreads over an additional 1,000 acres, with lakes, bogs, and woodlands.

Pentewan, 12 miles southwest of Fowey. www.heligan.com. ✆ **01726/845100.** £13 adults, £11 seniors, £6 children 5–17, £30 families. Apr–Sept daily 10am–6pm (last admission 4:30pm), Oct–Mar daily 10am–5pm (last admission 3:30pm).

Trelissick ★★★ GARDEN   This beautiful garden at Fal Estuary was first planted 200 years ago. In 25 acres of seaside terraces spilling down a hillside, hydrangeas, and camellias thrive next to gingkos and palms. The plantings didn't just delight the owner of the estate, Ronald Copeland, who was managing director of the Spoke china works in Stoke-on-Trent (p. 331) but inspired him as well: He used flowers from his garden in patterns on his china. Oak and beech woodlands stretch down to the River Fal and are laced with five miles of walking trails.

Feock, 25 miles southwest of Fowey. www.nationaltrust.org.uk. ✆ **01872/862090.** £9 adults, £4 children, £ 13–£22 families. Mid-Feb to Oct daily 10am–5:30pm, Nov to mid-Feb daily 11am–4pm.

Where to Stay & Eat

Ferry Inn ★ BRITISH   Just about all of the bright, plainly furnished rooms overlook the water from this prime perch on the west bank of the River Fowey, across the water from Fowey in the village of Bodinnick. Most atmospheric are the rooms in the original 400-year-old wing with beams, stone walls, and sloping floors. A nautical theme prevails in the pub downstairs, and in good weather the terrace provides a fine spot to enjoy a pint while watching the Fowey–Bodinnick ferry come and go. You can also keep an eye on the fishing boats, which bring in the haul that shows up in the excellent daily specials.

Bodinnick. www.oldferryinn.co.uk. ✆ **01503/220312.** 12 units. Doubles from £75, includes breakfast. **Amenities:** Bar; restaurant; free Wi-Fi.

Fowey Hall Hotel ★★   You'll feel like a guest in a private home the moment you step into the vast entrance hall of this handsome late-Victorian house perched above Fowey. Fireplaces, antiques, and comfortable furnishings combine with a casual atmosphere that is especially welcoming to kids, who are catered to not just with special meals but have their own dining room, as well as play programs, a game room, a zip line, and the company of a friendly dog. All of the rooms are large and nicely equipped with plump sofas and deep bathtubs; those in the old house are said to have been the inspiration for Toad Hall in Kenneth Grahame's *The Wind in the Willows*. Other rooms are in a coach house in the rear, so they don't have the sweeping sea views that those in the front have. A lovely oak-paneled restaurant is geared to grown-ups once the kids have retired, and the spa has an indoor heated pool.

Hanson Dr., Fowey, Cornwall PL23 1ET. www.foweyhallhotel.co.uk. ℂ **01726/833866.** 36 units. Doubles £210–245, includes breakfast. **Amenities:** Restaurant; babysitting; spa with indoor pool; billiard room; free Wi-Fi.

The Galleon Inn ★ BRITISH   Views of the river come with every table in this 400-year-old warehouse and its quayside terrace, now one of the best spots in town for lunch, dinner, and sandwiches throughout the day. Pub standards like fish pie and sausage are washed down with local ales and accompanied by live music on Friday evenings.

12 Fore St. ℂ **01726/833014.** Mains £6–£14. Daily noon–2:30pm; Mon–Sat 6–9pm, Sun 6–8:30pm.

The Old Sail Loft ★★ SEAFOOD   A 16th-century smugglers' haunt turned cozy snug provides plenty of oak beams and maritime relics, for an atmospheric meal that is well worth the 20 mile trip east along the coast from Fowey. The kitchen delivers delicious Cornish seafood chowder as a starter, a good choice of fresh fish, and some Cornish lamb and beef choices as well.

Quay St. East Looe. www.theoldsailloftrestaurant.com. ℂ **01503/262131.** Mains £13–£20. Jan–Apr and Nov–Dec Mon and Wed–Sat noon–2pm and 6–9pm; Easter–Oct Mon–Sat noon–2pm and 6–9pm.

PENZANCE & THE PENWITH PENINSULA ★★★

Penzance is 56 miles SW of Fowey

Land's End in the West of England is the moody Penwith Peninsula, a forlorn landscape of moors and pastures where the sea is never far from sight and the sound of crashing waves is ever present. Gilbert and Sullivan fans will forever associate the largest settlement on the peninsula with pirates. Actually, Spanish pirates razed Penzance in the 16th century, troops of Oliver Cromwell repeated the assault during England's 17th-century Civil War, and German bombers struck again during World War II. As a consequence, Penzance does not have a lot to show from it long past, but it's a friendly place with a salty charm all its own and is a good jumping off point for exploring England's westernmost point.

Essentials

GETTING THERE   There are daily **trains** and **buses** to Penzance from London. The train takes around 5½ hours from Paddington Station.

National Express buses make the long trip in 8½–9 hours from Victoria Coach Station. The A30 runs through the heart of Cornwall down to Penzance, where an unclassified road leads into the town itself.

VISITOR INFORMATION Penzance Tourist Office, at Station Approach, Penzance (www.purelypenzance.co.uk; ✆ **01736/362207**), is open Easter to September, Monday to Friday 9am to 5pm, Saturday 10am to 4pm; rest of year Monday to Friday 9am to 5pm.

Exploring the Area

In Penzance, **Chapel Street** ★★ leads from Parade Street down to the harbor, passing some nice 17th and 18th houses on the way. The most exotic facade is that of the elaborately painted and ornamented Egyptian House, at 6-7 Chapel St. The most remarkable view in Penzance is from the quays at the bottom of the street, across the water to St Michael's Mount (see below). At water's edge on the Victorian-era seaside promenade is the **Jubilee Pool** ★★ (www.jubileepool.co.uk), a triangular-shaped, sea-girt "lido" from 1935. The storm-buffeted pool is undergoing restoration, but when it reopens, you can swim in waters that are a wee-bit warmer and much calmer than those in the adjacent sea and dry off in the sun amid Art Deco porticos on the deck.

To the south, Penzance runs into the fishing port of **Newlyn** ★★. England's second-largest fishing fleet bobs in the harbor and the catch is often mentioned on restaurant menus as a guarantee of freshness. No longer are the nets loaded with pilchards, mature sardines that were a mainstay of the Cornish economy from the Middle Ages until overfishing nearly brought the industry to a standstill in the early 20th century. One of the last of the Cornish sardine factories is the Pilchard Works on Fore Street, where workers still can pilchards by traditional methods. The seascapes and quality of light in Newlyn were a draw for Victorian-era artists who became known as the Newlyn School. You can see some of their works back in Penzance at the **Penlee House Gallery and Museum** ★ (www.penleehouse.org.uk; ✆ **01736/363625**), in a private residence from 1865 that is open May to September daily 10am to 5pm, and October to April daily 10am to 4:30pm; £5 adults, £3 seniors and children. A joint ticket for Penlee House and Tate St Ives (p. 276) and the Barbara Hepworth Museum (p. 276) is £15.

Light and sea still inspire contemporary Newlyn artists, who show their work at the **Newlyn Art Gallery** ★ (www.newlynartgallery.co.uk; ✆ **01736/363715**); the gallery has two venues, one at the end of the green in Newlyn, and the other at The Exchange on Princes Street in Penzance.

Mousehole ★★★ (pronounced *Mou*-zel), a few miles west, is just about the prettiest village in all of Cornwall. You can almost forgive the friendly occupants of the stone cottages for their odd culinary tastes,

Sunset at Land's End, the southwestern tip of England.

such as Stargazy Pie, a terrifying-looking doughy concoction in which fish heads poke through the crust to "gaze at the stars." A sign on a house commemorates, Dolly Pentreath, who died at the age of 102 in 1777 and is said to be the last known monoglot speaker of Cornish.

The coast road continues its loop around the peninsula another few miles south then west to **Porthcurno ★**, a quiet little place known around the world, at least in some circles, as the hub of a submarine cable system that laid the groundwork for global communication. Vast underground tunnels here housed equipment that once transmitted communications through 14 undersea cables to points around the world. At the worthy, not nearly as dull as it sounds **Porthcurno Telegraph Museum ★**, old equipment and photographs show how telegraphy systems work, tell the story of submarine cable laying ships, and go a long way toward putting cell phones and the Internet in historical context. The museum is open April to October daily 10am to 5pm and at other times on weekends 10am to 4pm; £9 adults, £8 seniors, £5 children 5 to 15, and £22 for families.

Land's End ★★★, about 4 miles west, is the southwestern tip of England, once a place of much sentimental significance for sailors and seagoing passengers. This last sighting of British soil was so sacred to those who would be at sea for years and months, and indeed might never return, that it's been said that Land's End is to Cornwall what Jerusalem is to the Holy Land. It really is quite moving to stand atop the cliff and look across waters that stretch in one unbroken swath to the New World.

Minack Theatre, near Penzance.

The shopping arcade and theme park that share space with the scenic and historic point could easily spoil the effect, though a good blast of sea air helps restore the mood of this otherwise beautiful spot.

Minack Theatre ★★ THEATRE   Pity the poor actors who have to perform in one of the world's most spectacularly sited theaters, because they have to work so hard not to be upstaged by the backdrop of waves crashing onto the surrounding coast. Actually, sweeping views of the sea from this open-air amphitheater cut out of the side of a headland have been a perfect backdrop for performances of Shakespeare's *A Midsummer Night's Dream,* Gilbert and Sullivan's *Pirates of Penzance,* and many other plays and musicals since 1931. These days up to 750 spectators sit on grass- or rock-covered ledges to enjoy plays, operas, and dance pieces by international companies. You can also visit the theater outside of performances, and take a walk through the adjoining gardens.

9 miles west of Penzance in Porthcurno. www.minack.com. ⓒ **01736/810181.** Day visits Apr–late Sept daily 9:30am–5pm; Oct daily 10am–4:30pm; Nov–late Mar daily 10am–3:30pm. Opening times vary on days of performances. £5 adults, £4 seniors, £3 children 12–15, free for children 11 and under. Performances late Apr–late Sept. Theatre tickets £9–£12 adults, £5–£6 children 15 and under.

St Michael's Mount ★★★ CASTLE   A sea-girt island castle connected to the coast by a 152m (500-ft) causeway has been a monastery, a fortress, and for the past 350 years the home of the St Aubyn family. A Benedictine monastery founded in the 12th century was a daughter house of Mont St Michel in Normandy, and it's impossible to look at St Michael's without thinking of that more famous landmark across the English Channel. After the Dissolution of the Monasteries under

St Michael's Mount, founded in the 1100s.

Henry VIII, the mount's natural defenses and strategic position were well suited as a fortress that kept pirates and other marauders at bay; the beacon atop the church tower at the heights of the mount was lit in 1588 to warn of the advancing Spanish Armada. Royalist forces holed up on the mount during the Civil War but were forced to surrender after a long siege when fresh water ran low and the terraced gardens, now planted with palms and other exotic species, couldn't keep them supplied with food. The islet has evolved into a quirky and grand residence, with a dining room fashioned out of the monk's refectory, a cozy library tucked into the thick walled 12th-century monastic quarters, and some grand rococo salons. If the tide is out, you can walk across the causeway from Marazion in a few minutes; high tide renders the causeway impassible and creates work for boatmen who will ferry you across. Wear sturdy shoes to navigate the steep, rough castle steps.

St Michael's Mount, Mount's Bay. www.stmichaelsmount.co.uk. © **01736/710507.** Castle only £9 adults, £4 children 5–15, £13–£21 for families; gardens £6 adults, £3 children 5–15, free children 4 and under; castle and gardens £12 adults, £6 children 5–15, £18–£22 families. Castle Sun–Fri 10:30am–5pm; Jul–Aug to 5:30pm. Gardens mid Apr–late Jun Mon–Fri 10:30am–5pm; July–Aug Thurs–Fri 10:30am–5:30pm; Sept Thurs–Fri 10:30am–5pm.

Trengwainton Garden ★ GARDEN   The son of a Jamaican sugar plantation owner planted exotic species in a walled garden that he laid out to match the dimensions of Noah's Ark. Sir Edward Bolitho (1882–1969) and his gardeners expanded the gardens with rare species grown from seeds collected in Asia. Many of the plants flourished for the first time outside their native habitats, and today provide a colorful and exotic display for much of the year. The name, pronounced treng-*wain*-ton, means "house of the springs" in Cornish.

West of Heamoor, off the Penzance–Morvah Rd. www.nationaltrust.org.uk. ✆ **01736/363148.** £7 adults, £4 children 11 and under, £12–£20 families. Mid-Feb to late Oct Sun–Thurs 10:30am–5pm.

Where to Eat & Stay

The Abbey ★★★   The best hotel in Penzance is an enchanting place, full of old-fashioned English comforts and overlooking the harbor and St Michael's Mount. A fire burns next to plush sofas in the drawing room, the paneled dining room invites lingering over a leisurely breakfast, and a shady walled garden is laced with cobbled walkways. Seven guest rooms compliment the character of the 17th-century house with bold colors and overstuffed furnishings that exude an air of elegant relaxation. The world's first supermodel, Jean Shrimpton, created the Abbey, and it's now managed by her son Thaddeus.

Abbey St., Penzance. theabbeyonline.co.uk. ✆ **07930/347911.** 7 units. Doubles from £100, includes breakfast. Closed Jan 9–29. **Amenities:** Garden; free Wi-Fi.

The Ship Inn ★ BRITISH   One of the best things about staying in these rooms above an old pub (with some in a cottage next door) means you don't have to leave pretty Mousehole. Just gazing out the window into what's been called England's most beautiful harbor can keep you contented for hours. Guest rooms are light and airy, furnished in contemporary style with blonde wood and soothing fabrics. Downstairs, sandwiches and light fare are served next to an open fires, making this a good spot for lunch or dinner while exploring the coast.

South Cliff, Mousehill. www.shipinnmousehole.co.uk. ✆ **01736/731234.** Doubles £75–£100, includes breakfast. **Amenities:** Pub; free Wi-Fi.

The Turk's Head ★★ SEAFOOD   A wee bit of hyperbole aside, this charming old smuggler's lair might just be the oldest pub in Cornwall. It's bona fide fact that pirates used the place to stash loot 750 years ago, carting contraband through a secret tunnel from the harbor into the courtyard. Whether or not Turks really invaded Penzance in the 13th century during the Crusades and camped on the spot is more dubious, but little matter where the name comes from. The low-ceilinged rooms offer excellent fresh fish and seafood, along with the pub's own beer.

Chapel St., Penzance. www.turksheadpenzance.co.uk. ✆ **01736/363093.** Mains £10–£24. Daily noon–2:30pm and 6–9:30pm.

ST IVES ★★

10 miles NE of Penzance

It's easy to see why 19th-century artists began coming to what was then a small fishing village of white-washed stone cottages on a sheltered port.

The seaside village of St Ives.

The incredible light, majestic scenery, and cerulean-colored sea remain just as alluring, and fame has not spoiled the easygoing charm of one of England's most attractive and pleasant seaside getaways.

Essentials

GETTING THERE   There are no direct **trains** to St Ives, so it's necessary to change at St Erth, on the main line from London Paddington Station, which is just a short—and very scenic—ride to St Ives. National Express **buses** (www.nationalexpress.com; ✆ **0871/781-8181**) make the long haul from London Victoria Coach Station in about 8 hours. During the summer, many streets in the center of town are closed to vehicles, so it's best to leave your car in the public parking lot just outside the town.

Exploring the Area

The old heart of St Ives is known as "Downalong." Narrow cobbled lanes that lead to the sea are lined with cottages of white-washed granite. West Pier and, to the east, Smeaton's Pier, frame a harbor full of fishing boats and pleasure craft. The scene is especially picturesque when the tide goes out and the old quays front a ribbon of golden sand. Rising above it all is the tower of the 15th-century **church of St Ives.** Legend has it that the name comes from St Ia, a 5th-century Irish Christian missionary who floated here to the western end of England on a leaf. The church's Lady Chapel is decorated with two works by the sculptor Dame Barbara Hepworth, one of Britain's most noted 20th-century artists. Her presence in St Ives, where she lived for 45 years, put the town on the map as a center of the modern art world. She carved a Madonna and Child in memory of her eldest son, Paul, who died in a plane crash over Thailand in 1953 while serving with the RAF. Hepworth also sculpted the stainless steel Christmas Rose candlesticks and presented them to the church in 1972. Penzance has two fine sandy beaches, **Porthmeor** on the northwest side of town, and a little beyond, **Porthminster.**

The Barbara Hepworth Museum & Sculpture Garden, St Ives.

Barbara Hepworth Museum & Sculpture Garden ★★

MUSEUM   Dame Barbara Hepworth settled in this studio/house with her then-husband, the painter Ben Nicholson, in 1949, and she remained until her death in a fire in 1975, at the age of 72. Her house became the epicenter of British avant-garde art as other artists came to St Ives to visit her, many of whom settled nearby as well. Hepworth stipulated in her will that her studio and living quarters remain just as they were, so they now provide an evocative glimpse into her life and work. A small exhibit highlights Hepworth's life and career and chronicles the evolution of St Ives into an artists' colony. Her elegant living quarters and studio are filled with her work and that of friends, as well as her tools, drawings, and photographs. Just outside is a sculpture garden of her work.

Barnoon Hill. www.tate.org.uk/stives/hepworth. ✆ **01736/796226.** £7 adults, free for children 18 and under; £10 adults combined ticket with Tate St Ives; £15 joint ticket for Tate St Ives, Barbara Hepworth Museum, and Penlee House Gallery and Museum in Penzance. Mar–Oct daily 10am–5:20pm. Nov–Feb Tues–Sun 10am–4:20pm, with garden closing at 4:20pm or dusk, whichever is earlier.

Tate St Ives ★★

MUSEUM   The St Ives branch of London's Tate Gallery has no permanent collection but houses changing exhibits of modern art selected from the National Collection of British Modern Art. The stark white galleries usually show the work of artists who are in some way connected with St Ives and Cornwall. Aside from a piece or two by Hepworth, you'll probably also see paintings by Ben Nicholson (1894–1982), Hepworth's onetime husband and another longtime resident of St Ives. The museum has produced a downloadable Ben Nicholson walking tour of St Ives that shows off his homes and other sights of interest, including scenes that inspired his work.

Porthmeor Beach. www.tate.org.uk/stives. ✆ **01736/796226.** £8 adults, free for children 18 and under; £10 adults combined ticket with Barbara Hepworth Museum; £15 joint ticket for Tate St Ives, Barbara Hepworth Museum, and Penlee House Gallery and Museum in Penzance. Mar–Oct daily 10am–5:20pm; Nov–Feb Tues–Sun 10am–4:20pm. Closes occasionally to hang exhibits.

AROUND ST IVES

Adding to the moody atmosphere of the Penwith Peninsula that surrounds Penzance are prehistoric granite slabs and early Christian stone crosses that rise out of the stark landscapes. You'll find an early tomb at Lanyon Quoit, 11 miles west of St Ives on the B3306, where a huge granite slab rests on three upright stones. Most impressive are the ruins at Chysauster.

Chysauster Ancient Village ★ RUINS   From around 100 B.C. to A.D. 300, members of the Dummoni tribe lived in this village, in eight oval houses, each with a courtyard surrounded by thatched rooms. Stone walls, grinding stones, and other remains of their lives litter the grassy hillside. The purpose of a fogou, or underground passage is not known; it could have been a hiding place, a ceremonial chamber, or a cold store.

10 miles east of St Ives off B 3311. www.english-heritage.org.uk. ✆ **0370/333-1181.** £4 adults, £2 children 5–15, £10. Daily 10am–5pm.

Where to Stay & Eat

Alba Restaurant ★★ SEAFOOD/MODERN BRITISH   You can dine well here on Cornish beef or some of the juiciest chicken you're ever likely to taste, but that somehow doesn't seem right in an old lifeboat shed right on the wharf. Besides, seafood doesn't get much better. A dinner of fish soup, seared scallops and platter of Cornish cheeses shows off the local bounty to great effect, all the better when enjoyed in the upstairs room with views of the bay and coastline.

Old Lifeboat House, The Wharf. www.thealbarestaurant.com. ✆ **01736/797222.** Mains £12–£19. Daily noon–2:30pm and 5:30–9:30pm.

Pedn-Olva Hotel ★★   These dramatically perched rooms hanging over the sea are so snug they're called cabins, making it even easier to forget you're on dry land on this rocky outcropping between the town and Porthminster Beach. Rattan furnishings and light fabrics don't interfere with the airy sea views, all the better from a few choice rooms with balconies and the large communal terraces. The Lookout Bar lives up to its name, and is especially romantic when the crackle of a fire accompanies the sound of waves crashing below. A swimming pool hangs over the beach below.

West Porthminster Beach. pednolva.co.uk. ✆ **01736/796222.** 30 units. Doubles from £150, includes breakfast. **Amenities:** Bar; restaurant; pool; free Wi-Fi.

Primrose Valley Hotel ★★   An Edwardian villa a few steps from Porthminster Beach is well poised for a morning swim. Most of the chic, modern rooms have sea views, some from balconies, and all combine soft Italian leather chairs, oak tables, and hand-crafted bedsteads. A breakfast of farm fresh eggs and other local products is served in a similarly stylish lounge, where come evening the leather sofas seem tailor-made for sinking back and tasting one of the local ales on offer.

Porthminster Beach. www.primroseonline.co.uk. ℓ **01736/794939.** 9 units. Doubles £75–£170, includes breakfast. **Amenities:** Bar; free Wi-Fi.

Seafood Café ★ SEAFOOD   This bright room with lots of tile and plain tables on bare wood floor has all the charm of a fish market, and that's the point. Fish in the display case has just come off the boats; make your choice and the kitchen will prepare it for you to order, served with a sauce and side dish. Beef and free-range chicken are also farm fresh.

45 Fore St. www.seafoodcafe.co.uk. ℓ **01736/794004.** Mains £8–£14. Daily noon–3pm and 6–10pm.

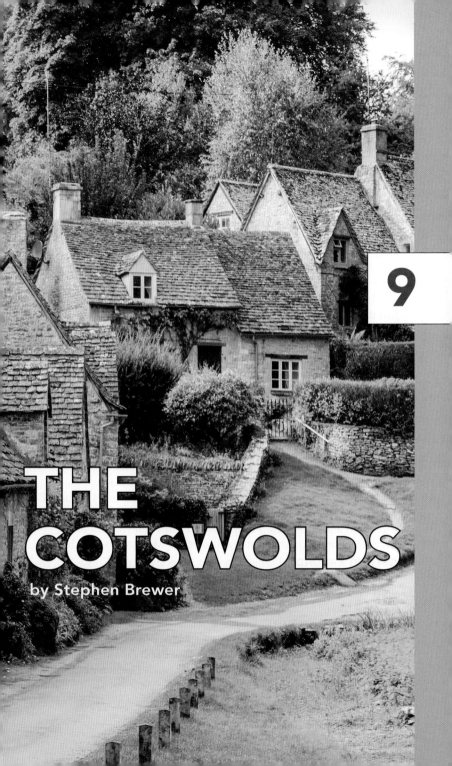

9

THE COTSWOLDS
by Stephen Brewer

These rolling limestone hills, steep escarpments, and meandering streams might just be the prettiest stretch of England. Medieval wool traders accented the scenery with beautiful villages of golden limestone, and beginning in the 19th century, appreciative artists and other aesthetically minded spirits put on another layer of veneer when they restored fine old manor houses and planted colorful gardens.

Most of the Cotswolds is farmland and protected as an Area of Outstanding Natural Beauty, keeping a lot of 21st-century encroachments at bay. Maybe the best thing the region offers is a chance to slow down a bit—settle onto the banks of a gurgling stream, enjoy a pint in front of a cracking pub hearth, pick through fresh produce at a country market, or just drift off to sleep in a four-poster bed in a creaky, centuries-old inn. It says a lot about the pace of life in the Cotswolds that this is prime walking country, and the region's rambling paths are among England's most popular hiking routes.

Essentials

GETTING THERE **Train** service from London's Paddington Station on the First Great Western line runs to the Cotswolds' town of Moreton-in-Marsh, a trip of 1½ hours. National Express **buses** from London's Victoria Coach Station serve several Cotswolds towns and villages, including Bourton-on-the-Water, Moreton-in-Marsh, and Stow-on-the-Wold. The trip takes 3 to 4 hours and there is no service on Sundays.

If you're **driving** from Oxford, take the A40 west to A424, near Burford. The A424 heads north to Stow-on-the-Wold and on to Chipping Campden and Broadway. From Stow-on-the-Wold you can follow A429 south to Bourton-on-the-Water and north to Moreton-in-Marsh.

GETTING AROUND Public transport is spotty in the Cotswolds, making it tricky to get around without a car. A few towns have decent **bus** links. Moreton-in-Marsh is a bit of a hub, with four-times-a-day service Monday through Saturday on the 21 route, operated by Johnson's Excelbus (© **01564/797070**), to and from Broadway, Chipping Campden, and other towns and villages. Buses on Pulhams Coaches (© **01451/820369**) 801 route provides hourly service between Moreton-in-Marsh and Stow-on-the-Wold, Lower Slaughter, and Bourton-on-the-Water. Distances are short so travel times are fairly quick, even with frequent

PREVIOUS PAGE: **Arlington Row, Bibury, one of England's most-photographed locales.**

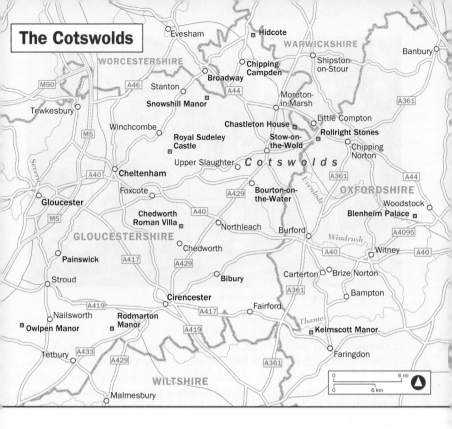

The Cotswolds

Evesham
Hidcote
WARWICKSHIRE
Banbury

WORCESTERSHIRE
Chipping Campden
Shipston-on-Stour

M50
A46
Stanton
Broadway
A44

Snowshill Manor
Moreton-in-Marsh
A361

Tewkesbury
Winchcombe
Chastleton House
Little Compton

M5
Royal Sudeley Castle
Stow-on-the-Wold
Rollright Stones

Upper Slaughter
Cotswolds
Chipping Norton

Cheltenham
A40
A361
A44

Foxcote
A429
Bourton-on-the-Water
OXFORDSHIRE

Gloucester
Woodstock

M5
Chedworth Roman Villa
A40
Northleach
Burford
Blenheim Palace

GLOUCESTERSHIRE
Chedworth
Windrush
A40
Witney
A40
A4095

Painswick
A417
A429
Carterton
Brize Norton

Stroud
Bibury
A361
Bampton

Cirencester
Fairford

A419
Nailsworth
Rodmarton Manor
A417
A419
Thames
Kelmscott Manor

Owlpen Manor
Tetbury
A433
A429
A419
A361
Faringdon

WILTSHIRE
Malmesbury

0 6 mi
0 6 km

stops: It's about 25 minutes from Moreton-in-Marsh to Broadway and 15 minutes from Moreton-in-Marsh to Stow-on-the-Wold. Service on all bus lines is severely curtailed on Sunday. For schedules, go to www.traveline.info; another good source for info on bus travel in the Cotswolds is www.escapetothecotswolds.org.uk. You can also get from town to town by **taxi** operated by companies such as **Cotswold Horizons** (*©* **01386/858599**) or **The Shire** (www.theshireprivatehire.com; *©* **0797/4813278**); expect to pay about £20 from Moreton-in-Marsh to Stow-on-the-Wold or Chipping Campden.

VISITOR INFORMATION Many towns have their own tourist offices, well stocked with maps and info about local attractions. They can be especially helpful in steering you to good walks in an area, and many also provide accommodation booking or can at least give you a list of hotels and B&Bs. While offices are geared to local interests, most also have some information for the entire region. For some advance planning, you might want to pay a visit to cotswolds.com and www.cotswold.gov.uk/visitors.

ORGANIZED TOURS Large tour companies operating out of London, Bath, and Oxford (see p. 114 for major firms) often offer a brief foray into

Burford, once a wealthy wool-producing center.

the Cotswolds. A walking or cycling tour provides a more in-depth and authentic look at the region. **Cotswold Walking Holidays** (www.cots woldwalks.com; ℂ **01386/833799**) offers 3- to 11-night tours, either guided or self-guided; rates include B&B accommodation and luggage transport from inn to inn and start at £215 per person. **Cotswold Country Cycles** (www.cotswoldcountrycycles.com; ℂ **01386/438706**) provides bikes, lodging, itineraries, and support for self-guided riding tours of 3 to 5 days that start at £225 per person.

BURFORD ★★

74 miles NW of London; 20 miles NW of Oxford

If you're approaching the region from Oxford or London, you'll officially cross into the Cotswolds via this unspoiled medieval town of golden stone. Burford was one of the first great wool centers, receiving a charter to trade in wool more than 900 years ago, and the industry bleated out its last breath during Queen Victoria's reign. The humble-looking, 12th-century **Tolsey** on High Street at one time made the town rich, for it was here that wool merchants paid their taxes. Strolling along the banks of the River Windrush as it passes beneath a stone bridge into the water meadows is a delightfully fitting introduction to the Cotswolds.

VISITOR INFORMATION The **Burford Tourist Information Centre** is at 33a High St. (www.oxfordshirecotswolds.org; ℂ **01993/823558**). It's open Monday to Saturday 9:30am to 5pm and Sunday 10am to 4pm.

Exploring the Area

In your wanderings around Burford keep an eye out for Sir Lawrence Tanfield (1551–1625) and his wife Elizabeth. Actually, don't: The unpopular lord and lady of an estate at Buckland Priory were often burned in effigy while they were alive and are said to take their revenge by flying around town in a burning coach; anyone who observes the spectacle will die on the spot. Other noted area residents include the fabled Mitford sisters, who grew up in a large house in nearby **Swinbrook,** a pretty village about a mile east of Burford. In the village churchyard are the simple graves of Nancy Mitford (1904–73), bestselling author of *Love in a Cold Climate* and other novels; Diana (1910–2003), an infamous fascist who was imprisoned with her husband, Oswald Mosley, for their political beliefs during World War II; and Unity (1914–48), a fascist supporter of Hitler who shot herself when England entered the war against Germany. Perhaps the best-known today are sisters Deborah, the late duchess of Devonshire (1920–2014), and Jessica (1917–96), who emigrated to America and became known for the *American Way of Death* and other exposes.

Church of St John the Baptist ★ CHURCH   Burford's magnificent church dates from 1175 and is almost cathedral-like in size, befitting the town's enormous wool-trade wealth. A close inspection of the church and surrounds suggest that the town of quaint lanes

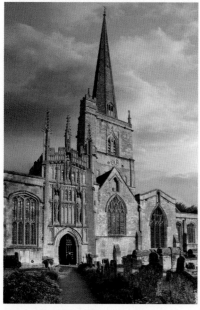

has not always been the gentle place it appears to be. A stone in the churchyard commemorates Athelhum, a giant who served King Aethelbald of Mercia and was slaughtered by Cuthred, King of the Wet Saxons, near the banks of the Windrush in 752. During the Civil War, in 1642, Oliver Cromwell's troops rounded up royalists known as the Burford Levellers and imprisoned them in the church, where they scratched their names and other graffiti into the stones. They were eventually led to the church roof and made to watch as their officers were executed in the yard below. Church Green. www.burfordchurch. org. © **01993/823788.** Free. Daily 9am–5pm.

Church of St John the Baptist, Burford.

Cotswold Wildlife Park ★ ZOO   As incongruous as it might be to see giraffes and rhinos roaming across the Cotswolds landscape against a backdrop of a stone Victorian manor house, these 65 hectares (160 acres) are hugely popular, especially with young visitors. A narrow-gauge railway chugs around the grounds from April to October, adding to the appeal. While it's hard to shake off the sense that the place is really just a big circus, the park's conservation programs are commendable.

A361, south of Burford. www.cotswoldwildlifepark.co.uk. ℂ **01993/823006.** £15 adults, £10 seniors and children 3–16. Apr–Oct daily 10am–4:30pm; Nov–Mar daily 10am–5pm, or dusk (last entry 1 hr. before closing).

Where to Eat & Stay

The Highway Inn ★★★   This 1480 inn has winding corridors and all sorts of enticing nooks and crannies, but there's a lot more here than well-worn flagstones and old world atmosphere. The bay windows with quilted cushions in the fire-warmed lounges and traditionally furnished guest rooms are relaxed, genuinely welcoming, and nicely equipped with beams and sloping old polished floors. Meals served in the tastefully cluttered bar and a medieval courtyard lean toward classic pub grub, with an upscale twist seen in venison pie and sausage and mash made with local produce.

117 High St., Burford. www.thehighwayinn.co.uk. ℂ **01993/823661.** 10 units. Doubles £85–£, includes breakfast. **Amenities:** Restaurant; bar; free Wi-Fi.

Lamb Inn ★   A perfect way to cap off a spin around Burford is a pub lunch in the stone-floored bar room of this old inn, in a 1420 weaver's cottage. Blazing hearths are warming on a chilly day, as are hearty servings of fish and chips, steaks, and huge sandwiches. A thoughtful selection of ales on tap accompanies the meals. The Inn also has a more formal dining room, candlelit at night, and 17 cozy bedrooms.

Sheep St. www.cotswold-inns-hotels.co.uk. ℂ **01993/823155.** Mains £10–£25. Daily noon–9:30pm.

BIBURY ★★

10 miles SW of Burford

Victorian poet, artist, and founder of the Arts and Crafts movement William Morris (1834–96) ordained this little assemblage of cottages on the banks of the tiny River Coln as England's most beautiful village. Morris, in fact, settled into a manor house nearby and regularly brought his many visitors over to admire **Arlington Row.** The row of pitch-roofed cottages was built alongside a gurgling stream in 1380 as a monastic wool store and converted into weavers' quarters and almshouses in the 17th century—it might just be one of the most photographed scenes in England. Henry Ford tried to buy the entire lot and ship it stone by stone, shingle by shingle back to Detroit. Residents have become inured to photographers, but aren't keen on you peering through the latticed windows into their living rooms. The 17th-century mill stands just across the water meadows.

Exploring the Area

Chedworth Roman Villa ★★ ANCIENT SITE   Romans were well established in the Cotswolds as early as the 1st century, and the roads they built to transport military supplies still run through the region. Even back then sheep rearing brought considerable wealth to the Roman settlers, as it would to medieval traders, and this large villa is at the center of what appears to have been an immensely prosperous Roman farm near the banks of the River Coln. The ruins came to light in 1864 when a gamekeeper found some fragments of flooring and pottery while trying to rout out a ferret. Excavations have unearthed elaborate mosaics, bath houses, parts of hypocausts (underground heating ducts), and latrines, suggesting that what might have begun as a simple farm dwelling in the 2nd century expanded over the next three centuries into a lavish residence. Many of the artifacts were carted off during Victorian-era excavations, but walkways provide close-up views of the elaborate mosaics, and many of the finds, including a charming carving of a hunter with his hound, are in the adjacent museum.

8 miles north of Bibury on A429. www.chedworthromanvilla.com or www.national trust.org.uk/chedworth-roman-villa. ℂ **01993/823006.** £9 adults, £5 children 8–16, £23 families. Daily 10am–5pm.

Kelmscott Manor ★★ HISTORIC HOME   Arts and Crafts Movement founder and grand old man of the cause William Morris came upon this handsome manor, built around 1600, while exploring the countryside, and admired the way it seemed to have "grown up out of the soil." He and Pre-Raphaelite painter Dante Gabriel Rossetti leased the house in 1871, but Rossetti did not take to country living and soon relinquished his share—but not before using the house as the romantic background for "Water Willow." Morris remained for the rest of his life. The house figures prominently in his socialist novel, *News from Nowhere,* and he was inspired by the manor's old ambiance, "the loveliest haunt of ancient peace," to fill the rooms with handcrafted furniture, textiles, and metalwork. Morris is buried in the grounds of nearby St George's Church. Access to the house is by timed ticket (last entry 4:30pm).

11 miles southeast of Bibury in Kelmscott, Lechlade (off the A417). www.kelmscott manor.org.uk. ℂ **01993/823006.** £9 adults, £5 students and children 8–16, £26 families. Apr–Oct Wed and Sat 11am–5pm.

St Mary's Parish Church ★ CHURCH   Everything about Bibury's pretty church is a bit extraordinary, including its extreme age, one of the oldest in the Cotswolds. A church has stood here since the 8th century, and what remains today, including pointed arches, carved stones, and buttresses, is mostly Saxon and Norman, with some beautiful 13th-century stained glass for good measure. The churchyard is also unique in being partly devoted to the former residents of another town: So-called Bisley Piece belongs to a village about 15 miles away that fell out of favor with the Pope on two occasions—once when the priest suspiciously fell into a well and drowned and again when a lethal brawl broke out in the churchyard. As a consequence, residents could not bury their dead in their own jurisdiction and were forced to bring them here to Bibury.

Cemetery Rd. Free. Usually open daily 9am–5pm.

Where to Eat & Stay

Swan Hotel ★★   Top choice for most idyllic Cotswolds setting might go to this vine-covered 17th-century coaching inn (with 14th-century origins) right on the banks of the River Coln. Riverside walks lead to impossibly picturesque Arlington Row, though the homey lounges are pleasant places to stay put with a book. Decor in the large, bright bedrooms steers away from predictable coziness with bold fabrics and dramatically dark walls, while the sound of the rushing river is a soothing tonic. The airy Brasserie is a pleasant change from the region's tradition-heavy dining rooms, with rattan furnishings set on tile floors and hearty two-course lunch and dinner menus as well as some a la carte choices in the evening.

Village center. www.cotswold-inns-hotels.co.uk. ✆ **01285/740695.** Doubles £160–£280, includes breakfast. **Amenities:** Restaurant; bar; free Wi-Fi.

The Swan Hotel, Bibury.

Arts & Crafts in the Cotswolds

Practitioners of the mid-19th century Arts and Crafts Movement thought they had found the promised land in the Cotswolds, where you'll find their work in any number of museums. The natural beauty, farm life, centuries-old stone masonry, and a tradition of craftsmanship were a perfect fit with their exaltation of hand-crafted work and return to an old-fashioned ways of working with materials. Textile designer and architect William Morris and the painters Edward Burne-Jones and Dante Gabriel Rossetti were among the most influential proponents of the movement, and by the 1870s they had found their way to the Cotswolds (see Kelmscott Manor, p. 285, and Broadway Tower, p. 297). Morris remained linked to the Cotswolds for the rest of his life, as he became internationally known for his wallpaper, textiles, furniture and stained glass. In 1902 Charles Robert Ashbee joined the established Cotswolds Arts and Crafts tradition when he opened his Guild of Handicraft in Chipping Campden (p. 301). He captured the philosophy of the movement when he said the workshops "seek not only to set a higher standard of craftsmanship, but at the same time, and in so doing, to protect the status of the craftsman."

PAINSWICK ★

23 miles W of Bibury

This top contender with Bibury for the title of "most beautiful town in the Cotswolds" is a cluster of mellow gray stone houses and inns dating from as early as the 14th century. The ironically named **New Street,** the so-called Queen of the Cotswolds, dates from 1450 and is lined with 15th-century limestone mansions.

St Mary's Church, built between 1377 and 1399, is steeped in legend. It's said that 99 massive yew trees, some 300 years old, grow in the churchyard, though well-meaning gardeners have never been able to grow the 100th, nipped in the bud by the devil himself. The church is free, and open April to September daily 9:30am to 6pm and October through March daily 9:30am to 4pm. The Sunday nearest September 19th is a bit quieter in Painswick than it once was—villagers still dance in a "clypping" circle around the church, though the ritual no longer ends in a drunken debauch. The china figurines of puppies standing atop pies you see in shop windows are not the cute mementoes you might mistake them for; they represent the "puppy dog pies" village bakers once prepared for medieval revelers.

VISITOR INFORMATION The **Painswick Tourist Information Centre** (www.painswicktouristinfo.co.uk; ✆ **07503/516924**) is staffed by volunteers who take enormous pride in introducing their village to visitors. One of the perks of working here is the address: Grave Digger's Hut, St Mary's Churchyard. They're around Monday and Wednesday through Friday from 10am to 4pm and Tuesday and Saturday from 10am to 1pm.

St Mary's Church, Painswick.

Exploring the Area

Owlpen Manor ★★ HISTORIC HOME   One of the most romantic houses in England lies in a secluded valley shaded by magnificent yew trees. The stone manor was built around 1200, rebuilt during the 16th century, and restored in the 1930s by Arts and Crafts architect Norman Jewson (1884–1975). Jewson brought the ruin, a so-called "Sleeping Beauty," back to its Tudor glory, preserving the paneled hall and elegant parlors where Queen Margaret of Anjou spent her last happy night in 1471, before her husband, King Henry VI (1421–71) and son, Prince Edward (1453–71) were murdered by the troops of Edward IV and she was exiled to France. She's still around, it's said, roaming the upper floors through passageways hung with rich tapestries and oil paintings.

Near Uley, 12 miles south of Painswick. www.owlpen.com. ✆ **01453/860261.** Open for group tours; call or write in advance to arrange visit. £26 guided tour with cream tea, £36 with 2-course lunch. Hours vary.

Painswick Rococo Garden ★ PARK/GARDEN   Around 1740 country gentleman Benjamin Hyatt designed the gardens of his mansion in the flamboyant rococo style that was then popular. His pleasure garden, with a statue of Pan and a pavilion devoted to Venus, did not go over well with locals, who claimed that the "squire riots here in vulgar love with a couple of orange wenches from the local-playhouse." Today the garden seems wholesome enough, enjoying lovely views of the countryside.

B4073, ½ mile north of Painswick. www.rococogarden.co.uk. ✆ **01452/813204.** £7 adults, £6 seniors, £3 children 5–16, and £18 families. Mid-Jan to Oct daily 11am–5pm.

Rodmarten Manor ★★ HISTORIC HOME   What Arts and Crafts architect Norman Jewson called the "last house of its size to be built in the old leisurely way" was completed in 1929 for stock broker Claude Biddulph and his wife, Margaret. The Biddulph's envisioned the house as a project to revive local craftsmanship, and their builders used local stone and wood felled on the estate. Many of the furnishings, from pottery to wall hangings and wrought-iron fittings, were crafted locally, as was much of the iron and lead work. The eight acres of gardens are a work of art as well, divided by walls and hedges into individual rooms.

Off the A433, in Rodmartonm 13 miles south of Painswick. www.rodmarton-manor. co.uk. ℓ **01285/841442.** £8 adults, £4 children 5–15. May–Sept Wed and Sat 2pm–5pm.

Where to Eat & Stay

Royal Oak ★   This atmospheric old inn with stone walls and ancient hearths is a good stop for simple pub food of the gammon-and-eggs, fish-and-chips variety. The standouts are the real ales from nearby Stroud Brewery, nicely savored in the sunny garden in good weather.

St Mary's St. www.theroyaloakpainswick.co.uk. ℓ **01452/813129.** Mains £8–£15. Mon–Sat 11am–3pm and 5:45–11pm, Sun noon–3pm and 6:45–11pm.

Wild Garlic Restaurant ★★   For a refreshingly innovative meal, it's well worth the 8-mile drive south from Painswick to the little village of Nailsworth, where this light and contemporary space is nicely blended into a centuries old, bow-windowed house. Everything is made on the premises, including the delicious bread and pasta. The chef's imaginative creations show up on a tapas menu and a short list of daily changing dishes that can be enjoyed on a tasting menu, a vegetarian tasting menu, or a la carte. Three comfortable and smartly decorated rooms are upstairs.

3 Cossack Sq., Nailsworth. www.wild-garlic.co.uk. ℓ **01453/832615.** Mains £16–£28; tasting menus £55. Wed–Sat noon–2:30pm and 6:30–9:30pm, Sun noon–2:30pm.

BOURTON-ON-THE-WATER ★

23 miles NE of Painswick

The River Windrush gurgles a course between green banks through this ridiculously pretty village, darting beneath five low bridges. The dreamy collection of 15th- and 16th-century stone cottages, willow trees, and lush riverside lawns can seem almost too bucolic to be true, but sorry to say, the gimmicky commercialism of the most touristic village in the Cotswolds will soon jolt you back to reality. A surefire antidote is a walk along a pastoral footpath into the quieter realms of the inaptly named Slaughters.

VISITOR INFORMATION   The **Bourton-on-the-Water Tourist Information Centre** (www.bourtoninfo.com; ℓ **01451/820211**) is a private

The River Windrush at Bourton-on-the-Water.

enterprise that dispenses information but is also after a share of your tourist dollar. The helpful staff sells everything from guidebooks to National Express bus tickets, as well as honey and other local products. They can also book accommodations. The center is open daily from 10am to 6pm.

Exploring the Area

Burton is home to some mildly interesting collections that will probably only appeal if an overload of pastoral scenery has become a bore. The quirkiest is the **Model Village at the Old New Inn,** High Street (www. theoldnewinn.co.uk/village.htm; ✆ **01451/820467**), a scale model (1:9) of Bourton-on-the-Water completed in 1937. Wandering through the somewhat time-tattered reconstruction might bring on an existential moment: Why did you just shell out the admission fee (£4 adults, £3 for seniors and children 4–13) to see a model of the real village just outside the gate? Though some gorgeous feathered creatures inhabit **Birdland** (www.birdland.co.uk; ✆ **01451/820480**), the storks, flamingoes, toucans, and other tropical species seem terribly out of place in parkland on the banks of the River Windrush; the stars among the 500 residents are the penguins. Admission is £9 adults, £8 seniors, £6 children, £28 families. It's open April through October daily 10am to 6pm; November through March daily 10am to 4pm (last admission 1 hr. before closing).

Cotswold Motoring Museum & Toy Collection ★★ MUSEUM
If motoring along the back roads of the Cotswolds has a romantic appeal, a pit stop at this wonderfully eclectic tribute to motorized travel is

The Cotswold Motoring Museum & Toy Collection, Bourton-on-the-Water.

mandatory. A true car buff might find the Jaguars, Austin Swallows, London taxi, and other vintage cars to be admirable but not terrifically extraordinary, but there's something amid the bric-a-brac to catch just about anyone's eye. Kids might not fully appreciate some of the vintage pedal cars and models of double-decker buses, but nostalgic adults certainly will.

Sherborne St. www.cotswoldmotoringmuseum.co.uk. ✆ **01451/821255.** £5 adults, £4 children 4–16, £13 families. Mid-Feb to mid-Dec daily 10am–6pm.

Where to Eat & Stay

Aside from the Lords of the Manor, where you will feel like one, overrun Burton-on-the-Water is not a terribly salubrious place to stay. You're better off heading to Stow-in-the-Wold or a less crowded village nearby.

Lords of the Manor Hotel ★★★   One of the Cotswolds' most luxurious retreats is far too posh for its small-village setting, but then again, the 17th-century manor house set amid rolling meadows has always been the fanciest for miles around. These days the huge guest rooms in the main house and surrounding barns are done up in chic style that almost goes over the top, with plush headboards, rich fabrics, and fancy wall coverings, all with high windows and fine moldings. Side-by-side freestanding tubs and private gardens with hot tubs scream romantic getaway, and the aura is enhanced in intimate lounges and the dining room glittering with crystal.

Upper Slaughter, 3 miles outside Bourton-on-the-Water. www.lordsofthemanor.com. ✆ **01451/820243.** 27 units. Doubles £249–£545, includes breakfast and a bottle of champagne. **Amenities:** Restaurant; bar; free Wi-Fi.

Shopping

Shopping is a popular pastime in Bourton-on-the-Water, with some high-quality goods on offer. **Cotswold Perfumery** on Victoria Street (www.cotswold-perfumery.co.uk; ✆ 01451/820698) is one of the few perfumeries in Europe that still make and sell their products on-site, and you can see the production on the 45-minute factory tour, which must be prebooked and costs £5 adults and £4 children 4 to 16. The delightful **Cotswold Pottery** on Clapton Row (www.cotswoldpottery. co.uk; ✆ 01451/820173) is the home and studio of ceramic artists John and Jude Jelfs. Their exceptional mugs, teapots, ornamental pots, and sculpture are on sale. The **Bourton Model Railway Exhibition & Toy Shop,** High Street (www.bourtonmodelrailway.co.uk; ✆ 01451/ 820686) carries a collection of die-cast vehicles, model trains and equipment, and has an enchanting exhibit in which 40 trains chug through elaborate landscapes and model cities. Admission to the latter is £3 adults, £2 seniors and children 5 to 15, £9 for families; it's open June to August daily 11am to 5pm, and September to May Saturday and Sunday 11am to 5pm.

A Side Trip to Upper & Lower Slaughter ★★

When the crowds in Bourton-on-the-Water get to be too much, get out of town—to Upper and Lower Slaughter. Don't be put off by the name: "Slaughter" is actually a corruption of an Old English word for "slothre" (for muddy place), a reference to the wetlands surrounding the villages. Houses in both villages are constructed of the usual russet-colored Cotswold stone, and they are enhanced with the cheerful little River Eye meandering right through their centers. Lower Slaughter's sturdy 19th-century **Old Mill** (www.oldmill-lowerslaughter.com; ✆ 01451/820052), rising above water meadows filled with fowl and meadows where sheep graze, once ground out flour and these days dispenses ice cream and tea. Entrance to the mill costs £3 for adults, and £1 for children 5 to 15; it's open

The Old Mill at Lower Slaughter, on the River Eye.

On Foot & Two Wheels

The **Cotswold Way** (www.nationaltrail.co.uk/cotswold) meanders for just over 100 miles from Chipping Campden (p. 301) in the north toward Bath (p. 240) in the south, taking in the best of the region's landscapes and traditional villages. This rustic **hiking** trail is one of the most popular in England, for good reason—the route not only winds through lush countryside but also past pubs and inns along the way, making it possible to enjoy a walk with a minimum of deprivation. You'll find an excellent list of walks on the Cotswolds Way and throughout the region at www.escapetothecotswolds.org.uk/walking; the site also lists free guided walks with the Cotswolds Voluntary Wardens organization. The narrow roads of the Cotswolds are well suited to **cycling.** Among many bike-and-gear rental shops is **Hartwells Cycle-Hire** (www.hartwells.supanet.com; ℰ **01451/820405**), located in Bourton on the Water. Rental rates are £14 a day, £10 half day.

March to October daily 10am to 6pm and November to February daily 10am until dark. Pretty as the little collection of stone and timber cottages in Upper Slaughter is, the scene is a bit of a contrivance—Sir Edward Lutyens (1869–1944), master of English country-house design, reconstructed them into their picture-perfectness.

You can drive the 2 miles to Lower Slaughter from Bourton-on-the-Water by heading west along Lansdowne Road then turning right onto the A436; after a short distance, you'll see a signpost pointing left into Lower Slaughter. To drive, though, means missing out on an easy yet inspiring walk. From Bourton-on-the-Water follow the dead-straight Fosse Way, route of an ancient Roman road; much of it covered with tarmac but closed to cars (**Note:** You're legally required to close each of the several gates that stretch across the footpath). From Lower Slaughter continue 1 mile to Upper Slaughter, passing sheep grazing in meadows, elegantly weathered houses crafted from local stone, stately trees arching over ancient millponds, and footbridges that have endured centuries of pedestrian traffic. If you're feeling energetic, you can follow a path from Lower Slaughter up to Stow-on-the-Wold, about 3 miles.

STOW-ON-THE-WOLD ★

4 miles NE of Bourton-on-the-Water

Straggling along the top of a 240-m (800-ft.) escarpment, this old wool town lies smack in the middle of the Fosse Way (A429), one of the Roman trunk roads that cut a swath through Britain. This location made Stowe one of the most important market towns of medieval England, famous for its sheep fairs. The animals were herded along narrow alleyways, known as "tures," into the market square, where as many as 20,000 sheep would change hands in a day. The scene is evoked during the spring and fall horse fairs, a colorful event that draws Romani people (or "Travelers") from all over the U.K. and Ireland. For the most part, though, Stow is a relatively quiet place, at most times spared the tourist crush. It's a pleasure to wander down the tures into the proud old square, where the 15th century Market Cross stands near the stocks where offenders were once pelted with eggs.

Exploring the Area

Chastleton House ★★ HISTORIC SITE   A prosperous Welsh wool merchant built this country house between 1607 and 1612 as a show-place to display his enormous wealth, and his descendants remained in residence for almost 500 years, until 1991. As the centuries passed the owners found themselves with diminishing funds to modernize or make extensive repairs, so there's a delightful unspoiled, time-warp flavor to the place. While the barrel-vaulted Long Gallery and paneled Great Hall are impressively grand, much of the house suggests centuries of homely domesticity—the kitchen ceiling is blackened by soot—and touring the old rooms is like stepping back into the 17th century. The extensive gardens include England's first ever croquet lawn.

Chastleton, 5 miles east of Stow-on-the-Wold via the A436. www.nationaltrust.org. uk/chastleton-house. © **01494/755560.** £10 adults, £5 children 5–15, £20 families. Apr–Sept Wed–Sat 1–5pm; Mar and Oct Wed–Sat 1–4pm. Access by timed ticket (180 each day). Last admission 1 hr. before closing.

Rollright Stones ★ HISTORIC SITE   This 4,000-year-old circle of 77 limestone blocks known as the King's Men is said to have been erected, like many similar prehistoric stone circles, for religious or cere-monial purposes. The much-weathered complex, also includes the King Stone and the Whispering Knights, four standing stones said to be part of a tomb. In-the-know locals will fill you in on the real story; that all the petrified remains of ancient residents come alive at midnight to dance and drink from a nearby spring. Anyone who comes upon the bacchanal dies or goes mad, hence the absence of eye-witness accounts.

Little Rollright, 8 miles northeast of Stow-on-the-Wold. www.rollrightstones.co.uk. No phone. £1 adults, 50p children 7–16. Daily sunrise to sunset.

Sudeley Castle & Gardens ★★ CASTLE   Most English castles are impressive and storied, but this sprawling 15th-century mansion, one of England's finest stately homes, is especially so. Sudeley has it all—lengthy royal connections, beautiful formal gardens, wealthy Victorian restorers, an American-born baroness in residence, plus a ruined abbey. The castle's most infamous moment occurred during a visit of Henry VIII and his bride Anne Boleyn to Sudeley in 1535, when Henry and his crafty minister Thomas Cromwell put into motion the Dissolution of the Monasteries—which explains why adjoining Winchcombe Abbey now lies in ruins. Henry's sixth wife and widow, Catherine Parr, lived at

Sudeley Castle & Gardens, near Stow-on-the-Wold.

Sudeley at the time of her death in 1548 and her marble tomb is in St Mary's chapel on the grounds. Gape at furnishings, tapestries, and paintings by Van Dyck and Turner that fill the paneled library, stone drawing room, elegant sewing room, state chambers, and other nooks and crannies. Elizabeth, Lady Ashcombe and her children and grandchildren (heirs of the 19th-century glove manufacturers who restored Sudeley) occupy parts of the castle; you may encounter a family member on a tour. Winchcombe, 12 miles west of Stow-on-the-Wold. www.sudeleycastle.co.uk. ℂ **01242/602308.** £15 adults, £14 seniors, £6 children 5–15, £38 families. Apr–Oct daily 10:30am–5pm (last admission 4:30pm).

Where to Eat & Stay

The Feathered Nest Country Inn ★★★   This relaxed and attractive country inn overlooks the Evenlode Valley from the edge of Nether Westcote, a tiny village near Stow-on-Wold. It won't be long after you set your bags down that you realize what a good value this beautifully redone mill is compared to many of its luxurious neighbors. The four nicely decorated guest rooms blend country comfort with amenities like fancy coffee machines and a stash of good reading matter. Downstairs, the woodsy bar and the heated terrace encourage lingering for many lazy hours, alongside villagers who stop in for a pint. Meals in the casual-yet-elegant dining room are as beautifully done as everything else here.
Nether Westcote. www.thefeatherednestinn.co.uk. ℂ **01993/833030.** 4 units. Doubles £180–£230, includes breakfast. **Amenities:** Restaurant; bar; free Wi-Fi.

The Old Butchers ★★   It's popular in Britain these days to talk about how blissfully rural towns like Stow have sold their souls to upscale tourism, but the down-to-earth fare served in a white-walled former butcher's shop might set the record straight. The new incarnation does the premises justice with steaks, chops, chunky game terrines, rich salamis, and some organ meats you've probably never encountered. The cholesterol is tempered with freshly caught fish and a few other seafood choices.

Park St. www.theoldbutchers.com. ℃ **01451/83100.** Mains £16–£26. Mon–Fri 6:30–9:30pm, Sat 6:30–10pm, Sun 6:30–9pm.

The Porch House ★★★ With timbers dating to the year 947, it would be easy for England's oldest inn to take a breather and rest on its laurels. But the creaky old place keeps getting better, with soothing guest rooms that blend old stone walls with vintage 1930s decor (like desks fashioned from sewing machine stands) and modern touches, such as freestanding bathtubs and large showers. The low-ceilinged pub rooms double as local gathering spots and serve delicious casual fare—though it's worth saving room for a steak dinner in the handsome dining room.

Digbeth St. www.porch-house.co.uk. ℃ **01451/87004.** 13 units. Doubles from £89–£159, includes breakfast. **Amenities:** Restaurant; bar; lounge; free Wi-Fi.

Shopping

While sheep were once big business in Stow, these days it's antiques. More than 60 dealers operate in the village and its environs, making Stow one of England's great antiques centers. **Antony Preston Antiques Ltd.** (℃ **01451/831586**) specializes in English and French furniture. **Baggott Church Street Ltd.,** Church Street (www.baggottantiques. com; ℃ **01451/830370**), is filled with furniture and paintings from the 17th to the 19th centuries. **Huntington's Antiques Ltd.,** Church Street (www.huntington-antiques.com; ℃ **01451/830842**) houses one of the largest stocks of quality antiques in England, showing them in 10 ground-floor rooms and a huge upstairs space. Shops tend to open Monday to Saturday 10am to 5pm, with limited hours in winter and on Sundays.

White Fleece & Golden Stone

Sheep and stone are forever linked in the Cotswolds. Medieval wool traders made fortunes exporting their much-in-demand commodity to the rest of England and the Continent. What better way to invest the profits than in a bit of salvation insurance? So they built so-called "wool churches," handsome edifices constructed from the yellow-colored limestone that is easily quarried throughout the region. These churches of Cotswold stone are still proud presences in the rolling landscapes, and it's not unusual to see the sheep that funded them grazing in green pastures nearby.

BROADWAY ★

9 miles NW of Stow-on-the-Wold

Of all the attractive Cotswolds villages, Broadway might be the proudest looking, with a formidably wide High Street that gives the town its name. In the days when Broadway was a major stop on the post road between London and Worcester, dozens of the handsome old houses lining the chestnut-tree lined avenue were inns where travelers would rest while their coachmen awaited fresh horses to make the climb up 1,000-foot-high Fish Hill; one of them, the Lygon Arms, still does a brisk business. Broadway famously inspired Arts and Crafts movement artists and craftsmen along with Peter Pan creator J. M. Barrie, composer Ralph Vaughn Williams, and legions of other creative souls. You might find it hard to find the magic among the onslaught of visitors, but take a walk down Broadway in the quiet of a morning or evening and you will see what the American expatriate novelist Henry James meant when he said that "Broadway and the land around it are in short the perfection of the English rural tradition."

VISITOR INFORMATION   The **Tourist Information Centre** is on Russell Square (www.beautifulbroadway.com; ✆ **01386/852937**). The office is staffed by friendly volunteers and is open year-round Monday to Friday 10am to 5pm and Sunday 2 to 5pm.

Exploring the Area

Ashmolean Broadway Museum ★ MUSEUM   A 16th century house on Broadway that was once a coaching inn showcases pieces on loan from Oxford's Ashmolean Museum. Works are grouped by century, so a walk up the glorious staircases and across the old floors is a bit of time travel. The 17th-century embroideries, 18th paintings by Gainsborough and Reynolds, 19th- and 20th-century pottery and textiles by Cotswolds craftspeople, and 21st paintings by local artists are atmospherically set against old fireplaces, rich paneling, and heavy beams and stonework.

65 High St. www.ashmoleanbroadway.org. ✆ **01386/859047.** £6 adults, £5 seniors, £2 children 5–15, £12 families. Tues–Sun 10am–5pm.

Broadway Tower ★★ OBSERVATION POINT   In 1798, Lady Coventry, wife of the 6th Earl of Coventry, decided to try a little experiment—if she were to build a whimsical tower outside Broadway on the crest of Fish Hill, overlooking the Vale of Eversham, would she be able to see a beacon lit atop her creation from her estate in Worcester, 22 miles away? She could, but better yet, the twin, 55-foot-tall towers of the mock Saxon castle afford stunning views across what seems to be half of England. The outlook over pastoral countryside, and the faux medieval aura of the place appealed to Arts and Crafts artists William

Broadway Tower, Broadway.

Morris and Edward Burne-Jones, who rented the tower as a summer retreat (displays in the tower rooms explore their work and their love of the Cotswolds). Another occupant was Sir Thomas Phillips, who went deeply into debt amassing the world's largest collection of books and manuscripts—he was so obsessed with owning a copy of every book in the world that a term "vello-maniac" was coined to describe his condition. In 1943 an RAF bomber on a training mission crashed into the hillside and a memorial commemorates the crew members, next to some lovely spots for a breezy picnic. There's an excellent cafe on the grounds. Middle Hill, A44 (1 mile SE of Broadway). www.broadwaytower.co.uk. © **01386/ 852390.** £5 adults, £4 seniors, £3 children 10–14, £13 families. Daily 10am–5pm.

Gordon Russell Design Museum ★★★ Sir Gordon Russell (1892–1980) developed a taste for furniture when he observed craftsmen at work in the repair studios of Broadway's Lygon Arms Hotel (see below), which his father owned. Russell opened workshops in Broadway in 1919, and oversaw the talented workers as they produced some of Britain finest 20th-century furniture, working with Arts and Crafts designs that became the vanguard of Modernism. The workshops are now filled with chests, cabinets, sideboards, and other pieces that more than 200 craftsman once produced to Russell's elegant designs and later those of his brother, Dick. Especially intriguing are the radio cabinets that Russell designed for the Murphy Radio Company, now icons of mid-century European design. 15 Russell Sq. www.gordonrussellmuseum.org. © **01386/854695.** £5 adults, £1 children 12–15. Mar–Oct Tues–Sun 11am–5pm; Nov–Feb Tues–Sun 11am–4pm.

Snowshill Manor ★★ MUSEUM This pleasant Cotswold manor house was once part of the vast holdings of Winchcombe Abbey, a Benedictine monastery that was founded in 798 as capital of the Anglo-Saxon capital of Mercia. As the final resting place of Kenelm, a royal prince who was martyred and became a wildly popular saint, the abbey was one of England's most popular medieval pilgrimage sites. Arts and Crafts architect and craftsman Charles Paget Wade (1883–1956) purchased Snowshill in 1919 as a place to store his remarkably eclectic, 22,000-piece collection. "Let nothing perish," he famously said, a motto that will ring true with every collector whose passion leans a bit toward hoarding. Wade lived in an adjoining cottage so he could fill the honey-colored stone manor with furniture, toys, tapestries, clothing, musical instruments, and paintings. It's all a tasteful mess—26 suites of Japanese Samurai armor are crammed into the Green Room—and it's head-clearing to step into the beautiful gardens. These, too, are Wade's work, a display of color and scent designed by Baillie Scott, an architect who also created the Blackwell Arts and Crafts manor in the Lake District (p. 422).

Snowshill, 3 miles south of Broadway. www.nationaltrust.org.uk/main/w-snowshill manor. *©* **01386/852410.** £9 adults, £4 children 5–15, free for children 4 and under, £22 families. Apr–June and Sept–Oct Wed–Sun noon–5pm; July–Aug Mon and Wed–Sun 11:30am–4:30pm. Admission by timed ticket. Last admission 4pm.

Where to Eat & Stay

A nice place in Broadway for a cup of tea is **Tisanes Tea Rooms,** 21 The Green (www.tisanes-tearooms.co.uk; *©* **01386/853296**). If you like the blended brew you're drinking along with a variety of sandwiches and cakes (served daily 10am–5pm) you can take a package or two home with you.

Dormy House Hotel ★★ A 17th-century farmhouse at the edge of an escarpment high above Broadway has taken on a glamorous new guise as a luxurious retreat full of big stone fireplaces, chic lounges, and a decadent spa where you can sip champagne through a straw while enjoying a manicure. Guest rooms, spread through the old house and adjacent buildings, are stylishly done in soothing colors and a mix of retro and modern touches that hint at mid-century glamour; you might find yourself sleeping in an atmospheric old attic, but the bed will be a minimalist take on a four poster and the beams will be white-washed. Dining is casual in the Potting Shed, and more formal in the Garden Room. The surrounding 400-acre Francombe Estate is laced with inviting walking trails.

Willersey Hill (take the A44 2 miles southeast of Broadway). www.dormyhouse.co.uk. *©* **01386/852711.** 48 units. Doubles from £230, includes breakfast. **Amenities:** Restaurant; bar; babysitting; gym; spa with indoor pool; room service; free Wi-Fi.

The Lygon Arms ★ You can't come to Broadway without at least stepping beneath the ancient stone mullion and through the front door

The Lygon Arms, Broadway.

of one of England's most famous old inns, and to stay here is keeping up with a 500-year-old tradition for travelers. The ground floor is a glorious maze of paneled nooks and crannies warmed by open fires, and the Great Hall is a wonderful century-old recreation of a Tudor banqueting room, complete with a minstrel's gallery. Most guest quarters are more banal, especially the perfect comfortable but bland rooms in the modern wing. To stay in style, request one the antiques-filled old rooms with beamed ceilings and open fires, like the Cromwell Suite, named after its most famous occupant, or the Charles I Suite, complete with a secret passage for a quick escape.

High St., Broadway. www.thehotelcollection.co.uk. ℰ **01386/852255.** 78 units. Doubles £105–£180. **Amenities:** 2 restaurants; cafe; bar; health club; pool (indoor); tennis courts; room service; spa; free Wi-Fi.

Shopping

Stop by **Snowshill Lavender** (www.snowshill-lavender.co.uk; ℰ **01386/ 854821**), on Hill Barn Farm, about 3 miles south of Broadway, to be transported to the South of France. Some 21 hectares (53 acres) of lavender are under cultivation—an ocean of lilacs, purples, and blues seems to stretch to the horizon. You can buy lavender soaps and oils in the shop, or munch lavender scones, cakes, and shortbread in the Lavender Tea Room. The shop is free, but admission to lavender fields (worth it for the visual and olfactory thrill) is £3 adults, £2 children under 16.

Snowshill Lavender at Hill Barn Farm, near Broadway.

CHIPPING CAMPDEN ★★

6 miles NE of Broadway

A century ago the historian G. M. Trevelyan observed that Chipping Campden's High Street "is the most beautiful village street now left in the island" and this may well still be the case. The long street still looks as it did in the 16th century, when wool merchants lined it with their fine stone houses, and the prospect hits a picturesque crescendo around the arched **Market Hall,** erected in 1627 to provide shelter for the local market.

VISITOR INFORMATION   The **Tourist Information Centre** is in the Old Police Station on High Street (www.chippingcampdenonline.org; ✆ **01386/841206**). It's open March through October, daily 9:30am to 5pm, and November through February, Monday through Thursday 9:30am to 1pm and Friday through Sunday 9:30am to 4pm.

Exploring the Area

The soaring tower of the **Church of St James** (www.stjameschurch campden.co.uk; ✆ **01386/841927**) is a beacon that's visible for miles around. Inside the huge edifice are the tombs and memorials of the wool merchants who once brought enormous wealth to the town, among them a 15th-century brass plaque commemorating William Grevel, "flower of the wool merchants of all England" (free admission; open Mar–Oct Mon–Sat 10am–5pm, and Sun 2–6pm; Nov and Feb Mon–Sat 11am–4pm and Sun 2–4pm). Gevel's house, a proud stone manor at the north end of High Street, was built in the 13th century and shows off what was then a new innovation in domestic architecture, chimneys—until then smoke escaped through a hole in the roof.

Court Barn Museum ★ MUSEUM Among the Arts and Crafts artisans choosing to locate in the Cotswolds was designer and entrepreneur Charles Robert Ashbee (1863–1942), a forward thinker who espoused socialism, homosexuality, a Jewish state, and equal rights for women. He moved his Guild of Handicraft, a collective that specialized in metal, ironwork and furniture, from London to Chipping Campden in 1902. Though the enterprise failed, Ashbee took his place among the artisans whose legacy is the focus of this small collection. Their work is nicely displayed next to story boards that trace the history and ongoing presence of artisans in the region. Replicas and some original work are on sale in the shop. The handsome barn was once part of the grand Campden House Estate, torched by Royalists during the English Civil War in 1643.

Church St. www.courtbarn.org.uk. © **01386/841951.** £5 adults, children 18 and under free. Apr–Sept Tues–Sun 10am–5pm, Oct–Mar Tues–Sun 10am–4pm.

Hidcote ★★★ GARDEN Shy and reclusive Major Lawrence Johnson (1871–1958) was a bit of an interloper in the elite English gardening circles, the heir to an American stock-broking fortune, but the gardens he created at his manor house just outside Chipping Campden are considered to be some of the finest in England. The poet Vita Sackville-West, whose gardens at Sissinghurst (p. 196) are often compared to these at

Hidcote manor & gardens, at Chipping Campden.

Hidcote, described Johnson's creation as "a jungle of beauty. I cannot hope to describe it in words." Touring the gardens is an adventure, since they are laid out as a series of rooms separated by topiary hedges. Narrow pathways open onto terraces and into secret gardens planted with species that Johnson brought back from the Andes, Africa, and the Far East.

Hidcote Bartrim. www.nationaltrust.org.uk/hidcote. ℂ **01386/438333.** £11 adults, £5 children 5–16, £26 families. Mar–Oct daily 10am–6pm, Nov–mid Dec and mid–late Feb weekends 10am–4pm.

Where to Eat & Stay

The Chef's Dozen ★★★ MODERN BRITISH   It's a tribute to what a nice town Chipping Campden is that it ranks a restaurant like this. Much of the lamb and beef is from nearby farms, the produce is locally grown, and pasta and bread is homemade. It all appears in innovative and fairly priced preparations on changing two- and three-course menus in an airy room where modern furnishings blend nicely with stone walls, polished wood floors, and wood-beamed ceilings.

High St. www.thechefsdozen.co.uk. ℂ **01386/840598.** Tasting menus £19, £25, and £38. Tues 6:30–9:30pm, Wed–Sat noon–2:30pm and 6:30–9:30pm.

The Cotswold House Hotel ★★★   This stately Regency house in the center of town, just opposite the old wool market, reveals some surprises behind its formal facade. A graceful spiral staircase leads to cozy old rooms done in imaginative contemporary style, with some plush armchairs and other old world touches thrown in, while out back, four suites are tucked into cottages facing groomed gardens. Walkways wind past secluded patios and lawns that will make you think you're in

A guest room at Cotswold House Hotel, Chipping Camden.

a country retreat and lead to an adults-only spa with an indoor pool and a relaxing hammam. A warmly lit bistro serves modern takes on British classics.

The Square. www.cotswoldhouse.com. *Ⓒ* **01386/840330.** 30 units. Doubles £150–£295, includes breakfast. **Amenities:** Restaurant; bars; spa with indoor pool; free Wi-Fi.

Noel Arms Hotel ★   The oldest inn in town exudes a warm, old-fashioned atmosphere, with fire-warmed lounges and a friendly bar full of chatty locals. Comfortable guest rooms furnished with a smattering of old heirlooms and more functional pieces spread across the creaky floors of the old coaching and into a house across a courtyard. The best room in the house is done up with a four-poster bed and heavy old antiques to look the way it did when Charles I allegedly spent a night or two back in 1657. The Conservatory is a choice spot for light meals and tea, while the dining room serves traditional fare and some of the best curries in the Cotswolds. Guests have use of the spa at the Cotswolds House across the street.

High St. www.chippingcampdenonline.org. *Ⓒ* **01386/840317.** 23 units. Doubles from £90–£160. **Amenities:** Restaurant; bar; free Wi-Fi.

Shopping

As you'll learn at the **Court Barn Museum** (see above) Charles Robert Ashbee brought a legion of craftspeople to Chipping Campden when he opened the Guild of Handicraft here in 1902. Many of the descendants of the metal and woodworkers and other artisans still work and live in the area. The **Old Silk Mill,** Sheep Street, is where the Guild of Handicraft was established in 1902 and has been revived with a series of craft workshops. One of them is **Hart Gold & Silversmiths** (www.hartsilversmiths.co.uk; *Ⓒ* **01386/841100**), where silver and gold is expertly smithed by descendants of George Hart, an original member of the Guild of Handicraft. Elsewhere, the Welch family has been crafting silverware, stainless steel, and cutlery for more than 50 years at the **Robert Welch Studio Shop,** Lower High Street (www.welch.co.uk; *Ⓒ* **01386/840522**).

10

THE HEART OF ENGLAND

by Stephen Brewer

E ngland reveals many facets in the Midlands, the region that is at the heart of the country geographically as well as in spirit. Shakespeare, the national treasure, was born here in Stratford-upon-Avon, a shrine that draws millions of devotees a year. Nearby, Warwick Castle is one of England's most beloved medieval monuments, while off to the west, Ironbridge gave rise to a momentous era in British history, the Industrial Revolution. Birmingham is emerging from its industrial past with energy and a bit of an edge, as becomes Britain's second-largest city. Yet another side of Britain comes into play along the Welsh borders, where green hills and lush valleys are dotted with half-timbered villages that seem to pop right off the pages of a story book.

STRATFORD-UPON-AVON ★★

91 miles NW of London

William Shakespeare was born in Stratford in 1564 and, after making a name for himself in London, died here 52 years later. Almost ever since, the place that began as a medieval settlement on the River Avon has been a one-industry town, where the spotlight is on the most revered author in the English language. While it's easy enough to find Romeo and Juliet iPhone cases and "To be or not to be" refrigerator magnets on the pretty streets and lanes, Stratford's shrines to the Bard, including his birthplace and several houses associated with him and his family, are reverently tasteful and sweep visitors back to the 16th and 17th centuries. The magic of Stratford is to become immersed in Shakespeare's life and times, an experience all the more potent if you take in one of the exquisite performances of his plays at the Royal Shakespeare Theatre.

Essentials

GETTING THERE The Chiltern Railways **train** service from London Marylebone to Stratford-upon-Avon takes about 2¼ hours. For information, go to **www.nationalrail.co.uk**. About three National Express **buses** (www.nationalexpress.com) run between London's Victoria Coach Station and Stratford daily. The trip takes about 3 hours. If you're

PREVIOUS PAGE: **Holy Trinity Church, Stratford-upon-Avon.**

The Heart of England

driving from London, take the M40 to junction 15 and continue to Stratford-upon-Avon on the A46/A439.

VISITOR INFORMATION The **Tourist Information Centre,** Bridge-foot (www.shakespeare-country.co.uk; ℂ **0870/160-7930**), provides any details you may wish to know about the Shakespeare houses and properties; it will also assist in booking rooms (see "Where to Stay," below). The center is open April through September, Monday to Saturday 9am to 5:30pm and Sunday 10am to 4pm; October through March, Monday to Saturday 9am to 5pm and Sunday 10am to 3pm.

The Royal Shakespeare Theatre

In Shakespeare's day, Stratford didn't have a theatre—the Bard's plays were performed in London. These days the red-brick **Royal Shakespeare Theatre** (*℗* **01789/403444;** www.rsc.org.uk) on the banks of the River Avon is the major showcase for the acclaimed **Royal Shakespeare Company (RSC),** with a season that runs from April to November. Offerings typically feature five Shakespearean plays, along with other classics and contemporary works. The RSC also stages productions in the smaller **Swan Theatre,** an intimate 430-seat space next door.

For **ticket reservations** book online or call *℗* **0844/8001110.** The box office is open Monday to Saturday 10am to 8pm, although it closes at 6pm on days when there are no performances. Seats range in price from £5 to £35. A small number of tickets is held for sale on the day of a performance.

Guided **Theatre Tours** focus on different aspects of the theatre, including backstage and front of the house. They last an hour to 75 minutes and cost from £7 to £10 for adults and £4 to £6 for children 17 and under. Advance booking is recommended.

You can take an elevator up the **Tower** (Mon–Fri 10am–6:15pm; Sat 10am–12:15pm and 1:30–6:15pm; Sun 10am–5pm) for a unique bird's-eye view of the town. Tickets cost £3 for adults and £1 for children 17 and under; the tower is closed when there are performances at the theatre.

The Royal Shakespeare Theatre along the River Avon, Stratford-upon-Avon.

Exploring the Area

Most of Stratford's historic attractions are administered by the **Shakespeare Birthplace Trust** (www.shakespeare.org.uk; *℗* **01789/204016**). The **Five House Pass** lets you visit five sights: Anne Hathaway's Cottage and Gardens; Hall's Croft; Harvard House; Mary Arden's Farm; Shakespeare's Birthplace, and Shakespeare's Grave and costs £24

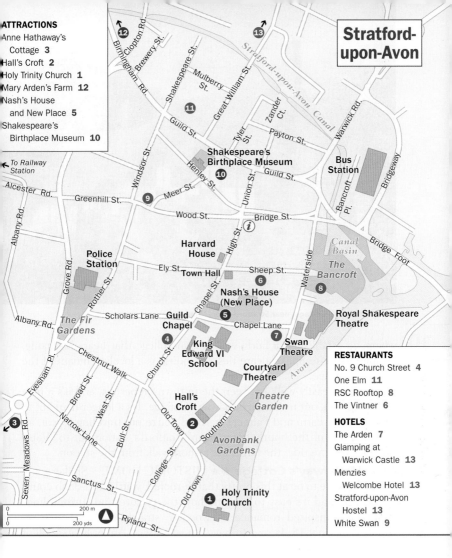

ATTRACTIONS

Anne Hathaway's
  Cottage **3**
Hall's Croft **2**
Holy Trinity Church **1**
Mary Arden's Farm **12**
Nash's House
  and New Place **5**
Shakespeare's
  Birthplace Museum **10**

Stratford-
upon-Avon

To Railway
Station

Shakespeare's
Birthplace Museum
10

Bus
Station

Police
Station

Harvard
House

Town Hall

The
Bancroft

Nash's House
(New Place)

Guild
Chapel

The Fir
Gardens

Royal Shakespeare
Theatre

King
Edward VI
School

Swan
Theatre

Courtyard
Theatre

Theatre
Garden

RESTAURANTS

No. 9 Church Street **4**
One Elm **11**
RSC Rooftop **8**
The Vintner **6**

HOTELS

The Arden **7**
Glamping at
  Warwick Castle **13**
Menzies
  Welcombe Hotel **13**
Stratford-upon-Avon
  Hostel **13**
White Swan **9**

Hall's
Croft

Avonbank
Gardens

Holy Trinity
Church

for adults, £22 for seniors and students, £14 for children 5 to 15, and £62 for families. The **Birthplace Pass** provides entry to Hall's Croft, Harvard House, Shakespeare's Birthplace, and Shakespeare's Grave and costs £16 adults, £15 seniors and students, £10 children 5 to 15, and £25 for families. Children 4 and under are free. Buy the passes at any of the Trust properties. While New Place and Nash House are closed for conservation work until April 2016, combination tickets include admission to Harvard House at 26 High St. Wealthy merchant Thomas Rogers built the house, with an elaborately timbered and carved facade, in 1596; his grandson, John Harvard, emigrated to the Massachusetts colony,

Anne Hathaway's Cottage, near Stratford-upon-Avon.

where he established a fairly well-known college that bears his name. Despite its loose Shakespeare ties, the house is a lovely remnant of the Elizabethan Age.

You can easily walk between the in-town properties, and it's a nice mile-long walk out to Anne Hathaway's Cottage. It's a longer haul out to Mary Arden's Farm and Palmer's Farm; if you're not traveling by car, an option is one of the hourly trains from Stratford's station out to Wilmcote, a 7-minute ride; the farms are a short walk from the station.

Anne Hathaway's Cottage ★★ HISTORIC HOME   Shakespeare wooed his wife to be at this pretty thatch-roofed, wattle-and-daub country cottage, and it's easy to imagine how the picturesque surroundings might have inspired romance. A wooden, straight-backed settee on which Will, only 18, is said to have snuggled with Anne, 8 years older and the daughter of a prosperous farmer, is among the original furnishings in the 12 rooms lit by latticed windows. The provenance of the painfully uncomfortable-looking piece is probably a bit of family yore invented by Hathaway descendants. Nor is the bedstead in the low-ceilinged upstairs bedroom the famous "second best bed" that Shakespeare bequeathed to Anne in his will, but it's probably the bed on which Anne was born. Beautiful gardens are often fragrant with plants popular in Shakespeare's time. The most enjoyable way to reach the cottage in on foot; it's a 1-mile walk across meadows along a well-marked path from Evesham Place in Stratford.

Cottage Lane, Shottery. www.shakespeare.org.uk. ⓒ **01789/292100.** £10 adults, £9 seniors and students, £6 children 5–15, £25 familes. Combination tickets available (see above). Mid-Mar to Oct daily 9am–5pm; Nov to mid-Mar 10am–4pm.

Hall's Croft ★★ HISTORIC HOME   Even without the Shakespeare connection, this comfortably furnished Tudor home would be an outstanding period piece. In 1607, Shakespeare's daughter Susanna married John Hall and the Bard presented the couple with a 107-acre parcel at the edge of town. In 1612 or 13 they built this two-story house with a large hall and parlor on the ground floor, a testament to the rise in middle class prosperity in 17th-century England. Hall was a highly respected physician, and a recreation of his consulting room shows off the instruments he would have used, while the garden is planted with the plants and herbs from which he concocted treatments.

Old Town St. (near Holy Trinity Church). www.shakespeare.org.uk. ☎ **01789/292107.** Admission by combination tickets (see above). Mid-Mar to Oct daily 9am–5pm; Nov to mid-Mar 11am–4pm.

Holy Trinity Church (Shakespeare's Tomb) ★   CHURCH A 13th-century parish church on the banks of the River Avon is probably the most-visited house of worship in England, for Shakespeare is buried in the chancel ("and curst be he who moves my bones") next to his wife, Anne, and other members of the family. You can also see the official registry records of the poet's birth and death, along with some other curiosities that include seats in the choir that are carved with mythical beasts and an enchanting scene of a domestic dispute between husband and wife. The knocker on the south porch was once well known to Stratford's miscreants—if an accused criminal managed to grab onto it before being apprehended he was automatically granted sanctuary in the church.

Old Town St. www.stratford-upon-avon.org. ☎ **01789/290128.** Church free; Shakespeare's tomb £2 adults, £1 students; or combination ticket (see above). Apr–Sept Mon–Sat 8:30am–6pm; Mar and Oct Mon–Sat 9am–5pm; Nov–Feb Mon–Sat 9am–4pm, Sun 12:30–5pm year-round.

Mary Arden's Farm & Palmer's Farm ★   FARM For decades, until the year 2000, visitors trooped through a timber-framed farmhouse with an old stone dovecote thinking it was the girlhood home of Shakespeare's mother, Mary Arden. It has since been discovered that Mary came

Shakespeare's tomb, Holy Trinity Church, Stratford-upon-Avon.

into this world (in 1537) in the red-brick farmhouse next door, so a visit now takes in the newly named Palmer's Farm and the actual Mary Arden House. Palmer's Farm is the grander of the two, with an impressive ingle-nook fireplace and comfortable Elizabethan furnishings; the exterior timbers reveal a bit of Elizabethan status consciousness—those facing the road are close together, suggesting the owner could afford large amounts of wood, while far fewer timbers, spaced farther apart, were used in the rear. Mary Arden's house is furnished with Edwardian and Victorian fussiness, just as the last owner left it upon her death in the 1970s. Surrounding both are barns, gardens, and pastures that bring an Elizabeth farm to life.

Station Rd., Wilmcote. www.shakespeare.org.uk. © **01789/293455.** £13 adults, £12 students and seniors, £9 children 5–15, £33 families. Combination tickets available (see above). Apr–Oct daily 10am–5pm.

Nash's House & New Place ★ HISTORIC HOME In 1610 Shakespeare retired to the second-largest house in Stratford, with 10 fireplaces and 5 large gables. Today the house is Stratford's most popular non-existing attraction, since it was torn down in 1759 (the properties are closed for conservation work and scheduled to reopen in April 2016). The destruction came about after the owner, the Reverend Francis Gastrell, chopped down a mulberry tree that Shakespeare had allegedly planted and angry townsfolk began throwing rocks through his windows; Gastrell tore the whole place down when Stratford increased his taxes. A mulberry tree that now grows in the garden is said to have sprouted from a cutting from Shakespeare's tree.

Upon Shakespeare's death, the house went to his daughter Susan Hall, who moved here from Hall's Croft (see above), then to her daughter, Elizabeth, who married the boy next door, Thomas Nash. His family home is filled with fine Elizabethan furnishings and hosts exhibitions that often reveal some juicy tidbits about Shakespeare— for instance, he was twice accused of being a tax dodge; a son-in-law did public penance when it was revealed he had fathered an illegitimate son; and though it's often been suggested that the Bard slighted his wife, Anne, when he left her the "second-best" bed, this was actually their matrimonial bed.

Chapel St. www.shakespeare.org.uk. © **01789/292325.** Admission by combination tickets (see above). Nov–Mar daily 11am–4pm; Apr–June and Sept–Oct daily 10am–5pm; July–Aug daily 10am–6pm.

Shakespeare's Birthplace Museum ★★ MUSEUM William Shakespeare was born in this fairly simple yet substantial wattle and daub house in 1564, when his father, John, was already well established as a glove maker. John's equipment is laid out in his ground floor workshop, where a guide will explain that it was then common practice for laborers to buy just one glove, an expensive purchase. The parlor, hall, and main bedroom are lined with attractively painted cloth, a stand-in for tapestries that only the very wealthy could afford, and furnished as they would have been when William grew up in these rooms and lived here in the early years of his marriage. A window is etched with the names of famous visitors, among them Sir Walter Scott and Charles Dickens, while the adjacent visitor's center pays homage to Shakespeare with stage and film presentations of his plays and a model of the Globe Theatre in London.

Henley St. www.shakespeare.org.uk. ℰ **01789/204016.** Admission by combination tickets (see above). Nov to mid-Mar daily 10am–4pm; mid-Mar to Jun and Sept–Oct daily 10am–5pm; July–Aug daily 9am–6pm.

Organized Tours

You'll pick up all sorts of tidbits about Shakespeare and Stratford (the plague years, the fires, the many famous visitors) as you stroll with one of the knowledgeable guides on a **Stratford Town Walk** (stratfordtown walk.co.uk). Just show up at the Swan Fountain next to the Royal Shakespeare Theatre by 11am weekdays and 11am and 2pm weekends. Cost is £6 adults, £5 seniors and students, £3 children under 16, free for children under 8. Tours last about 2 hours.

Outlying Attractions

Just north of Stratford are two of Britain's finest castles, **Warwick** and the ruined **Kenilworth.** Before stepping through the gates of Warwick Castle, take a stroll through the medieval town where in 1571 Robert Dudley, Earl of Leicester and the favorite minister of Elizabeth I,

Lord Leycester Hospital, Warwick.

established the **Lord Leycester Hospital** on High Street (www.lord leycester.com; ℂ **01926/491422**; £6, Tues–Sun summer 10am–5pm, winter 10am–4pm). He converted these half-timbered 14th-century houses into a home for old soldiers, "for the housing and maintenance of the needy, infirm or aged." The wonderfully photogenic steeped roofs and quaint porches are still home to retired service personnel and their spouses. Walk in the Elizabethan garden in the courtyard and take a look at the beamed hall where local officials held a banquet for King James I that put the town into debt for 10 years. Dining is still just as atmospheric in the hospital's oak-beamed **Brethren's Kitchen** tearoom (Tues–Sat 10am–5pm, Sun 11am–5pm; closed Jan.).

Take the A46 if you're driving; from Stratford-upon-Avon it's just 9 miles to Warwick and 14 miles to Kenilworth. Chiltern Railways trains run frequently between Stratford-upon-Avon and Warwick (22 min.); the station is a 10-minute walk from the castle. **Stagecoach** bus no. 16 departs Stratford-upon-Avon every hour during the day and goes to both castles. The trip to Warwick takes roughly half an hour, an hour to Kenilworth. Go to www.stagecoachbus.com for schedules.

Warwick Castle ★★★ CASTLE   There's never a dull moment at this mighty castle-cum-theme park, where soaring towers and crenellated battlements are perched on a rocky cliff above the River Avon. Madame Tussaud's wax artisans and a large entertainment company have conspired to bring history to life in what was begun in 914 on

Warwick Castle, begun in 914 A.D.

orders of Ethelfleda, daughter of Alfred the Great. The fortress was expanded for William the Conqueror and greatly enlarged into its present-day appearance by the Beauchamps, powerful 13th-century earls of Warwick.

In the Ghost Tower, murmurs and screams recreate a manservant murdering Sir Fulke Grenville, who converted the castle into a luxurious 17th-century country house, and in the dungeons, gruesome, corpse-littered displays re-enact torture, poisonings, and other ghastly deeds. Twelve elegant rooms are decorated as they would have been in 1898 and wax figures enjoy a weekend party—young Winston Churchill reads quietly and the countess of Warwick tries on a gown. Stone halls enlivened with mannequins, sounds and smells recreate a fateful morning in which the household of Richard Neville, a 15th-century earl of Warwick known as the Kingmaker, gets ready for the War of the Roses battle in which he died. Elsewhere on the grounds, a colossal catapult lobs rocks and fireballs and knights joust in reenactments. Whether you find the castle's many attractions to be a bit kitschy or highly entertaining, plan on spending the better part of a day here.

Warwick. www.warwick-castle.co.uk. © **0870/442-2000.** £21 adults, £15 children 4–16, £16 seniors, £72 families, free for children 3 and under; discounts for online tickets; Castle dungeon extra £8. Daily 10am–5pm.

Kenilworth Castle ★★   Even in splendid ruin, it's easy to imagine the majesty of one of England's largest and grandest medieval castles, founded in 1120. Henry III besieged the castle for 6 months in 1266, the longest siege on English soil, trying to quell the rebellious forces of the Earl of Leicester. The strong fortifications ensured the castle was not taken, and the king's forces were eventually forced to retreat after the rebels cut off the hand of the royal messenger. Elizabeth I made several visits under more peaceful circumstances, including a long stay in 1571, when the castle was home to her favorite courtier and alleged lover, Robert Dudley. The queen stayed in a purpose-built pavilion; took strolls in a specially designed garden, still the finest Elizabethan garden in England; and enjoyed grand dance parties in lavishly furnished apartments with huge windows and spectacular hearths. Enough remains to suggest the past might and grandeur, and the audio guide helps make sense of all the history that transpired here.

Kenilworth. www.english-heritage.org.uk. © **01926/852078.** £10 adults, £9 seniors, £6 children 5–16, free for children 4 and under, £25 for families. Daily 10am–6pm; Sept–Oct daily 10am–5pm and Nov–Feb daily10am–4pm.

Where to Stay

The Arden ★★★   Shakespeare connections run deep at this old house next to the RSC theatre—so close that theatregoers nip into the bar for a drink at intermission. It's said that Shakespeare wrote several of

Afternoon tea at The Arden, Stratford-upon-Avon.

his plays in the garden of a building that once stood on the spot, and the pretty present-day terrace is conducive to writing postcards or reading a play or two. Many rooms have river views and all are bright and elegant, with lots of cream-colored fabrics, soft-lined contemporary furnishings, huge comfortable beds, and enormous bathtubs (in many rooms). The bright and airy Waterside Brasserie and Champagne Bar serves modern British cuisine, and a handsome lounge is a snug spot for tea or a drink.

Waterside. www.theardenhotelstratford.com. ✆ **01789/298682.** 45 units. Doubles from £160. **Amenities:** 3 restaurants; 2 bars; room service; free Wi-Fi.

Glamping at Warwick Castle ★
You can't sleep in Warwick Castle, but you can do the next best thing and settle into a tent on the grounds. The 35 canvas structures aren't tents in the Boy Scouts sense of the word—they're fitted out with polished wood floors and antique-style furnishings that include grand Tudor-style four-poster beds. Bathrooms are down the grassy lane and communal, but hot water in the showers is plentiful. Campsite entertainment extends to jousts, medieval pageants, falconry, and the many other activities in the castle and on the grounds, to which a 2-day entry pass comes with overnight accommodation. A medieval banquet is held nightly (extra), and breakfast is included.

Glamping Village, Warwick Castle. www.warwick-castle.co.uk. ✆ **0871/6631671.** 35 units. Four-person tents from £160, includes breakfast and 2-day family pass to castle. **Amenities:** Free Wi-Fi in some areas.

Menzies Welcombe Hotel, Spa & Golf Club ★★
Many guests come out here to the countryside 10 minutes outside town for a round on the 18-hole golf course, but this Jacobean style manor from 1866 is also a good place just to get away from it all. Many of the gracious old guest rooms are quite large, with enough faux antiques to make you feel

you're a guest at an aristocratic house party—ask for a room in the main house, as those in the garden wing are pleasantly contemporary, but a lot less atmospheric. The spa has a huge indoor swimming pool and a soothing whirlpool that's open to the sky in even the most inclement weather. Warwick Rd. www.menzies-hotels.co.uk. ☎ **01789/295252.** 78 units. Doubles £78–£140. **Amenities:** 2 restaurants; bar; golf course; gym; indoor pool; room service; spa; tennis court; free Wi-Fi.

Stratford-upon-Avon Hostel ★   The hostelling experience ramps up several notches in this gracious Georgian mansion set on landscaped acres near the River Avon about 2 miles outside Stratford. Public areas are especially grand and well-furnished, and include a nice bar and restaurant that spill out onto a terrace. Guest rooms—most set up as doubles or family rooms and more than half with private bathroom—are a lot more utilitarian, and the steel-frame beds seem all the more functional when tucked against marble fireplaces and other architectural embellishments from the house's more glamorous days. Hemmingford House, Alveston. www.yha.org.uk/hostel/stratford-upon-avon. ☎ **0845/3719661.** 35 units. Doubles from £35. **Amenities:** Restaurant; bar; free Wi-Fi in public areas.

White Swan ★   For the full Shakespeare experience, tuck into a four-poster bed in one of the sloping-floored rooms of this old inn where the Bard used to drop by for a pint. The old beams of the 550-year-old house were probably creaking even back then, and what's now Stratford's longest-standing structure is atmospherically done up with old paintings and murals on the uneven walls and lots of nice antiques on the polished floors. Public rooms hit the full-on Elizabethan experience, with open fires and rich paneling, making the Swan a good stop for a drink. Rother St. www.white-swan-stratford.co.uk. ☎ **01789/297022.** 41 units. Doubles £119–£169, includes breakfast. **Amenities:** Restaurant; bar; room service, free Wi-Fi.

Where to Eat

Stratford is well-geared to feeding the hordes of day trippers trooping through the Shakespeare sights, with a few standouts for a quick bite. Everything, sandwiches, soup, quiche, baked goods, at **Haviland's Tea Room,** 4-5 Meer St., is top quality and well-priced (www.haviland stearoom.com; ☎ **01789/415477**). **McKechnies,** 37 Rother St., is known for its coffee and 17 types of tea, but most deserving of praise are the chunky farmhouse sandwiches (www.mckechniescafe.talktalk.net; ☎ **01789/299575**).

No 9 Church Street ★★ CONTEMPORARY ENGLISH   One of Stratford's finest, in a 400-year-old building in the center of town, offers a festive lunch or stylish evening out, which begin over drinks in an intimate downstairs lounge then move to a plain, homey room upstairs. The menu is as welcoming as the setting, with a seasonal, changing menu—beef rump with asparagus, grass-fed spring lamb, wild sea bass, an especially good value on lunch and pre-theatre menus.

9 Church St. www.no9churchst.com. 📞 **01789/415522.** Mains £12–£17. Tues–Sat noon–2:30pm, 5:30–9:30pm; every third Sun of the month noon–4pm.

The One Elm ★ ENGLISH   Many locals consider this sleek pub to be the best place in town for a steak, local and aged for 28 days, and just about everything else is also fresh and raised nearby, from free-range Cotswold chicken to the fish from local waters. You can also grab a sandwich or dine casually on a deli platter, or sit on the shaded terrace and nurse a pint from Warwickshire's Purity brewery.

1 Guild St. www.oneelmstratford.co.uk. 📞 **01789/404919.** Mains £10–£17. Mon–Sat 11am–10pm; Sun noon–3pm and 6:30–9:30pm.

RSC Rooftop Restaurant & Bar ★★ ENGLISH/CONTINENTAL The second-best views in town (after those from the theatre's tower) are from the floor-to-ceiling windows and terrace of this spot atop the Royal Shakespeare Theatre. The bright room is as pleasant as the swan-filled Avon below, and a simple menu offers a few non-fussy British classics at lunch and dinner, with pre-theatre seating; high tea and an enticing tapas menu at the bar. Non-theatre goers are welcome, but it's best to arrive after curtain time to avoid the crush.

In the Royal Shakespeare Theatre, Waterside. www.rsc.org.uk. 📞 **01789/403449.** Mains £13–£19; fixed-price menus available. Mon–Sat 11:30am–11pm; Sun noon–2:30pm.

The Vintner ★ ENGLISH/CONTINENTAL   It's said that William Shakespeare used to stop by this cozy spot for wine, and the low-ceilinged, heavy-beamed rooms haven't changed a bit—maybe because the place has been in the hands of the same family for 5 centuries. They still provide a popular place to gather over a drink or coffee, and though the menu accommodates modern tastes with some nice salads, the emphasis is on hearty roasts and fairly priced steaks.

4-5 Sheep St. www.the-vintner.co.uk. 📞 **01789/297259.** Mains £8–£15. Mon–Sat 9:30am–10pm; Sun 9:30am–9pm.

Shopping

Set within an antique house with ceiling beams, the **Shakespeare Bookshop,** 39 Henley St. (📞 **01789/292176;** www.shakespeare.org. uk; Wed–Sat 9:30am–5:30pm, Sun noon–5pm), across from the Shakespeare Birthplace Centre, is a fine source for textbooks and academic treatises on the Bard and his works.

Entertainment & Nightlife

Aside from attending a play at the **Royal Shakespeare Theatre** (see above), the best way to spend an evening in Stratford is to bend an elbow in a pub, the older and more half-timbered the better. The creaky old **Dirty Duck** (✆ **01789/297312;** daily 11am–11pm) has been a popular hangout for actors performing in Stratford since the 18th century, and the walls are lined with autographed photos of its famous patrons. The place was known more genteelly as the **Black Swan** until American GIs renamed it during World War II. Claimant to the oldest pub in Stratford is the **Garrick Inn,** at 25 High St. (✆ **01789/292186;** daily 11am–11pm), a handsome black-and-white timbered structure from the 1300s.

BIRMINGHAM ★

120 miles NW of London; 25 miles N of Stratford-upon-Avon

Brummies, as residents call themselves, like to talk about their city's cool vibe and increasing sophistication, but frankly, it's still a bit of a hard sell. With lots of brutal postwar building and industrial sprawl, plus a labyrinthine road system that slices through neighborhoods and discourages exploring on foot, England's second-largest city can be a challenge—or at best, lower on the list of places to visit in Britain. If you do find yourself here, though, you will discover pockets of striking Georgian and Victorian architecture, a network of enticing canals, troves of art, plenty of good food, and a few rapidly emerging cultural hotspots, like Digbeth. Birmingham's best years might be just around the corner with the proposed HS2: In a decade or so this high-speed rail line will make the journey time to and from London in just 45 minutes and is expected to bring a rush of new blood and energy to the city.

Essentials

GETTING THERE   **Virgin Trains** connect London Euston and Birmingham New Street every 15 to 30 minutes and take 1 hour 25 minutes. **CrossCountry** trains leave Manchester's Piccadilly Station nearly every hour for Birmingham New Street. The trip takes 1½ hours. **Chiltern Railways** trains from Stratford-upon-Avon arrive at Birmingham Moor Street every hour. For schedules and tickets, go to www.nationalrail. co.uk. National Express **buses** (www.nationalexpress.com) run between London's Victoria Coach Station and Birmingham Coach Station as often as every half hour; the trip takes about 2½ hours.

From London, the best route **driving** is via the M40, which leads onto the M42, the motorway that circles south and east of Birmingham. Once on the M42, any of the roads from junctions 4 to 6 will lead into the center. The drive takes about 2 to 2½ hours, depending on traffic conditions. Parking is available at locations throughout Birmingham.

Birmingham Airport (www.birminghamairport.co.uk), 8 miles east of the city center, handles **flights** to and from within the U.K. and the continent, as well as Newark and Orlando in the U.S.

VISITOR INFORMATION The Birmingham Visitor Centre, at the Library of Birmingham, on Centenary Square (www.visitbirmingham. com; ✆ **0870/2250127**), is open Monday to Friday 8am to 8pm, Saturday 9am to 5pm, and Sunday 11am to 4pm. It dispenses a wealth of information and will assist travelers in arranging accommodations, obtaining theatre or concert tickets, and planning itineraries.

GETTING AROUND You can get around the center of Birmingham on foot—the Bullring Shopping Centre, Birmingham Museum and Art Gallery, the cathedral, and New Street and Moor Street stations are all within walking distance of one another. But you'll probably want to hop on public transport to get to anywhere outside the immediate center—Digbeth, the Jewellery Quarter, and the Barber Institute, as well as Cadbury World and the Black Country Museum. Buses and commuter trains are operated by Network West Midlands; go to www.networkwestmidlands.com for info. Day-Saver tickets begin at £4, while single journeys are £2. Almost all buses stop outside New Street Station. An expanding tram line connects central Birmingham with the outskirts; you can use it to get from New Street to the Jewellery Quarter (www.travelmetro. co.uk); the fare is £2.

Taxis line up at various spots in the city center and at rail stations. You can also call radio-cab operators such as **TOA Taxis** or contact them online (www.toataxis.net; ✆ **0121/427-8888**).

Squares & Neighborhoods

Birmingham is a bit scattershot, stretching across neighborhoods that are crisscrossed by wide boulevards and highways. With a bit of navigating, you can find some places that especially show off the city in a good light.

VICTORIA SQUARE ★★

The city center blocks that show off the Industrial Revolution heydays cluster around this trim, planted square, where a statue of a female nude rising from a fountain is known as the "Floosie in the Jacuzzi." Standing nearby is a stern-looking Queen Victoria, who apparently was not fond of the Midlands and ordered that the blinds of her railway carriage be drawn when she was passing through the region. Among the pompous looking neoclassical buildings on the square are the Council House, an impressive example of the Italian Renaissance style that is still the meeting place for the Birmingham City Council, and the old Town Hall, now a concert hall and modeled after Rome's temple of Castor and Pollux.

JEWELLERY QUARTER ★★

By the time lovely St Paul's church went up on the square of the same name in 1779, the surrounding streets were already lined with jewelry workshops that turned out everything from gilt buttons to buckles and watch chains. By the middle of the 19th century Birmingham was

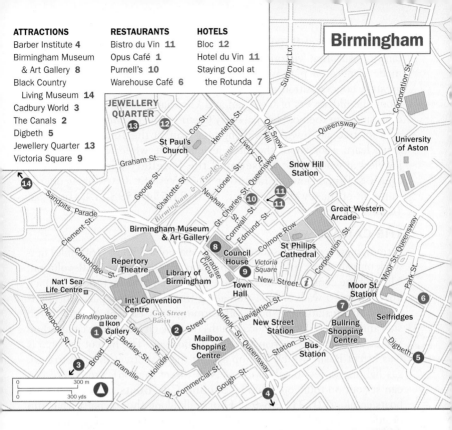

ATTRACTIONS
Barber Institute **4**
Birmingham Museum
   & Art Gallery **8**
Black Country
   Living Museum **14**
Cadbury World **3**
The Canals **2**
Digbeth **5**
Jewellery Quarter **13**
Victoria Square **9**

RESTAURANTS
Bistro du Vin **11**
Opus Café **1**
Purnell's **10**
Warehouse Café **6**

HOTELS
Bloc **12**
Hotel du Vin **11**
Staying Cool at
   the Rotunda **7**

Birmingham

Birmingham's famous fountain at Victoria Square.

producing most of Britain's silverware and fine jewelry, such an important industry that Victoria and Albert were urged to wear Birmingham-made bling as a patriotic gesture. The quarter still houses Europe's greatest concentration of jewelers, who offer their wares from shops along the old streets of Georgian and Victorian houses. You'll find a list of business in the booklet, *Jewellery Quarter: The Essential Guide*, available for free along with a walking tour map, at the Tourist Office, and you'll learn a lot about the city's jewelry trade while watching master jewelers at work at the **Museum of the Jewellery Quarter,** in the of Smith & Pepper jewelry factory at 75-79 Vyse St. (www.bmag.org.uk/museum-of-the-jewellery-quarter; ✆ **0121/554-3598**; £4, Tues–Sat 10:30am–4pm).

THE CANALS ★★★

Birmingham is crisscrossed with canals, part of a 250km (160-mile) network of waterways that were the highways of the Industrial Revolution. Many of the canals have been cleaned up, as have the factories that once lined them—a walk or boat ride along tree-lined quays past loft apartments and restaurants shows off Birmingham's elegant, cosmopolitan side and gives credence to local claims that the city has more canals than Venice and more trees than the Bois de Bologne. The hub of the area is Gas Street Basin, which laps up against the first street in town to have gas lighting (a few blocks west of New Street Station). From here you can set out on tours operated by **Second City Boats** (www.secondcityboats.co.uk; ✆ **0121/236-9811**) or walk along the towpaths that run beside the canals. For more evidence of Birmingham's sophistication, step into the **Ikon Gallery** on nearby Oozells Square (www.ikon-gallery.co.uk; ✆ **0121/248-0708**) featuring exhibitions of sound, film, mixed media, photography, painting, and sculpture.

DIGBETH ★

Anyone in search of the hip side of Birmingham should follow Digbeth Road southeast from the center into the same-named quarter, a swath of old industrial buildings that are slowly being gentrified. Ground zero is the **Custard Factory,** once the headquarters of Bird's, which manufactured a wildly popular powdered form of eggless custard. These days the vast premises on Gibb Street (www.custardfactory.co.uk; ✆ **0121/224-7777**) house art galleries, quirky shops, and cafes. Another artistic outpost is the **Eastside Projects,** 86 Heath Mill, Lane (www.eastsideprojects.org, ✆ **0121/771-1778**), another old factory now occupied by studios and galleries. At the other end of the cultural spectrum are a large number of Irish pubs—Digbeth is also known as the Irish Quarter. The most august is the **Dubliner** at 57 Digbeth High St. Bus 97A is one of several buses that run from the city center to Digbeth.

Exploring Birmingham

The historic center of Birmingham is **Victoria Square,** a 5-minute walk up New Street from New Street Station. A short walk the other way, south along Hill Street then east up Smallbrook Queensway, brings you to the Bullring, the shopping mecca at the city's commercial heart.

Barber Institute of Fine Arts ★★ MUSEUM   A 1930s stone-and-brick building looks more like a government office than a repository of fine art, but one inside the galleries hung with masterpieces you will feel as if you've stumbled into a mansion filled with a magnificent private collection. Which in a way it is: the museum is the vision of Lady Hattie Barber, who endowed the collection and building in memory of her husband Sir Henry Barber, an early 20th century real-estate developer. She succeeded in putting together what is considered to be the finest British museum outside of London. Only 120 works are on view, so you won't be overwhelmed as you stroll past portraits by Signorelli and Rubens—as well as "Portrait of a Man Holding a Skull" by Frans Halls, a somber reminder that no matter how much wealth we acquire we are all doomed to die. "Jockeys before a Race," by Degas (1878), is off the cuff and spontaneous, while George Bellow's dramatic "Nude: Miss Bentham" is one of two works in the museum by an American (the other is Whistler's "Symphony in White") and was considered groundbreaking when it was in unveiled in 1908; Andy Warhol once owned the painting.
University of Birmingham, just off Edgbaston Park Rd. www.barber.org.uk. © **0121/414-7333.** Free. Mon–Sat 10am–5pm; Sun noon–5pm. Bus: 61, 62, or 63.

Birmingham Museum & Art Gallery ★★ MUSEUM   This elegant 1885 hall, topped by a clock tower, is a monument to the Victorians. The Pre-Raphaelite painters of the period take center stage in galleries hung with works by Ford Maddox Brown, Dante Gabriel Rossetti, Edward Burne-Jones, and Holman Hunt. Looking at their works, you can't help but feel a tinge of sympathy for their good intentions gone awry. They called for a move back to the vivid colors and complex composition of medieval artists who worked before the painter Raphael introduced a more mannered approach, and they could manage, according to Charles Dickens, to make even the Holy Family look like slum dwellers and alcoholics. Another star attraction is the Staffordshire Hoard, with gold swords and other objects that comprise the most precious collection of Anglo-Saxon treasure and gold ever found. St Philip's Cathedral down the street on Colmore Row (www.birminghamcathedral.com; © **0121/262-1840**) is aglow in stained-glass windows by Pre-Raphaelite luminary Edward Burne-Jones (1833–98), who was born in Birmingham.
Chamberlain Square. www.bmag.org.uk. © **0121/303-1966.** Free; fees for special exhibitions. Mon–Thurs and Sat 10am–5pm; Fri 10:30am–5pm; Sun 12:30–5pm. Cathedral free. Mon-Fri 8:30am-6:30pm; Fri-Sat 9am-5pm.

The Birmingham Museum & Art Gallery.

Black Country Living Museum ★★ MUSEUM   The coal fields and factories that once surrounded Birmingham were known from the early 19th century as Black Country. One observer described the industrial sprawl as "black by day and red by night" and, according to Charles Dickens in "The Old Curiosity Shop," factory chimneys "Poured out their plague of smoke, obscured the light, and made foul the melancholy air." You can travel back to the era of long work weeks in grim conditions for low pay (some of the first labor strikes were staged here) as you plunge into mine shafts and step into a lime kiln. In a working man's village you can peruse the shelves of a chemist's shop and general store, moved here along with other houses and businesses, brick by brick, from surrounding towns. Among the many fascinating bits of machinery is the engine, invented surprisingly early, in 1712, by Thomas Newcomen to harness steam to power machinery. Vintage buses and trolleys traverse the 26 acres, and a trip through the Dudley Tunnel on an old canal boat is a spooky joy ride.

Tipton Rd., Dudley. www.bclm.co.uk. ✆ **0121/557-9643.** £17 adults, £8 children 5–16, £34–£47 families. Late Mar–Oct daily 10am–5pm; Nov–Dec Wed–Sun 10am–4pm (Jan–late Mar; check website).

Cadbury World ★ FACTORY TOUR   Clearly, the world loves chocolate. One of Britain's most popular attractions is this homage to the popular candy brand, the second largest confectionary company in the world. Don't expect the magical world of Willy Wonka's Chocolate Factory. Instead, you'll come away with a new appreciation for chocolate as a multibillion-dollar commodity as you follow a self-guided tour that begins with the origins of chocolate in the jungles of Aztec Mexico and comes to John's Cadbury's establishment of a company selling tea, coffee, and drinking chocolate here in Birmingham in 1824. Chocolate was then fairly exotic; the largest candy store in the world, crammed with the company products, is a testimony to its elevation to household staple—thanks in part to the company's mass-production techniques and the invention in 1914 of Dairy Milk (the precursor of the candy bar).

Linden Rd., Bournville. www.cadburyworld.co.uk. ℂ **0844/880-7667.** £16 adults, £12 seniors, £12 children 4–15, £45–£58 families. Late Jan–Dec Mon–Fri 10am–3pm (to 4:30pm in Aug); Sat–Sun 9:30am–4pm. Check website for changes in times.

Where to Stay

Most major chains operate in and around Birmingham, and since many are geared to business travellers, you can usually find some good weekend rates.

Bloc ★★   You might feel you've stepped into a train compartment, or if you're an optimist, into the cabin of a luxury liner, in these pod-like accommodations that barely fit a bed and a padded stool. Not an inch of space is wasted—certainly not on a closet, replaced here by pegs on the wall, while bathrooms are tiny but equipped with powerful showers. Fresh air is also in short supply, as windows do not open in favor of air conditioning, but Bloc is geared to guests who value price over luxury and aren't planning to spend time in the room except to sleep—good beds and linens and sound-proofing facilitate that. The Jewellery Quarter and St Paul's Square, just outside the door, are great places to wander.

Caroline St. www.blochotels.com. ℂ **0121/212-1223.** 73 units. Doubles from £45. **Amenities:** Free Wi-Fi.

Hotel du Vin ★★★   The Victorian-era Birmingham and West Midlands Eye Hospital lends itself surprisingly well to its new guise as one of the stylish outlets of this small British chain. Guest rooms named after famous wineries surround a courtyard and are as large as hospital wards but much more comfortable, with plush couches and lounge chairs, vast beds with good reading lights, and huge bathrooms with free-standing tubs and walk-in showers. Dark woods and earth tones give the air of a gentleman's club, though the lively bistro downstairs is decidedly French (see below). The cozy Cellar Bar has been carved out of storage vaults, alongside a large spa. Remnants of Victorian Birmingham, including the cathedral and art museum, are a short walk away.

Church St. www.hotelduvin.com. ℂ **08447/364250.** 66 units. Doubles £59–£90, includes breakfast. **Amenities:** Restaurant; 2 bars; spa; free Wi-Fi.

Staying Cool at the Rotunda ★★★   You'll be the envy of your Brummie friends when you take up temporary residence in these serviced apartments that occupy the top floors of the restored and iconic

A guest room at Staying Cool at the Rotunda, Birmingham.

1960s Rotunda high rise in the city center. Décor gives off an Austin Powers vibe: Think white leather couches, orange bucket chairs, and Plexiglas coffee tables. Curved floor-to-ceiling windows supply drama (Birmingham looks it best at night with its twinkling lights spread out at your feet), while iMacs, Poggi kitchens (with fridges full of breakfast food), and Gaggia coffee makers tend to practical needs. The Bullring Shopping Centre, another 60s-era relic, is just downstairs.

150 New St., Birmingham B2 4PA. www.stayingcool.com. ℭ **0121/643-0815.** 15 units. Doubles £99–£200, includes breakfast supplies. **Amenities:** Free Wi-Fi.

Where to Eat

A central spot for sandwiches is **Andersen & Hill,** in the Great Western Arcade, serving New York–style deli cuts as well as a fine selection of cheeses (www.andersonandhill.co.uk; ℭ **0121/236-2829,** Mon–Sat 10am–6pm/7pm on Thurs and Fri). **Peel & Stone,** in the Jewellery Quarter, under the railway bridge on Water Street, makes great sandwiches as well as excellent salads (peelandstone.co.uk; ℭ **0121/572-1713,** Mon–Fri 11:30am–3pm, Sat 10am–2pm).

Bistro du Vin ★★ FRENCH/MODERN BRITISH   The romantic dining room of the Hotel du Vin (see above) seems like such a Parisian standard that you can't help but to be whisked away from downtown Birmingham. The high ceilings, polished wood floors, and walls crammed with prints and paintings are bathed in flickering candlelight to provide the perfect setting for home-style French cooking. Bistro classics like escargots, steak frites, and roast chicken (along with some British

standards) are served by a knowledgeable staff well versed in the excellent wines. The well-stocked cheese trolley nicely tops off a meal.
Church St. www.hotelduvin.com. © **084473/64250.** Mains £14–£25. Mon–Sat noon–2:30pm, 5:30–10pm; Sun noon–4pm, 6–9:30pm.

Opus Café ★ MODERN BRITISH The kitchen at the bright and airy cafe of the Ikon Gallery (p. 322) serves breakfasts all day—British breakfast, that is, as in boiled egg with soldiers (toast points). Salads are meal size, and fish, chicken, and beef (braised in beer with bacon) are locally sourced. A two-course all-day menu at £10 is good prep for a walk along the city's canals, setting off from nearby Gas Street Basin.
Oozells Sq. www.cafeopus.co.uk. © **0121/248-3226.** Mains £7–£9. Mon–Sat 10am–8pm; Sun 11am–5pm.

Purnell's ★★★ MODERN BRITISH The mere mention of Glyn Purnell is enough to get foodies salivating, and Birmingham is rightfully proud of this accomplished chef's presence in the city. The décor, a soulless study in brown and black, is not likely to warm hearts, but just about everything that appears on the table will, from roasted duck liver to caramelized lamb shoulder to vanilla parfait; cooking is adventurous and masterful, and prices make for one of the best dining bargains in the land.
55 Cornwall St. www.purnellsrestaurant.com. © **0121/212-9799.** Menus from £32. Tues–Fri noon–4:30pm; Tues–Sat 7–9:30pm. Closed 1 week at Easter, last week in July, 1st week in Aug, and 1 week at Christmas.

The Warehouse Café ★ VEGAN CAFE A meal or snack at this funky, loft-like, white-walled cafe on the first floor of the Birmingham headquarters of Friends of the Earth is almost mandatory on a foray into the artsy quarter of Digbeth. You can do a bit of globe-trotting on the inspired menu with nods to Greek tzatziki, Moroccan couscous,

---

Bucket Dining in the Balti Triangle

Pakistani Kashmiri immigrants settled in Birmingham in the late 1970s, and they brought Balti with them. *Balti* literally means bucket, but it refers to a Kashmiri style of cooking meat and vegetables very fast over a hot flame; dishes are flavorful but not necessarily spicy and served with naan bread, not rice. There are now more than 50 *balti* houses in Birmingham's Balti Triangle (roughly within Ladypool Road, Stoney Lane, and Stratford Road), a 10-minute taxi ride south of the city center and on bus routes 6, 12, 31, 35, and 37. Most are bare-bones, BYOB affairs, and charge about £6 for a basic balti. Two of the oldest are **Adil,** 148-150 Stoney Lane (www.adilbalti.co.uk; © **0121/449-0335**), open Monday to Friday 5pm to midnight, and weekends noon to midnight, and **Al Faisals,** 136-140 Stoney Lane (alfaisal.co.uk; © **0121/449-5695**), open daily noon to midnight.

The distinctive Selfridge's store at Bullring shopping center, Birmingham.

Malaysian laksa, Italian risottos, and even an English trifle, and the laid-back surroundings encourage lingering over coffee or tea.

54-57 Allison St. www.thewarehousecafe.com. ℂ **0121/633-0261.** Mains £8–£9. Mon–Sat 11am–10pm; Sun 11am–6pm.

Shopping

Birmingham is the shopping hub for the Midlands, with a focus on department stores and international chains. The **Bullring,** in the heart of town near St Martin's Square (www.bullring.co.uk; ℂ **0121/632-1500**), is Europe's largest city-center retail area, with hundreds of stores. The star is **Selfridges** (www.selfridges.com), smothered in 15,000 aluminum discs that make it look like it's been bubble-wrapped. More upscale **Mailbox,** another urban shopping complex, is near the canals at Wharfside Street (www.mailboxlife.com; ℂ **0121/632-1000**). **Great Western Arcade** (www.greatwesternarcade.co.uk), just opposite Snow Hill railway station, houses smaller, independent stores amid Victorian elegance. Aside from the Jewellery Quarter you'll find distinctive shops in **Balti Triangle**, selling Indian textiles and food, and in **Digbeth,** especially in the **Custard Factory** (www.custardfactory.co.uk; ℂ **0121/224-7777**), with many galleries and vintage shops.

Entertainment & Nightlife

The Birmingham Visitor Centre (visitbirmingham.com) is a good source for what's happening on the city's active cultural scene and sells tickets. **Birmingham Symphony Hall,** Broad Street (www.thsh.co.uk;

☎ 0121/780-3333) is home to the highly acclaimed **City of Birmingham Symphony Orchestra,** and also hosts other classical music performances. The **Birmingham Royal Ballet** and visiting companies from around the world perform at the **Birmingham Hippodrome,** Hurst Street (www.birminghamhippodrome.com; ☎ **0844/338-5000**), while the **Birmingham Repertory,** one of the top theatre companies in England, performs at its theatre at Broad Street, on Centenary Square (www.birmingham-rep.co.uk; ☎ **0121/236-4455**). **New Alexandra Theatre,** Station Street (☎ **0121/643-5536**) hosts national touring companies, including productions from London's West End.

Birmingham's most atmospheric pubs by no accident happen to be in two of its most colorful neighborhoods: The **Old Crown,** in Digbeth at 188 High St. (www.theoldcrown.com; ☎ **0121/248-1368**) is Birmingham's oldest place to drink, dating to 1368, while **The Lord Clifden,** in the Jewellery Quarter at 34 Great Hampton St. (www.thelordclifden.com; ☎ **0121/523-7515**) hosts a wonderful collection of works by up and coming Birmingham artists.

As befits the home of Ozzy Osbourne, UB40, Duran Duran, and The Streets (aka local boy Mike Skinner), the Birmingham nightlife scene is especially lively. Among the popular venues are the **Hare and Hounds** pub, 106 High St. (hareandhoundskingsheath.co.uk; ☎ **0121/444-2081**), and The **02 Academy,** 16-18 Horsefair, Bristol St. (www.o2academybirmingham.co.uk; ☎ **0121/622-8247**).

Day Trips from Birmingham

COVENTRY ★
23 miles SE of Birmingham

The second largest city in the Midlands is best known for what's no longer there, a historic center once considered to be the finest concentration of medieval buildings in Britain. German bombers flattened Coventry on the night of November 14, 1940, when houses and industrial plants (many making munitions and aircraft) were engulfed in a firestorm so devastating that the term "coventrate" was coined to describe the act of completely destroying a city. What the Luftwaffe didn't achieve postwar architects did, replacing the ruins with Brutalist-style concrete office and housing blocks. A glorious exception is **Coventry Cathedral ★★**, rebuilt

Coventry Cathedral.

Coventry's Famous Naked Lady

Coventry's best-known citizen might be Lady Godiva, who took a legendary ride in the nude through town in the 11th century. As the story goes, the noblewoman agreed to the stunt if her wealthy landowner husband would revoke some of the taxes he imposed on his tenants. She forewarned the townsfolk to stay indoors and keep their shutters closed, but one fellow named Thomas couldn't resist looking—and has ever since been known as Peeping Tom. It's recorded fact that Lady Godiva and her husband, Leofric, were generous benefactors of several monasteries and that they regularly presented churches, St Paul's in London among them, with silver and gold ornaments. The long-haired beauty still rides through Coventry, in the guise of a statue on Broadgate in the center of town.

in the post-war years to incorporate the ruins of the 13th–14th-century original. Just beyond the stark, skeletal ruins is the new cathedral, over-powered by a 72-foot-tall tapestry of Christ, the most noted work of artist Graham Sutherland (1903–80). Entrance into the new cathedral becomes a symbolic journey from devastation to hope, the ultimate message of faith. A moving presence amid the stunning floor-to-ceiling stained-glass windows and sculptor Jason Epstein's "St Michael's Victory Over the Devil" are some crude crosses—one is fashioned from charred timbers that crashed to the floor during the bombing, others clumsily made by joining together medieval nails.

The cathedral, 7 Priory Row (www.coventrycathedral.org.uk; ℂ 024/7652-1200) is open Monday to Saturday from 10am to 5pm, and Sunday noon to 4pm; the ruins are open daily 9am to 5pm, and the tower is open during summer months when staff availability permits. Admission to the cathedral is £6 for adults; £5 for seniors and students; free for children. Tower admission is £3. Anyone can attend evensong, at 5:15pm (4pm on Sat), free of charge. The drive between Birmingham and Coventry takes about half an hour on A38 and the M6. Trains (nationalrail.co.uk) run between Birmingham New Street Station and Coventry every 15 minutes; the trip takes less than half an hour.

THE POTTERIES ★
46 miles N of Birmingham; 41 miles S of Manchester

Ceramic buffs might want to make a pilgrimage to **Stoke-on-Trent,** though it's necessary to leave behind any notions of cutesy crafts villages and cozy workshops. Stoke is a sprawl of six drab industrial towns (Tunstall, Burslem, Stoke, Fenton, Longton, and Hanley). Kilns were busy here in the 14th century, and Josiah Wedgwood (1730–95), perhaps England's most distinguished potter, helped propel the region into the industrial age. As many as 4,000 kilns, fueled by abundant local reserves of coal, once fired pieces fashioned from the clay that lay just below the ground. In fact, clay was once dug right out of the roads, giving us the phrase "pot hole." Dozens of factories manufactured everything from fine china place settings fit for kings and queens to porcelain toilets.

Most of the great kilns have disappeared, but shops, outlets, and museums remain. Among these is the **Potteries Museum & Art Gallery ★★**, Bethesda St., City Centre, Stoke-on-Trent, with the world's greatest collection of Staffordshire ceramics. Keep an eye out for the Staffordshire spaniels—these kitschy dog figurines were a Victorian staple and at one time no home was complete without a pair on the mantelpiece (www.stoke.gov.uk/museum; ✆ **01782/232323;** free; Mon–Sat 10am–5pm, Sun 2–5pm). At the **Wedgwood Museum & Visitor Centre ★**, Barlaston, Stoke-on-Kent, displays glisten with the famous company's output that includes a vase that Josiah Wedgwood created almost three centuries ago (www.wedgwoodmuseum.org.uk; ✆ **01782/371919;** £6 adults, £5 seniors and children 5–16, Mon–Fri 10am–5pm, weekends 10am–4pm). Many stores sell famous brands at discount prices, including **Portmeiron Factory Shop,** 473 King St., Longton, Stoke-on-Trent (✆ **01782/326661**), where the huge stock includes seconds (pieces that have minor flaws), and **Aynsley China,** Sutherland Road, Longton, Stoke-on-Trent (✆ **01782/339420**), with a wide selection of the U.K.'s favorite best-quality fine bone china.

The **Stoke-on-Trent Tourist Information Centre,** next to the train station in Stoke in Victoria Hall, Bagnall Street (www.visitstoke.co.uk; ✆ **01782/236000**), hands out a map of factories, museums, and shops; you can also download a handy map from the website. The office is open Monday to Friday 9am to 5pm, and Saturday 10am to

2pm. Getting to Stoke is easy—trains to and from Birmingham run about every half hour (nationalrail.co.uk) and the trip takes about 45 minutes. Stoke is just off the M6 motorway. Getting around the spread-out towns is a little more difficult if you are not traveling by car, though buses run from the rail station and tourist office to many of the potteries and museums.

THE WELSH MARCHES

The borderlands between England and Wales became known as the Welsh Marches, or the March of Wales, in the Middle Ages, and today comprise the counties of Herefordshire and Shropshire. This is the green heart of England, where lush river valleys and rolling hills, welcoming towns of half-timbered houses, and romantic old castles and manor houses are a pretty counterpoint to the industrial Midlands just to the east.

Essentials

GETTING THERE   London Midland trains run from Birmingham New Street Station to Shrewsbury about every half hour and the trip takes an hour. From Shrewsbury, Arriva trains on the Welsh Marches line connect to Ludlow and Hereford. For schedules and tickets, go to www.national rail.co.uk.

VISITOR INFORMATION   Hereford Tourist Information Centre (www.visitherefordshire.co.uk; ℂ 01432/268430) is located at 1 King St. and is open April to September daily 9:30am to 4:30pm, and October to March Monday to Friday 10am to 4:30pm. The **Shrewsbury Tourist Information Centre,** in Rowley's House Museum on Barker Street (www.visitshrewsbury.com; ℂ 01743/281200), is open May to September Monday to Saturday from 10am to 5pm, Sunday 10am to 4pm. From October to April, its hours are Monday to Saturday from 10am to 4pm. The Ludlow Visitor Information Centre is in the Assembly Rooms, 1 Mill St., and is open Monday to Saturday 10am to 8pm.

Exploring the Welsh Marches

The pleasure of being in this gentle countryside is to wander through the hills from one pretty market town to the next. By car, the place to begin is Shrewsbury, less than an hour west of Birmingham via the M54, and from there to follow the A49 south through Ludlow to Hereford. You can also follow the route by train, traveling to Shrewsbury and connecting to trains that link this trio of towns on the Welsh Marches line. You can also follow Offa's Dyke Path, a 177-mile walking trail along the 8th-century earthen dyke built on orders of Anglo-Saxon King Offa, which for many centuries marked the boundary between Wales and England; for more information go to www.nationaltrail.co.uk/offas-dyke-path.

SHREWSBURY ★★

48 miles W of Birmingham; 170 miles NW of London

This town near the Welsh border on the River Severn has seen its share of conflict over the years—including a siege in 1069 repelled by William the Conqueror—but a huge swath of black-and-white half-timbered buildings suggest nothing but the prosperity that came with the medieval wool trade. In your wanderings along enticing medieval lanes and alleyways (called "shuts," as they were closed off at night to keep out riffraff) you'll come upon a statue of Charles Darwin outside the library (formerly the school where the scientist was educated); the author of "On the Origin of Species" was born in Shrewsbury in 1809.

The center of town is the Square, where the 16th-century **Market Hall** housed produce stalls on the ground floor and a cloth exchange in the upper chambers. Atmospherically narrow **Grope Lane** is so called because the darkness created by the overhanging buildings required pre-street-lights pedestrians to grope their way along the narrow passageway, while **Fish Street** is a lovely assemblage of medieval houses. **Bear Steps** (named for a Tudor pub) will lead you to **St Mary's Church,** where the impressive 1340 Tree of Jesse window is a colorful depiction of the family tree of Christ, taken quite literally from the biblical reference (Isaiah 11:1) that Jesus is a shoot coming up from the stump of Jesse, the father of David. Two more streets of handsome old houses, **Dogpole** and **Wyle Coop,** lead down to the river and Shrewsbury Abbey. The crossing here, English Bridge, is one of two historic spans across the River Severn—the other is Welsh Bridge across town, and together the two say a lot about Shrewsbury's onetime strategic position.

Shrewsbury Abbey ★ ABBEY   The nave, porch, and aisles of a handsome church are all that remain of a vast Benedictine monastery that flourished near the banks of the River Severn from the end of the 11th century. The place became one of the England's medieval hotspots when the remains of 7th-century Welsh holy woman St Winifride were enshrined here. Pilgrims flocked to Shrewsbury in honor of Winifride's astonishing feat—her suitor, Caradoc, decapitated her when she spurned him to become a nun, but she miraculously came back to life when an uncle placed her head back on her shoulders. The monastery was dissolved by Henry VIII in the 1530s and slowly fell into ruin; even the grounds were desecrated when a road was built across them in the 1830s. You can still see stone pulpits and other remnants scattered amid foliage alongside the church, with the base of Winefride's ruined shrine still in place. Poet Wilfred Owen is among those whose names are inscribed on a tablet commemorating parishioners who lost their lives in World War I.

Abbey Foregate, Shrewsbury. www.shrewsburyabbey.com. ✆ **01743/232723.** Free; donations of £2 requested. Mon–Sat 10:30am–3pm, Sun 11:30am–2:30pm.

Shrewsbury Castle ★ CASTLE The red sandstone fortress that Norman earl Roger de Montgomery built in 1083 to secure the border with Wales is a rather bland shadow of its former self, having been severely remodeled 200 years ago by Thomas Telford. The Scottish architect and civil engineer so aggressively set about building roads, bridges, and canals that he was dubbed "The Colossus of Roads." Here in Shrewsbury he also laid the roadway through the abbey grounds (see above). If you decide to step into the castle precincts for a look through the Shropshire Regimental Museum's dry assortment of uniforms, medals, and weapons, keep an eye out for the American flag captured when the British burned the White House during the War of 1812.

Castle St., Shrewsbury. www.shrewsburymuseums.com/castle. ✆ **01743/361196.** £3 adults, £2 seniors, free for students and children 18 and under. Sept 10–Dec 22 and Feb 13–May 26 Mon–Sat 10:30am–4pm; May 27–Sept 9 Mon–Sun 10:30am–5pm. Closed Thurs, and Dec 23–Feb 12. Call ahead, as hours may change.

LUDLOW ★★

28 miles S of Shrewsbury; 40 miles W of Birmingham; 157 miles NW of London

A beautiful setting on two rivers backed by green hillsides and a remarkable jumble of medieval, Georgian, and Victorian houses come together to make this genteel market town a lovely place. In fact, Britain's popular poet laureate Sir John Betjeman gave Ludlow his seal of approval as "probably the loveliest town in England." Aside from taking in countryside views from the enormous ruined castle and following little lanes past half-timbered facades to the banks of the Rivers Teme and Corve, the thing to do in Ludlow is to eat, as the town attracts a disproportionate number of bakers, cheese mongers, and restaurateurs.

Ludlow Castle ★ CASTLE This spell-binding ruin, begun shortly after the Norman conquest and one of the first stone castles built in England, is the "very perfection of decay," according to 18th-century visitor Daniel Defoe. Enough remains of the massive red sandstone fortress to suggest its former might as the seat of lords who oversaw the borderlands between England and Wales. Powerful nobleman Roger Mortimer and King James I both spent considerable resources turning the castle into a luxurious palace, Catherine of Aragon spent her honeymoon here, and the little princes, sons of Edward IV, were held here before disappearing into the Tower of London. An especially evocative remnant is the Chapel of St Mary Magdalene, modeled after the Church of the Holy Sepulcher in Jerusalem, with one of England's last remaining circular naves. The **Castle Tea Room** operates out of several atmospheric venues within the castle, including a centuries-old scullery, a cozy, fire-warmed study, and a breezy terrace (open 10am–5pm, to 3pm in winter, and from 11am–closing on Sun).

Castle Square, Ludlow. www.ludlowcastle.com. ✆ **01584/873355.** £5 adults, £3 children 6–16, £14 families, free for children 5 and under. Daily 10am–5pm.

St Laurence Church ★★ CHURCH The wool trade was big business in medieval Ludlow, and 15th century merchants poured much of their wealth into renovating an already formidable Norman church as a way to ensure spiritual salvation while showing off material success. Wealthiest of the donors were the so-called Palmers, an elite guild whose membership was restricted to men who had made the pilgrimage to Jerusalem (and brought back a palm as proof of the feat). You can see a visual account of their journey in a magnificent stained-glass window in the north chapel they funded and in which, for a little extra insurance, six full time priests said mass for their souls. Far less pious are the choir stalls' misericords, or mercy seats, against which priests could lean during long services: Carvings depict witches, mermaids, a dishonest ale wife being dragged off to hell, and other scenes, real and fanciful, from everyday medieval life. The most esteemed person interred here is 15-year-old Prince Arthur, son and heir to King Henry VII who died in Ludlow not long after he arrived with his bride, Catherine of Aragon. Catherine, daughter of the Spanish monarchs Ferdinand and Isabella, went on to marry Arthur's younger brother Henry VIII, while Arthur's heart was placed in an undetermined spot in the church. The ashes of poet A.E. Houseman (1859–1936) were scattered in the churchyard; he evoked the surrounding countryside in his cycle "A Shropshire Lad."

College St., Ludlow. www.stlaurences.org.uk. ☏ **01584/872073.** Free. Summer 10am–5:30pm, winter 11am–4pm.

Stokesay Castle ★★★ ARCHITECTURAL SITE It's our good fortune that at the end of the 13th-century wool merchant Laurence of

The 17th-century gatehouse at Stokesay Castle, Ludlow.

The River Wye at Hereford.

Ludlow aspired to become a country squire. He built this harmonious, honey-colored, slate-roof manor in the lush Shropshire countryside it's now the finest fortified manor house in England. Later owners have been kind, adding only a paneled chamber here and there and an outrageously picturesque 17th-century gatehouse. The Great Hall is a medieval marvel, with a huge octagonal hearth and a staircase hewn from whole tree trunks that climbs toward the timbered roof. The steep castle walls and formidable north tower are probably a testament to Laurence's need to prove that a man's home is his castle—Welsh border battles had quieted down when the manor was built, and an intruder could have simply climbed in through one of the Great Hall's floor-length windows.

Stokesay, Craven Arms. www.english-heritage.org.uk. © **0370/333-1181.** £7 adults, £6 seniors, £4 children 5–15, £17 families. Late Mar–Sept daily 10am–6pm; Oct daily 10am–5pm; Nov–late Mar weekends 10am–4pm.

HEREFORD ★

24 miles S of Ludlow; 57 miles SW of Birmingham; 173 miles NW of London

As you approach this pretty market town you'll notice the famous white-faced Hereford cattle grazing in verdant pastures, while on the narrow lanes and squares carts sell cider that's just been pressed from apples right off the trees in the many orchards. You'll get the impression that Hereford is a fairly contented country town, and you need only step into the gloriously half-timbered Old House, a fine 17th-century mansion on High Town (© **01432/260694**), for proof that's been the case for a long time (free admission, open Tues–Sat 10am–5pm).

Hereford Cathedral ★★   If this great medieval monument seems unusually sturdy, there's a good reason. In 1056 Welsh invaders razed the Saxon church that stood here, and a couple of centuries later the Normans replaced it with an attack-proof version that has been ravaged over the centuries only by some ham-handed remodelers. Massive pillars and semicircular arches in the nave are a holdover from the Middle Ages, and in an adjoining fan-vaulted chantry is the **Mappa Mundi ★★★**, a map from 1290 that portrays the earth as flat and centered around Jerusalem. This is probably the most important medieval map in the world, as well as one of the age's finest illuminated manuscripts. Some 500 drawings superimposed on the continents present a picture of the world as it then existed, with depictions of around 420 cities and towns, Biblical events, plants, animals, birds and strange creatures, peoples of the world, and scenes from classical mythology. A 229-book **Chained Library ★** of medieval manuscripts (chained to rods on the back of the shelves) includes an 8th-century Anglo-Saxon gospel, and the cathedral possesses one of four original copies of the Magna Carta.

Cathedral Close, Hereford. www.herefordcathedral.org. © **01432/374200.** Free, donation of £5 suggested. Mappa Mundi and Chained Library £6 adults, £5 seniors and children 5–18. Cathedral Mon–Sat 9:15am–5:30pm, Sun 9:15am–3:30pm; exhibits daily 10am–5pm (4pm in winter).

Where to Stay

Castle Inn ★   Two adjoining Georgian villas next to the moat of Hereford's long-vanished castle and a nearby townhouse still have the air of private homes, with ornate plasterwork and other fine details, along with a beautiful garden. Guest rooms are traditionally plush, with handsome reproduction antiques and the occasional four-poster bed. A decanter of locally pressed cider brandy is a nice perk, a perfect nightcap after a meal in the Castle Restaurant downstairs.

Castle St., Hereford. www.castlehse.co.uk. © **01432/356321.** 24 units. Doubles from £150, includes breakfast. **Amenities:** Restaurant; bar; free Wi-Fi.

10

THE HEART OF ENGLAND

The Welsh Marches

The Feathers ★   You'll be sleeping amid a lot of history at this iconic Ludlow landmark, a popular gathering spot since the heavy Tudor beams and fanciful half timbering were put in place in 1619. You might also be sharing your quarters with a ghost or two—some guests even claim to have been dragged out of bed by their hair, others have awaken to find a gentleman and his hound at their bedside. Rooms are pleasantly comfortable, with traditional furnishings and enough beams and other quaint touches to keep things interesting, hauntings aside.

The Bull Ring, Ludlow. www.feathersatludlow.co.uk. ℂ **01584/875261.** 40 units. Doubles from £125, includes breakfast. **Amenities:** Restaurant; bar; free Wi-Fi.

Lion and Pheasant ★★★   The lower floors of these two old townhouses are a delightful warren of nooks and crannies that open into cozy lounges and hearth-warmed dining rooms (see below). Upstairs guest rooms are done in soothing neutrals that let the old beams, dormers, and fireplaces work their charms. Furnishings throughout are a tasteful blend of traditional (oak or wrought-iron beds in all rooms) with slight overtones of Scandinavian contemporary, and the white walls and fluffy duvets are accented with cheerful bursts of color. A view of the River Severn as it flows beneath English Bridge adds another flutter of drama.

49-50 Wyle Coop, Shrewsbury. www.lionandpheasant.co.uk. ℂ **01743/770345.** 22 units. Doubles from £99, includes breakfast. **Amenities:** Restaurant; bar; free Wi-Fi.

Ludlow Castle ★★★   Join the likes of Catherine of Aragon, James I, and other distinguished guests of this now-ruined castle, where a house on the grounds has been converted to three comfortable apartments. All

A guest room at Lion and Pheasant, Shrewsbury.

have sitting/dining rooms, fully equipped kitchens, two bedrooms, and one or two bathrooms—plus big bathtubs, powerful showers, and all sorts of other amenities that former castle occupants would have given up their kingdoms to enjoy. A stay comes with a chance to wander through the lovely gardens, along with entrance to the castle.

Ludlow Castle, Castle Sq., Ludlow. www.ludlowcastle.com. (C) **01584/873355.** 3 units. From £895 a week, £445 for 4 days. **Amenities:** Restaurant; free Wi-Fi.

Where to Eat

Arrive in Ludlow with an appetite, because the town is devoted to good eating. Some notable stops include **Mousetrap Cheese Shop,** 6 Church St. (www.mousetrapcheese.co.uk; (C) **01584/879556**) for an introduction to Shropshire and Herefordshire cheeses; they also have a shop in Hereford at 30 Church St. ((C) **01432/353423**). **Price and Sons,** 7 Castle St. (www.pricesthebakers.co.uk; (C) **01584/872815**) bakes bread on the premises and make excellent.

Café @ All Saints ★ CAFE/COFFEEHOUSE   You might feel a bit like you're in a church cafeteria as you work your way down the buffet line at Hereford's favorite cafe, and in a way you are. The lofty stone arches and timbered roof are part of a deconsecrated church. Cheese, milk, eggs, produce, and just about everything comes from farms around town, including the beef and pork, and the bread, scones, and other pastries are homemade. All this local bounty shows up in inventive pies, quiches, soups, and well-stuffed sandwiches, served at lunch only, though breakfast is excellent, too, as are the cakes and coffee.

All Saints Church, High St., Hereford. www.cafeatallsaints.co.uk. (C) **01432/370415.** Mains £4–£9. Mon–Sat 8am–5pm.

Lion and Pheasant ★★ CONTEMPORARY ENGLISH   The beamed and wood-floored dining areas of Shrewsbury's same-named hotel seem like a cozy pub and an airy Scandinavian country house at the same time. They're the setting for meals that are stylish and down to earth—though there's nothing unsophisticated about sea bass pan fried with chorizo or the locally sourced medallions of duck breast or steaks. Naturally, any meal should end with a selection of Shropshire cheeses.

49-50 Wyle Coop, Shrewsbury. www.lionandpheasant.co.uk. (C) **01743/770345.** Mains £19–£26. Daily noon–2:30pm and 6–10pm.

Mr. Underhill's ★★★ CONTEMPORARY ENGLISH/ MEDITER-RANEAN   Before dinner, you can fish just off the terrace along the banks of the River Teme as it flows beneath Ludlow's Castle, or just sit and enjoy a drink. As relaxing and casual as the setting is, eating in Ludlow's most famous restaurant, and the only one with a Michelin star, is serious business. Many diners come to Ludlow for the sole purpose of partaking of the nine-course ritual that begins between 7:15 and 8:00

and lasts the rest of the evening. You can spend the night, too, in one of the four well-appointed suites, though they're surprisingly expensive (from £220) given the extremely good value of dinner.

Dinham Weir, Ludlow. www.mr-underhills.co.uk. ✆ **01584/874431.** Fixed-price 8-course dinner £68–£75. Wed–Sun from 7:15.

IRONBRIDGE ★★★

135 miles NW of London; 36 miles NW of Birmingham; 18 miles SE of Shrewsbury

In 1709, Quaker ironmaster Abraham Darby, working at a water-powered blast furnace in the gorge of the Severn River, discovered a method for smelting iron by using coke as a fuel, rather than charcoal. The process made it much less expensive to manufacture iron, so rails, wheels, girders, beams, and other iron products could be mass-produced—the Industrial Revolution was underway. In 1779, Darby's grandson Abraham Darby III built the world's first iron bridge across the Severn, giving the area a new name, and soon the gorge was humming with industrial activity and littered with mines, pit mounds, spoil heaps, foundries, factories, workshops, warehouses, iron masters' and workers' housing, and public buildings. Today these industrial sites and historic properties are preserved as the **Ironbridge Gorge Museums.**

Essentials

GETTING THERE   The nearest **train** and long-distance **bus** station is in **Telford,** 5 miles north of Ironbridge and well connected to London and Birmingham. The **Gorge Connect** bus service links Telford Central Station to Ironbridge, a 20-minute ride. Fares are 50p per ride or £3 for an unlimited Day-Rover pass, useful as the bus connects all the major sights in Ironbridge. The catch is that the bus only runs on weekends and bank holiday Mondays April to October; buses run every 30 minutes or so between 9:30am and 3:54pm from Telford. Go to www.telford.gov.uk for more info. Alternatively, **Arriva** runs regular buses Monday to Friday to Ironbridge from Telford and Shrewsbury. See www.traveline.info for timetables. By **car,** Ironbridge can be approached by the M54 from Birmingham or Shrewsbury; once there, shuttle buses (1£ round-trip) make a circuit from well-marked car parks (2£ flat fee) to the sights.

VISITOR INFORMATION   The **Ironbridge Tourist Information Centre,** the Tollhouse (www.visitironbridge.co.uk; ✆ **01952/884391**), is open Monday to Friday 9am to 5pm, Saturday and Sunday 10am to 5pm.

Exploring Ironbridge

On even a short visit you'll want to take a good look at the Iron Bridge and walk across at least a portion of it, and you'll probably want to step into **Blists Hill Victorian Town,** if only for some authentic British refreshments (have a pint at the **New Inn** pub on High Street and fish and chips at **Fried Fish Dealers** on Canal Street). The **Museum of the Gorge** brings the importance of the region to light and explores the origins and world-changing consequences of the Industrial Revolution. A walk into the **Tar Tunnel** is an eerie but unusual experience, and a look at the **Hay Inclined Plane** shows off engineering ingenuity. What you see beyond these sights depends on your interests in various crafts (china in the **Coalport China Museum,** tiles in the **Jackfield Tile Museum,** pipes in the **Broseley Pipeworks,** iron-mongering in the **Coalbrookdale Museum of Iron**). Nine of the ten **Ironbridge Gorge Museums ★★** (www.ironbridge.org.uk; © **01952/433424**) are open March through October daily from 9am to 5pm; Broseley Pipeworks is open daily mid-May to mid-September from 1 to 5pm. The Tar Tunnel, Darby Houses, and Broseley Pipeworks close from November to March, and the other sites are open 10am to 5pm (Blists closes at 4pm). A passport ticket to all museums in Ironbridge Gorge is £28 for adults, £22 for seniors, £17 for students and children 5 to 18, £60 to £68 for families.

BLISTS HILL VICTORIAN TOWN ★★ Life as it once was in Shropshire is re-created in shops, pubs, a school, and a fairground, as well as in a foundry, print shop, sawmill, and other operations (£17 adults; £14 over 60; £12 children 5–18).

BROSELEY PIPEWORKS ★ Clay pipes were all the rage before rolled cigarettes came onto the scene in the late 19th century, and this pipe-making factory, abandoned 50 years ago, was once of Britain's largest suppliers (£6 adults; £5 over 60; £4 children 5–18).

COALBROOKDALE MUSEUM OF IRON ★ This is where it all began, in what remains of the blast furnace in which Abraham Darby perfected his method for smelting iron with coke, readily available in seams beneath the gorge. Displays demonstrate how the process works and how these ironworks launched the Industrial Revolution, while the glorious Boy and the Swan fountain, made on the premises for London's Great Exhibition in 1855, shows off the aesthetic side of iron-mongering (combined with Darby Houses: £10 adults; £9 over 60; £7 children 5–18).

COALPORT CHINA MUSEUM ★ One of Britain's finest manufacturers of china operated here between 1795 and 1926, and the company's huge kilns and impressive output—including the ostentatious Northumberland Vase, the largest piece the company ever made—are on display (£9 adults; £8 over 60; £6 children 5–18).

DARBY HOUSES ★ Abraham Darby lived in Dale House, overlooking the pool that powered his blast furnace. Nearby Rosehill House was home to generations of Darbys who oversaw the Coalbrookdale iron-works and where Abraham Darby III drew up the plans for his world-changing bridge. (combined with Coalbrookdale Museum of Iron: £10 adults; £9 over 60; £7 children 5–18).

ENGINIUTY ★   Hands-on displays of water power and horsepower will appeal to young and old, who'll also learn about X-rays, robotics, and other later inventions (£9 adults; £8 over 60 and children 5–18).

IRON BRIDGE & TOLLHOUSE ★★ The graceful span, the world's first major cast-iron structure, has become a symbol of the industrial revolution and affords great views up and down the gorge (free).

JACKFIELD TILE MUSEUM ★ Factories in the gorge were among Britain's largest producers of ceramic tiles and at the center of the world tile industry; sumptuously tiled rooms and an Edwardian tube station show off the output and artisans demonstrate tile pressing, decorating, and firing (£9 adults; £8 over 60; £6 children 5–18).

The world's first iron bridge, from 1779, at the River Severn, Ironbridge.

MUSEUM OF THE GORGE ★   The importance of the region's many industries come to the fore in exhibits that include a 40-foot-long model of Ironbridge Gorge as it appeared in 1796 (£5 adults; £4 over 60; £3 children 5–18).

TAR TUNNEL ★★   Late 18th-century engineers planned a tunnel to connect mine shafts to the banks of the River Severn, where coal could be loaded onto boats. Some 3,000 feet into the project they decided to abandon the idea when bitumen began bubbling to the surface—the thick, sticky black substance was ideal for waterproofing rope and caulking wooden ships, and was said to be a remedy for rheumatism. It still drips into the tunnel (£4 adults, £3 over 60 and children 5–18). The nearby **Hay Inclined Plane** was built to hoist boats along a railroad track from the Severn River to the Coalport Canal, a difference in elevation of 270 feet, using a combination of steam power and gravity (free).

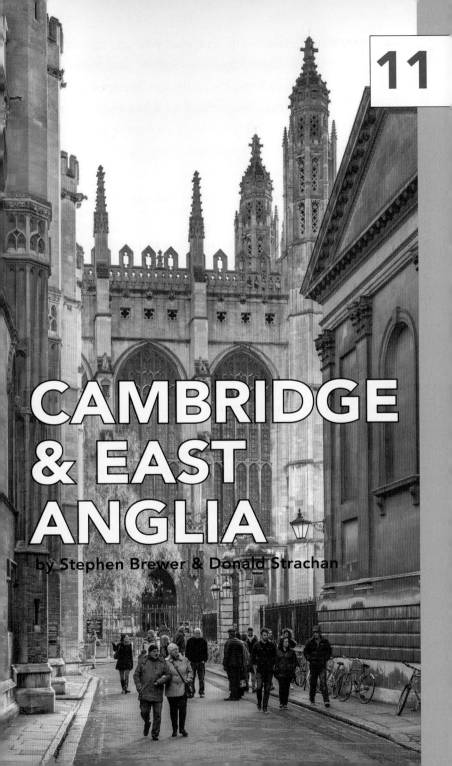

CAMBRIDGE & EAST ANGLIA

by Stephen Brewer & Donald Strachan

The farther north and east you go, East Anglia—Essex, Cambridgeshire, Suffolk, and Norfolk—the lower and flatter the landscape becomes; swathes of open fields, crisscrossed by dykes and ditches, turn to forest and heath until you come to the watery haven of the Norfolk Broads and then the coast.

East Anglia's most famous town is **Cambridge,** with its ornate colleges and chapels, while to the northeast is **Norwich,** the region's largest town, with a Norman castle and cathedral to show for its power and prosperity. Rising from the very flat landscapes are fine old wool towns—**Lavenham** and **Saffron Walden** are two of the prettiest—and many remarkable architectural landmarks, including the tall spire of Ely cathedral. Then there are those landscapes themselves—reed-lined waterways that are an adventure to explore by boat, long empty beaches, shimmering rivers, and broad skies that once inspired painter John Constable and will stir you, too.

CAMBRIDGE

55 miles N of London; 80 miles NE of Oxford

Though Cambridge traces its roots to a Roman fording place on the River Cam, the city is forever linked to the venerable university that has flourished on the river banks for eight centuries. Turreted college halls, magnificent chapels and old libraries, and the park-like "Backs" along the River Cam are as much a part of the city as its markets and busy little lanes. Spend time walking along King's Parade, floating on the river in a punt, admiring the medieval and Tudor monuments, or just sitting in one of the city's 100 pubs and a little of the fairy dust might rub off. You'll certainly envy the young scholars who get to spend several years here.

Essentials

GETTING THERE   Train trips between London's Kings Cross and Cambridge take 45 minutes to an hour while the trip from London's Liverpool Street is about 80 minutes. For schedules and information go to www.nationalrail.co.uk. Cambridge train station is one mile south of the center on Station Road; buses (Citi 1, 3, and 7) run about 15 minutes; National Express **buses** leave London's Victoria Station for Cambridge about every half-hour or so. Some buses make the trip in less than 2 hours, though others make more stops and can take considerably longer. The Cambridge bus station is near the city center, on Drummer Street.

PREVIOUS PAGE: **Approaching King's College Chapel, Cambridge.**

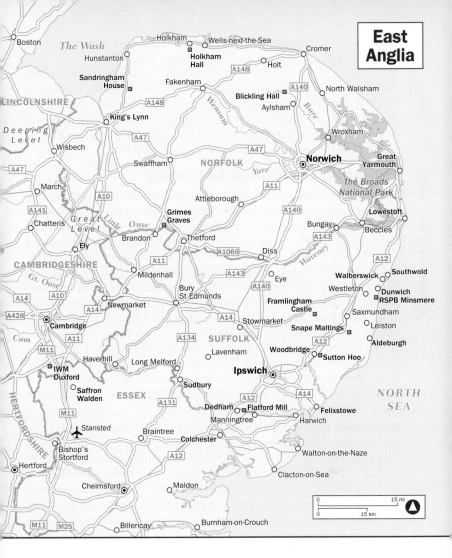

If you're **driving** from London, head north on the M11. From the northeast, use the A1; from the Midlands take the M6 to the A14.

VISITOR INFORMATION For information on attractions and public transport visit the **Cambridge Tourist Information Centre,** Peas Hill, CB2 3AD (www.visitcambridge.org; ℂ **0871/226-8006**). Staff can also book lodging. The center is open year-round, Monday to Saturday 10am to 5pm (Apr–Nov also Sun and bank holidays 11am–3pm).

GETTING AROUND City parking is expensive and the traffic in Cambridge can be unbearable. It's best to park outside the city center in one of the five well-marked Park and Ride sites. Parking is £1 for up to 18 hours, and Park and Ride round-trip bus tickets to the city center cost £3 from machines. Buses leave every 10 minutes (every 15 min. on Sun and bank holidays) and call at a number of stops around the city.

Walking is the easiest way to get around Cambridge. Keep in mind, though, that "Bicycling Safety 101" is not on the university curriculum and that the considerable brain power on display does not come into play when cycling, a common mode of transport for students. Be extremely mindful when steeping off curbs (look both ways) and when sauntering along paths you might be sharing with speeding cyclists.

Exploring Cambridge University

Scholars have been studying at Cambridge since the early 13th century, and the university began to grow quickly in the 16th century, when Henry VIII founded Trinity College and the curriculum expanded into the study of Greek, Latin, divinity, and mathematics. Reforms during the 19th century rearranged the university into something like the institution we know today, and two colleges for women were established: Girton in 1869 and Newnham in 1872. Cambridge University now consists of 31 colleges, all co-educational except three that remain female-only: Newnham, Murray Edwards College, and Lucy Cavendish. The colleges are all open to the public at certain times, but are almost all closed during May and June when students take exams. For a list of opening times and admission prices, go to www.cam.ac.uk. The main street through the city center parallel to the Cam is known alternately as Trumpington, King's Parade, Trinity, and St John's gives access to many of the colleges.

Emmanuel College ★ HISTORIC SITE   Sir Walter Mildmay, Elizabeth I's chancellor of the exchequer, was a Puritan, and he founded Emmanuel College in 1584 to educate Protestant ministers. Many early graduates emigrated to the colonies. Among them was John Harvard, who founded the famous university in Massachusetts that bears in name, modeled after Emmanuel. He is commemorated in a stained-glass window in the chapel, designed by Sir Christopher Wren and consecrated in 1677. Emmanuel's gardens are considered the prettiest in Cambridge, with a pool that the monk's once used for bathing—one of Europe's first. St Andrew's St. www.emma.cam.ac.uk. ✆ **01223/334200.** Grounds and chapel free.

King's College ★★ HISTORIC SITE   Henry VI was only 19 when he laid the cornerstone of a royal college in 1441. Admission was open to 70 graduates of Eton and for more than 400 years only Etonians could attend King's. **King's College Chapel ★★★** dates from Henry's time, begun in 1446. Work came to a standstill after the king was murdered in the Tower of London in 1471. Soon after Richard III took the throne in 1483 he commanded that "the building should go on with all possible dispatch," and during the reign of Henry VIII, masons finally put in place

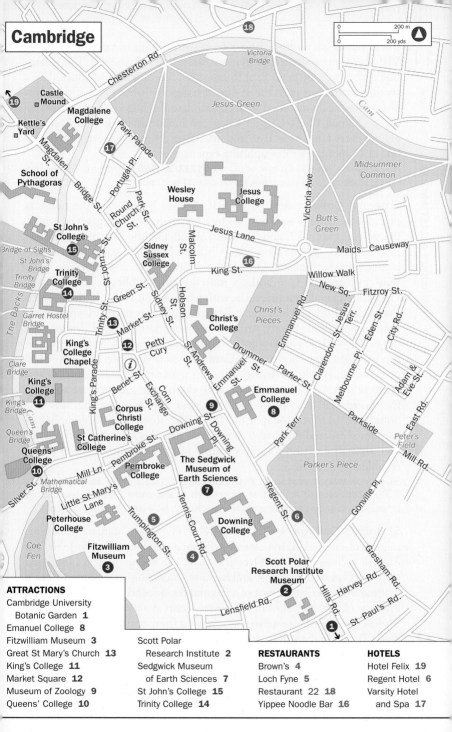

Cambridge

0	200 m
0	200 yds

18

Victoria
Bridge

Chesterton Rd.

Jesus Green

Cam

19
Castle
Mound

Kettle's
Yard

Magdalene
College

Magdalen
St.

Park Parade

Midsummer
Common

School of
Pythagoras

Bridge St.

Portugal Pl.

Park St.

Round
Church St.

17

Wesley
House

Jesus
College

Jesus Lane

Victoria Ave

Butt's
Green

St John's
College

15

Bridge of Sighs

St John's
Bridge

Trinity
Bridge

Trinity
College

14

Sidney
Sussex
College

Malcolm St.

King St.

16

Maids   Causeway

Willow Walk

New Sq.

Fitzroy St.

The Backs

Garret Hostel
Bridge

Green St.

Trinity St.

St John's St.

Sidney St.

Hobson St.

13

Market St.

12

Christ's
College

Christ's
Pieces

Emmanuel Rd.

Clarendon St.

Jesus Terr.

Eden St.

City Rd.

Clare
Bridge

King's
College Chapel

Petty
Cury

King's Parade

Benet St.

Corn
Exchange St.

St Andrews St.

Emmanuel St.

Drummer St.

Parker St.

Melbourne Pl.

Adam &
Eve St.

East Rd.

King's
College

11

King's
Bridge

Cam

Queen's
Bridge

Queens'
College

10

Corpus
Christi
College

St Catherine's
College

Pembroke St.

Mill Ln.

Silver St.

Mathematical
Bridge

Little St Mary's
Lane

Pembroke
College

Downing St.

Downing Pl.

9

Emmanuel
College

8

Park Terr.

Parkside

Peter's
Field

Gonville Pl.

Mill Rd.

Peterhouse
College

Coe
Fen

Trumpington St.

Tennis Court Rd.

Fitzwilliam
Museum

3

The Sedgwick
Museum of
Earth Sciences

7

5

Downing
College

Parker's Piece

Regent St.

6

4

Scott Polar
Research Institute
Museum

2

Hills Rd.

Harvey Rd.

Gresham Rd.

St. Paul's Rd.

Lensfield Rd.

1

ATTRACTIONS

Cambridge University
  Botanic Garden **1**
Emanuel College **8**
Fitzwilliam Museum **3**
Great St Mary's Church **13**
King's College **11**
Market Square **12**
Museum of Zoology **9**
Queens' College **10**

Scott Polar
  Research Institute **2**
Sedgwick Museum
  of Earth Sciences **7**
St John's College **15**
Trinity College **14**

RESTAURANTS

Brown's **4**
Loch Fyne **5**
Restaurant 22 **18**
Yippee Noodle Bar **16**

HOTELS

Hotel Felix **19**
Regent Hotel **6**
Varsity Hotel
  and Spa **17**

the beautiful fan vaulting, "the noblest stone ceiling in existence." Henry VIII also commissioned the glorious stained-glass windows. The *Adoration of the Magi,* by Peter Paul Rubens, is a recent addition, donated by a wealthy businessman in the 1960s. It hangs in the east end of the main chapel, specially modified to accommodate the huge canvas. Carols by the acclaimed King's Chapel Choir are broadcast worldwide from the chapel every Christmas Eve, and attending a King's evensong service is one of Cambridge's most uplifting experiences.

King's Parade. www.kings.cam.ac.uk. © **01223/331100.** £7 adults; £5 children 12–16, students, and seniors; free for children 11 and under.

Queens' College ★★ HISTORIC SITE Notice that the name is plural—the college was founded by English queens Margaret of Anjou, the wife of Henry VI, and Elizabeth Woodville, the wife of Edward IV, in 1448. Both queens have been vilified—Margaret as a scheming foreigner, Elizabeth as a gold-digging commoner—but no one can deny that they created Cambridge's most beautiful college. The Cloister Court is especially picturesque, with a handsome Tudor, half-timbered President's Lodge, while the red-brick Old Court houses Cambridge's first purpose-built library. Arched, wooden Mathematical Bridge connects the college's old section, known as the Dark Side, with the newer Light Side across the Cam. It's said that Sir Isaac Newton designed and built the bridge without the use of bolts and nuts. When some scholars decide to disassemble the bridge and recreate the feat they were unable to put it back together, and required the nuts and bolts seen in place today. Colorful as the story is, an accomplished carpenter erected the bridge a couple of decades after Newton's death and, though it's been rebuilt a couple of times, it's never been disassembled by students.

Silver St. www.quns.cam.ac.uk. © **01223/335511.** Late June to early Oct 10am–4:30pm admission £3 adults, free for children 11 and under (free admission other times). Oct daily 2–4pm (weekends 10am–4:30pm); Nov–late May daily 2–4pm.

St John's College ★★ HISTORIC SITE Lady Margaret Beaufort, mother of Henry VII, transformed the medieval hospital of St John into a small college in 1511. Over the years the college has accumulated some of Cambridge's finest architecture, including an impressive brick gateway with the Tudor coat of arms and the Second Court, another fine example of Tudor brickwork. The New Court evokes the romance of the Middle Ages, all the more so when viewed from across the River Cam at dusk. Don't let the effect deceive you, though, as the court is an 1834 creation and so unabashedly fanciful with its Gothic pinnacles and spires that the cupola is known as the Wedding Cake. The college's Bridge of Sighs is said to be inspired by the span in Venice's Doges Palace but bears no resemblance to that structure. The name also refers to the

Trinity College, founded by Henry VIII.

nervous sighs of students crossing the bridge for their exams. You can best see the bridge from the no less attractive Kitchen Bridge, fashioned from a single piece of limestone according to Wren's designs.

St John's St. www.joh.cam.ac.uk. ☎ **01223/338600.** £3 adults, £2 seniors and children 12–17, free for children under 12. Mar–Oct 10am–5:30pm; Nov–Feb Sat 10am–3:30pm.

Trinity College ★★ HISTORIC SITE   Cambridge's largest college, founded by Henry VIII, may also be its most storied. Sir Isaac Newton calculated the speed of sound by counting echoes as they traveled down the hallways outside his rooms in the Great Court, the largest enclosed courtyard in Europe. Lord Byron used to bathe naked in the Great Court's fountain with his pet bear, and it's a long-standing tradition to try to run the 341m (1,125 ft.) around the court in the 43 seconds that it takes the clock to strike 12 o'clock—the feat has never been accomplished as poetically as it is in the film *Chariots of Fire.* Alumni also include Alfred, Lord Tennyson; six British prime ministers; and two prime ministers of India, Nehru and Gandhi. Prince Charles graduated from Trinity in 1970, the first heir to the British throne to take a degree, and Trinity members have been awarded 32 Nobel Prizes. The novelist Vladimir Nabokov spent much of his time at Trinity daydreaming about a girl he would later immortalize in *Lolita* and claimed "Not once in my 3 years of Cambridge—repeat: not once—did I visit the University Library." He missed out: the 1695

CITY of science

Cambridge has long been a magnet for brilliant minds, and the little city has often led the way in scientific advances. Isaac Newton was a Lucasian professor of mathematics here from 1669 to 1703, a post that physicist Stephen Hawking now holds, and it's not by accident that Cambridge is known as "Silicon Fen" for its concentration of high-tech companies.

You can see specimens collected by Cambridge graduate Charles Darwin during his voyage on the Beagle in the 1830s, surrounded by the skeletons of giraffes and killer whales, at the **Museum of Zoology** on Downing Street (www.museum.zoo.cam.ac.uk; ℭ **01223/336650**) and they are. Admission is free and the museum is open Tuesday to Sunday 1:30 to 4:30pm (late Sept–early Apr 2–4pm). Darwin's mentor, botany professor John Henslow, founded the **Cambridge University Botanic Garden** (www.botanic.cam.ac.uk; ℭ **01223/336265**) on the site of a physic garden planted in 1761 to supply medical students with healing plants and herbs. A magnificent avenue of giant redwoods sprouted from seeds collected in California in 1851, the first ever brought to England, while a tropical rainforests thrives in the winter gardens. Admission is £5 adults, free for children under 17. The gardens, about half a mile south of the city center via Trumpington St., are open daily April to September 10am–6pm; February, March, and October 10am to 5pm; November, December, and January 10am to 4pm.

The **Scott Polar Research Institute** on Lensfield Rd. (www.spri.cam.ac.uk; ℭ **01223/336562**) is a cool place, especially if you have an interest in the expeditions of such frozen-terrain explorers as Captain Scott and Ernest Shackleton. Photographs from Scott's Terra Nova Expedition in 1912 are quite eerie, as the ill-fated explorers smile at us from the ice fields where they perished on their return from the South Pole; their frozen bodies were retrieved 8 months later, along with the letters and journals that are on display among their sleds, other gear, and clothing. The museum is free and open Tuesday to Saturday 10am to 4pm. At the **Sedgwick Museum of Earth Sciences** on Downing St. (www.sedgwickmuseum.org; ℭ **01223/333456**) 2 million rocks and fossils represent 4½ billion years of life, and standing over it all is *Iguanodon bernissartensis*, a gigantic, rhinoceros-shaped dinosaur. The museum is free, open Monday to Friday 10am to 1pm and 2 to 5pm, Saturday 10am to 4pm.

Wren masterpiece houses 1,250 medieval manuscripts, early Shakespeare editions, poet John Milton's handwritten copy of "Lycidias," books from Sir Isaac Newton's own library, and A.A. Milne's Winnie-the-Pooh manuscripts.

Trinity St. www.trin.cam.ac.uk. ℭ **01223/338400.** The Wren Library Mon–Fri noon–2pm, Sat 10:30am–12:30pm. Other areas are open at different times; ask at the porter's lodge. Free.

THE REST OF CAMBRIDGE

At the heart of Cambridge is vibrant **Market Square,** a cobbled expanse filled with stalls every day, and just opposite on Senate House Hill is the 15th-century **Great St Mary's Church.** The Dutch scholar and theologian Erasmus allegedly preached from the pulpit while visiting England in 1506; the German protestant reformer Martin Bucer (1491–1551) is buried in the church. There is a fine view of Cambridge from the top of the tower (www.gsm.cam.ac.uk; ✆ **01223/741716;** church free, tower £4 adults, £3 seniors, £2 children 5–16; £10 families; church daily 9am–5pm; tower summer daily 10am–4:30pm, winter until 4pm; Sun winter noon–4pm, summer noon–4:30pm). **Senate House Passage,** next to the church, leads to the Backs, the grand sweep of riverside lawns behind the colleges. The Wren Library, King's College Chapel, St John's College New Court, and other Cambridge landmarks are especially picturesque when viewed from the Backs.

Fitzwilliam Museum ★★★ MUSEUM   It's lucky for us that the 7th viscount Fitzwilliam (1745–1816) was such a fanatical collector. An alumnus of Cambridge's Trinity Hall College, Fitzwilliam enlarged his family's remarkable trove of Dutch paintings with masterpieces by Titian and other Italian masters, filled albums with etchings by Rembrandt and prints by other celebrated artists, and passionately gathered medieval manuscripts and music by early composers. He bequeathed them all to the university, along with funds to build the columned neoclassical monument in the town center that is one of Britain's finest

Interior, the Fitzwilliam Museum

museums outside London. Filling out Fitzwilliam's collection is a wealth of ancient artifacts, Impressionist paintings, and Flemish tapestries. The museum is comfortably small and rarely crowded, and a wander around reveals works that are both remarkable and unusual. The Lands-downe Relief, found near Hadrian's Villa outside Rome, illustrates Odysseus fighting off the sirens and other scenes from Greek mythology. The Macclesfield Psalter, a lavishly illustrated book of psalms created by East Anglian artists of the 1320s, became a cause celebre when it went up for sale in 2004 and British authorities barred its export to the Getty Museum in Los Angeles. Two sculptures of naked men riding panthers, the only surviving Michelangelo bronzes in the world, are a recent acquisition.

Trumpington St., near Peterhouse. www.fitzmuseum.cam.ac.uk. © **01223/332900.** Free; donations appreciated. Tues–Sat 10am–5pm, Sun noon–5pm. Guided tours Sat at 2:30pm (£6).

Organized Tours

The **Cambridge Tourist Information Centre** leads 2-hour walking tours of the city, from £8 to £15 for adults, and up to £7 for children under 12. Book tours by calling © **01223/457574** or visit www.visit cambridge.org.

Where to Stay

Hotel Felix ★ The Victorian-era facade and sweeping lawns suggests old world opulence, but beyond the grand entrance everything is fairly functional. The plain, contemporary design gives way to polished wood floors and some stylish flourishes, and the high-ceiling rooms in the old house are especially atmospheric—most accommodations are in a new wing and a lot more business-like, though sleek stone walled bathrooms with excellent showers are a luxurious touch throughout. The old parlors house a good restaurant, **Graffiti,** which in good weather spills onto a large terrace for drinks and afternoon tea.

Whitehouse Lane, Huntingdon Rd. www.hotelfelix.co.uk. © **01223/277977.** 52 units. Doubles from £215, includes English breakfast. **Amenities:** Restaurant; bar; access to health club; room service; free Wi-Fi.

Regent Hotel ★ This lovely Regency mansion dates from the 1840s and overlooks Parkers Piece, a 25-acre bit of greenery right in the center of town. Public rooms look over the green through gracious old bay windows, but the aesthetic steers away from period-piece traditional into a quietly contemporary aesthetic. Soothing guest rooms are done in pale tones enlivened with bright fabrics and handsome wall coverings; accommodation range in size and price, from extremely snug doubles to top floor suites that open to balconies beyond walls of glass.

41 Regent St. www.regenthotel.co.uk. © **01223/351470.** 22 units. Doubles £115–£145, includes breakfast. **Amenities:** Bar; free Wi-Fi.

Varsity Hotel and Spa ★★   The town and college take center stage here, since the floor-to-ceiling windows in most of the handsome, modern rooms afford fascinating glimpses over the towers, spires, and rooftops, and many look right down onto the river. The higher you go, the better the views, and the top-floor suites with balconies are especially dramatic, though even the standard doubles manage to be clubby yet light and airy, with dark furniture on polished floors and old prints on dramatic wallpaper. Guests can enjoy the rooftop terrace, as well as the adjacent gym and the spa with a Jacuzzi that looks out onto the River Cam. Thompson's Lane. www.thevarsityhotel.co.uk. ✆ **01223/305070.** 48 units. Doubles from £150, includes breakfast. **Amenities:** Restaurant; bar; free Wi-Fi.

Where to Eat

Aunties Tea Rooms, 1 St Mary's Passage (✆ **01223/315641**) is almost as much an institution as the marketplace out front, and serves sandwiches, breakfasts, and pastries; open Monday to Saturday 9:30am to 6:30pm, and Sunday 10:30am to 5:30pm. Two excellent stops for light fare are the **Norfolk Street Bakery,** 89 Norfolk St. (✆ **01223/660163;** daily 7:30am–5:30pm) and **The Table,** 85 Regent St., which also serves pizza and beer into the evening (thetablecambridge.co.uk; ✆ **01223/ 314230;** Wed–Sun 11am–9:30pm).

Browns ★   BRITISH/CONTINENTAL   A wing of the famous old Addenbrookes Hospital now houses an outlet of this gastropub chain, serving burgers, sandwiches, fish pies, and other casual fare that seems to be a hit with everyone who sets foot in Cambridge. Large groups of students add a bit of local color or create way too much noise, depending on your mood. Come for a late lunch and before the dinner crush to enjoy the wicker-and-ceiling-fan ambiance, a well-priced set menu (served until 6pm), and inexpensive cocktails. The shaded terrace is an especially alluring place to cool your heels during a round of sightseeing.
23 Trumpington St. www.browns-restaurants.co.uk. ✆ **01223/461655.** Mains £9–£19. Mon–Thurs 10am–10:30pm, Fri–Sat 10am–11pm, Sun 10am–10pm.

Loch Fyne ★   BRITISH   A 500-year-old former pub across from the Fitzwilliam Museum supplies a real treat in landlocked Cambridge— remarkably fresh seafood, including a good selection of oysters and Scottish salmon (this is part of a Scotland-based chain). Be aware that oysters here are lot more expensive than they are in many parts of the U.S. but well-priced two- and three-course set menus are a good value, as are fish and chips and some other fish-house standards.
37 Trumpington St. www.lochfyneseafoodandgrill.co.uk. ✆ **01223/362433.** Mains £8–£15. Daily 11:30am–10:30pm.

Restaurant 22 ★★ MODERN BRITISH   Unless you have a friend who lives in Cambridge, the parlors of a Victorian House just outside the city center near Jesus College offer the homiest dining experience you're likely to have. Guests squeeze into a dozen or so tables and are treated to a five-course set menu that changes every month. Many regulars come every month to enjoy the creative takes on British classics, with a choice of meat, seafood, and vegetarian dishes for each course, and anyone who walks in the door is treated like an honored guest.

22 Chesterton Rd. www.restaurant22.co.uk. ℰ **01223/351880.** Set menu £38. Tues–Sat from 7pm.

Yippee Noodle Bar ★ CHINESE   Noodle houses are common in British cities these days, but this sparse, cheerful room is a refreshing cut above the chains. Stir fries, heaping noodle platters, and spicy pork and chicken dishes are served at long communal tables with benches that are almost always packed with a mix of students and townsfolk.

7-9 King St. www.yippeenoodlebar.co.uk. ℰ **01223/518111.** Mains £8–£10. Mon–Fri noon–10:30pm; Sat–Sun noon–3pm and 5–10:30pm.

Shopping

In **Market Square,** stalls sell fruit and vegetables, clothes, books, and jewelry from Monday to Saturday, while on Sundays the focus turns to crafts plus homemade cakes, fresh bread, and organic food. There's been a bookstore since 1581 on the present site of the **Cambridge University Press bookshop,** 1-2 Trinity St. (www.cambridge.org; ℰ **01223/333333**), and **Heffers,** 20 Trinity St. (www.heffers.co.uk; ℰ **01223/568568**), is another Cambridge bibliophile institution.

Entertainment & Nightlife

The main venue for music and shows is the **Cambridge Corn Exchange,** 3 Parsons Court (www.cornex.co.uk; ℰ **01223/357851**), while the **Cambridge Arts Theatre,** 6 St Edward's Passage (www.cambridgeartstheatre.com; ℰ **01223/503333**), has some wonderful stage productions. For music, check out the **Trinity College Music Society** (www.tcms.org.uk; **01223/304-922**) which stages 20 concerts a year, from Renaissance to modern music, in such venues as Trinity College Chapel and the Wren Library.

If you want to spend the evening nursing a pint or two in atmospheric surroundings, a prime spot is **The Pickerel Inn,** near the river on Magdalene Street (ℰ **01223/355068**), said to have been serving for the past 600 years and the oldest pub in Cambridge. **The Eagle,** Benet Street, off King's Parade (ℰ **01223/505020**) was a popular hangout for American airmen during World War II—they carved their initials into the beams, and in the postwar years you'd often see Americans coming back for a nostalgic evening and trying to find their initials among the scrawls. **The Anchor,** Silver Street (ℰ **01223/353554**), enjoys a nice location on the Cam, with a riverside terrace in good weather.

Punting on the Cam near St John's College.

Outdoor Activities

If you don't mind risking a dunk in the river, you can rent a **punt** for an outing on the Cam, sitting back in one of the flat-bottomed wooden boats and gliding past the ivy-covered colleges and their immaculate gardens along the mirror-like river. All you have to do is put the long pole, about 5m (16 ft.), straight down into the shallow water until it finds the riverbed, then gently push and retrieve the pole in one deft, simple movement. Actually, it's easy once you get the knack, but watching inexperienced enthusiasts lose their pole or steer into the banks—or worse, lose their balance and pitch forward into the river—is a form of entertainment in Cambridge. Rent a punt from **Scudamore's Punting Company** (www.scudamores.com; ℭ **01223/359750**) for £25 an hour; you'll find rental stations at Magdalene Bridge and the boatyard off Mill Lane. Scudamore's also offers chauffeured punts, if you're nervous about propelling the boat yourself, for a minimum of £100.

To get around Cambridge like locals do, rent a **bike** from Station Cycles (www.stationcycles.co.uk; ℭ **01223/307125**), £7 for a half-day, £10 for a day. A £60 deposit is required. There are shops in the railway station parking lot and at Grand Arcade in Corn Exchange Street near the market. Both are open Monday to Friday 8am to 6pm (7pm on Wed), Saturday 9am to 5pm, and Sunday 10am to 4pm. **City Cycle Hire** in Newnham Road (www.citycyclehire.com; ℭ **01223/365629**) also has bikes for £7 per half-day, £10 per day.

A nice ride or **walk** follows a well-marked path up the river two miles to Grantchester (also a popular destination for punters). World

War I poet Rupert Brooke lived in Granchester when he was a student at Cambridge in the years just before the war and wrote nostalgically about the village in "The Soldier": "Stands the Church clock at ten to three? And is there honey still for tea?" You can find out for yourself at the **Orchard Tea Garden** (www.orchard-grantchester.com; ℰ **01223/551125**) near the church at 45-47 Mill Way. For something a little stronger, pop into the 400-year-old pub **The Green Man,** in the High St. (www.thegreenmangrantchester.co.uk; ℰ **01223/844669**).

Side Trips from Cambridge
ELY & THE FENS
Ely is 16 miles N of Cambridge

You'll see this small city, really just a market town on the River Ouse, long before you get there: The magnificent cathedral, the so-called ship of the Fens, rises high above the flat, marshy plains. From the 12th century the tall twin towers were a beacon for pilgrims who came to visit the shrine of Saint Etheldreda, and a powerful past unfolds as you walk along the lanes and riverside paths.

Buses operated by Stagecoach (www.stagecoachbus.com) link Cambridge and Ely and operate about every 20 minutes throughout the day; the trip takes 45 minutes. If you're driving from Cambridge, take the A10 north. The **Tourist Information Centre** is at Oliver Cromwell's House, 29 St Mary's St. (ℰ **01353/662062**; www.ely.org.uk). It's open April to October, daily 10am to 5:30pm, and November to March, Sunday to Friday 11am to 4pm, Saturday 10am to 5pm.

The nave of Ely Cathedral.

Ely Cathedral ★★ CATHEDRAL   Ely's mighty cathedral took root in the 7th century, with the arrival of Princess Etheldreda. The devout noblewoman was married twice but proudly remained a virgin. She was declared a saint when it was noticed that even 16 years after her death in 679 her body had not decomposed; her tomb, a marble Roman sarcophagus, became a place of pilgrimage. Soon after the Norman Conquest, a relative of William the Conqueror began to construct a cathedral that was completed in 1189. Funds from Etheldreda's pilgrims helped finance fan vaulting, gothic arches, fine carvings, and a magnificent Lady Chapel, built in honor of the Virgin Mary.

The cathedral survived Henry VIII's dissolution of the monasteries and the destruction of the Civil War but as the centuries passed was close to collapsing by sheer neglect. Victorian restorations added a painted ceiling and some gaudy stained glass, but the cathedral is still wonderfully medieval and many of the original flourishes remain. Rich carvings cover the facade and pillars at the base of the octagonal tower. A secession of finely crafted arches change from round to square along the massive nave, and medieval frescoes cover the Chapel of St Edmund. Etheldreda's tomb and shrine have long since disappeared, but the saint is honored with a simple memorial in the floor of the choir. Guided tours are included in the entrance fee from Monday to Saturday, with regular tours during the summer, fewer in the off season.

www.elycathedral.org. © **01353/667735.** £7 adults, £6 students and seniors, free for children 11 and under. Apr–Oct daily 7am–7pm; Nov–Mar Mon–Sat 7:30am–6pm, Sun 7:30am–5pm.

Ely Museum ★ MUSEUM Dinosaur bones and some Roman remains tell the town's long history, but most fascinating is a film, maps, tools, and old photographs depicting life in the fens, the swamps that once rendered Ely an island. A system of canals and dykes drained the fens in the 17th century, though the vast, flat lands long remained a water world laced with canals and dependent on fishing, waterfowl and eel catching, and harvesting reeds for thatch. It wasn't until the 20th century that modern drainage techniques assured dry land for farming.

Old Gaol, Market St. www.elymuseum.org.uk. © **01353/666655.** £5 adults, £4 students and seniors, £1 children 5–16. Summer Mon–Sat 10:30am–5pm, Sun 1–5pm; winter Mon–Sat 10:30am–4pm, Sun 1–4pm (closed Tues in winter).

Oliver Cromwell's House ★ HISTORIC HOME Few figures in English history are more controversial than Oliver Cromwell (1599–1658), who lived in this relatively modest house from 1636. The homey parlors and primitive kitchens are quite different from Hampton Court, where Cromwell took up residence as the Lord Protector of the Commonwealth from 1653 to 1658, after the Civil Wars left England a short-lived republic for the only time in its history. The many facets of this complex and enigmatic man, who attempted to instill democratic ideals through bloody means, come to light in the exhibits—his role in the execution of Charles I, savage treatment of the Irish, destruction of churches in the name of a puritanism, and virtual dictatorship. However history judges Cromwell, Royalists took their revenge in 1661, when his body was exhumed, beheaded, and hung from gallows in London.

29 St Mary's St. www.visitely.eastcambs. gov.uk. ✆ **01353/662062.** £5 adults, £4 seniors and students, £3 children 6–16, free for children 5 and under, £13 families. Apr–Oct daily 10am–5pm; Nov–Mar Sun–Fri 11am–4pm, Sat 10am–5pm.

A Tasty Pilgrimage at Ely

An outbuilding in the cathedral precincts that has been feeding pilgrims since the 13th century, **The Almonry Restaurant & Tea Rooms'** ★ (36 High St. www.elycathedral.org; ✆ **01353/666360**) medieval vaulting and beautiful gardens supply an atmospheric setting for sandwiches, pastries, home-cooked lunches and afternoon teas, pus evening roasts.

SAFFRON WALDEN
14 miles SE of Cambridge

It only makes sense that this pretty town is named after the saffron crocus. During the 16th and 17th centuries the flower was widely harvested in the surrounding fields and brought the town fame and fortune. Extracts from the stigma were used to make dye for East Anglia's textile-makers, and were used in medicines, perfumes, and aphrodisiacs. Saffron is one of the best-preserved medieval market towns in Britain, and many of the old facades are decorated with fine examples of pargetting, a decorative plastering effect in which images of birds, beasts, and foliage, along with entire scenes, are portrayed on facades. The half-timbered houses and brick Georgian mansions surround a ruined 12th-century castle and a common with an ancient turf maze, along which the faithful could try to pick their way to the end as a symbol of their struggle to reach heaven. Rising above it all are the tower and steeple of bright and airy **St Mary the Virgin Church** ★, the largest parish church in all of Essex (www.stmaryssaffronwalden.org; ✆ **01799/506024**). Open daily; £2, free for children under 18.

Greater Anglia **trains** run from Cambridge to Audley End (about 2 miles from Saffron Walden, and buses 59 and 301 connect the station with town; go to www.abelliogreateranglia.co.uk for timetables). **Buses** also run between Saffron Walden and Cambridge, Citi 7 Monday through Saturday and 132 on Sunday. If you're **driving,** Saffron Walden is just off the M11 at junction 10. The **Tourist Information Centre,** 1 Market Place (www.visitsaffronwalden.gov.uk; ✆ **01799 524002**), is open Monday to Saturday, 9:30am to 5pm.

Audley End ★ HISTORIC SITE   Grand as this house is, it was once a virtual palace three times its present size, the showplace of Thomas Howard, first earl of Suffolk (1561–1626). As an infant Howard inherited the house that his grandfather Thomas Audley, Lord Chancellor to Henry VIII, had converted from a Benedictine monastery. Lord Suffolk spent a fortune expanding and embellishing the mansion, largely to entertain King James I, whom he served as Lord Treasurer. It appears that Suffolk may have overspent, as he and his wife were eventually sent to the Tower of London for embezzlement. Though entire wings and courts were demolished over the years, in the 18th century architect Robert Adam created new reception rooms and landscape legend Capability Brown remodeled the grounds. The house's quirkiness offsets its rather cold ostentation—on a tour of Adams' ground-floor reception suite guides will explain that furniture in the great drawing room is smaller than usual, to offset the low ceilings, while columns in the more intimate Roman-themed drawing room are so close together that women in full dresses could not squeeze between them. A standout is the service wing, where the kitchen, dairy, larder, and laundry show that life downstairs was not as breezy it seems to be on *Downton Abbey.*

Audley End, Saffron Walden. www.english-heritage.org.uk. © **01638/667333.** £16 adults, £10 children, £42 families. Late Mar–Sept daily noon–5pm, grounds 10am–6pm; Oct daily to 4pm, grounds to 5pm; winter grounds only, Sat-Sun 10am–4pm.

Bridge End Garden ★ GARDEN   A couple of generations of Gibsons, a prominent Victorian family, spent much of the 19th century laying out their seven acres of gardens at the edge of town, creating seven interconnecting outdoor rooms—one walled, one filled with roses, another left as an untamed wilderness. Tucked amid the flowers and greenery are some fine pavilions and a challenging yew-hedge maze.

Bridge St. and Castle St. www.visitessex.com. © **01799/524002.**

Imperial War Museum Duxford ★★ MUSEUM   Duxford was an important air force base in both world wars, and the sprawling airfield is a fitting locale for a commemoration of the achievements of aerial warfare and general aviation. Exhibits are especially evocative of World War II, when Duxford was hugely important in the Battle of Britain, and the Spitfires and Hurricanes on display helped thwart German bombers determined to level London and other British cities. Americans arrived in 1943, taking off from Duxford and nearby fields for raids over German-held Europe in warplanes on display in the American Air Museum (reopening in spring 2016 after a complete revamp). More than 30,000 Americans lost their lives on missions from Duxford and other British bases. The AirSpace hangar shows off 30 historic craft, from World War I era biplanes to a supersonic Concorde, while a 1940s Operations Room, restored Officer's Mess, and archival films put a human spin on the base's important and colorful past. The museum's many events include some spectacular air shows. Duxforth is a 10-minute drive on the B184 from Saffron, and 12 miles south of Cambridge via the M11.

Duxford Airfield, Duxford. www.iwm.org.uk. © **01223/835000.** £18 adults, £14 seniors, £9 children 5–15, children under 5 free. Mid-Mar–Oct daily 10am–6pm, Nov–Mar daily 10am–4pm (last admission 5pm in summer, 3pm in winter).

DEDHAM & CONSTABLE COUNTRY ★

63 miles NE of London; 8 miles NE of Colchester

Dedham Vale was already known as "Constable Country" when the English landscape painter John Constable (1776–1837) was still alive. Nearly 200 years later, this Area of Outstanding Natural Beauty on the Essex–Suffolk border is still a magnet for art lovers. The classic itinerary takes in **East Bergholt,** the village where Constable was born; **Dedham,** the small market town where he went to school; and **Flatford Mill,** which he immortalized in his 1821 painting, "The Hay Wain," one of the Brits' favorite paintings. The glory of Dedham Vale remains what it was in Constable's time: A lazy river meandering through green fields past ancient woods and hedgerows under the huge East Anglian skies.

Essentials

You need a **car** to best explore this rural area: Take the A12 past Colchester, turn at East Bergholt, then on to Dedham. **Trains** leave three times an hour from London's Liverpool Street Station to Manningtree, about an hour away. It's a pretty 1-hour **walk** beside the River Stour from Manningtree to Flatford Mill. See www.dedhamvalestourvalley.org for more information on the Stour Valley Path.

Exploring Constable Country

The focal point of **Dedham** is a Georgian high street with independent shops and cafes and the **Dedham Grammar School,** Royal Square, where Constable was once a pupil. The school had a Royal Charter from Elizabeth I in 1575 and attracted wealthy families to the town in Georgian times, hence the many Georgian facades added to medieval buildings. At Dedham's heart is **St Mary's Church ★**, featured in several of Constable's works and where his painting of *The Ascension* is on permanent display. Many people from this part of Essex were among the Pilgrims to America; the far-rear pew is carved with memorials, including a celebration of historic links with Dedham, Massachusetts.

Flatford Mill & Bridge Cottage ★★ HISTORIC SITE/NATURAL ATTRACTION There is no public access inside Flatford Mill, but you can walk around the pond and along grassy footpaths by the river, providing opportunity to follow in Constable's footsteps or just have a picnic. It's possible to stand on the spot where he painted "The Hay Wain," though the terrain has sunk around 100 ft. in 200 years, so your view isn't quite the same as his. **Bridge Cottage,** owned by the National Trust, is a permanent exhibition about Constable and a cafe, and there's a small information center on the path from the parking lot to the mill. **River Stour Trust** boat trips leave from nearby (Apr–Oct weekends only;

www.riverstourtrust.org; ☏ **01787/313199**), or you can walk along the riverbank to Dedham or Manningtree (each under 1 hr. away).

Flatford, East Bergholt. www.nationaltrust.org.uk. ☏ **01206/298260.** Free parking. Cottage open weekends all year, daily Mar–Oct.

Sir Alfred Munnings Art Museum ★ MUSEUM   A short stroll from Dedham's pretty high street is this museum dedicated to the paintings of Sir Alfred Munnings (1878–1959), inside the house where he lived until his death. Munnings was a traditionalist, best known for his equestrian portraits, as well as for his work as an official war artist attached to the Canadian cavalry during World War I.

Castle House, Dedham. www.munningsmuseum.org.uk. ☏ **01206/322127.** £7 adults, £1 children 5–15. Apr–Oct Wed–Sun 2–5pm.

Where to Stay & Eat

The Sun Inn ★★   This 15th-century coaching inn has a prime location on Dedham's high street. Rooms ooze history, with low ceilings, antique armoires and ancient, undulating floors. Our favorite rooms are Constable and Elsa, both overlooking the pretty high street, the latter (named after the inn's "ghost") with a four-poster bed. Dining downstairs is open to guests and non-guests (booking advised). Menus change daily, and mix refined pub food (say, poached pollack with fennel) with Italian-influenced combinations of local produce, such as line-caught local cod with marjoram, capers, and chickpeas. Eat informally with a pint in the bar; or more formally in the restaurant. Mains cost £10 to £19.

High St., Dedham. www.thesuninndedham.com. ☏ **01206/323351.** 7 units. Doubles £120–£165, includes breakfast. **Amenities:** Restaurant; bar; free WiFi.

LAVENHAM ★

66 miles NE of London; 36 miles E of Cambridge; 11 miles S of Bury St Edmunds

This is the classic Suffolk "wool town"—the finest of a group of settlements that grew rich on the wool trade in the 1400s and 1500s. Lavenham has some of the best surviving examples of medieval architecture in England, full of half-timbered houses with the traditional Suffolk pink wash, but the jewel in the crown is the **Guildhall** on the main square. The huge **Church of St Peter and St Paul** has wonderful carvings on the misericords and chancel screen, as well as ornate tombs.

Seven miles away at **Sudbury,** is the former home of 18th-century artist Thomas Gainsborough. As founder of the English School of painting, he was much admired by fellow painter Constable, who once said, "I fancy I see a Gainsborough in every hedge and hollow tree."

Essentials

GETTING THERE   A **car** is the easiest way to reach Lavenham: From the Bury St Edmunds direction, take the A134 south then follow signs to

A half-timber house in traditional Suffolk pink wash, Lavenham.

Lavenham on the A1141. **Trains** offer a convoluted alternative, from London's Liverpool Street Station to Colchester with connections to **Sudbury,** then a connecting bus to Lavenham.

VISITOR INFORMATION The **Lavenham Tourist Information Centre,** Lady Street (www.heartofsuffolk.co.uk; ✆ **01787/248207**), is open from Easter to October daily 10am to 4:45pm; November to mid-December daily 11am to 3pm; and January through March weekends only 11am to 3pm.

Exploring Lavenham

The small center has plenty of antiques shops and lovely cafes. **Timbers ★**, High Street (✆ **01787/247218**), houses 24 antiques and collectables stalls, selling books, toys, military artifacts, glass, porcelain, and more. It's open daily.

Church of St Peter and St Paul ★ CHURCH   A village church large enough to be a cathedral: Building work on most of this ornate structure began in the late 1400s, and among its architects was John Wastell, who was involved with King's College Chapel and Great St Mary's in Cambridge (p. 360). Thanks to the riches of the wool trade, medieval Lavenham could afford the best. The interior décor took a bruising during the Reformation, when zealous iconoclasts destroyed statues and smashed almost all the original stained glass. The delicate stonework of the south porch survives, however.

Church St. ℂ **01787/247244.** Free. Open during daylight hours.

Guildhall of Corpus Christi ★ HISTORIC SITE   The exhibitions inside this marvelously creaky old timbered building explain how the textile industry once brought wealth to the area, but in the 19th century mechanized mills in the north produced cloth more cheaply and, like most of Suffolk, Lavenham fell back on agriculture. It caused poverty for generations, but it did save Lavenham and other villages from redevelopment, leaving its medieval center remarkably intact. The Guildhall's walled garden still houses the tiny village gaol.

Market Place. www.nationaltrust.org.uk/lavenham-guildhall. ℂ **01787/247646.** £5 adults, £3 children 5–15, £13 families. Apr–Oct daily 11am–5pm; Mar Wed–Sun 11am–4pm; Nov Sat–Sun 11am–4pm.

Where to Stay & Eat

If you're in the mood for fine dining, reserve ahead at **The Great House ★**, Market Place (www.greathouse.co.uk; ℂ **01787/247431**), where classic French cuisine makes use of local produce such as Lavenham lamb and Suffolk pork. Main courses cost £22 to £30; it's open for lunch Wednesday to Sunday and for dinner Tuesday to Saturday.

Swan Hotel ★   In a town of well-tended timbered buildings, the Swan Hotel stands out as one of the finest. There's an old-fashioned feel to the lodgings—think "olde England" rather than "boutique." Rooms are spread mazelike through its gently modernized interior, with plenty of aged beams on show. There's onsite fine dining, but we prefer the informal intimacy of the Airmen's Bar. This was a favorite drinking spot for US airmen during World War II, and fliers left still-legible graffiti on the timber and plaster walls. The airmen also left a running record of "the Boot": a speed-drinking contest using a glass boot filled with local ale. Returnees over the years have kept alive a tradition of signing the walls during USAF reunions—though the Boot is long gone.

High St. www.theswanatlavenham.co.uk. ℂ **01787/247477.** 45 units. Doubles £185–£305, includes breakfast. **Amenities:** 2 restaurants; bar; room service; spa; free Wi-Fi.

A Side Trip to Sudbury

Thomas Gainsborough was born at Sudbury in 1727, and by the time he died in 1788 he had become one of Britain's greatest painters. **Gainsborough's House ★** (46 Gainsborough St., Sudbury; www.gainsborough.org; ℂ **01787/** 372958. Admission £7 adults, Mon–Sat 10am–5pm; Sun 11am–5pm) built around 1520, holds the biggest collection of his paintings, drawings, and prints. The museum also hosts temporary exhibitions of other artists' work and runs art classes.

THE SUFFOLK COAST: SOUTHWOLD TO ALDEBURGH ★★

Southwold: 114 miles NE of London, 32 miles SE of Norwich; Aldeburgh: 104 miles NE of London, 44 miles S of Norwich

Suffolk's North Sea shores are characterized by tracts of coastal wetlands, heath, and saltmarsh, with vast skies that bathe the whole region in the serene light that painters love. Find a knoll and you can see for miles, with just the occasional copse or church spire to break up flatlands as far as the horizon. Look skywards to spot a wheeling marsh harrier or a flock of migrating geese.

There's a stylish air about **Southwold**'s small center. Between Easter and October, it's a popular weekend getaway with Londoners, and busy all summer—but joyously quiet otherwise. Why? Southwold has avoided the unwise overdevelopment that blights many resorts. The town Greens—patches of grass never rebuilt after the catastrophic 1659 "Great Fire of Southwold"—give it a leisurely feeling of space, as does its sandy beach, and the commons and marshes down to a quay-side beside the Blyth Estuary. It's genteel, gentrified (beach huts sell for more than $100,000), and a pristine taste of an old-time English seaside town.

Just to the south is the village of **Walberswick,** where a few neat row-houses cluster around a pretty green and a couple of pubs. A 1914 stay here inspired Art Nouveau pioneer Charles Rennie Mackintosh (p. 551). Things ended badly, however, when locals couldn't understand his accent and locked him up in Southwold on suspicion of being a German spy. Now a favorite celebrity second-home location, Walberswick is also fast becoming a kitesurfing hotspot thanks to brisk easterly winds.

Further down the coast is **Dunwich,** little more than a few cottages since the town fell into the sea several centuries ago. The beach is more pebbles than sand and you can walk the 10 miles to **Aldeburgh** along the coastal path, passing Maggi Hambling's **Scallop ★** sculpture en route. Aldeburgh is a yachting town, famous for its music festival (see below) and a magnet for Londoners chasing fresh air. Composer **Benjamin Britten** lived here, and is buried in St Peter and St Paul Church.

Essentials

ARRIVING   You really need a **car** to tour the Suffolk coast. If you're driving from the London area, take the M25 to the A12 and follow signs to any of the places mentioned above, which are all just off the A12. **Trains** do connect London to the coast, from Liverpool Street Station. Take a train to Ipswich, then onward on the Lowestoft line and get off at Saxmundham for Aldeburgh (6 miles away) or at Halesworth for Southwold (9 miles away). Local **buses** connect Saxmundham station with Aldeburgh and Halesworth with Southwold.

The Scallop by Maggi Hambling, near Aldeburgh.

VISITOR INFORMATION   There are **Tourist Information Centres** at 48 High St., Aldeburgh (www.suffolkcoastal.gov.uk/tourism; ✆ **01728/ 453637**) and 7 Child's Yard, Southwold (www.visit-sunrisecoast.co.uk; ✆ **01502/724729**). The Visit Suffolk website (www.visit-suffolk.co.uk) is excellent.

SPECIAL EVENTS   Aldeburgh was the home of composer Benjamin Britten (1913–76), best known for the opera "Peter Grimes." Many of his compositions were first performed at the **Aldeburgh Festival** (www. aldeburgh.co.uk; ✆ **01728/687110**), which he co-founded in 1948. The 2-week festival every June features internationally known performers. The silence of the Suffolk coast is briefly breached by **Latitude** (www.latitudefestival.co.uk), one of Britain's hippest outdoor rock and alt-arts festivals. Headliners have included The Black Keys and Damon Albarn. The Latitude site is by the A12 near Southwold.

Exploring the Suffolk Coast

The Suffolk coast puts your brakes on. Visitors just *slow down,* naturally, and there are several fine, gentle walks. From Southwold, it's a pretty 1-hour stroll along dunes and a quayside, then across the River Blyth by footbridge or an old-fashioned rowboat ferry (in season) to Walberswick. The signposted **Sailors' Path** links the old malthouses at Snape with Aldeburgh, via a 6-mile path along the River Alde through reed beds, woodland, and heath. This entire coastline, in fact, is a designated Area of Outstanding Natural Beauty, whose coastal heathlands, river estuaries, saltmarshes, and dunes are crisscrossed with some of southern England's finest rural walks. See www.suffolkcoastandheaths.org.uk.

In Southwold itself, the **Sailors' Reading Room** ★, East Cliff, opened in 1864 as a place for the town's fishermen and lifeboatmen to sit, talk, and catch up on daily news. A small room is packed with nautical memorabilia, including intricate model ships, and smells pleasantly of times past. Admission is free; it's open daily during daylight hours. You can also tour the inside of a working lighthouse, at the **Southwold Lighthouse** ★, Stradbroke Rd. (www.trinityhouse.co.uk; ✆ 01502/724729). It's unusual to find a 100-ft. lighthouse standing in the middle of a town, surrounded by houses, plus the coastal views from up there are of course, splendid. The lamp is visible 24 miles out to sea. Admission is by way of an insightful half-hour accompanied tour, costing £4 for adults, £3 children. Between April and October, it is usually open at least three days per week, more often during holiday periods.

Aldeburgh Museum ★ MUSEUM   The timber-framed **Moot Hall** ★★ building has been used as the meeting place for Aldeburgh's town council since about 1550—and it still is. Inside you can sit under the eaves of the council chamber, then view a small, eclectic collection. Exhibits include prehistoric and Anglo-Saxon archaeological finds, nautical models, Victorian pocket watches, old photos, and plenty more.

Market Cross Place, Aldeburgh. www.aldeburghmuseum.org.uk. ✆ **01728/454666.** £2 adults, free for children. June–Aug daily noon–5pm; Apr–May and Sept–Oct daily 2:30–5pm. Closed Nov–Mar.

Dunwich Museum ★ MUSEUM   This two-room museum tells the story of Dunwich, "the city that fell into the sea." Dunwich is now little more than one line of row-houses, but it was granted a Royal Charter in 1199, recognizing its importance as Suffolk's principal port. A massive New Year's storm in 1286 sealed off the natural harbor, and sealed Dunwich's fate. Business declined and coastal erosion gradually swallowed the rest. Population plunged from one-sixth of London's to today's community of fewer than 100 souls.

St James St., Dunwich. www.dunwichmuseum.org.uk. ✆ **01728/648796.** £1 donation. Apr–Sept daily 11:30am–4:30pm; Oct daily noon–4pm; Mar Sat–Sun 2–4:30pm. Closed Nov–Feb.

RSPB Minsmere ★ NATURE RESERVE/WALKING TRAIL   Avocets, marsh harriers, and booming bitterns are regularly spotted on this bird reserve, along with geese, ducks, swans, and wading birds. The reserve starts among the trees at the visitor center, and runs all the way down to the beach. There are lovely walks—and birdlife to enjoy—all year long, amid woodlands, wetlands, and coastal scenery.

Off A12, 5 miles southeast of Yoxford. www.rspb.org.uk. ✆ **01728/648281.** £8 adults, £4 children 5–18. Daily 9am–5pm (closes 4pm Nov–Jan).

Where to Stay

The best way to experience the Suffolk coast is by staying in a **vacation rental**—the area gets better the longer you linger. The usual "big names" offer properties here, but local specialists have superior portfolios, with seaside cottages available from a few days to several weeks. You'll find the best selection through **Suffolk Secrets** (www.suffolk-secrets.co.uk; ℂ 01502/722717), **Southwold Lettings** (www.southwoldlettings.com; ℂ 01502/725409), **Durrants** (www.durrantsholidaycottages.co.uk; ℂ 01502/723292), and **Best of Suffolk** (www.bestofsuffolk.co.uk; ℂ 01728/553099).

The Crown ★　This is one of several properties in the area owned by Adnams, the local brewer. But grungy it ain't: This handsome inn is the heart of Main Street Southwold. Rooms are more contemporary than the Georgian-style shell suggests, most in light wood and muted colors offset against splashes of bright fabric. The pub-style restaurant is pretty good, but there are even better places to eat in and around Southwold.

High St., Southwold. www.adnams.co.uk/hotels/the-crown. ℂ **01502/722275.** 14 units. Doubles £185–£255, includes breakfast. **Amenities:** Restaurant; bar; room service; free Wi-Fi.

Where to Eat

The **Aldeburgh Fish & Chip Shop ★★**, 226 High St., Aldeburgh (www.aldeburghfishandchips.co.uk), sells some of the best fish and chips in East Anglia. There's almost always a queue. It's open lunchtimes every day, and evenings Thursday through Saturday—turning up for an early lunch is the surest way to get served quickly. A hearty portion of cod, haddock, or plaice with chips costs around £6. Alongside fish, **Blythburgh pork**—from pigs raised outdoors along the banks of the River Blyth—is the outstanding local specialty.

The Westleton Crown ★★ GASTROPUB　From outside, this looks every bit the cutesy, traditional village pub. But out back, a glass-ceilinged restaurant opens onto a terraced back garden, with a menu that is modern and adventurous. Influences (but rarely ingredients) come from well beyond Suffolk's borders. Expect the likes of soy-marinated smoked pigeon with wasabi and pickled ginger followed by a slow-cooked Blythburgh pork "ribeye" with roast celeriac and crispy kale.

The Street, Westleton. www.westletoncrown.co.uk. ℂ **01728/648777.** Mains £14–£19. Daily noon–2:30pm and 6:30–9:30pm.

Shopping & Nightlife

Aldeburgh's beachfront has shacks selling fresh catch straight off a few day-boats. There's also a small smokehouse that sells its own haddock, kippers, and potted brown shrimps.

DRINKING & dining: PUBS ALONG THE SUFFOLK COAST

Southwold has some of Suffolk's most enticing watering holes, none more atmospheric than **The Lord Nelson ★★★**, East St., Southwold (www.thelordnelsonsouthwold.co.uk; ☎ 01502/722079). Regularly cited as one of Britain's best seaside pubs, the low-slung ceiling, friendly crowd, Adnams ales, and old-fashioned welcome are hard to beat. The nearby **Sole Bay Inn ★**, 7 East Green, Southwold (www.solebayinn.co.uk; ☎ 01502/7 23736), has a more family atmosphere (especially around mealtimes) plus a wider selection of Adnams keg (fizzy) beers. **The Harbour Inn ★★**, Black Shore, Southwold (www.harbourinns outhwold.co.uk; ☎ 01502/722381), is an old seafarers' pub where kitchen staff really know how to handle fish: Clam and smoked haddock chowder or a smoked trout "Caesar" salad are loaded with flavor. Across the river, **The Anchor ★**, Walberswick (www.anchoratwalberswick.com; ☎ 01502/722112), is more restaurant than pub, and has real flair with local seafood like Mersea oysters, plus a bottled beer menu that skips around Europe and North America. **The Ship at Dunwich ★★**, St James St., Dunwich (www.shipatdunwich.co.uk; ☎ 01728/648219), is a warrenlike 19th-century inn with Norfolk and Suffolk beers on tap. The menu is strong on pub classics such as Blythburgh gammon, egg, and chips, plus it does a fine Sunday roast lunch (reservations recommended).

Adnams Cellar & Kitchen ★ SHOP/BREWERY   Southwold's best-stocked shop sells drinkable souvenirs from the town brewer, in operation here since 1872. This is also the place to book guided tours of the traditional brewery or the much newer boutique distilling operation, which produces some of Britain's best vodka, gin, and (more recently) whisky. Both tours end with a 30-minute tutored tasting. 4 Drayman Square, Southwold. www.adnams.co.uk. ☎ **01502/725612.** Distillery and brewery tours (1½ hr. each) £10–12. Also at: 179b High St., Aldeburgh.

Snape Maltings ★ ENTERTAINMENT COMPLEX   These converted old malthouses and grain stores next to the River Alde host the annual **Aldeburgh Festival** (p. 365). Beside the concert hall, other buildings have been converted into cute upmarket shops selling ceramics, gift and design items, local crafts, and homewares. There's a farmers' market here on the first Saturday of every month. This is also the starting point for the **Sailors' Path** (p. 365) walk. Snape Maltings, beside the B1069 outside Snape. www.snapemaltings.co.uk. ☎ **01728/688303.** See www.alde burgh.co.uk for concert information.

Side Trips from the Suffolk Coast

Framlingham Castle ★ CASTLE   Unusually photogenic—and somewhat romantic thanks to its mere (artificial lake)—Framlingham is one of the few 12th-century castles still standing in East Anglia. Henry VIII's eldest daughter, the (Catholic) Mary Tudor took refuge here before succeeding her (Protestant) brother to the throne in 1553. Later in its 800-year history, Framlingham was used as a prison for enemies of the state and as a poorhouse for the destitute.

Church St., Framlingham. www.english-heritage.org.uk. © **01728/724922.** £7 adults, £4 children 5–15, £18 families. Apr–Sept daily 10am–6pm; Oct daily 10am–5pm; Nov–Mar Sat–Sun 10am–4pm.

Sutton Hoo ★★ HISTORIC SITE   These burial grounds of ancient Saxon kings lay undisturbed for 1,300 years until digs in the 1930s uncovered the treasures of Sutton Hoo. The discoveries are now a star part of London's **British Museum** (p. 66), but a trip to the original site provides fascinating context. A detailed exposition tells the story of England's colonization by Anglo-Saxon tribes—seafarers from the European continent—plus there's a room full of replica treasures found here, as well as original recent finds from nearby Rendelsham. You can walk out to the burial mounds themselves, including the one from which, in 1939, archaeologists pulled the remains of a 90-foot longboat and lavish treasures of a mysterious warrior king, possibly Raedwald of East Anglia.

Sutton Hoo, Woodbridge. www.nationaltrust.org.uk/sutton-hoo. © **01394/389700.** £8 adults, £4 children 5–15, £19 families. Mid-Mar to Oct daily 10:30am–5pm; Nov to mid-Mar Sat–Sun 11am–4pm.

NORWICH ★★

109 miles NE of London; 20 miles W of the North Sea

This river port tucked into hilly terrain in a crook of the River Wensum was one of the capitals of Norman England, with a mighty castle and magnificent cathedral to show for it. Then the medieval wool trade made Norwich hugely wealthy, so important it was England's second city. By the 19th century textiles that were machine-made in factories in the industrial north had knocked East Anglian wool out of the market and Norwich's river port was silting up. The city languished, but beautifully so, a backwater with trading halls, crooked houses, winding lanes, and sturdy churches from the medieval, Tudor, and Elizabethan heydays. The time-warp effect couples with geography to make Norwich seem all the more like a place apart—fens to the south and west separate Norwich from the rest of England, while the marshy Broads and flat landscapes that surround the city evoke the Low Countries just across the North Sea.

Essentials

GETTING THERE   **Trains** from London's Liverpool Street Station take just under 2 hours. If you're **driving** from London, take the M25, M11, and A11.

VISITOR INFORMATION   The **Norwich Tourist Information Centre** is in the Forum, 2 Millennium Plain, Bethel Street, NR2 1TF (www. visitnorwich.co.uk; ✆ **01603/213999**), open daily 9:30am to 5pm (except Sun in winter).

GETTING AROUND   You can walk anywhere you want to go in the compact old city, but you'll want to drive or take a bus out to the Sainsbury Center for Visual Arts, a few miles southwest of the city center. Buses are operated by First (www.firstgroup.com; ✆ **0871/2002233**) and leave from stops along St Stephen's Street and throughout the commercial center.

Exploring Norwich

Old Norwich is wedged fairly compactly between the castle and the cathedral, making it easy to ramble from one history-rich setting to another. The **Guildhall ★**, just below the castle on Gaol Hill, is one of many remnants of Norwich's enormous importance in the Middle Ages—it was one of the most important secular buildings in England when was completed in 1413, and it remains the largest and most important medieval civil building outside London. Cobbled **Elm Hill** has more Tudor houses than the whole of London; the quaint street was once the city's center of commerce, and wealthy residents had their own quays on the River Wensum at the bottom of the hill. The rivers loops around the old quarter, and one of the wealthiest merchant's houses, **Dragon Hall ★**, is on King Street (www.writers centrenorwich.org.uk; ✆ **01603/663-922**). The long, gloriously lopsided, and creaky old half-timbered house is Europe's only surviving medieval trading hall built by an individual, the cloth, wine, and spice merchant Robert Toppes. The name comes from 14 carved dragons that once adorned the massive oak beams that span the width of the Great Hall; one of the charming mythical creatures remains in place. Dragon Hall is home to the Writers' Center, Norwich, but is open occasionally for visits; check the website.

The area around the cathedral covers 44 acres, making it the largest cathedral close in England, and opens off **Tombland,** the Anglo-Saxon market square. The **Great Hospital ★**, near the river off Bishopgate, was founded in 1247 to house paupers, care for the sickly (treatments included bloodletting) and dispense a daily dole of bread and soup. The hospital still operates, and most of the medieval buildings are still in use.

Norwich Castle ★ CASTLE   This massive 12th-century Norman fortress atop a grassy knoll has withstood sieges and attacks, though a complete 19th century makeover in soft Bath stone makes the castle look more pretty than mighty. The ramparts, easily accessible from the streets below by elevator, provide lovely views into the countryside, while guided tours of the damp dungeons evoke the harshness of times

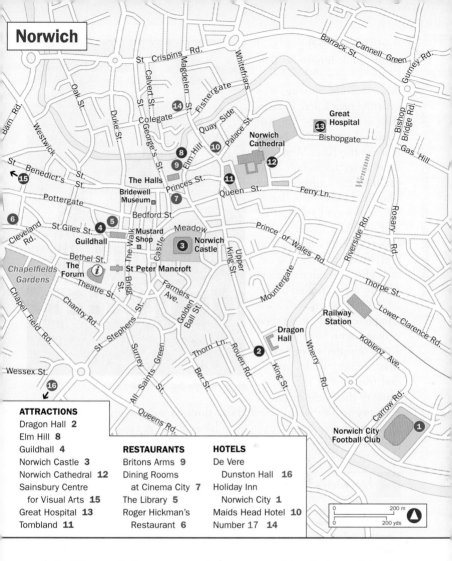

Norwich

ATTRACTIONS
Dragon Hall **2**
Elm Hill **8**
Guildhall **4**
Norwich Castle **3**
Norwich Cathedral **12**
Sainsbury Centre
 for Visual Arts **15**
Great Hospital **13**
Tombland **11**

RESTAURANTS
Britons Arms **9**
Dining Rooms
 at Cinema City **7**
The Library **5**
Roger Hickman's
 Restaurant **6**

HOTELS
De Vere
 Dunston Hall **16**
Holiday Inn
 Norwich City **1**
Maids Head Hotel **10**
Number 17 **14**

gone by. The castle houses several museums, with a few standouts in the somewhat staid exhibits—a Roman parade helmet, 2,000-year-old gold neck rings worn by Celtic tribes, and paintings of Norfolk landscapes by late 18th- and 19th century painters John Crome and John Sell Cotman.

Castle Meadow. www.museums.norfolk.gov.uk. ℂ **01603/493625.** £8 adults, £6 children 4–16. Mon–Sat 10am–4:30pm, Sun 1–4:30pm (until 5pm July–Aug).

Norwich Cathedral ★★★ CATHEDRAL   The enormous cathedral at one end of the medieval city was just about the most imposing building in the world when it was completed in 1145, less than 50 years after work began. Soft-gray and subtly pink limestone that lends a graceful, almost other-worldly quality was quarried near Caen, France, shipped across the English Channel, into the North Sea, up the River Wensum, then along a specially built canal to the cathedral site. The cathedral was large, tall, and meant to impress, and still lays claim to the largest cloisters in England and the second tallest spire.

The cathedral's finest feature was unveiled in the late 1400s, when craftsmen completed the rib-vaulted ceiling with more than 1,000 sculpted stone bosses that depict Bible stories and the lives of the saints, some of the finest medieval

Norwich Cathedral, completed in 1145.

masonry in the world (view them through magnifying mirrors placed along the nave, or better yet, with binoculars). A close look doesn't just provide a catechism lesson but also an irreverent glimpse of everyday

Norwich's Saintly Non-Saints

Monuments in Norwich Cathedral commemorate two extraordinary local women. Julian of Norwich is honored with two stained-glass windows and a statue on the west front. From 1393 to 1416 this devout woman (who was not a nun, as she is depicted in a window in the Bauchon chapel) took up solitary residence in a cell in nearby St Julian's Church. There she meditated and wrote *The Nature of Divine Love,* a sensible and practical treatise on the nature of sin, evil, and goodness that makes her the first woman to write in the English language. She must have been a good natured optimist to have asserted, "All

shall be well, and all shall be well, and all manner of thing shall be well." Edith Cavell is buried outside the east end of the cathedral. During World War I she was in charge of a nursing school in occupied Belgium, where she cared for wounded from both sides, famously commenting, "I cannot stop when there are lives to be saved." She also established an escape network that allowed more than 200 Allied soldiers to cross through enemy lines to neutral Holland. The Germans arrested Cavell and executed her on October 12, 1915. Army recruitment doubled when news of her death reached Britain.

medieval life and fantasy in which lords and ladies stand next to acrobats, priests tumble into the maws of hell, washerwomen chase off thieves, and otherworldly creatures cavort with devils. It's been said that this ceiling is like a snapshot in stone of the Mystery Plays that were once performed in the streets outside. Carvings on the undersides of the seats in the choir, so-called misericords, are a bestiary of dragons and griffins, along with plump Gluttony riding on the back of a sow. The cathedral's loftiest creatures are the famous peregrine falcons that nest on the 250-foot spire in the summer months.

62 The Close. www.cathedral.org.uk. ✆ **01603/218300.** Free; £4 suggested donation. Daily 7:30am–6pm.

Sainsbury Centre for Visual Arts ★★★ GALLERY   The core of this rich collection on the campus of the University of East Anglia are the works that Sir Robert and Lady Sainsbury, heirs to the British grocery store fortune, collected over 40 years. Pieces such as a fly swatter crafted for a Pacific Islander chief and a portrait of a youth painted on an Egyptian mummy reflect the Sainsbury's wide-ranging tastes, and the pleasure here is picking out similarities in disparate objects separated by time and place. A Modigliani portrait, *Head of a Woman,* bears striking resemblance to an Olmec head from Mexico, and Giacometti's *Diego,* a portrait of his brother sitting on a bed, resonates in another Olmec figure that's seated with legs splayed. It's easy to make comparisons since most works are displayed in one vast space, designed by Sir Norman Foster, without traditional separation into thematic. A portrait of Sir Robert by Francis Bacon says a lot about the creativity and spirit behind this

The Sainsbury Centre for the Visual Arts, near Norwich.

spectacular collection—blurred facial lines hover between the realism and abstraction that are typical of the artist but not of a formal portrait of a business leader.

University of East Anglia, Earlham Rd. www.scva.org.uk. © **01603/593199.** Free. Tues–Sun 10am–5pm. Bus: 22, 25, or 35 from the city.

Where to Stay

De Vere Dunston Hall ★★ This 19th-century mansion on 150 acres of parkland was built in the style of an Elizabethan manor house, with a forest of tall chimneys and a proud row of red-brick gables. The estate takes on another guise as a sprawling resort, with several new wings, a huge spa with an indoor pool, a gym, and a golf course. Some of the rooms in the old house have beams and four-poster beds that will make you feel as if you've dropped into a country-house party, but most accommodations are slickly conventional and have their own kind of appeal, and bridge the gap between traditional and conventional; those on the ground floor have French doors that open to private patios. Several restaurants include a lively grillroom.

Ipswich Rd. www.qhotels.co.uk. © **01508/470444.** 169 units. Doubles from £109; most rates include breakfast. **Amenities:** 3 restaurants; bar; bikes; 18-hole golf course; hot tub; indoor pool; sauna; steam room; spa; free Wi-Fi.

Holiday Inn Norwich City ★ You'll be leaving Norwich's medieval charm behind, but these refreshingly contemporary, light-filled and colorful rooms are well-poised at the edge of the city for exploring and are a very good value given the level of comfort. The cathedral is a short walk away along a river path that leads into medieval King Street; the train station and A47 (for drives into the Broads) are nearby; and Norwich's football stadium and the Riverside shopping complex are next door. Guests get free use of a nearby swimming pool.

Carrow Rd. www.ihg.com. © **877/410-667.** 150 units. Doubles from £60. **Amenities:** Restaurant; bar; free Wi-Fi.

Maids Head Hotel ★ In business since 1272, the Maids Head may well be the U.K.'s oldest continuously operated hotel. Elizabeth I is said to have stayed here, and the visit is commemorated in the four-poster Queen Elizabeth I Suite. Aside from the odd fireplace or old oak beam here and there, most of the decor is pretty conventional—if you need a bit of character, ask for the Filby Suite, a little raftered nest under the eaves overlooking the cathedral.

Tombland. www.maidsheadhotel.co.uk. © **01603/209955.** 84 units. Doubles from £89. **Amenities:** Restaurant; bar; room service; free Wi-Fi.

Number 17 ★★ A husband-wife team has beautifully redone an old printing mill near the cathedral with a lot of contemporary style. Rooms and family suites are soothingly done with light blonde floors and furnishings, accented with bright fabrics and thoughtful lighting. Many face a quiet courtyard that's tailor-made for relaxing after a day of sightseeing, and the large English breakfast is served alfresco, weather permitting.

17 Colegate. www.norwich.co.uk. ℭ **01603/764486.** Doubles from £85; includes breakfast. **Amenities:** Free Wi-Fi.

Where to Eat

The Britons Arms ★★ BRITISH   A medieval building on Elm Hill is the only surviving béguinage (religious refuge for women) in England from the Middle Ages. Now it's the atmospheric setting for breakfast, lunch or a snack in front of an open fire in winter and on a sunny terrace in summer.

9 Elm Hill. www.britonsarms.co.uk. ℭ **01603/623367.** Mains £10–£14. Tues–Fri 9:30am–5pm.

Dining Rooms at Cinema City ★ BRITISH   Norwich's knack for repurposing its old buildings comes to the fore in this odd mélange of medieval halls and elegant Georgian rooms. Art films are screened in one part of the complex and a friendly staff serves breakfasts, lunches and dinners in various nooks and crannies, some vaulted and flagstone-floored, others bright and high-ceilinged. An ambitious dinner menu includes some excellent seafood choices.

St Andrews St. www.picturehouses.co.uk. ℭ **07504/356378.** Mains £9–£18. Daily 10am–11pm.

The Library ★ BRITISH   If it's necessary to have a gimmick to bring in a crowd, it may as well be as high-minded as this one: a centuries-old public library has been lovingly preserved, with lots of polished paneling, pillars, and alcoves lined with fine old bookcases still filled with books. So there's no lack of reading matter while waiting for one of the delicious burgers, the house specialty; pastas and other dishes are also available, as are some well-priced lunch and dinner deals.

4A Guildhall Hill. www.thelibraryrestaurant.co.uk. ℭ **01603/616606.** Mains £9–£13. Daily 11am–10pm.

Roger Hickman's Restaurant ★★ BRITISH   The namesake head chef still oversees the finest dining experience in Norwich with a personal touch. The soft-hued, romantic room is a comfortably stylish setting for modern takes on classics that make the most of local ingredients, with lamb from the nearby Broads and seafood fresh from the coast, presented on two- and three-course menus and a tasting menu.

79 Upper St Giles St. www.rogerhickmansrestaurant.com. ℭ **01603/633522.** Fixed-price lunch £20 for 2 courses, £25 for 3 courses; fixed-price dinner £36 for 2 courses, £45 for 3 courses; tasting menu £60. Tues–Sat noon–2:30pm and 7–10pm.

Entertainment & Nightlife

The art deco **Theatre Royal,** Theatre Street (www.theatreroyalnorwich. co.uk; ℭ **01603/630000**) is Norwich's main venue for drama, music, and other entertainment. The smaller **Norwich Playhouse,** in a Georgina building at 42-58 St George's St. (www.norwichplayhouse.org.uk; ℂ **01603/598598**) stages drama and music with a bent toward family programs. The half-timbered **Maddermarket Theatre,** 1 St John's Alley (www.maddermarket.co.uk; ℂ **01603/620917**), is home to the amateur Norwich Players, who specialize in classical and contemporary drama. Norwich hosts the **Worlds Literature Festival** in June, with readings, talks, and workshops in various locations around town; for information, contact the Norwich Writers' Center (www.writerscentre norwich.org.uk; ℂ **01603/877177**).

The oldest pub in Norwich is the **Adam & Eve,** 17 Bishopgate (www.adamandevenorwich.co.uk; ℂ **01603/667423**), an alehouse since at least 1249. The **Fat Cat**, 49 West End St. (www.fatcatpub. co.uk; ℂ **01603/624364**) has a wide range of real ales including its own Fat Cat beer. It's said that Norfolk hero Horatio Nelson used to enjoy a drink at the **Maids Head Bar,** in the 750-year-old hotel of the same name in Tombland (www.maidsheadhotel.co.uk; ℂ **01603/209955**).

Shopping

Norwich's 900-year-old **food market** is still going strong in the center of town, on Gentleman's Walk; stalls operate Monday to Saturday, 8:30am to 5:30pm. Just opposite is the city's most atmospheric shopping mall, an ornate covered arcade from 1899. The most famous tenant, **Colman's Mustard Shop** (www.colmansmustardshop.com; ℂ **01603/627889**) is part museum, filled with displays of the company's famous products over the years, and the current output is on sale as well. More than 60 dealers operate out of **Tombland Antiques Centre,** 14 Tombland (ℂ **01603/619129**), a three-floor house opposite the cathedral.

Around Norwich

THE NORFOLK BROADS ★★
Wroxham: 7 miles NE of Norwich

Britain's largest protected wetlands, just north and east of Norwich, stretch for 188 square miles across an ecosystem of seven rivers and 63 shallow lakes, fringed with reed beds and grazing fields—all protected as the **Broads National Park** (www.broads-authority.gov.uk; ℂ **01603/ 610734**). Most of the wetlands are manmade, a byproduct of industrious medieval monks who dug peat out of the flat landscape and did a lucrative trade selling it for heating fuel. As sea levels rose over the years, the pits flooded, and 19th-century engineers helped things along by dredging and digging channels to create navigation lanes between the sea and inland cities. Leisure-seeking Victorians discovered the pleasure of drifting through the watery landscapes, and motor boaters, canoeists,

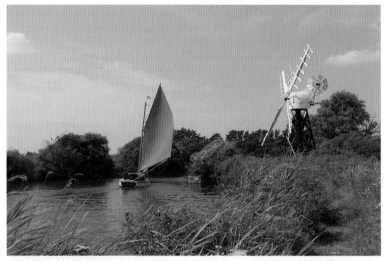

Sailing in Broads National Park.

and kayakers ply the waters today. One of the great delights of the Broads is spotting cormorants, kingfishers, harriers, swans, geese, otters, butterflies, and a bevy of other waterfowl and wildlife.

Wroxham, on the River Bure just 15 minutes from Norwich by train or car (on the A1151), is the unofficial capital of the Broads and a good place to rent a boat or board a cruise. **Barnes Brinkcraft,** Riverside Road, Wroxham (✆ **01603/782625**), has boats from £14 an hour to £240 a week, with the prices rising in the high season. **Bank Day Boats** (www.bannkboats.co.uk; ✆ **01692 582457**) at Wayford Bridge charges £48 a day. Alternatively, book a tour with **Broads Tours,** near Wroxham Bridge, or in Potter Heigham (www.broads.co.uk; ✆ **01603/782207** or 01603/670722). Trips start at £7 for 1-hour trips. For maps and other info, go to the **Broads Information Centre** at Hoveton/Wroxham, Station Road (✆ **01603/7560970**), open Easter to October, daily 9am to 1pm and 2 to 5pm. Other offices are at Potter Heigham, Ranworth, and Whitlingham. A good resource is www.enjoy thebroads.com, the website of the Broads Authority, a branch of the national park system that manages the Broads.

Not all of the attractions in the Broads are water-bound—there's a bit to see on dry land as well.

Bewilderwood ★ AMUSEMENT PARK   As much as you may want your young traveling companions to enjoy the natural spectacle of the Broads and its many wondrous creatures, they'll probably have the most fun crossing rope bridges and speeding down zip lines in this magic forest. The Sky Maze is a bonafide engineering marvel, a massive tree house 25 feet above the ground that twists and turns through a series of walkways, bridges, and spiral staircases.

Horning Rd., Hoveton. www.bewilderwood.co.uk. (C) **01603/783900.** £14 adults, £9–£12 children depending on height (free for children under 1m/3 ft.); £9 seniors. Daily Apr–Nov 10am–5:30pm or dusk, plus Feb school holidays.

Fairhaven Woodland & Water Garden ★★ GARDEN   Some of the loveliest gardens in Norfolk are the creation of the Second Lord Fairhaven, who bought this derelict estate in 1947. During the war the house had been used as a convalescent home for soldiers, the gardens and woodland used to conceal tanks, and waterways were blocked with sunken boats to prevent enemy seaplane landings. Over the next 30 years the lord created a charming woodland where little streams dart through groves of azaleas, rhododendrons, and species that thrive on the forest floor. The lord was especially keen on Candelabra Primula, a shade-loving plant that blooms in May and June and carpets the woods in color.

School Rd., South Walsham. www.fairhavengarden.co.uk. (C) **01603/270683.** £6 adults, £4 children 5–15. Daily Mar–Nov 10am–5pm, Dec–Feb 10am–4pm.

The Museum of the Broads ★ MUSEUM   The world of peat diggers, thatchers, and reed cutters unfolds with engaging detail in these canal-side boathouses that pay homage to life in the Broads since the Roman era. Racing yachts, punts, and all manner of other craft take center stage, and you can set out for a cruise aboard the Victorian steam launch *Falcon* on Tuesday to Thursday from 11am to 3pm.

The Staithe, Stalham. www.museumofthebroads.org.uk. (C) **01692/581681.** £5 adults, £3 children 5–15, £13 families. Boat trips £4 adults, £3 children. Daily Easter–Oct 10:30am–5pm. Closed in winter.

NORTH NORFOLK COAST ★★

Hunstanton is 105 miles NE of London; 53 miles N of Cambridge

A spectacular swath of beach, dunes, and salt marshes stretches between the old Victorian seaside resort of Cromer, 23 miles due north of Norwich, and Holkham, 36 miles to the west. While seaside towns with quays and wooden piers appear on the horizon now and then, this a place for walking and thinking, bird-watching, and relaxing. The scenery is most spectacular in the west, and the long beach at Holkham is especially inviting for a long, lonely walk. Just inland are some especially stately homes, including the queen's beloved holiday retreat at Sandringham.

Frequent **trains** on the Bittern Line connect Norwich with Cromer and Sheringham, another old-fashioned seaside town just to the west. If you're **driving** from Norwich, take the A140 to Cromer, then the A149 coast road west to Holkham. You'll find **Tourist Information Centres** along the coast at Sheringham, Railway Approach (www.sheringhamtown.co.uk; © **01263/824329**) and Wells-next-the-Sea, Staithe Street (www.wellsnextthesea.co.uk; © **01328/710885**).

Blakeney National Nature Reserve ★★ NATURE RESERVE   A 4-mile-long sand spit, backed by dunes, mud flats, and marshes seems to attract more birds and seals than human visitors. The spit hosts England's largest colonies of breeding seals, and in June and July hundreds of common seals give birth on the beach. The scene is repeated again in November and December when grey seals birth on the sands. The adjoining Cley Marshes Norfolk Wildlife Trust is another lovely spot—and is one of the first stops in England for geese, ducks, and wading birds as they head south from the Arctic.

Cley Rd., Blakeney. www.nationaltrust.org.uk. © **01263/740241.** Free, but National Trust pay parking lot.

Blickling Estate ★★ HISTORIC HOME   It's said that the headless ghost of Anne Boleyn, who by some accounts was born here, still roams the halls, and who could blame her? The Jacobean, redbrick mansion set amid meadows is simply lovely, decorated with fine tapestries and elaborate plasterwork. While Anne might recognize the Long Gallery and the grand staircase in the Great Hall, many of the rooms are from later periods. The Brown Room is especially sophisticated and stylish, redecorated with plush couches and armchairs in the 1930s for the 11th marquis of Lothian. The grounds are a delight to explore, with yew-hedge topiary, an orangery, and secret walled gardens tucked away here and there.

Blickling (off the A140 Norwich–Cromer Rd., near Aylsham). www.nationaltrust.org. uk. © **01263/738030.** House and gardens £14 adults, £8 children 5–15, £36 families; gardens only £9 adults, £5 children, £19 families. Late July to mid-Sept Wed–Mon 11am–5pm; mid-Sept to late July Wed–Sun noon–5pm.

Holkham Hall ★★ HISTORIC SITE   Much about the Palladian-style home of the earls of Leicester is over-the-top magnificent, especially the so-called Marble Hall (it's actually alabaster), modeled after the Temple of Fortuna Virilis in Rome and a 50-foot ceiling that suggests the Pantheon. Some of the rooms almost approach coziness, such as the several libraries that accommodate the earls' massive collections of manuscripts and early printed books. In the old kitchens, used until a new one was installed after World War II, cooks once fed a staff of 60 and prepared as many as 1,700 meals a month. The grounds roll across 25,000 acres of coastal terrain and include a vast deer park, a mile-long lake, and a wild and unspoiled beach.

Holkham (on the A149). www.holkham.co.uk. © **01328/710227.** Hall and museum £12 adults, £6 children 5–15, £33 families. Apr–Oct Sun–Mon and Thurs noon–4pm. Closed Nov–Mar; the park, with cafe and shop, is open year-round, free, to walkers.

Sandringham House & Gardens ★★ HISTORIC SITE   Queen Elizabeth gathers with the royal family for Christmas at this Victorian-era country house built in 1870 by the Prince and Princess of Wales, later King Edward VII and Queen Alexandra, on the estate that the prince's mother, Queen Victoria, purchased a few years before. The queen remains here for part of the winter, maybe because the atmosphere is a bit more relaxed than it is at the royal palaces (unlike most of those, Sandringham is a private home that the Windsor family actually owns) and the gardens provide plenty of space in which to get fresh air. Many of the reception rooms exude 19th and 20th-century comforts, and the house was one of the first in England to have gas lighting, flush toilets, and showers. The estate even once had its own time zone—Edward VII loved to hunt, and he had all Sandringham clocks set back by half an hour in the winter to give him more daylight hours outdoors. Lady Diana Spencer grew up in a house on the grounds.

Sandringham (off the A149). www.sandringhamestate.co.uk. 🕾 **01485/541571.** House, museum, and gardens £14 adults, £11 seniors, £7 children 5–15, £34 families. Apr to mid-Oct daily 11am–5pm.

Where to Eat

You can't come to this part of the world without making a stop at **Cley Smokehouse** ★ (www.cleysmokehouse.com; 🕾 **01263/740282**) on High Street in Cley next the Sea (pronounced Clee). Cley is 13 miles west of Cromer. The smoked seafood is legendary—lobsters, haddock, salmon, prawns, kippers, it's all delicious and packaged for a snack on the beach.

NORTHWEST ENGLAND

12

by Stephen Brewer,
Joe Fullman &
Donald Strachan

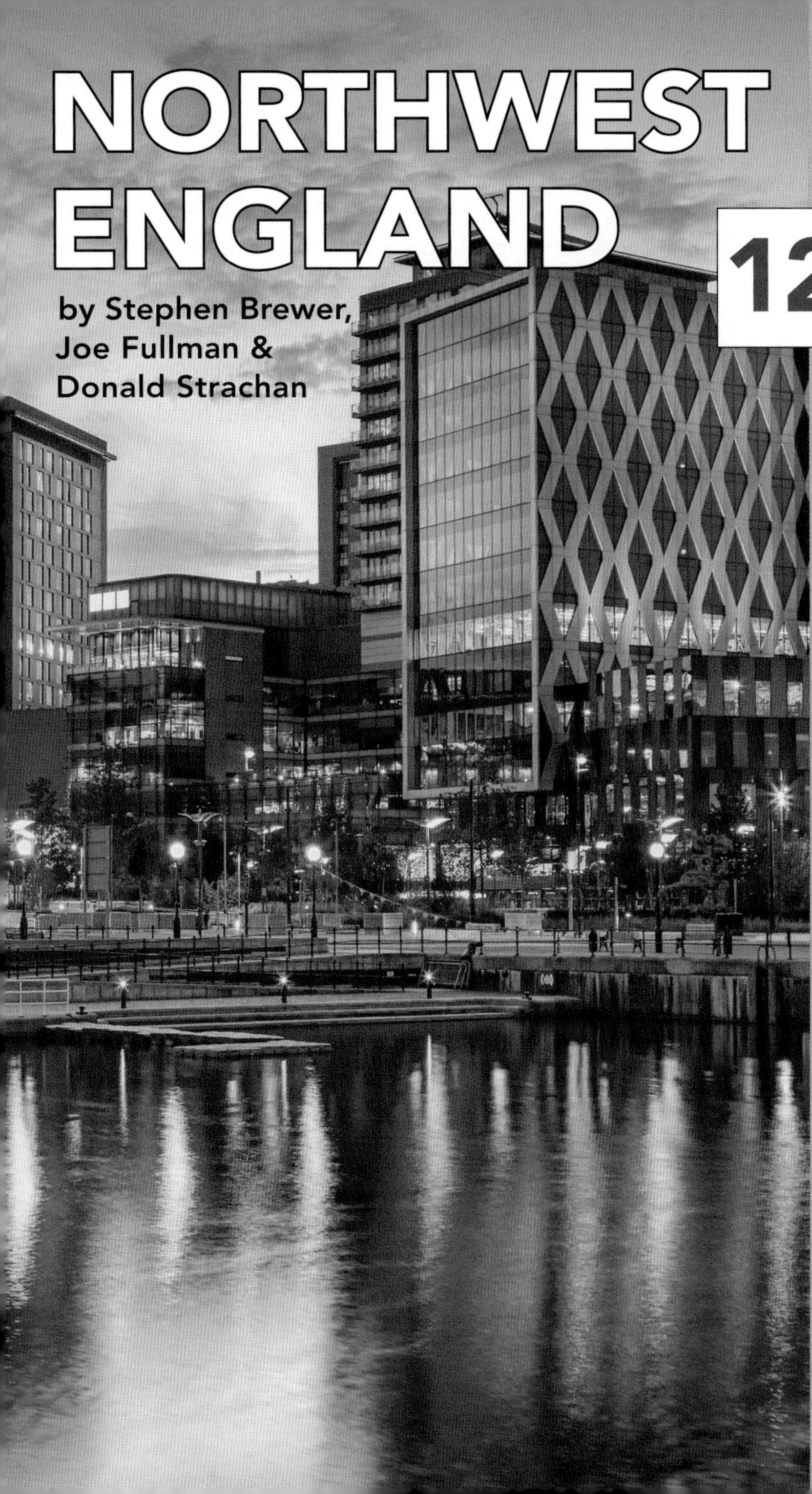

World-class cities within easy reach of the wonderful, unspoiled countryside of the Peak District National Park make the often-neglected northwest of England a must-see. If you want to get to know modern Britain, you'll find it here. The star turns are the twin (and traditionally rival) cities of Manchester and Liverpool, reasserting themselves after decades in the doldrums while remaining firmly tied to their industrial heritage. And there's more ancient history, too, at Chester and its Roman amphitheater.

It may not be Britain's prettiest landscape, but the 21st-century revival of Manchester's **Salford Quays**—new home to much of the BBC—makes for a fascinating case study in urban regeneration. Contrast today's cityscape with historical depictions of the area in the paintings of **L. S. Lowry**—many of them displayed in a state-of-the-art cultural center named after him.

Museums, especially art museums, are another strength of the region. Liverpool has some of the finest collections outside London, including the **Walker,** where the paintings cover seven centuries of art history and **Tate Liverpool,** for visitors with modern tastes. The Walker, as well as Manchester's **Whitworth Art Gallery** have almost unrivaled collections of British art, including several works by Turner, Constable, and Hockney. Antony Gormley's "**Another Place**" installation has raised the status of **Crosby** from unremarkable seaside town to globally significant art site, with its beach studded with 100 cast-iron casts of the sculptor's own body, faces turned to the horizon. It has to be seen to be believed.

Eating and drinking is a serious business here, too, whether that's a pint in one of Chester's reputedly **haunted pubs** or dinner cooked by a big-name chef at Manchester's **Michael Caines.** And the music and shopping scenes are England's best outside London.

MANCHESTER ★★

202 miles NW of London; 86 miles N of Birmingham; 35 miles E of Liverpool

One of the great Victorian manufacturing cities, the epicenter of England's Industrial Revolution and the world's largest cotton textile

PREVIOUS PAGE: **Salford Quays, Manchester.**

manufacturer was once known as "Cottonopolis." Along with enormous riches came smoke, grime, and working conditions so grim that Mark Twain commented that he wanted to move to Manchester in his old age because the transition from life to death would be seamless. Appalled visitors Karl Marx and Freidrich Engels were inspired to write the *Communist Manifesto*.

Gone are the smoke stacks and most of the soot and grime, but a commercial spirit remains, these days manifesting itself in shiny new high rises and shopping arcades. Popular sentiment that once found outlets in workers' movements and strikes focuses with foam-at-the-mouth rabidity on two football teams, Manchester United and Manchester City, and is channeled into a dynamic arts and music scene. Meanwhile, hulking Victorian and Edwardian warehouses and factories have been buffed and polished into offices, shops, and galleries, and entire factory districts and once-grimy docklands have been spiffed up. You'll see a lot in Manchester, and you'll have the jolting sensation of being pulled into the past and propelled into the future at the same time.

Essentials

GETTING THERE Frequent direct **trains** from London Euston to Manchester Piccadilly take just over 2 hours, costing around £70 for a round-trip. There are also direct trains from Birmingham (about 1½ hr.), Leeds (just under 1 hr.), York (about 1¼ hr.), and Edinburgh (about 3¼ hr.). Direct **National Express** (𝄡 **0871/781-8181;** www.nationalexpress.com) **buses** from London to Manchester take about 5 hours. There are also direct buses from Birmingham (2–3 hr.), Leeds (about 1 hr.), and Edinburgh (about 6½ hr.).

By **car,** Manchester is about 3½ hours from London, although traffic can be heavy on the M1 and M6 (the Midland Expressway will allow you to move more quickly past Birmingham).

Manchester International Airport (www.manchesterairport.co.uk; 𝄡 **08712/710-711**), 15 miles south of the center, handles flights to and from London and other U.K. cities, as well as many European and global destinations. From the U.S, British Airways and American serve Manchester with nonstop flights to and from New York's JFK, United to and from Newark, and Delta and Virgin to and from Atlanta and Orlando. Metrolink (www.metrolink.co.uk) connects the airport with the city center from a stop in the terminal; service costs £4 runs about every half-hour and the trip takes 45 minutes. Trains are much faster and cost the same, running from the airport to Manchester Piccadilly Station every 10 minutes; the trip takes about 20 minutes and costs £4.

GETTING AROUND The Metrolink tram system (www.metrolink.co.uk) runs through the city center and to many points beyond; fares begin at £3 and can be purchased at machines on the platforms. The same ticket can be used on buses (www.tfgm.com), though Metroshuttle buses make a free circuit around the city center every 10 minutes (the Tourist Office can supply a route map). Central Manchester is compact and you can walk to most sights, but you will probably use Metrolink to reach the Quays and other places that are slightly farther afield.

VISITOR INFORMATION **Manchester Visitor Information Centre,** Piccadilly Plaza, Portland Street (www.visitmanchester.com; 𝄡 **0871/222-8223**), is open Monday to Saturday 9:30am to 5:30pm, Sunday 10:30am to 4:30pm.

CITY LAYOUT Most of what you want to see is concentrated in and around the compact city center. You can get just about everywhere on foot, but carry a map to navigate the dense grid of streets as well as an umbrella—there's a reason Manchester is called "Rain City." On the north side is **Manchester Cathedral** and **Chetham's Library** and, east of them, a slightly bohemian warehouse district known as the Northern Quarter. Farther east is Piccadilly train station and gardens, and off Princess Street are the **Manchester Art Gallery** and, on Albert Square,

Manchester

Manchester (Victoria) Station

Chetham's Library **6**

National Football Museum **7**

Manchester Cathedral **4**

ANCOATS

Arndale Shopping Centre

8

5

Piccadilly Gardens

9

The People's History Museum **1**

John Rylands Library **2** **3**

Manchester Town Hall **12**

14 CHINATOWN

To Manchester (Piccadilly) Stn.

Granada TV Studios

Manchester Art Gallery

Museum of Science and Industry

10

Central Library

15 **16**

11

G-Mex Exhibition Centre **13**

Giants Basin

Deansgate Station **18**

CASTLEFIELD

Oxford Road Station

17

Whitworth Art Gallery **19**

Elizabeth Gaskill's House **20**

HULME

19

20

0   300 m
0   300 yds

ATTRACTIONS

Castlefield Urban
Heritage Park **18**
Chetham's Library **6**
Elizabeth Gaskill's House **20**
Imperial War
Museum North **17**
John Rylands Library **3**
The Lowry **17**
Manchester Art Gallery **14**

Manchester Cathedral **4**
Manchester Town Hall **12**
Museum of Science
and Industry **10**
Old Trafford Stadium **17**
National
Football Museum **7**
People's History Museum **1**
The Quays **17**
Whitworth Art Gallery **19**

RESTAURANTS

Michael Caines **16**
Mr. Thomas's Chop House **5**
The Oast House **2**
Ocean Treasure 235 **13**

HOTELS

Abel Heywood **8**
Castlefield Hotel **11**
Gardens Hotel **9**
Velvet Hotel **15**

the neo-Gothic City Hall. To the south is Castlefield, where old ware-houses line a network of canals and the **Museum of Science & Industry** occupies the world's first railway station. On the west side is **John Ryland's Library** and farther west, across the River Irwell, are the so-called Quays, where the **Imperial War Museum North** and the Lowry performing arts center are among the new landmarks.

Exploring Manchester

Manchester has succumbed to the latest craze for erecting a large Ferris wheel in the center of town. In this case, the 60m (197-ft.) **Wheel of Manchester** spins above Piccadilly Gardens (*C* **0161/8310-9918;** www.worldtouristattractions.co.uk; Sun–Thurs 10am–9pm, Fri–Sat 10am–midnight; £9 adults, £8 children 3–16); you'll get some panoramic views over the city, but eye-level views of the city's Victorian facades is more satisfying and you'll find a better aerial experience at the AirShard at the Imperial War Museum North (see below).

Elizabeth Gaskill's House ★★ HISTORIC SITE   Elizabeth Gaskell, the Victorian novelist and short story writer, spent her adult life in Manchester, and she wrote about the city's industrial-age society in *North and South* and other novels. In 1850 she and her minister husband purchased this large suburban villa, where they lived in bourgeoise comfort with their children and servants until Elizabeth's sudden death from a heart attack at the age of 55. The property went through several hands and was dilapidated until a recent restoration brought back original furnishings, paint colors, wallpaper designs, even the chintz that Gaskell had described as "such a pretty design with roses and pinks." Gaskell also wrote that she felt a bit guilty about her material good fortune and that she "must make the house give as much pleasure to others as she can." You might feel she did so as your step through the drawing and dining rooms where the Gaskells entertained Charles Dickens and Harriet Beecher Stowe. Charlotte Bronte was a frequent guest but so shy that she hid behind the voluminous draperies to avoid other visitors.

84 Plymouth Grove. www.elizabethgaskellhouse.co.uk. *C* **0161/273-2215.** £5 adults, £4 seniors and students, children under 16 free. Wed, Thurs, and Sun 11am–4:30pm. Bus: 197.

Imperial War Museum North ★★ MUSEUM   Packaging has everything to do with the experience here: on the banks of the Manchester ship canal, in an industrial zone flattened in World War II bombings, architect Daniel Libeskind has created an aluminum clad statement on the absurdity of war. Three undulating pavilions are cobbled together to form what looks like a splintered globe, suggesting the shattering effect of conflict. Inside are six bunker-like silos that focus on various conflicts since World War I, with sloping walls and floors that create the sensation of a world gone mad. Dramatic, totally immersing surround-sound visual presentations of the blitz of 1941 and other war scenes are

Imperial War Museum North, Manchester.

projected onto bare, 27-foot-high walls behind such mementoes as twisted girders from the World Trade Center. War-inspired drama doesn't end when you ascend the AirShard to enjoy the views of Manchester spread out 100 feet below—the elevator shakes and jolts on the way up, and search lights bore through the mesh walkways underfoot.

The Quays, Trafford Wharf Rd. www.north.iwm.org.uk. © **0161/836-4000.** Free. Daily 10am–5pm. Bus X50; tram stop MediaCity.

Manchester Art Gallery ★★★ GALLERY   To experience the best of this small but impressive collection, enter through the neoclassical portico from the 1820s and head straight upstairs, where the galleries are filled with works by Pre-Raphaelite artists. These works seem to capture the essence of 19th-century Manchester with their radical approach, earnest workmanship, and expression of morality and righteousness. *Work* by Ford Maddox Ford (1873–1939) is probably the most emblematic, a reflection of Victorian society with its depiction of workers digging a modern sewage system as ragamuffins, itinerants, and the leisured class look on. Even *Autumn Leaves* by John Everett Millais, at first glance a colorful landscape, is a bit of social dogma, suggesting inequality in its portrayal of girls of different classes and a whiff of decay in a depiction of dead leaves. William Etty's enormous *Ulysses and the Sirens* in the 1830s, was deemed indecent and tasteless for its portrayal of naked women surrounded by corpses as they bewitch sailors as; little did moralists realize that Etty considered the work to be a righteous statement on the "importance of resisting sensual delights."

Mosley St. www.manchestergalleries.org. © **0161/235-8888.** Free. Daily 10am–5pm, Thurs until 9pm.

John Rylands Library, Manchester.

City of Book Worms

Since 1653 scholarly Mancunians have been retreating to **Chetham's** (Long Millgate; www.chethams.org; ℂ **0161/834-7961;** Mon–Fri 9:30am–12:30pm and 1:30–4:30pm), the oldest surviving public library in the English-speaking world. Textile merchant Humphrey Chetham provided for a collection of books to cover the "whole range of available knowledge," with the proviso that librarians "require nothing of any man that cometh into the library" (you may still enter for free to admire the stacks, reading rooms, and adjoining cloisters). Among those taking advantage of the volumes, picturesquely shelved behind iron gates, was Friedrich Engels, who penned his grim observations of life in Manchester in *The Condition of the Working Class in England* here in the 1840s. By the 1890s

Manchester was enormously prosperous, though a bit sooty, a hub of textile manufacturing and industry, and wealthy widow Enriqueta Augustina Rylands decided to build a library to commemorate her late husband, a cotton magnate. **John Rylands Library ★**, Deansgate (www.library.manchester.ac.uk; ℂ **0161/305-0555;** Sun–Mon noon–5pm, Tues–Sat 10am–5pm), is a pompous but glorious pile of bricks and arches that's heavily neo-Gothic with elements of the Arts and Crafts movement thrown in. On display are some of the world's rarest manuscripts, including 2nd-century fragments of the Bible on papyrus and parchment, a Guttenberg Bible, some of the earliest printed works from the presses of William Caxton, and first editions of *Ulysses* and other works.

Manchester Cathedral ★ MUSEUM   The mellow, moss-covered stones of Manchester's central place of worship don't impart the gravitas of other great English cathedrals, but the church is a pleasing medieval presence in the modern city. The fact it's still standing is a something of

Football Fix

You'll have better luck arranging an audience with the Queen than getting a ticket to see Manchester United play, but you can do the next best thing and take a guided tour of the **Old Trafford Stadium,** Sir Matt Busby Way, Old Trafford (www. manutd.com; ✆ **0161/866-8000**). The 80-minute visit includes a look at the changing rooms and other areas that even fans don't see. To bring yourself up to speed on the game and the sport, peruse photos, trophies, and other memorabilia in the team museum (the audio guide really helps make sense of the English passion for the sport). Tours cost £18 adults, £12 seniors and children, £54 family of four. The museum is open daily 9:30am to 5pm, and tours are given from 9:40am to 4:30pm. You will learn everything you've ever wanted to know about football at the **National Football Museum,** Urbis Building, Cathedral Gardens (www. nationalfootballmuseum.com; ✆ **0161/ 870-9275;** free; daily 10am–5pm, opens at 11am on Sun, guided tours hourly 11am–4pm), where thousands of photographs and accompanying text chronicle the sport in an exhaustive and at times less than scintillating way; most engaging are film clips of interviews with such legends as George Best and other players and enthusiastic spectators.

a miracle, given that it took a direct hit during World War II bombings. The so-called Fire Window commemorates the calamity with a wall of flaming, swirling red hued panels that, ironically, was damaged in the 1996 IRA bombing. While the window infuses the nave, the widest in England, with some gloriously spiritual light, carvings on the seats in the choir stalls will pull you right back into secular realms. A woman scolds her husband for breaking a pot, and men hover over a backgammon board, a rebuke to the church fathers who had deemed the game detrimental to church attendance.

Victoria St. www.manchestercathedral.org. ✆ **0161/833-2230.** Free. Daily 8am–7pm. Tram stop: Victoria.

Museum of Science and Industry ★★★ MUSEUM   The world's first train station, built in 1830 for the Liverpool and Manchester Railway, is the centerpiece of a tribute to the city's many scientific achievements. Manchester also dug the first commercially viable canal and led the way in such 20th century innovations as aviation and computing (the latter in 1948, as you'll see, with a massive piece of office equipment called "Baby.") Little wonder it's said, "What Manchester does today, the rest of the world does tomorrow," and proof is here in a walk-through Victorian sewer, huge turbines that once powered the city's textile mills, and rows of giant steam locomotives. Manchester's old market hall now houses the Air and Space galleries, where a 1909 Avro biplane and a World War II Spitfire show how the city has also been a big player in aviation.

Liverpool Rd. www.mosi.org.uk. ✆ **0161/832-2244.** Free (small charges for some elements). Daily 10am–5pm.

Manchester's Museum of Science and Industry is housed in an 1830 train station.

Stepping Into Manchester's Industrial Past

Manchester got its start in the Castlefield district as Mamucium, a Roman fort and settlement that gave the city its name and stood on a grassy knoll above the River Irwell on the road between Chester and York. Castlefield did not rev up again until the Industrial Revolution took root here in the 18th century, when canals were dug to connect Manchester and the rest of the Midlands with the north. Cobbled canal-side paths, massive brick warehouses built to store coal and goods, and a network of railways are preserved in a 17-acre outdoor **Castlefield Urban Heritage Park,** where the **Museum of Science and Industry** (p. 389) tells the backstory of the momentous events that transpired in industrial-age Manchester. Much of the industrial might centered on the nearby **Quays,** the docklands that flourished with the opening of the Manchester Ship Canal in the 1890s to connect the city with Liverpool and the sea; more than 5,000 ships a year sailed in and out the docks, while quayside factories manufactured textiles and other goods for export. The **Imperial War Museum** (p. 386) and other flashy new landmarks rise out of the former docklands, including the **Lowry,** a performing arts center named for Manchester artist L.S. Lowry (1887–1976), whose scenes of the industrial north fill several galleries. You'll find another visual tribute to Manchester's past in the Victorian-era Gothic Revival style **Town Hall,** Albert Square (✆ **0161/ 234-5000;** free; Mon–Fri 9am–5pm), where Pre-Raphaelite painter Ford Maddox Brown (1821–93) decorated the Great Hall with a cynical eye, portraying a Roman youth kicking an African servant and John Kay, inventor of the fly shuttle that revolutionized the textile industry, fleeing an angry mob. Workers are celebrated in The **People's History Museum,** Left Bank (www.phm.org.uk; ✆ **0161/838-9190;** free; daily 8am–5pm, Sun from 10am), where posters, political cartoons, and photos fill a former pumping station to celebrate the ordinary working stiff.

Whitworth Art Gallery ★★ GALLERY Light-filled galleries shake off their Edwardian mustiness with lots of space and walls of glass, an appropriate setting for contemporary works such as Cornelia Parker's *The Distance,* in which life-sized papier-mache figures of

Rodin's *The Kiss* are entwined in a mile-long length of string. Some of the 11 Picassos are the first works of the artist ever to be purchased by a museum and *Moonlight on Lake Lucerne* is among more than 50 works by J. M. W. Turner. Taking his place among Francis Bacon, Lucian Freud, David Hockney and other 20th-century British artists is Manchester's own L.S. Lowry, whose industrial scenes and local landscapes brought him much unwanted fame; you can see more of his work in the Lowry (p. 395). Local lore has it that the artist kept a suitcase near his front door so he could tell unwanted visitors that he was just leaving on a trip; one enthusiastic fan insisted to accompany Lowry to the station, and the artist was forced to board a train he had no intention of taking.

Whitworth Park. www.whitworth.manchester.ac.uk. ℭ **0161/275-7450.** Free. Mon–Sat 10am–5pm, Sun noon–4pm.

Where to Stay

Abel Heywood ★★ The Northern Quarter is Manchester's most creative neighborhood, with lots of independent shops and bars occupying the old warehouses and sweatshops; among them is this nicely refurbished pub with rooms. The downstairs pub rooms are woodsy and old world British, while guest quarters are modern and not quite as edgy as the slogan "no ordinary hotel" might have you believe. Colorful ceramic tiles in the bathrooms, lively wall coverings, and digital illustrations add a bit of flair to rooms that are otherwise standard, with some nice touches that include large desks and cozy lounge chairs.

Potato Wharf, Manchester M3 4NB. www.abelheywood.co.uk. ℭ **0161/819-1441.** 15 units. Doubles £60–£115. **Amenities:** Restaurant; bar; free Wi-Fi.

Castlefield Hotel ★ The surroundings, on the banks of a canal in Manchester's old industrial district, could not be more atmospheric, though the accommodations are pleasantly no-nonsense and business-like, with low-slung beds and wood cabinetry, desks, and leather club chairs. The complex also encompasses a huge health club, and guests can use the gym, swimming pool, steam room, and sauna, making this an especially relaxing place for a retreat while enjoying the city center. The ground floor Castlefield Lounge is a popular bar/restaurant.

Liverpool Rd. castlefield-hotel.co.uk. ℭ **0161/832-7073.** 48 units. Doubles £50–£100. **Amenities:** Restaurant; bar; fitness center with pool; free Wi-Fi.

Gardens Hotel ★ One of Manchester's prime locations right on Piccadilly Gardens might warrant a grander hotel, but this modest one delivers an admirable amount of standard, no-frills comfort at very good value. Beyond the uninspiring entrance is a crisply modern lobby and lounge while the updated guest rooms upstairs are nicely done with neutral tones and fluffy duvets on the beds. Be careful when booking, though, as a few rooms have brick-wall views and some have no

A guest room at Velvet Hotel, Manchester.

windows at all (and are priced accordingly), while those in the front and rear are bright and have some decent city views through tall windows. 55 Picadilly. www.gardenshotelmanchester.com. ☏ **0161/236-5155.** 101 units. Doubles £30–£60, includes breakfast. **Amenities:** Bar; free Wi-Fi.

Velvet Hotel ★★★ The notion of designer flair in a hip area does not always promise taste and comfort, though these beautiful room and suites in Manchester's gay village deliver both, with individually decorated accommodations that are truly tastefully done with chaise longues, tall polished headboards, gilt mirrors, and some impressive chandeliers throughout. All the rooms are extra large, and multilevel suites are almost loftlike. In some lower-floor rooms you can risk street noise (obliterated by double glazing) for the sake of a balcony, perfect for watching the parade of bar hoppers below.
2 Canal St. www.velvetmanchester.com. ☏ **0161/236-9003.** 19 units. Double £75–£165. **Amenities:** Restaurant; bar; free Wi-Fi.

Where to Eat

Culinary Manchester is still partial to the Dickensian-style fare that once kept the city burghers popping out of their waistcoats. Just about every other kind of cuisine is also available, including some excellent Asian food and lots of really mediocre Italian fare (with some notable exceptions in both categories). The city's young professionals like to eat on the run, and all sorts of excellent casual eateries line the streets to satisfy them. **Bakerie,** 43-45 Lever St. (bakerie.co.uk; ☏ **0161/236-9014**) serves sandwiches, soups, and cheese and meat platters that you can wash down with wine and follow up with some excellent dessert choices. **Slice,** 1a Stevenson Sq. (slicepizza.co; ☏ **0161/236-9032**) makes superb crusts on the premises, with a tempting variety of toppings and available in the portions to go. Should a homesickness fueled craving hit you, head to **Byron Burgers,** 115 Deansgate (byronhamburgers.com;

© 0161/832-1222). **Leo's Fish Bar,** in the Northern Quarter at 12 Oldham St. (www.leosfishbar.com; © 0161/237-3999) fries up what may be the best fish and chips in town. Stop by the **Pancho's Burritos** stall in the Arndale Food Market (panchosburritos.co.uk) for all sorts of Mexican fare made from family recipes; they also run a sit-down restaurant in the Quadrangle, on Chester St. (© 0161/235-0712).

The swankiest spot for tea is the **Midland Hotel,** Peter St. (www. qhotels.co.uk; © 0161/236-3333) where you might be so swept up in the vaguely exotic, Moorish ambiance of the Octagon Lounge that you'll want to hang around for cocktails, too. If you're feeling escapist, the **Richmond Tea Rooms** (www.richmondtearooms.com) transport you into a fantasy world via an over-the-top Alice in Wonderland theme.

Michael Caines ★★ MODERN BRITISH AND EUROPEAN It would be easy to write this fancy dining experience off as part of a posh chain (with branches in Chester, Exeter, and elsewhere) or a money-maker for a celebrity chef resting on his laurels, but none of it would be true. Rather, as Mancunians out for the best dinner in town do, succumb to the pleasure of descending into the chic polished underbelly of the Abode Hotel and enjoying Caines' creative takes on the freshest ingredients from the region, served in tasting menus (some very reasonably priced) or a la carte. Lamb roasted with herbs and pan-fried scallops are perennial favorites, but you won't go wrong with the specials on offer, followed by inspired desserts and paired with an excellent wine selection.

107 Piccadilly. www.michaelcaines.com. © **0161/200-5678.** Mains £21–£26. Mon–Sat noon–2:30pm and 6–10pm.

Mr. Thomas's Chop House ★★ TRADITIONAL ENGLISH A perfectly preserved Victorian pub is tiled in jade and brown, with plenty of dark woodwork and warm hearths to create what's known as a "cozy boozer." It's easy to imagine yourself among mustachioed 19th-century burghers as you sit back and tuck into traditional British food that spurns any concerns about fat and calories: corned beef hash that simmers for 10 days, onion soup cooked for 36 hours and so thick you can eat it with a knife and fork, homemade steak and kidney pie served with chips, mushy peas, and a jug of gravy. The same management also runs **Sam's Chop House,** another Victorian charmer serving similarly heavy fare just around the corner off Cross Street on Back Pool Fold.

52 Cross St. www.tomschophouse.com. © **0161/832-2245.** Mains £10–£25. Mon–Thurs noon–3pm and 5–9:30pm; Fri–Sat noon–10pm, Sun noon–8:30pm.

Oast House ★★ Don't think this charming old relic has anything to do with Manchester—it was moved here brick by brick, timber by timber, from Kent, where these odd-looking structures for drying hops are a common sight. The old drying room and warm-weather patio provide an atmospheric place to sit back and enjoy casual food of the burger and kebab ilk prepared on a grill outside and, paying homage to the oast house provenance, served with an astonishing selection of casked and bottled beers. The rotisserie chicken is done to juicy perfection, and a filling deli board, is an excellent lunch or midafternoon snack. Crown Sq., Spinningfields. theoasthouse.uk.com. ✆ **0161/829-3830.** Mains £10–£14. Sun–Wed noon–midnight, Thurs noon–1am, Fri–Sat noon–2am.

Ocean Treasure 235 ★ CHINESE   Manchester is home to the largest Chinese population in Britain outside London, and Mancunians are almost as ardent about the places to eat Chinese food as they are about football (well, not quite). Top contender is this oasis of subtle lighting, and sleek furnishings in an old warehouse. Despite the modern surroundings, food is strictly old-fashioned Cantonese of the crispy duck, king prawn variety, available in a dizzying array of banquet and dim sum menus, or served a la carte. The steamed dumpling platters are delicious and a healthful meal in themselves. You might not feel totally transported to the Far East as the adjoining casino can keep noise levels from squealing partiers high, then again, what's more Chinese than that? 2 Watson St. www.oceantreasure235.co.uk. ✆ **0161/839-7631.** Mains £8–£14. Daily 2pm–midnight (Sat until 1am).

Shopping

Central Manchester is packed with shops, especially around **King Street, St Ann's Square, Market Street,** the **Avenue,** and the **Arndale Centre,** an urban shopping mall that was part of a city renewal scheme after a 1996 IRA bomb tore much of the center apart. If you wish to get away from chain stores, follow Oldham Street from Piccadilly Gardens into the **Northern Quarter,** home to plenty more retro boutiques, record stores, including the fashion emporium **Afflecks,** 52 Church St. (www.afflecks.com; ✆ **0161/839-0718**) and the gift store **Oklahoma,** 74-76 High St. (✆ **0161/834-1136**). The excellent **Manchester Craft Centre,** 17 Oak St. (www.craftanddesign.com; ✆ **0161/832-2474**), a good source for jewelry and crafty trinkets sold from stalls in a Victorian market building.

Arndale Market, off High St. (www.manchester.gov.uk/markets; Mon–Sat 9:30am–6pm and Sun 11am–5pm), is among the food stalls are many outlets selling sandwiches and other food to go. Manchester's **Real Food Market** (✆ **0161/234-7356**) takes place on the second and fourth weekend (Fri–Sat 10am–6pm) of the month in Piccadilly Gardens, offering products from local farms and producers.

Entertainment & Nightlife

Bridgewater Hall, Lower Mosley Street (www.bridgewater-hall.co.uk; ✆ **0161/907-9000**) is home to the Hallé Orchestra, BBC Philharmonic, and Manchester Camerata, and the 2,400-seat concert hall also hosts a wide variety of other events, from pop concerts to comedy acts.

The Royal Shakespeare Company, Donmar, and other visiting groups often perform at the **Lowry Theatre** (www.thelowry.com; ✆ **0843/208-6000**) at Salford Quays, with two main theatres and a studio space; surrounding galleries are hung with the works of Manchester artist L. S. Lowry, who painted scenes of England's industrial north. The city's other major theater is the **Royal Exchange** (www.royalexchangetheatre.org.uk; ✆ **0161/833-9833**), where Britain's largest theatre-in-the-round occupies a glass capsule suspended within the Great Hall of the Exchange on St Ann's Square.

Manchester has given birth to the Bee Gees, the Hollies, and Herman's Hermits, and in more recent years The Smiths, New Order, Oasis, and The Stone Roses. Big names perform in the 21,000-seat **Manchester Arena** at Hunts Bank (www.men-arena.com; ✆ **0161/950-5000**), while smaller venues include the University of Manchester's **Manchester Academy and Club Academy** on Oxford Rd. (manchesteracademy.net; ✆ **0161/275-2930**), **Night & Day,** 26 Oldham St. (www.nightnday.org; ✆ **0161/236-1822**), and **O2 Apollo,** Stockport Rd., Ardwick Green (www.o2apollomanchester.co.uk; ✆ **08444/777-677**). To keep with the music scene, go to Manchester After Dark, www.manchesterad.com.

Cloud 23, 303 Deansgate (www.cloud23bar.com; ✆ **0161/870-1600**) is the loftiest place in Manchester to enjoy a cocktail, served with views from the 23rd floor of the Hilton Hotel. Drinking, a very popular local pastime, is usually done in more down-to-earth surroundings, or even underground at **The Temple** (✆ **0871 230 3668**), in a Victorian-era public toilet at 110 Great Bridgewater St. **Peveril of the Peak**, alongside an old industrial canal at 127 Great Bridgewater St. (✆ **0161/236-6363**) is another Victorian-era institution with a huge selection of ales is on tap. Another old favorite is 200-year-old The **Briton's Protection,** 50 Great Bridgewater St. (britons-protection.com; ✆ **0161/236-5895**), an especially good stop if you want to sample some of the 300 kinds of whiskey on tap. Another popular Castlefield spot is **Dukes 92,** at 2 Castle St. (www.dukes92.com; ✆ **0161/839-3522**). The former stables of the duke of Bridgewater offers outdoor seating and is famous for its cheese platters and fine selection of beer.

Gay Manchester

Manchester has the largest gay scene outside of London, with most the bars and other venues centered in the so-called Gay Village on and off Canal Street. Two of the oldest and still most popular are Churchill's, 37 Charlton St. (✆ **0161/236-5529**) and Napoleon's, 35 Bloom St. (www.napoleons.co.uk; ✆ **0161/336-8800**). The largest gay bar in town, G-A-Y, 10 Canal St. (www.g-a-y.co.uk), is an offshoot of the London club of the same name and is especially pleasant when its huge roof terrace opens for the season.

Side Trips from Manchester

Just to the east of Manchester is the surprisingly rural **Peak District National Park** ★★ (www.peakdistrict.gov.uk), 555 square miles of wild and beautiful landscapes of heaths, dales, and craggy hills. Remember, though, this is Britain, where national parks encompass more than wilderness: Tucked amid the fields and woods are attractive villages and some of England's most stunning country houses. If you're relying on public transportation, settle for an outing by train and bus, passing through some beautiful patches of countryside, to Chatsworth. If you're driving, head through Eyam to Chatsworth, and from there to medieval **Haddon Hall** or Elizabethan **Hardwick Hall. Eyam** is a collection of lovely gray-stone cottages in the green folds of the Derbyshire Dales with a sadly heroic past. During the plague of 1665, villagers voluntarily quarantined themselves to avoid spreading the disease elsewhere. About half of the 800 residents died, many are buried in the churchyard of the 12th century village chapel. So-called plague stones still stand on the outskirts of the village, marking boundaries that could not be crossed.

Chatsworth ★★ HISTORIC HOME   If you're feeling in need of a *Downton Abbey* fix, the ancestral seat of the Duke of Devonshire is arguably the finest country house in all of Britain. The house has always been meant to impress, ever since the countess of Shrewsbury, a.k.a. Bess of Hardwick, had a Tudor mansion built above the River Derwent in the 1560s. Extensions have added a long, handsome Palladian facade, and elaborate gardens enhance the grandeur with a cascade, gravity-fed

The Wellington bedroom at Chatsworth, Derbyshire.

fountains, greenhouses, grottoes, and 100 acres of parkland. A mere 30 or so staterooms are open to the public, leaving the family 100 other rooms in which to roam. Most elaborate is the Painted Hall, a grandiose, two-story spectacle full of statuary, frescoes depicting the life of Julius Caesar, and twin staircases. By comparison the extraordinary art collection, displayed in well-appointed salons, seems almost homey, all the more so since many of the masterpieces are tied to the family in one way or the other. John Singer Sargent's *Acheson Sisters* is a portrait of the granddaughters of a former Devonshire duchess; *Skewball Mare* is by Lucian Freud, who has also painted several members of the family. Also on the vast estate are working farms, shops, and restaurants.

Bakewell, Derbyshire. www.chatsworth.org. ℂ **01246/565300.** £22 adults, £20 seniors and students, £16 children, £68 families. House late Mar to early Nov daily 11am–5:30pm; garden late Mar to early Nov 11am–6pm. 40 miles east of Manchester via the A623. By public transport, take the train to Sheffield and bus 218 from there.

Haddon Hall ★★ HISTORIC HOME On a night in 1563, so the story goes, the beautiful young Dorothy Vernon slipped away from a ball at Haddon Hall, her childhood home, and fled through the gardens to meet her lover, George Manners, and the two were whisked away in a carriage and eloped. The story has inspired novels, operas, and even a 1924 silent film with Mary Pickford. But this remarkable stone manor house, built in the 11th century for an illegitimate son of William the Conqueror, is romantic even without the story of two young lovers. They did indeed live happily ever after and their descendants still reside in the best-preserved medieval manor house in Britain, with a banqueting hall, minstrels' gallery, long gallery, and frescoed chapel.

Bakewell, Derbyshire. www.haddonhall.co.uk. ℂ **01629/812855.** £12 adults, £11 seniors, £6 children, £35 families. Apr and Oct, Sat–Mon daily noon–5pm; May–Sept daily noon–5pm. Haddon Hall is 5 miles SW of Chatsworth on B6012 and A6.

Hardwick Hall ★★ HISTORIC HOME If you're driving, you might want to continue on from Chatsworth to what's considered to be one of the finest Elizabethan houses in England. That's what Bess of Hardwick did around 1571 when she was led to believe that her fourth husband, the Earl of Shrewsbury (whom she described as a "knave and a scoundrel") was having an affair with Mary Queen of Scots, whom Elizabeth I had placed under house arrest at Chatsworth. Bess retired to Hardwick and, obviously believing that spending the earl's fortune was the best revenge, magnificently transformed the house into a glass palace. Many of the light-filled rooms are hung with tapestries that Bess and Mary worked on together at Chatsworth, along with other tapestries and embroideries that are known as the Hardwick Hall Textiles and comprise one of the finest such collections in the world. The 30 acres of gardens and orchards surrounding the house are also lovely.

Doe Lea, Chesterfield, Derbyshire. www.nationaltrust.org.uk. ℂ **01246/565300.** £13 adults, £6 children, £37 families. Mid-Feb to Oct Wed–Sun 11am–5pm. Hardwick Hall is 17 miles west of Chatsworth via A617.

Blackpool Tower and beach.

A Day at the Beach

Let's see, where shall it be? The South of France or Blackpool? For Mancunians, it's often the latter. The nation's most famous beach resort, Blackpool is a cross between Miami Beach and Las Vegas, but it's probably closest to Coney Island. Sands washed by Irish Sea waters that are chilly even in summer stretche for 6 miles beneath an often-gray sky. Entertainment is decidedly on the lower-brow end of the scale and pleasure central is **Pleasure Beach** (www.pleasurebeach resort.com), a vast 125-ride amusement park dating from 1896. **Blackpool Tower** (www.theblackpooltower.co.uk) is another late-19th century relic that's exactly half as tall as the Eifel Tower and houses a Victorian ballroom, a circus, an indoor adventure playground, a corny dungeon experience, and an observation platform. The resort gets especially festive during the **Blackpool Illuminations** (www.visitblackpool.com/site/illumina-tions), from late August or early September to November each year, when hundreds of neon figures and twinkling lights illuminate the promenade—a kitschy ploy to extend the season, but a heck of a lot of fun, like so much else in Blackpool.

CHESTER ★

220 miles NW of London; 40 miles SW of Manchester; 19 miles S of Liverpool

A walk through what appears to be at first glance a pleasant county seat is a bit of a head spin, as a different era of history seems to unfold on almost every street corner. The walls and ruins of a vast amphitheater are Roman; the cathedral is sturdily medieval; and the facades of the Rows and many other shops and houses are handsomely, half-timbered Tudor (though often with Victorian touch-ups). Though the general aspect is

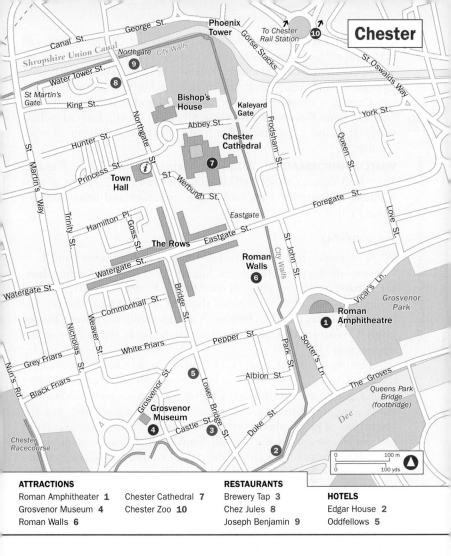

ATTRACTIONS

Roman Amphitheater **1**

Grosvenor Museum **4**

Roman Walls **6**

Chester Cathedral **7**

Chester Zoo **10**

RESTAURANTS

Brewery Tap **3**

Chez Jules **8**

Joseph Benjamin **9**

HOTELS

Edgar House **2**

Oddfellows **5**

county-life British, and the Cheshire countryside is picturesquely rural, Ancient Rome is the trump card here. Even the street plan is Roman, and the four main roads of the Roman garrison town of Deva Victrix now bisect the town center as Eastgate, Northgate, Watergate, and Bridgegate.

Essentials

GETTING THERE Direct **trains** from London's Euston Station to Chester take 2 hours, costing around £70 for a round-trip. There are also direct trains from Manchester (1½ hr.) and Liverpool (40 min.). There are a few direct **National Express** (www.nationalexpress.com,

✆ 0871/781-8181) **buses** between London and Chester, taking just over 6 hours; most services require a change at Birmingham. There are also direct buses from Manchester (about 1 hr.) and Liverpool (50 min.). Consult www.traveline-northwest.co.uk for public transport routes.

Chester is about 3½ hours northwest of London, mainly via the M1 and M6. From Birmingham it's about 80 miles (1½ hr.), from Manchester about 45 miles (just under 1 hr.), and from Liverpool about 28 miles (40 min.).

VISITOR INFORMATION Chester **Visitor Information Centre,** Town Hall Square (www.visitchester.com; ✆ 0845/647-7868), is open Monday to Saturday 9am to 5:30pm, Sundays and bank holidays 10am to 5pm.

Exploring

When it comes to street planning, things haven't changed much in Chester over the past 2,000 years. The center of town is still the **Chester Cross,** at the junction of Northgate, Eastgate, Watergate, and Bridge Streets—all laid out along the grid of roads that bisected the town when it was a Roman fortress. A medieval addition is the **Chester High Cross,** a red-sandstone crucifix standing in the middle of the intersection.

Fanning out from Chester Cross along Chester's four main streets is the **Rows,** one of the world's most extraordinary shopping centers. dating in large part to the 1200s, when Chester was a major port with bustling docks along the River Dee. Parts are Victorian restorations, but the assemblage of half-timbered buildings is a real stunner. Originally, shops and warehouses lined the ground floors, with living quarters above. These days the premises are almost strictly commercial. Gone, too, are "all the rogues, and fools, and drunkards in the country" who, according to one aristocratic observer, inhabited the various nooks and crannies, though you'll probably still be able to find a few wandering about town.

ROMAN AMPHITHEATER ★★

The Romans built the largest amphitheater in Britain as an assembly point for troops and perhaps as a grounds for military training. The sheer size, 98m by 87m (322 ft. by 285 ft.) suggests that military commanders of the 20th Legion may have planned to use Chester as a base from which to invade Ireland. Given the extensive seating that could accommodate 8,000 spectators, it's also likely it was used for gladiatorial contests, cock-fighting, and other entertainment, with a vast underground network of dungeons. The amphitheater fell into disuse in the 4th century, was used as a dump and as a grounds for medieval bear-baiting contests, and only came to light in 1929. Excavations continue, though many of the ruins lie beneath houses from the 17th through 19th centuries. A clever trompe l'oeil mural helps provide the illusion of what the theater looked like in its entirety. The entrance is off Little John Street, and the amphitheater can be visited during daylight hours; admission is free.

Roman Walls ★★★

The best way to soak in the ancient ambiance of Chester is with a walk along Britain's largest remaining circuit of Roman walls—they're about 2 miles in length, though the Roman originals have been added to, knocked down, and reinforced over the past two millennia. Saxon Queen Aethelflaed had them strengthened in 907 to ward off raiding Vikings. The Normans built a wooden castle that was fortified in stone in the 13th century, though the scant remains do little to suggest the fierce battles when Norman conquerors set out from here on a scorched earth policy that left more than 150,000 dead, or Welsh when warriors ravaged the surrounding countryside right up to the city gates. Victorians added the Eastgate Clock, the second largest timepiece in Britain after Big Ben, to commemorate Queen Victoria's Jubilee in 1897. You can walk the walls in the company of shills dressed as gladiators who congregate near the entrances and offer their services as guides, but make the circuit at your own leisurely pace. The best place to start is Northgate, since it's the highest section and affords a nicely orienting overview of the city.

Guarding the Roman walls and Eastgate Clock at Chester.

Chester Cathedral ★ CHURCH

If you look beyond the Victorian, faux-Gothic redo of parts of the main church—and overlook entirely the ghastly 20th-century bell tower—you can easily step into the Middle Ages. This monastery complex was established in 1092 on the site of a Roman altar and flourished for centuries, housing as it did a shrine to popular Werburgh, Chester's patron saint. The 7th-century Anglo-Saxon princess and Benedictine abbess was not left in peace—her casket was regularly hoisted to the top of the city walls during raids to ward off invaders. Legend has it the tactic proved especially effective when 11th-century Welsh king Gruffydd ap Llwelyn was struck blind at the spectacle. The 12th century cloisters are utterly charming, as are the carvings in the choir stalls; several depict still-popular fairy tales, including that of Reynard the fox playing dead in the mud to attract birds, whom he snaps in his jaws. The carvings of geese relate to St Werburgh's most popular miracle, in which a flock of wild geese that were devouring crops flew away at her bidding; when she discovered that her servants had slain one to eat, she resurrected the bird and sent it on its way, too.

Abbey Square. www.chestercathedral.com. © **01244/324756.** Free, donations accepted. Mon–Sat 9am–5pm, Sun 1–4pm.

Chester Zoo ★★ ZOO   One of the largest zoos in the U.K. is also one of the world's best, an especially hospitable place for endangered species. Many of the 9,000 residents, belonging to 442 species, benefit from the zoo's extensive conservation efforts and captive breeding programs, and you'll often see cubs and other babies frolicking near their moms. The Cheshire landscape has been transformed into some exotic-looking natural habitats: Chimpanzees and monkeys live on specially designed islands, elephants roam through rainforests, jaguars leap across savannahs, while humans look on from monorails and boats.

Upton-by-Chester, 2 miles south of center. www.chesterzoo.org. © **01244/380280.** Admission varies by season; in school holidays: £15 adults, £12 children 3–15, monorail and boats extra. Daily from 10am, check website for closing times.

Grosvenor Museum ★ MUSEUM   Viewing the collection of Roman tombstones here is not quite as morbid as you might imagine, as the weather worn stones depict some utterly delightful characters among the shepherds, horsemen, headless warriors, and obscure gods. Many of the stones look a little the worse for wear, as they were used to shore up the city walls in times of battle. Similarly engaging are the watercolors of Louise Rayner (1832–1924), a local resident who intricately depicted street scenes of Victorian-era Chester and other British cities.

27 Grosvenor St. www.cheshirewestandchester.gov.uk. © **01244/402033.** Free. Mon–Sat 10:30am–5pm and Sun 1–4pm.

Where to Stay

Edgar House ★★★   You can't find a more welcoming setting in Chester than this lovely 19th-century house tucked into the city walls. The sound of the gurgling River Dee, a perfect tonic for relaxation and sleep, is a standard amenity in the large, bright rooms that are done with a blend of traditional English style and contemporary simplicity, with carefully designed and commodious bathrooms. Even the obvious design flourishes, along the lines of copper bathtubs and some dramatic wall coverings, are relatively low-key, as is the pleasant fire-warmed lounge.

22 City Walls. www.edgarhouse.co.uk. © **01244/347007.** 6 units. Doubles from £149, includes breakfast. **Amenities:** Restaurant; bar; free Wi-Fi.

Oddfellows ★★   The handsome Georgian facade is misleading, and, as the name warns, stepping through the gracious entrance can be like falling down the rabbit hole into a warren of clutter. It may all be way too far over the top for some tastes—stags heads and vintage typewriters hanging from the walls, huge lamps reflecting off astro turf on the terrace, florid parrots and foxes papering the public rooms. Rooms tend to be a little bit more sedate and come in various shapes and sizes, including some tucked away in attics and cottages. Beyond all the knickknacks there are real comforts in all of them, such as homey lounge chairs and plush headboards, along with some nice touches that include illustrations by local children's book illustrator Randolf Caldecott.

20 Lower Bridge St. www.oddfellowschester.com. ⓒ **01625/441794.** 18 units. Doubles from £79, includes breakfast. **Amenities:** Bar; restaurant; free Wi-Fi.

Where to Eat

Brewery Tap ★★ BRITISH   Beers from Chester's own Splitting Feathers brewery is on tap, and the hearty fare is local, too, with many of the ingredients coming from within a few miles of town. Pigs fed with leftover grains from the brewery supply the thick pork chops with honey-glazed vegetables, roast ham sandwiches, and pork and apple sausages, served with mashed potatoes and onion gravy. Even the onion soup is topped with Cheshire cheese. The vast 16th–17th-century banquet hall lends a pleasantly regal air to a homey meal.

52-54 Lower Bridge St. www.the-tap.co.uk. ⓒ **01244/340999.** Mains £7–£10. Mon–Sat noon–11pm, Sun noon–9:30; food served until 9:30pm, 9pm on Sun.

Chez Jules ★★ FRENCH   Step beyond the Tudor facade and the red-checked table cloths will whisk you off to Paris, as will the *bouef* bourguignon, duck confit and other bistro classics. Reasonably priced two- and three-course daytime menus make this a top spot for lunch, while flickering candlelight and French-accented service, combined with excellent cooking, are the ingredients for a romantic dinner.

71 Northgate St. www.chezjules.com. ⓒ **01244/400014.** Mains £9–£13. Mon–Sat noon–10:30pm, Sun noon–9:30pm.

Have a Pint with a Spirits Chaser

Chester's pubs, many dating from the 17th and 18th centuries when the city was a busy port, are said to have some regulars who simply refuse to leave. The **Boot Inn,** Eastgate Street (ⓒ **01244/ 324435**) was once Chester's most popular brothel, and ghostly female voices still ring through the place long after last call. At **Ye Olde King's Head,** 48 Lower Bridge St. (ⓒ **01244/ 324855**) shadowy phantoms roam the upstairs rooms and leave messages on mirrors. Watch your back at the **Falcon Inn** (ⓒ **01244/342060**), Lower Bridge Street, where a poorly treated barmaid of times past supposedly still hurls glasses around the room.

Joseph Benjamin ★★★ MODERN BRITISH/EUROPEAN   The Wright Brothers have really taken off in Chester—puns aside, brothers Joe and Ben Wright are committed to creating delicious food from top-quality ingredients in their deli-cum-coffee house-cum restaurant next to the city walls. Pastries, sandwiches and snacks are available throughout the day, and three evenings a week a small but satisfying seasonal menu is offered, with the emphasis on local meat and produce. The free-range rotisserie chicken, a menu fixture in any season, is delicious, as are any of the dishes with grass-fed lamb.

140 North Gate St., Chester. www.josephbenjamin.co.uk. ℂ **01244/344295.** Mains £13–£18. Tues–Wed 9am–5pm, Thurs–Sat 9am–midnight, Sun 10am–5pm.

LIVERPOOL ★★

219 miles NW of London; 103 miles NW of Birmingham; 35 miles W of Manchester

Like Manchester, **Liverpool** has re-emerged over the past few decades to become a world-class city, enjoying a proud cultural and economic reawakening and reclaiming its extraordinary maritime heritage.

It began life as a small fishing village in the 12th century and would remain as such for several hundred years. Its population started to expand in the 1600s and by the late 18th century it had grown to national prominence through its sugar, spice, tobacco, and above all, slave trade with the Americas. Under Queen Victoria, it became Britain's biggest commercial seaport and a vibrant cosmopolitan place.

Unfortunately, the 20th century saw a major reversal of the city's fortunes. The Great Depression hit it hard, the Luftwaffe destroyed much of the center, and the rise of containerization after the World War II put most of the docks out of business. Despite the brief spot-light of international attention that shone on Liverpool during the Beatles' 1960s heyday, the city wouldn't begin the process of regenera-tion until the late 20th century. Since then, sustained investment has transformed Liverpool's waterfront and center and seen the opening of a glut of new galleries, museums, shopping complexes, and hotels. In 2004, much of the waterfront was designated a UNESCO World Heritage Site, while the naming of Liverpool as the European Capital of Culture 4 years later gave the international stamp of approval to the city's re-emergence.

Essentials

GETTING THERE   Frequent **trains** from London's Euston Station to Liverpool Lime Street Station take just over 2 hours direct but more usu-ally 2½ hours, with a change at Crewe. There are also direct trains to Liverpool from Birmingham (about 1¾ hr.), Manchester (about 1 hr.), Chester (about 45 min.), Leeds (about 1¾ hr.), and York (about 2¼ hr.).

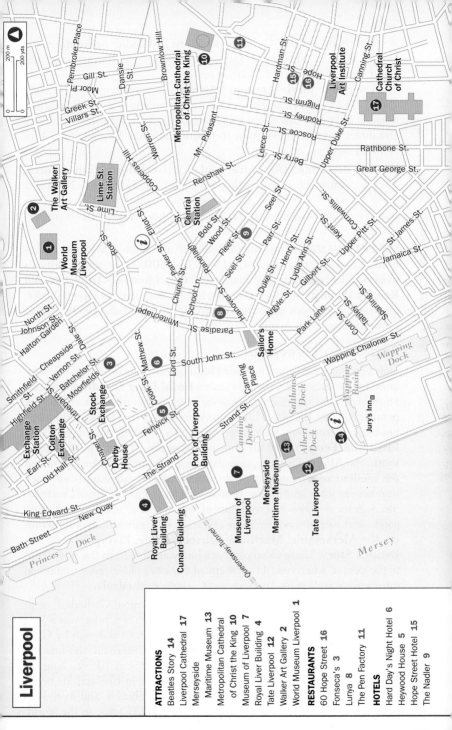

Liverpool

ATTRACTIONS

Beatles Story **14**
Liverpool Cathedral **17**
Merseyside
  Maritime Museum **13**
Metropolitan Cathedral
  of Christ the King **10**
Museum of Liverpool **7**
Royal Liver Building **4**
Tate Liverpool **12**
Walker Art Gallery **2**
World Museum Liverpool **1**

RESTAURANTS

60 Hope Street **16**
Fonseca's **3**
Lunya **8**
The Pen Factory **11**

HOTELS

Hard Day's Night Hotel **6**
Heywood House **5**
Hope Street Hotel **15**
The Nadler **9**

Liverpool is about 3¾ hours northwest of London by **road,** mainly on the M1 and M6; about 1¼ hours northwest of Birmingham; and about 45 minutes west of Manchester.

Liverpool **John Lennon Airport** (www.liverpoolairport.com; © **0871/521-8484**), serving mainly European and a few U.K. destinations, is linked by bus to central Liverpool and Manchester. There are also direct buses from **Manchester International Airport** (p. 384) to central Liverpool.

VISITOR INFORMATION Liverpool Tourist Information Centre, Anchor Courtyard (www.visitliverpool.com; © **0151/233-2008**), is open 10am to 5:30pm from April to September, until 5pm the rest of the year. There are also information desks at John Lennon Airport and on Platform 7 at Lime Street Station.

SPECIAL EVENTS The Grand National at Sefton's **Aintree Racecourse** (www.aintree.co.uk; © **0151/523-2600**) every April is Britain's most popular horserace, and a major TV event. Liverpool's **International Beatles Week** (www.cavernclub.org/beatleweek) attracts about 100,000 fans and bands from more than 20 countries for a 7-day celebration in various venues each August.

Exploring Liverpool

Down on the waterfront, the **Pier Head** boasts some of Liverpool's best-loved buildings, notably the Edwardian **Royal Liver Building.** The two 18-ft. high Liver (pronounced "*Lie*-ver") birds on its towers have become popular icons of the city. This is also where you'll find some of the city's newest constructions, including the angular, modernist stylings of the **Liverpool Ferry Terminal** and the **Museum of Liverpool.** To the south, the **Albert Dock** represents both the heart of old Liverpool and the modern regenerated, tourist-friendly city. These waterfront brick warehouses were built in the 1840s at the height of Liverpool's mercantile majesty to store vast volumes of tobacco, tea, textiles, and other goods, and are now home to some of the city's favorite attractions, including the **Merseyside Maritime Museum, Tate Liverpool,** and the **Beatles Story.** There's also plenty to lure you away from the waterfront to the center, where you'll find many of the city's older, more traditional museums as well as its Anglican and Catholic **cathedrals.**

Liverpool Cathedral ★ CATHEDRAL Liverpool Cathedral, or to give it its full title, the Anglican Cathedral Church of Christ, was a long time in the making. Began in 1904 to a Gothic revival design by Giles Gilbert Scott, it was eventually completed in 1978. Today, the fine red sandstone building holds a number of records: at 186m (619-ft.) long, it's the longest cathedral in the world and the largest in England. Its organ has nearly 10,000 pipes, the most found in any church, and its tower's bells are the highest (66m/219 ft.) and heaviest (31 tons) in the world.

Ferry Cross the Mersey, with the Royal Liver Building, Liverpool.

Ferry Cross the Mersey

It's from Pier Head that you can catch the famous **Ferry Cross the Mersey** ★★ (www.merseyferries.co.uk; ② **0151/236-7676**), which serves as both a locals' shuttle service and a tour boat offering the best views of Liverpool's skyline. Round-trip River Explorer tickets are £10 adults, £7 children 5 to 15, and £27 families. This includes entry to **U-Boat Story,** Woodside Terminal (www.u-boatstory.co.uk; ② **0151/330-1000**), a real German submarine housing interactive displays and archive film footage. You can also get joint tickets (£14 adults, £9 children, £38 families) for **Spaceport,** Seacombe Terminal (www.spaceport.org.uk; ② **0151/330-1444**), which has various space-themed galleries and a planetarium.

Alternatively, Mersey Ferries also runs **Manchester Ship Canal Cruises** ★★ from Pier Head along the 35-mile canal that helped shape the city of Manchester, as far as Salford Quays (p. 382). Trips take 6 hours, followed by a 2½-hour stopover and then a 1 hour return coach journey. They cost £39.

It's free to enter the main body of the cathedral, although you pay extra to ascend its tower (2 elevators, then 108 stairs) for views over the city. St James' Mount. www.liverpoolcathedral.org.uk. ② **0151/709-6271.** Free admission to cathedral; ticket for audioguide, and access to the tower costs £6 adults, £5 seniors, students, and children, £15 families. Daily 8am–6pm.

Merseyside Maritime Museum ★★ MUSEUM   Filled with ship models, maritime paintings, and an assortment of nautical paraphernalia, this 5-story museum is devoted to the seafaring that turned Liverpool

IN THE FOOTSTEPS OF THE fab four

These days there's an entire industry devoted to catering to the thousands of Beatles pilgrims who come each year to visit the band's home city, encompassing exhibitions, tours, a festival (p. 406), and even a hotel (p. 411). In the **Museum of Liverpool** (p. 409), you can get a 15-minute overview of the band's career at "The Beatles Show" in the Wondrous Place gallery. Pier Head and Albert Dock are each home to a memorabilia-filled **Beatles Story ★** (www.beatlesstory.com; ✆ **0151/709-1963**). They're open daily April to October 9am to 7pm, 10am to 6pm the rest of the year; tickets cost £15 adults, £12 seniors and students, £9 children ages 5 to 16.

Of the many Beatles tours on offer, the best are **Cavern City Tours ★**

(www.cavernclub.org/beatles-tours; ✆ **0151/236-9091**). Tickets for the 2-hour bus-and-club tour cost £17. For truly ardent fans, **Pool of Life ★** (www.pooloflifetours.com; ✆ **0776/276-9296**) offers both full-day Beatles Tours (£115 per person) or custom tours lasting from 2 hours to 2 days.

To tour both **Mendips ★** and **20 Forthlin Road**—Lennon and McCartney's childhood homes, restored to how they would have looked in the 1950s—book a place on a minibus from the city center (www.nationaltrust.org.uk/beatles; ✆ **0151/427-7231**); there's no independent access. Tickets cost £23 adults (£7 children). Tours run Wednesday to Sunday from mid-March to November and fill well in advance.

The Beatles Story, Liverpool.

from a seaside village into a global trading hub. It covers all aspects of the maritime experience, from life at sea to the growth of the port itself. The "Seized!" galleries in the basement reveal the shady, shadowy world of smuggling, while the "Titanic and Liverpool" exhibition traces the links between the world's most famous ship and the city where it was designed. Elsewhere, there are displays on shipbuilding, the Battle for the Atlantic in the Second World War, and mass emigration. Things take a more somber turn on the third floor, where the **International Slavery Museum** explores the dark underbelly of Liverpool's maritime glory.

Albert Dock. www.liverpoolmuseums.org.uk/maritime. ✆ **0151/478-4499.** Free. Daily 10am–5pm.

Metropolitan Cathedral of Christ the King ★ CATHEDRAL

Liverpool's Roman Catholic home lies around a half-mile northeast of Liverpool Cathedral. Sir Edward Lutyens came up with the original design, which was begun in 1933. The Second World War put a stop to construction, and in its aftermath it was decided that Lutyens' design was too costly to complete, so Sir Frederick Gibbert came up with the space-age alternative you see today. Inside it's bathed in colored light from the stained glass of the central lantern tower. You can get an idea of what the original might have looked like by visiting the crypt, the only part of Lutyens' design to have been completed.

Mount Pleasant. www.liverpoolmetrocathedral.org.uk. ✆ **0151/709-9222.** Free admission to cathedral; crypt £3. Daily 7:30am–6pm.

Museum of Liverpool ★★ MUSEUM

This white, stone-clad building—which is vaguely reminiscent of a ship—uses technologically advanced displays to retell the history of the great port city. It's divided into a number of themed areas—Global City, People's Republic, City Soldiers, the Great Port, History Detectives, and Wondrous Place—which together examine Liverpool's role on the world stage, particularly the period when it sat at the heart of a great mercantile empire, its subsequent industrial decline, and the lives and creative endeavors of its

The Museum of Liverpool.

people, from pop music to footballing triumphs. It's all very modern with lots of videos, computer wizardry, and giant projected images.

Pier Head. www.liverpoolmuseums.org.uk/mol. © **0151/478-4545.** Free. Daily 10am–5pm.

Tate Liverpool ★★ MUSEUM   One of four Tates (the others are in London and Cornwall), this is home to an ever-arresting collection of modern and contemporary art displayed in a bright, swanky space. Expect to encounter artists of the caliber of Picasso and Jackson Pollock, as well as some less-celebrated names. As with all the Tates, there's plenty for families to do in the form of trails, events, a play area and activities, as well as a great shop filled with lavishly illustrated books.

Albert Dock. www.tate.org.uk/liverpool. © **0151/702-7400.** Free admission except special exhibitions. May–Sept Tues–Sun 10am–5pm; June–Aug daily 10am–5pm.

Walker Art Gallery ★★ GALLERY   Named after Sir Andrew Walker—a wealthy local brewer and one time mayor of Liverpool, who largely paid for its construction in the 1870s—the Walker is one of the largest and most prestigious art collections outside of London. The huge collection includes a wealth of European art dating back to 1300. The painting galleries are particularly strong on British artists, holding works by Turner, Constable, Stubbs, as well as some Pre-Raphaelites and several 20th-century artists, including Lucian Freud and David Hockney and even a Banksy (in the form of a sculpture donated by the artist). The museum's acclaimed sculpture gallery focuses principally on European works from the period between the 18th century and World War I.

William Brown St. www.liverpoolmuseums.org.uk/walker. © **0151/478-4199.** Free. Daily 10am–5pm.

World Museum Liverpool ★ MUSEUM   "World" is a fitting description for this six-floor extravaganza where you'll find galleries dedicated to everything from dinosaurs (plenty of life-size casts) and ancient civilizations (look out for the Egyptian mummies) to the natural world (there's an aquarium and a Bug House with live giant insects), world cultures, and Space—where you can watch effects-heavy shows about the cosmos at the **Planetarium.**

William Brown St. www.liverpoolmuseums.org.uk/wml. © **0151/478-4393.** Free. Daily 10am–5pm.

Where to Stay
EXPENSIVE

Hope Street ★★   The city's foremost boutique hotel has a winning industrial-heritage-meets-modern-chic vibe. So the exposed brickwork and cast-iron columns of the 19th-century building (originally a carriage builders) have been augmented with polished oak floors, lavish fittings, plump beds, and fine linens. Many of the rooms have great city views and the restaurant, the **London Carriage Works,** is a draw in itself.

40 Hope St. www.hopestreethotel.co.uk. ✆ **0151/709-3000.** 89 units. Doubles £120–£250. **Amenities:** Restaurant; bar; gym; room service; in-room treatments; free Wi-Fi.

MODERATE

Hard Day's Night ★   This centrally located tribute hotel to the city's most famous musical sons is surprisingly comfortable. Spread across a fine-looking 19th-century building, the rooms vary in size but are of a high quality with luxurious bathrooms and attractive decor. However, there's no escaping the relentless theming with memorabilia, paintings and photographs everywhere, and hits piped constantly into the public areas. Your enjoyment will depend on how big of a fan you are.

Central Buildings, North John St. www.harddaysnighthotel.com. ✆ **0151/709-3000.** 110 units. Doubles £90–£180. **Amenities:** Restaurant; bar; room service; free Wi-Fi.

INEXPENSIVE

Heywood House ★★   One of the best bargains in town, the Heywood provides three levels of accommodation: standard "comfy" rooms; superior "plush" rooms; and the top choice, "balcony" rooms with terraces overlooking the city. All offer a good standard of solid comfort and amenities at very reasonable prices. Note that there are no eating facilities, but there are plenty of decent cafes and restaurants nearby.

11 Fenwick St. www.heywoodhousehotel.co.uk. ✆ **0151/224-1444.** 35 units. Doubles £55–£115. **Amenities:** Free Wi-Fi.

The Nadler ★   The Liverpool outpost of this minichain occupies a lively spot among a glut of bars and clubs. It can get noisy on weekends, but the triple-glazed windows should ensure you get your 8 hours' sleep. Housed in a converted mid-19th century warehouse, the rooms are attractively laid out. There's no bar or restaurant but each room has a small kitchenette. Continental breakfast can be delivered to your room.

29 Seel St. www.thenadler.com/liverpool.shtml. ✆ **0151/705-2626.** 106 units. Doubles £53–£160. **Amenities:** Free Wi-Fi.

Where to Eat

60 Hope Street ★★★ MODERN ENGLISH   This family-run, fine-dining stalwart is perhaps the city's most vaunted gastronomic experience. The walls are even kept free of art so as not to distract you from the task in hand—sampling some of the best modern British cooking around. The menu changes regularly, but expect the likes of lemon sole meunière, cider-cured sea trout, and roasted rump of Cumbrian lamb with sweetbreads. The downstairs bistro serves a fixed-price menu and is a little more informal.

60 Hope St. www.60hopestreet.com. ✆ **0151/707-6060.** Mains £18–£33. Mon–Sat noon–2:30pm and 5–10:30pm, Sun noon–6pm.

Spanish tapas at Lunya, Liverpool.

Fonseca's ★★ INTERNATIONAL   This ever popular, bustling deli (downstairs) and bistro (upstairs) has a changing menu of locally sourced favorites. It's great for lunch on the go, serving takeout sandwiches, soups, and salads, or for something more substantial, such as beef bourgignon, pan-fried seabass, or vegetable curry.

12 Stanley St. www.delifonseca.co.uk. ℂ **0151/255-0808.** Mains £12–£19. Mon–Thurs 8am–9pm, Fri–Sat 8am–9:30pm, Sun 9:30am–5pm.

Lunya ★★★ SPANISH   The sheer variety of tapas on offer at this Catalan–Spanish place is the main draw. With well over 50 cold and hot tapas on the menu, there's something for everyone. All the classics—albóndigas, fried calamari, patatas bravas—are there alongside some more unusual choices. Look out for the Catalan Scouse, their signature mix of vegetables, minced lamb, and chorizo.

18 College Lane, Liverpool One. www.lunya.co.uk. ℂ **0151/706-9770.** Tapas £5–£11. Mon–Thurs 9am–9pm, Sat 9am–10pm, Sun 10am–8:30pm.

Pen Factory ★★ ENGLISH   Run by the former proprietor and chef of the old bistro at the Everyman Theatre, this occupies the Annexe next door. The bare brickwork and exposed light fittings give it a semi-industrial look, but it has a lively ambience and serves great, simple food—soups, quiches, sandwiches (including "crisp butties"), and salads—plus a few mains offered with an impressive range of craft beers.

13 Hope St. www.pen-factory.co.uk. ℂ **0151/709-7887.** Mains £8–£12. Mon–Sat 9am–late, Sun 10am–11pm.

Shopping

Liverpool's rebirth has included the creation of the vast, retail-led **Liverpool One complex** ★ (www.liverpool-one.com) near the Albert Dock. Home to about 170 mainly familiar high-street names such as John Lewis and Topshop, it's one of the U.K.'s largest shopping centers.

The nearby **Metquarter** (www.metquarter.com) opened on Whitechapel in 2006 and has been dubbed "the Bond Street of Liverpool." It houses mainly upscale boutiques. More bohemian shopping can be found along villagey **Lark Lane** (www.larklaneguide.com). For all your Beatles memorabilia, head to **The Beatles Shop,** 31 Matthew Street (www.thebeatleshop.co.uk; ✆ **0151/210-2895.**).

Entertainment & Nightlife

The **Liverpool Philharmonic Hall** ★, Hope Street (www.liverpoolphil.com; ✆ **0151/210-2895**), is home to one of the best orchestras outside London, while the city's well-respected theatrical venue, the **Everyman Theatre** ★, Williamson

A portion of Antony Gormley's "Another Place" sculpture installation at Crosby.

Square (www.everymanplayhouse.com; ✆ **0151/709-4776**), specializes in experimental works, often by British playwrights.

Art-house and independent films are shown at the **FACT (Foundation for Art and Creative Technology) Centre,** 88 Wood St. (www.fact.co.uk; ✆ **0871/902-5737**), which also contains galleries where avant-garde art, video, and photography exhibitions are staged.

The Liverpool rock, pop, and dance music scenes continue to thrive, particularly in the Ropewalks district. **Nation,** Wolstenholme Square (✆ **0151/707-1309**), hosts the world-famous **Cream** ★ (www.cream.co.uk) dance night, typically held four times a year and attracting superstar DJs. For listings at Nation and elsewhere, see www.anightinliverpool.com or pick up flyers around town.

A Side Trip to "Another Place"

The coastal town of **Crosby** to the north of Liverpool is where globally renowned sculptor Antony Gormley—also behind the **Angel of the North** (p. 463)—has sited his art installation, "**Another Place**" ★★★ (www.sefton.gov.uk). Along 2 miles of Crosby's beach as far as about a half-mile out to sea, stand 100 cast-iron casts of Gormley's own body, sunk to various depths in the sand and appearing to stare out to the horizon in silent expectation.

THE LAKE DISTRICT

by Stephen Brewer

L ittle wonder this compact region is high on just about everyone's list of favorite spots. The tallest mountain and largest lake in England are here, and that's just the beginning. Shimmering little lakes, dramatic mountain valleys, craggy peaks, and welcoming stone villages comprise a landscape that has captivated travelers since the Romantic poets rhapsodized about the Lakes in the early 19th century. Ever since, travelers have beaten a path here to walk in the hills, boat on the waters, and just take in the magnificent valley-and-peak scenery.

The Lake District retreats of some of Britain's great artistic lions—William Wordsworth's cottage, Beatrix Potter's farm, John Ruskin's manor—are big attractions, too, putting a fine polish on all the natural beauty. Every year more than 16 million visitors venture into the Lake District, where more than 885 square miles are protected as the Lake District National Park, helping preserve the hills, mountains, forests, and lakes in some semblance of their pristine beauty and serenity.

Essentials

GETTING THERE   Virgin Trains operate seven **daily trains** from London Euston to Oxenholme Lake District station; local trains connect the station to Windermere, where you can continue by local buses to other Lake District towns. The trip takes from 2½ to 3½ hours. A direct train also links Manchester and Oxenholme, and the trip takes an hour. For more information, go to nationalrail.co.uk. National Express **buses** run from London's Victoria Coach Station, to Windermere; for schedules and fare info, go to www.nationalexpress.com.

If you're **driving** from London, head north on the M1 and the M6 past Liverpool until you reach the A685 junction heading west to Kendal. From Kendal, the A591 continues west to Windermere.

GETTING AROUND   Buses operated by **Stagecoach** link the main Lake District towns, with fairly frequent service that is curtailed on weekends. For timetables and information, go to www.traveline.info.

Staff at Visitor Information Centers can also provide schedules and route information, along with a booklet, *The Lakes Connection*. They are usually eager to dispense advice about getting around the region without a car. An especially convenient route for sightseeing is Stagecoach's **555 Lakeslink,** which runs at least a couple of times an hour during the

PREVIOUS PAGE: **A Lake District panorama.**

summer and stops at Windermere (with connections to Bowness); Brockdale (for the Lake District National Park Visitor Centre); Rydal Water (for Rydal Mount, Wordsworth's home); Grasmere; and Keswick.

In summer, Stagecoach's open-top **Lakeland Experience** runs between Windermere and Grasmere. Another handy Stagecoach route, the **Coniston Rambler,** 505, connects Windermere with Hawkshead, while the Kirkstone Rambler, 517, travels between Windermere and Glenridding, for Lake Ullswater steamers. The **Cross Lakes Shuttle** runs from Ferry house on the western shore of Lake Windermere to Hawkshead and Coniston, connecting with the ferry from Bowness; service runs in summer only. Tickets are available on the buses, as is the Explorer's pass, good for a day (£10) or 3 days (£22).

VISITOR INFORMATION The Lake District National Park Visitor Centre (www.lakedistrict.gov.uk; ✆ **01539/446601**) is located on the lakeshore at Brockhole, on the A591 about 2 miles north of Windermere. Aside from dispensing a plethora of information about the region, including detailed hiking routes and boat and bus schedules, the center is also part museum and part amusement park. It houses exhibits on the geology of the lakes, the background of the national park, and the history of Lake District travel, and on the grounds are a beach for swimming, a marina for boat rentals, and 10 acres of formal gardens. Many towns in the region also have Tourist Information Centres.

ORGANIZED TOURS Experienced guides of **Keswick Ramblers** (www.keswickramblers.org.uk; ✆ **017687/71292**) lead full-day walks of varying degrees of difficulty almost every day, with bus transportation to routes that are not within easy walking distance of Keswick; rates are £20 person, £10 under 16, payable on the day of the walk and walks must be booked in advance; there's a booking form on the website. The **Lake District National Park** also leads walks in the region (www.lakedistrict.gov.uk; ✆ **01539/724555**); a list of walks, with meeting points, degree of difficulty, and fee (usually about £5), appears on the website, where you can also fill out a booking form.

If you're in the Lake District without a car, an excellent way to see a lot of scenery in a short amount of time is with **Mountain Goat** (www.mountain-goat.com; ✆ **015394/45161**). Half-day and full-day tours often combine lake cruises and drives in a van through mountain scenery, with stops at villages and local sights. Tours begin in Windermere, sometimes with pickups in other towns; fees run from about £40 for a full-day tour, £20 for a half-day.

The Lakes in Brief

The Lake District National Park spreads over 885 square miles of forests, fields, towns, villages, mountains, and, of course, lakes. Within the park is Britain's tallest mountain, Scafell Pike, soaring to 978m (3,210 ft.)—modest by world summit standards, but an impressive presence

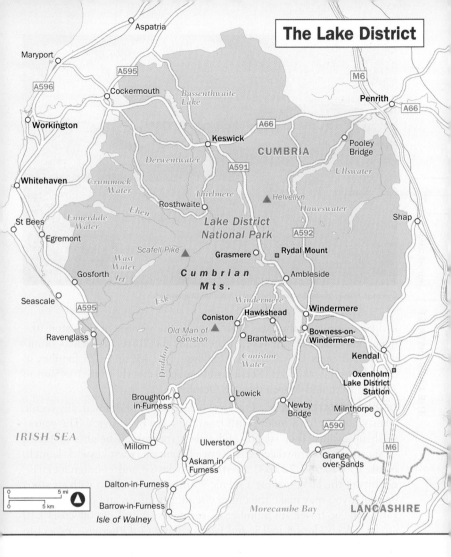

The Lake District

Aspatria
Maryport
A596
A595
Cockermouth
Bassenthwaite Lake
M6
Penrith
A66
Workington
Keswick
A66
CUMBRIA
Pooley Bridge
Derwentwater
A591
Whitehaven
Crummock Water
Thirlmere
Helvellyn
Ullswater
Haweswater
Ehen
Rosthwaite
Ennerdale Water
St Bees
Lake District National Park
Shap
Egremont
A592
Scafell Pike
Grasmere
Rydal Mount
Gosforth
Wast Water
Irt
C u m b r i a n   M t s .
Ambleside
Seascale
A595
Esk
Windermere
Windermere
Ravenglass
Coniston
Hawkshead
Bowness-on-Windermere
Old Man of Coniston
Brantwood
Duddon
Coniston Water
Kendal
Oxenholm Lake District Station
Broughton-in-Furness
Lowick
Newby Bridge
Milnthorpe
A590
IRISH SEA
Millom
Ulverston
Grange-over-Sands
M6
0   5 mi
0   5 km
Askam in Furness
Dalton-in-Furness
Barrow-in-Furness
Isle of Walney
Morecambe Bay
LANCASHIRE

nonetheless. Among the 20 or so lakes in the region are the largest in England, Lake Windermere, 11 miles long and a mile across at its widest point, and the deepest, Wastwater, hitting depths of 74m (243 ft.).

THE LAKES

CONISTON WATER ★★   About 5 miles long and ½ mile wide, the district's third-largest lake once provided surrounding abbeys with fish. The placid waters and green hillsides offered up enough solace and scenery to satisfy 19th-century man of letters John Ruskin, whose home, Brantwood, commands a rise above the shoreline. The Coniston Launch (www.conistonlaunch.co.uk; ✆ **01768/775753**), a timbered steamer,

Coniston Water, viewed from John Ruskin's home, Brantwood.

makes a circuit of the lake, with stops at the villages of Coniston (the major settlement on the lake), Waterhead, and Torver, as well as Brantwood, and costs £11 adults, £5 children 5 to 15, and £25 families of 2 adults and 3 children. Service runs roughly hourly from 10:45am to 4:45pm from mid-March through October.

DERWENTWATER ★★★ One of the district's most dramatically scenic lakes stretches for 3 miles south from the town of Keswick. The waters wash up against four islands and reflect the rugged heights of Friar's Craig and the Borrowdale Fells. Keswick Launch (www.keswick-launch. co.uk; ⓒ **017687/72263**) alternates clockwise and counterclockwise circuits of the lake, making a scenic 90-minute round trip with six stops en route; you may make the entire circuit, getting on and off as often as you wish, or travel any number of segments. A full circuit costs £10 adults, £5 children 5 to 15, and £24 for families. Otherwise, expect to pay about £2 per segment. Boats run every half-hour, from 9am to 4:30pm in late March and late November; from 9am to 6pm from April through June and September through October; from 9am to 8pm in July and August; and 9am to 5pm in early November.

LAKE WINDERMERE ★★ England's largest lake, about 11 miles long and dotted with 11 islands, has been a favorite with travelers since a railway line opened to Windermere, the largest town on the lake, in 1847. Adjacent Bowness-on-Windermere is the lake resort, with marinas and ferry docks. Windermere Lake Cruises Ltd. (www.windermere-lake cruises.co.uk; ⓒ **01539/443360**) offers freedom tickets that allow you to hop on and off boats as often as you wish; 24-hour tickets cost £12 adults, £6 children 5 to 15, £34 families (2 adults, 3 children). The

Hiking above Derwentwater.

Walker's Special is good for 1 day and allows you to hike segments of the lakeshore paths; the segment between Wray's Castle and Ferry House is especially scenic. Tickets are £10 adults, £6 children 5 to 15, and £28 for families. In summer boats run approximately from 9:15am to 6:45pm and in winter from 10am to 4pm.

ULLSWATER ★★★   The second-largest lake in the district stretches for 9 miles beneath dramatic mountain rises. Paths cross the forests and rolling green fields along the shores, and the best way to explore the lake is to combine a hike and a boat ride on the **Ullswater Steamers** (www. ullswater-steamers.co.uk; ✆ **017684/82229**) that operate between Pooley Bridge in the north, Howtown on the east, and Glenridding in the south. A good outing is to take a boat from Glenridding halfway up the lake to Howtown and walk back. Round-the-lake tickets that lets you hop on and off for a day are £13 adults, £7 children 5 to 15, and £28 families; you can also purchase segment tickets—for instance, Glenridding to Howton is £6 adults, £3 children. From April through October, six to nine boats makes the circuit between 9:45am and 4:45pm, with curtailed service at other times.

SCENIC WONDERS

AIRA FORCE ★★   The most dramatic of the Lake District's waterfalls plunges 70 feet into a river that flows into Ullswater. A half-mile-long trail from the Aira Force pier (a stop for Ullswater steamers, see above) leads to the falls through a magnificent forest of cedar, spruce, and pines.

BORROWDALE & BUTTERMERE VALLEYS ★★★   These side-by-side valleys just west of Keswick offer welcoming hills, rushing streams, and

A sailboat on Ullswater.

Aria Force.

colorful moors to satisfy any Lake District walker. Bleak, boulder-strewn Honister Pass connects the two valleys, providing one of the most dramatic drives in the Lake District. You can get a nice feel for the gentler side of local beauty with a 4-mile hike around little Buttermere Lake, accessible by bus number 77/77A from Keswick.

FRIAR'S CRAG ★★ John Ruskin went so far as to call the vista across Derwentwater into the surrounding hills and forests from this cliff top

Walking in Borrowdale Valley.

one of the three best scenes in Europe. Medieval monks gave the promontory its name when they paused to take in the vista on their way to the lakeshore for the short row out to nearby St Herbert's Island. The crag is less than a mile outside Keswick, an easy stroll along the lake.

THE PEAKS ★★★   The Lake District's best view with the least exertion may be from this 1,200-foot-high Latrigg Peak, an easy 15-minute walk from the Gale Road, just north of Keswick. Views extend down the beautiful Borrowdale Valley. The most dramatic Lake District peaks, though, are **Blencathra, the Helvellyn range, Langdale Pikes, Scafell Pike,** and **Skiddaw;** challenging routes ascend all of them. Scafell Pike is the tallest mountain in England and rises to 978m (3,209 ft.).

STOCK GHYLL FORCE ★   This powerful cascade, admired from a viewpoint a 15-minute walk from the little lakeside community of Ambleside, near Windermere, is not just spectacular but was at one time an economic boon. Beginning in the 14th century the 70-foot falls drove 12 water wheels, which in turn powered factories and mills that produced everything from cattle feed to fabric. Daffodils carpet the route in spring.

TARN HOWS ★★   Even a steady stream of scenery-seekers can't detract from the beauty of this little lake near Coniston. The clear waters are fed by rushing streams and surrounded by woodlands and hills, with the Helvellyn range and Langdale Pikes in the background. A path of about 1¾ miles circles the lake, a popular spot since the Victorian era and accessible by the road between Coniston and Hawkshead or on a 5-mile hike from the jetty at Monk Coniston on Coniston Water.

Tarn Hows in autumn.

WINDERMERE & BOWNESS ★★

274 miles NW of London; 10 miles NW of Kendal; 55 miles N of Liverpool

Though they're forever linked, these are two distinct towns: one right on the water, Bowness-on-Windermere, and one perched on a hillside about half a mile above the shores, Windermere. Bowness has all the trappings of a good-natured resort, with marinas, yacht clubs, and ferry landings, while Windermere is a more somber place of tidy slate-roofed cottages and Victorian-era row houses. The attention in both is squarely on Lake Windermere, the largest body of water in England, stretching for more than 11 miles between forested slopes. The two towns have been the gateway to the Lake District since trains began pulling into Windermere in 1847. You won't find much of the solitude that William Wordsworth was talking about when he wrote, "I wandered lonely as a cloud . . ." but it's easy to get out onto the water and escape the crowds, and these towns are appealing. Yet another town, Ambleside, is a pleasant village on the lakeshore about 4 miles north of Windermere.

VISITOR INFORMATION　**Windermere Tourist Information Centre** is on Victoria Street (www.golakes.co.uk; ✆ **01539/446499**). It's open November through March, Monday to Saturday 9:30am to 4:30pm and Sunday 10am to 4pm, and April through October daily 9:30am to 5pm.

Exploring the Area

Blackwell ★★ HISTORIC SITE　With the arrival of trains in 1847, Windermere became a popular getaway for wealthy residents of

The dining room at Blackwell.

Manchester and Liverpool. Among them was Sir Edward Holt, a Manchester brewer and one-time mayor, who in 1901 commissioned architect Mackay Hugh Baillie Scott (1865–1945) to build a holiday retreat. Baille Scott put his theories of light, texture, and space to work and created this magnificent house set in terraced gardens as a showpiece for Arts and Crafts, the late 19th-century artistic movement that promoted traditional crafts. The mosaic floors, carved wood panels, leaf-shaped door handles, and other hand-crafted decorative details are a delightful manifesto against mass production; Sir Edward's initials are even hand-carved into the downspouts. Visitors are encouraged to linger and enjoy the bright, airy rooms as Sir Edward and his family did, lounging on window seats and snuggling up in the inglenooks surrounding the tiled fireplaces. It's hard to imagine a better way to spend a rainy day than dividing your time between the excellent cafe and the paneled, grand-yet-intimate Great Hall, once described as "a whole village of rooms in one."

Just off the A5074, 2 miles south of Bowness. www.blackwell.org.uk. ℂ **01539/446139.** £8 adults, free for children under 16 and students. Daily 10:30am–5pm (4pm Nov–Feb).

Lakeland Motor Museum ★ MUSEUM Though these serene landscapes seem ill-matched with speed racing, father-and-son team Sir Malcolm and Donald Campbell each set water speed records on the lakes. They also set land records, and replicas of their boats and cars pay tribute to these achievements that kept the Campbells in the public eye from the 1920s until Donald's 1967 death in the crash of his speedboat on Coniston Water. The museum's quiet surroundings near the lake are an appropriate setting for old-fashioned gas pumps, vintage MGs and Bentleys, and vintage photos of motoring the lakes in the early 1900s.

Old Blue Mill, Backbarrow. www.lakelandmotormusuem.co.uk. ✆ **01539/530400.** £8 adults, £5 children 5–15, £23 families. Daily 9:30am–5:30pm.

World of Beatrix Potter ★ ENTERTAINMENT COMPLEX *Peter Rabbit* creator Beatrix Potter was a longtime Lake District resident, and judging by the lines outside this kid-oriented tourist trap, it appears that her popularity eclipses that of William Wordsworth and his fellow Lake poets. Little ones love to slip through the garden gate, wander through the vegetable patches inspired by Potter's tales, and have a nibble in the Beatrix Potter Tea Room. Mr. Jeremy Fisher, Mrs. Tiggy-winkle, and other characters who make appearances as animated-puppets and romp in sophisticated 3-D tableaux are admittedly pretty cute, and some well-narrated film footage of the landscapes that inspired the tales admirably honor Potter's conservation efforts.

The Old Laundry, Bowness-on-Windermere. www.hop-skip-jump.com. ✆ **01539/488444.** £7 adults, £4 children 4–16, £19 families. Easter–Oct daily 10am–5:30pm (to 4:30pm rest of year).

Outdoor Activities

You can rent canoes, kayaks, paddle boards, and bikes from **Windermere Canoe Kayak,** on the Bowness waterfront on Ferry Nab Road (www.windermerecanoekayak.com; ✆ **01539/444451**) and from the **Lake District National Park Visitor Centre** in Brockhole (www.lakedistrict.gov.uk; ✆ **01539/446601**). The **Low Wood Watersports & Activity Centre,** 3 miles north of Windermere on the A591

Kayaking on Lake Windermere.

(www.elh.co.uk; ✆ **01539/439441**) is the place for sailing, kayaking, waterskiing, and power-boating rentals and instruction.

GRASMERE ★★

282 miles NW of London; 9 miles NW of Windermere

This village on the gentle lake of the same name is so pretty that you can almost forgive Wordsworth for giving into a bit of hyperbole when he referred to his surroundings as "the loveliest spot that man hath ever known." The poet takes center stage here in the homes where he spent most of his adult life, and he remains in Grasmere for eternity beneath a modest tombstone in the village churchyard. Despite its Wordsworthian connection, Grasmere realizes that man cannot live by poetry alone and also makes wickedly good gingerbread, invented here in 1854.

VISITOR INFORMATION **Grasmere Tourist Information Centre,** Town Hall, Highgate (www.golakes.co.uk; ✆ **01539/797516**), is open March through October, Monday to Saturday 10am to 5pm, and November through February, Monday to Saturday 10am to 4pm.

Exploring the Area

A mandatory stop is the **Grasmere Gingerbread Shop** (www.grasmere gingerbread.co.uk; ✆ **01539/435428**) by the gate of St Oswald's Church. Local baker Sarah Nelson invented Grasmere Gingerbread in 1854, and the spicy-sweet cross between a cookie and a cake has been a hit with visitors ever since. You can also stock up on Kendal Mint Cakes, a peppermint flavored sweet that hill walkers have been toting along as a pick-me-up ever since it began appearing in Lake District shops in the 1880s. Sir Edmund Hillary and his team nibbled them when they successfully ascended Mt. Everest in 1953.

Dove Cottage, the Wordsworth Museum ★★ HISTORIC HOME From 1799 until 1808, poet William Wordsworth lived in this white-washed cottage with a tangle of pink roses clinging to the walls. He settled into the cramped rooms with his sister, Dorothy, and later the household expanded to include his wife, Mary, her sister, Sara, and their first three children. The Wordsworths also entertained a steady stream of visitors, including many of the literary giants of the day—Sir Walter

Approaching Grasmere lake and village.

Scott, Charles and Mary Lamb, and Wordsworth's close friend and fellow poet, Samuel Taylor Coleridge. Wordsworth wrote some of his finest poetry here, working in front of the fire and in the garden behind the cottage. Given how crowded the cramped rooms must have been, his poem, "I Wandered Lonely as a Cloud" might have been a work of wistful thinking. A guide leads a brief tour, then leaves visitors free to explore at their leisure. In the Wordsworth Museum behind the cottage is a treasure trove of Wordsworth memorabilia, including the largest collection of the poet's papers and letters in the world.

On the A591, south of the village of Grasmere. www.wordsworth.org.uk. ℂ **01539/ 435544.** Dove Cottage and museum £8 adults, £5 children 5–16, £17 families. Daily 9:30am–5:30pm (to 4:30pm Nov–Feb).

Rydal Mount ★★ HISTORIC HOME William Wordsworth was enjoying considerable success by 1813, when he moved his family into this large house on a hillside overlooking Lake Grasmere and Rydal Water. He lived here until his death in 1850, and his descendants still live in the house, preserving the flagstone-floored dining room, large drawing room and library, several bedrooms, and the attic study just as they were in the poet's day. Wordsworth designed much of the four-acre garden, and in all but the coldest weather he worked in the rustic garden house. When his beloved daughter Dora died of tuberculosis in 1847, he planted an adjoining hillside with daffodils, now known as Dora's Field.

Off the A591, 1½ miles north of Ambleside. www.rydalmount.co.uk. ℂ **01539/ 433002.** House and gardens £7 adults, £6 seniors and students, £3 children 5–15, £18 families. Mar–Oct daily 9:30am–5pm; Nov–Dec and Feb Wed–Sun 11am–4pm.

Shrewd Dealings in the Grass

Dora's Field next to Wordsworth's home Rydal Mount, awash in spring color might evoke the poet's famous poem "Daffodils," "When all at once I saw a crowd, / A host of daffodils. / Beside the lake, beneath the trees, / Fluttering and dancing in the breeze." Or maybe you'll remember that often-quoted line from "Imitations of Immortality," "Though nothing can buy back the hour / Of splendor in the grass, of glory in the flower." The scene is a testament to the fact that Wordsworth did more than write beautiful poetry. He was a crafty businessman as well, and he purchased the field to out-maneuver his landlady, from whom he rented Rydal Mount. In 1825 Lady Anne Fleming announced she was going to sell the house to relatives, so Wordsworth bought this adjoining plot and made it known he was going to build on it, blocking the view from Rydal Mount. The ploy worked, and safely settled in Rydal Mount, the poet gave the land to his daughter Dora.

Wordsworth Graves at St Oswald's Church ★ CHURCH William Wordsworth died in his bed at Rydal in 1850, just a couple of weeks past his 80th birthday, of a cold that turned into pleurisy. His simple grave in the yard of the 13th-century church that he had known since boyhood is especially touching. His wife, Mary and daughter, Dora, are buried nearby, as are other family members and Hartley Coleridge, the son of Wordsworth's friend and fellow poet Samuel Taylor Coleridge. Eight yew trees that Wordsworth planted shade the graves. His tombstone, naturally, is inscribed with a line from his poem Imitations of Immortality, "There was a time when meadow, grove, and stream, / The earth and every common sight, / To me did seem appareled in celestial light, / The glory and the freshness of a dream."
Church Stile, Grasmere. Free. Daily 9am–5pm.

CONISTON ★

263 miles NW of London; 12 miles W of Windermere

This little village was at one time a copper-mining center, but these days scenery steals the show. The Old Man of Coniston rises to a height of 2,600 feet behind the village, while long, tranquil Coniston Water stretches 5 miles south. Hiking the 7 miles to the top of the Old Man and back or ascending other nearby heights is one reason to come to Coniston, and another is to step aboard the vintage steam yacht *Gondola* to cross the lake and pay tribute to one of the region's greatest admirers at Brantwood, home of the 19th-century man of letters John Ruskin.

VISITOR INFORMATION **Coniston Tourist Information Centre,** Ruskin Avenue (www.conistontic.org; ✆ **01539/441533**), is open from April (or Easter, whichever is earlier) to September, daily 9:30am to 5pm, and from October to March (Easter), daily 10am to 4pm.

Exploring the Area

Brantwood ★★ HISTORIC SITE   John Ruskin (1819–1900) was one of the greatest figures of the Victorian age, an art critic, philosopher, social thinker, painter, author, and patron and friend of many of the other great men and women of his day. This complex man felt an affinity for the Lake District since his childhood visits and he retired to this large house on Coniston Water in 1872, and remained until his death. Among the many renovations he undertook was the waterfall and stream in the gardens; he also enlarged the harbor, where it's still possible to arrive by boat. Rooms are filled with paintings by the Pre-Raphaelites and other artists Ruskin admired, as well as his own watercolors. Ruskin is buried in the churchyard of St Andrew's Church in Coniston.

East shore of Coniston Water. www.brantwood.org.uk. ✆ **01539/441369.** £8 adults, children 16 and under free. Mid-Mar to Nov daily 10:30am–5:30pm; Dec to mid-Mar Wed–Sun 10:30am–4pm.

Gondola ★★★ HISTORICAL SITE/CRUISE   This elegant steam yacht began plying the waters of Coniston Water in 1859, showing off the beauty of the lakes to travelers arriving on the new railway line. The *Gondola* did service until 1936 and re-emerged in 1980, with upholstered salons and decks polished to a high gloss. The National Trust operates the vintage vessel for sailings across the lake to Brantwood, a fitting way to approach the grand home. The boat also cruises the entire lake, and you can disembark at Monk Coniston for a 5-mile round-trip walk to Tarn Hows, a pretty little lake tucked into mountain scenery (p. 421).

Coniston Pier/Boat House. www.nationaltrust.org.uk/main/w-gondola. ✆ **015394/ 32733.** Cruises run £11–£21 for adults, £6–£10 children 5–16, £28–£31 families. Apr–Oct 4 daily sailings: Mon–Fri 11am, noon, 1, and 2:30pm; Sat–Sun 11am, 1, 2:30, and 3:30pm. Times may vary according to weather conditions.

Ruskin Museum ★ MUSEUM   John Ruskin's secretary and friend W. G. Collingwood established this museum in 1901 and the eclectic collections, displayed almost randomly, do justice to the far-reaching interests of the honoree. Displayed among Ruskin's correspondence and sketchbooks are tools used in the region's copper mining industry, pre-historic artifacts, and a dry stone wall constructed from centuries-old techniques. Several cases are filled with locally made linen and lace, a cottage industry that Ruskin instigated, along with wood carving. Book jackets and manuscripts pay tribute to a no-less popular Lake District literary figure, Arthur Ransom (1884–1967), whose children's stories set in the Lakes were at one time a staple of every British childhood. Another section honors local racing champion Donald Campbell, who died in a speedboat accident on Coniston Water in 1967; his crash helmet and overalls are on display, along with a tail fin of his Bluebird K7 craft that fatally propelled him across the lake at 250 mph.

Off Yewdale Rd., Coniston. www.ruskinmuseum.com. ☏ **015394/41164.** £6 adults, £3 children 6–16, £16 families. Early Mar to mid-Nov daily 10am–5:30pm; mid-Nov to early Mar Wed–Sun 10:30am–3:30pm.

Outdoor Activities

Coniston Boating Centre on Lake Road (www.lakedistrict.gov.uk; ☏ **01539/441366**) rents canoes, kayaks, and windsurfing gear and offers instruction as well.

HAWKSHEAD ★

288 miles NW of London; 9 miles W of Windermere

The best approach to this little village is by the scenic, 10-minute crossing on the car ferry between Bowness and Ferry House. The poet William Wordsworth was a regular rider back in his late-18th-century school days when he attended the grammar school in Hawkshead. Once you reach the village the spotlight is on Beatrix Potter, whose lush illustrations hang in her husband's law offices and whose farm, Hill Top, is in the surrounding countryside. Though the pleasant little lanes and stone cottages are submerged in touristic cuteness, it's still easy to see how this lovely setting amid fields, hills, and woodlands inspired Potter to spend much of her adult life crusading to preserve its natural beauty.

VISITOR INFORMATION **Hawkshead Tourist Information Centre,** Main Street (www.hawksheadtouristinfo.org.uk; ☏ **01539/436946**), is open from April (or Easter, whichever is earlier) to September, daily 9:30am to 5pm, and from October to March (Easter), daily 10am to 4pm.

Beatrix Potter Gallery ★ GALLERY In 1913, Beatrix Potter married local solicitor William Heelis, whose 17th-century-era law offices now house an extensive collection of Potter's original illustrations, watercolors, and sketches for the ever popular *Tales of Peter Rabbit* series. Potter's distinctive work, especially the watercolors, not only shows off her talent but also her beautiful imagination and love of animals and the countryside. Along with letters and diary entries, they also shed light on the details of Potter's privileged and rather quirky life, including her childhood menageries and her adult travels with a pet hedgehog "in a little basket and bunnies in a wooden box."

Main Street. www.nationaltrust.org.uk/main/w-beatrixpottergallery. ☏ **01539/ 436355.** £5 adults, £3 children 5–17, £14 families. Discount for Hill Top Farm with ticket. Mid-Feb to Oct Sat–Thurs 11am–5pm (closes at 3:30pm mid-Feb to mid Mar). Hours can vary; check website.

Hill Top Farm ★★ HISTORIC HOME Beatrix Potter bought Hill-top Farm, 2 miles outside Hawkshead, with the proceeds from the *Tale of Peter Rabbit* in 1905. She lived here until she moved to the larger, more comfortable Castle Farm after her marriage in 1913, though she

Hawkshead village, former home of Beatrix Potter.

kept a studio and workshop at Hill Top throughout her life. It's easy to see how the cottage, with its herb and vegetable gardens and tangle of wildflowers out front inspired her ever-popular stories of frolicsome bunnies, mice, and squirrels. What also comes to the fore amid her paintings and personal items is her work as a conservationist. Potter and her husband, William Heelis, purchased numerous farms throughout the Lake District and became experts on breeding Herdwick sheep, indigenous to the region. They preserved vast tracts of land that might have otherwise fallen prey to developers. Upon Potter's death in 1943 she left more than 4,000 acres to the National Trust, helping ensure the establishment of the Lake District National Park.

Near Sawrey, Hawkshead. www.nationaltrust.org.uk/main/w-hilltop. ℂ **01539/ 436269.** £10 adults, £5 children 5–16, £24 families. Discount at Beatrix Potter Gallery with Hill Top ticket. Mid-Feb to Oct Sat–Thurs 10:30am–4:30pm (closes at 3:30pm mid-Feb to mid-Mar). Shuttle bus from Hawkshead or Ferry House.

Hawkshead Grammar School ★   Even when William Wordsworth attended classes here from 1779 to 1787, this school was a well-known Lake District landmark, founded in 1585 and one of the best academic institutions in the north of England. Wordsworth and many other students boarded with local families to study at the school, where instruction was largely in Greek and Latin and stressed ancient history, as well as mathematics and the sciences. Guides colorfully evoke the days when classes ran from 6am to 5pm, plus compulsory church attendance, and boys were allowed to smoke and drink beer. They show off the initials "W.W." carved into one of the old desks, explaining that pupils were encouraged to leave their mark in this way.

Hawkshead. www.hawksheadgrammar.org.uk. £3. Apr–Oct Mon–Sat 10:30am–1pm and 1:30–5pm.

KESWICK ★★

294 miles NW of London; 22 miles NW of Windermere

The northernmost town in the Lake District has a sturdy, workaday look, as befits a long legacy of mining and trading—the market square has been a lively center of commerce for 700 years. As lively and pleasant as Keswick is, most folks want to get out of town, into the spectacular Borrowdale and Buttermere mountain valleys or onto the open waters of the Derwentwater, one of the loveliest lakes in the region.

VISITOR INFORMATION **Keswick Tourist Information Centre,** at Moot Hall, Market Square (www.keswick.org; ✆ **01768/772645**) is open late March to late November, daily 9:30am to 5:30pm, and late November to late March, daily 9:30am to 4:30pm. The center arranges bookings of outdoor activities for all levels of experience and ability.

Exploring the Area

Castlerigg Stone Circle ★★★   These large stones were laid out 5,000 years ago in a valley beneath some of the highest peaks in the Lake District. Their purpose and the significance of their placement is a matter of ongoing debate, though the stones have been associated with the autumnal equinox and other solar and lunar events. It's also believed that the stones may have been a meeting place where residents engaged in religious ceremonies before a ritual exchange of stone axes. Even the exact number of stones in the circle is not certain, as smaller "packing" stones, used to support the larger stones, have risen to the surface. The official count remains at 38, with a suggestion that there could be 40.

1½ miles east of Keswick. www.english-heritage.org.uk/visit/places/castlerigg-stone-circle. Free. Daylight hours.

Castlerigg Stone Circle, near Keswick.

Cumberland Pencil Museum ★   The Lake District is not only blessed with some of Britain's most beautiful scenery but can also claim the world's largest pencil, 26 feet long and weighing a whopping 984 pounds. While the pencil is, literally, pointless, it's presence here is not. Keswick was fated to leave its mark on pencil-making when some 16th-century shepherds found graphite in the surrounding hills and discovered it was great for scratching identification marks on sheep. Displays tell the story of the local industry, with some intriguing insights into the manufacture of secret spy pencils and other great moments that continue to make Derwent, the company behind the museum, one of the world's leading pencil manufacturers. The shop is a dream come true for artists and anyone who wants to stock up on a fine array of colored pencils.

Southey Works. www.pencilmuseum.co.uk. £5 adults, £4 children 16 and under, £13 families. Late Apr to mid-July and Sept–Oct daily 9:30am–5pm, mid-July to Aug daily 9:30am–6pm, Nov–Dec daily 11am–4pm.

Honister Slate Mine ★★ HISTORIC SITE   Slate was big business when this mine opened in the 18th century, and as you don a hard hat and descend a low, sloping tunnel, guards will explain that slate from mines like this one was used mostly for roofing, flooring, and gravestones. It doesn't take long to understand that mining was hard and dangerous work, but you can have a bit for fun on the adjacent Via Ferrata, or Iron Way. The series of cables, rungs, and ladders outside the mine follows an old miner's path up a steep mountainside; the views are stupendous and a safety cable assures a safe ascent and descent.

Honister Pass, Borrowdale. www.honister-slate-mine.co.uk. ✆ **01768/777230.** Mine tours from £13 adults, from £8 children 15 and under; Via Ferrata Classic from £35 adults, from £25 children 10–15; Via Ferrata and zipline from £40 adults, from £30 children 10–15. Daily 9am–5pm, dependent on weather conditions.

The Lake Poets

Around the turn of the 19th century the Lake District gave rise to the so-called Lake Poets, a group of creative souls whose unifying bond was an appreciation for pastoral landscapes and an emotional rather than purely rational reaction to the world around them. Leader of the pack was William Wordsworth, who along with his sister Dorothy, spent his life in the Lake District. Other members were Charles Lamb and Thomas De Quincey, and aside from Wordsworth the most enduringly popular poet of the group was Samuel Taylor Coleridge (1772–1834), to whom the Lakes seemed to bring little solace. Probably suffering from bipolar disorder, he suffered long periods of depression and manic episodes, and probably wrote some of his best-known poetry, such as "Kubla Kahn" and "The Rime of the Ancient Mariner," while under the influence of the opiates he took for relief. Even a climb up 3,210-foot Scafell Pike, the tallest mountain in Britain, didn't calm the savage beast in his soul; he wrote "Dejection: An Ode" around the same time.

Entertainment & Nightlife

Keswick's 400-seat **Theatre by the Lake** (www.theatrebythelake.co.uk; ✆ **01768/774411**) produces a year-round program of drama productions. It is best to buy tickets in advance, particularly in the summer.

Where to Stay in the Lake District

EXPENSIVE

Inn on the Lake ★★   It's easy to feel like a Victorian gent or lady while sitting on the lawn of this grand old hostelry overlooking Ullswater, 13 miles north of Windermere. Its perch in Glenridding at the southern edge of the lake has to be one of the best locations in all the Lake District, and the adjacent landing dock is well poised for excursions. The big downstairs lounges don't attempt to be anything other than comfortably traditional, nor do the high-ceilinged guest rooms, where lake views fill the big windows.

Glenridding. www.lakedistricthotels.net/innonthelake. ✆ **017684/82444.** 47 units. Doubles from £200, includes breakfast. **Amenities:** Restaurant; bar; free Wi-Fi.

Linthwaite House Hotel ★★★   A hilltop Edwardian residence from around 1900 still has the intimate feel of a private home, with a well-executed dash of designer flair to keep the hominess from feeling stodgy. Fires crackle in the sitting rooms and a lovely conservatory stocked looks across 14 acres of sloping lawns and gardens to the lake. Large guest rooms are comfortably eclectic, with contemporary touches that don't detract from a casual-yet-elegant, lived-in feel that encourages you to sit back in one of the comfy armchairs and take in the views—or just to drift off to sleep amid countryside quiet in the supremely comfortable beds. The excellent restaurant serves modern British cuisine.

Crook Rd., Bowness-on-Windermere. www.linthwaite.com. ✆ **01539/488600.** 27 units. Doubles £200–£285, includes breakfast. **Amenities:** Restaurant; bar; room service; free Wi-Fi.

MODERATE

Miller Howe ★★   It's tempting to settle in and not venture out again from this Edwardian-era lakeside residence, where the surroundings manage to be both sumptuous and relaxed enough that you won't feel like a rube hanging out in hiking gear. Sink into a sofa in one of the three beautifully decorated, light-filled salons or spend hours looking across Lake Windermere to the Langdale Pikes. Guest rooms tastefully combine antiques, contemporary pieces, and Arts and Crafts flourishes and have balconies, many facing the lake; some suites are rather romantically set in a gardener's cottage on the five acres of well-tended lakeside grounds. If you time it right, you can settle into dinner just as the sun is setting across the shimmering waters.

Rayrigg Rd., Windermere. millerhowe.com. ✆ **01539/42536.** 15 units. Doubles from £ 105, includes breakfast. **Amenities:** Restaurant; bar; free Wi-Fi.

Wordsworth Hotel & Spa ★★   Two acres of lawns and gardens provide a welcome retreat in busy Grasmere, and this handsome old stone country house was once the hunting lodge of the Earls Cadogan, the wealthy owners of much of what is now London's Kensington neighborhood. The premises have been embellished with a spa and an indoor swimming pool, while guest quarters vary considerably in size and décor and range from viewless courtyard-facing rooms to character-filled timbered attics with views of the surrounding mountains. Tea in the conservatory is popular with visitors on the Wordsworth trail.

Stock Lane, Grasmere. www.thewordsworthhotel.co.uk. ℂ **01539/435592.** 36 units. Doubles £118–£240, includes breakfast. **Amenities:** Restaurant; bar; exercise room; Jacuzzi; heated indoor pool; room service; sauna; free Wi-Fi.

INEXPENSIVE

Ivy Guest House ★★   This stately Georgian house in the center of Hawkshead stands out grandly amid the surrounding cottages, but the lounges and guest rooms are geared to homey comfort. A wood fire burns in the grate, and the nice sized, high-ceilinged bedrooms upstairs are all about solid comfort, with four-poster beds in most; two can accommodate families, and dogs are welcome for a small fee. The in-town location makes this a good choice for travelers without cars, since amenities are near at hand, bus service connects with other Lake District towns, and some good countryside walks begin just outside the front door.

Hawkshead. www.ivyguesthousehawkshead.co.uk. ℂ **01539/36204.** 11 units. Doubles £80, includes breakfast. **Amenities:** Free Wi-Fi.

Littletown Farm Guest House ★   It's hard to stay put in this handsome old farmhouse a few miles outside Keswick, where the surrounding fells lure you out for long walks. When you return, drinks are served in homey lounges and an enclosed garden, while the bedrooms upstairs are nicely done with wood floors, brass beds, and a welcome minimum of cuteness. Hats off to the gracious owners for the latter, as it might have been tempting to capitalize on the fact that Beatrix Potter used the farm as the setting for the *Tale of Mrs. Tiggy-Winkle.*

Littletown, Newlands, Keswick. www.littletownfarm.co.uk. ℂ **017687/78353.** 8 units. Doubles from £82, includes breakfast. **Amenities:** Bar; free Wi-Fi.

Rooms at the Apple Pie ★★   The rooms above the pub concept takes on a twist in these pleasant accommodations in an old stone house adjoining the Apple Pie, one of the best bakeries for miles around. Guest quarters are pleasantly no-frills, with furnishings picked out of an Ikea catalogue and some nice amenities that include a communal fridge and discounts on the pool and spa at a swanky hotel nearby. Top floor rooms come with the add-on coziness of sloping ceilings. Breakfast is not included, but it's served downstairs all day at a 10% discount.

Ambleside. www.roomsattheapplepie.co.uk. ℂ **01539/433679.** 8 units. Doubles £52–£75. **Amenities:** Free Wi-Fi.

The Jumble Room, Grasmere.

Where to Eat

EXPENSIVE

Holbeck Ghyll ★★ MODERN BRITISH   The former hunting lodge of the Earl of Lonsdale is now the setting for the finest dining in the Lake District, in a richly paneled room overlooking Lake Windermere. Local lamb and game are paired with farm-grown produce and an excellent selection of wines. Lunch and dinner are offered on a two-course menu, and dinner on three set menus. For the ultimate experience dinner guests can book a luxurious rooms upstairs, with attractive dinner with bed and breakfast rates.

Holbeck Lane, Windermere. www.holbeckghyll.com. ☎ **01539/432475.** Lunch from £30, dinner £68–£133. Noon–1:30pm and 7–9pm.

The Jumble Room ★★★ ECLECTIC   The Lake District is still a place for poetic souls, judging by the quirky décor (lots of bright colors, 1950s kitsch, and mismatched furnishings) and similarly eclectic cooking that could best be described as global. Stilton or beef crostini, Hungarian flatbread, South African spice lamb, or just plain fish and chips are among the mishmash of temptations. This is one of the most pleasant evenings spots in Grasmere, and popular for weekend lunches.

Langdale Rd., Grasmere. www.thejumbleroom.co.uk. ☎ **01539/435188.** Mains £17–£22. Fri–Sun noon–3pm; Mon and Wed–Sun 5:30–9:30pm.

MODERATE

The Drunken Duck Inn ★★★ MODERN BRITISH   A popular fixture in the beautiful landscape between Coniston and Hawkshead is this beamed, antiques-filled pub. You can stop by and taste the house-brewed

Barngates Ales in front of the fire, but the main reason to come is to enjoy creative takes on old British classics like pork belly or beef rump with turnips. Grounds surround a small lake, and the 16 rooms above the inn set a new standard for how luxurious pub accommodations can be. You cannot reserve at lunch, when you'll have to arrive early or late to avoid the lines; and dinners book up weeks in advance in high season.
2½ miles north of Hawkshead, off the B5286, Barngates. © **01539/436347.** www.drunkenduckinn.co.uk. Mains £11–£26. Daily noon–4pm and 6:30–9:30pm.

Lucy's on a Plate ★ MODERN BRITISH   A pine-floored room and a sunny warm-weather garden are cheerful surroundings for some genuinely inventive cooking based on local produce. The ever-changing menus ranges through pastas and Moroccan tagines to chargrilled rib-eye and fresh mussels. The cakes are legendary, and served along with sandwiches and snacks in a fire-warmed cafe throughout the day.
Church St., Ambleside. www.lucysofambleside.co.uk. © **01539/432288.** Mains £14–£22. Daily 10am–9pm.

The Pheasant ★ BRITISH   A former coaching inn near the north-western tip of Bassenthwaite Lake oozes British coziness. It's the real thing, in business for 200-some years, with well-worn fireside armchairs and time-burnished paneling. Light fare is served in a cozy bar room, casual meals in a bright bistro, and more formal dinners and Sunday lunches in the natty Fell Restaurant, with fine linens and handsome old prints. Afternoon tea is laid out in the antiques-filled lounge. The menus are as traditional as the surroundings, with a slant toward grilled fish and roasted fowl, and service is old-school polished.
Bassenthwaite Lake, Cockermouth. www.the-pheasant.co.uk. © **01768/776234.** Mains £12–£22. Bistro daily noon–4:30 and 6–9pm; restaurant Tues–Sat 7–9pm, Sun noon–2pm.

INEXPENSIVE

Hole in t' Wall ★★ PUB   The oldest pub in Bowness, dating back to 1612, is officially named New Hall, but everyone knows it by the name that refers to the opening made to connect the original ale house with an adjacent blacksmith's shop. Charles Dickens is among the long list of appreciative customers, who soak in the stone walls and darkened beams while enjoying a pint and meal next to the open fires. The food matches the surroundings, with hearty meals of slow-cooked lamb shank or fish pie on offer, alongside sandwiches and other lighter pub fare.
Lowside, Bowness-on-Windermere. © **01539/443488.** Mains £8–£14. Mon–Sat 11am–11pm, Sun noon–10:30pm.

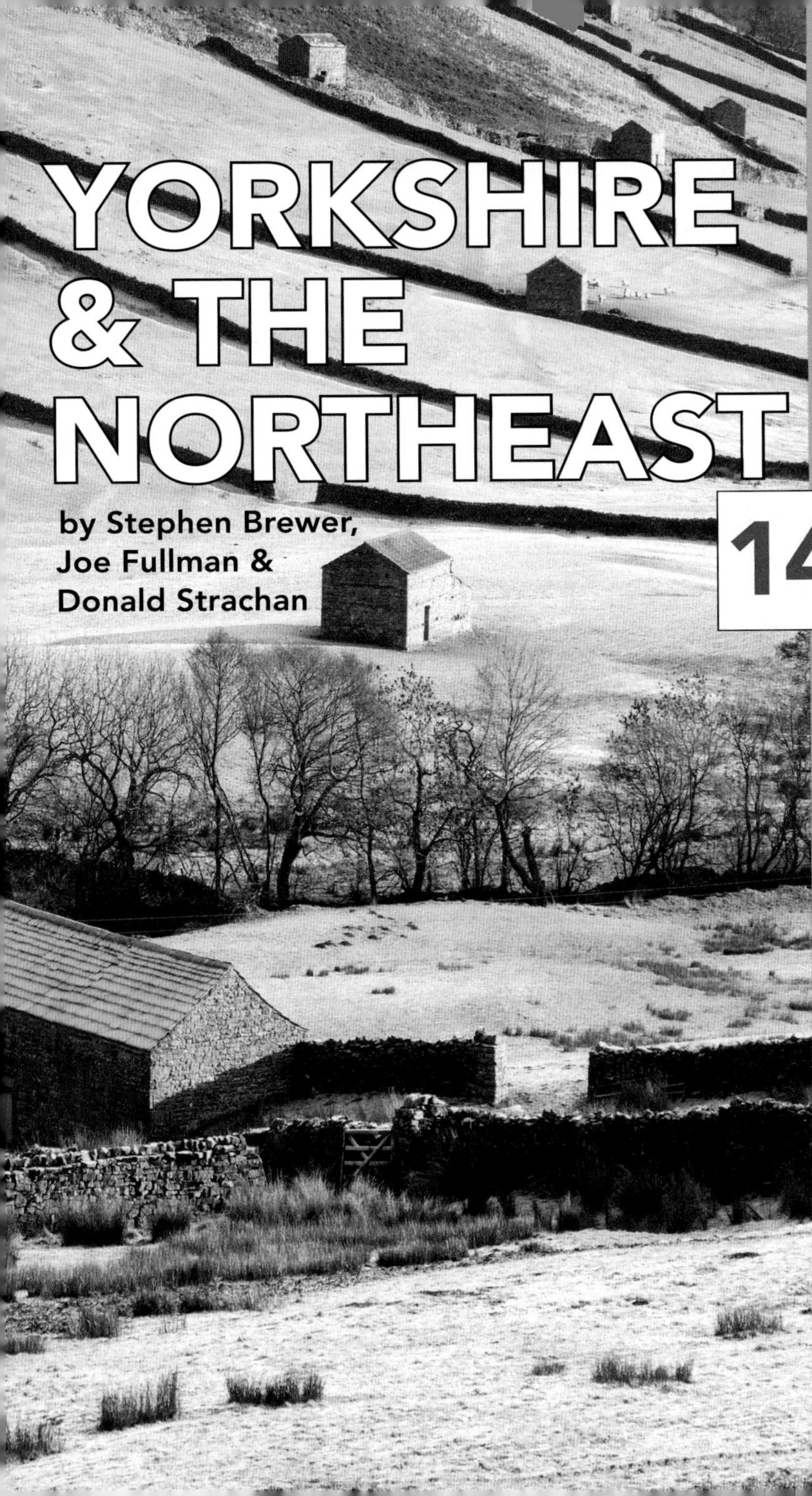

YORKSHIRE & THE NORTHEAST

by Stephen Brewer,
Joe Fullman &
Donald Strachan

14

Roman ruins, lonely abbeys, castles, stately homes, museums, and literary shrines are just some of the attractions on offer in Yorkshire and the more northern regions of County Durham and Northumberland. Together with historic York, they are also jumping-off points for exploring the wild and remote beauty that characterizes both the interior of England's northeast and its incredible shoreline—which includes the old port of Whitby, Gothic inspiration for the original "Dracula" tale.

A thoroughly modern British city reawakening from a post-industrial slumber, **Newcastle** is as hip and happening a destination as you'll find in the U.K. It has earned a reputation for its shopping and nightlife, but there's also an array of contemporary museum spaces including **BALTIC,** over the River Tyne in Gateshead. Travel back in time west of the city with a visit to the fortified remains of **Hadrian's Wall,** which once protected Roman Britain from the wild tribes to the north.

There's almost limitless countryside to explore, and the **Yorkshire Dales** is justly revered by walkers. Its scenery was praised by Wordsworth and painted by Turner, and inspired Charles Kingsley's "The Water Babies."

The double whammy of Northumberland's **Alnwick Castle**—which doubled as "Hogwarts" in two Harry Potter movies—and the **Alnwick Garden,** one of the world's most exciting contemporary gardens, makes the town of Alnwick much more than just a base for exploring the Northumberland coast. It's an added bonus that **Lindisfarne Priory** and spectacularly sited **Bamburgh Castle** are just a short drive away. It's also a short hop from here onward to Edinburgh and the rest of Scotland.

YORK ★★★

Still encircled by its 13th- and 14th-century walls—which are around 2½ miles long with four gates—York is a picturesque historical tapestry. There was a Roman York (Hadrian came this way), then a Saxon York, a Danish York, a Norman York (William the Conqueror slept here), a medieval York, a Georgian York, and a Victorian York, center of a flourishing rail empire. Today, you can still walk the footpath of the medieval walls and explore much of the 18th-century city.

PREVIOUS PAGE: **Frost on fields in Upper Swaledale, Yorkshire Dales National Park.**

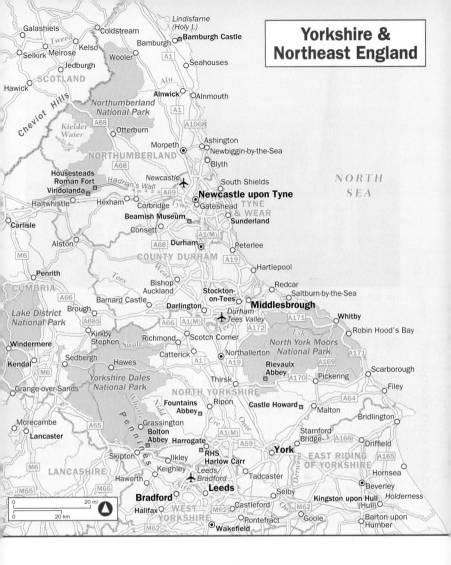

Yorkshire & Northeast England

Essentials

GETTING THERE   Frequent **trains** from London's King's Cross to York take just under 2 hours. There are also direct trains to York from Manchester, Birmingham, and Edinburgh, as well as from **Manchester International Airport** (p. 384).

    Daily London to York **National Express buses** (www.national express.com; ✆ **0871/781-8181**) take 5 hours and up; most require a change at Leeds.

The York skyline, with 13th-century York Minster in the background.

York is 3½ hours north of London by **road,** not far off the main M1. From Manchester to York it's about 1½ hours, from Birmingham 2 hours, and from Edinburgh 4 hours.

VISITOR INFORMATION   The **York Visitor Information Centre,** 1 Museum Street (www.visityork.org; ℭ **01904/550099**), is open Monday to Saturday from 9am to 5pm (until 5:30pm in July and Aug), and on Sundays from 10am–4pm.

TOURS & SPECIAL EVENTS   The **Association of Voluntary Guides** (ℭ **01904/550098;** visitor center, see above) runs free tours from Exchange Square (10:15am daily, plus 2:15pm and 6:45pm in summer). The **Ebor Festival,** in August, is highlight of the flat-racing season at the prestigious **York Racecourse** (www.yorkracecourse.co.uk). In February, York also sees a 9-day **Viking Festival,** organized by Jorvik (see below).

Exploring York

Mighty **York Minster** makes the city an ecclesiastical powerhouse equaled only by Canterbury (p. 180). Steps away from it, **Treasurer's House ★**, Minster Yard (www.nationaltrust.org.uk/treasurers-house-york; ℭ **01904/ 624247**) conceals Roman remains in its cellar—those of a road. You can also tour its 13 period rooms full of antiques, ceramics, textiles, and paintings, the Edwardian servants' attics, and a sunken garden. Interactive exhibitions make it child-friendly. In February and November (closed most of Dec and Jan), visits are by guided tour only (Sat–Thurs 11am– 3pm); March to October you can explore at your own pace (Sat–Thurs 11am–4:30pm). Adults pay £8, children £4.

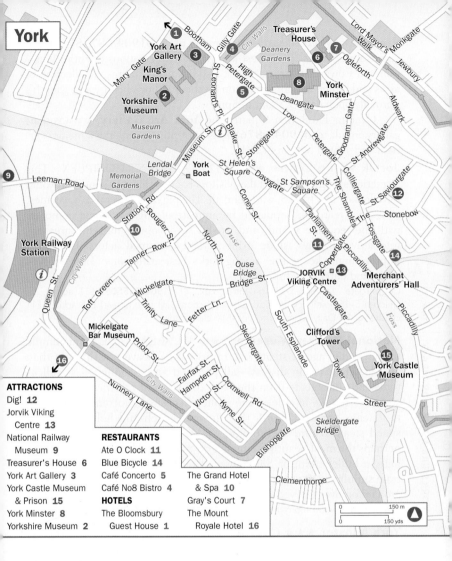

York

1

York Art Gallery 3

King's Manor

Yorkshire Museum 2

Museum Gardens

Mary Gate

St Leonard's Pl.

Museum St.

Bootham

Gilly Gate

Gilly Gate

High Petergate

Blake St.

Stonegate

York Art Gallery

4 City Walls

Treasurer's House

Deanery Gardens

6

7

Lord Mayor's Walk

Monkgate

Ogleforth

Jewbury

5

8 York Minster

Deangate

Low Petergate

Goodram Gate

Aldwark

St Andrewgate

St Saviourgate

12

Stonebow

Lendal Bridge

York Boat

St Helen's Square

St Sampson's Square

Davygate

Coney St.

Parliament St.

The Shambles

The Fossgate

Collergate

Piccadilly

14

Merchant Adventurers' Hall

Leeman Road

9

Memorial Gardens

Ouse

11

Coppergate

13

JORVIK Viking Centre

York Railway Station

Station Rd.

Rougier St.

Tanner Row

North St.

Ouse Bridge

Bridge St.

10

Mickelgate

Toft Green

Trinity Lane

Fetter Ln.

Skeldergate

South Esplanade

Castlegate

Clifford's Tower

Tower

15

York Castle Museum

Fossa

Piccadilly

Queen St.

City Walls

Mickelgate Bar Museum

Priory St.

Fairfax St.

Hampden St.

Victor St.

Cromwell Rd.

Kyme St.

Bishopgate

Skeldergate Bridge

Street

16

City Walls

Nunnery Lane

Clementhorpe

0   150 m
0   150 yds

ATTRACTIONS

Dig! 12

Jorvik Viking
  Centre 13

National Railway
  Museum 9

Treasurer's House 6

York Art Gallery 3

York Castle Museum
  & Prison 15

York Minster 8

Yorkshire Museum 2

RESTAURANTS

Ate O Clock 11

Blue Bicycle 14

Café Concerto 5

Café No8 Bistro 4

HOTELS

The Bloomsbury
  Guest House 1

The Grand Hotel
  & Spa 10

Gray's Court 7

The Mount
  Royale Hotel 16

On Coppergate, the **Jorvik Viking Centre** (see below) offers up a reconstruction of the Viking city that once stood on the site; its nearby sister attraction, **Dig!** gives you the chance to plunder excavation pits for clues as to how people lived in Roman, Victorian, medieval, and Victorian times, accompanied by an archaeologist. There are further archeological treasures, plus rare animals, birds, and fossils, at the **Yorkshire Museum** ★ (www.yorkshiremuseum.org.uk; ✆ **01904/687687**) within the city's free botanical **Museum Gardens.** Museum opening times are generally 10am to 5pm daily; kids go free, adult tickets are £8, or £12 if you also visit the **York Castle Museum & Prison** ★,

Eye of York (www.yorkcastlemuseum.org.uk; ☏ **01904/687687**). At the site of York Castle, this is best known for its recreations of entire Victorian and Edwardian streets, but it also has period rooms, a collection of arms and armor, and an exhibition on the building's history as a gaol. It's normally open daily 9:30am to 5pm.

Over in Exhibition Square, the **York Art Gallery** (www.yorkart gallery.org.uk; ☏ **01904/687687**) is currently undergoing a major overhaul and should reopen in 2016.

Jorvik Viking Centre ★★ ENTERTAINMENT COMPLEX   This attraction's "time capsule" takes visitors back to this very spot as it would have looked in A.D. 975, warts and all: The pig sties, fish market, latrines, and other features, populated by animatronic figures, come complete with the requisite sounds and smells. An adjoining museum area has interactive displays, static exhibits, and costumed actors. Continual improvements keeps this among York's best attractions. Tickets allow unlimited entry for a full year.

Coppergate. www.jorvik-viking-centre.co.uk. ☏ **01904/615505.** £11 adults, £7 children 5–15; joint tickets with sister attraction Dig! (see above) £15 adults, £11 children 5–15. Daily 10am–5pm (Dec–Mar closes 4pm).

National Railway Museum ★★★ MUSEUM   This giant temple to the golden age of steam is a trainspotters' heaven, with more than 100 locomotives on display—all polished and gleaming—as well as thousands of objects from the past 200 years of rail travel. If time is short, try to take in at least the replica *Rocket* (the locomotive that set the steam age in motion), the *Mallard*, which still holds the world speed steam record at 126mph, the Art Deco *Duchess of Hamilton,* perhaps the most beautiful engine ever made, and bringing things up to date, a bullet train, or *Shinkansen,* from Japan. Elsewhere there are train simulators to enjoy, a miniature railway, and various special events are laid on over the year.

Leeman Rd. www.nrm.org.uk. ☏ **08448/153139.** Free. Daily 10am–6pm.

York Minster ★★★ CATHEDRAL   York's superb Gothic cathedral traces its origins from the early 7th century but the present building is from the 13th century, with, like Lincoln's cathedral, three 15th-century towers. The central tower is lantern shaped in the Perpendicular style; the fit can climb its stone spiral staircase for panoramic views, at an extra charge. Don't miss the medieval stained glass, or, in the Undercroft beneath the central tower, the foundations of the Roman buildings where Emperor Constantine lived while he began his rise to greatness.

Chapter House St. www.yorkminster.org. ☏ **0844/939-0011.** £10, adults, free for children 15 and under; combined ticket with tower £15 adults, £5 children 8–16, children under 8 not admitted to tower. Mon–Sat 9:30am–5:30pm, Sun noon–3:45pm; free 60–90 min. guided tours Mon–Sat 9am–3pm.

Where to Stay

The Bloomsbury Guest House ★　The main drawback to staying here is mainly the location on a busy road (the double glazing does block out most of the noise), around a 15-minute walk from the center. The upsides are the attractive 19th-century red-brick house prettily adorned with flower baskets, high-ceilinged, tastefully decorated rooms with large beds and well-equipped bathrooms, and the friendly owners.

127 Clifton. www.bloomsburyhotel.co.uk. ℂ **01904/380038.** 9 units. Doubles £75–£90, includes breakfast. **Amenities:** Free Wi-Fi.

The Grand Hotel & Spa ★★　In sight of the cathedral, this luxury hotel—York center's only five-star offering—occupies a grand building which was once the headquarters of the North Eastern Railway. The splendid Edwardian construction—all red brick and cream stonework—offers a supreme level of comfort. All the bedrooms have high ceilings, large beds, and marble bathrooms, and there's a whisky lounge, a good restaurant, and a spa.

Station Rise. www.thegrandyork.co.uk. ℂ **01904/380038.** 107 units. Doubles £130–£340. **Amenities:** Restaurant; bar; babysitting; gym; indoor swimming pool; room service; spa; free Wi-Fi.

Gray's Court ★★★　For a hotel that's pretty much right in the center of town by the Minster, this feels strangely secluded. Indeed, as one of the city's oldest buildings—built in the 11th century as a home for the Minster's treasurers—it almost seems to inhabit a different time zone to the rest of the city. The place is redolent of history (kings have stayed here over the centuries) with a Jacobean oak-paneled gallery, a Georgian

A room at Gray's Court hotel, York.

dining room, and antiques everywhere. The seven individually deco-rated, and extremely characterful bedrooms come with period furniture and plenty of old school charm. Food is served all day.

Chapter House St. www.grayscourtyork.com. ℂ **01904/612613.** 8 units. Doubles £170–£240, includes breakfast. **Amenities:** Restaurant; bar; free Wi-Fi.

Mount Royale ★★   Although just a few minutes south of the railway station, this hotel occupying twin, ivy-clad Victorian properties has something of a country-house vibe. The rooms vary in size, but are all very well turned out. The finest come with four-poster beds, antiques, and views overlooking the gardens. Even the most basic rooms are still of a good standard. The restaurant, **Oxo's ★**, turns out a superor British menu.

119 The Mount. www.mountroyale.co.uk. ℂ **01904/628856.** 30 units. Doubles £125–£200, includes breakfast. **Amenities:** Restaurant; bar; babysitting; gym; outdoor swimming pool; room service; spa; free Wi-Fi.

Where to Eat

Ate O Clock ★ MEDITERRANEAN   This quirky little place located down a narrow alleyway is adorned with sculptures of eagles and an assortment of clocks (all set to 8 o' clock, of course) and serves a "Medi-terranean menu with a twist of Scouse." For the uninitiated, this trans-lates into the likes of risotto of blue swimming crab, polenta-coated fishcakes, and pan-fried duck with walnut potato cake. The 3-course "B4Ate" set menu is good value at £20.

13a High Ousegate. www.ateoclock.co.uk. ℂ **01904/644080.** Mains £15–£18. Tues–Fri noon–3pm and 6–9:30pm, Sat noon–2:30pm and 5:30–9:30pm.

Blue Bicycle ★★ INTERNATIONAL   It may look refined now, but in the early 20th century, this building was a brothel—the madam would apparently leave a blue bicycle outside to let her clients know it was open for business. Although homage is paid to the venue's past in the form of pictures of scantily clad women on the menu, these days the only appe-tites being sated are for locally sourced, expertly prepared bistro food. There also have a few self-catering apartments available.

33 Fossgate. www.thebluebicycle.com. ℂ **10904/673990.** Mains £16–£24. Daily 6pm–9:30pm; Thurs–Sun also noon–2:30pm.

Café Concerto ★★ MODERN ENGLISH   Right by the Minster, this cozy little place has run with the "concerto" theme, so expect walls papered with scores, instruments used as decorations, and crockery adorned with musical notes. The food, which runs the gamut from hearty "Yorkshire breakfasts" to soup and baguettes and a dinner menu of Brit-ish classics (such as sausage, mash, and onion gravy), also hits the right notes. An apartment is available for short-term lets.

21 High Petergate. www.cafeconcerto.biz. ℂ **01904/610478.** Mains £13–£17. Daily 9am–9pm (closed Sun and Mon evenings in winter).

Café No8 Bistro ★ INTERNATIONAL/ENGLISH   This is a long-time favorite with the locals—so much so that it underwent a major expansion a couple of years ago. It always seems busy, a testament to the great location by the city walls, the convivial atmosphere, and a menu that champions local ingredients. It serves everything from breakfasts and sandwiches to a half-dozen main courses, such as deep fried hake and slow-booked beef terrine.

18 Gillygate. www.cafeno8.co.uk. ✆ **01904/653074.** Mains £13–£18; fixed-price 2-course dinner Fri–Sat £25. Mon–Fri noon–10pm, Sat–Sun 10am–10pm.

Shopping

Don't miss the cobbled **Shambles ★**; voted Britain's most picturesque street in the Google Street View awards, it's lined by wooden-framed buildings that lean so far across the narrow alley that some of their roofs almost touch. Once the city's meat-butchering center, it's now home to shops and cafes, many selling jewelry (a highlight of York shopping). York's antiques dealers tend to congregate on or around **Gillygate;** for independent one-off stores, try **Stonegate.**

York is also a great place to shop for food, with several delis and

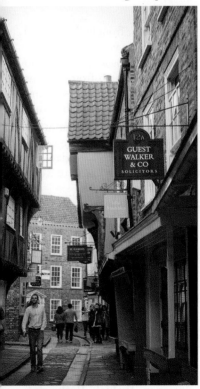

local food stores: Try **Demijohn,** 11 Museum Street (www.demijohn.co.uk; ✆ **01904/637-487**), for handmade British spirits, oils, and vinegars bottled to order; **Henshelwoods,** 10 Newgate (www.deliyork.co.uk; ✆ **01904/673877**), for award-winning cheeses and Italian specialties; **Hairy Fig,** 39 Fossgate (www.thehairyfig.co.uk; ✆ **01904/677074**) for "on tap" vinegars, oils, fig vodka, and more. York also has a daily open-air **market** with more than 100 stalls. For more foodie treats try the **Balloon Tree Farmshop and Café,** at Gate Helmsley between York and Bridlington (www.theballoontree.co.uk; ✆ **01759/373023**).

Entertainment & Nightlife

York is said to have a pub for every day of the year—more per square mile, some claim, than any city in the country—but it's lively rather

Shambles, York.

than rowdy, except around the Micklegate area (including Rougier Street). Stick to laid-back **Goodramgate** and the **Swinegate** area, where you'll find a good mix of traditional pubs and swanky bars. The **Coney Street** area is the most upmarket. The oldest pub in town, **Ye Olde Starre Inne,** Stonegate (☏ **01904/623063**), has a beer garden with Minster views.

HARROGATE & AROUND ★

About 22 miles west of York and 7½ miles north of Harewood House, the enchanting Victorian spa town of **Harrogate** is most famous as the home, since 1919, of the original **Bettys Café Tea Rooms.** Prior to that, in Georgian times, it attracted nobility and other wealthy visitors to its iron-, sulfur-, and salt-rich waters, which continue to be bottled and sold. Despite Dickens's description of it as "the queerest place with the strangest people in it leading the oddest lives," the town continues to be considered one of the U.K.'s most desirable places to live, with the added bonus for plant lovers of the **RHS Garden Harlow Carr** (see below) on its outskirts.

Essentials

GETTING THERE   Harrogate is just over a half-hour from both York and Leeds by direct **train.** National Express **buses** (www.nationalexpress.com; ☏ **0871/781-8181**) travel from Leeds to Harrogate in around 50 minutes. It'll take twice as long and cost twice as much from York, as services travel via Leeds. By **road,** York–Harrogate is 22 miles (40 min.) via the A59. For buses in and around the Dales, see **www.dalesbus.org**.

VISITOR INFORMATION   The **Harrogate Tourist Information Office,** Royal Baths, Crescent Road (www.visitharrogate.co.uk; ☏ **01423/537300**), is open April to October Monday to Saturday 9am to 5:30pm, Sunday 10am to 1pm; November to March hours are Monday to Saturday 9am to 5pm.

SPECIAL EVENTS   Harrogate's **Great Yorkshire Show** (www.great yorkshireshow.co.uk), in early July, features cattle parades, sheep-shearing, pole-climbing, and more.

Exploring Harrogate

You can learn all about the history of the spa town in the **Royal Pump Room ★** (www.harrogate.gov.uk; ☏ **01423/556188**), where you can still find Europe's strongest sulfur wells and taste their waters. Open Tuesday to Saturday 10am to 5pm, it costs £4 for adults, £2 for children. You might visit the free **Mercer Art Gallery ★** (same website and phone as the Pump Room), about 100 yards away, with mainly 19th- and 20th-century works; it's open Tuesday to Saturday 10am to 5pm, Sunday 2 to 5pm. The town's highlight is its Victorian **Turkish Baths ★★**

Harrogate's Turkish Baths.

Fountains Abbey & Studley Royal Park, Harrogate.

(www.turkishbathsharrogate.co.uk; ☏ **01423/556746**), with Moorish arches and screens, painted ceilings, and terrazzo floors. Splurge on a treatment or just relax in the steam room. There are women's, men's, and mixed-session times (entry £18–£29).

Some 12 miles north of Harrogate is the cathedral city of Ripon, site of Britain's largest monastic ruin, **Fountains Abbey** within Studley Royal Park (see below). **Ripon Cathedral ★** (www.riponcathedral.info; ☏ **01765/603462**) has one of the country's oldest Saxon crypts, survivor of a church founded on the site by St Wilfrid in the 7th century, plus medieval wood-carvings thought to have inspired "Alice in Wonderland" author Lewis Carroll. It's free, and open daily 8:30am to 6pm.

Fountains Abbey & Studley Royal Park ★★★ HISTORIC SITE Founded on the banks of the Silver Skell by Cistercian monks in 1132, the dramatic ruins of Fountains Abbey now form the breathtaking focal point of the Georgian water gardens of Studeley Royal, created around the ruins in the 18th century and dotted with neoclassical statuary and follies. Together they're a UNESCO World Heritage site. The site also comprises a Cistercian corn mill—the last to stand in the U.K.—a medieval deer park populated by three breeds of wild deer, an exhibition on the abbey's history, and a play area for kids.

Fountains, Ripon, North Yorkshire. www.fountainsabbey.org.uk. ☏ **01765/608888.** £11 adults, £6 children 5–16. Abbey and gardens Apr–Sept daily 10am–5pm, rest of year (except Fri Nov–Jan) 10am–5pm; deer park open daily during daylight hours.

This National Park occupying the western half of North Yorkshire consists of some 700 square miles of hills and water-carved valleys filled with dramatic white-limestone crags, fields bordered by dry-stone walls, fast-flowing rivers, isolated sheep farms, and clusters of sandstone cottages. The main dales are, in the south, **Ribblesdale, Malhamdale, Airedale, Wharfedale,** and **Nidderdale;** and in the north, **Wensleydale, Swaledale,** and **Teesdale.** Harrogate makes a good base for exploring the park, as does **Grassington,** 26 miles northwest. This pretty stone-built village is ideal for touring **Upper Wharfedale,** one of the most scenic parts of the Dales—the **Dales Way** footpath passes through the heart of the village. The **Grassington National Park Centre,** Hebden Road (www.yorkshiredales.org.uk; ✆ **01756/751690**), has information and maps. **Bolton Abbey ★** (www.boltonabbey.com; ✆ **01756/718000**) is worth a detour, its ruins set in beautiful grounds with moorland paths. Access is £8 per vehicle.

RHS Garden Harlow Carr ★★ GARDEN   This Royal Horticultural Society garden was created to complement the Yorkshire landscape of which it is a part, with the emphasis on water, stone, and woodland. Seasonal trails, a log maze, woodland dens, and observation beehives make it an unexpectedly fun place to bring kids.

Crag Lane, Harrogate. www.rhs.org.uk/gardens/harlow-carr. ✆ **01423/565418.** £9 adults, £5 children 6–16. Mar–Oct daily 9:30am–6pm (until 4pm in winter).

Where to Stay & Eat

Acorn Lodge ★   This superior B&B on a tree-lined lane near the center of Harrogate makes a pleasant base for exploring the town and countryside. The bedrooms are elegant—more boutique hotel than traditional B&B—and the bathrooms come with either power showers or whirlpool baths. The friendly owners cook up a mean breakfast.

1 Studley Rd., Harrogate. www.acornlodgeharrogate.co.uk. ✆ **01423/525630.** 7 units. Doubles £89–£110, includes breakfast. **Amenities:** Free Wi-Fi.

Bettys Café Tea Rooms ★ ENGLISH TEA/CONTINENTAL   The original incarnation of the famous Yorkshire institution first began serving its tempting pastries in 1919. Today, it offers more than 300 types of bread, cakes, and chocolates (from around £4), as well as around 50 kinds of tea and coffee. Breakfasts, snacks, sandwiches, and afternoon teas are offered—try to get a seat overlooking the Montpelier gardens—and there's a separate cafe where a full daytime and evening menu is served.

1 Parliament St., Harrogate. www.bettys.co.uk. ✆ **01423/814070.** Mains £9–£14. Daily 9am–9pm.

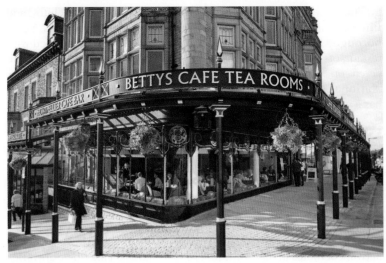
Betty's Café Tea Rooms at Harrogate.

The Lawrance ★★   A great minibreak option, the Lawrance offers a choice of 19 one, two, and three-bedroom apartments spread over three centrally located properties. Each comes with a kitchen, living room, and bathroom and are very well equipped—with dishwashers, washing machines, cooking facilities, closets, and DVD players—and are pretty stylish to boot. Weekly cleaning is included.

Kings House, Kings Rd., Harrogate. www.thelawrance.com. ✆ **01423/503226.** 19 units. £80–£265 (2-night minimum). **Amenities:** Room service; free Wi-Fi.

Yorke Arms ★★ MODERN BRITISH   It's a bit of a drive—albeit through lovely rolling countryside—to the Michelin-starred Yorke Arms. Consistently voted one of the country's top restaurants, the setting, in an ivy-clad medieval building, is idyllic. The cooking, based on creative combinations of seasonal ingredients, top notch. The prices, as you'd expect, are on the expensive side. But for an occasional treat, it's well worth it. Country-style rooms are also available from £170.

Ramsgill-in-Nidderdale (18 miles NW of Harrogate). www.yorke-arms.co.uk. ✆ **01423/755243.** Mains £24–£35. Mon–Sat noon–2pm and 7–9pm; Sun noon–2pm.

WHITBY & AROUND ★★

With its mixture of Gothic and seaside charms, Whitby is the undisputed jewel of the 45-mile North Yorkshire coastline. Today, this coast has an active, if waning, fishing industry, with some ports doubling as traditional seaside resorts. **Bridlington,** 36 miles south of Whitby, and **Filey,** 26 miles south, are fairly low key, with kid-friendly beaches. **Scarborough,** 19 miles north of Bridlington, has a lively seafront lined with restaurants and shops. The remains of a medieval **Scarborough Castle** perch on its headland. Inland from Whitby, **North York Moors National Park** (see below) is England's largest expanse of moorland. It has a wild beauty, especially in summer when purple heather blooms.

Essentials

GETTING THERE   By **train,** Whitby is about 4¾ hours from London King's Cross with changes at both Darlington and Middlesbrough. The best way to arrive, however, is aboard the **North York Moors Railway** (www.nymr.co.uk) from Pickering, where you can relax in carriages pulled by historic steam engines across an otherworldly landscape. Whitby is a 1-hour, 50-mile car **drive** from York, via the A64 and A169.

The **Moorsbus** (www.northyorkmoors.org.uk/moorsbus) operates a network of routes in the North York Moors National Park; there are buses into the park from York, Scarborough, Middlesbrough, and Whitby. The scenic **Esk Valley Railway** (www.eskvalleyrailway.co.uk) between Whitby and Middlesbrough also takes you into the heart of the park.

VISITOR INFORMATION   The **Whitby Tourist Information Centre,** Langborne Road (www.visitwhitby.com; ℭ **01723/383636**), is open daily from 10am to 4:30pm. **The Moors National Park Centre,** Lodge Lane, Danby, Whitby (www.northyorkmoors.org.uk; ℭ**01439/772737**), is open April to October daily 10am to 5pm; mid-February to March and November and December it's open daily 11am to 4pm; January to mid-February hours are 11am to 4pm.

Exploring Whitby

The charming harbor town of **Whitby** began life as a religious center in the 7th century, with an original Saxon monastery replaced in the 12th century by **Whitby Abbey** (see below). The town subsequently became a prominent whaling port and then an active smugglers' port. Among famous explorers to push off from its beaches were Captain James Cook, who circumnavigated the globe twice in ships made by local craftsmen; learn about him in the **Captain Cook Memorial Museum,** Grape Lane (www.cookmuseumwhitby.co.uk; ℭ **01947/601900**), which is open daily from April to October from 9:45am to 5pm (11am–3pm in Feb and Mar). Admission is £5 adults, £3 children. Ask at the tourist office about the **Captain James Cook Heritage Trail,** taking in other North Yorkshire sites up the coast from Whitby.

About 5 miles south along the coast, the village of **Robin Hood's Bay** was once a notorious smugglers' port (it has no link with the eponymous Nottinghamshire outlaw). Tucked into a deep ravine, its Lower Bay is a mix of quirky, old-fashioned shops and inns bordering a huge wild beach abounding in rock-pools. Buy fish and chips to eat on the beach or alfresco treats from Picnics on New Road, or a van parks up on the beach to sell farm ice-cream, tea and coffee, and rental deckchairs.

Whitby Abbey ★★★ RUINS Looming ominously over the historic port from the East Cliff, this breathtaking ruin replaced a Saxon monastery that occupied the same site. Caedmon, the first identifiable English-language poet, was a monk here, and Bram Stoker was inspired by it in the writing of "Dracula," much of which is set in the town. The excellent visitor center, which has great features for children, fills you in on this and more.

Abbey Lane, Whitby. www.english-heritage.org.uk/visit/places/whitby-abbey. ✆ **0870/333-1181.** £7 adults, £4 children 5–16. Apr–Sept daily 10am–6pm, Oct–Mar Thurs–Mon 10am–4pm.

NORTH YORK MOORS NATIONAL PARK ★★

With beautiful rolling moorland dotted with early burial grounds, ancient stone crosses, and ruined abbeys, this 554-square mile national park is hugely popular among walkers and lovers of the great outdoors.

If you're heading up from York, don't miss Castle Howard (see below). North of it, the market town of **Pickering** is one of the gateways to the Moors, which are crisscrossed by an extensive network of public bridleways and footpaths. Noteworthy trails include **Lyke Wake Walk** (www.lykewake.org), a 40-mile east-to-west trek right across the Moors, linking the hamlets of Osmotherly and Ravenscar via a path established by 18th-century coffin bearers. The more challenging **Cleveland Way** (www.nationaltrail.co.uk/ClevelandWay) follows the park's perimeter for 109 miles from Helmsley to Saltburn-by-the-Sea.

The delightful market town of **Helmsley** serves as a great base for exploring the Moors, with superb accommodations, a ruined medieval **castle,** and easy access to the atmospheric nearby ruins of **Rievaulx Abbey** ★ (www.english-heritage.org.uk/visit/places/rievaulx-abbey), one of the country's wealthiest monastic institutions until it was dissolved by Henry VIII. It's open from April to September 10am until 6pm daily (until 5pm in Nov) and costs £6 adults, £4 children.

Castle Howard ★★★ HISTORIC HOME This 18th-century palace designed by **Sir John Vanbrugh,** of Blenheim Palace (p. 171) fame, occupies dramatic grounds with lakes, fountains, gardens, and an adventure playground. Boat trips on the lake and kids' trails and quiz sheets make it a great family bet. Begun in 1699 for the 3rd Earl of Carlisle, Castle Howard has a striking facade topped by a painted and gilded dome, and, inside, a chapel with stunning 19th-century stained-glass windows by Sir Edward Burne-Jones. Paintings on display include a portrait of Henry VIII by **Holbein** and works by Rubens and Reynolds.

Castle Howard. www.castlehoward.co.uk. ✆ **01653/648333.** House and gardens £14 adults, £9 children 5–15. Apr–Oct daily 10am–5pm.

Castle Howard, North York Moors National Park.

Where to Stay & Eat

Humble Pie and Mash ★★ TRADITIONAL BRITISH Offering a welcome alternative to Whitby's ubiquitous fish-and-chip outlets, this quaint establishment in a restored 16th-century shop turns out a mouth watering array of homemade pies in flavors both conventional (steak and ale) and not so conventional (black pudding and sausage), served with a mash, mushy peas and either gravy or parsley sauce for just £6.

163 Church St., Whitby. www.humblepienmash.co. ✆ **07919/074954.** Mains £6. Mon–Sat 12:30–8:30pm, Sun 12:30–5pm.

La Rosa ★★ The eight themed rooms at this hotel have been decorated in an impish, joyful way, with flea market finds, vintage wallpapers and zany knick-knacks. There's also an apartment that sleeps six (and comes with its own dressing up box), a retro tearoom, and 7 miles away in the the National Park, an equally "through the looking glass" campsite made of vintage caravans and recycled objects.

5 East Terrace, Whitby. www.larosa.co.uk. ✆ **01947/606981.** 9 units. Doubles £85–£135 double, includes breakfast. **Amenities:** Bar; tearoom; free Wi-Fi.

Magpie Café ★★ SEAFOOD Occupying an 18th-century building, the city's most celebrated fish-and-chip emporium operates a proper sit-down restaurant as well as a takeout service. Its reputation has made it ferociously popular, but it's worth braving weekend queues to get a plateful of battered-to-perfection fish served with chunky chips. In addition to the standard choices of cod, haddock, and plaice, there are a few more unusual fishes to try, including turbot, monkfish, and brill.

14 Pier Rd., Whitby. www.magpiecafe.co.uk. ℂ **01947/602058.** Mains £9–£20. Daily 11:30am–9pm.

Shepherd's Purse ★ This value guesthouse can be found in Whitby's cobbled old town. The seven rooms, which are laid out around a courtyard, exude a cozy, old-world charm with four-poster (or brass) beds, local furniture and fabrics, and fresh flowers. True, it's a bit creaky, and there's no soundproofing against the ever-present seagulls, but it makes a good base from which to explore the town and beyond.

Sanders Yarde, Whitby. www.theshepherdspurse.com. ℂ **01947/606981.** 7 units. Doubles £65–£185 double. **Amenities:** Free Wi-Fi.

DURHAM ★★

19 miles south of Newcastle; 270 miles N of London; 75 miles N of York

Bill Bryson, author of *Notes from a Small Island* and other bestsellers, said it best: "If you have never been to Durham before, go there at once. Take my car, it's wonderful." More cynical Tobias Smollett, the 18th-century Scottish novelist, observed, "The city of Durham appears like a confused heap of stones and brick, accumulated so as to cover a mountain, round which a river winds its brawling course. . . . The cathedral is a huge gloomy pile." But back to Bryson, the one you should trust: "Durham, I think, as anybody who has ever stepped out of the railway station and looked across the valley will appreciate, is one of the most beautiful cities in the world." You, too, will have the same experience if you arrive by train and look out across the valley to see the town clamoring up the hillside to the cathedral and castle on the top. The urge to explore this inviting British scene up close is nearly irresistible.

Essentials

GETTING THERE The train journey from Newcastle to Durham only takes 15 minutes. If you're coming from London, the trip from King's Cross takes about 2¾ hours. There are also direct trains from Manchester and Birmingham. Daily **National Express** (www.national express.com; ℂ **0871/781-8181**) buses to Durham from London take 6 to 7½ hours. By car, follow A1 south from Newcastle to Durham; the trip takes about 20 minutes. London to Durham by car is a straightforward 270-mile run up the M1, then the A1, taking you 4½ hours or more.

VISITOR INFORMATION **Durham Tourist Information Centre** is at 2 Millennium Place (www.thisisdurham.com; ℂ **0191/384-3720**).

Exploring Durham

A jumble of houses and towers packed higglety pigglety along winding lanes beckons from the banks of the River Weir. Just head up Silver

Street, through the Marketplace, then up Saddler Street and Owensgate to the Palace Green, with Durham Castle on the north side and Durham Cathedral to the south. This is about a 15-minute walk that introduces you to the delights of small town British life, enlivened with the presence of hundreds of university students who probably won't be acting in a terribly scholarly manner if you catch them making their rounds of pubs.

Durham Castle ★ CASTLE William the Conqueror ordered the construction of a castle at Durham, in 1072. The need was obvious. Troublesome Scots were lurking just across the border, ready to invade. Then there was what is rather innocently called the "Harrying of the North," in which William tried to subdue his unruly northern subjects through force and sheer maleficence, starving as many as 100,000 locals to death in the years just after the conquest. As more and more of William's appointed overlords were murdered, the castle was more heavily defended with wood and stone, built atop a mound that commands an almost impregnable rise above the River Weir.

Though much of the castle is now used as what must be one of the world's most romantic dormitories for the University of Durham, tours show off the Norman chapel, a moody assemblage of stone vaulting from 1078, and a larger, more bombastic church from 1540. The castle's 14th-century Great Hall was once the largest in the land; though its been shortened over the centuries, it is still a grand setting for college meals. Also a bit revised over the centuries is a magnificent grand staircase that was designed to "float," resting only on unseen crossbeams in the walls—it became necessary to shore it up with posts. Intricate carvings remain, including one of a strange object that your guide will explain is supposed to a pineapple, an exotic fruit that the 16th-century artist had probably read about but never seen.

Palace Green. www.dur.ac.uk. ☎ **0191/374-3800.** Guided tour only, £5 adults, £4 seniors and children up to 16, £12 families. During school term daily 1:15, 2:15, 3:15, and 4:15pm.

Durham Cathedral ★★★ CHURCH When the Normans began construction of a cathedral at Durham in 1093 they had several goals in mind. One was to provide a suitable resting place for Cuthbert, the wildly popular saint who had been an early bishop of

Construction began on Durham Cathedral in 1083.

It's only fitting that St Cuthbert and the Venerable Bede lie near each other in Durham Cathedral, as they were two of the most luminous figures in northern England during the Dark Ages. Cuthbert (634–687) was a monk, bishop, and, eventually, hermit whose wisdom and knack for healing earned him the nickname "Wonder Worker of Britain." His miraculous powers even affected Alfred the Great, who claimed that visions of Cuthbert inspired him in his victory over the Danes. Much of what we know about Cuthbert comes from Bede (672–735). The monk, scholar, and linguist, known as the Father of English History, translated many early church writings into the vernacular, helping establish Christianity in England. Among his many theological and historical works is his *Lives of St Cuthbert*.

the north; another was to make a show of power over the defeated Saxons and the Scots—or as Sir Walter Scott later said, the cathedral was "half church of god, half castle 'gainst the Scot." In just 40 years craftsmen created one of the great architectural masterpieces of Europe. More than 400 feet long, it was one of the first buildings in the world to be covered with a stone roof on such an enormous scale, made possible by rib vaulting that allows for airy heights and a feeling of lightness. Cathedral builders throughout Europe mimicked the style for the next 400 years.

Cuthbert is now buried beneath a simple slab; his shrine that was described as "one of the most sumptuous in all England, so great were the offerings and jewels bestowed upon it," was destroyed under Henry VIII's dissolution of the monasteries. The Venerable Bede, a monk from nearby Monkwearmouth, is interred in the Galilee Chapel, in a simple tomb that honors this humble scholar. Parts of the cathedral were used to depict Hogwarts in the Harry Potter films. Americans may want to seek out the stars and stripes on the crest of George Washington's family, whose ancestral home is in nearby Washington.

Palace Green. www.durhamcathedral.co.uk. © **0191/386-4266.** Free; guided tours £5. Mon–Sat 7:30am–6pm, Sun 7:45am–5:30pm.

Around Durham

Barnard Castle ★ MUSEUM What might be the most romantic ruined castle in all of England is a 12th-century concoction of jagged walls teetering above the gorge of the River Tees. Very little remains of the once fearsome stronghold against the Scots, though the ruins you see are not just the ravages of time and weather: 17th-century politician Sir Henry Vane bought the castle and had the stones carted off to enlarge his nearby castle at Raby. But even in tatters, Barnard's towers and Great Hall evoke the wonder of the Middle Ages and are so evocative that Sir Walter Scott was inspired to set his 1813 romantic poem *Rokeby* here.

Scar Top, Barnard Castle. www.english-heritage.org.uk. ℂ **0191/370-4000.** £5 adults, £4 seniors, £3 children 5–15, £12 families. Apr–Sept daily 10am–6pm, Oct 10am–5pm, Nov–Mar, weekends 10am–4pm.

Beamish, the Living Museum of the North ★★★ MUSEUM

Recreating rural life in northeastern England in the midst of rural north-eastern England might seem a bit redundant. Yet these 300-plus acres, deep in the countryside 12 miles northwest of Durham, are fascinating to explore, and so authentic that you will probably forget that a lot of the houses and buildings were moved here from other places. Your wanderings, via vintage trams gathered from nearby towns and cities, take you through rolling countryside to an early-19th-century pit village, where a school, chapel, and numerous machinery buildings surround a mine shaft that can be toured; a turn-of-the 20th-century town, with shops, a pub, and tearooms; a World War II era farm; and Pockerley Old Hall, the home of well-to-do tenant farmers that has commanded a green hilltop here since the 12th century. An 1893 steam-powered carousel, a narrow-gauge railway, farm animals and draft horses, and some genuine old-time dining experiences—including fish-and-chips fried in beef drippings over a coal burner—ensure a satisfyingly informative day and a really good time.

Beamish. www.beamish.org.uk. ℂ **0191/370-4000.** £19 adults, £14 seniors, £11 children 5–16, £35–£49 families. Apr–Oct daily 10am–5pm; first 3 weeks. Nov and early Jan–Mar Sat–Sun and Tues–Thurs 10am–4pm, plus some of Dec.

Bowes Museum ★ MUSEUM   John Bowes (1811–85), the illegitimate son of an earl and a gardener's daughter, clearly believed that living

Beamish Living History Museum.

well was the best revenge. Shunned by Victorian society, he went to Paris and took up with an actress, who later became the Countess of Montalbo. They spent their happy marriage collecting racehorses, along with jewels, porcelain, Old Masters paintings, clocks, and textiles, then built a magnificent chateau to show off their treasures to the public. Some of Canaletto's most colorful and detailed scenes of Venice's Grand Canal are here, as is El Greco's *Tears of St. Peter,* a soulful work that Bowles reluctantly bought on the advice of a dealer who said it might be important one day. A couple of years ago the holdings became even more renowned when it was discovered that a portrait thought to be a relatively worthless copy was a masterpiece by Anthony Van Dyck. His *Portrait of Olivia Boteler Porter* has been beautifully restored and is now a star attraction, though the piece that catches most eyes is an elegant silver automaton of a swan that enticingly moves its head, glides across a pond of glass, and, in a grand finale, swallows a silver fish.

Barnard Castle. www.thebowesmuseum.org.uk. ✆ **01833/690606.** £11 adults, £10 seniors, £6 students. Daily 10am–5pm.

Where to Stay

Bannatyne Hotel ★ The surroundings, in a commercial district on the fringes of the city center, don't evoke Durham's considerable charm, but there is plenty else going for these extremely good-value lodgings. Contemporary furnishings in the comfortable rooms are of the no-nonsense variety, and an adjoining health club offers such luxuries as a swimming pool, steam room, and whirlpool. A cafe serves breakfast as well as sandwiches, a few well-prepared entrees, and drinks all day, and is especially welcome in the evening when the bus or 20-minute walk into the center of town might be more than you want to undertake.

Hurworth on Tees, Darlington, County Durham DL2 2DU. www.rockliffehall.com. ✆ **01325/729999.** 61 units. Doubles from £65. **Amenities:** Restaurant; bar; swimming pool; free Wi-Fi.

Durham Castle ★ Durham's most notable accommodation is its famous fortress, where you can choose to live like a commoner or royalty, depending on your tastes and budget—in Spartan rooms (some with private bathrooms) or in two grand state rooms. The modest option is only available when Durham University, which uses the castle as a dormitory, is not in session; the two-room Chaplain's Suite and more opulent Bishop's Suite are available year round. All guests are served breakfast in the medieval Great Hall, and get a free castle tour.

Palace Green, Durham DH1 3RN. www.dur.ac.uk. ✆ **0191/334-4106.** 72 units. Doubles £77–£98; suites £150 and £195, includes breakfast. **Amenities:** Bar/lounge.

The Townhouse ★★ While Durham's cathedral and castle suggest medieval austerity, this beautiful Georgian residence in the center of town is all about opulence. In some rooms free-standing bathtubs are placed in front of fireplacces; one room resembles a ship's cabin while another is decked out like a luxurious train compartment. Two rooms are set in the garden and have outdoor hot tubs. Meals are served in a fittingly opulent salon full of gilt and brocade, and you can enjoy a drink on a terrace above the River Weir.

34 Old Elvet. www.thetownhousedurham.co.uk. ✆ **0191/384-1037.** 11 units. Doubles £99–£250, includes breakfast. **Amenities:** Restaurants; bar; free Wi-Fi.

Where to Eat

Durham's large student population keep the pubs busy. The most atmospheric is probably the **Shakespeare Tavern** on Saddler Street (www.shakespearedurham.com; ✆ **0191/384-3261**), dating to 1190 and claiming to be one of the smallest pubs in England (it *is* ridiculously narrow) and one of the most haunted. For something a little more refined, step into pretty **Tealicious Tearoom** (tealicioustearoom.co.uk; ✆ **0191/3401393**) at 88 Elvet Bridge for a slice of delicious homemade cakes or the famous pork pie. In Barnard Castle, **Penny's Tea Rooms** (www.pennys-tearooms.co.uk; ✆ **0183/3637634**) is a local institution.

Bistro 21 ★★ MODERN BRITISH/EUROPEAN   You'll have to venture about a mile outside Durham city center to enjoy a meal in this large stone house, part of the servant's wing of an 18th-century country estate, where homey, white-washed rooms with simple pine floors overlook the River Weir. Vegetables grown in the courtyard accompany such regional specialties as wild sea bass and steaks of locally grown beef. Fixed-price menus are an especially good.

Aykley Heads House, Aykley Heads, Durham. www.bistrotwentyone.co.uk. ✆ **0191/384-4354.** Mains £15–£23. Mon–Sat noon–2pm and 6–10pm.

Oldfield's Noted Eating House ★★ MODERN BRITISH/EUROPEAN   Fans of the television show *Portlandia* might be reminded of the episode in which a restaurant provides a complete dossier on the chicken they serve—warm-hued walls here are covered with portraits of suppliers, accompanied by words of appreciation. Whether or not you care to know where your beef comes from, it's delicious, expertly braised, and accompanied by Yorkshire pudding. You can also enjoy slightly lighter fare, along the lines of bangers and mash and meaty sandwiches served on homemade bread.

18 Claypath. oldfieldseatinghouse.com. ✆ **0191/370-9595.** Lunch and early dinner: 2 courses £14, 3 courses £16; dinner mains £16–£17. Daily noon–10pm.

Rose and Crown ★★ BRITISH   If you're venturing east from Durham to visit the Bowes Museum in Barnard Castle (see above), lunch at this old village pub is almost mandatory. Cheese is made just down the road, and accompanies farmhouse ham from Cumbria; you can savor both in delicious salads, a ploughman's platter, or in sandwiches served on crusty baguettes. Lunch is served in the welcoming bar, while dinner service moves into an oak paneled room softened with candlelight. Romaldkirk, Barnard Castle. www.rose-and-crown.co.uk. ✆ **01833/650213.** Mains £7–£10. Daily noon–2:30pm and 6:30pm–9pm.

Shopping

Durham's Victorian-era **Indoor Market** houses 50 or so vendors and is open Monday–Saturday 9am to 5pm. Some shops and stalls are charmingly traditional, such as Humbies candy shop, while others are quirkily impractical—none more so than **Get Dressed For Battle** (gdfb.co.uk), where you can stock up on chainmail, battleaxes, and whatever other gear your tour of British castles and battlefileds might inspire you to buy.

NEWCASTLE & GATESHEAD ★

Newcastle: 283 miles N of London; 145 miles NE of Manchester; 121 miles S of Edinburgh

The River Tyne separates these two cities, for all practical purposes the same place, linked in spirit and quite literally so by seven bridges. The showiest of the spans is the **Gateshead Millennium Bridge ★**, a rainbow-arched crossing for pedestrians and cyclists that dramatically tilts on schedule to accommodate ship traffic. Crossing the bridge, between the riverside Quays district in Newcastle and the so-called Arts Quarter in Gateshead, is a popular pastime for Geordies (as residents are called—to some an elegant reference to support for George II, for others a nod to safety lamps designed by George Stephenson that miners once

The pedestrian-only Gateshead Millennium Bridge connects Newcastle & Gateshead.

wore). Yet the real local charm is in the stone-and-brick blocks of Georgian and Victorian facades that recall the cities' past as a prosperous center of shipping, shipbuilding, and coal mining. A century ago a local brewer captured the essence of the area's proud working class traditions in a bottle, with Newcastle Brown Ale, one of the most popular beers in the U.K. and an export that puts the city on the map for many Americans.

GETTING THERE   By direct **train**, Newcastle is about 3 hours from London King's Cross. There are also direct trains from Manchester, taking about 2½ hours, and from Edinburgh, taking about 1¾ hours. Daily **National Express buses** (www.nationalexpress.com; ✆ **0871/781-8181;**) from London to Newcastle take 6½ hours and up. Nexus (www.nexus.org.uk) operates city buses and the Metro light railway/underground system. From London, expect a **drive** of about 4¾ hours (283 miles), most of it up the main M1/A1.

VISITOR INFORMATION   **Newcastle Tourist Information Centre,** Central Arcade (www.newcastlegateshead.com; ✆ **0191/277-8000**), is open Monday to Friday 9am to 5:30pm, Saturday 9am to 5:30pm, Sunday 11am to 5pm. **Gateshead Tourist Information Centre,** Gateshead Heritage Centre at St Mary's (www.newcastlegateshead.com; ✆ **0191/478-4222**) is open Tuesday to Sunday 10am to 4pm.

Exploring Newcastle & Gateshead

A walk around Newcastle should begin in the Georgian and Victorian blocks that fan out from **Grey's Monument** and are known collectively as the Monument and also as Grainger Town—the latter for Richard Grainger, the early 19th-century architect and real-estate developer who put together what is still considered some of the finest architecture in Britain. The monument itself is a column topped with a statue of Charles, the Second Earl Grey, known for lending his name to the popular tea blend but also an ardent political reformer who abolished slavery in the British empire. In the monument's shadow are such fine Newcastle landmarks as the **Theatre Royale** and **Grainger Market ★**, where butchers and fishmongers now share space under the glass arcades with jewelers and fashion designers. From the Monument, Grey Street curves gracefully downhill toward the river, creating a pleasant cityscape that inspired 20th-century poet laureate Sir John Betjeman to enthuse, "I shall never forget seeing it to perfection, traffic-less on a misty Sunday morning. Not even Regent Street, even old Regent Street London, can compare with that descending subtle curve." You may well agree as you make your way down to **Quayside**, the once bustling former docklands where cobbled lanes follow the north and south banks of the River Tyne. These days the quays are not the haunt of sailors and prostitutes but of "stags and hens"—the weekend partiers who descend upon Newcastle from around northern England.

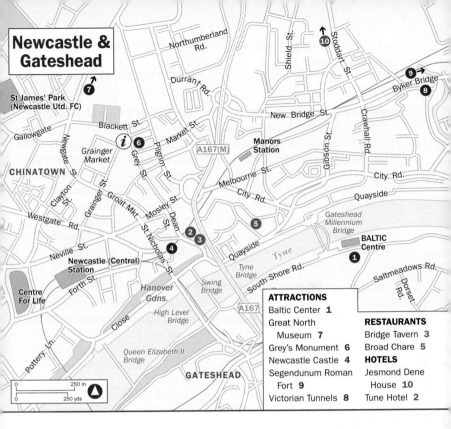

Newcastle & Gateshead

St James' Park
(Newcastle Utd. FC)

Northumberland Rd.

Shield St.

Stoddart St.

Byker Bridge

Gallowgate

Blackett St.

Durrant Rd.

New Bridge St.

Crawhall Rd.

Market St.

Manors Station

Gibson St.

City Rd.

CHINATOWN

Grainger Market

Grey St.

Pilgrim St.

A167(M)

Melbourne St.

City Rd.

Quayside

Newgate St.

Clayton St.

Grainger St.

Groat Mkt.

Mosley St.

Dean St.

St Nicholas St.

Westgate Rd.

Neville St.

Gateshead Millennium Bridge

BALTIC Centre

Newcastle (Central) Station

Quayside

Tyne

Saltmeadows Rd.

Tyne Bridge

South Shore Rd.

Dorset Rd.

Centre For Life

Forth St.

Hanover Gdns.

Swing Bridge

High Level Bridge

Close

A167

Pottery Ln.

Queen Elizabeth II Bridge

GATESHEAD

ATTRACTIONS	
Baltic Center **1**	
Great North	**RESTAURANTS**
Museum **7**	Bridge Tavern **3**
Grey's Monument **6**	Broad Chare **5**
Newcastle Castle **4**	**HOTELS**
Segendunum Roman	Jesmond Dene
Fort **9**	House **10**
Victorian Tunnels **8**	Tune Hotel **2**

0   250 m
0   250 yds

BALTIC Centre for Contemporary Art ★ MUSEUM   The looming presence of a former riverside industrial site, a flour mill, is not all that's reminiscent of London's Tate Modern. Britain's second-largest showcase for contemporary art has even hosted the Tuner Prize, an honor that's been afforded to the Tate since 1984. The center has no permanent collection, but hosts rotating exhibits of contemporary artists, among them Antony Gormley, Anish Kapoor, and Sam Taylor-Wood. Exhibits often play off local themes, such as American sculptor Chris Burden's 1/20 scale model of the Tyne Bridge, looming just outside the windows.
Gateshead Quays, South Shore Rd. www.balticmill.com. ✆ **0191/478-1810.** Free. Daily 10am–5pm.

Great North Museum ★ MUSEUM   A handsome neoclassical building on the campus of the University of Newcastle houses a curiosity cabinet of collectibles that sweep through ancient history, with two excellent mummies, and the natural sciences, with tanks of sharks and pythons. Large-scale standouts are a recreation of Hadrian's Wall that points out every fort and guardhouse along its 73-mile length, providing an excellent introduction if you're planning on seeing the real thing, and magnificent recreations of a Tyrannosaurus rex and an African elephant.

Barras Bridge. www.twmuseums.org.uk. © **0191/208-6755.** Free. Metro: Haymarket.

Newcastle Castle ★ MUSEUM   The pile of stones that gave the city its name looks a bit woebegone these days, rising as it does out of the sprawl of the railway station and tracks. With a little imagination, and informed by the heritage center inside, you might be able to picture the fort the Romans built here to guard over the River Tyne and the wooden castle ("New Castle") erected by a son of William the Conqueror after one of many campaigns against the Scots. The current keep dates to 1177, and the fortified entrance, Black Gate, was added in 1250. The Great Hall and Chapel are solidly medieval and are said to be haunted.

Castle Garth. newcastlecastle.co.uk. © **0191/230-6300.** £4 adults. Daily 10am–6pm. Metro: Central Station.

Segedunum Roman Fort, Baths & Museum ★ MUSEUM   Surrounded by suburban sprawl, these remains of a Roman fort and a section of Hadrian's Wall are not as evocative as what you'll encounter of the Roman presence farther west at Vindolanda and Housesteads (p. 463–464), but they're transporting nonetheless, and only a metro ride away from the center of Newcastle. The Romans built a complex overlooking a crossing in the River Tyne here around A.D. 125 to protect the easternmost sections of the wall, at the far reaches of the empire. Excavations include the foundations of a huge cavalry barracks and an altar inscribed by a 3rd-century garrison commander. The main attraction is the reconstructed remains of a bathhouse in its entirety, with changing rooms, cold, warm and hot bathing chambers, and lavatories. Until the 1970s the site was buried beneath houses of shipyards workers; most of the ongoing excavations did not come to light until the 1990s.

Buddle St., Wallsend. www.twmuseums.org.uk. © **0191/278 4217.** £6 adults, £4 seniors and students. June–Aug daily 10am–5pm, Sept–Oct daily 10am–4pm, Nov–Mar daily 10am–2:30pm, Apr–May daily 10am–4:30pm. Metro: Wallsend.

Tynemouth Castle and Priory ★ MUSEUM   A sense of forlorn isolation surrounds these weather-battered ruins on the shores of the North Sea near the mouth of the River Tyne. Walking among tombstones and jagged walls of a priory and castle, taking in the sweeping views of the wind-buffeted coast and sea, it's easy to imagine just how hard life here could have been, and a risky business, too. Seafaring Danes attacked repeatedly, massacring monks and nuns, until a castle was heavily fortified in the 11th century, then eventually left to decay. The grounds were used as a coastal defense until the end of the 20th century.

Pier Rd., Tynemouth. www.twmuseums.org.uk. © **0191/278 4217.** £5 adults, £4 seniors, £3 children 5–15. Metro: Tynemouth.

Victorian Tunnels ★ MUSEUM Beneath your feet in Newcastle runs one of the world's first subways, a 2½-mile-long wagon way dug out in 1842 to transport coal to the banks of the Tyne, where it was loaded into ships. Though the tunnel was not used for transport after the 1860s, it came back into service as an air raid shelter during World War II. You can traverse the low, narrow, white-washed passageways on 2-hour tours that are informative and surprisingly entertaining. Guides will explain the Victorian heydays when the city flourished with dockyards and factories, adding fascinating bits like how Newcastle was the first city in the world to install electric street lighting—the manufacture of incandescent bulbs was once big business here. They also show off parts of the tunnels fitted with the beds and crude toilets that provided safe accommodation during World War II bombings, though Newcastle was spared the devastation that leveled many other British industrial cities.

> ### Angel of the North
>
> A 66-foot-tall sculpture spreads her 177-foot wingspan atop a hillside on the southern outskirts. Sculptor Antony Gormley has described the Angel of the North as "a focus for our hopes and fears." Some critics have alternately described so-called "Rusty Rita" a piece of vulgar rubbish and others deemed her to be a monument akin to the Eifel Tower and Statue of Liberty; you can decide for yourself when approaching by train or by car along the A1.

Entrance at Stepney Bank, Arch 6 in Byker Bridge. ouseburntrust.org.uk. ☏ **0191/261 6596.** £6 adults, £3 children under 12. Thurs 6:30pm, Fri 10:30am and 1:30pm, Sat 10am, 1, and 3pm, Sun 1pm, some Wed 10:30am or 1:30pm. Metro: Byker.

ALONG HADRIAN'S WALL

The barren moors that stretch to the west of Newcastle seem quiet and bucolic, but for almost 2,000 years they were a war zone, a buffer that kept barbarians and, for centuries after the Norman Conquest, fractious Scots at bay. Roman emperor Hadrian, determined to protect his holdings in Britain, instructed legionnaires to construct a 73-mile fortification across the north, and large portions of **Hadrian's Wall** ★★★ still stand, one of the most remarkable artifacts from the ancient world. Just outside the pretty market town of **Hexham,** 24 miles west of Newcastle, forts and sections of the wall evoke the long-ago Roman presence.

Housesteads Roman Fort & Museum ★★ HISTORIC SITE This huge fort, known as Vercovicium, was completed soon after construction of Hadrian's Wall began in 122. More than 800 men were housed in the compound, part of a total garrison of 10,000 legionnaires who were stationed at 15 forts along the wall. The foundations of barracks, the commandant's villa, and primitive latrines (the most popular spot for photos in the compound) provide a sense of what an outpost of civilization this was in such barren, godforsaken terrain. You'll get a overview of the extent of the wall by following a path up the escarpment that looms above the fort. An even better place to see the wall is at **Walltown Crags** ★★★, 7 miles west off B6318, where a large, still-intact section rises and falls across the empty landscape.

Housesteads Farm, Haydon Bridge. www.english-heritage.org.uk. © **0870/333-1181.** £5 adults, £3 children 5–16. Daily 10am–6pm (4pm in winter).

Roman Vindolanda & Roman Army Museum ★★ HISTORIC SITE   A fort first took shape at Vindolana ("White Enclosure") around A.D. 90 and was extended several times, though the compound appears to have been abandoned, at least for a time, with the completion of Housesteads. Among the ruins of a bathhouse, barracks, and temple is a large and lavish dwelling whose size, along with fragments of elaborate wall paintings, suggest a palatial residence built to house Emperor Hadrian and his imperial party when they came north in 122. The most remarkable artifacts unearthed at the fort—from a pit where waste from the compound was discarded—are thousands of wooden writing tablets. Ground conditions have proven to be an excellent preservative, and much of the writing is intact, providing a wealth of information—fort rosters, letters to soldiers from home, correspondence between officers. These are the top treasures in the adjoining **Roman Army Museum,** though a wealth of other material includes some fascinating everyday objects such as shoes, bags, and buckets, all fashioned from leather.

Vindolanda: southeast of Twice Brewed, just off the B6318; museum: west along the B6318. www.vindolanda.com. © **01434/344277.** £6 adults, £4 children 5–18; museum £5 adults, £3 children. Daily 10am–6pm, depending on season.

ALNWICK, THE COAST & HOLY ISLAND

The farther north you go from Newcastle the more scenic the coastline becomes. Especially lovely, with dunes and sandy beaches and few manmade incursions, is a stretch that runs north from the Coquet Estuary just southeast of **Alnwick** ★, a pretty market town of the River Ain about 35 miles north of Newcastle and 5 miles inland from the North Sea.

Seeing the Wall

The B6318, an old military road built in the 18th century to link Carlisle and Newcastle, follows the length of Hadrian's Wall; in fact, in places engineers ran the roadway right on top of the wall. Along the road are many viewpoints and turnouts where you can park and walk into some of the notable ruins. Traveling west from Newcastle, you'll see especially scenic sections of the wall around **Heddon-on-the-Wall** (where the village church is built of stone from the wall); between Sewingshields and Housesteads; and at **Walton Crags.** By car from Newcastle, follow A69 10 miles west to Heddon-on-the-Wall, and there get onto B6318 and continue west as far as **Vindolanda** (see above); Vindolanda is about 25 miles west of Heddon-on-the-Wall and 35 miles west of Newcastle.

A scenic coastal spot and a good place to walk on the beach is **Bamburgh Castle** ★ (www.bamburghcastle.com, open daily 10am–5pm, £11 adults, £5 children), 17 miles north of Alnwick, where a fortress of some sort has commanded a volcanic outcropping since the 5th century; the huge Norman castle that spreads across bluffs high above dunes is home to the heirs of a Victorian industrial fortune.

Alnwick Castle ★★★ CASTLE   This gloriously romantic, richly towered and turreted castle may be readily recognizable upon first sight—set high above a ravine of the River Ain, it's been a popular subject of painters for centuries, among them J. M. W. Turner and Canaletto. More to the point, any child will know the crenelated medieval profile as "Hogwarts" in the first two Harry Potter movies, where the castle doubles as the fictional school. Almost since the Norman Conquest, the castle has stood in one form or another. It's also been home to some of England's most famous nobles. Among them was Henry Percy, a valiant knight who led a campaign against the Scots, earning his nickname Hotspur for his speed in the saddle, then against Henry IV (he was slain in battle, but not, as Shakespeare has it, by young Prince Hal, the Prince of Wales). A later heir, Henry Percy, Sixth Earl of Northumberland, was betrothed to Ann Boleyn but forced to give her up, paving the way for the advances of Henry VIII. The castle is currently the second largest inhabited castle in England, after Windsor, and is the seat of the Duke and Duchess of Northumberland, who are a viable presence in the lavish staterooms, where family photos sit beneath canvases by Canaletto and, the castle treasure, "Ecce Homo" by Titian. Tours take in a few staterooms as well as the library and dining room. Special events, such as Harry Potter-themed wizardry shows, liven things up for kids.

Alnwick. www.alnwickcastle.com. ℰ **01665/511100.** £15 adults, £12 seniors, £8 children 5–16, £39 families (discounts online). Daily 10am–6pm Apr–Oct.

Alnwick Garden ★★★ GARDEN   Renowned gardens have flourished next to Alnwick Castle since 1750, when Capability Brown laid out formal plantings as part of his overall design of the castle park. The gardens had fallen into disrepair by the 1990s, when Jane Percy, the Duchess of Northumberland, undertook a restoration and created what's said to be the most ambitious garden project in Britain since World War II. The centerpiece is an Ornamental Garden, where flower-bordered pathways follow small streams that flow from a central fountain. A **treehouse** ★ is said to be the largest in the world, reached by rope bridges and suspended walkways, where trees grow through the floor next to a roaring fire in the **Treehouse Restaurant** (see below). Behind closed gates is a **Poison Garden** ★, planted with belladonna, foxglove, and other plants known for their ability to kill. As the duchess has said, "I felt that most children I knew would be more interested in

A tour of the Alnwick Garden Poison Garden.

hearing how a plant killed, how long it would take you to die if you ate it and how gruesome and painful the death might be."

Denwick Lane, Alnwick. www.alnwickgarden.com. ℭ **01665/511-350.** £12 adults, £10 seniors, £4 children 5–16, £30 families (discounts online). Apr–Oct daily 10am–6pm, Nov–Dec daily 11am–5pm.

Barter Books ★★ LANDMARK   You won't risk of having nothing to read in Alnwick, as the town's Victorian-era railway station is the setting for one of Europe' largest and most celebrated secondhand bookshops. Regulars exchange books, hence the name, though cash sales are also encouraged. Owners Mary and Stuart Manley invite customers to linger around glowing hearths and in cozy seating areas beneath 40-foot-long murals of famous writers and other relevant themes. Browsing through the mother lode has turned up some remarkable finds, including a World War II poster proclaiming "Keep Calm and Carry On" that has since circulated around the world in meme form.

Alnwick Station. www.barterbooks.co.uk. ℭ **01665/604888.** Summer 9am–7pm, winter 9am–5pm (until 7pm Sat).

Lindisfarne Priory ★★★ LANDMARK   One of the most dramatic sights in all of England might be the appearance of Holy Island, or Lindisfarne, seeming to rise from the waves just off the coast north of Alnwick. St Aidan established a monastery on the island, some 3 miles long and 1½ miles wide, in 635 and the stone complex soon became a center of learning and an active force of Christianity in the north. St Cuthbert was the prior of Lidisfarne from 665 until he retreated to his hermitage in 684, and he was buried here until Viking raiders destroyed

Lindisfarne Castle on Holy Island.

the community in 875; Cuthbert's remains were toted around northern England until they found a permanent resting place in Durham Cathedral (p. 454) in 1104. The romantic ruins that now rise above the windswept island are not of Cuthbert's time but are all that remain of a Benedictine priory built on the spot in the 12th century, dissolved and left to ruin under Henry VIII. Nearby **Lindisfarne Castle** ★★ is a 16th-century Tudor creation, though in the early 20th century architect Sir Edwin Lutyens converted the primitive structure into an atmospheric retreat. Well-known garden designer Gertrude Jekyll created the walled garden.

Part of visiting Lindisfarne is the adventure of getting there—this is a tidal island, reached across flats that are accessible only at low tide; crossing times are prominently posted and must be strictly followed.

Lindisfarne Priory. www.english-heritage.org.uk. ✆ **0870/3331181.** £6 adults, £5 seniors, £3 children. Apr–Sept daily 9:30am–6pm, Oct–Mar weekends 10am–4pm. Lindisfarne Castle. www.nationaltrust.org.uk. ✆ **01289/389244** £7 adults, £4 children 5 to 17, £17 families. Mar–Oct, opening times vary with tides, either 10am–3pm, 10am–4pm, 11am–5pm, or noon–5pm; open some winter weekends.

Where to Stay

Hogs Head Inn ★ Harry Potter fans might only find it natural that this modern motor inn on the outskirts of Alnwick takes it name from the pub in the wizarding village of Hogsmeade. But guests looking for magic charm might be disappointed to find extremely large, spotless rooms, with comfortable if bland contemporary furnishings that don't bear a trace of resemblance to the rough-hewn tables in the fictional Hogs

A room at the Jesmond Dene House hotel.

Head. Pullout sofas and a lot of extra floor space are well-geared to families. The in-house pub is pleasantly clubby, with meat-heavy lunches and evening meals served in front of a roaring fire; some good-value half-board deals are often available on the website.

Hawfinch Dr., Alnwick. www.hogsheadinnalnwick.co.uk. © **0191/5803610.** 53 units. Doubles £89–£109, includes breakfast. **Amenities:** Restaurant; bar; free Wi-Fi.

Jesmond Dene House ★★★ A lovely stone Arts and Crafts style house in a leafy Newcastle suburb is a former school, but in its current incarnation is a gracious retreat surrounded by gardens only minutes from the city center. In the spacious guest rooms, rich paneling and leaded windows are offset with modernist furnishings and contemporary art, along with lush wall coverings and handsome textiles; rooms in a tasteful modern extension lack the original detailing but are similarly comfortable and sophisticated. Meals in the restaurant, with a focus on locally sourced fish and meat, are exceptional.

Jesmond Dene Rd. www.jesmonddenehouse.co.uk. © **0191/212-3000.** 40 units. Doubles from £120. **Amenities:** Restaurant; bar; free Wi-Fi.

Matfen Hall Hotel, Golf & Spa ★★ A gracious old Victorian Gothic country manor deep in the countryside is a handy base for exploring Hadrian's Wall and is an easy drive from Newcastle and the coast. Lord and Lady Blackett house their guests in commodious, traditionally furnished rooms in the old manor and in a pleasant but less character-filled new extension. There's plenty here to keep you entertained on the vast grounds—a spa, a large indoor pool, a golf course, and walking trails through gardens and the surrounding woods and farm lands. Formal dining is in the Library Print Room, while more casual fare is available in the Conservatory and Keeper's Lodge.

Matfen. www.matfenhall.com. ☏ **01661/880-6500.** 53 units. Doubles £130–£300, includes breakfast. **Amenities:** 3 restaurants; bar; golf; spa; pool; free Wi-Fi.

Tune ★ This chain with many outlets in Asia goes Spartan with a high tech gloss, providing as much comfort as possible while eliminating expensive hotel extras. Some of these you might miss—overhead lighting is harsh; the only comfortable perch is the bed, a few hooks suffice for a closet, and the lowest-priced rooms don't have windows. No rooms have telephones, and TV, extra towels, and daily housekeeping might be extra, depending on the rate. What you do get is an excellent mattress, covered with a fluffy, cloud-like duvet, and a hot, powerful shower. The location in Quayside is well-poised for eating, drinking, and exploring Newcastle.

Proctor House, 23-29 Side. www.tunehotels.com. No phone. 103 units. Doubles from £40. **Amenities:** Free Wi-Fi.

Where to Eat

Bridge Tavern ★★ MODERN BRITISH An on-premises microbrewery, with the product dispensed directly from the taps, is the draw at this 200-year-old Quayside hideaway tucked beneath the stanchions of the Tyne Bridge. Exposed pipe and brick combined lend a touch of industrial chic to the welcoming, mens-club surroundings, where you can nibble your way through crispy pigs' ears and fried mussels to a full-blown casual meal of fish and chips or steak and fries.

7 Akenside Hill. www.thebridgetavern.com. ☏ **0191/261-9966.** Mains £9–£14. Mon–Thurs noon–midnight, Fri–Sat noon–1am, Sun noon–11pm.

Broad Chare ★★★ MODERN BRITISH Though the slogan, "Proper pub, proper beer, proper food," might raise a suspicious eyebrow (why do they need to reassure us?), the wood-floored, plain-walled room in Newcastle's Quayside lives up to its claims. The attention goes well beyond excellent local beers to fine food; though you might need a translator to help you through a menu of such homey offerings as bubble and squeak and spicy black pudding, it's all pretty straightforward and served in hearty portions. Reservations are recommended for dinner.

25 Broad Chare. www.thebroadchare.co.uk. ☏ **0191/211-2194.** Mains £15–£19. Mon–Sat noon–10pm, Sun noon–5pm.

Olde Ship Inn ★ TRADITIONAL BRITISH If you're driving from Alnwick up to Lindisfarne, the tiny harbor at Seahouses is a nice place to breathe in some sea air and enjoy a pint at this traditional pub. The wooden floor is ships' decking, and every inch of wall space is taken up with ships' figureheads, diving helmets, ships in bottles, and other nautical bric-a-brac. The centerpiece is a replica of the lifeboat *The Grace Darling,* named after the daughter of a Victorian-era lighthouse-keeper's

The Alnwick Garden Treehouse.

daughter who saved 13 people from a shipwreck. Soup, sandwiches, and a few seafood dishes are available, as well as steak and ale pie and some other old pub standards. Guest rooms and apartments are available.

Seahouses. www.seahouses.co.uk. © **01665/720200.** Mains £10–£11. Mon–Sat 11am–11pm, Sun noon–11pm.

Treehouse ★ MODERN BRITISH/EUROPEAN   A meal could take second place to a one-of-a-kind setting like this. The food is excellent, with an emphasis on seasonal specials made from local fish and seafood and Northumberland beef and lamb, but it tastes all the better because you're dining 60-feet up in the treetops above the Alnwick Garden (p. 465), surrounded by rough-hewn walls, higgledy-piggledy windows, big beams, and the twisting limbs of lime trees snaking past your table.

Denwick Lane, Alnwick. www.alnwickgarden.com. © **01665/511-852.** Mains £14–£24 (dinner). Daily 11:30am–2:45pm; Thurs–Sun 7–11pm; 6:30–9pm June–Sept and Mon when bank holiday.

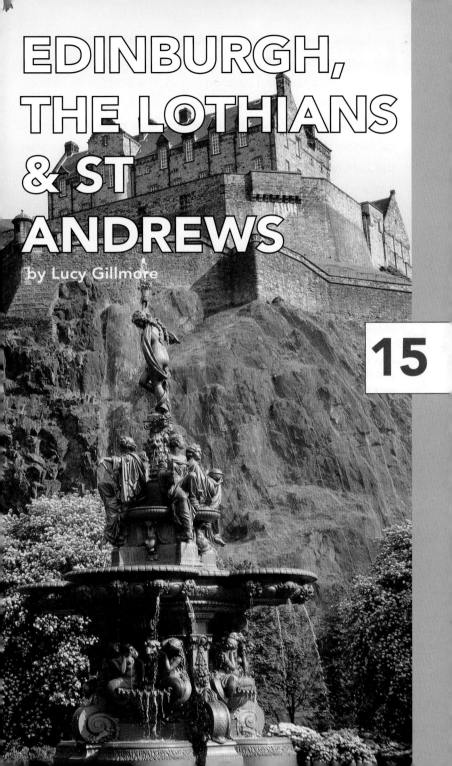

EDINBURGH, THE LOTHIANS & ST ANDREWS

by Lucy Gillmore

15

f cities were movie stars, Edinburgh would be Katharine Hepburn, or, as this is Scotland, Tilda Swinton. The Scottish capital is a cool, classic and cultured beauty. The Scottish Parliament, tucked in the shadow of extinct volcano, Arthur's Seat, might be strikingly modern, but Edinburgh feels more like a historical film set than a contemporary political powerhouse—even after the 2014 referendum for Scottish independence. The capital was a staunch "no" vote, for the record.

Surprisingly compact and built around a series of hills, Edinburgh is peppered with tiny neighborhoods, each with its own distinct character and charm. Dipping in and out of these is one of the best ways to explore the city, and to shake off the crowds. Away from the main arteries there are pockets of peace where it feels almost sleepily provincial. All you can hear is the rumble of cars on cobbles as you breathe in the heady scent of hops and soak up the history seeping out of the stonework.

Edinburgh is also, of course, host to one of the biggest cultural shindigs in the world. Come the summer, that famous reserve melts away and the low-key capital cranks it up a gear. Thousands of visitors from all over the world flock to the Edinburgh Festival and Fringe Festival. The Royal Mile becomes a rippling river of ticket touts, street performers and face-painters and the whole city turns into a vast open-air arena.

Essentials

GETTING THERE Edinburgh Airport (www.edinburghairport.com; ✆ **0844/448-8833**) is 7½ miles west of the city center. Double-decker **Airlink** buses (www.lothianbuses.com; ✆ **0131/555-6363**. £4 one-way, £7 round-trip) make the round-trip from the airport to Edinburgh city center every 10 minutes, letting you on and off at Haymarket or Waverley train stations. The journey takes around 25 minutes You can also take the swanky new **tram** into town. They run every 8 to 12 minutes from the airport to York Place via Haymarket train station and Princes Street and the fare is £5 one-way, £8 return. You buy your ticket from the machine at the stop. There's a busy **taxi** stand at the airport and a ride into town costs around £20, depending on traffic.

Edinburgh has two **train** stations—**Haymarket** in the West End and **Waverley**, the main station in the city center at the east end of Princes Street. **Virgin Trains East Coast** (www.virgintrainseastcoast. com; ✆ **03457/225-111**) link London's King's Cross with Waverley

PREVIOUS PAGE: **Edinburgh Castle viewed from Princes Street Gardens.**

station, depart London every hour or so, take about 4½ hours and cost from £134 round-trip, with frequent online promotions. **Scotrail** (www.scotrail.co.uk; ✆ **0330/303-0111**) operates the Caledonian Sleeper service—overnight trains from London with sleeper berths. One-way fares cost from £66. There's a taxi stand in Waverley station and Edinburgh's bus station is only a short walk away.

The least expensive way to travel between London and Edinburgh is by **bus,** but it's a 9½ hour journey. **MegaBus** (www.megabus.com; ✆ **0900/1600-900**) is the cheapest option with one-way fares costing from £13. **National Express** (www.nationalexpress.com; ✆ **0208/458-3096**) has one-way fares costing anywhere between £17 and £68. Busses depart from London's Victoria Coach Station to Edinburgh's **St Andrews Square Bus Station.**

If you're **driving,** Edinburgh is 46 miles east of Glasgow and 105 miles north of Newcastle-upon-Tyne in England. No express motorway links Edinburgh with London, which lies 393 miles to the south. The M1 from London takes you part of the way north, and then becomes the A1—otherwise known as the "Great North Road"—leading drivers along the coast to enter Edinburgh from the east. Allow 8 hours or more if you're driving from London. A city bypass, the A720, circles Edinburgh and routes from all other directions meet this road, making it easy to enter the city from whichever point suits you. The M8 links Edinburgh with Glasgow and connects with the city on the west side of the bypass, while the M90/A90 travels down from the north over the Forth Road Bridge.

VISITOR INFORMATION Edinburgh's main **Tourist Information Centre** (www.visitscotland.com; ✆ **0845/225-5121**: Mon–Sat 9am–9pm in summer, 9am–5pm winter and Sundays year round) is at the street level of Princes Street Mall, next to Waverley train station and the Balmoral Hotel. Staff can also help book a place to stay and sightseeing tickets. There's also an info desk at Edinburgh Airport (✆ **0131/473-3690**).

GETTING AROUND Many of Edinburgh's attractions are scattered around a small area along or around the Royal Mile, Princes Street, or one of the major streets in New Town. As such it's easy to explore on foot.

Edinburgh's **bus** system is operated by **Lothian Buses** (www.lothianbuses.com; ✆ **0131/555-6363**); its frequent, inexpensive service covers every corner of the city. The fare for a one-way journey of any distance is £1.50 for adults, 70p for children aged 5 to 15, free for children under 4. A **Day Saver Ticket** allows 1 day of unlimited travel on city buses at a cost of £3.50 for adults and £2 for children. You need to have the exact change to buy tickets. Route maps and timetables can be downloaded from Lothian Buses' website or found at one their travel shops on either Waverley Bridge or Hanover Street. Both offices are open

Monday through Friday 9am to 6pm and Saturday 9am to 5.30pm. The Waverley Bridge Travel shop also opens on Sunday from 10am to 5:30pm and is open until 7pm Monday and Thursday.

You can hail a **taxi** or pick one up at any of Edinburgh's numerous taxi stands. Meters begin at £2.10 and increase £2 every ⅔ mile. Taxi stands are at Hanover Street, North St Andrews Street, Waverley Station, Haymarket Station, Lothian Road, and Lauriston Place. Fares are displayed in the front of the taxi, including extra charges for night drivers or destinations outside the city limits. To call a taxi, try **City Cabs** (☏ **0131/228-1211**) or **Central Radio Taxis** (☏ **0131/229-2468**).

Most residents don't **drive** around the center of Edinburgh; public transport is very good, the city's traffic system is tricky, and parking is expensive and difficult to find. Metered parking is available (exact change required) but some zones are only for permit holders; vehicles with no permit are towed away and Edinburgh's traffic wardens are notoriously active in handing out tickets. A yellow line along the curb indicates no parking. Major parking lots are at Castle Terrace, convenient for Edinburgh Castle, Lothian Road, and the West End; and St John Hill, convenient for the Royal Mile and St James Centre (entrance from York Place), close to the east end of Princes Street.

The cobbled streets in the New and Old Towns can make **cycling** a challenge, as does the fact that the city is hilly. That said, there's a network of bike paths round the city that many love. Bike rental companies include **Leith Cycles** (www.leithcycleco.com; ☏ **0131/467-7775**) rentals start at £12 for a half-day and include a helmet, lock, map, and puncture repair kit. Children's bikes, trailers, and tag-alongs can also be rented.

CITY LAYOUT   Edinburgh is a compact city, at its center the Old and New Towns, separated by the grassy divide of Princes Street Gardens. The **Royal Mile** forms the spine of the **Old Town** snaking downhill from Edinburgh Castle to the Palace of Holyroodhouse. A labyrinth of ancient wynds (small lanes) and steep stone stairways spreads out on either side, while to the south is the **Grassmarket,** a wide, open street where criminals were once hung on the gallows. Today cafes, pubs, and shops line this historic thoroughfare, spilling out onto its pavements in summer.

To the north of Old Town is the Georgian **New Town,** a masterpiece of neoclassical town planning, its broad avenues, leafy squares and elegant crescents created between 1765 and 1850 in response to overcrowding in the dark and claustrophobic Old Town. Peppered with gourmet restaurants, buzzing bars, smart shops and attractions, such as the **National Portrait Gallery,** the New Town rolls down to the village-like **Stockbridge** with its cafes, delis and boutiques. From here you can walk along the city's narrow meandering river, the Water of Leith to **Dean Village** (another rural pocket) and the **National Gallery**

Edinburgh & Environs

of Modern Art. Or head in the other direction and you'll emerge in the revamped docklands of Leith with its Michelin-starred restaurants and gastropubs.

Between the city center and Haymarket is the **West End** where there are a cluster of performance spaces such as **Usher Hall** and the **Traverse Theatre.** Edinburgh's **Southside** is mostly residential, with the sprawling park known as the **Meadows,** Edinburgh University, as well as suburbs such as Marchmont.

> ### World Heritage Edinburgh
>
> Edinburgh's Old and New Towns have been designated a UNESCO World Heritage site, in recognition of their historical and architectural importance. **Edinburgh World Heritage** (www.ewht.org.uk) provides a wealth of information to help visitors make the most of their time here. You can follow a range of themed trails, such as *Walk in the Footsteps of Robert Louis Stevenson,* around the Heritage Site; pick these up at the Tourist Information (p. 473) or download them from Edinburgh World Heritage's website, along with accompanying podcasts.

The Neighborhoods in Brief

OLD TOWN   The **Royal Mile** is the backbone of the Old Town, a medieval thoroughfare snaking along the spine of the volcanic crag that supports **Edinburgh Castle** to the flat land of Holyrood Park—home to the **Palace of Holyroodhouse** and the imposing **Arthur's Seat.** English author Daniel Defoe described the Royal Mile as "the largest, longest, and finest street for buildings and number of inhabitants in the world." Little has changed today, and you haven't really experienced Edinburgh until you've explored the Old Town's dark, history-soaked streets.

NEW TOWN   North of the Old Town, Edinburgh's New Town is one of the largest Georgian developments in the world, a network of elegant squares, terraces, and circuses. It stretches from Haymarket in the west to Abbeyhill in the east and from Canonmills at its northern perimeter to Princes Street, its main artery, along the southern tier. The **West End Village** north of Shandwick Place is peppered with chic shops and gastropubs. While technically outside New Town, Edinburgh's **West End** leads along Lothian Road where you'll find many of the city's theatres, cinemas, and nightclubs.

BRUNTSFIELD   This suburb to the southwest of the Old Town is fringed by **Bruntsfield Links,** the park where James IV gathered his Scottish army before marching to their devastating defeat at Flodden in 1513. It's also the site of the mass graves of the city's plague victims. Today, the main thoroughfare, Bruntsfield Place, is lined with quirky boutiques and bustling cafes.

STOCKBRIDGE   Northwest of New Town, Stockbridge is one of Edinburgh's hidden gems. Once a village on the outskirts of the city, it was

The Royal Mile.

incorporated into Edinburgh in the 19th-century, yet still retains a village feel. This is an upmarket area with a bohemian edge and is known for its delis, cafes and galleries, and its proximity to the **Water of Leith** and Edinburgh's **Botanic Gardens.**

LEITH   Once a down-at-heel area, the revamped **Port of Leith,** the city's major harbor, opens onto the Firth of Forth. The port might not flex the maritime muscle it used to, but the regeneration has given it a new lease of life, the waterfront now lined with fish restaurants and lively pubs. Today, cruise ships dock at Leith's Ocean Terminal and although this isn't an area in which many visitors stay, it's one of the best places in the city to eat and a must-see for anyone wanting to glimpse the often overlooked maritime side of Edinburgh past and present.

[Fast FACTS] EDINBURGH

ATMs   There are ATMs all over Edinburgh and most are open 24/7.

Babysitters   A reliable service is provided by Super Mums (www.supermums. co.uk; ✆ **0131/225-1744**).

Business Hours
Banks are usually open Monday through Friday 9am to 5pm; some also open on Saturdays from 10am to 3pm. Stores generally open Monday through Saturday 9 or 10am to 6pm;

on Thursday some stores open until 8pm. Offices generally open Monday through Friday 9am to 5pm.

Doctors & Dentists
If you have a dental emergency, go to the **Chalmers**

Dental Centre, 3 Chalmers St. (☎ **0131/536-4800**), which has a walk in clinical service. Children under 16 will be treated at the Children's Department of the **Edinburgh Dental Institute** on Lauriston Place (☎ **0131/536-4920**). On evenings and weekends, call the **Lothian Dental Advice Line** ☎ **0131/536-4800** or **NHS 24** on ☎ **111.** You can seek advice from NHS Lothian's Lauriston Building, 1 Lauriston Place (☎ **0131/536-1000**). However, the city's 24-hour Accident and Emergency Department is located at the **Royal Infirmary of Edinburgh,** 51 Little France Crescent, Old Dalkeith Road (☎ **0131/536/1000;** www.nhslothian.scot.nhs.uk).

Emergencies Call ☎ **999** for the police, an ambulance, or firefighters.

EXPLORING EDINBURGH
Along the Royal Mile

The Old Town's **Royal Mile ★★★** is, in fact, 1 mile and 107 yards long and stretches from Edinburgh Castle all the way down to the Palace of Holyroodhouse. It's made up of a chain of linked streets: Castlehill, Lawnmarket, High Street, and Canongate and is lined with a mix of museums, churches and shops selling cashmere, tweed and whisky—and a fair bit of tartan tat—to the tourists who flock here. Walking its length you'll see some of the most fascinating parts of the old city, including a section of the **Flodden Wall** if you veer off along St Mary Street. Built in the 16th century, this 1.2m-thick (4 ft.) structure used to mark the city limits. The point where a fortified gateway once stood as it crossed the Royal Mile was known as the World's End. Today a pub of the same name now stands near the spot.

Holyrood Park, which opens out at the bottom of the Royal Mile, is a dramatic landscape, characterized by rocky crags, a loch, sweeping meadows, and a tiny ruined chapel. The 250m-high (820 ft.) peak of **Arthur's Seat ★★★** is the park's crowning glory, rewarding all who climb with heart-stopping views over Edinburgh and the Pentland Hills and Firth of Forth beyond.

Edinburgh Castle ★★★ HISTORIC SITE   Few locations in Scotland have lore equal to that of Edinburgh Castle. The very early history is somewhat vague, but in the 11th century, Malcolm III and his Saxon queen, later venerated as St Margaret, founded a building on this spot. There's only a fragment of their original pile in St Margaret's Chapel, which dates principally to the 1100s. After centuries of destruction, demolitions, and upheavals, the buildings that stand today are basically those that resulted from the castle's role as a military garrison over the past 300-odd years. It still barracks soldiers. And many of the displays are devoted to military history, which might limit the place's appeal for some. The castle vaults served as prisons for foreign soldiers in the 18th century, and these great storerooms held hundreds of Napoleonic soldiers in the early 19th century. Some prisoners made wall carvings still seen today.

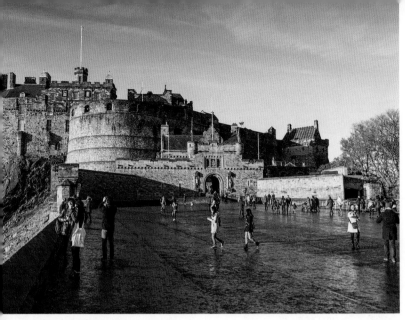
Edinburgh Castle entrance.

However, it is not all about war. Visitors can see where Mary, Queen of Scots gave birth to James VI of Scotland (later James I of England) in 1566. Scottish Parliaments used to convene in the Great Hall of the castle. Another highlight for visitors is the Scottish Crown Jewels, used at the coronations, along with the scepter and sword of state of Scotland and the infamous Stone of Scone.

It's not the easiest attraction to navigate if you have a disability—there are cobblestones, steep hills and the chapel and prisons have narrow entrances. But there is a mobility vehicle and a number of wheelchairs.

Castlehill. www.edinburghcastle.gov.uk. ℂ **0131/225-9846.** £16 adults, £13 seniors (60+), £10 children 5–15, free for children under 5. Apr–Sept 9:30am–6pm, Oct–Mar 9:30am–5pm last admission 1 hr. before closing.

Gladstone's Land ★ HISTORIC SITE   Dip into this 17th-century merchant's house on the Royal Mile, one of the few surviving Old Town tenements (many were pulled down and rebuilt in the 1800s) to get a real feel for the living conditions at this time—of the wealthier classes. There's a reconstructed shop at street level and upstairs an apartment, decorated in the original style with period furnishings and a glorious painted ceiling dating back to 1620. The top two floors can be rented through the National Trust for Scotland as a holiday apartment.

477B Lawnmarket. www.nts.org.uk. ℂ **0131/226-5856.** £7 adults, £5 seniors and children. Apr–June and Sept–Nov daily 10am–5pm; July–Aug daily 10am–6:30pm.

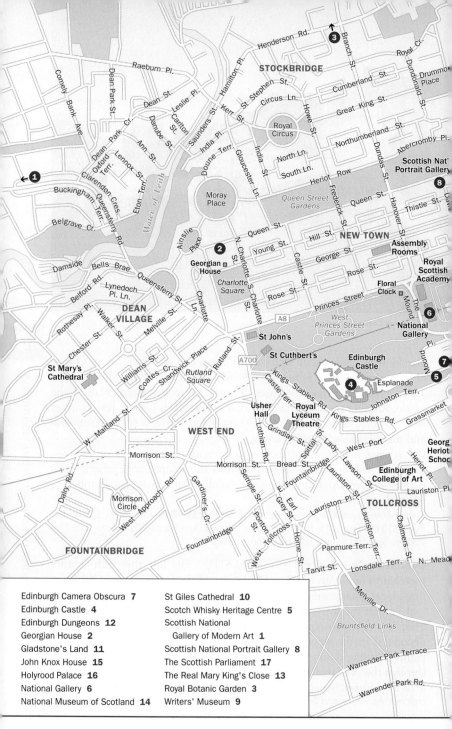

Edinburgh Camera Obscura **7**

Edinburgh Castle **4**

Edinburgh Dungeons **12**

Georgian House **2**

Gladstone's Land **11**

John Knox House **15**

Holyrood Palace **16**

National Gallery **6**

National Museum of Scotland **14**

St Giles Cathedral **10**

Scotch Whisky Heritage Centre **5**

Scottish National
  Gallery of Modern Art **1**

Scottish National Portrait Gallery **8**

The Scottish Parliament **17**

The Real Mary King's Close **13**

Royal Botanic Garden **3**

Writers' Museum **9**

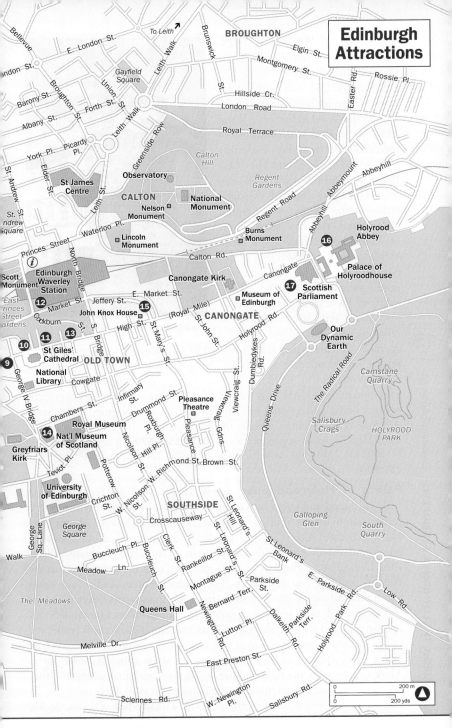

Edinburgh Attractions

To Leith ↗

BROUGHTON

Bellevue

E. London St.

Brunswick

Elgin St.

Montgomery St.

London St.

Easter Rd.

Rossie Pl.

Barony St.

Broughton St.

Forth St.

Leith Walk

Union St.

Hillside Cr.

St.

York Pl.

Albany St.

Picardy Pl.

London Road

Royal Terrace

Gayfield Square

Greenside Row

Calton Hill

Regent Gardens

Abbeymount

Abbeyhill

St Andrew St.

Elder St.

St James Centre

Observatory

CALTON

Nelson Monument

National Monument

Regent Road

Abbeyhill

Holyrood Abbey

16

St. Andrew Square

Waterloo Pl.

Lincoln Monument

Burns Monument

Calton Rd.

Palace of Holyroodhouse

Princes Street

Scott Monument

Edinburgh Waverley Station

Canongate Kirk

Canongate

17 Scottish Parliament

East Princes Street Gardens

12

Market St.

Jeffery St.

E. Market St.

Museum of Edinburgh

Cockburn St.

John Knox House

15

High St.

St. Mary's St.

(Royal Mile)

St John St.

CANONGATE

Holyrood Rd.

Our Dynamic Earth

11 **13**

Bridge

Dumbiedykes Rd.

Camstane Quarry

10

St Giles' Cathedral

OLD TOWN

National Library

Cowgate

Viewcraig St.

The Radical Road

9

George IV Bridge

Chambers St.

Infirmary St.

Drummond St.

Pleasance Theatre

Viewcraig Gdns.

Queens Drive

Salisbury Crags

HOLYROOD PARK

Royal Museum

14 Nat'l Museum of Scotland

Roxburgh Pl.

Pleasance

Hill Pl.

W. Richmond St.

Brown St.

Greyfriars Kirk

Nicolson St.

Teviot Pl.

Potterrow

Crichton St.

University of Edinburgh

W. Nicolson St.

SOUTHSIDE

St Leonard's Hill

St Leonard's St.

Galloping Glen

South Quarry

George Sq. Lane

George Square

Crosscauseway

Clerk St.

St Leonard's Bank

St Leonard's St.

E. Parkside Rd.

Low Rd.

Walk

Buccleuch Pl.

Buccleuch St.

Rankeillor St.

Parkside St.

Meadow Ln.

Montague St.

Holyrood Park Rd.

The Meadows

Queens Hall

Newington Rd.

Bernard Terr.

Lutton Pl.

Dalkeith Parkside Terr.

Melville Dr.

East Preston St.

Sciennes Rd.

W. Newington Pl.

Salisbury Rd.

0   200 m
0   200 yds

John Knox House ★ HISTORIC SITE Arguably the most picturesque dwelling house in Edinburgh's Old Town, the John Knox House is characteristic of the "lands" that used to flank the Royal Mile. Its interior is a showcase of medieval craftsmanship, including a frescoed ceiling in The Oak Room. And John Knox himself is an important figure, the acknowledged father of the Presbyterian Church of Scotland, the Protestant tenets of which he established in 1560. While some regard him as a prototypical Puritan, he actually proposed progressive changes in the ruling of the church and in education. Knox lived at a time of great religious and political upheaval; he

The John Knox House.

spent 2 years as a galley slave and later lived in exile in Geneva. Upon his return, he became minister of St Giles and worked to ensure the Reformation's success in Scotland. Even if you're not overly interested in the firebrand reformer (who may have never lived here anyway), this late-15th-century house still merits a visit. Today Knox's house is joined to the Scottish Storytelling Centre, with its bright cafe and performance space.

43-45 High St. www.tracscotland.org. ⓒ **0131/556-9579.** £5 adults, £4 seniors, £1 children 7 and up, under 7 free. Mon–Sat 10am–6pm (Sun noon–6pm July–Aug).

Palace of Holyroodhouse ★★★ HISTORIC SITE The Royal Mile is topped and tailed by a castle and a palace. While the former is a fortress drenched in military history and housing an arsenal of weapons, Holyrood, the Queen's official residence in Scotland, is all lightness, grace, and charm. Holyrood started life as an Augustinian abbey built by King David I of Scotland in 1128. It morphed over the centuries into the elegant building you see today. The complimentary audio tour takes about an hour as you wind through the State Apartments heavy with tapestries and still used for official functions, but it's Mary Queen of Scots' apartments and the Darnley rooms that give the biggest thrill (you'll see the place where her lover Rizzio was murdered). In terms of access, the Great Staircase has 27 steps and there's a steep spiral staircase up to Mary Queen of Scots bedchamber (with no wheelchair access). Other areas are accessible and manual wheelchairs are available.

Canongate. www.royalcollection.org.uk. ⓒ **0131/556-5100.** £11 adults, £10 seniors/students, £7 under 17, free under 5, £30 families, with complimentary audio tour. Nov–Mar 9:30am–4:30pm; Apr–Oct 9:30am–6pm.

Palace of Holyroodhouse, an official residence of Queen Elizabeth II.

National Museum of Scotland ★★ MUSEUM   With a subject matter as broad as "Scotland," the resulting collection was always going to be a bit of a mish-mash. There are dinosaurs, meteorites, the jaws of a sperm whale, and frocks—in fact, some 12,000 objects make up the museum (including the adorable Hillman Imp, one of the last automobiles manufactured in Scotland). It's a bit like a stroll through a living encyclopedia, but worth dipping into for the magnificent Victorian Grand Gallery alone. Plus there's a cafe, brasserie, shop, regular events, and, up on the roof, The Tower Restaurant, a fine dining spot from restaurateur royalty James Thomson, with stunning views of the Castle.
Chambers St. www.nms.ac.uk. ✆ **0300/123-6789.** Free. Daily 10am–5pm, closed Dec 25, Dec 26 noon–5pm, Jan 1 noon–5:30pm.

Edinburgh's Camera Obscura ★ OBSERVATION POINT   This is Edinburgh's oldest purpose-built tourist attraction. An optician, Maria Short, added the white Victorian Outlook Tower to the building in 1853 and topped it with a periscope, which throws a revolving image of Edinburgh's streets and buildings onto a circular table in the top chamber. You can pick people up on a piece of paper as they walk up to the castle—while the guide shares tales of the city's landmarks and history. The other five floors are crammed with interactive optical illusion exhibits—great fun for kids.
Castlehill. www.camera-obscura.co.uk. ✆ **0131/226-3709.** £14 adults, £12 seniors and students, £10 children 5–15. July–Aug daily 9am–9pm; Sept–Oct and Apr–June daily 9:30am–7pm; Nov–Mar daily 10am–6pm.

St Giles' Cathedral ★★ CATHEDRAL   This moodily magnificent cathedral standing sentinel on the Royal Mile is also known as the High

Kirk of Edinburgh, and is one of the most important churches in Scotland. Its oldest parts date to 1124, but after a fire in 1385 many sections were rebuilt and altered during its 19th century restoration. The brooding stone exterior features a distinctive crowned spire and graceful flying buttresses. Don't skip Thistle Chapel. Built in 1911 and dedicated to the Knights of the Thistle, Scotland's order of chivalry, this intricate space houses beautiful stalls and detailed heraldic stained-glass windows.

High St. www.stgilescathedral.org.uk. ℂ **0131/225-9442.** Free (£3 donation suggested). May–Sept Mon–Fri 9am–7pm, Sat 9am–5pm and Sun 1–5pm; Oct–April Mon–Sat 9am–5pm and Sun 1–5pm.

Scotch Whisky Heritage Centre ★ MUSEUM/ENTERTAINMENT COMPLEX   A theme-park style barrel ride spins you through the whisky-making process at this popular attraction. After you are "taught" how to sample a wee dram, the tour finishes in a bar housing the world's largest whisky collection.

354 Castlehill. www.scotchwhiskyexperience.co.uk. ℂ **0131/220-0441.** £14 adults, £12 seniors and students, £7 children 6–17, £35 families. Daily Sept–May 10am–5:30pm; June–Aug 10am–6pm.

The Scottish Parliament ★★ ARCHITECTURE   Like it or loathe it, this bold and controversial modern building stands opposite the Palace of Holyroodhouse at the east end of the Royal Mile and embodies a strong statement of Scotland's past, present, and future. Designed by the late Spanish architect Enric Miralles, who died before his vision was completed, this unique building cost a cool US$893 million. The abstract motif repeated on the facade facing the Canongate was apparently inspired by Raeburn's painting of *Rev. Walker skating on Duddingston*

The Scottish Parliament building, opened in 2004.

Loch, which hangs in the National Gallery of Art. To understand the philosophy behind the architecture and to enter the debating chamber, a guided tour is a must.

Canongate. www.scottish.parliament.uk. ✆ **0131/348-5200.** Free. Mon, Fri, and Sat 10am–5pm; Tues–Thurs 9am–6:30pm.

New Town

Georgian House ★ ARCHITECTURE   Robert Adam designed this Georgian gem at the heart of Charlotte Square in 1796. The gracious drawing and dining rooms filled with antique furnishings, china, and artwork capture the elegance of the era while the servants' quarters give a sense of below-stairs life.

7 Charlotte Sq. www.nts.org.uk. ✆ **0131/226-3318.** £7 adults, £6 children, students, and seniors, £17 families. Mar and Nov daily 11am–4pm; Apr–June and Sept–Oct daily 10am–5pm; July–Aug daily 10am–6pm.

National Gallery Complex ★★ GALLERY   The grand columned buildings of this imposing museum complex, slap bang in the middle of Princes Street Gardens, have real stage presence—and are a fitting home for Scotland's small but carefully chosen collection of fine art from the early Renaissance to the end of the 19th century, including important works from Raphael, Rembrandt, Rubens, Velazquez, El Greco, Van Gogh, and Cézanne, as well as a dedicated Scottish collection.

The Mound. www.nationalgalleries.org. ✆ **0131/624-6200.** Free; fees for some temporary exhibitions. Fri–Wed 10am–5pm; Thurs 10am–7pm.

Scottish National Gallery of Modern Art ★★ MUSEUM   A (decapitated?) head emerges from the pavement at the entrance of Modern One, a grand Neoclassical building dating back to 1825. Across the road is Modern Two, originally a 19th-century orphanage. Together, the galleries in both buildings showcase an impressive, sometimes kooky, permanent collection, from works by Picasso and Matisse to Damien Hirst and Tracey Emin, along with a series of changing exhibitions. The head in front of Modern One, by the way, is one of Antony Gormley's six Times' sculptures, a series of cast-iron, life-size figures rising out of the river and pavement. It's the sculpture park that's the biggest draw,

15

EDINBURGH, THE LOTHIANS & ST ANDREWS

Exploring Edinburgh

Edinburgh has many claims to bookish fame including being the world's first **UNESCO City of Literature** (www.cityofliterature.com) and home to the biggest literary shindig in the world, the **Edinburgh International Book Festival** (www.edbookfest.co.uk) each August. From Robert Burns to Ian Rankin, Sir Walter Scott to JK Rowling, this is a city steeped in the written word. Even the flagstones outside **The Writers' Museum** ★ (www.edinburghmuseums.org.uk; 𝄢 **0131/529-4901**), a 17th-century hidden gem in Lady Stair's Close off the Lawnmarket, are inscribed with inspirational quotes from poets and authors. The treasure trove of portraits, relics, and manuscripts belonged to three of Scotland's greatest writers: Robert Burns (1759–96), Sir Walter Scott (1771–1832), and Robert Louis Stevenson (1850–94) and is open Monday to Saturday 10am to 5pm, and on Sundays in August noon–5pm. To delve deeper into the city's literary heritage hit the streets with **Edinburgh Literary Tours'** walking tour (£10) or an evening **Lost World Literary Pub Crawl** (£8); www.edinburghbookloverstour.com for both.

however, featuring works by Henry Moore and Barbara Hepworth. Slightly off the beaten tourist track—not that anywhere in Edinburgh is much of a schlep—the Scottish National Gallery of Modern Art is just above the Water of Leith, the little river that tumbles through the city. 73-75 Belford Rd. www.nationalgalleries.org. 𝄢 **0131/624-6200.** Free. Daily 10am–5pm.

Scottish National Portrait Gallery ★★ GALLERY This grand red sandstone Arts & Crafts building dates back to 1889; it was the first purpose-built portrait gallery in the world. Today, its mix of intimate rooms, and light-filled contemporary spaces are strung with images, from paintings to photographs, of famous and not-so-famous Scots. It's a wonderful place to dip into to marvel at the ornate Great Hall, the detailed frieze of notable persons in chronological order and external decorative statues of Scottish poets and monarchs. 1 Queen St. www.nationalgalleries.org. 𝄢 **0131/624-6200.** Free. Daily 10am–5pm, until 6pm Aug.

Organized Tours

Every city seems to have a hop on, hop off open-top **bus tour** these days and they can be a fun introduction to the main sights. **Edinburgh Bus Tours** (www.edinburghtour.com; 𝄢 **0131/220-0770**) has a range of routes and themes, starting on Waverley Bridge and lasting around an hour. Tickets cost £14 for adults, £13 for seniors and students, and £6 for children aged 5 to 15.

There's no shortage of literary and ghost tours nowadays but back in 1985 when a group of history teachers set up **Mercat Tours** (www.mercattours.com; 𝄢 **0131/225-5445**) they were ground-breaking.

View of Edinburgh from Calton Hill, with the Dugald Stewart Monument in foreground.

Thirty years on and a clutch of awards later they're still going strong—as are two of the original tours: "Secrets of the Royal Mile" and "Ghosts and Ghouls." Tickets start at £11 for adults and £6 for children 5 to 15 (no children under age 5).

Outdoor Activities

Calton Hill ★★★ MONUMENT   Edinburgh is said to have been built, like Rome, on seven hills—although which hills is disputed. Calton Hill is one, with its medley of monuments at the summit including the unfinished (the money ran out) 19th-century **Scottish Monument** designed to replicate the Parthenon in Athens. The **Nelson Monument** contains relics of the man himself and is crowned by a large time ball to enable vessels on the Firth of Forth to set their chronometers accurately, while the **Dugald Stewart Monument,** modeled after the Tower of the Winds in Athens, boasts one of the best view in the city. **Calton Old Cemetery** (enter via Waterloo Place), dating from the 1700s, is also worth a detour. It's the resting place of many famous Scots including the philosopher David Hume. The **Scottish-American Soldiers Monument** is crowned with a statue of Abraham Lincoln to remembers the Scots who fought for the Union during the American Civil War.

Calton Hill can be entered via Waterloo Place and Royal Terrace. Free except for the Nelson Monument (£4). Oct–Mar Mon–Sat 10am–3pm; April–Sept Mon–Sat 10am–7pm, Sun noon–5pm.

EDINBURGH'S famous FESTIVALS

Summer in the city is a festival frenzy. However, there are festivals peppered throughout the year, kicking off with **Hogmanay** (www.edinburghshogmany.com; ☎ **0844/573-8455**) the capital's world-famous 3-day New Year's Eve revelries. Show-stopping events include a torchlight procession and one of the biggest street parties in the world on Princes Street (ticket-only—it's a sell-out so book early. The spectacular firework display at midnight over the castle can be seen all over the city).

In the spring, the **Edinburgh International Science Festival** (www.sciencefestival.co.uk; ☎ **0131/553-0320**) takes place each April, followed by the **Leith Festival** for 10 days in June (www.leithfestival.com; ☎ **0131/555-4104**) and the **Edinburgh International Film Festival** (www.edfilmfest.org.uk; ☎ **0131/623-8030**) at the end of the month. July sees the **Edinburgh Jazz & Blues Festival** heralding the start of festival season proper (www.edinburghjazzfestival.com; ☎ **0131/473-2000**).

The summer's clutch of world-class festivals celebrating theatre, music, opera, dance, comedy, street theatre, literature and art, to name but a few, all started with the **Edinburgh International Festival** (www.eif.co.uk; ☎ **0131/473-2000**) in 1947. It attracts major international stars in all those fields, from jazz artist Chick Corea to movie star Juliette Binoche in the title role of *Antigone*. The box office at **The Hub,** an old church on Castle Hill is open daily year-round.

The **Edinburgh Festival Fringe** (www.edfringe.com; ☎ **0131/226-0026**), or "the Fringe," was created at the same time as an opportunity for anybody—professional or amateur—to put on a show wherever they can find an empty stage or street corner. The Fringe is the biggest arts festival in the world with street performers, comedy, offbeat theatre and late-night cabaret. The box office is at 180 High St. (the Royal Mile).

One of the most exciting August spectacles is the **Royal Edinburgh Military Tattoo** (www.edintattoo.co.uk; ☎ **0131/225-1188**), which takes place over 3 weeks every night except Sundays on the floodlit esplanade in front of Edinburgh Castle. First performed in

Royal Botanic Garden Edinburgh ★★ PARK/GARDEN   Edinburgh is a green city dotted with parks, but the jewel in the crown is the Botanic Gardens. Established in the 17th century, today the 70-acre site is a haven of tranquility. Highlights include the **Chinese Hillside,** its slopes bushy with the largest collection of wild-origin plants outside China; the rock garden (5,000 plants at any one time); and the steamy **Victorian Palm House.** The cutting-edge, eco-designed visitors center houses a cafe upstairs that spills outside, and exhibition space, a shop, and a nursery. **Inverleith House,** an 18th-century mansion in the grounds, hosts temporary art exhibitions. There are guided garden tours at 11am and 2pm during the summer, or just while away an hour or two lying on the grass with a picnic.

Arboretum Place. www.rbge.org.uk. ☎ **0131/248-2909.** Gardens free; glasshouses £5 adults, £4 seniors, under 15 free. Daily (except for Dec 25 and Jan 1), Nov–Jan 10am–4pm, Feb and Oct 10am–5pm, Mar–Sept 10am–6pm.

1950, the Tattoo features the precision marching of the Massed Band of Her Majesties Royal Marines and other regiments from around the world, along with Highland dancing, motorcycle displays, and the heart-stirring massed pipes and drums bands, concluding with the poignant spectacle of the Lone Piper playing high up on the castle ramparts. The Tattoo Office is at 32 Market St. behind Waverley station.

Other festivals during August include the **Edinburgh International Book Festival** (www.edbookfest.co.uk; ✆ **0845/373-5888;** see the box on p. 486); the **Edinburgh Art Festival** (www.edinburghartfestival.com; ✆ **0131/226-6558**) and the **Edinburgh Comedy Festival** (www.edcomfest.com).

Tickets for many shows at the International Festival and Military Tattoo sell out months in advance, so book early. Ways to save money include opting for lower-priced preview shows at the start of the festival and the Fringe's 2-for-1 ticket deals that can be bagged on the first Monday and Tuesday of the festival. The Fringe also operates a Half Price Hut by the National Gallery Complex on the Mound.

The Royal Edinburgh Military Tattoo takes place every August.

Especially for Kids

There are dungeons, a castle or two and giant pandas, what more could kids want? And, when they need to let off steam, there are plenty of parks and beaches nearby. A wild scramble up **Arthur's Seat** is always a good bet or for a breath of salty air, head to the town beach at **Portobello** for fish and chips on the seafront or an ice-cream on the sand.

Craigmillar Castle ★ CASTLE   Dubbed Edinburgh's other castle, Craigmillar is one of Scotland's best preserved medieval castles with plenty of nooks and crannies to explore and large lawns for picnicking. At its heart is a late 14th-century tower whose labyrinthine interior is filled with a complex of rooms including a Great Hall and Queen Mary's Room where the Queen of Scots is said to have stayed. A large complex of buildings grew around the tower, however, much of these are now merely picturesque ruins.

Arthur's Seat at Holyrood Park.

Craigmillar Castle Rd. www.historic-scotland.gov.uk. ☎ **0131/661-4445.** £6 adults, £3 children. Apr–Sept daily 9:30am–5:30pm; Oct–Mar Sat–Wed 9:30am–4:30pm. Take any bus to the Royal Infirmary, it is a ½ mile walk to the castle.

Edinburgh Dungeons ★ THEME PARK This 80-minute roller-coaster of a journey through a 1,000 years of Scottish history with a cast of costumed actors is a highly staged, Disney-style attraction. From body snatchers Burke and Hare to cannibalism in the caves of Galloway it's funny, scary, and a little corny, and not ideal for very young children.
31 Market St. www.thedungeons.com. ☎ **0871/423-2250.** £17 adults, £16 students and seniors, £13 children 5–15. Open daily. Hours vary; check website.

Edinburgh Zoo ★★ ZOO Giant Pandas Tian Tian (Sweetie) and Yang Guang (Sunshine) are so popular that you have to book a timed viewing slot to see them. The penguins, splashing about in the largest outdoor penguin pool in Europe with a waterfall feature and water shoot, are also a big hit. Scotland's largest animal collection is on the western edges of the city and spreads over 32 hectares (79 acres) of hillside park-land with views towards the Pentland Hills. The zoo is home to more than 1,000 animals including many endangered species.
134 Corstorphine Rd. www.edinburghzoo.org.uk. ☎ **0131/334-9171.** £18 adults, £16 seniors and students, £14 children 3–14, £58 families. Apr–Sept daily 9am–6pm; Oct and Mar daily 9am–5pm; Nov–Feb daily 9am–4:30pm.

The Water of Leith ★

Meandering along the 12-mile wooded trail that hugs the **Water of Leith,** a ribbon-like river that tumbles from the Pentland Hills down to

underground EDINBURGH

Tall tales of an underground city have been circulating for years, not all of which are unfounded. Abandoned railway tunnels lead under New Town, a legacy of old train lines that once linked the ports along Edinburgh's coast with Waverley station. However, it's in Old Town that tales of underground Edinburgh take on a mythical status. It's long been rumored that a network of secret tunnels spread out from Edinburgh Castle, one of which leads under the Royal Mile to the Palace of Holyroodhouse. However, more grounded in the real world are stories of bricked over streets. In the late 18th and early 19th centuries as the fortunes of Old Town declined, anyone with the funds to do so fled its cramped unhygienic closes for the wide-open streets of the blossoming New Town. Most of the dilapidated housing around the Royal Mile was demolished, and in the case of streets such as Mary King's Close, the lower levels were simply built over and tales of underground streets with resident ghosts passed into urban legend.

In the late 1990s, the old street level sections of Mary King's Close were rediscovered and are, today, one of Edinburgh's spookiest tourist attractions. Hidden beneath the City Chambers, you enter **The Real Mary King's Close ★★** (www.realmarykingsclose.com; ✆ **0845/ 070-6244**) via Warriston's Close off the Royal Mile. Costumed actors lead you back to the 17th century through a haunted underground warren of old houses where people lived and worked for centuries. You learn about Mary King herself and the last man to leave her close, whose ghost is believed to still occupy his old house (Nov–Mar Sun–Thurs 10am–5pm and Fri–Sat 10am–9pm, and Apr–Oct daily 10am–9pm). Admission is £13 for adults, £12 seniors and students and £8 for children 5 to 15.

The Water of Leith.

the now swank docklands in Leith to meet the Firth of Forth, you could easily forget that you were in the heart of the city (www.waterofleith.org. uk). You can dip in and out, following the brown signposts from the visitor center in Balerno (pick up a map here or download it from the website) as the track passes landmarks such as Murrayfield Stadium, the Modern Art Galleries, Dean Village, Stockbridge, and the Royal Botanic Gardens. **Dean Village** is a picture-perfect little pocket, the old grain milling buildings converted into apartments, the high arched **Dean Bridge** (1833) designed by Thomas Telford. Dip into **Warriston Cemetery** an overgrown oasis—now a designated nature reserve—designed in 1842 with catacombs, Gothic arches and moss-blanketed war graves. Think tree-shaded pathways, scampering squirrels, and blackberry picking among the tombs.

Leith ★

Leith is the hub of Edinburgh's long maritime history. Archaeological excavations discovered medieval wharfs dating back to the 12th century, while today cruise ships still dock at Ocean Terminal. For years a dilapidated area, over the last couple of decades the Shore has been revamped and is now a chic spot sprinkled with gastropubs, Michelin-starred restaurants and even a boutique hotel, the cobbled waterfront scattered with interpretive boards depicting old harbor life.

The biggest tourist draw is the **Royal Yacht Britannia ★** (www. royalyachtbritannia.co.uk; © **0131/555-5566**) moored at Ocean Terminal. Launched on April 16, 1953, this 125m (410 ft.) luxury yacht sailed more than a million miles before she was decommissioned in 1997. Onboard, an audio tour takes you around the five levels including

Interior of the Royal Yacht Britannia, Leith.

the decks where Prince Charles and Princess Diana strolled on their honeymoon, the Royal Apartments, engine room, and captain's cabin. It costs £14 for adults, £13 for seniors and £9 for children and is open daily November to March 10am to 3:30pm; April to September 9:30am to 4:30pm and October 9:30am to 4pm.

Where to Stay

Edinburgh has a dizzying array of accommodation. Now, along with the traditional no-frills options such as **Ibis** (www.accorhotels.com; ✆ **0131/ 240-7000**) and **Premier Inn** (www.premierinn.com; ✆ **0871/527-8368**) you can find two outposts of German budget design chain, **Motel One** (www.motel-one.com; ✆ **0844/693-1077**) both just a stone's throw from Waverley Station and with rooms from £69. Then there is the budget airline equivalent of the hotel chain: **Tune Hotel Haymarket,** directly opposite the train station and tram stop, is the perfect crash pad if you've an early or late flight. Using the low-cost airline model, rooms start at £25 and you just pay for any extras you need, such as TV, Wi-Fi— and towels (www.tunehotels.com; ✆ **0131/347-9700**).

Hostels are no longer a bare-bones option. Many are now spruced up, sleek alternatives to the traditional guesthouse with private rooms as well as dorms. **Edinburgh Central,** a five-star hostel and part of the Scottish Youth Hostel Association, at 9 Haddington Place, along Leith Walk (www.syha.org.uk; ✆ **0845/293-7373**) has single en suite rooms from £37 and double and twins from £54.

Added to this you have the meteoric rise of **Airbnb** (www.airbnb. co.uk) and there's never been so much choice for visitors. Of course, during the busiest times of the year—the summer festival season from late July to early September and Hogmanay (New Year)—you still need to book as far in advance as possible and prepare for sharp price rises. Surfing the **Edinburgh Principal Hotel Association** website, www. stayinedinburgh.net you can often get great deals. Other useful sites include **Edinburgh Festival Rentals** (www.edinburghfestivalrentals. com; ✆ **0131/221-1646**) and **Festival Flats** (www.festivalflats.net; ✆ **01620/810-620**).

If you have an early flight and want a more characterful option than the airport Hilton, **The Bridge Inn** in the tiny village of Ratho (27 Baird Rd, EH28 8RA; www.bridgeinn.com; ✆ **0131/333-1320**) is a gourmet bolthole which feels a million miles away from the city but is actually just 20 minutes by car from the center of Edinburgh and 10 minutes from the airport. Four charming double rooms start at £80 with breakfast.

NEW TOWN

Expensive

The Balmoral ★★★ As soon as the doorman ushers you from fre-netic Princes Street into the elegant marble foyer, you're enveloped in a chic cocoon filled with eclectic artwork and fresh flowers. The Victorian

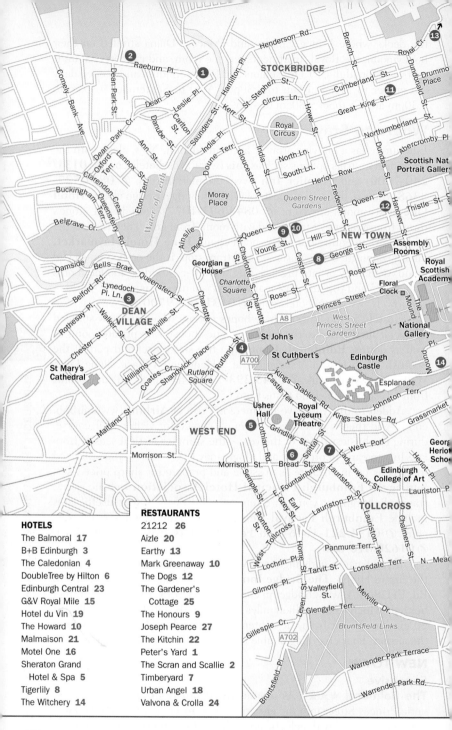

STOCKBRIDGE

NEW TOWN

Scottish Nat
Portrait Galler

Assembly
Rooms

Royal
Scottish
Academy

Floral
Clock

National
Gallery

West
Princes Street
Gardens

DEAN
VILLAGE

St Mary's
Cathedral

St John's

St Cuthbert's

Edinburgh
Castle

Esplanade

Georgian
House

Charlotte
Square

Moray
Place

Rutland
Square

Usher
Hall

Royal
Lyceum
Theatre

Grassmarket

WEST END

West Port

Georg
Heriot
Scho

Edinburgh
College of Art

TOLLCROSS

Queen Street
Gardens

Royal
Circus

Bruntsfield Links

HOTELS

The Balmoral **17**
B+B Edinburgh **3**
The Caledonian **4**
DoubleTree by Hilton **6**
Edinburgh Central **23**
G&V Royal Mile **15**
Hotel du Vin **19**
The Howard **10**
Malmaison **21**
Motel One **16**
Sheraton Grand
  Hotel & Spa **5**
Tigerlily **8**
The Witchery **14**

RESTAURANTS

21212 **26**
Aizle **20**
Earthy **13**
Mark Greenaway **10**
The Dogs **12**
The Gardener's
  Cottage **25**
The Honours **9**
Joseph Pearce **27**
The Kitchin **22**
Peter's Yard **1**
The Scran and Scallie **2**
Timberyard **7**
Urban Angel **18**
Valvona & Crolla **24**

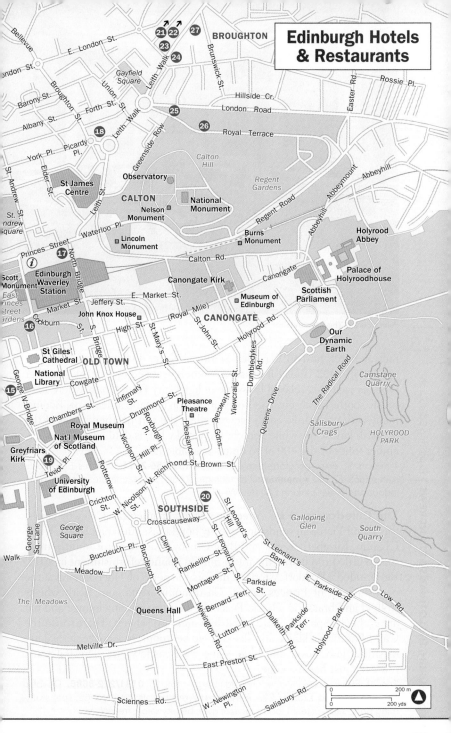

Edinburgh Hotels & Restaurants

495

Palm Court at The Balmoral.

railway hotel, next to Waverley Station with its distinctive clock tower, opened in 1902. Today, it boasts a Michelin-starred restaurant, Number One, as well as a relaxed brasserie; a light, airy Palm Court where harp music soothes away city cares over afternoon tea; and a sleek spa. Rooms, many with panoramic castle views, reflect the soft heathery tones of the Scottish landscape while Scotch, the whisky bar, is daubed in the earthy amber tones of the 400 or so drams available here.

1 Princes St. www.roccofortehotels.com. ⓒ **0131/556-2414.** Doubles £180–£565, suites £665–£2,350. **Amenities:** 2 restaurants; 2 bars; spa; sauna; steam room; gym; indoor pool; valet parking £27; free Wi-Fi.

The Caledonian ★★   Affectionately nicknamed the Caley by locals, this grand Victorian sandstone railway hotel (past guests include Charlie Chaplin, Elizabeth Taylor and Bing Crosby) was, to put it bluntly, more than a little tired before the multi-million pound refurbishment in 2012. Re-branded a Waldorf Astoria, it mirrors the perks of The Balmoral at the opposite end of Princes Street. Gastronomic restaurant (with whisky trolley) and brasserie: check. Peacock Alley, the buzzing lounge and bar area: check. Spa (the U.K.'s first by Guerlain): check. There's also the Caley Bar for cocktails, and sleekly chic bedrooms in a cool color palette of smoky grey, silver and blue, some with castle views. The Balmoral, however, just has the edge.

Princes Street. www.thecaledonianedinburgh.com. ⓒ **0131/222-8888.** Doubles £175–£689, suites £255–£2,249. **Amenities:** 2 restaurants; bar; lounge; spa; swimming pool; sauna; steam room; Jacuzzi; gym; beauty salon; free Wi-Fi.

Moderate

The Howard ★★   If you've been nursing a secret "Downton" fantasy this discreet Georgian townhouse could be the answer. Each room gets butler service; he'll unpack your suitcase, whisk away crumpled clothing for pressing or organize a private whisky tasting. There's no tea tray in the room—ring for the butler and he'll make you a fresh pot. It's more small, luxury than boutique hotel, spread throughout three Georgian town-houses. Bedrooms are on the traditional side (read slightly old-fashioned); terraced suites have their own entrance right onto one of the grandest cobbled streets in Edinburgh's New Town.

34 Great King St. www.thehoward.com. ℂ **0131/557-3500.** Doubles £125–£265, suites £215–£425. **Amenities:** Restaurant; drawing room; bar service; butler concierge and room service; valet parking; free Wi–Fi.

Sheraton Grand Hotel & Spa ★★   Its big, its modern, it's a Shera-ton. With a signature Sweet Sleeper bed—a giant marshmallow of a mattress—a good night's sleep is virtually guaranteed. And then there's the spa, One Spa. The open-air rooftop hydrotherapy pool is still a win-ner, as is the Roman-style thermal suite with its sauna, steam room, trop-ical showers, hammam, and tepidarium. The sleek new lobby has a communications hub with free Wi–Fi and PCs, while staff are as slick and professional as you'd expect in the Sheraton's U.K. flagship—especially the bartenders, whose knowledge of gin is encyclopedic.

1 Festival Sq. www.sheratonedinburgh.co.uk. ℂ **0131/229-9131.** Doubles £170–£675, suites £320–£1,200, includes breakfast. **Amenities:** Restaurant; bar; spa; indoor swimming pool; rooftop hydrotherapy pool; sauna; steam room; gym; loaner PCs; free Wi–Fi.

Tigerlily ★★   Tigerlily is not for shrinking violets. The 33 rooms and suites in this refurbished Georgian townhouse ooze sex appeal, seduc-tively outfitted in bright Designers Guild fabrics, four poster beds, lucite chairs and statement wallpapers. There are pre-loaded iPods, plasma screen televisions—and GHD hair straighteners. If the basement night-club, Lulu's is all a little too pink and disco-balled, check into the Black Room in the eaves, with its wicker egg chair and black toilet paper. It's fabulously over-the-top. Breakfast in the dimly lit restaurant booths does feel a little "morning after the night before."

125 George St. www.tigerlilyedinburgh.co.uk. ℂ **0131/225-5005.** Doubles £105–£275, suites £150-£470. **Amenities:** Restaurant; bar; nightclub; complimentary gym and swimming pool access; room service; free Wi–Fi.

Inexpensive

B+B Edinburgh ★★   There's a lot to recommend this cross between a bed-and-breakfast and boutique hotel. Set in a grand, Grade II listed 19th-century building, designed for newspaper owner John Ritchie Find-lay is one thing, each floor has a different color scheme (heather, bracken—you get the gist). Beds are comfy, furniture funky (think lucite chairs), and some rooms have freestanding bathtubs. The only disappointment is the dentist's waiting room-style scratchy carpets. At the front, rooms face the castle, but views at the back—of pretty Dean Village to the Forth and hills of Fife—are equally good. The first-floor library, with two-story-high bookshelves stacked with an eclectic collection of tomes, is the "wow" factor. The bar, walls lined with framed front pages of "The Scotsman," is a cozy spot for a dram. For every six nights you stay, you get one free.

3 Rothesay Terrace. www.bb-edinburgh.com. © **0131/225-5084.** Doubles £75–£140, includes breakfast. **Amenities:** Breakfast room; bar; library; lounge with free tea and coffee and newspapers; complimentary bike hire; free Wi–Fi.

OLD TOWN

Expensive

The Witchery ★★★   This flamboyant and fabulously gothic haven is all your historical fantasies rolled into one. James Thomson opened this restaurant with rooms in 1979 in a clutch of 16th-century buildings tucked away beneath the castle and it's still, more than three decades later, the ultimate romantic retreat. There are nine suites scattered through a higgledy-piggledy warren of buildings. Outfitted with antiques, ornately carved four–posters, rich brocades and velvets, hedonistic tubs for two, and the odd suit of armor, it's the antidote to years of mealy mouthed minimalism. Breakfast can be taken in the equally theatrical restaurant (all wood–paneling and candlelight at night) but why struggle out of bed when they'll bring a gourmet breakfast hamper to your suite? If it's fully booked, try Prestonfield (www.prestonfield.com;

The Semphill Suite at The Witchery.

C **0131/225-7800**) Thomson's second hotel and mini country estate on the outskirts of the city.

Castlehill, The Royal Mile. www.thewitchery.com. *C* **0131/225-5613.** Doubles £325–£360, includes breakfast and a bottle of champagne. **Amenities:** Restaurant; free Wi-Fi.

Moderate

G&V Royal Mile Hotel ★★   The Carlson Rezidor Hotel Group took over this modern five-star design hotel from the Missoni fashion label and some changes have been made. Fashion designer Judy R Clark and 21st-century kilt legend Howie Nicholsby redesigned the uniforms, while Glasgow-based Timorous Beasties was put in charge of the crockery and linen. Rooms have been renamed in twee *Brave*–style (wee, bonnie, braw, and muckle) but other than that, it's indistinguishable from the old hotel. Colors are still bright, patterns bold and thankfully Cucina, the fabulous restaurant set up by Giorgio Locatelli (love its Prosecco on tap), is still on property. The G&V stands for George & Victoria, with a nod to the area's royal heritage.

1 George IV Bridge. www.gandvhotel.com. *C* **0131/220-6666.** 136 units. Doubles £115–£500, suites £450–£1,000. **Amenities:** Restaurant; lobby bar; spa; room service; free Wi-Fi.

Hotel du Vin ★★   This boutique chain revolving around, and reveling in, wine is as inspired an idea today as it was when the first property opened in Winchester in 1994. With rooms named after wines and champagnes, an encyclopedic wine list, monthly Saturday wine tastings, and a giant wine glass chandelier in reception, there's no getting away from the grape. The other trademark features include the contemporary conversion of an historic building (in this case a mental asylum); a relaxed French bistro (with affordable prix-fixe menu); a bar, and, with a nod to Scotland, a whisky snug, with leather wingback chairs and a smattering of tasteful tartan. The building is a warren, and rooms vary. Many have luxurious freestanding tubs; those in the older part have sloping ceilings and beams; some look inward over the inner courtyard. For a view of Arthur's Seat, splash out on a luxury suite with terrace.

11 Bristo Place. www.hotelduvin.com. *C* **0844/736-4255.** 47 units. Doubles £99–£180, suites £150–£350. **Amenities:** Restaurant; bar; whisky snug; tasting room; room service; free Wi-Fi.

Inexpensive

DoubleTree by Hilton ★   The grand 19th St Cuthbert's Co-operative building, with its eye-catching dome, was converted in March 2014 into a Hilton Doubletree. That's good news for travelers. The Bread Street Brasserie now has a cool Parisian feel with its grey and turquoise palette and high-backed banquettes. Deluxe rooms and suites have views of the castle, while on the first Thursday of the month the penthouse becomes the Skybar and guests can swan around sipping cocktails gazing out at the rooftop panorama. Perhaps the most important new feature, however, is the signature warm chocolate chip cookie at check in.

34 Bread St. Old Town. www.doubletree.com. ℂ **0131/221-5555.** 138 units. Doubles £69–£239, suites £194–£364. **Amenities:** Restaurant; bar; 24-hr. business center; free Wi-Fi in public areas; fee in-room.

The Grassmarket Hotel ★★ Designer Jim Hamilton is a playful fellow and his sense of fun infuses this hotel. Rooms are divided into cosy (single), snug (double), and comfy categories—double, triple, and quad. All the amenities the hotel-savvy guest expects are here (rainfall showers and iPod docking stations), along with a few they probably don't, including comic strip Dandy wallpaper, a magnetic city map across one wall, and complimentary Tunnocks teacakes, for the big kid in you. In the lobby are bookshelves stacked with games and comic books. You can grab a cappuccino here, but for breakfast you need to stumble next door to Biddy Mulligans pub.

94-96 Grassmarket. www.thegrassmarkethotel.co.uk. ℂ **0131/220-2299.** 42 units. Doubles £68–£345. **Amenities:** Free Wi-Fi.

LEITH
Moderate
Malmaison ★★ This grand 19th-century building in the Scottish baronial style opened in 1885 as a Seaman's mission, housing up to 56 sailors—with room for 50 more, after a shipwreck, in the attic. It was also a "house of ill-repute" at one time, apparently. Now a design hotel, it's a respectable part of the spruced-up waterfront, its brasserie and bar buzzing, with guests spilling out onto the cobbled street. Opt for a room at the front overlooking the port, if possible, as rooms at the back are darker, and with no view to speak of. The hotel might lack a city center location, but transport links are quick and easy, and this vibrant area is now a destination in itself.

1 Tower Place. www.malmaison.com. ℂ **0131/468-5000.** 100 units. Doubles £175–£205, suites £245–£295. Bus 16 or 22. **Amenities:** Restaurant; bar; gym; room service; free Wi-Fi.

Where to Eat

Gone are the days when jokes about deep-fried Mars Bars and haggis were *de rigeur* whenever Scottish cuisine was mentioned. The country's natural larder is stocked with wild venison from ancient Highland estates, heather-fed lamb, Aberdeen Angus beef and salmon from its rushing rivers. Add shellfish from the chilly waters off the Scottish coast—langoustines (aka Dublin Bay Prawns), oysters, mussels and plump hand-dived scallops along with fish such as halibut, bream, and sea bass and the chefs have all the ingredients they need to create a gastronomic extravaganza. Fresh vegetables include asparagus, kale, and, of course, potatoes—the spuds grown in Ayrshire's sandy soils are unparalleled for their fluffy texture.

A dining room at 21212.

A good guide to grab for more dining ideas is **The List** magazine's comprehensive **Eating & Drinking Guide** updated annually and featuring reviews of hundreds of restaurants, bars, and cafes in Edinburgh. It is available to buy or check out the reviews online.

NEW TOWN
Expensive
21212 ★★★ CONTEMPORARY FRENCH   The concept is simple: a choice of two starters, a set soup course, a choice of two mains, a set cheese course, and so on. But the works of art presented to awed diners at 21212, however, are anything but simple. Michelin-starred chef Paul Kitching takes the wow factor and lets it spiral into outer space. Along with his open-kitchen theater, the dramatic restaurant design features a giant moth-themed carpet, crystal chandelier, and cool gray color scheme. The four-story Georgian townhouse also has a private dining "pod" with cherub-laced Caravaggio print wallpaper. But the food is the star. Each course is a multi-faceted explosion of flavors: a cauliflower cheese starter for instance, was an invention of Gruyere risotto, black pudding, apple, walnuts and sultanas, roasted onion, cauliflower, and Branston pickle—with foam. What are you waiting for? Book a table.
3 Royal Terrace. www.21212restaurant.co.uk. ✆ **0131/523-1030.** 5-course dinner £69, 2-course lunch £22 on weekdays. Tues–Sat noon–1:45pm; Tues–Thurs 7–9pm; Fri–Sat 6:45–9:30pm.

Mark Greenaway ★★★ PROGRESSIVE BRITISH   The pudding man cometh. When Mark Greenaway opened his eponymous restaurant in the New Town, waistbands groaned at the prospect. Deconstructed desserts—such as the Knot Chocolate tart, composed of custard jelly, frozen cookies, crème fraiche parfait, salted caramel, and kumquat puree—are the chef's stock in trade, and few do them better. He's also a master of the savory, like his signature Loch Fyne crab cannelloni with smoked cauliflower custard, lemon pearls, herb butter, and baby coriander. The surroundings are subtly dramatic: Think dark teal walls and crisp white tablecloths with a statement brass cluster chandelier. For a less formal meal, head down the hill to his second eatery, Bistro Moderne by Mark Greenaway (www.bistromoderne.co.uk; ✆ **0131/225-4431**) for French brasserie classics with a Scottish twist.

69 North Castle St. www.markgreenaway.com. ✆ **0131/226-1155.** Mains £21–£29, 3-course market menu £22, 8-course tasting menu £65. Tues–Sat noon–2:30pm, 5:30–10pm.

Moderate

The Honours ★★ BRITISH BRASSERIE   Martin Wishart's Michelin-starred eponymous restaurant down in Leith's revamped docklands might be on the formal side, but at his city center brasserie everything loosens up. Designer Ian Smith's interiors jump from Las Vegas to Dubai via Paris: bold and gold geometric brasserie bling with a dash of razzle dazzle (think: bright turquoise banquettes, a broad black-and-white striped tiled floor, and honey-hued walls). The name, incidentally, is a nod to Sir Walter Scott, who lived nearby and rediscovered the Scottish Crown Jewels known as the Honours of Scotland, which had gone missing for a century. (They had been hidden, it turns out, from the pesky English in an old oak chest in Edinburgh Castle.) The menu features a traditional lunchtime prix-fixe menu, with oysters and scallops and a lengthy grill section. Along with Donald Russell grass-fed and dry-aged beef, there's a select-breeds option that includes Black Angus cattle from Creekstone Farm and Short-horn cattle from the Glenarm Estate. Whatever you do, don't miss the sublime crab cappuccino (served, thankfully, in a large bowl instead of a coffee cup), with chunks of succulent crab submerged in a creamy bisque and topped, of course, with foam.

58A North Castle St. www.thehonours.co.uk. ✆ **0131/220-2513.** Mains £17–£33. Tues–Sat noon–2:30pm, 6–10pm.

Inexpensive

The Dogs ★★★ BRITISH REVIVAL   David Ramsden's shabby-chic little joint (old wooden pews and an eclectic collection of tongue-in-cheek dog memorabilia) on the first floor of a grand Georgian townhouse keeps pulling them in with its off-beat menu—devilled ox liver, offal toast, and Arbroath smokie fishcakes with vanilla sauce—and prices that won't mug your wallet. For dessert, don't miss the legendary lemon posset with an oat and ginger biscuit.

110 Hanover St. www.thedogsonline.co.uk. ✆ **0131/220-1208.** £10–£17. Daily noon–4pm, 5–10pm.

OLD TOWN
Moderate

Timberyard ★★★ MODERN BRITISH   The foodie Radford family's latest venture, Timberyard is housed in a sprawling 19th-century costume and props warehouse. The main event is an industrial-scale dining area with metal columns, rough-hewn floor, and tartan rugs flung over

Casual dining at The Dogs.

chairs. There's also a butchery, smokehouse, private dining in the Shed, and open-air seating in the south-facing Yard. The imaginative menu features dishes such as raw venison, burnt oak oil, shallot, mustard, and buckwheat alongside smoked beef loin, shallot, burnt ramson, cauliflower, kohlrabi, and mustard. Andrew and Lisa Radford's son Ben heads up the kitchen, while his brother Jo performs bartender alchemy, conjuring seasonal cordials along with herbal tonic for the gin and homemade cola, and ginger beer from herbs grown in the kitchen garden.

10 Lady Lawson St. www.timberyard.co. ☏ **0131/221-1222.** Mains £16–£22; 8-course set menu £55, paired drinks an extra £35. Tues–Sat noon–2pm, 5:30–9:30pm.

SOUTHSIDE
Moderate

Aizle ★★ SCOTTISH BISTRO   There's no menu here, just a list of ingredients from which your four-course tasting menu will be conjured. Yes, it's gimmicky, but it's fun and adds a sense of adventure to your dining experience. Our most recent list featured foraged wildflowers sea aster, sea plantain, pink purslane, mead, miso, feuilletine (sweet patisserie flakes), and bee pollen. It all turned out well and the *boudin blanc* with purslane, celeriac, and slivers of pear was exquisite. The decor is a little more shabby than chic—or possibly done up in a hurry—but the culinary mystery tour is magical. Aizle, by the way, rhymes with hazel (and is the old Scots word for spark or ember).

107-109 St Leonard's St. www.aizle.co.uk. ☏ **0131/662-9349.** 4-course tasting menu £35. Wed–Sun 6–10pm.

STOCKBRIDGE
Moderate

The Scran & Scallie ★★ GASTROPUB   The rise of the gastropub might be old news (although Scotland could still do with a few more), but when two Michelin-starred chefs (Tom Kitchin and Dominic Jack) start playing with the concept, they take it to a new level. This is gastropub with attitude. (*Scran* means grub and *Scallie* is scallywag). Alongside the traditional fish and chips, you'll find forgotten classics such as sheep's heid (old Scots spelling) Scotch broth and hearty dishes such as braised *hogget* shoulder (a young sheep—older than a lamb, but not as old as mutton). Design-wise, it's also up a notch, with a nod to Scandinavia (Tom's wife is Swedish) mixed in with Scottish tweeds, mismatched chairs, exposed brickwork, rough wooden floors, a wood-burner, and a scattering of sheepskin rugs.

1 Comely Bank Rd. www.scranandscallie.com. © **0131/332-6281.** Mains £10–£19. Mon–Fri noon–3pm, 6–10pm; Sat, Sun noon–10pm.

Inexpensive
Peter's Yard ★★ SWEDISH BAKERY Swede Peter Ljunquist established his first artisanal bakery and cafe in the city's Southside Quartermile conversion, a hard-angled vision of glass and pale wood, softened by the mounds of freshly baked bread. In 2012, he opened a second spot in village-y Stockbridge, adding sourdough pizzas, traditional open-topped sandwiches (like herring with oat crumble, potato, crème fraiche, and boiled egg on Swedish rye bread), cardamom buns and hot chocolate, which patrons consume at communal wooden tables or wrapped in cozy blankets at the tables outside.

3 Deanhaugh St. www.petersyard.com. © **0131/332-2901.** Pizza £10, sandwiches £5–£6. Mon–Fri 8am–9pm; Sat, Sun 9am–9pm.

CANONMILLS
Inexpensive
Earthy ★★ CAFE DELI/NEW BRITISH "Forage. Nourish. Share" is the tagline at Earthy. The staff are called Earthlings, the word "mission" is bandied about, and the cheerily painted distressed furniture is made from reclaimed timber and wind-damaged trees. The cafe is open for breakfast, lunch, dinner, all-day grazing, and takeaways. Whether you're slurping organic sweet potato soup with coconut and cardamom; munching carrot cake; or savoring a plate of seared East Lothian venison fillet with salsify, figs, buttered spinach, and a dark chocolate and chili sauce (£17), share the love and share the food.

1-6 Canonmills Bridge. www.earthy.uk.com. © **0131/556-9696.** Mains £6–£17. Mon–Sat 9am–5pm, Sun 9am–5pm, Tues–Sat 6–9pm.

EAST END
Moderate
The Gardener's Cottage ★★ BRITISH Chefs Edward Murray and Dale Mailley's communal dining hotspot is in a 19th-century stone cottage in the wooded Royal Terrace Gardens. The country flavor of this bothy (rustic shelter) is enhanced by the old wooden tables, jars of wildflowers, mismatched china, church chairs, and an old record player churning out jazz. The daily changing menu, scrawled on a blackboard,

features seasonal and local ingredients—so local in fact, that some of the herbs and vegetables are plucked from the resto's own patch, for delicious dishes such as mackerel tartare with rhubarb and sea vegetables.

1 Royal Terrace Gardens. www.thegardenerscottage.co. ℂ **0131/558-1221.** 6-course set dinner menu £30, lunch a la carte mains £15–£17. Sat–Sun 10am–2:30pm, 5–10pm; Mon, Thurs, Fri noon–2:30pm, 5–10pm.

Inexpensive

Joseph Pearce ★★ SWEDISH GASTROPUB Entrepreneurial Swedish couple Anna and Mike Christopherson have five bohemian bars and eateries but Joseph Pearce is my fave. Decor is eclectic with a retro chic vibe, junk shop chairs, soaring ceilings, comfy sofas and frilly lampshades. It's all very family-friendly: in the back there's a stack of high chairs, toys, and games. The eatery also hosts events from knitting nights to cult film and music nights. Food-wise it's a step up from your traditional gastropub grub, with a menu that includes Swedish meatballs with feta, mint and green bean salad, or a catfish fillet marinated in lemongrass and ginger with polenta fritters and caper salad. In August, swing by for traditional Swedish crayfish parties.

23 Elm Row. www.bodabar.com. ℂ **0131/556-4140.** Mains £10–£13. Sun–Thurs 11am–midnight, Fri–Sat 11am–1am.

Urban Angel ★ CAFE Urban Angel, a light and airy neighborhood cafe in the lively East End, puts an emphasis on organic foods and delivers on taste. Perennially popular with the breakfast crowd, the all-day brunch features a raw chocolate smoothie (cacao, raw almond milk, banana, and vanilla), porridge, and French toast with free-range bacon and maple syrup. Lunch from noon to 5pm is a mix of little plates (falafel balls in a curry and coconut emulsion as an example) and bigger plates, such as raw superfood salad. If you fancy an early supper, blackboard specials change every day.

1 Forth St. www.urban–angel.co.uk. ℂ **0131/556-6323.** Breakfast £4–£9, mains £8–£17. Mon–Fri 8am–8pm; Sat–Sun 9am–5pm.

Valvona & Crolla ★★ ITALIAN The Contini family are Edinburgh deli royalty—and this local institution, established in 1934, is reassuringly old school. It feels like stepping back in time, with hams dangling from the high ceiling, old wooden shelves crammed with Scottish and Italian delicacies that include the family specialty, a spicy fonteluna sausage, the recipe created in their Italian mountain village a thousand years ago. At the back of the long, narrow shop, the space opens out into a cafe where you can tuck into traditional rustic fare, made from recipes handed down over the years and washed down with a fine vintage plucked from the shelves for the shop price plus £6 corkage. There's a wine recommendation next to each dish in case you're daunted by the staggering array to choose from.

19 Elm Row. www.valvonacrolla.co.uk. ℂ **0131/556-6066.** Mains £10–£16. Mon–Thurs 8:30am–6pm; Sat–Sun 8am–6:30pm; Sun 10:30am–4pm.

Leith

Expensive

The Kitchin ★★★ MODERN BRITISH   After stints in a clutch of three-Michelin-starred restaurants in London, Paris, and Monte Carlo, Tom Kitchin came home and opened his own restaurant in an old whisky warehouse in the rejuvenated Leith docklands in 2006. Just 7 months later, at the age of 29, he became the youngest chef-proprietor to be awarded a Michelin star. Other notches on his belt include a string of TV appearances. His philosophy, From Nature to Plate (also the name of his first book), focuses on Scotland's abundant natural larder. Don't miss the signature surf and turf starter, pig's head and langoustine. Main courses of note include Ox (boudin of Inverurie ox tongue with braised ox shin, bone marrow potato, Parisienne carrots, and Perthshire girolles) and Lamb (a selection of Highland lamb with raw vegetable salad and black olive jus). The restaurant is intimate and understated, despite the chef-y window onto the kitchen.

78 Commercial St. www.thekitchin.com. ℂ **0131/555-1755.** Mains £28–£36, 3-course set lunch £29. Tues–Sat 12:15–2.30pm; Tues–Thurs 6:30–10pm; Fri–Sat 6:30–10:30pm.

Shopping

The best places to shop are Edinburgh's "village" neighborhoods. George Street, in New Town, is a high-end high street, crowned at its eastern edge off St Andrews Square with a large branch of **Harvey Nichols** and a cluster of stylish shops within teetering distance along **Multrees Walk.**

In the Old Town, the **Royal Mile** is strung with shops selling cashmere, tweed and specialist whisky stores as well as a fair few stocked with tartan tat, but swing down **Cockburn Street** and **Victoria Street** and you'll stumble upon quirky boutiques. **Grassmarket** is tops for vintage clothes and, **Bruntsfield** for chic boutiques and cafe culture. Also swell: **West End Village,** a string of Georgian streets between The Caledonian hotel and Haymarket which even has its own website: www.westendedinburgh.org) promoting its independent boutiques. **Stockbridge,** meanwhile, is peppered with delis and specialist food stores, such as **IJ Mellis** cheesemonger (www.mellischeese.co.uk; ℂ **0131/226-6215**), a real hub for food lovers. It's also home to an increasingly popular farmers market every Sunday, giving the jauntily striped stalls of the original Saturday **farmers market** (www.edinburghfarmersmarket.co.uk) on Castle Terrace every Saturday morning a run for its money.

FOOD & DRINK

Demijohn ★★   The demijohns (large glass bottles) in this self-styled liquid deli are full of fragrant oils, vinegars, liqueurs, artisan wines and meads which are decanted into an Italian glass bottle of your choice.

You're encouraged to try before you buy. You might not want to sip Perthshire rapeseed oil or Elderflower Vinegar, but Sloe Gin or Bramble Scotch Whisky Liqueur? 32 Victoria St. ✆ **0131/225-3265.** www.demijohn.co.uk.

CASHMERE, TARTANS & KILTS

21st Century Kilts ★★ Contemporary takes on the kilt are the specialty of this tiny New Town store. From camouflage to Harris Tweed, PVC to denim, owner Howie Nicholsby has it all. Passion for men's skirts runs in the family: his father, Geoffrey is one of the most famous kiltmakers in Edinburgh, counting Sean Connery and Mel Gibson among past clients. For a traditional hand-sewn, made to measure kilt head to his High Street store, Geoffrey's Kilts. 48 Thistle St. www.21stcenturykilts.com. ✆ **0131/220-9450.** 57 High St. www.geoffreykilts.co.uk. ✆ **0131/557-0256.**

Anta ★★★ In 2012 designers Annie and Lachlan Stewart opened their sleek flagship store on George Street over in the New Town. Provenance is key for this brand and everything from the cushions to the capsule clothing collection is made in Scotland: the yarn for the tweeds, carpets and tartan cabin bags comes from the Western Isles and is woven in the Borders, the furniture is made from Scottish oak, while the signature ceramics are hand-decorated in the Highlands. 117-119 George St. www.anta.co.uk. ✆ **0131/225-9096.**

Hawico ★★★ This stalwart might have been producing the finest cashmere in its Scottish Borders mills for over a century, but there's not a whiff of the heritage brand about this bright, light, sleekly minimalist store which oozes class and has price tags to match. The collections and accessories are displayed with precision and artistry. 71 Grassmarket. www.hawickcashmere.com. ✆ **0131/225-8634.**

Walker Slater ★★ Specialists in Scottish tweed sounds stuffy and old-fashioned. However, this is anything but. Think a Ralph Lauren vibe in the stylishly bare-boarded stores on Victoria Street. Contemporary bespoke tailoring sits alongside rugged knitwear and linens. 18-20 Victoria St. (Menswear), 46 Victory St. (ladieswear). www.walkerslater.com. ✆ **0131/220-2636.**

Entertainment & Nightlife

Edinburgh has a year-round, vibrant cultural scene. The West End is the cradle of theater and music, with the innovative **Traverse Theatre** (www.traverse.co.uk; ✆ **0131/228-1404**) as well as the grand Victorian **Royal Lyceum Theatre** (lyceum.org.uk; ✆ **0131/248-4848**), and, for concerts, the classic and acoustically excellent **Usher Hall** (www.usherhall.co.uk; ✆ **0131/228-1155**). Nearby, the **Filmhouse** (www.filmhousecinema.com; ✆ **0131/228-6382**) offers the best in independent and art-house cinema, while for comedy **The Stand** ★★ is an Edinburgh stalwart showcasing local talent as well as big name acts (5 York Place; www.thestand.co.uk; ✆ **0131/558-7272**).

The bar and pub scene is equally vibrant from olde-worlde pubs to glitzy cocktail bars. Alongside whisky, gin is now basking in the spotlight. Edinburgh Gin (1a Rutlant Pl.; www.edinburghgindistillery.co.uk; ✆ 0131/656-2810) is created in copper stills under the city's pavements in the West End. During the day you can take a tutored tasting; at night it turns into a funky cocktail bar.

When it comes to **bars and pubs,** the **Grassmarket** in Old Town and **Broughton Street** in New Town are buzzing, as is the waterfront in the port of **Leith.** The cocktail is king in Edinburgh, and one of the best places to sip one in the New Town is **Bramble ★★** (16A Queen St.; www.bramblebar.co.uk; ✆ 0131/226-6343). This tiny boho basement bar is all exposed brickwork, dimly lit nooks and crannies and bartenders conjuring up margaritas in teacups and delicate lavender martinis. The **Voodoo Rooms ★★** (19A W. Register St.; www.thevoodoorooms.com; ✆ 0131/556-7060) offer live music, cabaret, and 60-specialty tequilas in a string of bars and ballrooms in a historic building down a little alley just off Princes Street. The main first-floor bar and restaurant is a glamorous affair with booths, banquettes, huge arched windows, and soaring ceilings ornately decorated with gold leaf.

And for a nightcap? A dram of course. There's no shortage of whisky bars and olde-worlde pubs with an eye-watering range of malts. Rustic **Whiski Rooms ★★** (4-7 North Bank St.; www.whiskirooms.com; ✆ 0131/225-7224) has a shop stocking around 500 whiskies, a bar, bistro, and tasting room—where along with traditional tastings, whisky is matched with cheese and chocolate. You can take a whisky flight in the bar or try a whisky cocktail or just relax with the perfect dram.

There's no distinct gay quarter in Edinburgh but the city's oldest gay bar is **CC Blooms** (22-24 Greenside Place; www.ccbloomsedinburgh.com; ✆ 0131/556-9331), while **The Regent** (2 Montrose Terrace; www.theregentbar.co.uk; ✆ 0131/661-8198), is a cozy traditional pub. Also check out Edinburgh's "Pink Triangle" around the top end of Leith Walk and **Broughton Street.**

SIDE TRIPS FROM EDINBURGH

Armed with a road map or a train timetable it's easy to explore historic towns, tourist attractions, and seaside resorts just a day trip from Edinburgh. If you don't fancy the DIY method, tour companies for everything from a 1-day trip to Rosslyn Chapel and the Scottish Borders to a 5-day tour of the Highlands, include **Rabbie's** (www.rabbies.com; ✆ 0131/226-3133), **Highland Experience** (www.highlandexperience.com; ✆ 0131/226-1414) and, for the personal touch, **Afternoon Tea Tours** (www.afternoonteatours.co.uk; ✆ 07873/211-856).

Falkirk Wheel ★★★ ARCHITECTURE   When an ambitious project was proposed to re-link the Union and Forth & Clyde canals, the

The Falkirk Wheel is the world's only rotating boat wheel.

major obstacle to overcome was the fact that one canal lay 35m (115 ft.) below the other and the flight of 11 locks that once joined them had been demolished. The solution, the Falkirk Wheel, is an impressive feat of modern engineering. Boats enter from one canal and the wheel, which operates according the Archimedes' principle of water displacement, rotates and discharges them into the other canal. Visitors can hop aboard a boat to experience this, the world's only rotating boat wheel, or spend time in the visitor center to find out how it was created and how it works.

Lime Rd. Tamfourhill, Falkirk. www.thefalkirkwheel.co.uk. ⓒ **08700/500-208.** Boat rides £9 adults, £5 children 3–15. Mar–Oct daily 10am–5:30pm; Nov–Mar Wed–Sun 11am–4pm. Approximately 23 miles from Edinburgh, with frequent train service between Edinburgh and Falkirk and regular buses from the town center.

Rosslyn Chapel ★★★ CHAPEL Catapulted into the limelight by Dan Brown's international bestseller *The Da Vinci Code* and the subsequent movie, this holy site, one of the alleged sites of the Holy Grail, has long been the subject of legend and lore. Every inch of this historic masterpiece, founded by Sir William St Clair in 1446, is adorned with elaborate stonework, depicting everything from devils to dragons, knights to farmer's wives, and angels playing the bagpipes. By far the most celebrated piece is the Apprentice Pillar, which an apprentice mason carved after being inspired by a dream.

Chapel Loan, Roslin (6 miles south of Edinburgh). www.rosslynchapel.org.uk. ⓒ **0131/440-2159.** £9 adults, £7 seniors, children 18 and under free. Oct–Mar Mon–Sat 9:30am–5pm, Sun noon–4:45pm; Apr–Sept Mon–Sat 9:30am–6pm, Sun noon–4:45pm.

The Forth Railway Bridge linking North and South Queensferry.

South Queensferry ★

Bridges are a relatively modern invention (and some of the high-tech new ones in this vicinity are gorgeous). Boats were the historic means of transport, which is how this tiny settlement got its name. Saint Margaret, Queen of King Malcolm III, used to cross the water here in the "Queen's Ferry." Another boat will take you from here to wildlife-rich **Inchcolm Island ★★**, home to the ruins of a 13th-century abbey. Trips aboard *The Maid of the Forth* (www.maidoftheforth.co.uk; ℂ **0131/331-5000**) depart from Hawes Pier from April to October (check the website for times); £19 for adults, £9 for children. If you're puckish, the **Hawes Inn** (www.vintageinn.co.uk; ℂ **0131/331-1990**) on the waterfront in South Queensferry was featured in Robert Louis Stevenson's *Kidnapped*. Catch a bus from Edinburgh's St Andrews bus station to South Queensferry, or a train from Waverley to Dalmeny station, a short walk from the High Street.

Hopetoun House ★ HISTORIC SITE Set amid beautifully landscaped grounds, *a la* Versailles, Hopetoun is Scotland's greatest mansion by famed architect Robert Adam and a fine example of 18th-century architecture. Seven bays extend across the slightly recessed center, and the classical style includes a complicated tympanum, as well as hood molds, quoins, and straight-headed windows. The reception rooms are filled with 18th-century furniture, paintings and statuary; from the roof there are panoramic views of the Firth of Forth. There's also a nature trail, deer park, Stables Museum and formal gardens to explore.

10 miles from Edinburgh off the A904. www.hopetoun.co.uk. ℂ **0131/331-2451.** £9 adults, £8 seniors, £5 children 16 and under, £25 families. Easter–Sept daily 10:30am–5pm (last admission 4pm).

Linlithgow ★

Mary Queen of Scots was born in **Linlithgow Palace** in 1542. Today, it's an eerily evocative ruin surrounded by sweeping parkland on the side of a loch while Linlithgow itself, a royal burgh, is one of West Lothian's most picturesque historic towns and an easy day trip from Edinburgh, 18 miles to the east. You can picnic in the parkland or for a treat, book at table at the perennially popular **Livingston's ★** in a converted stable block tucked away off the High Street. (www.livingstons-restaurant. co.uk; ✆ **01506/846-565**). **Trains** run every half-hour between Edinburgh and Linlithgow; the journey takes 20 minutes, and a round-trip fare costs £8 adults and £4 children.

Linlithgow Palace ★★ HISTORIC SITE   A devastating fire swept through the palace in 1745 and today it stands a magnificent roofless ruin, yet still imbued with a haunting power and grandeur. Wander the old royal rooms and Great Hall, gaze up at the pink-tinged walls soaring five stories high and supported by flying buttresses. From the ramparts there are panoramic views over the loch, and for a picture-perfect walk round the loch the palace forms a majestic backdrop.

Off High St., Linlithgow. www.historic-scotland.gov.uk. ✆ **01506/842-896.** £6 adults, £4 seniors, £3 children 16 and under. Apr–Sept daily 9:30am–5:30pm; Oct–Mar daily 9:30am–4:30pm.

North Berwick ★

Once dubbed the Biarritz of the North, this little seaside town, hugging a rocky promontory where the Firth of Forth meets the North Sea, might not have the old-world glamour of the French Atlantic resort, but it was once a tourist hotspot complete with tidal swimming pool built on the

North Berwick.

Side Trips

beach in 1840 for local bathing beauties. Today, it's still popular with weekenders in search of fish and chips and bracing sea air. It's just a 44-minute drive from Edinburgh along the coastal strip lined with dune-backed beaches, wildlife reserves and golf courses.

Gazing seawards the volcanic **Bass Rock,** emerges wild and white from the waves, the breeding ground each spring for the world's largest colony of gannets. Boat trips on the old wooden boat, Sula, chug out of the little harbor each day or you can spy on the birds via the live webcams in the state-of-the-art **Scottish Seabird Centre ★** (www.seabird.org; *(C)* **01620/890-202**) on the seafront. The center opens daily year-round from 10am closing at 6pm in the summer and between 4 and 5:30pm in winter. Admission costs £9 for adults and £5 for children aged 3 to 15.

Trains between North Berwick and Edinburgh run roughly every hour. The journey takes a half-hour and a day-trip costs £7 for adults, £for children.

If you overnight in the area, **Greywalls Hotel ★★** is an elegant country house hotel designed by Edwardian architect Edward Lutyens in 1901 and visited by Edward VII, who is said to have admired the views across the Firth of Forth. A stroll in the beautiful gardens created by

The gannet colony on Bass Rock, North Berwick.

Two Castles in a Single Day

The coastline heading east from Edinburgh is strung with pretty dune-backed beaches and guarded by fairy-tale castles. **Gullane, Bents,** and **Yellowcraig** are lovely sweeps of sand, but **Seacliff,** a couple of miles from North Berwick, comes with a burnt-out mansion dating back to 1750, a tiny harbor carved out of the rocks in 1890 and said to be the smallest in Scotland and a ruined 14th-century castle. Perched above a sheer cliff face, **Tantallon Castle ★** (www.historic-scotland.gov. uk; ℭ **01620/892-727**) dates back to the 1350s. It has endured a number of sieges, and the sturdy gun in the east tower is an exact replica of the one used to defend the castle in the 15th and 16th centuries. It is open April to September daily 9:30am to 5:30pm,

October-March daily 9:30am to 4:30pm; £5 adults and £3 children.

Midway between North Berwick and Gullane is **Dirleton,** one of the prettiest villages in Scotland and home to a 13th-century castle (www.historic-scotland. gov.uk; ℭ **01620/850-330**). Abandoned in 1663, **Dirleton Castle ★** looks like a fairy-tale fortification with its towers, arched entries, and oak ramp mimicking the old drawbridge. The castle was partially destroyed by Cromwell in 1650, but you can still see the remains of the Great Hall and kitchen, as well as the Lord's Chamber. The gardens date from the late 19th and early 20th century and are one of its highlights. Dirleton Castle is open April to September daily 9:30am to 5:30pm and October to March daily 9:30am to 4:30pm; £6 adults and £3 children.

15

EDINBURGH, THE LOTHIANS & ST ANDREWS

Side Trips

The ruins of Tantallon Castle, near North Berwick.

Gertrude Jekyll helps work up an appetite for dinner in gourmet French restaurant, **Chez Roux** (Muirfield, Duncur Rd., Gullane; www.greywalls.co.uk; ℭ **01620/842-144.** Doubles £240–£335)—the twice-baked cheese soufflé is legendary. Georgian **Glebe House ★** (4 Law Rd; www.glebehouse-nb.co.uk; ℭ **01620/892-608;** Doubles £120) dates back to 1780 and was originally the home of the pastor of the nearby Presbyterian Church. Today it's an elegant bed-and-breakfast near the center of town and close to the sea.

ST ANDREWS ★★

14 miles SE of Dundee; 51 miles NE of Edinburgh

There's more to St Andrews than golf. As sacrilegious as that might sound to those who've travelled halfway round the world to visit the medieval royal burgh where golf was first played in the 1400s, St Andrews is also home to the oldest and most prestigious university in Scotland—the place where the Duke and Duchess of Cambridge (William and Kate) first met. Add a magnificent ruined cathedral and a clifftop castle, a cluster of cobbled streets and a clutch of gorgeous beaches—and there are plenty of other reasons to swing by.

Essentials

GETTING THERE **Trains** from Edinburgh to Leuchars run every half-hour and take about an hour. From there a connecting bus takes you on the 8-mile, 11-minute journey to St Andrews. A one-way fare with **ScotRail** (www.scotrail.co.uk; ✆ **0330/303-0111**) is £17 and a round-trip fare is £25. The journey by **car** also takes an hour. Head northwest along the A90 and cross the Forth Road Bridge. Continue north exiting at junction 8 and follow the A91 west to St Andrews.

VISITOR INFORMATION A **Tourist Information Centre** is located on 70 Market St. (www.visitstandrews.com; ✆ **01334/472-021**) and opens April to July Monday to Saturday 9:15am to 5pm, Sunday 10am to 5pm. July to September it closes at 6pm, and 5pm on Sundays. From September to April it opens Monday to Saturday 9:15am to 5pm.

Exploring St Andrews

Tooling around the medieval streets, clambering over a ruined castle or going for a wild, wind-whipped walk along West Sands: St Andrews is easy to explore on foot. The 2-mile, seemingly endless stretch of **West Sands** is backed by grassy dunes and bordered by one of the most famous golfing greens in the world. This is where the opening scenes of the iconic movie *Chariots of Fire* were filmed. **East Sands,** by the old harbor behind the cathedral, is smaller, more family-friendly and a good place to join the **Fife Coastal Path** (www.fifecoastalpath.co.uk). On a Sunday one of the university's oldest traditions takes place along the harbor wall: the red-gowned students' post-chapel pier walk.

Known as Scotland's "Oxbridge," the **University of St Andrews** was founded in 1410 and is the third oldest in Britain. It dominates the town and its ancient stone buildings and quadrangles dot the streets: landmarks such as the tower and church of **St Salvator's College** (1450) and the courtyard of **St Mary's College,** which dates back to 1538. The three main thoroughfares, North Street, South Street, and Market Street in the middle, are threaded together by tiny cobbled alleys and run parallel to each other, meeting at the ruined cathedral.

Golf aficionados head to the other end of town for the hallowed **Old Course ★★** along with the iconic **Royal and Ancient** clubhouse and, on Bruce Embankment the recently revamped (re-opening June 2015) **British Golf Museum ★** (✆ **01334/460046;** www.britishgolf museum.co.uk) which takes you through 500 years of golfing history.

St Andrews Castle ★ CASTLE   This atmospheric 13th-century ruin teeters on the cliff-edge as the waves crash far below. At one time a bishop's palace and later a prison, its bottle dungeon carved 7m (23 ft.) down into the rock, was said to be the worst in Scotland. The castle was the scene of the trial and burning at the stake of religious reformer George Wishart in 1546, watched by Cardinal Beaton. A group of vengeful reformers murdered Beaton 3 months later and took control of the castle for almost a year. Both attacking Catholic forces and the sieging reformers dug underground passages to attack each other, a perfect example of medieval siege warfare.

The Scores. www.historic-scotland.gov.uk. ✆ **01334/477-196.** Castle only £6 adults, £3 children. Combined castle and cathedral tickets £7 adults, £4 children 5–15. Apr–Sept daily 9:30am–5:30pm; Oct–Mar daily 9:30am–4:30pm.

St Andrews Cathedral ★ CATHEDRAL   Poised on the edge of the coast by the old harbor, the evocative ruins of what was once Scotland's most important cathedral are among the most significant in the country. The cathedral was founded in 1160 and consecrated in 1318 in the presence of Robert the Bruce. The relics of St Andrew, Scotland's patron saint, were once enshrined in its high altar. Today the remaining ruins strike a dramatic pose against the North Sea, and highlights include the 12th-century St Rules Tower and cathedral museum.

Off Pends Rd. www.historic-scotland.gov.uk. ✆ **01334/472-563.** Cathedral only £5 adults, £3 children. Combined castle and cathedral tickets £7 adults, £4 children 5–15. Apr–Sept daily 9:30am–5:30pm; Oct–Mar daily 9:30am–4:30pm.

Hitting the St Andrews Links

St Andrews Links is made up of seven public courses, most famously the **Old Course,** established in 1552 and the oldest golf course in the world. This fabled course hosted the British Open in 2015. The other courses are young whipper-snapper, the **New Course,** which opened in 1895; the **Jubilee Course,** opened in 1897, in honor of Queen Victoria's Diamond Jubilee; the **Eden,** opened in 1914; the **Strathtyrum,** the most far-flung, opened in 1993; **Balgove,** a 9-hole course ideal for children, families, and beginners and the newest addition, the **Castle Course** which opened in 2008. There's no handicap limit on any of the courses, except the Old Course—max 24 men, 36 ladies, and a handicap certificate is required to play. All courses are maintained by the **St Andrews Link Trust** (www.standrews.com; ✆ **01334/466-666**) and the website outlines the procedure you need to follow to book a round.

Swilcan Bridge, with the Royal and Ancient Clubhouse and Hamilton Hall, at the 18th hole of the Old Course, St Andrews.

The **Royal and Ancient** ★ (www.randa.org; © **01334/460-000**), the world's most prestigious golf club, founded in St Andrews in 1754 by a group of noblemen, professors, and landowners, and which to this day governs the rules of golf everywhere except the U.S, was for almost three centuries an "old boys' club" but in 2014 it finally opened its doors to women. The Links Clubhouse is far less stuffy and 400 yards from the first tee of the Old Course. It's open year-round to golfers and non-golfers and offers lockers, showers, and changing facilities. There's also a bar and restaurant on site.

Where to Stay

With a world-famous golf course and historic university it's not surprising that there's no shortage of accommodations, from upmarket resort hotels to streets lined with B&Bs for the steady stream of year-round visitors.

EXPENSIVE

Old Course Hotel ★★★ This large golden-stoned golf and spa resort sticks out like a sore thumb as you approach St Andrews along the A91. It's a golfers' favorite for obvious reasons—it looms over the 17th fairway of the Old Course—although it's not actually connected to it. (The hotel does have its own championship course, The Duke's, nearby.) A traditional five-star resort, it ticks all the right boxes: gourmet restaurant, swimming pool, spa. Rooms are on the traditional side apart from the Deluxe Suites. Think a dramatic color palette of rich reds and black and white stripes, plus private balconies looking over the Old Course to the sea.

Old Station Rd. www.oldcoursehotel.co.uk. ✆ **01334/474-371.** 144 units. Doubles £175–£330, suites £300–£1,175. **Amenities:** 4 restaurants; 4 bars; pool (indoor); spa w/Jacuzzi; children's activities; concierge; babysitting; free Wi-Fi.

Peat Inn ★★   This gourmet hideaway is on all well-travelled foodies' radars. In a bucolic setting 6 miles from St Andrews, the village of Peat Inn took its name from the 18th-century coaching inn it grew up around, giving this Michelin-starred restaurant with rooms its quirky address: Peat Inn, Peat Inn. After indulging in Geoffery Smeddle's six-course tasting menu, dished up in an intimate series of small dining rooms, you meander back through the pretty gardens to the eight individually designed suites. Peat Inn, www.thepeatinn.co.uk. ✆ **01334/840-206.** 8 units. Suites £195–£225, includes breakfast. **Amenities:** Restaurant; bar; room service; free WiFi.

MODERATE

Hotel du Vin ★★   In 2014 St Andrews got its first, long overdue, boutique hotel. Hotel du Vin might be a mini-chain but it's the most exciting development to hit the hotel scene here. The wine-themed group has jazzed up the tired old Scores hotel overlooking the glorious golden sweep of West Sands beach. There's the signature French bistro and cozy bar and, with a nod to tradition, they've kept student haunt Ma Bells pub in the basement—with a makeover. Rooms range from standard to sea-view suites with comfy custom-made leather sleigh beds, fabulous bathrooms (monsoon showers or roll-top tubs). Another nod to the golfing set: Caddy Rooms with bunk beds for the cash-strapped/budget conscious. 40 The Scores. www.hotelduvin.com. ✆ **08447/489-269.** 36 units. Doubles £155–£228, suites £215–£268. **Amenities:** Restaurant; 2 bars; free Wi-Fi.

INEXPENSIVE

Cambo Estate ★★   A 10-minute drive down hedgerowed lanes from St Andrews is Cambo. Now famous for its annual snowdrop festival, the estate, tucked away in the trees, was first occupied by John de Cambo in the 12th century. You can bed down four-poster-style in the Yellow Room in the stately home's B&B, check in to a holiday cottages or an antique-peppered apartment or, from May to October, snuggle up in the Snow-drop tents. In a woodland glade close to the beach, each has a comfy bed, fire-pit and fairy lights: glamping has reached St Andrews' perimeters (4 night-breaks from £185). Cambo House, Kingsbarns. www.camboestate.com. ✆ **01333/450-313.** 5 units. Doubles £110–£144, includes breakfast. **Amenities:** Children's play area; tennis court; woodland walk and gardens; basketball court; barbecue; babysitting; free Wi-Fi.

Where to Eat

The streets are crammed with cafes and pubs and a clutch of gourmet food shops such as Italian deli **Rocca** (33 Bell St.; www.roccadeli.com;

☎ **01334/473130**) and **Mitchell's** (110-112 Market St. www.mitchells deli.co.uk; ☎ **01334/441396**) which also has a buzzing shabby chic cafe, two great cheese shops: **The Old Cheese Shop** (141 South St.; oldcheeseshop.co.uk; ☎ **01334/477355**) and **IJ Mellis** (149 South St. mellischeese.net; ☎ **01334/471410**) along with old favorites such as **Fisher and Donaldson** (13 Church St.; www.fisheranddonaldson.com; ☎ **01334 472201**) famous for its fudge donuts, and **B. Jannetta** (31 South St.; www.jannettas.co.uk; ☎ **01334/473-285**), which has more than 50 flavors of ice cream including Tablet (vanilla mixed with grainy, deliciously addictive Tablet or Scottish fudge)—so there's no excuse not to picnic on the beach. For high-class fish and chips head to **Cromars** (1 Union St.; www.cromars.co.uk; ☎ **01334/475555**) which specializes in locally caught fish and suggests local craft beers or champagne as an accompaniment.

Balgove Larder ★★ FARM SHOP/CAFE These low-slung old stone farm buildings on the outskirts of St Andrews have been transformed into a rustic chic deli, gourmet cafe and on-site butcher selling beef, game and pork from the estate. As well as fresh fruit and veg, you can buy a range of local produce including cheeses, oatcakes and delicacies such as haggis Scotch eggs. In the summer there's a pop-up restaurant in the barn.

Balgove Farmhouse, Strathyrum Estate. www.balgove.com. ☎ **01334/898-145.** Mon–Sat 9am–5pm, Sun 10am–5pm.

Rocca ★★ SCOTTISH/ITALIAN You'll need to book ahead to get a table at the restaurant where the Head Chef won TV gold: Jamie Scott was 2014 Masterchef champion. The setting is sublime, overlooking the 18th fairway, the Royal and Ancient and West Sands beach—especially at sunset. The menu is Scottish with an Italian twist featuring starters such as Pata Di Castagne, chestnut pasta, porcini mushrooms, thyme and shaved parmesan and main courses such as Perthshire Hare: biroldo sausage, hot pot, white carrots and civet sauce.

The Links. www.roccarestaurant.com. ☎ **01334/472-549.** Mains £21–£30. Mon–Sat 6:30–9:30pm, Fri–Sat 12:30–2pm.

The Seafood Restaurant ★★ SEAFOOD This glass box seemingly suspended above the cliff overlooking West Sands beach has the architectural wow factor. Its regularly changing set menus more than match the setting, with starters such as East Neuk Crab Velouté, crab bonbon, citrus crème fraîche and tarragon and mains of lemon sole, floured and roasted on the bone with brown shrimp beurre noisette, spinach and samphire. The restaurant has an equally transparent sustainable seafood policy: serving fish in season, proud of its provenance and fishing methods.

Bruce Embankment. www.theseafoodrestaurant.com. ☎ **01334/479-475.** Fixed-price lunch £22 for 2 courses, £26 for 3 courses; fixed-price dinner £49 for 3 courses. Mon–Sat noon–2:30pm, Sun 12:30–3pm; daily 6–9pm.

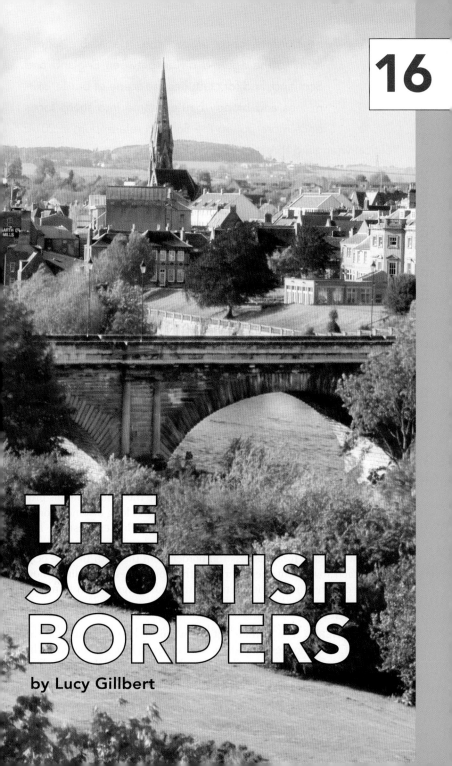

THE SCOTTISH BORDERS

by Lucy Gillbert

The Borders, once tagged the "debatable lands" forming the age-old divide between England and Scotland, and for centuries the scene of border skirmishes and bloody battles, came into sharp focus once more during the Scottish referendum in 2014. Political wrangling threatened to redraw a line that had become smudged. This gently rolling landscape dotted with sturdy stone towers and fortified farmhouses designed to defend against marauders still bears the scars of its turbulent history, but had been dozing peacefully, out of the spotlight, for years.

As it slumbered, however, tourists sped past, on their way to the Highlands and the "real" Scotland. Yet the Borders is as rich in history and natural attractions as the Scottish Highlands but with the added advantage of being off-radar, barely observed by northbound crowds.

This understated region is crammed with castles and stately homes to discover; the shadow of Mary Queen of Scots greets you at every turn and literary connections jump off each page. In fact, the novelist responsible for kick-starting tourism to the Highlands, Sir Walter Scott, lived here and you can visit his former home, **Abbotsford** just outside Melrose. Add the glorious ruins of four great 12th-century abbeys, **Dryburgh, Melrose, Jedburgh,** and **Kelso**—now linked by walking and cycling routes—and you've got plenty to keep you busy for a few days.

Long distance hiking routes include **The Southern Upland Way,** which weaves its way through the Borders, while the Pentland Hills provides trails on Edinburgh's doorstep. There are also long distance horse-riding trails celebrating a unique aspect of the Borders history. The Common Ridings evolved in response to the Borders Reivers, looters and rustlers who made forays across the border from the 13th to 17th centuries. Each town sent men to patrol the boundaries, a tradition now celebrated each summer with Return to the Ridings festivals in 11 towns.

Essentials

GETTING THERE The Borders got a new **rail** link to Edinburgh at the end of 2015—the longest new domestic railway to be constructed in the U.K. for more than 100 years. The new rail line stops at Galashiels before terminating at Tweedbank near Melrose. The journey takes 55 minutes

PREVIOUS PAGE: **Overlooking the market town of Kelso.**

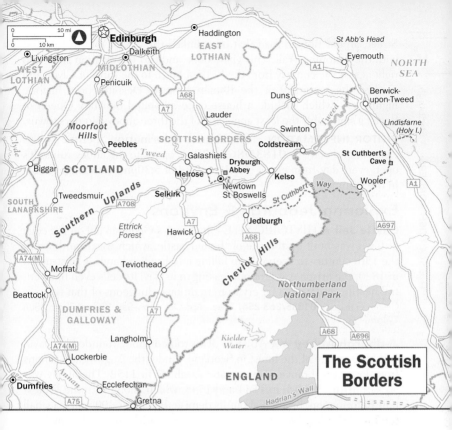

from Edinburgh Waverley (www.nationalrail.co.uk; ✆ **08457/484-950**). A handy site is **Traveline Scotland** for public transport time-tables and fares (www.travelinescotland.com; ✆ **0871/200-2233**). There are daily **buses** from Edinburgh to Jedburgh operated by **National Express** (www.nationalexpress.com; ✆ **08717/818-181**); the journey takes 1 hour 40 minutes, and the fare is £10 one-way, £19 round-trip. Perryman's Buses (www.perrymansbuses.co.uk; ✆ **01289/308-719**) operates a direct service from Edinburgh bus station to Jedburgh and Kelso. The service, the no 51/52 takes just under 2 hours to reach Kelso.

If you are **driving** from Edinburgh, join the A68 at the east side of the city bypass (A720) and follow this until the junction with the A6091, which leads west to Melrose. For Kelso fork left north of Lauder onto the A697. At Whiteburn, fork right onto the A6089, which leads to Kelso.

JEDBURGH ★

48 miles SE of Edinburgh; 57 miles N of Newcastle-upon-Tyne; 13 miles S of Melrose

Jedburgh is a low-key little market town, divided by the River Jed and built around its 12th-century Augustinian abbey. It's also close to Dere

Street, an old Roman road that once linked the city of York in England with the Antonine Wall. This giant stone and turf fortification stretched right across the country from the Firth of Forth to the Firth of Clyde and marked the boundary of the Roman Empire. Despite these historic highlights—which include a house once inhabited by Mary Queen of Scots, it's probably the least appealing of the three abbeys Borders towns.

VISITOR INFORMATION   The **Tourist Information Centre** (www. visitscotland.com; ℂ **01835/863-170**) is opposite the abbey ruins. It's open every day, from either 9 or 10am to 4 or 5:30pm, with longer hours in the summer.

Exploring Jedburgh & Environs

Castle Jail ★ HISTORIC SITE   Jedburgh's Georgian jail on the edge of town was built on the site of the old castle, which was torn down in the 15th century to keep it from falling into English hands. Constructed in 1820, the prison was groundbreaking in its day; its cells even had central heating and were a far cry from traditional dungeons of that time.

Castle Gate. ℂ **01835/863-254.** Free. Apr–Oct Mon–Sat 10am–4:30pm; Sun 1–4pm.

Jedburgh Abbey ★★ ABBEY   This ruined abbey, founded by David I in 1138, is one of the finest in Scotland. Under the Augustinian canons from Beauvais, France, it was made an abbey in 1152. The abbey was sacked by the English in 1544 and 1545, which, along with the Protestant Reformation, brought about its demise. For about 300 years, a small section of the building was used as the town's parish church, but by 1875 the ruins lay empty. Teams of architects have since restored the original

Jedburgh Abbey, founded in 1138.

medieval design and, although roofless, the abbey is fairly complete. Highlights include the late-12th-century west front, the magnificent nave, and the almost complete cloister.

Abbey Place. www.historic-scotland.gov.uk. *C* **01835/863-925.** £6 adults, £4 seniors, £3 children 15 and under. Apr–Sept daily 9:30am–5:30pm; Oct–Mar daily 9:30am–4:30pm.

Mary Queen of Scots' Visitor Centre ★ HISTORIC HOME In 1566 Mary Stuart spent a month in Jedburgh, where she almost died of a mysterious ailment after a tiring 23-mile ride from a visit to the Earl of Bothwell at Hermitage Castle. In a later lament—commenting on the emotional agonies of the last 20 years of her life—she wrote, "Would that I had died at Jedburgh." The house where she lived during this time is now crammed with paintings, engravings, and articles relating to Mary's life and death, including a lock of her hair and her death mask. You can also stroll in Mary's footsteps in the pear tree garden that joins the house—a reminder of the days when Jedburgh was famous for its fruit.

Queen St. *C* **01835/863-331.** Free. Mar–Nov Mon–Sat 9:30am–4:30pm; Sun 10:30am–4:30pm.

Near Jedburgh

Harestanes Countryside Visitor Centre ★ NATURE RESERVE This lovely courtyard conversion is just north of Jedburgh and houses a tearoom serving homemade cakes and a design shop stocked with local crafts. There are marked trails through the wooded grounds and guided walks along with family friendly activities, from Easter treasure trails to photography and basket-weaving workshops.

Ancrum. www.scotborders.gov.uk/harestanes. *C* **01835/830-306.** Free. Apr–Oct daily 10am–5pm.

Hermitage Castle ★ CASTLE Follow in the footsteps of Mary Queen of Scots, who traveled from Jedburgh in 1566 to the bedside of her lover, the Earl of Bothwell (1535–78), who lay wounded by English troops. Still mired in the misty gloom of the 1300s, this isolated medieval castle, close to the Anglo-Scottish border, is steeped in stories of murder and intrigue. Its original owner, Lord Soulis, was accused of devil worship and boiled alive by the angry townspeople. The castle was restored in the early 1800s and is now a prime spot to soak up some of the region's most turbulent history.

On an unclassified road (the castle is signposted) between the A7 and B6399, 10 miles south of Hawick. www.historic-scotland.gov.uk. *C* **01387/376-222.** £5 adults, £4 seniors, £3 children 15 and under. Apr–Sept daily 9:30am–5:30pm.

Monteviot House & Gardens ★ GARDEN Dripping in wisteria, roses and clematis, this charming country house, perched above a curve in the River Teviot, is still Lord Lothian's family home and only open to the public for 1 month a year (July). It's a wonderful architectural hodge-podge dating to the 18th century. The tranquil, 12-hectare (30 acres) garden is open from Easter to October. You can spend a lovely hour or so in the formal gardens, divided into a series of "rooms" such as the rose garden, river garden and Oriental-style garden and woodland.

Off the B6400, which leads east off the A68 north of Jedburgh. www.monteviot.com. ℰ **01835/830-380.** Garden £4 adult, under 16 free; house £5 adult, under 16 free. Garden open Apr–Oct daily noon–5pm; house July only daily 1–5pm.

Where to Eat & Stay

Just over the road from the Jedburgh Abbey on Abbey Place, the **Clock Tower Bistro** (www.clocktowerbistro.com; ℰ **01835/869-788**) is the best place in the center of Jedburgh for lunch or dinner, while the **Abbey View Café Bookshop** (ℰ **01835/863-873**) is a charming spot next door dishing up homemade cakes and coffee.

Ancrum Craig ★ From the Gold Room of this lovely 18th-century farmhouse turned stately Victorian home, you can gaze out large bay windows over lovely landscaped grounds. The other two rooms are the charming Heather Room looking onto the courtyard of the original farmhouse and the large, sunny Blue Room. In the grand drawing room you can relax in front of a roaring fire on chillier evenings.

Ancrum, Jedburgh. www.ancrumcraig.co.uk. ℰ **01835/830-280.** 3 units. Doubles £80–£100, includes breakfast. **Amenities:** Free Wi-Fi.

KELSO ★★

44 miles SE of Edinburgh; 12 miles NE of Jedburgh; 15 miles E of Melrose

Kelso is postcard pretty, its large cobbled square once the region's cattle market. Today, there's a bustling farmers market here on the fourth Saturday of the month. Sir Walter Scott called it "the most beautiful, if not the most romantic, village in Scotland," and it's still one of the most picturesque of the Borders' market towns. Lying at the point where the River Teviot meets the River Tweed, every other shop seems to sell fishing tackle. The town grew up around the abbey, now merely a crumbling shell. As well as the abbey there are two magnificent historic properties nearby, **Floors Castle** and the **Mellerstain House**, both of which were partially designed by the great architect William Adam.

Exploring the Area

Floors Castle ★★ CASTLE High upon the banks of the Tweed, Floors Castle is the magnificent home of the 10th Duke of Roxburghe and Scotland's largest inhabited castle, first created in 1721 by William Adam who was invited to extend the original building. A second Scottish architect, William Playfair, was then commissioned in the mid-19th century to remodel Floors into the grand masterpiece it is today. The breathtaking interiors are embellished by an outstanding art collection. A guided tour meanders through a succession of rooms including the Drawing Room, complete with 17th-century tapestries, and the

Floors Castle, Kelso.

sweeping ballroom with its long views of the Roxburghe estate. In the surrounding grounds there are riverside walks, a children's play area, and the holly tree that marks the spot where Scottish King James II was killed in 1460.

Off the A697, 1¾ miles north of Kelso. www.roxburghe.net. ✆ **01573/223-333.** £9 adults, £8 seniors, £5 children 5–16, under 5 free. Easter weekend and May–Sept daily 10:30am–5pm. Oct 10:30am–3:30pm.

Kelso Abbey ★ ABBEY   You can wander at will through this grand roofless ruin. Once a great ecclesiastical center, Kelso Abbey was reduced to rubble by the English in the late 16th-century. Although it might not be as impressive as other ruins in this region, it is the oldest (1128) and was probably the largest and richest. The remains of the west transept tower suggests the abbey's massive construction, and it, along with the west front are flanked by buttresses crowned by rounded turrets.

Bridge St. www.historic-scotland.gov.uk. No phone. Free. Apr–Sept daily 9:30am–4:30pm, Oct–Mar Sat–Wed 9:30am–4:30pm.

Mellerstain ★★ HISTORIC SITE   This golden-hued Georgian gem is the seat of the earls of Haddington and one of the most famous William and Robert Adam-designed mansions in Scotland. William built two wings in 1725, while his son, Robert, designed the main building 40 years later. One of Mellerstain's enduring legacies is the "Household Book" of Lady Grisell Baillie (1665–1746), the estate's most famous resident, a detailed account of 18th-century customs and social life. Another highlight is the opulent library with its exquisite plasterwork. The

525

William and Robert Adam–designed Mellerstain, near Kelso.

surrounding parkland was laid out in 1725 by William Adam, with sweeping views out towards the Cheviot Hills from the terraced garden.

5 miles northwest of Kelso off the A6089. www.mellerstain.com. ✆ **01573/410-225.** £9 adults, £4 children, under 5 free. Easter weekend, May–Sept Fri–Mon 12:30–5pm.

Outdoor Activities

Designed by Dave Thomas, one of Britain's leading golf-course architects, the par-72, 7,111-yard **Roxburghe Golf Course** (www.roxburghe.net; ✆ **01573/450-331**) is the only championship course in the region. Guests of the Roxburghe Hotel (see below) can most easily get tee times, but the course is also open to non-members.

Where to Eat & Stay

The best places to eat are **The Cobbles** (www.thecobbleskelso.co.uk; ✆ **01573/223-548**) a modern gastropub at 7 Bowmont St., and **Pharlanne** delicatessen (✆ **01573/229-745**) at 13 Bridge St.

The Old Priory B&B ★ This wonderful B&B and rambling family home, just around the corner from the abbey, has an incredibly warm and welcoming atmosphere. It's full of character and dates back to 1796—think shuttered sash windows, antiques, a large drawing room with old wooden floors, comfy sofas, books and games and an airy breakfast room where each morning you can tuck into a slap-up spread. There's also a lovely walled garden. The family suite, with original fireplace, has a twin room linked to a master double bedroom.

Woodmarket, Kelso. www.theoldpriorykelso.com. ✆ **01573/223-030.** 3 units. Doubles £85, suite £95–£160, includes breakfast. **Amenities:** Free Wi-Fi.

COLDSTREAM

The small town of Coldstream sits on the banks of the River Tweed where it forms the boundary between Scotland and England, 9 miles northeast of Kelso, and is famous for giving its name to the British army's oldest continually existing Corps—the Coldstream Guards. Part of the Queen's personal troops, the Coldstream regiment was founded more than 360 years ago and was the only one to survive the disbanding of Cromwell's New Model Army in 1661; it still undertakes active service. Learn all about this iconic regiment at the **Coldstream Museum ★** (*© 01890/882-630*) on Market Square. The museum is free and open March to September Monday to Saturday 9:30am to 12:30pm and 1 to 4pm and Sunday 2 to 4pm, and October Monday to Saturday 1 to 4pm.

Other places to visit in the town include **Henderson Park,** which stands high above the banks of the Tweed and features a monument commemorating Coldstream's connection with the guards. Take time for a riverside walk to the tiny old village of **Lennel,** 1 mile northeast of Coldstream, or the **Hirsel Estate** (www.dandaestates.co.uk; *© 01555/851-536*; off the A697 as it leads into Coldstream) for a small museum, woodland walks, and a tearoom.

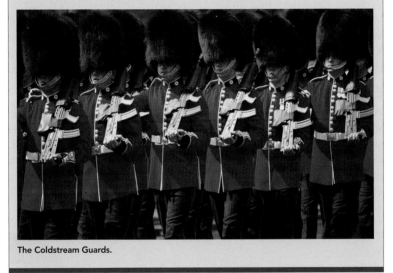

The Coldstream Guards.

The Roxburghe Hotel & Golf Course ★★ This gorgeous late-19th-century mansion is surrounded by 81 hectares (200 acres) of woodland and well-tended gardens. It was originally the Roxburghes' family home on the banks of the trout-filled River Teviot, but in 1982 it was converted into a luxurious hotel. The old stable block now houses six modern guest rooms (dogs allowed—perfect for those here for outdoor pursuits), however the 16 rooms in the main house have the most class. Think four-poster beds, luxurious drapes and a dash of classic chintz. There are roaring fires at every turn: in reception, the hallway, in the masculine book-lined bar and in the elegant drawing room. The hotel offers a whole host of activities from archery to fishing and boasts its own golf course. This could well be country house hotel-perfection.

Off the A698 at Heiton near Kelso. www.roxburghe-hotel.net. © **01573/450-331.** 22 units. Doubles £225–£265, suites £305–£345, includes breakfast. **Amenities:** Restaurant; bar; golf course; croquet lawn; spa; room service; free Wi-Fi.

MELROSE ★★

37 miles SE of Edinburgh; 70 miles NW of Newcastle-upon-Tyne; 40 miles W of Berwick-upon-Tweed

Melrose, in the shadow of the Eildon Hills, is the chicest of the Borders towns, with a clutch of lovely little shops to poke around, delis to dip into and cafes where you can quaff a cappuccino. Its rose-tinged ruined **abbey** is home to the heart of Robert the Bruce, which lies in a sealed casket. Nearby **Dryburgh,** the most romantic of the Borders' great abbeys, is the burial place of Sir Walter Scott. His former home **Abbotsford House** is just outside Melrose itself. The **Southern Upland Way** passes through Melrose, and a day's hike on the section along the River Tweed outside town is one of the most delightful and scenic walks in Scotland.

VISITOR INFORMATION   **Melrose Tourist Information Centre** at 4 Abbey St. (www.visitscotland.com; © **01896/822-283**), is open April to October Monday to Saturday 10am to 5pm and Sunday 1pm to 5pm.

Exploring the Area

Abbotsford House ★★★ HISTORIC HOME   From the sleek, state-of-the-art visitor center you can just glimpse the turrets of this grand Scottish baronial mansion designed by Sir Walter Scott himself. Before continuing to the house, it's well worth viewing the exhibition and listening to the short film, which puts his life and work into perspective and highlights not only his professional achievements, but his qualities

Abbotsford House at Melrose, built by Sir Walter Scott.

Melrose Abbey, established in 1136.

as a man. It's a moving tribute and one that leaves you feeling that this might well be the greatest Scot ever. After his literary works, Abbotsford, built on the banks of the Tweed in 1822, is thought to be his most enduring achievement. The audio tour, with an actor narrating as Scott, is a wonderfully atmospheric way to explore the house filled with artifacts he collected, from the grand entrance hall to his study and his old writing desk. His library contains 9,000 rare volumes, while the dining room overlooking the Tweed is where Scott died on September 21, 1832.

Off the B6360, 2 miles west of Melrose. www.scottsabbotsford.co.uk. ☎ **01896/752-043.** £9 adults, £5 child 5–17, £28 families. Mar–Apr 10am–4pm; May–Sept 10am–5pm; Oct 10am–4pm.

Melrose Abbey ★★ ABBEY   The view from the top of the tower over Melrose and the surrounding countryside is worth the steep schlep up the spiral stone staircase. These evocative ruins are all that's left of the ecclesiastical community established here by Cistercian monks in 1136. Sir Walter Scott was instrumental in getting the crumbling remains repaired and restored in the early 19th century, writing: "If thou would'st view fair Melrose aright, go visit in the pale moonlight." However, it's in the sunshine that the abbey's sandstone shell has a rosy glow. Elongated windows, carvings, and delicate tracery still exist along with the ground plans of two large cloisters to the north and west of the abbey. A plaque marks the spot where it's believed the heart of Robert the Bruce lies buried. Don't miss the carving of the bagpipe-playing Melrose pig and the museum filled with medieval artifacts unearthed on the grounds.

Abbey St. www.historic-scotland.gov.uk. ☎ **01896/822-562.** £6 adults, £4 seniors, £3 children 5–15. Apr–Sept daily 9:30am–5:30pm; Oct–Mar daily 9:30am–4:30pm.

A walk along **THE BORDERS: ST CUTHBERT'S WAY**

Follow in the footsteps of 7th-century St Cuthbert along the Scotland–England border by walking all or part of the 62½-mile St Cuthbert's Way, which stretches from Melrose across the border into England to the Holy Island of Lindisfarne on the Northumberland coast. St Cuthbert began his ministry in Melrose in about A.D. 650 and was later appointed Bishop of Lindisfarne, where he died and was buried in 687. Following Cuthbert's death, the community he created on the island produced one of the greatest legacies of the Anglo-Saxon period, the Lindisfarne Gospels. This marked walk starts at Melrose Abbey and passes many places linked to Cuthbert's life and legend including prehistoric relics, Roman ruins, and historic castles. The complete walk takes around 4 to 5 days to complete, or you can meander along the first part from the abbey into the nearby Eildon Hills. Visit the Melrose Tourist Information Centre for more details or see www.stcuthbertsway.info.

Thirlestane Castle ★ CASTLE   Thirlestane has been owned by the Maitland family since 1218. Over the centuries the castle has been added to and today strikes a fairytale pose of towers and turrets against the backdrop the Leader valley. The interior is a feast of ornamental plasterwork and ancestral portraits, the old nurseries are crammed with Georgian, Edwardian, and Victorian toys. A taste of life below stairs can be glimpsed among the cast-iron ranges of the old kitchen. A tour includes the room where Bonnie Prince Charlie slept in 1745.

10 miles north of Melrose off the A68. www.thirlestanecastle.co.uk. ℂ **01578/722-430.** £8 adults, £7 seniors, £4 children 5–15, £20 families. June Tues–Thurs 10am–3pm; July–Aug Sun–Thurs 10am–3pm. Grounds open until 5pm.

Where to Eat & Stay

In the center of Melrose there are two inns where you can bed down or tuck into traditional pub grub. The 18th-century black and white **Burts Hotel** (www.burtshotel.co.uk; ℂ **01896/822-285**), with flowery window boxes on the town's Market Square, or sister property the **Townhouse Hotel** (www.thetownhousemelrose.co.uk; ℂ **01896/822-645**) also with traditional black and white exterior but more contemporary and with a modern brasserie. Sprinkled among the bookshops, antique stores and interior designer shops are a smattering of delis and cute cafes such as **Apples for Jam** (ℂ **01896/823-702**) on the High Street, which pegs itself a "gallery and kitchen" with gourmet teas and coffees. If you're packing a picnic, stop at award-winning **Millers of Melrose** (ℂ **01896/822-015**) and stock up on beef and haggis pies.

In St Boswells, 5 miles south of Melrose, **The Mainstreet Trading Company** (www.mainstreetbooks.co.uk; ℂ **01835/824-087**) is a stylish emporium, part bookshop, part rustic cafe, and in a separate building across the courtyard, a thriving deli and homeware store: a real one-stop-shop from husband and wife team Rosamund and Bill de la Hey.

Buccleuch Arms ★★ This rambling, award-winning gastropub (crowned Scottish Inn of the Year 2015) on the main road between Melrose and Dryburgh is one of the best places to stay in the Borders. Dating back to 1836, the décor is eclectically shabby chic, the entrance hall with its bare floorboards and elegant antique sofas and chairs a cozy place to lounge in front of an open fire. The 19 rooms are individually designed, some with luxurious tweed drapes and headboards. The relaxed restaurant, the Blue Coo Bistrot, has a funky feel, with mismatched tables and chairs peppered through three connecting rooms—giant gilt framed pictures, a painted antler chandelier and quirky mix of kitsch memorabilia scattered around. The menu highlights local produce, and beef is a specialty; the different cuts—outlined on the cow stencil—described in detail. It's all washed down with a local beer. Breakfast is also worth a mention for the signature eggs en cocotte and kippers.

The Green, St. Boswells, Melrose. www.buccleucharms.com. ℂ **01835/822-243.** 19 units. Doubles £110–£130. **Amenities:** Restaurant; bar; free Wi-Fi.

A Side Trip to Dryburgh Abbey ★★

Amble 6 miles southeast of Melrose off the B6356 to the ruins of the Borders' fourth great abbey, **Dryburgh**. On the way take a short detour to the signposted **Scott's View ★** a famous vantage point above the Tweed Valley overlooking Sir Walter's beloved Eildon Hills.

Dryburgh Abbey ★★ ABBEY Wandering among the ancient headstones and clambering over the crumbling walls of the most secluded of all the ruined Borders abbeys, it's impossible not to be moved by its haunting beauty. Surrounded by gnarled yew trees and cedars of Lebanon said to have been planted by knights returning from the Crusades, Dryburgh's ravaged remains stand in peaceful solitude on a wide loop of the River Tweed. The gentle ruins are a place to soak up the peace and solitude that epitomized a monk's life. Sir Walter Scott was buried in Dryburgh's north transept after he died in 1832.

Off the B6356, Dryburgh. www.historic-scotland.gov.uk. ℂ **01835/822-381.** £6 adults, £4 seniors, £3 children 5–15. Apr–Sept daily 9:30am–5:30pm; Oct–Mar daily 9:30am–4:30pm.

WHERE TO STAY

Dryburgh Abbey Hotel ★ Set in 10 acres of parkland, right next to the abbey ruins on the banks of the Tweed (fishing is an obvious attraction) this country house hotel is a tranquil and traditional—if a little tired—rural retreat. It was built in 1845 as the home of Lady Grisell

Dryburgh Abbey.

Baillie and haunted by the "gray lady," who had an ill-fated affair with a monk leading to his execution and her suicide. There's an indoor pool and sauna and roaring log fires for when it's "dreich" outside.

Dryburgh Abbey. www.dryburgh.co.uk. © **01835/822-261.** 38 units. Doubles £125–£180, suites £210–£320, includes breakfast. **Amenities:** Restaurant; bar; pool (indoor); sauna; room service; free Wi-Fi.

SELKIRK ★

40 miles SE of Edinburgh; 73 miles SE of Glasgow.

One of Scotland's oldest Royal Burghs, Selkirk teeters above the Ettrick Valley, one of the Borders' most beguiling landscapes. The town itself is low-key, but the surrounding countryside is bucolic and the area has connections with Sir Walter Scott and William Wallace. Bowhill, one of the region's finest country houses, stands on the western fringes of town. The great explorer Mungo Park was born near Selkirk in 1771. Park was a doctor who won fame exploring the River Niger, where he drowned in 1806. A gleaming white statue of the explorer stands at the east end of High Street, opposite the old surgeon's hall where Park trained.

Exploring the Area

Bowhill ★★ HISTORIC SITE   This archetypal Scottish country estate is set against some of the Borders' most stunning scenery. The magnificent 18th-century mansion is the family seat of the Scotts of Buccleuch, relatives of Sir Walter Scott, who referred to the house as "Sweet Bowhill" in the poem "The Lay of the Last Minstrel." It was King Robert the Bruce himself who gave the land to the family in the 14th

The countryside around Selkirk.

century, while the origin of the name Buccleuch is steeped in romance. During the 10th century King Kenneth III was hunting in the forest when he was charged by a deer or "buck" in a ravine or "cleuch." John Scott saved the king's life by grabbing the deer by the antlers and ever since the Scotts were called Buccleuch. Bowhill's art collection includes works by Canaletto, Gainsborough, and Reynolds and is as grand as the house itself, which also contains fine French furniture, porcelain, tapestries and mementos of Sir Walter Scott. The surrounding country estate features a fabulous children's adventure playground and five trails that range from a gentle stroll around the loch to a 7-mile woodland hike. Details of Bowhill's ranger-led activities can be found in the Visitor Centre.

Off the A708, 3 miles west of Selkirk. www.bowhillhouse.co.uk. ✆ **01750/222-04.** House £10 adults, £9 seniors, £4 children 3–16; Estate £5 adults, £4 seniors and children. House Aug daily and some bank holidays 11:30am–4pm. Estate Apr–May and Sept Wed–Mon 10am–5pm; July–Aug daily 10am–5pm.

PEEBLES ★

23 miles S of Edinburgh; 53 miles SE of Glasgow; 20 miles W of Melrose

The royal burgh of Peebles stands on the banks of the River Tweed, one of Scotland's most famous salmon fishing rivers. Cradled by the Pentland Hills, Glentress Forest, and the Tweed Valley, this county town has a host of outdoor activities on its doorstep, from walking to mountain biking to fishing. The surrounding countryside is also home to ancient estates such as Traquair, whose roots reach back to the times when royal hunting parties plundered the region's great forests.

Peebles is also a writer's town. Robert Louis Stevenson lived here for a while and the town was also home to Sir John Buchan (Baron Tweedsmuir, 1875–1940), a Scottish author who was appointed Governor-General of Canada and is remembered chiefly for his World War II novel *The 39 Steps,* which Hitchcock made into a film in 1935.

Essentials

GETTING THERE The nearest **train** station is Edinburgh Waverley 23 miles away; contact **National Rail Enquiries** for train timetables and fares (www.nationalrail.co.uk; ✆ **08457/484-950**). **First** (www. firstgroup.com; ✆ **08457/484-950**) operates **bus** no. 62, a direct service from Edinburgh to Peebles that runs roughly every half-hour; the journey takes about an hour. For more information contact **Traveline Scotland** (www.travelinescotland.com; ✆ **0871/200-2233**).

If you're **driving** from Edinburgh, join the A702 from the city bypass (A720); take a sharp left onto the A703, which leads into the A701 until Leadburn, where the road reverts to the A703 and heads south to Peebles.

VISITOR INFORMATION The **Tourist Information Centre** (www. visitscotland.com; ✆ **01721/723-159**) is on High Street. It's open daily 9am to 5pm most of the year, with reduced hours in winter.

Exploring the Area

Peebles is an attractive market town, with a broad High Street lined with Victorian buildings and smattered with small, independent stores, a butcher, a baker and a deli. The Chambers Institute just off High Street houses a great little museum, **The John Buchan Story ★** (www.johnbuchanstory.co.uk; ✆ **01721/723-525**), worth dipping into to learn more about this underrated author. Peebles' striking **war memorial** stands in the courtyard opposite the Institute, and bears the names of the 225 men from Peebles who lost their lives in World War I.

Neidpath Castle, near Peebles.

Riverside walks leading into the countryside start on the banks of the Tweed as it flows through of town. Follow the river west for 1 mile to 12th-century **Neidpath Castle** ★ (www.neidpathcastle. co.uk; ✆ **01875/870-201**). Standing above the river, this romantic old building is privately owned but tours can be organized through the estate office.

Peebles is close to some of southern Scotland's most picturesque countryside including the **Pentland Hills** ★ to the northwest (www. pentlandhills.org), featuring more than 60 miles of signposted trails threading their way past the remains of ancient forts and cairns with visitor centers, off the A702 north of Penicuik and east off the A70 near Balerno. **Glentress Forest** (www.glentressforest.com) immediately northeast of Pebbles is laced with bike trails for all abilities and accessible off the A72 east of town. For details on the forest and bike rentals, contact **The Hub in the Forest** (www.glentressforestlodges.co.uk; ✆ **01721/721-736**).

Dawyck Botanic Garden ★ GARDEN   The Royal Botanic Garden Edinburgh (p. 488) owns and runs this glorious botanical garden in the Borders. A woodland garden sprawling across 25 hectares, it was once part of the Dawyck Estate. Highlights include the spring snowdrop display around the cascading Scrape Burn falls, an Azalea Terrace that bursts into life in late spring and the Beech Walk, which leads to views of Dawyck House and turns from vibrant green to a golden blaze of color in the fall. A program of guided walks around Dawyck runs throughout the season; contact the garden for details on dates and times.

Stobo, off the B712 near Bellspool, 8 miles south of Peebles. www.rbge.org.uk. ✆ **01721/760-254.** £6 adults, £5 seniors, children free. Feb and Nov 10am–4pm; Mar and Oct 10am–5pm; April–Sept 10am–6pm.

Kailzie Gardens ★★ GARDEN   As well as exploring the wild woodland walks and formal walled garden at Kailzie, from Easter until the end of August you can watch ospreys nesting in the Tweed Valley Forest Park on the live webcams placed high in the forest canopy. The gardens themselves are a feast of color during the spring and summer months. In the walled garden you can meander grassy paths between a glorious display of roses and shrubs, dipping into greenhouses showcasing fragrant wisteria along with exotic fuchsias and begonias. Old pathways lead through woodland, carpeted in spring with snowdrops, daffodils and bluebells and around a duck pond rich in bird life. The rustic restaurant, located inside an old stable building, is a great place to eat even if you aren't visiting the gardens. If you can't bear to leave there is a self-catering cottage here along with a cozy bunkhouse.

Kailzie on the B7062, 2½ miles southeast of Peebles. www.kailziegardens.com. ✆ **01721/720-007.** £5 adults, £4 seniors £1 children 5–16. Apr–Oct daily 11am– 5:30pm; Nov–Mar daily daylight hours.

Little Sparta ★★ GARDEN Artist Ian Hamilton Finlay created what has been called the "only original garden" created in Britain since 1945, which blends poetic and sculptural elements with a perfectly manicured landscape. For his inspiration he turned to the gardens created by great poet-philosophers from Epicurus to William Shenstone. Finlay died in 2006, but Little Sparta, with its metaphors ranging from the French Revolution to Scottish fishing fleets, is his legacy to the world. The garden contains some 275 sculptures made mostly of stone, wood, and metal. Little Sparta is not suitable for children under 10.

Stonypath (off the A702), 17 miles northwest of Peebles. www.littlesparta.org.uk. ✆ **07826/495-677.** £10. June–Sept Wed, Fri, and Sun 2:30–5pm.

Traquair House ★ HISTORIC HOME Dating from the 10th century, Traquair is one of Scotland's most romantic old houses. Once surrounded by ancient forests, this staunchly Stuart household has strong connections to Mary Queen of Scots and the Jacobite uprisings. One of the most poignant exhibits is an ornately carved oak cradle in the King's Room, in which Mary rocked the infant James VI.

Tours of the house lead visitors through a property rich with history and collections of portraits, books, and furniture, while in the museum you can see a letter signed by Mary Queen of Scots and a wall painting dating from the early 16th century. The surrounding grounds are an informal 40-hectare (100-acre) spread of woodland walks, a maze, craft workshops, and walled gardens. Traquair Ale is brewed on-site, in the old-fashioned way in original oak vessels. If you'd like to stay overnight in Scotland's oldest inhabited house, check into one of the three elegant rooms, which cost £190 for bed and breakfast.

The High Drawing Room at Traquair House.

Off the A72 at Innerleithen, 6 miles east of Peebles. www.traquair.co.uk.
T **01896/830-323.** £9 adults, £8 seniors, £4 children 3–16, £23 families. Apr–Sept daily 11am–5pm; Oct daily 11am–4pm; Nov weekends only 11am–3pm.

Where to Eat & Stay

Cringletie House Hotel ★   This 19th century Victorian mansion is a vision of towers and turrets set on 28 acres of well-manicured grounds, which are carpeted with snowdrops in spring and feature a 17th-century walled garden. Apart from the cutesy teddy bears propped up on the pillows, these individually designed rooms with far-reaching views of the surrounding countryside have plenty to recommend them, including original fireplaces, freestanding tubs and, in the suites, a complimentary dram each night. The spa cottage sleeps 2 to 6 and has a hot tub. Dinner is served in the elegant Sutherland Restaurant, which is open to both guests and non-guests and features a spectacular painted ceiling.
Edinburgh Rd, Peebles, off the A703 2½ miles north of Peebles. www.cringletie.com.
T **01721/725-750.** 13 units. Doubles £99–£199, suites £179–£299, includes breakfast. **Amenities:** Restaurant; bar; croquet lawn; putting green; free Wi-Fi.

The Horseshoe Inn ★★ FRENCH/SCOTTISH   This award-winning restaurant with rooms was once the local village hostelry. Today, it's still decked out in traditional style but its gourmet credentials are now stellar. You can tuck into starters such as rabbit pie with parsnip remoulade or skate terrine, salt cod brandade and dandelion, while mains such as grilled turbot, gurnard, pink fur potato, crab, bouillabaisse sauce and purple broccoli sit alongside duck breast, potato terrine, carrot puree and pak choi. And if you just want to stumble to bed after eating your fill, the inn also has eight bedrooms in a converted schoolhouse that cost £120 to £145 per night available Wednesday to Saturday night.
Off the A703 at Eddleston, 5 miles north of Peebles. www.horseshoeinn.co.uk.
T **01721/730-225.** Set 3-course lunch £25, Dinner £40, 4-course £50, 6-course tasting menu £50 per person. Wed–Sun noon–2:30pm, 7–9:30pm.

Windlestraw Lodge ★★   This secluded Edwardian country house on the banks of the Tweed is a luxurious retreat, just an hour south of Edinburgh but a million miles away from the hurly burly of city life. The house features charming rooms with wrought iron bedsteads, neutral color palettes and roll-top tubs. From the McIntosh room, you can recline on a chaise longue and gaze out over the surrounding hills. The gourmet restaurant uses produce sourced from farms all over the Borders as well as homegrown herbs, with a set four-course dinner each night. Large peaceful gardens look out over the Tweed Valley, a ready-made adventure playground where you can go walking, fishing, and cycling.
Off the A72 (Galashiels Rd.), Walkerburn, 8½ miles east of Peebles. www.windle straw.co.uk. *T* **01896/870-636.** 6 units. Doubles £170–£210, includes breakfast. **Amenities:** Restaurant; bar.

17

GLASGOW, THE WEST COAST & THE SOUTHERN HEBRIDES

by Stephen Brewer

These days a lot of old industrial cities claim to be coming back from the brink to enjoy new life and vitality. In Glasgow, that's really true, though Scotland's largest city never really lost its edge. Many of the 19th- and 20th-century shipyards and factories are shuttered, but elegant Georgian merchants' houses and grand Victorian piles remain, as does Scotland's oldest medieval cathedral and rows of tenements built to house the working class. They all speak legions about this city's down-to-earth values and an unpretentious worldliness, as much in evidence in old pubs as it is in glitzy shops, sophisticated bars and clubs, and outstanding museum collections. Glaswegians are well aware that a lot of the world considers Edinburgh to be more elegant, but they really don't care. As they like to say, the only good thing to come out of Edinburgh is the train to Glasgow.

Glasgow makes an ideal jumping off point for the Herbridean Islands just offshore. There are few better places to experience Scotland in all its rugged beauty. They're discussed later in this chapter.

Essentials

Glasgow is 47 miles west of Edinburgh, 216 miles north of Manchester, and 404 miles north of London.

ARRIVING   Glasgow Airport (www.glasgowairport.com; ✆ **0870/040-0008**) is 10 miles west of the city. The easy-to-use airport handles flights to and from London Heathrow and Gatwick and many other airports. **First** (www.firstgroup.com; ✆ **0141/423-6600;** adults £6.50 one way/£9 round-trip, kids £4 one way/£5.50 round-trip) operates shuttle bus no. 500 between the airport and several stops in Glasgow, with a final stop at Buchanan Street bus station. This 24-hour service runs up to every 10 minutes; the ride takes 25 minutes. Pay on the bus. A taxi to the city center costs about £20.

Glasgow's second airport, **Prestwick** (www.glasgowprestwick.com ✆ **0871/223-0700**) is on the Ayrshire coast, 33 miles southwest of the city center, and serves flights from across Europe. Connections to Glasgow are on **ScotRail** to Central Station (www.scotrail.co.uk;

☎ 0845/601-5929) and the X77 **Stagecoach** bus (www.stagecoach bus.com; ☎ 01292/613-500) to Buchanan Street bus station.

Glasgow's main **train** station is **Central Station** on Gordon Street. **Virgin Trains** (www.virgintrains.co.uk; ☎ 08719/744-222) operates a regular service between London Euston and Glasgow Central. The journey time is approximately 4½ hours. Caledonian Sleeper service operated by ScotRail (www.scotrail.co.uk; ☎ 0845/601-5929) runs overnight trains with sleeper berths to and from London.

Glasgow's **Queen Street Station** stands on the north side of George Square and serves the north and east of Scotland, with ScotRail trains arriving from and departing to Edinburgh every 15 minutes until 11:30pm. The journey takes 50 minutes. You can also travel to Highland destinations from this station as well as Aberdeen and Stirling.

Buchanan Street Bus Station is 2 blocks north of Queen Street Station on Killermont Street. **National Express** (☎ 08717/818-178; www.nationalexpress.com) operates a service from London's Victoria coach station. **Megabus** (www.megabus.com; ☎ 0871-266-3333) also operates a service between London Victoria and Buchanan Street. Buses take between 8½ and 11 hours to reach Glasgow, depending on the number of stops; low fares may compensate for the extra time. **Scottish Citylink** (www.citylink.co.uk; ☎ 08705/505-050) operates frequent bus service between Glasgow and Edinburgh; the journey is 1 hour 20 minutes but can be much longer during rush hour.

If **driving** from England, Glasgow is reached via the M74, which becomes the A74 as it leads into the city. From Edinburgh, the M8 joins the two cities and travels directly through the heart of Glasgow.

GETTING AROUND   While it's easy to navigate the city center on foot, you'll need to rely on public transport to visit attractions in the West End, along the river, and in other parts of the city.

Glasgow is serviced by **First buses** (www.firstgroup.com; ☎ 0141/423-6600). Services run frequently throughout the day, but are greatly curtailed after 11pm. Pick up schedules at the Travel Centre at the **Buchanan Street Bus Station** on Killermont Street (Mon–Sat 6:30am–10:30pm, Sun 7am–10:30pm) or download them from First's website at www.firstgroup.com/ukbus/glasgow. One-way fares are £1.20 for short journeys (usually up to 5 stops) and £2 for longer trips anywhere within the city. Pay on the bus, exact change required. A day pass for unlimited travel costs £4.30, and a week pass is £17.

The bright orange cars of Glasgow's single-line **subway** (underground) make a circular route with 15 stops. Hence the name, "Clockwork Orange." Trains run every 4 to 8 minutes and operate Monday through Saturday 6:30am to 11:30pm and Sunday 10am to 6pm. Tickets can be bought at any subway station and one-way fare is £1.60 adults

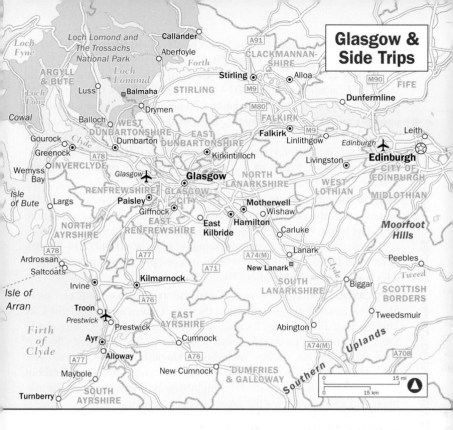

and 70p children; round-trip tickets are £3 adults, £1.35 children. Trains make the entire circuit in 24 minutes. Inner Circle trains travel in a counterclockwise direction, Outer Circle trains travel in a clockwise direction. Aside from spending some extra time underground, it doesn't really matter which direction you go in, as you'll get to your stop eventually. For more information, go to www.spt.co.uk.

You can hail **taxis** on the street or call **Glasgow Taxis** (www.glasgowtaxis.co.uk; ℂ **0141/429-7070**). When a taxi is available on the street, a "taxi" sign on the roof is lit a bright yellow. Meters start at £2.20 and increase by £1 every kilometer.

Driving around Glasgow can be hard, and really unnecessary for a sightseeing visit. The city is a warren of one-way streets, and parking is expensive and difficult to find. Metered parking is available at 60p 12 minutes in the city center, 2 hours maximum, exact change required. A yellow line along the curb indicates no parking, and some zones are marked permit holders only—your vehicle will be towed if you have no permit. Multistory parking lots, open 24 hours a day, are at Anderston Cross, Cambridge, George, Mitchell, Oswald, and Waterloo streets.

You'll pay £1.40 an hour for the first 3 hours, £2.40 thereafter, £1.50 on Sunday, and £2.50 for the overnight.

Bikes can be rented at **Gear of Glasgow,** 19 Gibson St. in the West End (gearbikes.com; ✆ **0141/339-1179**). Rates range from £15 for a half-day or £20 for a full day to £70 for a week; a driver's license or passport must be left as a deposit. You can also try the city's bike-sharing **Nextbike** system (www.nextbike.co.uk), available at stands throughout the city. You'll register via an app or hotline (✆ **020/816-69851**) and pay a £10 deposit. Prices are £1 for every 30 minutes up to 4 hours, and £10 for 5 to 24 hours after that.

VISITOR INFORMATION Glasgow City Marketing Bureau (GCMB) provides a wealth of info on its website, peoplemakeglasgow.com. In the city, stop by the Glasgow Information Centre in the Buchanan Galleries at 10 Sauchiehall St. (www.visitscotland.com; ✆ **0141/204-4400**), open Monday to Saturday from 9am to 6 or 7pm year-round, and Sundays from April to September (10am–6pm).

CITY LAYOUT Glasgow is spread out, and its neighborhoods can seem like lands apart. You can walk from the City Centre and Merchant City into the East End, though it's a bit of a trek from the City Centre out to the West End and to the cluster of museums along the River Clyde. A good transportation system, including a single-line underground (subway), makes it easy to get around. In the city center, streets are laid out in a grid that, in a bit of a stretch, might suggest Manhattan. When asking for an address, ask for the cross streets as well.

The Neighborhoods in Brief

THE EAST END & MEDIEVAL GLASGOW Most of Glasgow's history has transpired in what is now considered the East End. The city began here along the banks of the River Clyde and, in the Middle Ages, expanded up the hill where the **Cathedral of St Kentigern** was completed in 1197. **Glasgow Green,** common land since 1178, stretches from the riverbanks toward **Glasgow Cross,** the junction of High Street and four other main thoroughfares of the old city.

THE CITY CENTER & MERCHANT CITY Glasgow spread west of High Street in the 18th century, and so-called tobacco barons built elegant townhouses and warehouses in what is now known as Merchant City. As the city expanded, George Square and the blocks around Central Station became the city center, and remain so today. Many of the shop-lined streets are for pedestrians only.

THE WEST END In the Victorian era, Glasgow spread farther west, this time into what is now a lively neighborhood that is home to the University of Glasgow and the Kelvingrove and Hunterian Museums, all housed in grand neo-Gothic and baroque quarters on the edge of **Kelvingrove Park.**

ALONG THE CLYDE   Glasgow once shipped its manufactured goods around the world from docks on the River Clyde, amid shipbuilding yards and factories. These days the shores are lined with museums, office complexes, and apartment blocks.

THE SOUTHSIDE   About 3 miles south of the city center, largely residential Southside gives way to Pollok Country Park. Highland Cattle graze within sight of beautiful Pollok House.

[Fast FACTS] GLASGOW

Business Hours   Most **offices** and **banks** are open Monday through Friday 9am to 5pm; some banks also open on Saturday. Many have 24-hour ATM machines. **Shops** are generally open Monday through Saturday 9:30am to 6pm, with many city center shops remaining open until 7pm on Monday through Wednesday. On Thursday stores remain open until 8pm; many also open on Sundays from 11am to 5 or 6pm.

Currency Exchange
Most city center banks operate a *bureaux de change*. There are also currency exchanges at Glasgow Airport and Central Station, where you'll also find ATM machines.

Dentists   If you have an emergency, go to the Accident and Emergency Department of **Glasgow Dental Hospital & School,** 378 Sauchiehall St. (www. gla.ac.uk/schools/dental; ☎ 0141/232-6323). Appointments are necessary. Hours are Monday through Friday 8:30am to 5:15pm; at other times, call **NHS 24,** operated by the National Health Service (☎ 08454/242-424; www.nhs24.com). You can also call NHS 24 in an emergency.

Doctors   The major hospital is the **Glasgow Royal Infirmary,** 82-86 Castle St. (www.nhsggc.org. uk; ☎ 0141/211-4000).

Embassies & Consulates
See "Fast Facts: England & Scotland" (p. 667).

Emergencies Call ☎ 999 in an emergency to summon the police, an ambulance, or firefighters.

Pharmacies   There are branches of Boots (www. boots.com) in most of the main shopping malls and at 200 Sauchiehall St. (☎ 0141/332-1925), open Monday through Wednesday and Friday and Saturday 8am to 7pm, Thursday 8am to 8pm, and Sunday 10:30am to 5:30pm.

Police   In an emergency, call ☎ 999. For other inquiries, contact police headquarters at ☎ 0141/ 532-2000.

Post Office   The main branch is at 47 St Vincent's St. (☎ 0845/722-3344). It's open Monday through Saturday 9:30am to 5:30pm.

Safety   Glasgow is the most dangerous city in Scotland, but it's relatively safe when compared with cities of its size in the United States. Drug use is a big problem here, and with it comes muggings and other crimes. As in any big city stay alert and watch your wallet and other belongings.

EXPLORING GLASGOW

Glasgow's attractions are spread around the city. It's easiest to approach them in clusters: City Center, Merchant City, and East End in one go, West End in another, the riverside museums as a separate trip.

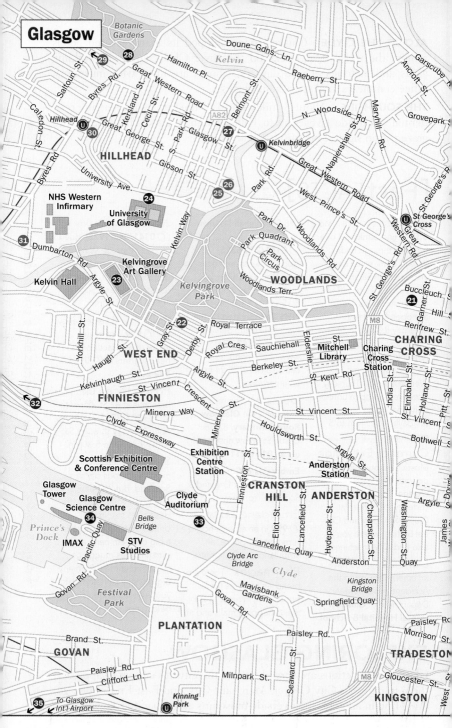

Glasgow

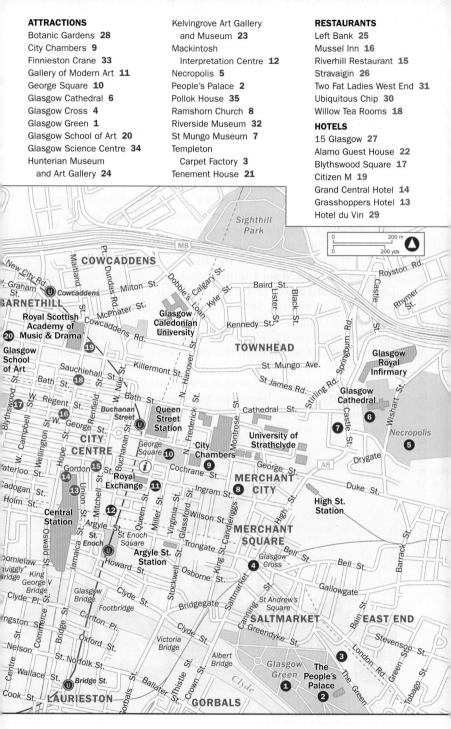

ATTRACTIONS
Botanic Gardens **28**
City Chambers **9**
Finnieston Crane **33**
Gallery of Modern Art **11**
George Square **10**
Glasgow Cathedral **6**
Glasgow Cross **4**
Glasgow Green **1**
Glasgow School of Art **20**
Glasgow Science Centre **34**
Hunterian Museum
    and Art Gallery **24**

Kelvingrove Art Gallery
    and Museum **23**
Mackintosh
    Interpretation Centre **12**
Necropolis **5**
People's Palace **2**
Pollok House **35**
Ramshorn Church **8**
Riverside Museum **32**
St Mungo Museum **7**
Templeton
    Carpet Factory **3**
Tenement House **21**

RESTAURANTS
Left Bank **25**
Mussel Inn **16**
Riverhill Restaurant **15**
Stravaigin **26**
Two Fat Ladies West End **31**
Ubiquitous Chip **30**
Willow Tea Rooms **18**

HOTELS
15 Glasgow **27**
Alamo Guest House **22**
Blythswood Square **17**
Citizen M **19**
Grand Central Hotel **14**
Grasshoppers Hotel **13**
Hotel du Vin **29**

The East End & Medieval Glasgow

Glasgow's long history makes itself known in the eastern end of the city, rather spookily so in the Cathedral Precinct. The dark hulking mass of the medieval cathedral, the city's oldest structure, rises next to a steep green hillside littered with the soaring monuments of the **Necropolis ★**, a Victorian city of the dead. If you're a Goth, you've found your place. Volunteer give free tours of the Necropolis two or three times a week; go to www.glasgownecropolis.org for schedules and a list of major monuments and to book a place; black attire is de rigueur, of course.

The medieval city stretched from here south to river, surrounding **Glasgow Green ★**. This sprawling greensward where sheep once grazed has, over the centuries played host to Bonnie Prince Charlie's 18th-century Jacobite army that tried to restore the Stuarts to the British throne, early-20th-century suffragette meetings, and 21st-century rock concerts. Facing the green is the elaborate, vaguely Moorish-looking brick **Templeton Carpet Factory,** which once supplied carpets for the Taj Mahal and Houses of Parliament and now houses the Bavarian-owned West brewery (p. 565). In 1888 James Templeton was granted permission to build his factory on the green, provided he erect a structure befitting the prestigious surroundings. So, he modeled the facade on the Doges' Palace in Venice. It collapsed during construction, killing 29 women in the adjacent weaving sheds; the statue atop the highest pinnacle of a woman holding flowers is a memorial to the victims.

Just to the west of the green is the junction of the four main streets of the medieval city at the **Glasgow Cross.** The seven-story **Tolbooth Steeple** to one side of the Cross towers above an area that is a bit more

The Victorian-era Necropolis, Glasgow.

salubrious than it was when a prison stood at its base. Witches, thieves, and murderers were often hung from a platform attached to the tower.

Glasgow Cathedral ★★★ CATHEDRAL Glasgow's oldest structure and Scotland's only complete medieval cathedral was consecrated in 1197 and dedicated to St Mungo, the city's patron. The sixth-century missionary, also known as Kentigern, spent 13 years converting Glaswegians. These efforts, along with the deprivations of a life of fasting and prayer in a rock cell, wore the poor fellow out to such an extent that he was forced to wear a bandage to support his chin. Mungo lies amid a forest of pillars in a vaulted crypt

Stained glass in Glasgow Cathedral, consecrated in 1197.

beneath the church. The fact he has lain here peacefully through the centuries, and that the church's beautiful nave and timbered roof are intact, is due, in part, to the courageous intervention of the faithful. During the destruction of churches during the 16th century Reformation, congregants linked arms around the cathedral to prevent mobs from smashing the place to bits.

Cathedral Square. www.glasgowcathedral.org.uk. © **0141/552-6891.** Free. Apr–Sept Mon–Sat 9:30am–6pm, Sun 1–5:30pm; Oct–Mar Mon–Sat 9:30am–4pm, Sun 1–4pm.

People's Palace ★★ HISTORIC SITE It's only fitting that this red sandstone pavilion built in 1898 as a cultural center for the enlightenment of slum dwellers in the East End should now trace the history of Glaswegians from 1750 through the present day. Photographs of tenements show how grim life has been for many, and provide some fascinating glimpses in such everyday realities as going to the "steamie," or communal laundry. Glasgow-trained artist Ken Currie's evocative mural of the Canton Weaver's Massacre in 1787 captures Scotland's first major labor dispute that came to a bloody end when troops fired on strikers in a village just outside Glasgow, killing six. Plenty of joyous moments are captured, too, including dances at the Barrowland Ballroom and outings aboard steamers down the Firth of Clyde. In the adjoining Winter Gardens, you can enjoy a cup of coffee amid a jungle of tropical plants, and in the forecourt of the palace is the magnificent Doulton Fountain. Sir Henry Doulton, founder of the famous tableware firm, presented what is still the world's largest terracotta fountain to Glasgow in 1887 to commemorate Queen Elizabeth's Golden Jubilee.

Glasgow Green. www.glasgowlife.org.uk. ℓ **0141/276-1625.** Free. Tues–Thurs and Sat 10am–5pm; Fri and Sun 11am–5pm.

St Mungo Museum of Religious Life & Art ★ MUSEUM Glasgow's patron saint is nicely honored with a wide-ranging look at world religions. The Hindu snake demon Naga Rassa and dancing skeletons from Mexico's Day of the Dead celebrations share space with crosses, stained glass, menorahs, and other religious artifacts. What comes through are the themes—birth, death, renewal—and the message of hope that lie at the core of all religions.

2 Castle St. www.glasgowlife.org.uk. ℓ **0141/276-1625.** Free. Mon–Thurs and Sat 10am–5pm; Fri and Sun 11am–5pm.

City Center & Merchant City

It seems that anybody who's anybody in Scotland sooner or later ends up in stone effigy in vast **George Square,** laid out in 1781 and by most calculations the city center. Novelist and poet Sir Walter Scott (1771–1832) surveys the scene from atop a 24m (80-ft.) column in the center of the square and around him is a statuary Who's Who of Scottish achievement: poet and favorite son Robert Burns (1759–96), inventor of the steam engine James Watt (1736–1819), and chemist Thomas Graham (1805–69), to name but a few. King George III (1738–1820) is here, as are Queen Victorian and her beloved prince consort Albert (the pair are

Glasgow's central George Square.

Glasgow's Love Letters Murder Case

Among the elite interred in the overgrown churchyard of Ramshorn Church is the man who might be Glasgow's most beloved murder victim, Pierre Emile L'Angelier (died 1857). The apprentice nurseryman had the misfortune of entering into an affair with socialite Madeline Smith (1835–1928). When Smith became engaged to a more suitable match, she demanded that L'Angelier return her passionate love letters. He refused, and she likely poisoned him. Despite overwhelming evidence, including Smith's revealing letters found in L'Angelier's lodgings and proof that she had purchased a bottle of arsenic, the case was resolved as "not proven." This uniquely Scottish verdict means there's not enough evidence to find the accused guilty or not guilty. Smith left Scotland under a cloud of scandal and eventually settled in New York City, where she died at the ripe old age of 93. Director David Lean told the story in his 1950 film *Madeline*, starring his wife, Ann Todd.

astride horses, as if they've just trotted out for a bit of air). Fine weather can bring hundreds of workers from the surrounding offices out to the greens to soak up the sun. The sight of armies of shirtless, pasty-skinned accountants may well send you into the dark depths of the nearest pub—or into the **City Chambers** for a look at the mosaics and grand marble staircases; free guided tours are conducted daily at 10:30am and 2:30pm.

From the 17th through mid-19th centuries Glasgow's tobacco lords, traders who made their fortunes importing and exporting tobacco, as well as spices, sugar, and slaves, lived in mansions near their warehouses just south of the Square, in the blocks now known as Merchant City. **Merchant's Steeple,** completed near the River Clyde on Bridgegate in 1665, wasn't just a show of might but also served as a lookout to watch the comings and goings of ships laden with cargo from the Far East and New World. The merchants would descend from their perch into the since-demolished guildhall where they would do their trading and sort out the city's commercial interests. Here they agreed to join the Crown to help crush the rebellious American colonists, who threatened their lucrative tobacco trade, and they repeatedly raised funds to deepen the Clyde and make the river more navigable. These dredging schemes signaled the neighborhood's decline, as the shipping and shipbuilding that made Glasgow into one of the great centers of the Industrial Revolution shifted to the riverbanks alongside deeper stretches of the Clyde to the west. Many of the tobacco lords are spending eternity in the churchyard of nearby **Ramshorn Church,** on Ingram Street, the city's oldest burial ground, once rather optimistically known as "Paradise."

Gallery of Modern Art ★ GALLERY   In 1778 tobacco lord William Cunninghame had this ridiculously pompous townhouse designed to resemble a grand public building. In its current guise, the neoclassical edifice is a showcase for changing exhibitions of some of Scotland's top contemporary artists, among them Galswegians Douglas Gordon, best known for his eerily altered photographs and video projections, and Ken Currie, whose paintings explore the dark depths of illness, aging, and social inequities. They take their place alongside David Hockney and other internationally acclaimed artists. Out front is a much-beloved statue of the Duke of Wellington, the plastic traffic cone on his head a symbol of Glaswegian defiance of authority. The police have long since stopped removing the irreverent millinery, because every time they do so it reappears.

Royal Exchange Sq. www.glasgowlife.org.uk. ℅ **0141/287-3005.** Free. Mon–Wed and Sat 10am–5pm; Thurs 10am–8pm; Fri and Sun 11am–5pm.

Glasgow School of Art ★★★ HISTORIC STRUCTURE

Charles Rennie Mackintosh is Glasgow's local boy made good. He was born in Glasgow in 1868, studied at the Glasgow School of Art, and designed some of the city's most distinctive landmarks. His masterpiece is the school's main building, completed in 1907. The striking design leans toward the Art Nouveau, with a sparse stone facade of huge windows to light the north-facing studios, with subtle hints of turrets, arches, and ironwork to suggest a Scottish castle. A fire ripped through the structure in May 2014, destroying studios and the piece de la resistance, the galleried library. Restoration is underway with an indefinite date for completion. In the meantime, students lead engaging tours to point out the highlights of the exterior and escort you up the light-filled staircases of the new Reid Building across the street to a gallery filled with Mackintosh furniture. The master's straight-backed chairs are easy on the eye but it might be torture to sit in one, though that's certainly not allowed. The center also leads 2-hour architectural walking tours (£20 adults) throughout the year.

167 Renfrew St. www.gsa.ac.uk. ℅ **0141/353-4500.** £10 adults, £8 seniors, £5 under 18. Tours daily 11am, 2, and 3:15pm, plus 11:30am July–Sept.

Tenement House ★★ HISTORIC HOME

A voyeuristic look into the home life of shorthand typist Agnes Toward says a lot about early-20th-century domesticity in Glasgow. In local parlance tenements aren't the squalid fleapits of American industrial cities but small apartments like this that went up across the city to house the growing and upwardly mobile population. Folks like Miss Toward lived in relative comfort in cramped but well furnished rooms, with coal fires, indoor plumbing, and gas lighting. Fortunately for us, Miss Toward was a bit of a pack rat, and many of the scraps she saved, including wartime rationing leaflets, are on view in a ground floor reception flat. You'll also learn the ins and outs of tenement life so you'll never again have to wonder what a "hurly" is.

145 Buccleuch St. www.nts.org.uk. ℅ **0844/493-2197.** £7 adults, £5 seniors and children, £12–£17 families. Mar–Oct daily 1–5pm (11am–5pm July–Aug).

Local Hero: Charles Rennie Mackintosh

Get ready to meet internationally celebrated artist, architect, and designer Charles Rennie Mackintosh (1868–1928). Not only are the buildings he designed some of Glasgow's favorite landmarks, but you probably won't get out of town without a Mackintosh teacup or dish towel in your baggage. Mackintosh achieved considerable success early in his career and was already a noted architect by age 21. He gentlemanly claimed that his wife, the glass and textile designer Margaret Macdonald, "has genius, I only have talent." Mackintosh's headquarters for the *Herald* newspaper on Mitchell Lane in the City Center, aka "The Lighthouse" for its iconic tower, houses the **Mackintosh Interpretation Centre ★** (www.glasgow.gov.uk; ☎ **0141/276-5360**). Photographs, architectural renderings,

and Mackintosh-designed furniture bring the master's genius, er, talent, to light. Another place to wallow in Mackintosh-infused design is the **Willow Tea Rooms** (www.willowtearooms.co.uk; ☎ **0141/332-0521**) at 217 Sauchiehall Street, opened in 1904. Makcintosh and Macdonald designed every aspect of the still-operating premises: exterior, interior, furnishings, tableware, cutlery, even the waitresses' uniforms (p. 560). Mackintosh abandoned architecture in 1914, eventually moved to France to paint, and died in London at age 60. The **Charles Rennie Mackintosh Society** (www.crmsociety.com) has info on Mackintosh-related properties around the city. They also sell a Mackintosh Trail ticket for £16 that includes admission to sights and public transportation between them.

The West End

By the 19th century, Glasgow was caught up in the full-thrust of the industrial revolution, and the City Center was becoming unbearably crowded and sooty. Those who could afford to do so began resettling in mansions and terrace houses in the West End, where **Kelvingrove Park** was laid out along the banks of the River Kelvin. **Glasgow University** followed suit in 1870, moving from High Street to settle into a faux-Gothic campus that looks like an Oxfordian dreamscape, or Hogwarts. The West End is still *the* place to live, preferably in a red sandstone townhouse surrounded by flowery gardens. The **Kelvingrove** and **Hunterian** museums supply a heady dose of culture, while 25,000 students infuse the pretty streets with a bohemian vibe. Shop-lined Breyers Road cuts a swath through the West End, easily reached from the City Center on the Underground to Hillhead or Kelvinhall stations.

Hunterian Museum & Art Gallery ★★★ MUSEUM   The oldest museum in Scotland (opened in 1803) is a wondrous, sometimes oddball, treasure-trove divided into several buildings. It was founded by William Hunter (1718–83), a physician and anatomist, who seems to have had an interest in just about everything. On display in the Victorian era, high-vaulted timber-roofed galleries are (among other fab items): a 2,000 year-old coin that bears a portrait of Cleopatra; a 17th-century map of the world that a Jesuit missionary prepared for Chinese Emperor

Kangxi; dinosaur fossils; Viking plunder; and a 350-million-year-old shark. Despite the shiny displays and high-tech lighting, you'll feel as though you're exploring a fusty old curiosity cabinet. Across the avenue is the Hunterian's art gallery, which holds the largest collection of works by Scottish-American painter James McNeill Whistler (1834–1903). The main gallery also displays 17th century paintings (Rembrandt to Rubens) and 19th century art by the Scottish Colourists and so-called "Glasgow Boys", such as Hunter, Cadell and Fergusson. Temporary exhibits, culled from Scotland's largest collection of prints, are in the second floor print gallery. A final lure: the home of architect Charles Rennie Mackintosh and his wife, Margaret, painstakingly recreated. Tours of these sparse, pleasing, and surprisingly contemporary rooms are by timed ticket only. University of Glasgow, University Ave. www.hunterian.gla.ac.uk. ✆ **0141/330-5431** or 0141/330-4221. Free. Mon–Sat 9:30am–5pm. Subway: Hillhead.

Kelvingrove Art Gallery & Museum ★★★ MUSEUM The Hunterian may be the oldest museum in Scotland, but the Kelvingrove is the country's most visited, its attendance numbers the greatest in the UK, outside of London's museums. Set in a magnificent, faux Spanish baroque palace, built for the 1901 Glasgow International Exhibition, its collection spans from 17th century Dutch and Flemish masters through the French Impressionists and colorful works by the so-called Glasgow Boys (local painters who began to gain fame at the same time as Renoir and his gang) and beyond. Among the Kelvingrove's "Mona Lisas" are Rembrandt's 1655 painting *Man in Armor,* in which a pensive young man seems to be contemplating his mortality in light of an upcoming battle; and Salvador Dali's *Christ of St. John of the Cross,* which shows Christ floating across a darkened sky. The museum also has delightful touches of whimsy. Where else can you see a RAF Mark 21 Supermarine Spitfire suspended above an Asian elephant named Sir William? Wandering

Going Green

As Glaswegians began to move west in the 19th century, city fathers had the foresight to create two tranquil green spaces in the West End. The **Botanic Gardens,** at 732 Great Western Rd., were laid out in 1841 to supply the University of Glasgow with plant material for research, though the glass-dome Kibble Palace greenhouse always seemed more like a pleasure palace than a laboratory. The city bought the parcel in 1981 and opened it to the public. Greenhouses filled with exotic plants and tropical rainforests are surrounded by lawns and gardens. Nearby **Kelvingrove Park,** a 85-acre strip of greenery straddling both banks of the River Kelvin, opened in 1852. The lawns and shaded groves were meant to entertain the middle classes moving to the West End and also to provide a bit of relief to those remaining behind in the crowded city center. The Botanic Gardens (www.glasgowbotanic gardens.com; ✆ **0141/276-1614**) are open daily 7am to dusk, greenhouses from 10am to 6pm. Entry is free.

An installation at the Kelvingrove Art Gallery & Museum.

through the sumptuously tiled halls you'll come upon a working hive of bees, a leather satchel worn by a medieval monk, and a complete set of armor for a man and horse. The latter is a nice counterpoint to the famed Rembrandt painting; making comparisons like this is one of the pleasures of spending an afternoon here. This remarkable collection is refreshingly manageable, so you can peruse it in an hour or two, with luck as the Kelvingrove organ belts out some music (at 1pm Mon–Sat and 3pm Sun).

Argyle St. www.glasgowlife.org.uk. © **0141/276-9599.** Free. Mon–Thurs and Sat 10am–5pm; Fri and Sun 11am–5pm. Subway: Kelvinhall.

Along the Clyde

According to a popular saying, the Clyde made Glasgow and Glasgow made the Clyde. The river made the city into a great medieval trading power and later a shipbuilding center—the *QE2* was launched here in 1967, and the Clyde would be just another trickle if Glasgow hadn't put it on the map. Though most of the riverside industry has died out, the Clyde is coming back into its own, with shiny new riverside apartment and office buildings, the **Clyde Auditorium** (called the "Armadillo" for its shape), and two flashy museums, the **Glasgow Science Centre** and the **Riverside Museum.** You can follow a riverside path, the **Clyde Walkway,** from King Albert Bridge, at the western end of Glasgow Green, for 1¾ miles downstream toward the museums, traversing some urban wasteland. But it's far more satisfying to experience the river from the water on a Clyde cruise (see above), hopping on and off to explore a museum or two. One of the most impressive riverside sights is the

The Glasgow Science Centre & IMAX theater.

out-of-service **Finnieston Crane,** a giant, 53m tall (174 ft.) cantilever crane dating back to the 1920s that was once used to load steam locomotives and heavy cargo onto ships. Its hulking presence speaks volumes about the city's industrial past.

Glasgow Science Centre ★★★ MUSEUM/PLANETARIUM   This gleaming titanium-clad, crescent-shaped landmark resembles the hull of a ship, a reference to the adjacent basin where ships were once brought to have barnacles scraped off their hulls. You can learn all about marine invertebrates inside the Science Mall, as well as ship engineering, and just about anything else having to do with science and technology. Sections on health and the human body are especially enlightening. The adjacent Planetarium and IMAX put on spectacular shows, but the biggest thrill is a trip up the 100m (328 ft.) tall Glasgow Tower. The entire tower turns, making it the tallest rotating structure in the world. Ironically, given the center's devotion to cutting-edge technology, the tower is often closed for repairs.

50 Pacific Quay. www.gsc.org.uk. ✆ **0141/540-5000.** £11 adults, £9 children and seniors, Planetarium and IMAX £3 extra, Tower £4 extra. Bus 90 from Union St.

Riverside Museum ★★★ MUSEUM   The zigzag roof of this new landmark by star architect Zaha Hadid represents waves on the River Clyde, while its long, linear shape is supposed to evoke a tunnel that connects the city and the river. The lime green interior seems a bit less inspirational, more like a trolley barn—which, come to think of it, is the ideal setting for the trolleys, buses, cars, planes, even skateboards and wheelchairs that entertainingly celebrate the glories of transport, the

The Riverside Museum and the tall ship Glenlee, Glasgow.

subject of the museum. Stepping aboard vintage 1930s buses and looking into old house trailers (called caravans here) means pleasantly indulging in some nostalgia, and the experience is made all the richer by enlightening taped commentary. A Pakistani talks about arriving in Glasgow in the 1950s, getting a job as a bus driver, and encountering his first-ever first snowfall. Several Glaswegian ladies of a certain age recall their evenings at dance halls and rushing to catch the last homeward-bound streetcars of the night. The three-masted tall ship *Glenlee,* launched in Glasgow in 1896, is berthed outside. Onboard you'll encounter what might be the most haunting story of all: One of the ship's hands sailed around Cape Horn three times, survived multiple typhoons and hurricanes at sea, took up flying, and was with Amelia Earhart when her plane disappeared over the Pacific in 1937.

100 Pointhouse Pl. www.glasgowlife.org.uk. ℂ **0141/2872720.** Free. Museum: Mon–Thurs, Sat 10am–5pm, Fri and Sun 11am–5pm. SV *Glenlee:* thetallship.com. ℂ **0141/357-3699.** Free. Feb–Oct daily 10am–5pm, Nov–Jan daily 10am–4pm. Subway: Patrick Station or Bus 100 from the north side of George Sq.

Southside

You have less incentive to venture across the Clyde into the largely residential Southside these days now that the **Burrell Collection** is closing for long overdue repairs (reports suggest the roof is in danger of collapsing). It will be at least several years before the Burrell reopens.

Pollok House ★★ HISTORIC HOME/GALLERY The Maxwell clan lived at the Pollok Estate for 700 years, and since 1752 they resided in this handsome country house designed by William Adam, the most famous architect of his day. End-of-the-line Dame Anne Maxwell donated the mansion to the city of Glasgow in 1966, giving the rest of us a chance to vicariously enjoy a posh lifestyle. Time in the lavish interiors seems to have stood still since the 1930s, not a bad place to be stuck amid glamorous drawing rooms, a 7,000-book library, and plush bedrooms. The Maxwells had a taste for Spanish painting, and their Goyas and El Grecos are part of one of the best collections of Spanish art in the U.K. The vast Edwardian kitchen is now an atmospheric tea room. As you nibble on a home-baked scone think about the times when a staff of 48 toiled down here in service to a household of three. The estate is now 146-hectare (361-acre) Pollok Country Park. A well-manicured section is planted in the house's formal gardens, famous for their rhododendrons, while the rest of the acreage is given over to woods and meadows where a herd of Highland cattle graze.

Pollok Country Park, 2060 Pollokshaws Rd. www.nts.org.uk/Property/Pollok-House. ✆ **0844/493-2202.** House £7 adults, £5 seniors and children, £12–£17 families. Daily 10am–5pm. 3 miles south of the city center. First buses 45, 48, or 57.

Organized Tours

Open-top bus tours operated by **City Sightseeing Glasgow** (www.city sightseeingglasgow.co.uk; ✆ **0141/204-0444**) are a good way to get to know the city. A complete tour, accompanied by a detailed, informative, and often witty taped commentary, takes about 1 hour and 15 minutes, and you can get off at any of the 15 stops along the way then get back on. One-day tickets (good until the last tour of the day of purchase) are £13 adults, £12 seniors and students, £7 children 5 to 15, and £28 for families; 2-day tickets are £15 adults, £14 seniors and students, £8 children, and £32 families. The 2-day ticket is well worth the small extra investment. On the first day take the full tour to get a city overview, then use the buses to visit the far-flung museums along the River Clyde and in the West End. Buses depart from stop no. 1 at George Square from 9:30am until 4:30pm and run every 15 minutes from April to October and every half-hour November to March.

It seems only proper to admire the city from the river that once fueled its economy. A **Glasgow City Cruise** (www.clydecruises.com; ✆ **01475/721281**) operates a 1-hour trip between Broomielaw Pontoon in the City Center and the Riverside Museum, showing off historic sights and new riverside development. Tickets are £10 adults, £5 children, and £27 families. Departures are hourly from 11am at Broomielaw and 11:25am from the Riverside Museum.

GreetinGlasgow (www.greetinglasgow.com; ✆ **07751/976-935**) leads walking tours around Merchant City and the East End, taking in the main sights and rich history. Tours last 1 hour and 20 minutes and cost £8 per person (under 14 free). Tours depart daily at 10am and 2pm, from Doulton Fountain for the East End tour and George Square for the Merchant City tour. It's necessary to reserve in advance.

WHERE TO STAY

In Glasgow, lodging options come down to the choice of two neighborhoods: the City Center and the West End. The many excellent hotels and guest houses in both put you within easy reach of the sights and amid everything that's good about life in this vibrant city.

City Center

Blythswood Square ★   This row of elegant Georgian era townhouses long served as the headquarters of the old Royal Scottish Automobile Club, and even lots of contemporary style doesn't detract from an old world clubby atmosphere of grand staircases, pillars, and Art Deco flourishes. The huge, high-ceilinged guest rooms in the old houses are especially bright and airy, despite their relentless purple and gray color schemes and black-fabric chandeliers—front-facing views into the colorful gardens in the square brighten things up considerably. Smaller rooms in a new wing in the rear are quieter but otherwise have a lot less to recommend them. There's a lively restaurant and bar, and the spa has steam rooms, saunas, and two small pools, though it's complimentary to guests only at off hours.

11 Blythswood Sq. www.townhousecompany.com. ✆ **0141/248-8888.** 88 units. Doubles £165–£285. **Amenities:** Restaurant; bar; 2 pools (indoor); health club and spa; room service; free Wi-Fi.

Citizen M ★★   Go ahead—you won't be the first guest who's said "Beam me up, Scotty" when stepping into the futuristic-looking lobby where black clad "ambassadors" walk you through the self check-in process. If you've ever wondered what sleeping quarters on the *Starship Enterprise* might be like, you'll find out upstairs, where all the compact, cubical-like guest rooms are exactly the same (no anxiety about an upgrade here). A bedside tablet controls the blinds, temperature, lamps, free movies, and some very romantic mood lighting, but you're probably better off experiencing this *Jetsons*-worthy lodging on your own. Floor space is limited; square beds are exactly the width of the room, demanding that one half of a twosome sleep on the inside; and you put on an X-rated floor show when you step into the glassed-in, room-facing shower pod. For a bit of space, the sprawling lounge-restaurant-bar downstairs is artfully furnished with couches and worktables.

60 Renfrew St. www.citizenmglasgow.com. ✆ **0141/404-9485.** 198 units. Doubles £70–£100. **Amenities:** Restaurant; bar; room service; free Wi-Fi.

Grand Central Hotel ★★   Everything about these grand Edwardian-era spaces and comfy guest rooms exudes a hint of glamor and the romance of the bygone age of travel—including what must be the longest hotel corridors in the world (along with the world's second-largest crystal chandelier cascading down a grand staircase). Vintage railway scenes decorate the contemporarily styled bedrooms, some of which overlook the tracks of adjacent Central Station through heavily soundproofed windows. Photos of Frank Sinatra and other globe-trotting guests hang in the darkly welcoming lobby, and a marble floored Champagne Bar overlooks the station concourse. For one more bit of historic provenance, consider that in 1927 John Logie Baird transmitted the first television pictures from London to a receiver in the hotel.

99 Gordon St. www.thegrandcentralhotel.co.uk. © **0141/240-3700.** 186 units. Doubles £80–£165. **Amenities:** Restaurant; 2 bars; room service; free Wi-Fi.

Grasshoppers Hotel ★★★   The worn lobby and stark elevator don't prepare you for the pleasure of stepping into this welcoming and stylish sixth-floor lair high above Central Station. Soothing rooms are geared to tasteful, pared-down luxury. Handmade Scandinavian furnishings are clean-lined, Italian lighting is warm and efficient, and handmade mattresses are topped with Egyptian cotton sheets and feather-down pillows. Breakfast and weeknight dinners are served family-style in a kitchen-dining room that's as warm and inviting as everything else about this place.

87 Union St. www.grasshoppersglasgow.com. © **0141/222-2666.** 30 units. Doubles £90–£120, includes breakfast. **Amenities:** Restaurant; bar; free Wi-Fi.

West End

15 Glasgow ★★   Design buffs will be in their element in this exquisitely redone Victorian townhouse where the tiled and pillared entry and beautiful period details are enhanced by a soothing and starkly contemporary aesthetic and many luxurious overtones. Stylish as it all is, design doesn't trump comfort. Quiet bedrooms are equipped with plush headboards and fine linens, and the communal drawing room overlooking the square is outfitted with big couches. Breakfast is delivered on a tray to your room, a nice way to start a day of sightseeing—Kelvingrove Park, the West End and City Center are an easy walk away.

15 Woodside Pl. 15glasgow.com. © **0141/332-1263.** 5 units. Doubles £99–£215, includes breakfast. **Amenities:** Free Wi-Fi.

Alamo Guest House ★★   Remember the Alamo, because intimate Glasgow lodgings don't get much more welcoming than this rambling Victorian house on a quiet cul-de-sac at the edge of Kelvingrove Park. The fireplaces, elaborate moldings and big bay windows are homily atmospheric, and nice iron bedsteads and other antiques are scattered among the comfortable rooms. Rooms vary considerably in size and price; the seven with shared facilities are especially good value, since they're just a step or two to a beautifully done and well-maintained bathroom. The surrounding greenery is soothing, and big city attractions, including the West End museums and restaurants, are just around the corner.

46 Gray St., G3 7SE. www.alamoguesthouse.com. © **0141/339-2395.** 12 units. Doubles £52–£105, includes breakfast. **Amenities:** Free Wi-Fi.

Hotel du Vin ★★★ Devonshire Gardens has always been one of Glasgow's most posh addresses, and these five connected, beautifully decorated townhouses do justice to the neighborhood. A warren of corridors and wooden staircases lead off a series of soothing, clubby lounges to similarly welcoming rooms and suites. Bold, deep colors and wall coverings offset acres of Victorian-era woodwork, fireplaces, and large bay windows, and handsome classic furnishings hit just the right tone. Plenty of nice flourishes include deep bathtubs and walk-in monsoon showers. Some of the grander suites have their own conservatories and saunas, but any room here sets you up in style.

1 Devonshire Gardens. www.hotelduvin.com. *©* **0141/339-2001.** 49 units. Doubles £160–£335. **Amenities:** 2 restaurants; bar; exercise room; free Wi-Fi.

WHERE TO EAT

Glasgow's longtime standby for a quick bite is **Peckham's** ★ (www.peckhams.co.uk; *©* **0141/553-0666**), housed in an Art Deco building on Glassford Street in Merchant City; this shop and branches, including one at 124-126 Byres Rd. in the West End, serve sandwiches and other light fare late into the evening (closed Mon). **Riverhill Coffee Bar** ★, next to Central Station at 24 Gordon St. (www.riverhillcafe.com; *©* **0141/204 4762**) has worked its way into the hearts of Glaswegians with excellent city-roasted Deer Green coffee and a short eat-in/eat out menu, with cheese topped scones, chorizo bagels, and crayfish sandwiches; it's open Monday to Friday 8am to 5pm, Saturday 9am to 5pm, and Sundays 10am to 5pm.

City Center & Merchant City

Mussel Inn ★ SEAFOOD You can almost smell the sea air in this breezy two-level room operated by shellfish harvesters in western Scotland. That translates to the freshest oysters in town—like the mussels (sold by the kilo or half kilo in a choice of preparations), they're cultivated in plankton-rich sea lochs. Equally fresh are the chowders, fish stew, and especially admirable seafood pasta. They grill a good burger here, too, but really, that would be a desecration to the sea gods. Lunch specials are a remarkably good deal.

157 Hope St. www.mussel-inn.com. *©* **0141/572-1405.** Mains £7–£23. Mon–Fri noon–2:30pm and 5–10pm, Sat noon–10pm, Sun 12:30–10pm.

Riverhill Restaurant and Bar ★★ MODERN SCOTTISH Even the breakfast menu in this small, eclectic room is imaginative—potato nan stuffed with bacon, masala beans with fried eggs—and by the time lunch and dinner roll around, the kitchen is preparing cheddar and potato pierogis (Eastern European dumplings), curries, light-as-a-feather gnocchi with braised rabbit, and aromatic Indian fish bakes. The quick bites, like hummus on flatbread or old-fashioned fish fingers, are elevated a notch or two above the ordinary, too. The coffee bar around the corner serves similarly imaginative small plates, plus sandwiches and pastries.

3 West Nile St. www.riverhillcafe.com. ✆ **0141/248-3495.** Mains £10–£15. Mon–Wed 8am–10pm, Thurs–Sat 8am–late, Sun 10am–6pm.

Willow Tea Rooms ★ SEAFOOD   Glasgow's most famous spot for tea is a stop on the Charles Rennie Mackintosh pilgrimage route. The architect and his designer wife, Margaret Macdonald, redesigned the four floors for proprietor Kate Cranston in 1901, taking control of every detail right down to the last teaspoon. Their tastes still shine in the white and gray interiors with hints of rose, purple, and silver. Light and basic Scottish fare is served all day and includes scrambled eggs with smoked salmon and better-than-it-sounds Cullen Skink (a thick, creamy soup of smoked haddock, potatoes, and onions). A three-tiered cake stand is laden with sandwiches, scones, and pastries. The willow-motifs you see all around aren't arbitrary: Look at the address: Sauchie-hall is a combo of two old Scots words for *saugh*, willow, and *haugh*, meadow.

217 Sauchiehall St. www.willowtearooms.co.uk. ✆ **0141/332-0521.** Light mains £5–£9. Mon–Sat 9am–4:30pm, Sun 11am–4:30pm.

West End

The Left Bank ★ MODERN SCOTTISH   This split level space seems to capture all the upscale-yet-still-bohemian vibe of the West End. So does the eclectic menu that dips into some South Asian exoticism while also sticking to the basics—take your pick, depending on your mood, Goan chicken with curry leaf sauce or beer-battered North Sea haddock. Brick walls, neutral tones, and worn wood floors are welcoming in an easygoing way, so much so that the neighborhood folks sitting at tables with kid or laptops, or both, seem to be in no hurry to move on. A daily brunch and an all-day menu of salads, burgers, and noodle dishes are good enough reasons to linger in the bright, sunlit spaces. A few more substantial fish and meat dishes are added in the evenings, when excellent cocktails are served from a concrete-sculpted bar.

33-35 Gibson St. www.theleftbank.co.uk. ✆ **0141/339-5969.** Mains £8–£16. Mon–Fri noon–midnight, Sat–Sun 10am–midnight.

Stravaigin ★★ SCOTTISH   Haggis—you have to try it sooner or later. No better place to do so than this attractive, straightforward room with plain wood tables and straight-backed chairs where the menu focuses on all things Scottish, with some exotic global flourishes thrown in. A small plate of haggis, neeps and tatties—that's lamb's heart, liver, and lungs, minced with onion, spices, and a few other ingredients and served with turnips and potatoes—washed down with a wee draught of single malt should satisfy your curiosity. Thus fortified, you might want to backpedal into something as conventional as lamb livers simmered in

Madeira or even beer-battered fish and chips. A similarly intriguing, Scots-oriented menu is available in the casual cafe upstairs.

28 Gibson St. www.stravaigin.co.uk. © **0141/334-2665.** Dinner mains £13–£25. Mon–Fri 9am–1am, Sat–Sun 11am–1am.

Two Fat Ladies West End ★★ MODERN SCOTTISH/SEAFOOD Glaswegians are adamant about their picks for best seafood in town, and this intimate space often comes out on top. The name has nothing to do with the proprietors' physique but is a reference to the slang term for the bingo number that happens to be the same as the address of this charmingly ornate Fat Ladies original (there are several Fat Ladies in Glasgow). Many of the ingredients are straight from Scottish waters, and cooked to perfection. Hand-picked scallops, the halibut or other local fish prove that "fresh" is the element that really matters when it comes to what the establishment calls "seriously fishy" dishes. If that's *too* fishy for your landlubber taste, excellent locally-sourced beef and pork dishes are also on offer. Two Fat Ladies at the Buttery, in the Finnieston neighborhood, is all rich paneling and tartan-plaid upholstery, well suited to business lunches or romantic evenings.

88 Dumbarton Rd. www.twofatladiesrestaurant.com. © **0141/339-1944.** Fixed-price lunch/pre-theatre £16–£21. Mon–Sat noon–3pm and 5:30–10:30pm, Sun 1–9pm. Buttery: 652-654 Argyle St. © **0141/221-8188.**

Ubiquitous Chip ★★★ SCOTTISH   The plant filled, stonewalled nooks and crannies of a former undertaker's stables give off an easygoing vibe that seems to suggest "we're so solidly good we don't have to put on airs." That's true, and since 1971 this fab place, as much a mandatory Glasgow stop as the nearby Kelvingrove and Hunterian museums, has celebrated local produce and Scottish cuisine that, as they claim, is inspired by "aunties, grannies and even folklore." Perhaps the venison haggis might be a bit too folkloric, but Aberdeen beef and Orkney salmon are surefire hits. The bar serves generous cocktails and snacks, but they don't include the fries (chips here) that inspired the name, a snide reference to what at one time passed as haute cuisine in Glasgow.

12 Ashton Lane, off Byres Rd. www.ubiquitouschip.co.uk. © **0141/334-5007.** Mains £16–£27. Mon–Sat noon–2:30pm, Sun 12:30–3pm; daily 5–11pm.

SHOPPING

By the look of things, Glaswegians are consummate consumers. In the U.K., only London has more shops. Most of this trade transpires along pedestrian streets and malls in the City Center and Merchant City. The main shopping venues are Buchanan Street, a long pedestrian thoroughfare that runs north to south through the City Center; Argyle Street, stretching east from Central Station; Sauchiehall Street, rather refreshingly lowbrow with bargain shops and outdoor vendors, running which leads east from Royal Exchange Square through Merchant City to High Street. Shopping malls include Buchanan Galleries, off Buchanan Street, with an enormous branch of the **John Lewis** department store; **Princes Square,** with many designer shops behind an early 19th-century blonde sandstone facade, also off Buchanan Street; and **St Enoch Shopping Centre** under the biggest glass roof in Europe, off Argyle Street, to the east of Central Station.

The **Argyll Arcade** at 30 Buchanan St. was built in 1827 and is Europe's oldest covered shopping arcade. The largest group of retail **jewelers** in Scotland is clustered beneath the vaulted glass roof, making this the place to shop for high- quality diamond jewelry, watches, and wedding rings. The **Italian Centre,** a small complex off Ingram Street in Merchant City, is nicknamed "mini-Milan" for its designer outlets.

Elsewhere in the city, independent, quirky shops are located along or close to Bryes Road and Great Western Road in the West End. **De Courcy's Arcade** on Cresswell Lane is heaven for vintage clothing.

For a real slice of Glaswegian market life, stop by **The Barras** (theglasgowbarras.com; Sat–Sun 10am–5pm), on a large patch of ground between London Road and Gallowgate in the East End. This legendary market has been operating for nearly a century, with hundreds of traders who ply everything from clothes to collectibles.

If kilts and tartans are on your shopping list, **Hector Russell ★★** (110 Buchanan St.; www.hector-russell.com; ✆ **0141/221-0217**) is one of Scotland's oldest and most prestigious kiltmakers, and turns out beautiful Highland wear, along with more practical, reasonably priced tweed jackets, tartan-patterned accessories, and beautiful cashmere sweaters.

Antiques & Collectibles

You'll have to do some elbowing and careful picking at **Victorian Village ★** (93 W. Regent St.; victorianvillageglasgow.com; ✆ **0141/332-0808**), but you can almost find a well-priced treasure or two in this warren of little stalls. You might hit pay dirt if you're looking for 19th-century jewelry, a specialty here. Everything in the **Glasgow School of Art Shop ★★★** (p. 550), including the books, cards, stationery, sterling-and-enamel jewelry, even the coffee and beer mugs is tasteful, with designs based on the work of Charles Rennie Mackintosh and Margaret McDonald. If you're in the market for a larger Mackintosh-inspired piece, try furniture maker **Bruce Hamilton** (www.bruce hamilton.co.uk; ✆ **01505/322-550**), who crafts high-quality reproductions of Mackintosh-designed furniture.

Scottish history is a specialty at **Caledonian Books ★★**, a jam-packed West End second-hand shop (483 Great Western Rd.; www.caledoniabooks.co.uk; ✆ **0141/3349663**), but you can pick your way through stacks of out-of-print literature on just about everything else. **Henderson** ★ (www.hendersonjewellers.co.uk; ✆ **0141/331-2569**) at the Willow Tea Rooms (p. 560) offers delicate silver jewelry based on Mackintosh designs, as well as glassware and other tasteful knickknacks.

ENTERTAINMENT & NIGHTLIFE

Glasgow is one of the most happening cities in the U.K. For detailed info on all entertainment options, check listings at **www.list.co.uk**.

The Performing Arts

King's Theatre, 297 Bath St., City Center (www.ambassadortickets.com; ✆ **0844/871-7648**) stages plays, musicals, and comedies and in winter an annual pantomime. The **Theatre Royal,** 282 Hope St., City Center (www.ambassadortickets.com; ✆ **0844/871-7647**), resplendent with Victorian Italian Renaissance plasterwork and glittering chandeliers, hosts touring productions by national theatre companies from across the U.K. Glasgow's beloved Victorian-era **Citizens Theatre,** 119 Gorbals St., Southside (www.citz.co.uk; ✆ **0141/429-0022**) stages its own productions and hosts touring companies, favoring emerging theatre companies. The ornate **Pavilion Theatre,** 121 Renfield St., City Center (www.paviliontheatre.co.uk; ✆ **0141/332-1846**), specializes in mainstream music concerts and comedy.

The **Tron Theatre,** 63 Trongate, East End (www.tron.co.uk; ✆ **0141/552-4267**), occupies the former Tron Church, with its famous dome by architect Robert Adam and presents contemporary drama, dance, and music events. For a real slice of bygone Glasgow nightlife, catch a show at the **Britannia Panopticon,** 113-117 Trongate, East End (www.britanniapanopticon.org; ✆ **0141/553-0840**), the oldest surviving music hall in the U.K. where Stan Laurel first trod the boards in 1906. Even though the building is in need of restoration, it still plays host to a number of cabaret, comedy, music, and film events—be warned that this old charmer has no heating so bundle up for winter performances.

The **Theatre Royal** and **Tron Theatre** (see above) both host performances by **Scottish Opera** (www.scottishopera.org.uk; ✆ **0141/248-4567**), while **Scottish Ballet** (www.scottishballet.co.uk; ✆ **0141/331-2931**) is based at the **Tramway** on the Southside, although most of its Glasgow performances are held at the **Theatre Royal.** The **Glasgow Royal Concert Hall,** 2 Sauchiehall St., City Center, is home to the **Royal Scottish National Orchestra** (www.rsno.org.uk; ✆ **0141/226-3868**), and alongside its performances you can catch folk, world, country, and rock and pop concerts in its 2,475-seat auditorium. **City Halls,** Candleriggs, East End, is home to the **BBC Scottish Symphony Orchestra** (www.bbc.co.uk/orchestras/bbcsso; ✆ **0141/552-0909**); the **Scottish Chamber Orchestra** (www.sco.org.uk;

favorite PUBS & BARS

Bon Accord ★★ A large selection of malts from across Scotland and live music will help you pass happy hours at this amiable institution. There's no better place to sip a pint of hand-pumped real ale. The knowledgeable bar men claim to dispense 900 different kinds of beer a year (153 North St. www.bonaccordweb.co.uk. ℭ **0141/248-4427.** Mon–Sat noon–midnight, Sun noon–11pm).

Curler's Rest ★ The West End's favorite local invites you to sink back into one its deep sofas and enjoy one of the five ales, 19 specialty beers, and three ciders on tap. The fish and chips are first rate (256-260 Bryes Rd. www.curlersrestglasgow.co.uk. ℭ **0141/341-0737.** Daily noon-midnight).

Delmonicas ★ This stylish Merchant City gay-bar and

pre-club stop is jam-packed most evenings and hosts quiz and DJ nights and karaoke (68 Virginia St. ℭ **0141/552-4803.** Open daily noon–midnight).

Drygate ★★★ A former factory just down the hill from the cathedral is

Drygate micro-brewery, beer hall and restaurant, Glasgow.

ℭ **0131/557-6800**) also regularly performs at this elegant Victorian venue. Adjacent to City Halls on Candleriggs is the **Old Fruitmarket** where jazz, pop, and world music gigs regularly rock the roof.

The Stand, 333 Woodlands, West End (www.thestand.co.uk; ℭ **0844/335-8879**) is Glasgow's premiere comedy club. In March, the Glasgow International Comedy Festival (www.glasgowcomedyfestival.com) blazes across many city venues.

The Club & Music Scene

Glasgow's most famous nightclub, **The Arches** ★ (253 Argyle St.; www.thearches.co.uk; ℭ **0141/565-1035**) recently lost the "night" part of that appellation when its late-night operating license was revoked amid reports of drug use on the premises. The space beneath Central Station continues to operate in its other guises as an experimental theatre, cutting-edge event space, and cafe-bar. Tickets are £7 to £20. **Barrowland** ★★ (Gallowgate; www.glasgow-barrowland.com; ℭ **0141/552-4601**) is a legendary holdover from the 1930s Golden Age of dance halls and is now the city's most celebrated concert hall, now a micro-brewery, beer hall and restaurant, where you can sample the "experimental" brews and enjoy a burger while watching the brew masters at work (85 Drygate, East End. www.drygate.com. ✆ **0141/2128815.** Daily 11am–midnight).

The Pot Still ★★★   Glasgow's most famous whisky pub claims has 483 varieties on hand, served in convivial surroundings (154 Hope St. www.thepotstill.co.uk. ✆ **0141/333-0980.** Mon–Thurs noon–11pm, Fri–Sat noon–midnight).

The Scotia Bar ★   One of Glasgow's old timers, established in 1762, is a woody, low-ceilinged place that will make your feel at right at home. Lots of writers, actors, and singers do, and many of them take the stage for some of the city's best low-key entertainment (112-114 Stockwell St. www.scotiabar.net. ✆ **0141/552-8681.** Mon–Sat noon–midnight, Sun noon–11pm).

Waterloo Bar ★★   The oldest gay bar in town attracts a crowd that seems to have been there from the beginning. Each night of the week celebrates the music of a different decade (306 Argyle St. ✆ **0141/248-7216.** Open daily noon–midnight).

West ★★   The former wool-winding room of Glasgow's iconic Templeton Carpet Factory is now in the hand of some of Scotland's most respected brewers, and you can sample their output as you sit in a Bavaria-worthy beer hall and look down into the brew house below. German/Scottish dishes accompany a fine selection of premium beers brewed according to German purity laws of 1516 (Glasgow Green. www.westbeer.com. ✆ **0141/550-0135.** Beer hall and restaurant daily 11am–9pm; bar daily 11am–11pm, Fri–Sat to midnight).

filling its 1,900 seats with big names as well as emerging talent. Cover charges run £11 to £26. There's someone onstage every night at **King Tut's Wah-Wah Hut ★** (272-A St Vincent St.; www.kingtuts.co.uk; ✆ **0141/221-5279**), a 300-seat venue that hosted Blur, Travis, Radiohead, and other legends before they became legends. Cover £5 to £18.

Other musical watering holes include **Nice 'n' Sleazy ★** (421 Sauchiehall St.; www.nicensleazy.com; ✆ **0141/333-0900**), the unpretentious fave of students at nearby Glasgow School of Art, with reasonable cover charges, inexpensive beer, and Mexican food to accompany the alt music and open mic events. Cover from £3. **Sub Club ★** (22 Jamaica St.; www.subclub.co.uk; ✆ **0141/248-4600**) is an underground venue near Central Station where the top DJs and a stellar sound system guarantee the best dance nights. Cover £3 to £10.

Òran Mór ★★ (Bryes Rd.; www.oran-mor.co.uk; ✆ **0141/357-6200**) stages theatre and music events beneath the glorious ceiling mural of a repurposed Victorian church. A standout is A Play, A Pie and A Pint, a 45-minute-long lunchtime treat that features new talent and includes a pint and a pie. Cover free to £6.

SIDE TRIPS FROM GLASGOW

When Glaswegians want a quick fix of sea air, they head 35 miles or so west to the rugged Ayrshire coast. That also happens to be the place to pay homage to national poet **Robert Burns,** at his birthplace in Alloway. Loch Lomond provides a freshwater getaway, and some of Scotland's most beautiful and romantic scenery surrounds the famous lake.

South of Glasgow

Two intriguing sights are just beyond the spread of Glasgow's southern suburbs and easy to reach by train and bus.

National Museum of Rural Life ★ MUSEUM   Nothing about this well-done assemblage of displays, and a working farm, is coy or nostalgia laden. Tractors, threshers, and other equipment in a huge barn-like pavilion show the move to mechanized farming and its effect on what was once an agricultural society. A 1950s era farm captures a time when machines like these were starting to replace manpower and horsepower; cows, pigs, chickens, and sheep are reared as they would have been in ways that, even half a century ago, required considerably more labor—as you might realize when you milk one of the cows.

11 miles south of Glasgow. Wester Kittochside, Philipshill Rd., East Kilbride. www. nms.ac.uk. ℂ **0300/123-6789.** £7 adults, £5 seniors, £4 children, £19 families. Daily 10am–5pm. First bus no. 31.

New Lanark ★★★ HISTORIC SITE   In 1799 Welsh social reformer Robert Owen took control of cotton mills powered by falls in the Clyde

New Lanark historic site.

and established a community that would greatly improve workplace conditions. He did away with child labor and cruelly long work weeks, improved safety, and provided health care, care, education, and housing. Profits soared, though most of Owens' innovations would not be legislated into common practice for at least another century. Working machinery, a school, the company store, and the homes of Owen and a worker show what life was like in this enlightened place.

25 miles southeast of Glasgow, New Lanark Rd., off the A73. www.newlanark.org. ✆ **01555/662322.** £9 adults, £7 seniors, £6 children, £25–£35 families. Apr–Sept daily 10am–5pm, Oct–Mar daily 11am–5pm. Train from Glasgow Central to Lanark station, connected by bus with New Lanark.

Ayr ★

35 miles southwest of Glasgow

The largest and most popular resort on Scotland's west coast braces itself against the breezy Firth of Clyde at its confluence with the River Ayr. **ScotRail** trains from Glasgow's Central Station (www.scotrail.co.uk; ✆ **08457/484-950**) whisk you to Ayr in 50 minutes. Ayr's **Tourist Information Centre** is at 22 Sandgate (www.ayrshire-arran.com; ✆ **0845/225-5121**). It's open year-round from 9am to 5 or 6pm Monday to Saturday, and Sunday from 10 or 11am to 5pm.

First order of business is to stroll along the town's noted seaside mile, past Georgian and Victorian houses that have seen some better days. Another walk, this one along the River Ayr, will introduce you to the local reverence for Scotland's unofficial national poet Robert Burns (1759–96). He was baptized in the **Auld Kirk of Ayr.** Looking out at the river from the gloomy old churchyard, you can see the setting for Burns' poem "Twa Brigs," in which the 13th-century **Auld Brig o' Ayr,** just north of the church, argues with the new bridge (completed in 1788) downstream, calling him a "conceited gawk."

Alloway ★

2 miles south of Ayr

A Burns pilgrimage hits high gear in the pretty village where the poet was born in 1757. From Ayr, follow the A77 south, or take Stagecoach bus 57 (www.stagecoachbus.com; ✆ **01292/613-500**) from the seafront. A pleasant, well-marked route leads around the village to such spots as the tiny thatch-roofed gardener's cottage—the "auld clay biggin"—where the poet entered the world and lived until he was seven. The cottage and other Burns sights in the village are part of the **Robert Burns Birthplace Museum ★** (www.burnsmuseum.org.uk; ✆ **0844/493-2601;** Jan–Mar and Oct–Dec 10am–5pm daily, Apr–Sept 10am–5:30pm; £9). A handsome stone and timber gallery near the cottage houses the world's largest collection of Burns memorabilia, including a cast of his skull, his desk and spectacles, and some 500 manuscripts.

The admission price includes a ride in the electric carts that run along the paths between the sights.

Burns set part of his famous "Tam o' Shanter" in the ruins of **Alloway Auld Kirk,** where you can pause to read the poem, chiseled on the gravestone of the poet's father, William. The **Burns Monument ★** is the grandest building in town, a pillared Grecian-style pavilion from 1823 that houses a statue of the poet—one of many around the world, and they're plotted on a map with the boast that there are more statues to Burns on the planet than to any other writer. From gardens surrounding the monument you can see the River Doon slipping beneath the **Brig o' Doon,** the romantic-looking 13th-century stone span you may have just seen mentioned in your graveyard reading of "Tam o' Shanter."

Troon ★

6¾ miles north of Ayr and 31 miles southwest of Glasgow

The lively little windswept resort town has a huge sailing marina, six golf courses, and 1¾ miles of sandy beaches that stretch along both sides of the harbor. Troon takes its name from the curiously shaped promontory on which it sits, once called Trwyn, the Cymric word for "nose," which later became Trone, and finally Troon.

The **Royal Troon Golf Club** on Craigends Road (www.royaltroon.co.uk; ✆ **01292/311-555**) is one of the world's finest championship courses, founded in 1878 and eight-time host of the British Open. The 7,175-yard, par-71 **Old Course** is the more famous, while the 6,289-yard, par-71 **Portland** is, by some estimates, even more challenging. Visitors can play between mid-April and mid-October, on Monday, Tuesday, and Thursday; greens fees are £205 for a day tariff that includes a round on both the Old Course and Portland or £150 for just a round on the Old Course. Mind what you wear: Shirts must have collars and be tucked into tailored trousers or shorts.

ScotRail trains from Glasgow's Central Station (www.scotrail.co.uk; ✆ **08457/484-950**) bound for Ayr stop at Troon en route. The journey from Glasgow takes around 40 minutes.

Scottish Maritime Museum ★ MUSEUM   Irvine harbor, 6 miles north of Troon, was once a major port and is now a major stop for maritime history buffs. A shipyard worker's tenement is restored to its 1920s state, and a collection of machinery, ships models, lifeboats, and other paraphernalia are stashed in a glorious glass-roofed Victorian shed. Out on the harbor are moored the SY *Carola,* built on the Clyde in 1898 and the oldest seagoing steam yacht in Great Britain, and the MV Kyles, a steam-engine cargo coaster launched in 1872, making it the oldest Clyde-built vessel still afloat. If you're feeling energetic, you can walk between Troon and Irvine on a well-marked coastal path.

Linthouse Building, Harbour Rd., Irvine. www.scottishmaritimemuseum.org. ✆ **01294/278-283.** £8 adults, £6 seniors and children 5–14. Apr–Oct daily

10am–5pm. From Troon, follow A78 north. Trains from Glasgow Central bound for Ayr and Troon stop at Irvine train station.

Turnberry ★

This small town has a big name for its **Turnberry Golf Courses.** The 7,204-yard, par-70 is one of the most exacting courses yet devised, with the added challenge of buffeting winds. The par-72 Kintyre frames glorious views of the Ailsa Craig island. Greens fees start at £115 on Ailsa and £55 on Kintyre. If you're exploring the coast by car, you might want to head 10 miles south of Turnberry past the little town of Girvan to the forlorn seaside ruins of **Carleton Castle.** According to local legend, laird of the castle Sir John Cathcart married and murdered seven women in order to get his hands on their money. He was foiled when his eighth wife, May, realized what he was up to and pushed him off the cliff to his death. It's said that Cathcart's desperate screams can still be heard; the tale is the inspiration for "The Ballad of May Colvin."

Culzean Castle & Country Park ★★★ CASTLE   One of Scotland's finest stately homes may also be its most romantic. In the late 18th-century the Kennedy clan asked fashionable Scottish architect Robert Adam to revamp a medieval seaside castle and told him to go to town. Adams' formal designs are almost playful. The house seems to teeter on the edge of the cliff, the effect enhanced by a viaduct that crosses a precipice to the entrance. Inside, the two main spaces are circular, a sweeping grand staircase that ascends in graceful double arcs and a vast oval salon. Engaging as the interiors are, the surrounding 228-hectare (563-acre) park is just as magical, with ponds, pagodas, an orangerie,

Culzean Castle & Country Park, near Turnberry.

beaches, woodlands, and an enchanting walled garden. Then-general Dwight D. Eisenhower stayed at Culzean during World War II.

4 miles north of Turnberry and 12 miles south of Ayr, off A719 near Maybole. www. nts.org.uk. ✆ **0844/493-2149.** £16 adults, £12 seniors and children 5–15, £30–£38 families; country park only £10 adults, £8 seniors and children 5–15, £25 and £18 families. Castle open Apr–Oct daily 10:30am–5pm; park open year-round daily 9:30am–sunset. Bus no. 57 from Turnberry or Ayr.

Souter Johnnie's Cottage ★ HISTORIC HOME   This was the 18th-century home of the village cobbler, John Davidson (Souter Johnnie), who, with his friend Douglas Graham of Shanter Farm, was immortalized by Burns in *Tam o' Shanter*. Burns met the men, who you'll encounter in the form of life-size sandstone statues, when he spent a summer in the village. Burns described "scenes of swaggering riot and roaring dissipation," but Davidson remained sober enough to use the tools on display and amass the fine furniture in the cottage rooms.

Main Road, in Kirkoswald, 3 miles west of Turnberry via A77. www.nts.org.uk. ✆ **0844/493-2147**). £4 adults, £3 children and seniors, £7 families. Apr–Sept Fri–Tues 11:30am–5pm.

Loch Lomond & the Trossachs ★★★

Balloch is 19 miles north of Glasgow

The largest of Scotland's lochs packs a wallop of scenic splendor. The river-fed loch stretches for 24 miles between forested heights, none more imposing than Ben Lomond on the eastern shore, rising to 968m (3,176 ft.). Surrounding the lakes are woodland glens, braes (hills), and smaller lochs, all protected as 720-square-mile **Loch Lomond and the Trossachs National Park** (www.lochlomond-trossachs.org). A commonwealth of "elfs, fawns, and fairies" is how one 18th-century observer described this region of shimmering waters, moors, and woodlands, the romantic setting for Sir Walter Scott's 1810 poem *The Lady of the Lake* and his novel *Rob Roy*. If you drive from Glasgow, you might want to pull off at **Dumbarton Castle ★** (www.historic-scotland.gov.uk; ✆ **01389/732-167**; Apr–Sept 9:30am–5:30pm daily, Oct–Mar Sat–Wed 10am–4pm; £5 adults, £3 children), the mighty fortress at the center of the ancient kingdom of Strathclyde, supposedly visited by Merlin. The climb up the 500 steps to the perch on a volcanic rock beside the Firth of Clyde provides head-spinning views. The castle is 20 miles northwest of Glasgow off the A814 at Dumbarton.

You'll probably catch your first glimpse of Loch Lomond at Balloch. On a fine day it might seem like you're in the company of the entire population of Glasgow, but you can soon get out onto the soothing lake waters on **Sweeney's Cruisers** (www.sweeney.uk.com; ✆ **01389/752-376**), departing from Sweeney's Shipyard off Balloch Road in the town center. As you cruise, keep an eye out for the ruins of **Lennox Castle** on Inchmurrin, one of the loch's 30 islands; Robert the Bruce planted the

Loch Lomond, Scotland's largest loch.

island's yew trees to ensure a suitable supply of wood for the bows of his archers. **Loch Lomond Shores** (www.lochlomondshores.com; ℗ **01389/751-035**), an unabashedly touristic enclave on the eastern edge of town off Ben Lomond Way, is also the departure point for cruises; you can rent bikes, kayaks, and canoes as well.

Along the nearby shores, the 81-hectare (200-acre) **Balloch Castle Country Park** ★ surrounds **Balloch Castle** (www.lochlomond-trossachs.org; ℗ **01389/722-600**; 8am–dusk daily; free), an 1808 Gothic style replacement for the 13th century original. The walled garden shields an impressive display of rhododendrons and azaleas in late May and early June. The park is about 1 mile east of town.

A regular train operated by **ScotRail** (www.scotrail.co.uk; ℗ **0845/601-5929**) runs between Glasgow Queen Street and Balloch stations. The journey takes around 45 minutes. **Scottish Citylink** (www.citylink.co.uk; ℗ **08705/505-050**) and **First** (www.firstgroup.com; ℗ **0871/200-2233**) run several buses a day to Balloch from Glasgow; the trip takes 45 minutes. The **National Park Gateway Centre** at the Loch Lomond Shores (www.lochlomond-trossachs.org; ℗ **01389/722-600**) is open daily from 9:30am to 6pm with extended hours in summer. The **Tourist Information Centre** (℗ **08707/200-607**) in the town center on Ballach Road is open daily from 9:30am to 6pm in the summer and 10am to 5pm November to March.

EXPLORING THE AREA

While you can reach some places in the national park by bus, a car makes touring much easier.

DRYMEN ★ This lakeshore village 5 miles northeast of Balloch was at one time known for the famous visitors to **Buchanan Castle ★★**, the ancient fortress of the Duke of Montrose. Hitler's deputy, Rudolf Hess, was imprisoned here in 1941 after he flew solo to Scotland to negotiate a peace agreement with Britain, and other illustrious guests have included the Shah of Iran and King Victor Emmanuel of Italy. The roof was removed in 1955 to avoid paying tax, and the castle fell into the romantic ruin you see today. Both Drymen and Balmaha can be reached via bus no. 309 from Balloch, operated by McColls Coaches (www. mccolls.org.uk; © **01389/754-321**).

BALMAHA ★ Things quiet down a bit here on the eastern shore 4 miles west of Drymen. Excellent walking trails lead into the surrounding countryside from the **National Park Centre** (© **01389/722-100**), open daily from Easter to October 9:30am to 4pm and weekends only the rest of the year. The Balmaha Millennium Forest Path following a circular route via loch shores and deep forest is especially scenic. You can board a vintage wooden ferry for a loch cruise at the **Balmaha Boatyard** (www.balmahaboatyard.co.uk; © **01360/870-214**).

LUSS ★★ A settlement stood here on the western shores of Loch Lomond, 8⅔ miles north of Balloch off the A82, as early as the 7th century. The storybook collection of sandstone and slate cottages is largely an 18th-century town improvement scheme that mercifully preserved the Dark Ages memorial slabs in the churchyard. The **Luss Visitor Centre** (© **01436/860-240**) is open daily from 10am until 7pm in summer and from 10am until 4pm in winter. You can reach Luss from Balloch by boats operated by **Loch Lomond Waterbus services** (www. lochlomond-trossachs.org; © **01389/754-321**).

ABERFOYLE ★ Sir Walter Scott set his romantic poem *The Lady of the Lake* in this pretty village, 19 miles northeast of Balloch via A81 and A811. His evocative verses even lured Wordsworth and Coleridge away from their beloved Lake District (p. 414) for a visit. Wordsworth was so inspired he wrote *To a Highland Girl.* Queen Victoria was so enchanted by the beauty of the region that she had a holiday home built on nearby Loch Katrine. You can admire the same moor, woodland, and mountain views she did from aboard the small steamer **SS *Sir Walter Scott*** (www.lochkatrine.com; © **01877/332-000**); regular sailings between Trossachs Pier and Stronachlachar depart from Easter to late October. **The Lodge, Forest Visitor Centre** (©**01877/382-258**), a mile north of Aberfoyle along the A821, is the starting point for hikes through the **Queen Elizabeth Forest Park ★**. The Lodge is open daily from 10am to 5pm; with earlier closings from October to April.

CALLANDER ★ Most visitors come to little Callander, 11 miles west of Aberfoyle on A81, to set off on dozens of trails into the Trossachs. Walks are detailed in the "Callander Paths" leaflet you can pick up at The **Rob**

Roy & Trossachs Visitor Centre (www.robroycountry.com; © **01877/ 330-342**; daily 10am–6pm July–Aug, 10am–5pm Mar–June, 10am–4pm Sept–Feb) in a converted church in Ancaster Square off Callander's Main Street. Even if you're not hiking, you can enjoy the film narrated by Sean Connery extolling the beauties of the region. These include the **Falls of Leny** and the stunning scenery around **Glen Finglas.**

THE WEST COAST & THE SOUTHERN HEBRIDES

As soon as the Kintyre peninsula, just 12 miles across the channel from Ireland, begins its northward sweep, a certain enchantment takes hold. Golden eagles sore over Arran's craggy mountains, seals and otters swim along the shores of sea lochs and bays, deer and wild sheep scramble across moors and glens on Jura. Throw in some dramatically poised castles on Mull, add the peaty single malt whiskeys of Islay, and top it all off with the freshest seafood you'll ever taste and you begin to understand the great allure of these lands.

INVERARAY ★★

57 miles NW of Glasgow

Inveraray is splendidly poised on the upper shores of Loch Fyne. The town is especially lovely when seen from the east, as you approach from Glasgow, with its trim collection of white houses arranged tidily on a finger of land jutting out into the loch. The little resort town does not have a lot to see and do, and that's just fine. Sitting on a bench and looking across the sparkling waters of the loch can fill a few happy hours.

Essentials

GETTING THERE The Citylink-926 Service (www.citylink.co.uk; © **08705/505-050**) operates **buses** out of Glasgow to Inveraray. The journey takes about 2 hours. If you're **driving** from Glasgow, follow the A82 north and east to its junction with A83 for the final leg east to Inveraray.

VISITOR INFORMATION The **Tourist Information Centre** is on Front Street (www.inveraray-argyll.com; © **01499/302-063**). It's open from June to mid-September, daily 9am to 6pm; with reduced hours the rest of the year.

Exploring the Area

When the Duke of Argyll revamped his castle in the 18th century, he went all out and redid the whole town as well. That explains the remarkably orderly arrangement of white houses with black trim and black-slate roofs. The duke built cottages for workers, a woolen mill, and a pier to boost the export of herring pulled from the loch (herring appear on the town coat of arms, and the town motto translates as "May a herring always hang to thee.") Another town symbol is a **Celtic burial cross** imported from the Hebrides island of Iona that now stands next to the lakefront in the center of town. A nice place to take it all the

Inveraray Castle.

surrounding natural beauty is the **Ardkinglas Woodland Garden** ★ (www.ardkinglas.com; ✆ **01499/600-261**), where conifers and rhododendrons thrive on a 12,000-acre estate at the head of Loch Fyne 4 miles east of town. Admission is £5 for adults, £15 for families; it's open daily from 9am to 5pm. At **Crarae Garden** ★ (www.nts.org.uk; ✆ **0844/493-2210**), 8 miles southwest of Inveraray, cliffs, a gorge, and a rippling stream on a wooded hillside alon Loch Fyne are planted with rare Asian species and in a scene reminiscent of a Himalayan woodland valley. Admission is £7 adults, £5 children 5 to 16, £12 to £17 families. The gardens are open year-round daily 9:30am to sunset.

Inveraray Castle ★★ CASTLE The dukes of Argyll, chiefs of the Clan Campbell, have occupied their hereditary seat since the early 15th century. But their gray-green stone castle, all crenulations and pointy-roofed turrets, is a wildly romantic 18th-cenutry Gothic Revival version of what the 5th duke thought an ancestral seat should look like. The Victorian Room pays homage to Princess Louise, the daughter of Queen Victoria and Prince Albert, who married the 9th duke in 1871. While salons and staterooms are appointed with some excellent art works and dainty 18th-century French furniture and old porcelain, the standout is the remarkable, 1,300-piece collection of arms, from battle axes to muskets. It's on display in the Armory Hall beneath a 21m (69 ft.) ceiling, the highest in Scotland. The castle has a shop and a tea room.
Main St. www.inveraray-castle.com. ✆ **01499 302381.** £10 adults, £8 seniors, £5 children 5–16. Daily 10am–5pm.

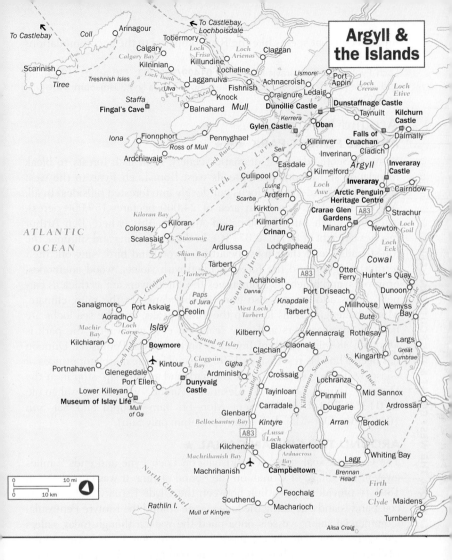

Inveraray Jail ★★ MUSEUM Ever wonder what it was like to be locked up in a small cell with a lunatic or be strapped to a whipping table? Well, you'll learn more than you ever wanted to know about the ins and outs of the British penal system in an exhaustive tour of recreated cells, torture chambers, and a Victorian-era courtroom. The setting is realistic enough, a formidable complex of three-foot-thick stone walls that served as Inveraray's prison from 1820 to 1889. Sound effects (jangling keys, screams, the sound of footfalls) accompany your visit, as do taped commentary of prisoners' stories and extracts from 19th-century trials. You'll leave on a bright note, with a visit to a modern cell that seems like the Ritz compared to the accommodations of yore.

Loch Fyne. www.inverarayjail.co.uk. ✆ **01499/302-203.** £10 adults, £9 seniors and students, £7 children, £29 families. Apr–Oct daily 9:30am–6pm; Nov–Mar daily 10am–5pm.

Around Inveraray

ARGYLL FOREST PARK ★★★

Some of Scotland's most dramatic scenery, from lush forests to bleak moorlands and mountains, spreads west from Loch Fyne to the west coast, where fjord-like sea lochs cut deeply into forested hillsides. In all, Argyll Forest Park covers an area of 24,000 hectares (59,000 acres), extending north into the so-called Arrochar Alps, where Ben Arthur reaches a height of 877m (2,877 ft.). In the early spring and summer, the forest trails are at their most beautiful—woodland birds sing out their territorial rights, and the forest is filled with violets, wood anemones, primroses, and bluebells. Sometimes the wildflowers are as thick as carpets. Ferns and mosses also grow in abundance in the rainy climate. More challenging trails lead up the loftier peaks, and the sea lochs are habitats for sea otters and gray seals. An easy gateway to the park is Dunoon, 38 miles south of Inveraray on the Cowal Peninsula. Dunoon has been a holiday resort since 1790, created for the merchant princes of Glasgow. To pick up info about the park and a trail map, stop in at the Dunoon Tourist Centre, 7 Alexandra Parade (www.visitcowal.co.uk; ✆ **01369/703-785**; Apr–Sept Mon–Fri 9am–5:30pm and Sat–Sun 10am–5pm, Oct–Mar daily 9am–5pm, 4pm only Sun).

AROUND THE CRINAN CANAL ★

The Crinan Canal starts at Ardrishaig on Loch Fyne and ends 9 miles away at the village of Crinan on the Sound of Jura. It was completed in 1801 to provide a quick link between the Clyde Estuary and the west coast and islands, avoiding the long voyage around the Kintyre Peninsula. Commercial sailing vessels once plied the waters, though today sailors and yachters navigate the canal purely for recreation. Even staying on dry land along the towpath is a picturesque outing that leads past 15 locks, seven bridges, two lighthouses, and numerous lock-keepers' cottages.

The varied landscapes of Knapdale spread south from the canal. Part of the flat lands are covered by Knapdale Forest. The **Taynish National Nature Reserve** (www.nnr-scotland.org.uk/taynish; ✆ **01546/603-611**), near the village of Taynish, is a breeding ground for up to 20 species of butterflies and on the migratory routes of many rare birds. **Moine Mhor,** or "Great Moss" (www.nnr-scotland.org.uk/moine-mhor; ✆ **01546/603-611**), best approached from the tow path near Bellanoch, is a water world of pools and bogs that are home to hen harriers and ospreys in the summer, and geese and swans in winter.

A swing bridge along the Crinan Canal.

Kilmartin Glen, just north of the canal, was 1,500 years ago the center of the Gaelic Kingdom of Dalriada. More than 800 ancient sites and monuments, including standing stones, burial tombs, and forts, litter the grassy glen. At the **Kilmartin House Museum** (www.kilmartin.org; ✆ **01546/510-278**) is £5 for adults, £4 for seniors, and £2 for children, you can see archaeological finds and get maps and information to help you locate the most important monuments. The museum is open March to October daily from 10am to 5:30pm, November to December daily from 11am to 4pm; closed from Christmas to the end of February.

From Inveraray, drive along Loch Fyne to Lochgilphead and follow the A83 south into the region. The **Tourist Information Centre** on Lochnell Street in Lochgilphead (www.heartofargyll.com; ✆ **01546/602-344**) is open from April to October, Monday through Friday 10am to 5pm, and Saturday and Sunday noon to 5pm.

Arduanie Gardens ★★ PARK/GARDENS   As if the setting on the southern slopes of the Arduaine Peninsula next to the Bay of Jura weren't spectacular enough, these 20 acres are laced with a colorful display of Tibetan poppies, Himalayan lilies, and other species that thrive in temperate zones around the world, especially eastern Asia and South America. The gardens were planted around the turn of the century as part of the Arduanie House estate, now the adjacent Loch Melfort Hotel (see below). Horticulturalist brothers Edmund and Harry Wright nurtured them back to robust health in the 1970s and 80s. Barriers of hearty evergreens protect the gardens from sea gales, allowing many different species of rhododendrons to thrive among ferns, mosses, and tender plants that carpet slopes besides ponds and streams. Well-maintained paths weave through the gardens and end at a breezy bluff above the sea. Arduaine, 15 miles north of the Crinan Canal on A816. www.nts.org.uk. ✆ **01852/200366.** £7 adults, £5 seniors and children 5–16, £12–£17 families. Daily 9:30am–sunset.

Where to Stay & Eat

Crinan Hotel ★★★   Frances Macdonald, one of the operators of this 1930s lodge perched at the point where the Crinan Canal flows into Loch Crinan, is a well-known landscape artist, and it's easy to see where she gets her inspiration. Sparkling blue water and achingly green hill-sides fill every window, and views extend out to the Hebrides. Being in the light, airy bedrooms is a lot like floating across the loch on a boat, and a top floor lounge is filled with dizzying crow's nest outlooks. Downstairs are comfy sitting rooms and a cozy pub room where fishermen and yachters gather to chat over meals of local seafood. The village is a good starting point for walks along the Crinan Canal Towpath.
Crinan. www.crinanhotel.com. ✆ **01546/830261.** 20 units. Double from £100, inclu-des breakfast. **Amenities:** 2 restaurants; bar; free Wi-Fi.

Loch Fyne ★★   The Loch Fyne chain of popular restaurants operates around the U.K., but none can compare to the fresh-from-the source experience in this attractive room of white stone walls. Oysters, mussels, and much of the other seafood on the menu has just been hauled out of the loch a few steps away. Even breakfast can be a feast of Loch Fyne kippers and house-smoked salmon. A shop sells Loch Fyne's famous smoked fish.
Clachan, 8 miles east of Inverary. www.lochfyne.com. ✆ **01499/600264.** Mains £11–£28. Mon–Thurs 9am–5:30pm, Fri–Sun 9am–7:30pm.

Loch Melfort Hotel ★★   When diamond and tea merchant James Arthur Campbell designed his house in 1898, he wanted to take advan-tage of views far across Asknish Bay to the islands off the west coast. Next to the mansion he planted what have become some of the finest seaside gardens in Scotland. Five character-filled rooms are in the old house, while the rest are in an atmospheric motor-lodge-like extension. Just about all take advantage of the views from terraces and balconies. Dinner in a large sea-facing room begins and ends with drinks in the gracious lounges, making you feel like you're a guest at a private Scottish retreat.
Arduaine, 15 miles north of the Crinan Canal on A816. www.lochmelfort.co.uk. ✆ **0843/886-0233.** 25 units. Doubles £75–£135, includes breakfast. **Amenities:** 2 restaurants; bar; beach; free Wi-Fi.

THE ISLE OF ARRAN ★★

So many glens, moors, lochs, sandy bays, and stretches of rocky coast are packed onto this small island near the mouth of the Firth of Clyde that

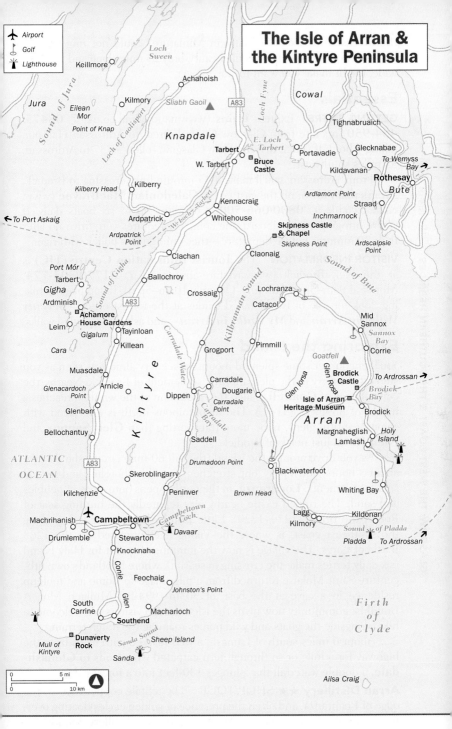

The Isle of Arran & the Kintyre Peninsula

Airport
Golf
Lighthouse

Loch Sween

Keillmore

Jura

Sound of Jura

Eilean Mór

Point of Knap

Kilmory

Achahoish

Sliabh Gaoil

A83

Knapdale

Cowal

Loch Fyne

Tighnabruaich

Glecknabae

Portavadie

Kildavanan

Rothesay

Bute

To Wemyss Bay

Tarbert

W. Tarbert

E. Loch Tarbert

Bruce Castle

Kilberry Head

Kilberry

Kennacraig

Ardlamont Point

Inchmarnock

Straad

To Port Askaig

Ardpatrick

Ardpatrick Point

Whitehouse

Skipness Castle & Chapel

Skipness Point

Ardscalpsie Point

Port Mór

Tarbert

Gigha

Ardminish

Clachan

Ballochroy

A83

Achamore House Gardens

Leim

Gigalum

Tayinloan

Killean

Cara

Crossaig

Claonaig

Lochranza

Catacol

Sound of Bute

Kilbrannan Sound

Carradale Water

Sound of Gigha

Muasdale

Arnicle

Glenacadorch Point

Dippen

Glenbarr

Bellochantuy

Grogport

Pirnmill

Carradale

Dougarie

Carradale Point

Carradale Bay

Saddell

Goatfell

Glen Iorsa

Glen Rosa

Brodick Castle

To Ardrossan

Brodick Bay

Isle of Arran Heritage Museum

Brodick

Arran

Margnaheglish

Lamlash

Holy Island

ATLANTIC OCEAN

A83

Skeroblingarry

Peninver

Drumadoon Point

Brown Head

Blackwaterfoot

Whiting Bay

Kilchenzie

Machrihanish

Campbeltown

Drumlemble

Stewarton

Knocknaha

Davaar

Campbeltown Loch

Lagg

Kilmory

Kildonan

Sound of Pladda

Pladda

To Ardrossan

Feochaig

Conie Glen

Johnston's Point

South Carrine

Macharioch

Southend

Dunaverty Rock

Mull of Kintyre

Sanda Sound

Sheep Island

Sanda

Firth of Clyde

Ailsa Craig

0   5 mi
0   10 km

the overused moniker "Scotland in Miniature" could not ring truer. A single day on this speck of scenic beauty, only 25 miles long and 10 miles wide, might make you want to stay forever.

Essentials

GETTING THERE   Express **trains** (www.nationalrail.co.uk; ✆ 08475/484-950) operate from Glasgow Central direct to Ardrossan Harbour, taking 1 hour. If you're **driving** from Glasgow, follow A737 to Ardrossan, 33 miles southwest.

From Ardrossan, you'll make a 45-minute ferry crossing to Brodick, Arran's main town, on the east coast. **Caledonian MacBrayne** (www.calmac.co.uk; ✆ 0800/066-5000) operates up to six boats daily. If you're bringing a car onboard, the company requires you arrive no later than 30 minutes before departure—they enforce this policy with rigor.

VISITOR INFORMATION   The **Tourist Information Centre (TIC)** is at the Pier, Brodick (www.ayrshire-arran.com; ✆ 01770/303-774; Mon–Sat 9am–5pm, Sun July–Oct only 10am–5pm). If you plan on hiking, look for one of two detailed guides at the tourist office—*Seventy Walks in Arran* and *My Walks in Arran*—and ask about guided walks.

Exploring the Island

You'll encounter some splendid mountain scenery almost as soon as you step off the ferry in the pleasant little settlement of Brodick. Nearby, the conical peak of **Goatfell** (called the "mountain of the winds"), reaches a height of 869m (2,851 ft.). The mountainous north is also laced with some beautiful glens, none more transporting than **Glen Sannox** and **Glen Rosa,** just north of Brodick.

As you drive around the island (the full 60-mile circuit should take about 3 hours) you'll pass long stretches of pebbly shoreline and several small settlements. **Lochranza,** in the north, opens onto a bay of pebbles and sand. The ruined castle nearby was reputedly the hunting seat of Robert the Bruce (1274–1329). Little **Lamlash,** on a pretty bay along the southeast coast, is where the Viking fleet prepared for the 1263 Battle of Largs. The village is now the jumping off point for Holy Island (six daily ferries make the crossing in season), where Scotland's own 6th-century Saint Molaise returned from a pilgrimage to Rome and took up residence in a cave at the base of 303m (994-ft.) Mullach Mor. A Buddhist community now owns the islet, though visitors are welcome to hike alongside the goats and wild ponies roaming the rough terrain.

About 6 miles south of Lamash, a well-marked path leads from the highway for a mile or so through fern-carpeted woodlands to **Glenashdale,** a double waterfall that plunges 130-feet into a forest gorge.

Arran Distillery ★★ SHOP/TOUR   The telltale copper roofs at the edge of Lochranza, and often the presence of golden eagles floating overhead, signals the presence of Arran's prestigious distillery, founded in

Goatfell Mountain on the Isle of Arran.

1995. The operation carries on a long island tradition from the early 19th century when more than 50 Arran distillers were producing what many connoisseurs consider to be among the best of Scottish single malts. The malts are said to acquire their taste from the pure waters of Loch na Davie and the combo of sea breezes, mountain air, and the warm flow of the Gulf Stream. Judge the quality of the output with a draught or two, offered in a tasting room/shop and at the end of an engaging tour. Lochranza. www.arranwhisky.com. © **01770/830264.** £8, £20, and £65, based on tour length and tastings. Mar–Nov daily 10am–5:30pm. Winter hours vary.

Brodick Castle ★★ CASTLE   If the historic home of the dukes of Hamilton looks familiar, it's because you've seen it on the back of 20-pound notes issued by the Bank of Scotland. Aristocracy has lived here at the base of Goatfell Mountain since the Dalriada Irish, a Celtic tribe, founded their kingdom in the 5th century. The red-sandstone castle dates from the 13th century, though a 19th-century redo is in the style of a grand Victorian hunting lodge. The sitting rooms and bedrooms seem almost homey once you get past the 87 sets of stag horns in the main hall and grand staircase. The ghost of one of the dungeon inmates, a woman locked away to starve to death as she succombed to the plague, still haunts the paneled hallways. The specter of a white stag is said to roam the beautiful gardens, laced with streams and waterfalls and overlooking Brodick Bay. His presence supposedly foretells the death of a chief of the Hamiltons; the castle has long since passed out of their hands, which may explain the presence of so many deer in the fern-carpeted woodlands.

1½ miles north of the Brodick pier head. www.nts.org.uk. ℰ **0844/493-2152.** Castle and gardens £13 adults, £9 seniors, students, and children aged 6–16, £23–£30 families. Castle: Apr–Oct daily 11am–4pm (until 3pm in Oct); park: year round, daily 9:30am–sunset.

Isle of Arran Heritage Museum ★ MUSEUM A snuggly furnished cottage, blacksmith shop, and 1920s schoolroom recall island life over the centuries. The well-done archaeology room reaches into the far distant past to tell the story of 5,000-year-old Clachaig Man, whose remains were unearthed on the island, and delves into the significance of the Machrie Stone Circle and other remnants of early Arran inhabitants. Geology exhibits explain what brings rock hounds from around the world to Arran to scour the terrain for some incredibly rare igneous specimens.

Rosaburn, 1½ miles north of the Brodick ferry piers. www.arranmuseum.co.uk. ℰ **01770/302-636.** £4 adults, £3 seniors, £2 children, £9 families. Apr–Oct daily 10:30am–4:30pm.

Where to Stay & Eat

Auchrannie House Hotel ★★ The dowager duchess of Hamilton would probably be pleased to see what's become of her Victorian mansion. She and just about everyone else should certainly be impressed with the two large indoor swimming pools, saunas, and other resort amenities that are a lot fancier than anyone might expect to find on the little island. Rooms in the old manor house are especially atmospheric, while new outbuildings on the estate house bright, spacious, and handsomely styled rooms, along with 30 "lodges" with kitchens. Three dining rooms include a delightful conservatory where diners enjoy nice views of swaying palm trees through the glass panes.

Auchrannie Rd., Brodick. www.auchrannie.co.uk. ℰ **01770/302-234.** 64 units. Doubles £82, includes breakfast. **Amenities:** 3 restaurants; bar; 2 pools (indoor); gym; spa; sauna; free Wi-Fi.

Brodick Bar ★ SEAFOOD/SCOTTISH Don't let the plain, tartan-themed decor deceive you: this is one of the best places on the island for a good meal, and in the unlikely event you're tired of fresh seafood you're in luck. Specialties include Arran lamb and beef, along with hand-dived scallops, local shellfish, and just-caught fish.

Alma Rd. brodickbar.co.uk. ℰ **01770/302169.** Mains £9–£24. Mon–Sat noon–2:30pm and 5:30–10pm; bar until midnight.

Creelers Seafood Restaurant ★★ SEAFOOD/SCOTTISH The island's well known smokehouse is the place to stock up on cured salmon and scallops. The adjacent dining room in old farm buildings near Brodick Castle uses the products and all manner of local seafood in imaginative dishes you probably won't encounter elsewhere. Locally caught haddock is topped with a sauce of smoked haddock and fresh mussels, and smoked salmon comes with warm potato salad—all made with ingredients brought fresh to the kitchen door every morning.

Home Farm, 1 mile north of Brodick. www.creelers.co.uk. *℗* **01770/302-810.** Mains £12–£18. Tues–Sat 12:30–2:30pm and 6–9pm.

Shopping

Arran Aromatics (www.arranaromatics.com; *℗* **01770/302-595**), in an old dairy farm near Brodick Castle, sells high-end toiletries and cosmetics made on Arran, including some fragrances for the home that will make your visit last long after you leave the island. The **Old Byre Showroom,** Auchencar Farm (www.oldbyre.co.uk; *℗* **01770/840-227**), 5 miles north of Blackwaterfoot along the coastal road in Machrie, is a good source for sheepskin, leather, and tweeds, but its biggest draw is the large selection of locally produced woolen sweaters.

THE KINTYRE PENINSULA ★★

The longest peninsula in Scotland seems like an island, for the most part surrounded by water, often approached by ferry, and seemingly lost in a sleepy world of its own. Kintyre drops 60 miles south from the old fishing village of Tarbert, where a wee slip of land connects it to the rest of Scotland. The southern end of the peninsula looks toward Ireland across 12 choppy miles of the Mull of Kintyre, immortalized by local resident Paul McCartney, and the east coast faces Arran. This scenic sliver of land is wonderfully isolated, and its quiet glens and woodlands rise and fall above pebbly shorelines that are largely unspoiled.

Essentials

GETTING THERE & GETTING AROUND **Loganair** (www.flybe.com; *℗* **0871/700-2000**) makes two scheduled 45-minute **flights** a day from Glasgow Airport to Campbeltown, the chief town of Kintyre. From Glasgow, the trip by **Scottish Citylink buses** (www.citylink.co.uk; *℗* **08705/505050**) to Tarbert, Campbeltown, and other towns along the peninsula takes about 4 to 5 hours (schedules vary seasonally).

The most efficient way to travel to and around Kintyre is by **car.** Though Tarbert, at the northern end of the peninsula, is due west of Glasgow, the drive takes you a bit out of your way, but scenically so, quite a way north along the scenic shores of Loch Lomond then back south along Loch Fyne. From Glasgow, take the A82 up to Loch Lomond and cut across to Arrochar and over the "Rest and Be Thankful" route to Inveraray (the A83). Then drive down along Loch Fyne to Lochgilphead and continue on the A83 south to Tarbert, which is the gateway to the peninsula. Allow about 2½ hours for the trip. The two-lane A83 follows the western coast of the peninsula to Campbeltown, while the scenic but much slower single-track B842 drops down the eastern shore (take

Take the Low Road

The **Kintyre Way** ★★ is one of Scotland's most scenic long-distance walks. It stretches for 89 miles, beginning at Tarbert in the north of the peninsula and rambling all the way down to the village of Southend. Hikers generally complete the route in 4 to 7 days. Some of the miles that traverse hill terrain can be difficult, although nothing to challenge the serious hiker.

Most of the walk is a gentle ramble through low-lying terrain along the rugged coastline, taking in castles, woodlands, and wildlife along the way. Pep Cars taxi service (www.pepcars. co.uk; ✆ **01880/730369**) will transport luggage from point to point along the route. Pick up a map of the trail at any local tourist office or visit www.kintyre way.com.

your time along this road, yield to sheep, and use the turnouts to accommodate oncoming traffic).

Tarbert ★

103 miles west of Glasgow

The name of this sheltered harbor derives from a Gaelic word meaning isthmus, because this is where the Vikings used to drag their boats from Loch Fyne across the mile-wide neck of land that connects the Kintyre Peninsula to the rest of Scotland. Some of the fishermen who live in the pretty village houses beneath the ruined castle of Robert the Bruce still haul herring and shellfish out of the waters of Loch Fyne (see Inveraray, p. 573), but these days the docks are mostly crowded with pleasure craft.

Campbeltown ★

37 miles south of Tarbert, 140 miles southwest of Glasgow

This fishing port at the southern tip of the Kintyre Peninsula is charmingly old fashioned. So much so that the way locals refer to it simply as the "wee toon" makes perfect sense. The 14th-century Celtic **Campbeltown Cross** ★ stands picturesquely next to quays that are crowded with fishing boats and yachts. Similar scenes are captured in a decent collection of paintings by Scottish artists in the **Campbeltown Museum** (www.museumsgalleriesscotland.org.uk; ✆ **01586/559-017**), in the center of town on St John's Street. Among them are canvases by William McTaggart, who was born in Campbeltown in 1835 and went on to become one of Scotland's best-known landscape painters. He returned to Campbeltown continually, drawn by the light and scenery, and it's been said that being in Kintyre is like stepping into his paintings. (You'll also see them at the National Galleries of Scotland and other museums.)

Cambeltown's **Wee Picture House,** 20 Hall St. (www.weepic tures.co.uk; ✆ **01586/553-800**) occupies an Art Deco building from

1913 and is believed to be the oldest surviving purpose-built cinema in Scotland.

The **Tourist Information Centre** is at MacKinnon House, The Pier (www.visitscottishheartlands.com; ✆ **01586/552-056**). Hours vary, with longer summer hours, but you can mostly count on it being open 10am to 5pm Monday to Saturday and 11am to 4 or 5pm on Sundays.

Some of Scotland's most famous golf courses are near Campbeltown. About 5 miles east are the historic **Machrilhanish Golf Club** (www.machgolf.com; ✆ **01586/810-277**) and **Machrihanish Dunes** (www.machrihanishdunes.com; ✆ **01586/810000**). The 18-hole **Dunaverty Golf Course** (www.dunavertygolfclub.com; ✆ **01586/830-677**) is outside Southend.

Southend & the Mull of Kintyre ★★

Southend is 10 miles south of Campbeltown

Land's end on Kintyre is near the village of Southend. A debate has been raging for centuries about the origins of the footprint-shaped indentations on a rock near the town's old chapel. Some claim the prints mark the spot where St Columba first set foot on Scottish soil. Others suggest that they mark the spot where ancient kings were crowned. Just about everyone agrees that some of the most savagely beautiful seascapes in Scotland surround the lighthouse south of town on the Mull of Kintyre. Let Paul McCartney's lyrics inspire you as you make the trip out to the desolate point along a single track road: "Mull of Kintyre, Oh mist rolling in from the sea, My desire is always to be here, Oh Mull of Kintyre."

WHERE TO STAY & EAT

Two places for live music are next door to each other on Cross St. in Campbeltown. **The Feathers Inn** (✆ **01586/554-604**) hosts groups on Thursday nights, while **the Commercial Inn** (✆ **01586/553-703**) has live music on Fridays and alternate Saturdays. They're open from noon to 1am.

Torrisdale Castle Estate ★★★   The romantic 19th-century castle that Naill and Emma Macalister Hall and their family call home is perched in meadows and woodlands above the eastern shore, and they share these colorful surroundings with guests in a castle apartment and four lodges and cottages on extensive grounds. The apartment in the former servant's quarter is especially comfortable, with three bedrooms and sitting rooms (as well as a secret chamber) occupying the former kitchens, wine cellar, and store rooms. A wood-fired hot tub and sauna next to a gurgling stream are unexpected luxuries, while a tannery in the former laundry building uses centuries-old natural methods to produce sheepskin and deer-hide rugs and cat mats that are great souvenirs.

Main St., Campbeltown, PA28 6AB. www.torrisdalecastle.com. ✆ **01583/431233.** 5 units. Doubles from £225 a week; shorter stays available. **Amenities:** Free Wi-Fi.

Ugadale Hotel ★★ Once upon a time, well-to-do Glaswegians arrived by steamer to spend summer months at this grand hotel overlooking the sea. After some decades of neglect and weather-induced battering, the sea-facing resort has been redone top to bottom and is looking better than ever. Large rooms are smartly done in wood, brass, and plaids to provide lodging for golfers on two superb courses, the Machrilhanish Golf Club and Machrilhanish Dunes, and they are the most comfortable base for miles around for anyone else exploring the southern peninsula. Even if you're not golfing or staying elsewhere, the Old Clubhouse, the hotel's casual restaurant, is tops for a pub lunch.

Machirhanish, 5 miles east of Campbeltown. www.machrihanishdunes.com. ✆ **01586/810001.** 22 units. Doubles from £149, includes breakfast. Gold and meal packages available. **Amenities:** 2 restaurant; 2 bars; free Wi-Fi.

THE ISLE OF GIGHA ★

3 miles W of Kintyre's western coast

It's easy to get the feeling that the world has passed this 6-mile long islet by. The Vikings stored their loot here after plundering the west coast of Scotland, and cairns, ruins, and legends speak of times when the island might have been a little busier than it is now. The **Ogham Stone** is one of only two standing stones in the Hebrides that bears an Ogham inscription, a form of script used in the 6th-century Scottish kingdom of Dalriada. The ruins of the **Church of Kilchattan** date back to the 13th century. Quiet is how the 100 or so islanders like it. To keep things that way, in 2002 they formed the Isle of Gigha Heritage Trust (www.gigha.org.uk) and bought Gigha in its entirety for £4 million. Islanders now celebrate March 15, when the purchase was completed, as "Independence Day."

Walking is what brings most visitors to Gigha, along with the island's glorious garden. **Ferries** link Gigha with Tayinloan, halfway up the west coast of Kintyre on the A83. Sailings are daily on the hour during the summer, and take about 20 minutes; boats arrive at **Ardminish,** Gigha's main hamlet. For ferry schedules, contact Caledonian McBrayne, www.calmac.co.uk; ✆ **0800/066-5000**). Gigha has no tourist office, but you'll find a wealth of information at www.gigha.org.uk.

Achamore House Gardens ★★ PARK/GARDEN These 20-hectares (49-acres) are the creation of the late Sir James Horlick. Aside from being an astute businessman who made a fortune from the soothing malted bedtime drink that bears his name, he was also one of the world's great horticulturalists. He bought Achamore House, along with rest of Gigha, in 1944, because he was interested in growing exotic plants in the island's favorable microclimate. He surrounded Achamore House with roses, hydrangeas, rhododendrons, and azaleas, as well as pines from Central America, conifers from Australia, and other rare specimens.

Paths wind through the gardens into woodlands and up ridges overlooking the mountains and sea, and a 2-acre walled garden is often ablaze with color.

1 mile outside Ardminish. www.gigha.org.uk. ✆ **01583/505-400.** £5. Daily–dusk.

Where to Stay & Eat

Gigha Hotel ★   Gigha's only hotel and pub occupies an 18th-century farmhouse near the ferry landing. The small rooms plain and cozy, as befits the island's down-to-earth lifestyle, and their best assets are the lovely views of the sea and the rugged countryside. Even if you're not overnighting on the island, you should stop in for a pub lunch or a drink, both of which come with a chance to talk with the islanders, many of whom have chosen to relocate to this tranquil place from elsewhere. A shop next door sells a nice selection of handmade crafts, woolens, and souvenir mugs and plates decorated with the Gigha tartan.

Isle of Gigha. www.gigha.org.uk. ✆ **01583/505-254.** 13 units. Doubles £80–£120, includes breakfast. **Amenities:** Restaurant; bar; free Wi-Fi.

THE ISLE OF ISLAY ★★

16 miles W of the Kintyre Peninsula

The southernmost island of the Inner Hebrides (the name is pronounced "*Eye*-la"), is a serene and unspoiled place of moors, salmon-filled lochs, sandy bays, and rocky cliffs. The stark beauty doesn't reach the standards of Arran, Kintyre, or Mull, but that's not saying Islay is anything less than lovely. Plus, the tiny island, only 20 miles at its widest point and 25 miles long, is home to eight distinguished distilleries, offering the chance to drink some of the world's finest single malts at the source.

Essentials

GETTING THERE Caledonian MacBrayne (www.calmac.co.uk; ✆ **08705/650-000**) provides a daily **ferry** service from Kennacraig on the Kintyre peninsula to Port Askaig, on the northeastern coast of Islay. In the summer there are up to four ferries a day. The journey takes about 2 hours. By **air,** Flybe makes the short hop from Glasgow to Islay's little airport between Port Ellen and Bowmore (www.flybe.com).

VISITOR INFORMATION   The Islay Tourist Information Centre is on The Square, Bowmore (www.islayinfo.com; ✆ **01496/810-254**). Opening hours are: April to June, Monday to Saturday 10am to 5pm, Sunday 2 to 5pm; July and August, Monday to Saturday 9:30am to 5:30pm, Sunday 2 to 5pm; September and October, Monday to Saturday 10am to 5pm.

Port Ellen ★

Islay's principal port, on the south coast, is most visited for the string of distilleries along the coast just north of town. A nice time out from the whisky circuit is a visit to the **Kildalton churchyard** in lovely country-side about 7½ miles to the northeast. The 8th century **Kildalton Cross ★**, one of Scotland's finest early works; the hard stone is richly carved with biblical scenes that are still a vivid work of pictorial story telling: the Virgin cradles the child, Abraham is poised to sacrifice Abel, and David fights a lion. At the **Oa Nature Reserve,** 8 miles south of Port Ellen, spectacular, windswept headlands overlook the Mull of Oa.

The Oa Nature Reserve ★★★ PARK/GARDEN   The 1,931-hectare Oa Peninsula, where impoverished tenant farmers once worked the scrappy land and illicit whisky smugglers hid their stashes in sea caves, is now designated a Special Protected Area. Sheer cliffs are home to golden eagles and other rare sea birds, while Highland cattle and long-horn sheep graze on the rippling grasslands and moors. At the edge of the bluffs stands a forlorn stone tower, the **American Monument,** commemorating lives lost at sea in two incidents. On February 5, 1918, 9 months before the end of World War I, a German U-boat sunk the *Tuscania,* a luxury liner converted to a troop ship, with the loss of 230 lives. Eight months later, on October 6, another 400 lives were lost when the troop ship HMS *Ontario* collided with the steamship HMS *Kashmire.*

Oa peninsula, 8 miles south of Port Ellen. www.rspb.org.uk. ℂ **01496 300118.** Always open.

Bowmore ★

Islay's pint-sized capital is unusually orderly, built in 1770 along wide, gridlike streets on orders of Daniel Campbell the Younger, overlord of the island. If the tidy streets seem to inspire good behavior, the town's Round Church does so in spades, providing no corners where the devil can hide. All this righteousness doesn't put a damper on whisky-making, big business at the town's Bowmore Distillery.

Loch Gruinart ★, 8 miles north of Bowmore, is the winter home for wild geese and also haven for many rare sea birds, otters, common and grey seals, hares, red and roe deer. The 1,215 hectares (3,000 acres) of moors and farmland around the loch are protected as the **Loch Gruinart Nature Reserve** (www.rspb.org.uk; ℂ **01496/850-505**); the visitor center is open daily, 10am to 5pm.

Finlaggan (finlaggan.com), 7 miles northwest of Bowmore off A846, is a pretty but godforsaken-looking place with a storied and important past. The stone ruins clustered on an islet in a little loch were at one time home to the lord of Clan Donald, who ruled the islands and large sections of the West Coast; walking around the overgrown ruins might remind you of "Ozymandias," Shelley's poem about long-vanquished power, depending on how many distillery stops you've made. A visitor center is open April through September Monday through Saturday 10:30am to 4:30pm and Sunday 1:30pm to 4:30pm, with reduced hours October through March.

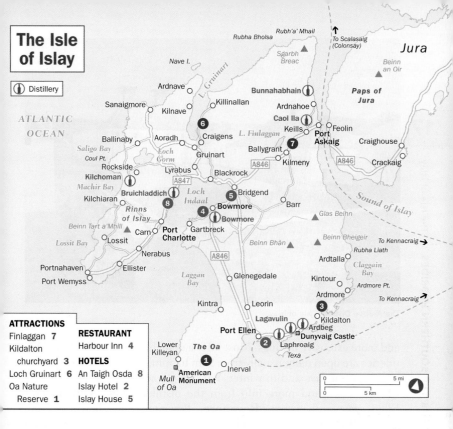

The Isle of Islay

ⓘ Distillery

ATLANTIC OCEAN

Jura

Paps of Jura

Beinn an Oir

Rubh'a' Mhail

Rubha Bholsa

Sgarbh Breac

Nave I.

L. Gruinart

To Scalasaig (Colonsay)

Ardnave

Sanaigmore

Kilnave

Killinallan

Ardnahoe

Bunnahabhain ⓘ

Caol Ila ⓘ

Keills

Feolin

Port Askaig

Craighouse

Craigens

Aoradh

Ballinaby

Saligo Bay

Coul Pt.

Rockside

Kilchoman ⓘ

Machir Bay

Kilchiaran

Bruichladdich ⓘ

Rinns of Islay

Beinn Tart a'Mhill

Lossit Bay

Carn

Lossit

Nerabus

Portnahaven

Ellister

Port Wemyss

L. Finlaggan

6 Craigens

Loch Gorm

Gruinart

Lyrabus

Blackrock

Ballygrant

Kilmeny

A846

Crackaig

Sound of Islay

7

A847

Loch Indaal

Bridgend

5

8

4 Bowmore

Bowmore

Gartbreck

Port Charlotte

Barr

Glas Beinn

Beinn Bheigeir

Beinn Bhàn

Ardtalla

Rubha Liath

To Kennacraig →

Claggain Bay

Ardmore Pt.

To Kennacraig ↗

Laggan Bay

Glenegedale

Kintour

Ardmore

3

Kintra

Leorin

Lagavulin

Port Ellen

Lower Killeyan

The Oa

Ardbeg

Kildalton

Dunyvaig Castle

Laphroaig

2

Texa

1 American Monument

Inerval

Mull of Oa

0 ____ 5 mi
0 ____ 5 km

ATTRACTIONS
Finlaggan **7**
Kildalton
  churchyard **3**
Loch Gruinart **6**
Oa Nature
  Reserve **1**

RESTAURANT
Harbour Inn **4**

HOTELS
An Taigh Osda **8**
Islay Hotel **2**
Islay House **5**

Port Charlotte ★

Much of southern Islay curves around Loch Indaar, with trim, proud little Bowmore holding court on the eastern shore and Port Charlotte lying directly across the waters on the western shore. The picturesque port town is the place to bone up on island history, at the **Museum of Islay Life ★** (www.islaymuseum.org; ℂ **01496/850-358;** £3 adults, £2 seniors, and £1 kids 5–16) in an old church. Among a predictable showing of whisky stills and ships' figureheads are a charmingly random mishmash of Victorian bedroom sets, photos of shipwrecks, and fossils. From Easter to October, the museum is open Monday through Saturday 10am to 4pm.

Visiting the Distilleries ★★

Islay's peat-flavored single malts made by the antiquated pot-still method puts the island on the world map. Boatloads of aficionados come ashore to visit the Islay's eight working distilleries, all of which offer tastings and tours and sell their products onsite. At all expect to pay about £6 for a tour, and £15 for a basic tasting, with prices increasing for lengthier tours

The Ardbeg Distillery, Isle of Islay.

and more extensive tastings. Most offer a draught to visitors for free. Distilleries are open daily, usually from 9am to 5pm, sometimes with shorter hours on Sundays and in winter. You can get an overview at www.islay whiskies.com, and more info from the distillery sites (**Ardbeg,** Port Ellen, www.ardbeg.com; **Bowmore,** Bowmore, www.bowmore.com, ✆ **01496/810-441; Bruichladdich,** Bruichladdich, www.bruich laddich.com, ✆ **01496 850 190; Bunnahabhain,** Port Askaig, www. bunnahabhain.com, ✆ **01496/840-646; Caol Ila,** Port Askaig, www. malts.com; **Kilchoman,** Bruichladdich, kilchomandistillery.com; **Lagavulin,** Port Ellen, www.malts.com, ✆ **01496/302-749; Laphroaig,** Port Ellen, www.laphroaig.com, ✆ **01496/302-418**).

Remember, whether you visit one distillery or all eight, Scotland has strict laws against driving while intoxicated. Most distilleries will give you a takeaway sampler in lieu of a tasting.

Shopping

The **Islay Woollen Mill** ★, Bridgend (www.islaywoollenmill.co.uk; ✆ **01496/810-563**; Mon–Sat 9am–5pm) has been making country tweeds and accessories for more than a century. The mill shop sells items fashioned with tweeds created for Mel Gibson's *Braveheart* as well as smart Shetland wool ties, Jacob mufflers and ties, flat caps, travel rugs, and scarves. **Islay House Square,** next to Islay House in Bridgend, occupies what was once servants' quarters and workshops for the manor house; it now houses a brewery, photography galleries, a marmalade shop, and other distinctive business.

Where to Stay & Eat

An Taigh Osda ★★★   You would have to be inured to charm if you didn't feel immediately at home in this gracious Edwardian-era seaside home where Paul and Joan have perfected the art of inn keeping. Attractive rooms are appointed with wool carpets and tasteful furnishings that do justice to the house's fine old bones. Unbroken vistas of Loch Indaal outside most of the tall windows provide a show of scenic drama. Guests can dine in house on a three course menu accompanied by good wines and followed with an excellent selection of local whiskies.

Bruichladdich. www.antaighosda.co.uk. *©* **01496/850587.** 5 units. Doubles from £150, includes breakfast. 3-course dinner £35. **Amenities:** Restaurant; lounge-bar; free Wi-Fi.

Harbour Inn ★ SEAFOOD/PUB FOOD   Workers from nearby Bowmore Distillery gather at this old-fashioned pub, with stone walls, a fireplace, and wooden floors, so the selection of single malts must be pretty good. They also hang around for the sure-handed and inventive preparations of fresh-from-the-docks seafood.

Main St., Bowmore *©* **01496/810-330.** Mains £17–£26. Daily noon–2:30pm and 6–9pm. Bar until 1am.

Islay Hotel ★   You couldn't find a more convenient base for touring Islay's famous trio of distilleries just outside Port Ellen. The large, bright rooms just beyond the ferry landing are also well poised for exploring the rest of the island, and are nicely done in sporty pine furnishings, and light colors and fabrics. The excellent restaurant downstairs spills out onto a terrace in good weather; it's not unusual to come upon an impromptu music session in the adjoining whisky bar/pub.

Charlotte St. theislayhotel.com. *©* **01496/300109.** 13 units. Doubles from £120, includes breakfast. **Amenities:** Restaurant; bar; free Wi-Fi.

Islay House ★★   One of Scotland's finest manor houses, once the home of the Campbell clan, puts a sophisticated spin on the notion of a bed and breakfast. The large and gracious old bedrooms are beautifully redone with period furnishings and retain original architectural details. All overlook the sea and the wooded grounds, where a two-acre walled garden is not only a horticultural masterpiece but also feeds the island with fresh produce. You could not outdo the Peat Cutter bar for grand surroundings in which to sample a dram or two of island whiskies.

Bridgend. www.islayhouse.co.uk. *©* **01496/810702.** 10 units. Doubles from £175, includes breakfast. **Amenities:** Bar; free Wi-Fi.

THE ISLE OF JURA ★

⅔ mile E of Islay

The red deer on Jura—Scotland's largest animals, at around 1.2m (4 ft.) in height—outnumber people by about 25 to 1. As it should be, since the name comes from the Norse *jura* for "deer." Only about 250 hearty souls live on the 27-mile-long island, and they're surrounded by a dramatic landscape of mountains, soaring cliffs, and moors.

Jura's only road, the A846, begins at Feolin (little more than the anchoring place for the ferry from Islay) and runs up the east coast of the island as far as the village of Lussa-given. Most walkers head for the so-called **Paps of Jura,** the three steep conical mountains of quartzite on the uninhabited western side of the island. The highest, Beinn-an-Oir (or "mountain of gold" in Gaelic), reaches 786m (2,575 ft.). The island's hamlet capital, **Craighouse,** has Jura's only shop, church, and hotel/pub, along with a whisky distillery (www.isleofjura.com; ℡ **01496/820-385**). Guided distillery tours are offered April to September, Monday through Friday at 11am and 2pm. Advance booking is required.

From Port Askaig, on Islay, **ferries** make the 5-minute trip across the Sound of Islay to Feolin at the southern tip of Jura about every half-hour during the summer. Boats are operated by **ASP Ship Management Ltd** (www.islayinfo.com/jura-ferry.html; ℡ **01496/840-681**).

> ### Orwell on Jura
>
> Novelist and critic George Orwell (1903–50) spent much of 1946 and 1947 in a remote island cottage on Jura, and the landscapes appear to have inspired him in a strange way: Rather than observing simple, old-fashioned Hebridean life and natural beauty, Orwell completed his dystopian novel *1984* while on Jura. Perhaps the overpowering presence of the Paps of Jura and the ever-present howl of winter winds found their way into Orwell's evocation of Big Brother and omnipresence government surveillance. He died of tuberculosis shortly after the novel was published to widespread acclaim.

MULL ★★

90 miles NW of Glasgow

The third-largest island in the Hebrides is said to be a land of ghosts, monsters, and the wee folk, and even for those of us who aren't superstitious, the wild landscapes, mountains, and shimmering sea lochs loom large. The island's highest peak, **Ben More,** soars to 961m (3,153 ft.), and roe deer, polecats, and feral goats roam the moors and woodlands. Little wonder that many islanders and their appreciative visitors consider Mull to be the most beautiful of all the Hebridean islands; it might be the wettest, too, so bring a rain coat.

Essentials

GETTING THERE & GETTING AROUND It's a 45-minute trip by **car ferry** from the mainland town of Oban (100 miles northwest of Glasgow) to Craignure, on Mull. For departure times, contact **Caledonian Mac-Brayne** (www.calmac.co.uk; ℡ **0800/066-5000**). There are five or six sailings per day. **Bowmans Coaches Mull** (www.bowmanstours.co.uk; ✆ **01680/812-313**) connect with the Craigmure ferry at least three times a day and will take you to Fionnphort and Tobermory.

VISITOR INFORMATION The **Harbour Visitor Centre** in Tobermory provides information and will help with booking accommodation and boat trips (www.tobermory.co.uk; ✆ **01688/302-182**). It's open from Easter to October, Monday through Friday from 9am to 6pm.

ORGANIZED TOURS **Sea Life Surveys,** Beadoun, Breidwood, Tobermory (www.sealifesurveys.com; ✆ **01688/302-916**), will take you out to see whales, dolphins, and seals on tours that range from all-day whale-watching trips to 2-hour seal-watching cruises. From the Ulva Ferry Piers, on the west side of Mull, you can cruise to the lonely **Treshnish Isles,** a sanctuary for puffins, guillemots, and seals. The *Turus Mara* (www.turusmara.com; ✆ **01688/302-916**), carries up to 60 passengers on half-day visits from April to September, at £45 to £55. The Treshnish Isles are murky, muddy, and boggy, and so bring dry clothes, boots, and a sense of humor.

Outdoor Activities

BIKING Two rental outlets are On Yer Bike, at Inverinate, Salen near Aros, not far from Tobermory (✆ **01680/300-501;** Easter–October only) and **Brown's,** on High Street in Tobermory (www.browns tobermory.co.uk; ✆ **01688/302-020**). Both are open daily from 8:45am to around 5:30pm.

GOLF At the isolated 9-hole **Craignure Golf Course** (www.craig nuregolfclub.co.uk), 22 miles west of Tobermory, you're requested to deposit £15 greens fees into an honesty box. **Tobermory Golf Club** (www.tobermorygolfclub.com; ✆ **01688/302-741**) is a 9-hole course with hilly terrain, and wind that poses a challenge offset by what must be some of the best views of any course in the world.

HIKING Mull is wonderful for hiking. The tourist office sells two books, *Walks in North Mull* and *Walks in South Mull* that provide detailed options for routes with historic, scenic, ethnographical, or geological interest.

Craignure ★

The sea approach to the island's main ferry port provides a quintessentially Scottish view of lonely Duart Castle rising above the sea and moors. Adding to the romance is that somewhere on the seabed lies the *Florencia,* a Spanish galleon that went down laden with treasure.

Duart Castle ★ CASTLE In 1791 the dukes of Argyll sacked the 13th- century home of the fiery MacLean clan and the castle lay in ruin until 1911. That's when Sir Fitzroy, the 26th chief of the MacLeans and grandfather of the present occupant, began restoring

Colorful Tobermory on the Isle of Mull.

what was essentially a piles of stones. He must have been a romantic, as the silhouette of turrets, ramparts and gables seem to leap right out of medieval legend. You might run into one of the MacLeans, who reside at the castle on and off, as you walk through the Great Hall, kitchens, and bedrooms.

On the eastern point of Mull 3 miles east of Craignure. www.duartcastle.com. ℰ **01680/812-309.** £6 adults, £5 seniors and students, £3 children, £14 families. Apr Sun–Thurs 11am–4pm; May to mid-Oct; daily 10:30am–5pm.

Tobermory ★★

21 miles northwest of Craignure

One of the most sheltered harbors in Scotland is the unofficial capital of Mull, where brightly painted houses face a flotilla of bobbing boats. The little **Mull Museum** ★ (www.mullmuseum.org.uk; ℰ **01688/301-100**) in an old bakery on Main Street is the place to bone up on island history. It's free, and open Easter to mid-October, Monday to Friday from 10am to 4pm, and sometimes on Sundays in the summer. The **Tobermory Malt Whisky Distillery** (ℰ **01688/302-645**), gives tours by appointment only.

Dervaig ★

8 miles west of Tobermory

The name of the loveliest village on Mull means Little Grove. The **Old Byre Heritage Centre** ★ (www.old-byre.co.uk; ℰ **01688/400-229**) houses 25 charming scale models, painstakingly made by a local historian, that illustrate the history of Mull from the first settlers to the Highland Clearances. Admission is £3 for adults, £2 for seniors and students, and children 5 to 12. It's open from April to October, Wednesday through Sunday from 10:30am to 6:30pm.

Fionnphort ★

50 miles south of Dervaig, 35 miles southwest of Craignure

The drive down the west coast along single-track road across the windy western flanks of **Ben More,** Mull's tallest summit, is so spectacular that islanders often go out of their way to make the tip. The road ends at tiny Fionnport, where passenger ferries depart for the 1-mile trip to the Isle of Iona, one of the most visited places in Scotland.

Iona ★★

⅛ mile west of Mull

This tiny piece of rock, only 1 by 3½ miles, sheltered the first Christian settlement in Scotland, whose inhabitants preserved learning that might otherwise have been lost in the Dark Ages. The island was owned by the dukes of Argyll from 1695, but in order to pay £1 million in real-estate taxes, in the 1970s the 12th duke was forced to sell Iona to Sir Hugh Fraser, former owner of Harrods department store. Fraser secured Iona's future and made it possible for money raised by the National Trust for Scotland to be turned over to the trustees of the restored abbey. The only village on Iona, **Baille Mor,** sits in the most sheltered spot, allowing some trees and garden plots to be cultivated.

    Though the island attracts nearly 1,000 visitors a week in high season, it remains a peaceful and spiritual place. It's easy to appreciate the fact that from this tiny island Celtic Christianity spread through Scotland and to Europe beyond. A very few parts of the Benedictine **Iona Abbey ★** date from the 13th century, as it was more or less left to ruin when the monks gathered up their libraries and left the island during the 15th century Scottish Reformation. The abbey was rebuilt in the mid-20th century. A few relics of the settlement founded here by St Columba in A.D. 563 also remain, among them several stone crosses. The abbey is run by Historic Scotland (www.historic-scotland.gov.uk), which leads tours and runs a coffee shop daily from 9:30am to 4:30pm in winter, and from 9:30am to 5:30 in summer. Admission is £7 adults, £6 students and seniors,

Iona Abbey, Isle of Iona.

£4 children 5 to 15. You can wander freely around the island, and make the easy ascent to the top of **Dun-I** to contemplate the ocean and the landscape as though you were the only person on earth.

STAYING ON IONA

The **Iona Community** (www.iona.org.uk; ☎ **01681/700-404**) maintains a communal lifestyle in Iona abbey and offers full board and accommodation to visitors. From March to October, the community leads a series of seminars, each lasting from Saturday to Saturday. The cost of a week's full board during one of these seminars is about £300 per person; there are significantly discounted rates for students and children. The abbey also opens to guests from late November to mid-December, although no seminars are offered then. The per-week price is the same as in summer. Guests are expected to contribute about 30 minutes per day to the execution of some kind of household chore. The daily schedule involves a wake-up call at 8am, communal breakfast at 8:20am, a morning religious service, and plenty of unscheduled time for conversation, study, and contemplation. Up to 44 guests can be hosted at one time, in bunk-bedded twin rooms with shared bathrooms.

Staffa ★

6¼ miles north of Iona

This tiny island was abandoned 170 years ago, though visitors continue to come ashore to visit **Fingal's Cave ★★**, known in Gaelic as *An Uamh Ehinn*, or "musical cave." Over the centuries, the sea has carved a huge cavern in the basalt, the crashing waves and swirling waters created an

Fingal's Cave, Isle of Staffa.

eerily harmonious sound that could pass for a symphony, with heavy use of drums and bass, of course. The music inspired Mendelssohn to write the *Fingal's Cave Overture*: Turner painted the cavern and Keats, Wordsworth, and Tennyson all praised it in their poetry.

Entrance to the cave is free, but for boat passage from Fionnport on Mull or Iona you'll pay about £30 for adults and £15 for children aged 13 and under. Between March and October the boat runs twice daily from Iona, at 9:45am and 1:45pm, and from Fionnphort at 10am and 2pm. The trip lasts about 3 hours, including about 1 hour ashore. Rubber-soled shoes and warm clothing are recommended. Reservations are important; telephone **Mrs. Carol Kirkpatrick,** whose husband, David, operates the boat, at *Tigh-na-Traigh* (House by the Shore), Isle of Iona (www.staffatrips.co.uk; © **01681/700-358**).

WHERE TO STAY & EAT

Gannet's Restaurant ★ SCOTTISH   It's hard not to be reeled into this simple little seaside place that claims "the only thing frozen is the fisherman." All the fish and seafood come off the restaurant's own boat. You can savor the freshness with a cold shellfish platter, the contents of which have been caught that day, and in hearty seafood stews.

The Pier. Tobermory. www.thecafefish.com. © **01688/301253.** Mains £10–£18. Mar–Oct daily 10am–11pm.

Glenforsa Hotel ★   The woodsy side of Mull comes to the fore in this log, seaside lodge on the secluded east coast. Pine-paneled rooms with crisp white linens and draperies are rustically elegant, as are the lounges looking beyond tall evergreens to the Sound of Mull. Many guests fly their own planes onto the hotel's grass airstrip to fish for salmon, and the lovely grounds and panoramic upstairs sitting room are prime spots for bird watching and observing otters and seals on the shore.

Salen, by Aros. www.glenforsa.co.uk. © **01680/300-377.** 15 units. Doubles £95, includes breakfast. **Amenities:** Restaurant; bar; room service; free Wi-Fi.

Glengorm Castle ★★   You'd be surprised at just how easy it is to feel at home in the Great Hall of a castle, sitting next to a roaring fire, sipping a single malt, and looking over the Sound of Mull. That's the point at this 1860 castle/county house, home to the Nelson family and welcomingly furnished with an eclectic mix of heirlooms and comfy couches and armchairs. Bedrooms range in size from large to enormous and are appointed with period pieces, handsome wall coverings, and paintings. The views from most seem to extend forever. A turn of the century stone pool next to the shore provides a dip that's a little less bone-chilling than a swim in the sea.

On the B8073, Tobermory. www.glengormcastle.co.uk. © **01688/302-321.** 5 units. Doubles £135–£210, includes breakfast. A £30 discount applies after the first night. **Amenities:** Bar; pool; library; coffee shop; Wi-Fi (in Great Hall only; free).

Sheiling Holidays ★ You won't be living in luxury, but these tents are carpeted, have firm beds, and are framed with extra thick canvas to keep out the wet and chill. A communal toilet block is sparkling clean, as are the shared cooking facilities. A seat at the campfire comes with views over the Sound of Mull, Loch Linnhe and the Firth of Lorne.

Outside Craigmure. www.shielingholidays.co.uk. From £37 a night, minimum 2 nights. **Amenities:** Communal kitchen; Wi-Fi (free, in some areas only).

THE HIGHLANDS & THE ISLE OF SKYE

by Lucy Gillmore

Mist-shrouded mountains, gloomy glens blanketed in pungent pine forests, swollen lochs and wild heather-sprung moors: a vast ancient landscape grazed by herds of magnificent red deer, and golden eagles wheeling far above. Rushing rivers swim with trout and salmon while a mythical monster lurks in the region's most famous loch. Add a scattering of gnarled castles, Bonnie Prince Charlie connections at every turn, one of Scotland's bloodiest massacres and the grand ancestral home of Shakespeare's "Macbeth" and you've got all the ingredients for a jam-packed, history-soaked road-trip.

This is the tartan-clad Highlands of romantic imagination. The region is also a giant outdoor adventure playground, with slopes to ski, Munros to bag and coastline to kayak, while for those who hanker after gentler pursuits there's a Malt Whisky trail to meander. Scotland's most famous bard, Robert Burns, hailed from the Borders, but even he penned a poem claiming "My Heart's in the Highlands."

INVERNESS ★

156 miles NW of Edinburgh; 134 miles W of Aberdeen

Inverness is the gateway to the Highlands. That makes it sound rather grand. However, it's essentially a provincial capital with a small town feel. At the end of the **Great Glen,** which slices disagonally across Scotland from the southwest coast at Fort William to Inverness in the northeast, this royal burgh has a pretty historic center and is built on the banks of the River Ness. From here you can explore **Loch Ness, Culloden Battlefield** and **Cawdor Castle.**

Essentials

GETTING THERE Inverness Airport (www.hial.co.uk; ✆ 01667/464-000) is about 15 minutes' drive east along the A96 from the city center. The tiny airport is mainly a domestic hub. The flight time from London's Gatwick is 1¾ hours. **Trains** arrive at Inverness station in the city center (Station Square, off Academy St.) from London, Glasgow, Edinburgh and Aberdeen and from the north and west coasts. The train from Edinburgh and Glasgow takes 3½ hours from either city.

PREVIOUS PAGE: **Snow capped mountains and a path in Glencoe.**

Scottish Citylink (www.citylink.co.uk; ☎ 0871/266-3333) has daily **bus** service from Edinburgh and Glasgow (a 4-hr. trip each way). The bus station is near the train station at Farraline Park, off Academy Street.

It's a 3½ hour **drive** from Edinburgh, along the M9 north to Perth, and then the Great North Road (the A9) to Inverness—one of the most notorious roads in Scotland and an accident hotspot. This is the main route north so traffic is heavy. Add trucks with a lower speed limit into the mix and as the road veers back and forth from single lane to dual carriageway, drivers stuck behind the trucks get frustrated which can lead to dangerous overtaking—if you're driving take care.

VISITOR INFORMATION The comprehensive VisitScotland tourist information center is at Castle Wynd, off Bridge Street (www.visitscotland.com; ☎ 01463/234-353); open Sept–June Mon–Sat 9am–5pm, and Sun 10am–4pm; until 6 or 6:30pm in the summer.

SPECIAL EVENTS The July **Highland Games** feature traditional sporting events such as tossing the caber along with Highland dancing and piping bands (www.invernesshighlandgames.com; ☎ 01463/785-006).

Exploring Inverness

Inverness is a bustling little town straddling the River Ness, with a pretty center and picturesque riverfront. There's not much to see in the town itself, but it's a handy jumping off point for nearby attractions. This is one of the oldest inhabited areas in Scotland, with a handful of key archaeological sites. On **Craig Phadrig** the remains of a vitrified fort are

Inverness.

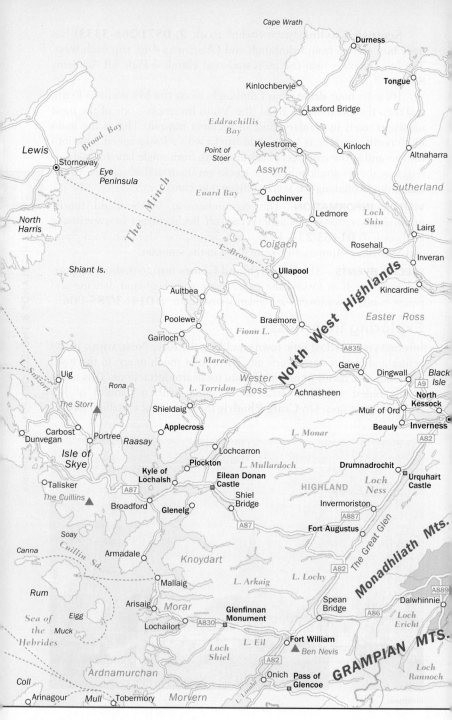

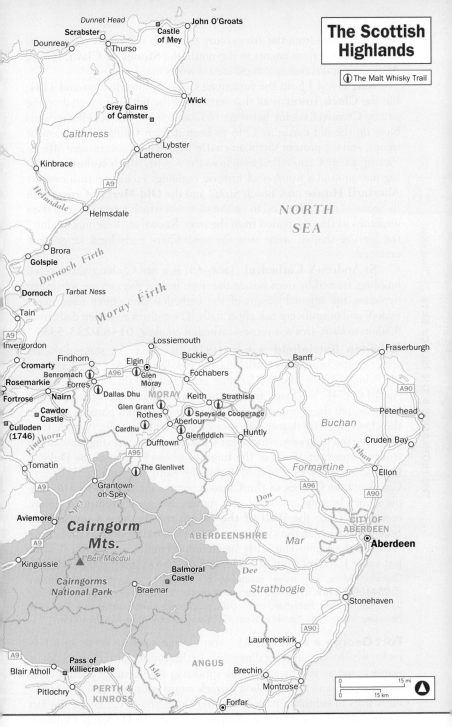

The Scottish Highlands

ⓘ The Malt Whisky Trail

believed to date from the 4th century B.C. while one of the most important prehistoric monuments in the north, the **Stones of Clava,** Bronze Age cairns and standing stones, are 6¼ miles to the east.

King David I built the first stone castle in Inverness around 1141, but the **Clock Tower** is all that remains of the fort later erected on the site by Cromwell's army between 1652 and 1657. The rebellious Scots blew up the old castle in 1746 to keep it from falling to government troops, and the present Victorian **castle** houses local government offices. Pick up a City Center Trail map from the tourist, which outlines a walking tour around a number of historic buildings including 16th-century **Abertarff House** on Church Street and the **Old Mercat Cross,** with its Stone of the Tubs, said to be the stone on which women rested their washtubs as they ascended from the river. Known as "Clachnacudainn," the lozenge-shaped stone was the spot where early local kings were crowned.

St Andrew's Cathedral (1866–69) is a neo-Gothic twin-towered building, framed by trees beside the river. Inside, you can see a painting depicting the original design of the cathedral (the spires were never added) and magnificent oak choir stalls. The cathedral is open daily from 9:30am to 6pm. (www.invernesscathedral.co.uk; ✆ **01463/233-535**).

Culloden Battlefield ★★★ HISTORIC SITE   A state-of-the-art visitor center brings this battlefield site vividly to life. At Culloden, Bonnie Prince Charlie and the Jacobite army suffered their final defeat on April 16, 1746. You listen to accounts from characters caught up in the battle before the 4-minute long battle immersion film plunges you into the chaos, the 360 degree film projected on all four walls. A guide then takes you out onto eery, windswept Culloden Moor, weaving tales as you trudge through the Field of the English, where 52 men of the Duke of Cumberland's forces who died during the battle are supposedly buried. Check out the **Graves of the Clans,** communal burial places with simple stones bearing individual clan names; the great **memorial cairn,** erected in 1881; the **Well of the Dead;** and the huge **Cumberland Stone,** from which the victorious "Butcher" Cumberland is said to have reviewed the scene. The battle lasted only 40 minutes; the prince's army lost some 1,200 men out of 5,000, and the Duke's army 300 of 9,000. Culloden Moor, 6¼ miles southeast of Inverness. www.nts.org.uk/culloden. ✆ **0844/493-2159.** Battlefield free; visitor center £11 adults, £9 seniors and children 5–15, £26 families. Battlefield open daily year-round; visitor center daily Feb–Mar, Nov–Dec 10am–4pm, Apr–May, Sept–Oct 9am–5:30pm; June-Aug 9am–6pm.

Fort George ★★ MUSEUM   Fort George is still an active army barracks, which adds an extra dimension to this historic attraction. Soldiers wander past as you meander this sprawling 18th-century coastal complex, dipping into the recreated barrack rooms with their tableaux of soldiers' lives in centuries past. Built after the Battle of Culloden, the fort was occupied by the Hanoverian army of George II. Dr. Samuel Johnson and James Boswell visited here in 1773 on their Highland trek. From the ramparts you can often spot dolphins in the Moray Firth. Highlights include the Robert Adam-designed garrison chapel and the Queen's Own Highlanders Regimental Museum, with objects from 1778 to the present.

Ardersier, 11 miles northeast of Inverness. www.historic-scotland.gov.uk. © **01667/460-232.** £9 adults, £7 seniors £5 child. Apr–Sept daily 9:30am–5:30pm; Oct–Mar daily 9:30am–4:30pm.

Inverness Museum & Art Gallery ★ MUSEUM   This quirky little museum in the center of town is so low-key that you might be tempted to overlook it in favor of the flashier attractions outside town, but it is worth dipping into (it's free after all) even if just for the stuffed Scottish wild animal tableaux. Other exhibits focus on the social and natural history, archaeology, art, and culture of the Scottish Highlands.

Castle Wynd, off Bridge St. www.inverness.highland.museum. © **01463/237-114.** Free. Apr–Nov Tues–Sat 10am–5pm; Nov–Mar Thurs–Sat 10am–5pm.

Where to Stay

EXPENSIVE

Culloden House ★   Bonnie Prince Charlie slept here. This grand Georgian Grade A-listed mansion with its stunning, ivy-clad Adam facade incorporates the castle in which Bonnie Prince Charlie slept the night before the Battle of Culloden. Today, it's a magnificent country house, surrounded by 40 acres of sweeping lawns, woods and parkland, with a croquet lawn, tennis court and a walled garden. Relax in the library bar with a dram or in front of the fire in the elegant drawing room. Bedrooms are cozy with period features but are on the old-fashioned side. The fine dining restaurant focuses on the best local ingredients.

Culloden. www.cullodenhouse.co.uk. © **01463/790-461.** 28 units. Doubles £270–£320, suites £395, includes breakfast. **Amenities:** Restaurant; bar; tennis court; croquet lawn; sauna; spa; room service; free Wi-Fi.

Rocpool Reserve ★   This is the closest Inverness comes to a design hotel—even if that design is in a 20th-century time warp, with harsh black and red tones and busy carpets. Still, it's the most stylish place to stay in a town with little competition. The 19th-century residence turned boutique hotel is uphill from the city center in a quieter residential area. The modern bedrooms are divided into Hip, Chic, Decadent, and Extra Decadent with a color palette veering from espresso to cappuccino (yes, 50 shades of brown). Two rooms have outdoor hot tubs, and other luxurious touches include velvet robes and double showers. The restaurant (not to be confused with the Rocpool p. 605) is a Chez Roux (as in famous French chef, Albert Roux). The food is sublime, the atmosphere much less-so. Main courses cost between £19 and £24.

Culduthel Rd. www.rocpool.com. © **01463/240-089.** 11 units. Doubles £195–£395. **Amenities:** Restaurant; bar; room service; free Wi-Fi.

MODERATE

Bunchrew House Hotel ★ Location, location, location: Venture down the gracious tree-lined driveway and prepare to be wowed. This gorgeous Scottish baronial mansion, all turrets and dusky pink paintwork, lounges on the shore of Beauly Firth and is the ancestral home of the Fraser and the McKenzie clans. Surrounded by 8 hectares (20 acres) of landscaped gardens, you can taste the salty sea air as you wander the pebbled beach. Inside there's a cozy bar and wood-paneled drawing room with a roaring log fire. This is real old-school country house territory, with creaking floorboards and bags of character. The bedrooms are also old-school: comfortable and traditional, but they could do with updating.

Bunchrew, Inverness (on the A862). www.bunchrew-inverness.co.uk. © **01463/234-917.** 16 units. Doubles £140–£280, includes breakfast. **Amenities:** Restaurant; bar; room service; free Wi-Fi.

Glenmoriston Townhouse Hotel ★ This Victorian townhouse hotel has a picturesque position on the tree-lined riverside with lovely views, and is just a short walk into town. It's also home to a cocktail and whisky bar and two of the town's best restaurants: **Abstract** (see below), and the buzzing bistro, **Contrast**. Bedrooms are smart, modern, but slightly dated (leather bucket chairs and a camel and red color palette).

20 Ness Bank. www.glenmoristontownhouse.com. © **01463/223-777.** 30 units. Doubles £75–£269, includes breakfast. **Amenities:** 2 restaurants; bar; room service; free Wi-Fi.

Where to Eat
EXPENSIVE

Abstract ★ FRENCH/SCOTTISH This fine dining restaurant offers a six-course tasting menu plus canapés—showcasing the best Scottish produce and peppered with tempting morsels such as Chef's Haggis (Ross-shire lamb, sweetbreads, black pepper and turnip) and Gairloch crab ravioli (brown crab, saffron pasta, bisque puree and heritage tomato). The Chef's Table is another option: a front-row seat onto the kitchen, a five-course menu and the chance to chat with the head chef. A set three-course menu is also available.

20 Ness Bank. www.glenmoristontownhouse.com. © **01463/223-777.** 3-course set menu £45; tasting menu £55 per person. Chefs table £55 Tues–Sat 6–10pm.

Rocpool ★★ MODERN SCOTTISH This is without doubt the best restaurant in town—reflected by the fact that you have to book weeks ahead to get a table on the weekend. This buzzing waterfront brasserie has sleek interiors and a gorgeous menu, and its arrival injected a shot of adrenaline into the sleepy culinary scene. Dishes are based around those foodie buzz words: local and seasonal, featuring venison from Speyside, scallops from the West Coast and razor clams from Fortrose, with starters such as Cromarty crab with risotto of roasted butternut squash, toasted pumpkin and sunflower seeds. Check out the great lunch and early evening menu deals.

1 Ness Walk. www.rocpoolrestaurant.com. ✆ **01463/717-274.** Mains £13–£25; lunch menu £16 for 2 courses; early evening menu (5:45–6:30pm) £18 for 2 courses. Mon–Sat noon–2:30pm and 5:45–10pm.

MODERATE

Café 1 ★ MODERN SCOTTISH   The field-to-plate ethos here is helped by the fact that the owner breeds his own sheep and cattle. Hebridean sheep and Highland cows appear in the restaurant's signature dishes such as the Holly House Highlander Ultimate Burger in a brioche bun with sun-blushed tomato mayo, melted gruyere, caramelized red onion, maple bacon and hand-cut chips (£14).

75 Castle St. www.cafe1.net. ✆ **01463/226-200.** Lunch mains £8 for 1 course, £10 for 2 courses; dinner mains £10–£24; 3-course dinner £32. Mon–Sat noon–2:30pm, Mon–Fri 5–9:30pm, Sat 6–9:30pm.

INEXPENSIVE

The Dores Inn ★ GASTROPUB   A picturesque 8-mile drive outside Inverness, in the little village of Dores on Loch Ness, this pretty whitewashed pub serves great pub grub. The tiny bar (where you can listen to impromptu jam sessions some evenings) opens into two small dining rooms, rustic chic with a wood-burning stove. Tuck into fish and chips or large bowls of mussels and then go for a walk along the beach.

Dores. www.thedoresinn.co.uk. ✆ **01463/751-203.** Mains £10–£16. Daily noon–8:45pm.

Shopping

Inverness, like many small Scottish towns, is marred by a modern shopping mall. The **Eastgate Shopping Centre** is an uninspiring place in the center of town with the usual chain stores, while the **Victorian Market** (constructed in 1870) on Academy Street, could be a quaint tourist attraction but feels unloved, peppered with boarded up shopfronts. One place to check out inside, however, is **Boarstone Tartans,** 14-16 Victorian Market (www.boarstonetartans.co.uk; ✆ **01463/239-793**) a Highland dress specialist selling kilts, jackets, tartan trousers, shooting coats and deerstalker hats. The hunting, shooting, fishing fraternity, meanwhile, makes a beeline for **Grahams** at 37-39 Castle St. (www.grahamsonline.co.uk; ✆**01463/233-178**). This Inverness stalwart, established in 1857, is the place to come for everything from fishing tackle and permits to wallet-busting Le Chameau rubber boots.

Another highlight is **Leakey's Bookshop and Café,** Scotland's largest secondhand bookstore, in an old 18th-century church on Church Street (✆ **01463/239-947**). Filled to the rafters with old books, this cavernous space is fabulous for rummaging. You could lose hours among the shelves jam-packed with musty paperbacks and rare leather-bound tomes.

Entertainment & Nightlife

Inverness is rowdy on the weekends. The attractive riverfront is lined with hotels and restaurants—which are often fully booked. You need to reserve a table for dinner, sometimes weeks in advance.

One of the most popular places in town is **Hootananny,** Church Street (www.hootananyinverness.co.uk; ✆ **01463/233-651**), three packed floors of bars, pubs and live music from traditional Scottish ceilidhs to local bands. A much smaller venue but a legendary part of the Inverness scene is the **Market Bar,** 32 Church St. (✆ **01463/220-203**) down a narrow alley and up some backstairs. This tiny dive is standing room only for the local musicians who play in the scruffy, friendly little bar.

The **Gellions Pub,** 8-14 Bridge St. (www.gellions.co.uk; ✆ **01463/233-648**) is also legendary with nightly live music and ceilidhs, while the **Castle Tavern,** 1 View Place (www.castletavern.net; ✆ **01463/718-178**) perched on top of the hill near the castle has great views and and outdoor beer garden.

The cultural hub of Inverness is **Eden Court** (www.eden-court.co.uk; ✆ **01463/239-841**), Bishops Road, next to the cathedral. This contemporary theatre complex also has a cafe, bar and restaurant.

Side Trips from Inverness
BEAULY ★

Beauly, 12 miles west of Inverness on the A862, is a pretty little village, with the picturesque ruins of a monastery at one end. French monks first settled here in the 13th century and gave the town its name: literally, "beautiful place."

Dating back to around 1230, ruined **Beauly Priory ★** (✆ **01463/782-309**) is one of three priories built for the Valliscaulian order left, an austere body that drew its rules from the Cistercians and Carthusians. Some of the intricate windows and arcades remain intact.

Beauly is a pleasant place to walk around, with antique shops, galleries and boutiques. **Corner on the Square** (www.corneronthesquare.co.uk; ✆ **01463/783-000**) is a gourmet deli and cafe, **Iain Marr Antiques** a few doors down, a treasure trove of antique glass and silverware (www.iain-marr-antiques.com; ✆ **01463/782-372**), while **Campbell & Co.** at Highland Tweed House (www.campbellsofbeauly.com; ✆ **01463/782-239**) is an institution, run by the same family from 1858 until 2015. The new owners, the Brooke and Sugden textile families, have vowed to maintain its traditions, its excellence in tweed tailoring and the unique atmosphere of this old-fashioned store.

If you're here in early August, the **Black Isle Show** (www.blackisleshow.info; ✆ **01463/870-870**), one of the largest agricultural shows in Scotland, is held annually on the showground between Beauly and Muir of Ord. It's a great day out featuring everything from show-jumping to gun-dog displays and you can wander among pens of rare-breed sheep, shaggy Highland "coos" and marquees squawking with chickens.

ALONG LOCH NESS ★★

It's not the deepest loch (that's Morar), nor the longest (that title goes to Loch Lomond), but Loch Ness contains the largest volume of water of any Scottish loch, more, in fact, than all the lakes in England and Wales put together. It's also the most famous. The Loch Ness Monster or "Nessie" is one of Scotland's most enduring myths and biggest tourist attractions. Since the 1930s visitors have been traipsing to this mysterious loch 23 miles long and 600 feet deep in search of that elusive monster.

Though the legend dates back to the 6th century, things kicked off in earnest in 1933 after a local man, George Spicer, told newspapers he'd seen a prehistoric beast crossing the road and disappearing into the water. Renowned naturalist Sir Peter Scott even gave the monster a fancy Latin name, *Nessitera rhombopteryx,* although sceptics later pointed out that it was an anagram for "monster hoax by Sir Peter S." And there have been many hoaxes over the years, but still the sightings continue, with their blurred film footage and photographs.

In the summer, you can take boat cruises down Loch Ness from both Fort Augustus and Inverness. If you're driving, the A82 snakes along the northern side of the loch between Fort Augustus and Inverness (with plenty of scenic photo ops) and in high season is clogged with traffic.

Drumnadrochit ★

The bucolic village of Drumnadrochit is the home of the **Loch Ness Centre and Exhibition** (see below), a pretty village green and a buzzing whitewashed pub, **Fiddler's** (www.fiddledrum.co.uk; ℂ **01456/450/678**) with tables spilling out onto the terrace in summer.

Loch Ness Centre & Exhibition ★ MUSEUM   An attraction that could so easily be cheesy is, in fact, cleverly done and more interesting than you might think. Of course, there are Nessie toys in the gift shop, but the attraction itself is far more grown-up, taking you on a geological journey from A.D. 565 to the present with the help of photographs, audio, and film footage, exploring the myths and folklore around the "monster" and listening to firsthand accounts. Details of the scientific expeditions on the loch and archive newspaper cuttings are particularly interesting.
Drumnadrochit. www.lochness.com. ℂ **01456/450-573.** £7 adults, £6 students and seniors, £5 children aged 6–18, under 6 free, £22 families. Easter–Oct daily 9:30am–5pm (July–Aug to 6pm); Nov–Easter daily 10am–3:30pm.

Urquhart Castle ★★★ RUINS   A short 8-minute film whisks you through 1,000 years of turbulent Scottish history, then the curtains part

The ruins of Urquhart Castle, overlooking Loch Ness.

and there, perched on a promontory overlooking Loch Ness are the ruins of largest medieval castle in the Highlands. That it has the "wow" factor goes without saying. Coach-loads of summer tourists agree, so get there early or you might not get in at all. The smart modern visitor center with its contemporary cafe, gift shop and theatre is excellent. You can wander at will using the interpretation boards, but it's well worth taking the free half-hour guided tour. You'll learn how Clan Grant was given the castle by the Scottish king in return for keeping the unruly Macdonalds in check. With the Jacobite uprisings and the castle in ruins by the end of the 17th century, they cut their losses and headed back to Speyside.

Loch Ness. www.historic-scotland.gov.uk. ℗ **01456/450-551.** £8 adults, £6 seniors, £5 children 5–15. Apr–Sept daily 9:30am–6pm; Oct daily 9:30am–5pm; Nov–Mar daily 9:30am–4:30pm.

WHERE TO STAY

Loch Ness Lodge ★★   This luxurious B&B is by far the best place to stay on Loch Ness. The modern, baronial-style lodge is tucked into the hillside, surrounded by beautiful grounds overlooking the loch. The seven bedrooms are all named after Scottish lochs and glens. Assynt has a modern four-poster decked out with oyster silk and a touch of tweed along with a roll-top tub. Affric, meanwhile, incorporates the turret into its design. All the rooms come with glorious views. Downstairs, the drawing room, with its roaring log fire is sumptuous, with a relaxed country-house vibe. There's also a hot tub and sauna, and a therapy room where you can indulge in a range of treatments.

Brachla, Loch Ness-side. www.loch-ness-lodge.com. ℗ **01456/459-469.** 7 units. Doubles £175–£330, includes breakfast. **Amenities:** Restaurant; spa; free Wi-Fi.

Fort Augustus ★

There's no longer a fort here. This pretty village at the other end of the loch from Inverness, 36 meandering miles along the A82 in fact, is now more famous for its staircase of locks. General George Wade, of road- and bridge-building fame, made his headquarters here in 1724, and in 1729 the government constructed a fort on the banks of the loch, naming it Augustus after William Augustus, the Duke of Cumberland and son of King George II. The Jacobites seized the fort in 1745 and controlled it until their defeat at Culloden. Long since destroyed, Wade's fort was turned into the Fort Augustus Abbey. A Benedictine order was installed in 1867, and the monks ran a Catholic secondary school on the site for years—later at the center of an infamous child abuse scandal.

Fort Augustus is one of the best places to see the locks of the **Caledonian Canal ★** in action. In the heart of the village, the locks are a popular attraction when boats pass through. Built between 1803 and 1822, the canal runs right across the Highlands, almost in a straight line, from Inverness in the north, to Corpach, near Fort William. The canal is 60 miles long, with 22 man-made miles and the rest natural lochs.

To tackle the locks yourself, hire a boat from **Caley Cruisers,** Canal Road, Inverness (www.caleycruisers.com; ✆ **01463/236-328**) for a week or 3-day break. Cabin cruisers for two to six people are available from March to October—you don't need to have much marine experience and are given a full briefing. The waters of Loch Ness can be a little choppy, but the canal is calm and doesn't pose any of the dangers of cruising on the open sea. A week's rental ranges from £725 to £2,667; fuel, taxes and insurance are extra.

AVIEMORE ★

129 miles N of Edinburgh; 29 miles SE of Inverness; 85 miles N of Perth

Outdoor activity center Aviemore, located on the River Spey in the heart of the **Cairngorms National Park ★★★**, was established as a year-round resort in 1966. Although the center of Aviemore is often lambasted as ugly, it's no worse than many French ski resorts, and it's a bustling little place with outdoor sports shops and buzzing cafes. Visitors make a beeline here to ski in winter and hike in summer—or to bag a Munro. Munros are Scottish mountains over 914m (3,000 ft.) and Munro-bagging (climbing and ticking off the 282 summits) is a national sport.

The Cairngorms is the largest national park in Britain, covering 4,500 sq km (1,467 sq. miles)—almost 10 per cent of Scotland in fact. An Area of Outstanding Natural Beauty, it's home to 55 summits over 900m, including five of the U.K.'s six highest peaks and 43 Munros. Here you'll find a quarter of Scotland's native woodland and 25% of its threatened species. The park encompasses wild mountain tundra, heathered moorland and on the lower slopes, the ancient Caledonian pinewoods. This is the home of Britain's largest mammal, the red deer and its most majestic bird of prey, the golden eagle. Rushing rivers, icy lochs, and dense pine forests are dotted with farms and small hamlets. It's an open-air adventure playground, networked with cycling and walking trails and offering kayaking, canoeing, wildlife-watching, horse-riding and fishing. For maps, advice on walks and other information, contact **Cairngorms National Park Authority,** 14 The Square, Grantown-on-Spey (www.cairngorms.co.uk; ✆ **01479/873-535**).

Essentials

GETTING THERE   Aviemore is on the main Inverness–Edinburgh **railway** line. It's a half-hour journey from Inverness, 3 hours from Edinburgh and Glasgow. For train times in Aviemore, call ✆ **01479/810-221.**

Aviemore is also on the main Inverness–Edinburgh **bus** route. The trip from Edinburgh takes about 3 hours. Frequent buses also arrive throughout the day from Inverness (trip time: 40 min.). For schedules, call ✆ **0871/266-3333**, or visit www.citylink.co.uk.

If you're **driving** from Edinburgh, after crossing the Forth Bridge Road, take the M90 to Perth, and then continue along the A9 to Aviemore.

VISITOR INFORMATION   The **VisitScotland Tourist Information Centre** is on Grampian Road (www.visitaviemore.co.uk; ✆ **01479/810-930**). It's open year-round from Monday to Saturday 9am to 5pm, and on Sunday 10am to 4pm. July and August it is open Monday to Saturday until 6:30pm and 9:30am to 6pm on Sunday.

Exploring the Area

Climb on board a vintage steam train with the **Strathspey Railway ★**, Dalfaber Road (www.strathspeyrailway.co.uk; ✆ **01479/810-725**), and chug along the valley of the River Spey between Boat of Garten and Aviemore. The round-trip takes about an hour. Trains run between April and October but check the website for the schedule.

You can also travel to the top of Cairngorm Mountain on the highest funicular railway in the U.K. The **Cairngorm Funicular Railway ★** (www.cairngormmountain.co.uk; ✆ **01479/861-261**) cranks up to the top where there's a visitor center, viewpoint and the highest restaurant (over 3,500 ft.) in the country. From there you can take a guided mountain bike descent or guided walk. A day ticket costs adult £11, senior £10 and child £7.

One of the most charming attractions in the area is the **Cairngorm Reindeer Centre ★**, Reindeer House, in Glenmore (www.cairngormreindeer.co.uk; ✆ **01479/861-228**). While visiting the area in 1952, Swedish reindeer herder Mikel Utsi realized how similar it was to the reindeer's natural habitat in Lapland, and that it also had a plentiful supply of lichen, their native food. Utsi brought over a handful of Swedish

A resident of Cairngorm Reindeer Centre, near Aviemore.

reindeer and the rest is history. Alan and Tilly Smith now own the Cairn-gorm Reindeer Herd and today the herd of around 150 roams across the mountains. You can hike up the mountain slopes with a herder and feed the reindeer each morning at 11am. It costs adult £13, senior £10, child £7. During the summer months (June, July, and Aug) you can also go trekking for half a day with the reindeer (£55). At Christmas the reindeer go on the road, making guest appearances around the country, but a few stay in the paddock and there's a wonderfully old-fashioned feeling to the grotto here.

Where to Stay

Hilton Coylumbridge Aviemore ★   This is a sprawling resort spread over 26 hectares (65 acres). Dogs are welcome, children are welcome (there's a Fun House and plenty of outdoor family activities) and there are endless things to do, from tackling the dry ski slope or climbing wall to relaxing with a massage in the Thai Lodge Spa. Along with the smart modern hotel rooms, there are a number of luxury self-catering lodges in the grounds; each accommodates up to eight people.

Coylumbridge. www.hiltonaviemore.com. © **01479/810-661.** 88 units. Doubles £109–£159, suites £148–£241, includes breakfast. **Amenities:** 2 restaurants; 5 bars; babysitting; 2 pools (indoor); gym; spa; room service; free Wi-Fi.

Lazy Duck ★   The story started with a cozy 8-bed hostel on this 6-acre family smallholding, the next chapter saw the addition of the Woodman's Hut, a tiny eco-retreat in the woods sleeping two with a wood-burner, outside shower and incredibly chic compost toilet hidden in the trees. And then the Duck's Nest fluttered down. Another little wooden hut, this one is beside the pond paddled by rare-breed ducks. This too has a skylight for stargazing, outside bush shower and wood-burner, but it also has Wi-Fi and an outdoor wooden hot tub.

Nethy Bridge. www.lazyduck.co.uk. 🕿 **01479/821-092.** 3 units Doubles £95–£115. **Amenities:** Sauna, wood-fired hot tub, free Wi-Fi.

Where to Eat

Active Cafaidh ★ CAFE   Above an outdoor clothing and equipment shop in Aviemore, this cafe is a blast of fresh Highland air dishing up hearty soups, yummy cakes, gourmet platters of local meats and cheeses and, if your waistband can take it, that traditional Alpine dish, tartiflette, made with cream, cheese, bacon, onion and potato.

Grampian Rd. www.activeoutdoorpursuits.com. 🕿 **01479/780-000.** Daily 8:30am–5:30pm.

The Druie Restaurant Café ★ SCOTTISH   This rustic chic cafe with a cozy wood-burning stove is in the same old stone building as the gourmet deli and farm shop on the Rothiemurchus estate, just down the road from Aviemore. It's a great place for a steaming bowl of homemade soup and crusty bread for lunch or gooey cake and coffee after a hike. It's now also open for evening meals, with main courses such as pan-roast grouse breasts with fennel, pear, radicchio, hazelnuts and orange.

Rothiemurchus Center, www.rothiemurchus.net. 🕿 **01479/810-005.** Dinner mains £12–£18. Daily 9:30am–5:30pm, 6:30–9pm.

Old Bridge Inn ★ SCOTTISH   This friendly old-world pub on the banks of the Spey has a great atmosphere, roaring log fire and gastropub grub along with regular live music in the evenings. Think twice-cooked pork belly with toffee apple puree, red cabbage, celeriac and roast potatoes or Scrabster lemon sole, puy lentils, confit chicken wings, pak choi and Shetland black crisps.

23 Dalfaber Rd. www.oldbridgeinn.co.uk. 🕿 **01479/811-137.** Lunch mains £4–£12. Dinner mains courses £10–£17. Mon–Thurs noon–2pm, Fri–Sun noon–3pm; Sun–Thurs 6–9pm, Fri–Sat 6–10pm.

NAIRN & CAWDOR CASTLE ★

172 miles N of Edinburgh; 91 miles NW of Aberdeen; 16 miles E of Inverness

A favorite family seaside resort on the sheltered Moray Firth, Nairn (from the Gaelic for "Water of Alders") is a royal burgh at the mouth of the Nairn River. Its fishing harbor dates back to 1820 and was constructed by Thomas Telford, while golf has been played here since 1672—and still is today.

Essentials

GETTING THERE   Nairn can be reached by **train** from the south, changing at either Aberdeen or Inverness. For train times and fares check

Follow the road signs for the **Malt Whisky Trail** ★★ (www.maltwhiskytrail.com) a bucolic tourist route linking eight distilleries and one cooperage from the Moray coast through the rolling hills of Speyside. There are more than 50 distilleries sprinkled through this picture-perfect sweep of lush, rolling countryside. The ones on the trail include Benromach, a friendly little distillery on the coast near Forres, the historic distillery Dallas Dhu, Cardhu, Glenfiddich, Glen Grant, Strathisla and Glen Moray. At **The Glenlivet** (www.theglenlivet.com; ℂ **01340/821-720**) you can take an exclusive Spirit of the Malt tour and tasting or fill your own bottle straight from the cask, cork, cap and label it. At the **Speyside Cooperage,** meanwhile, you can watch the fiery barrel-making process. A good place to spend the night is the pretty little village of Aberlour on the banks of the River Spey, the fastest-flowing river in Britain. The long distance walking route, the **Speyside Way,** meanders along its banks. Aberlour is the home of Walkers Shortbread and the **Aberlour** distillery. **The Mash Tun** (www.mashtun-aberlour.com; ℂ **01340/881-771**) is a quirky little stone pub with five rooms named after local distilleries. In May each year the **Spirit of Speyside Whisky Festival** (www.spiritofspeyside.com) features a host of whisky themed events and many distilleries normally closed to the public fling open their doors.

National Rail Enquiries (www.nationalrail.co.uk; ℂ **08457/484-950**). If you're driving from Inverness, take the A96 east to Nairn.

VISITOR INFORMATION The **Tourist Information Centre** is in the community centre at 62 King St. (www.nairncc.co.uk; ℂ **01667/453-476**) and is open all year Monday to Thursday 8:30am to 10pm, Friday to Saturday 8:30am to 5pm, Sunday 9am to 9pm.

Exploring Nairn

Nairn is a little seaside town, with a beautiful sandy beach and promenade. The harbor area is also worth exploring, as is **"Fishertown"** just to the south, with its narrow streets of fishermen's cottages.

Nairn is also a famous golfing destination, with two 18-hole championship golf courses. The **Nairn Golf Club,** Seabank Road (www.nairngolfclub.co.uk; ℂ **01667/453-208**), was established in 1887 and is one of the finest traditional links courses in the world. The **Nairn Dunbar Golf Club,** Lochloy Road (www.nairndunbar.com; ℂ **01667/452-741**) traces its history back to 1899.

Cawdor Castle ★★ CASTLE Cawdor Castle has been home to the thanes of Cawdor since the early 14th century. Although the castle was constructed two centuries after his time, it has been romantically linked to Shakespeare's *Macbeth*, once the thane of Cawdor. The castle has all the architectural ingredients you'd expect: a drawbridge, an ancient tower, and fortified walls. Its severity is softened by pretty gardens and rolling lawns. Inside, grand rooms are decked out with paintings by Sir

Joshua Reynolds, antique furniture, and historical artifacts. The grounds include five woodland nature trails, a 9-hole golf course, a putting green, a picnic area and a restaurant.

Off the A96, Cawdor. www.cawdorcastle.com. ✆ **01667/404-401.** £11 adults, £10 seniors and students, £7 children, free for children 4 and under. May–Sept daily 10am–5:30pm.

Where to Stay

Boath House ★★★   Don and Wendy Matheson restored this fabulous Georgian mansion from 1825 and turned it into a gourmet destination with eight gorgeous, individually designed bedrooms. Scattered through the house, the bedrooms seamlessly blend the contemporary with the past, with roll-top baths, a peppering of antiques and lush fabrics. Room 3 is the master bedroom where original owner, Sir James Dunbar once slept. It has twin slipper baths as well as a walk-in shower, room 4 has a four-poster bed while room 6 is in a separate stone cottage. The hotel has a Michelin-starred restaurant (see below) and lush gardens where swans and ducks swim on a lake stocked with trout. You can also indulge in an Ayurvedic spa treatment.

Auldearn, Nairn. www.boath-house.com. ✆ **01667/454-896.** 8 units. Doubles £260–£365, includes breakfast. **Amenities:** Restaurant; gym; spa treatments; free Wi-Fi.

Cawdor Cottages ★   Lady Isabella Cawdor, married to the Thane of Cawdor, was once a stylist for magazines such as Elle and Vogue. Her creative hand shows in these five self-catering cottages on the Cawdor Castle estate. From the sumptuous 19th-century Drynachan Lodge to the tastefully renovated crofters' cottages, these are some of the best self-catering options in the Highlands. Gardener's Cottage, with views of the River Findhorn, has a log fire and sleeps six; Achneim, was once a gamekeeper's cottage, sleeps two in a brass bed and has sweeping views over the Moray Firth. They all come with a welcome basket.

Cawdor. www.cawdor.com ✆ **01667/402-402.** 3-night stays from £370.

Where to Eat

The Boath House ★★★ CONTEMPORARY SCOTTISH   Michelin-starred magic is dished up in the elegant antique-scattered dining room of this luxury Georgian retreat (see above). After canapés in the drawing room, as you gaze out through the French windows over sweeping tree-studded lawns, you'll be savoring a menu created from the organic vegetables, herbs and fruit from the walled kitchen garden along with meat and from a nearby organic farm, locally foraged wild mushrooms and fish from the West Coast. Head chef Charlie Lockley is a keen advocate of the Slow Food movement. You can also indulge in a gourmet afternoon tea.

Boath House, Auldearn. www.boath-house.com. ✆ **01667/454-896.** 2-course lunch £24, 3-course lunch £30; fixed-price 6-course dinner £70, 3-course menu £45. Daily 12:30–2pm and 7–8:30pm.

Cawdor Tavern ★ MODERN SCOTTISH   This olde-worlde country pub in a pretty village was once the carpenter's shop for Cawdor Castle. You can sup a pint of ale or sip a single-malt whisky in the oak-paneled bar or tuck into traditional pub grub such as fish and chips, steak and Orkney ale pie or venison sausages in the cozy restaurant in front of an open fire. There are also tables outside during the summer.
Cawdor. www.cawdortavern.co.uk. ✆ **01667/404-777.** Lunch mains £9–£22; dinner mains £10–£22. Mon-Fri noon–2:15pm, Sat-Sun noon–5pm; dinner daily 5–9pm.

Shopping

Nairn has a pleasant town centre lined with cafes, delis, antique shops and the independent **Nairn Bookshop** at 97 High St. (www.nairnbookshop.co.uk; ✆ **01667/455-528**). Just outside Nairn, in the village of Auldearn is a rambling antiques emporium in an old church which is always worth a rummage, **Auldearn Antiques,** Dalmore Manse (www.auldearnantiques.co.uk; ✆ **01667/453-087**).

Also east of Nairn on the A96 is **Brodie Countryfare** in Brodie (www.brodiecountryfare.com; ✆ **01309/641-555**). This shopping complex and cafe stocks everything from Scottish knitwear to jams and chutneys. It's well worth continuing along the A96 to Elgin (22 miles east of Nairn), where Scottish cashmere producer since 1797, **Johnstons of Elgin,** Newmill (www.johnstonscashmere.com; ✆ **01343/554-000**), has a lovely visitor centre: mill, cafe, and luxury shopping complex.

Entertainment & Nightlife

Nairn has its own theatre, **The Little Theatre**, King Street (www.nairndrama.org.uk; ✆ **01667/455-899**), which stages productions throughout the year. In September the town hosts the **Nairn Book & Arts Festival** (www.nairnfestival.co.uk; ✆ **01667/453-476**), with author events, films, exhibitions, plays, and music.

THE BLACK ISLE PENINSULA ★
Cromarty: 23 miles NW of Inverness (via Kessock Bridge)

Despite its name the Black Isle isn't an island—or black. Just over the Kessock Bridge from Inverness, it's a lush, wooded peninsula with a rugged coastline and pretty beaches. The name is thought to come from the fact that, as snow usually doesn't settle here in winter, the promontory looks black while the surrounding countryside is white. In summer, however, the land is green and fertile, with fields of broom and whin, bordered by salt mudflats and scattered coastal villages. The peninsula has been inhabited for 7,000 years, as the 60-odd prehistoric sites testify, and Pictish kings, whose thrones passed down through the female line, once ruled the land. Subsequently, it was the Vikings who held sway, and the existence of many gallows hills testifies to their harsh justice.

Essentials

GETTING THERE   The nearest **train** station is Inverness. **Stagecoach** (☎ **01463/233-371,** or visit www.stagecoachbus.com runs a **bus** service from Inverness (nos. 26, 26A) bus station stopping at North Kessock, Munlochy, Avoch, Fortrose, Rosemarkie, and Cromarty.

If you're **driving**, take the A9 north from Inverness over the Kessock Bridge and follow signs for Munlochy and Fortrose. It's about 23 miles from Inverness to Cromarty (on the western tip of the Black Isle).

VISITOR INFORMATION   Ask at the **Inverness Tourist Information Centre** (p. 601) for details on the Black Isle, because the peninsula is often included on a day tour from the city.

North Kessock ★

The village just over the bridge is a well-known vantage point for watching bottlenose dolphins, which live in the Moray Firth—and are reputed to be the most northerly group of bottlenose dolphins in the world. Or, you can look out over the Firth from the **Dolphin and Seal Centre ★** (www.wdcs.org.uk; ☎ **01463/731-866**), just to the north of the village off the A9, and run by the Whale and Dolphin Conservation Society. It's open daily from June to September from 9:30am to 4:30pm.

Fortrose ★ & Rosemarkie ★

In the sleepy village of Fortrese you can wander around the ruins of **Fortrose Cathedral ★**. Founded in the 13th century, the cathedral was dedicated to Sts Peter and Boniface and you can still see fine detailing in the 14th-century remains. If the stones scattered about don't seem adequate to fill in the gaps, it's because Cromwell's men took many of them to help build a fort in Inverness. There are no formal opening hours; you can wander through the ruins at any time.

Fortrose adjoins **Rosemarkie,** the next village along. The two villages share the **Fortrose & Rosemarkie Golf Club** (www.fortrose golfclub.co.uk; ☎ **01381/620-529**) established in 1888. Set on the Chanonry Ness, the course juts out into the Moray Firth with fabulous views across to **Fort George** on the other side. The golf course is the site of the **Chanonry Point Lighthouse** at the 4th hole, which was designed by Alan Stevenson (the uncle of writer Robert Louis Stevenson) and began operating 1846. This is also a good place for dolphin spotting.

The charming village of Rosemarkie has been inhabited since the Bronze Age. A center of Pictish culture, the town saw the arrival of the first Christian missionaries, and it's reported that St Moluag founded a monastery here in the 6th century. The **Groam House Museum ★** on the High Street (www.groamhouse.org.uk; ☎ **01381/620-961**) tells the story of the region from prehistoric times. The museum's prize exhibits are 15 carved Pictish stones, some dating back to the 8th century A.D. The pride of the collection is the **Rosemarkie cross-slab ★**, decorated with enigmatic Pictish symbols. Visitors can also learn about the legendary prophet Brahan Seer, who was buried alive at Chanonry Point. The museum is open daily April to October Monday to Friday 11am to 4:30pm, Saturday and Sunday 2 to 4:30pm. Admission is free.

Rosemarkie is not just of historical interest, however, it's a lovely little seaside spot with a good beach, popular with families and dog-walkers, a bistro on the shore and a gourmet deli in the village.

WHERE TO EAT & STAY

The Anderson ★   This award-winning little restaurant with rooms on the corner of Cathedral Square in Fortrose dates back to 1840, although the wine cellar is said to be another 200 years old. Downstairs is the whisky bar and restaurant where you can relax in front of a roaring fire before tucking into salmi of pheasant, a rich hunter's stew with bacon, porcini and shitake mushrooms (£17) or turbot and scallops, flame-grilled Scottish turbot with West Coast scallops and blackberry sauce £18. The nine quirky rooms, some with four-posters, sleigh beds and roll-top baths can be on the small side but they have character.

Union St. www.theanderson.co.uk. ℂ **01381/620-236.** Doubles £99–£109, includes breakfast. **Amenities:** Restaurant; bar; free Wi-Fi.

Crofters Bistro ★   This relaxed bistro on the seafront in Rosemarkie dishes up great brasserie-style food and is always buzzing. Try the crispy fried whitebait with tartar sauce, beer battered fish with handcut chips or venison burger with cranberry jelly.

11 Marine Terrace, Rosemarkie. www.croftersbistro.co.uk. ℂ **01381/620-844.** Mains £9–£16. Wed–Sat 11am–3pm and 5:30–8:30pm, Sun 12:30–3pm and 5:30–8:30pm.

Cromarty ★

Cromarty is a picturesque village at the tip of the peninsula, where the North and South Sutors (the high rocky outcrops) guard the entrance to the Cromarty Firth, the second-deepest inland-waterway estuary in Europe. The village, with its lanes of cottages that seem to hunch against the north winds, was once a flourishing port, and the clutch of larger 18th-century merchants' houses are testament to this. In more recent times, the coast was home to a large facility for the manufacture and maintenance of North Sea oil platforms. The remnants of this industry can still be seen in the waters of Cromarty Firth, on the northern side of the town. In fact, on a boat trip with **Eco Ventures ★**, Victoria Place (www.ecoventures.co.uk; ℂ **01381/600-323**) you can get up close to the giant legs of one of the old platforms. The 2-hour wildlife-watching trips are one of Cromarty's highlights, the dolphins leaping around the boat a truly magical experience (Adults £27, children 5–12 £20).

Cromarty is also noteworthy as the birthplace of Hugh Miller in 1802. Born in a little thatched cottage, Miller worked as a stonemason as a young man, but came to be recognized as an expert in the field of geology, as well as a powerful man of letters in Scotland. **Hugh Miller's Cottage ★**, Church Street (www.nts.org.uk; ✆ **01381/600-245**) contains many of his personal belongings and collections of geological specimens. From 23 March to October, it's open daily from noon to 5pm; in October on Tuesday, Thursday, and Friday from noon to 5pm; £7 for adults, £5 for students and seniors, and £17 per family.

SUTHERLAND & THE FAR NORTH ★

Sutherland is off-the-beaten-track—and off many tourists' radars. This is the far-flung northern Highlands, although ironically the name is derived from "southlands," the Vikings' term for all the country under Caithness. The joke is that there are more sheep here than people—with a population of around 13,000 in an area of 2,300 square miles, that's probably true.

Bordered to the north and west by the Atlantic and to the east by the North Sea, it's a land of heather-swept moorland, bleak mountains and mysterious lochs. The area isn't overloaded with attractions, although there are one or two castles to visit. What there is is a vast empty landscape to explore. This is perfect roadtrip territory.

Sutherland bore the brunt of the notorious 19th-century Highland Clearances, when many residents were driven out of their ancestral crofts. Some made their way to the New World. In remote glens, you can still see the ruins of the crofting villages they left behind.

Dornoch ★

63 miles northwest of Inverness and 219 miles northwest of Edinburgh

Motoring north on the A9, one of the most picturesque settlements along the way is Dornoch, famous for its ancient cathedral and golf club. This tiny town on the coast is also known for its sandy beaches backed by wild dunes and perfect for windswept walks.

The **Tourist Information Centre** is on The Square (www.visit dornoch.com; ✆ **01862/810-400**). It's open year-round Monday to Saturday 9:30am to 5pm and Sunday 10am to 3pm. From Inverness bus station (✆ **01463/233-371**), Stagecoach and Scottish Citylink run **buses** to Dornoch: The journey takes 60 to 90 minutes.

EXPLORING DORNOCH

The Royal Burgh of Dornoch is famous for its golf club on the sheltered shores of Dornoch Firth. The **Royal Dornoch Golf Club ★**, Golf Road (www.royaldornoch.com; ✆ **01862/810-219**), is the northernmost first-class course in the world, founded in 1877 with a royal charter granted by Edward VII in 1906. Golf was first played here, in fact, by monks in 1614.

Dornoch Cathedral ★, Castle Street, was built in the 13th century and partially destroyed by fire in 1570. Its fine 13th-century stonework remains intact. The cathedral is famous for its modern stained-glass windows—three are in memory of Andrew Carnegie, the American steel magnate—and more recently for the fact that Madonna had Rocco, her son with Guy Ritchie, christened here. The cathedral is open daily from 9am to dusk.

In the cathedral's cemetery, where the marketplace used to be, is the **Plaiden Ell,** a medieval measure for cloth. In one of the gardens is the 1722 **witch's stone,** marking the spot where the last burning of a condemned witch to take place in Scotland.

Poking around shops such as the **Dornoch Bookshop** and the **Jail on Castle Street** (www.jail-dornoch.com; ℂ **01862/810-555**) opposite the cathedral whiles away an hour or so. Housed in a converted jail, this craft centre sells jewelry and pottery, along with knitwear, tartans and tweeds. On the other side of the Dornoch Firth you have **Anta**'s (www.anta.co.uk; ℂ **01862/832-477**)—think tasteful contemporary tartan rugs, pottery, blankets and homeware. It also has a lovely little cafe.

At **Embo ★**, about 3 miles north of the beaches of Dornoch, are the remains of two funereal vaults believed to date from around 2000 B.C. Another 1¾ miles north of Embo are the shores of lovely **Loch Fleet,** where there's a meager ruin of **Skelbo Castle** on a lonely grassy mound. At one time, in the 14th century, Skelbo was a powerful fortification.

WHERE TO STAY & EAT

Dornoch Castle Hotel ★   Once the residence of the bishops of Caithness, this rambling hotel dates back to the 15th century. It was set alight during clan feuding, turned into a school, jail, court house, and hunting lodge before being converted, in the middle of the 20th century, into a hotel. Today, it's all winding stairs, mazlike corridors, and impenetrable cellars—and 24 characterful bedrooms split between the original building and an extension overlooking the garden. For a splurge, check into the Old Courtroom with its hand-carved four-poster bed, log fire and view of the cathedral. The restaurant serves mussels from Dornoch Firth, salmon from Loch Duart, and lamb and beef from local farms.
Castle St. www.dornochcastlehotel.com. ℂ **01862/810-216.** 24 units. Doubles £99–£260, includes breakfast. **Amenities:** Restaurant; bar; free Wi-Fi.

Links House ★★★   This is a definite step up—more like a giant leap in fact—from the usual hotels in the northeast of Scotland. Of course, it has a price tag to match. Oozing luxury and class, the elegant manse next to the Royal Dornoch golf course is the baby of American businessman

Dinner at Links House, Dornoch.

Todd Warnock, who restored the dilapidated building. The eight opulent bedrooms are named after Scottish salmon rivers: Brora, Beauly, Shin, Oykel, Helmsdale, Cassley, Conon and Carron and are decorated with antiques and hand-picked artwork reflecting the local landscape or Scottish field sports, while bathrooms are clad in sumptuous Italian marble. As well as a golf course on the doorstep, the hotel arranges activities such as salmon and trout fishing, deer stalking, grouse shooting, hill-walking and tours of the Highlands' castles and historic sites. After a day on the go you can curl up in front of a log fire in the library with a dram as you flick through some of the tomes on the area. Gourmet dinners are served in the contemporary dining room with its huge stone fireplace and antler chandelier, after which you can step outside with a cigar from the humidor and relax in front of the open-air fireplace on the terrace.

Golf Rd. www.linkshousedornoch.com. ℂ **01862/811-279.** 8 units. Doubles £270–£360, includes breakfast. **Amenities:** Library bar; restaurant; free Wi-Fi.

Golspie ★

Just north of Dornoch, Golspie has a crescent-shaped sandy beach but its main attraction is the magnificent Dunrobin Castle.

Dunrobin Castle ★★ CASTLE   This glorious castle, all turrets and spires, looks like it's jumped straight out of the pages of a fairytale. Home of the earls and dukes of Sutherland, Dunrobin is the largest of the great houses in the northern Highlands, dating in part from the early 13th century. Some of the castle's 189 rooms are open to the public—the ornately furnished dining room, a billiard room, and the room with the gilded four-poster bed where Queen Victoria slept when she visited in 1872.

Dunrobin Castle, Golspie.

The formal gardens were laid out in the manner of Versailles. There's a museum in the grounds, which contains many relics from the Sutherland family. Falconry displays are at 11:30am and 2pm most days.
Golspie. www.dunrobincastle.co.uk. © **01408/633-177.** £11 adults, £9 students and seniors, and £6 children 5–16, £29 families. Apr–May and Sept–Oct Mon–Sat 10:30am–4:30pm, Sun noon–4:30pm; June–Aug daily 10am–5pm. Last entrance 30 min. before closing.

Tongue ★

257 miles NW of Edinburgh; 101 miles NW of Inverness

Leaving the coast and slicing diagonally up to the far north of Scotland along the A836, you sweep through a vast empty landscape of bleak moorland crouching beneath brooding mountain peaks, to Tongue. The rugged north coast is wild and untamed. It's here you'll find the tallest cliffs on the mainland and the highest waterfall. The mighty cliffs of **Clo Mor** soar 920 ft./281m near Cape Wrath (known for its large colonies of puffins) while the **Eas-Coul-Aulin** waterfall plummets 650 ft./200m. At the **Falls of Shin,** you can watch salmon leap, while towering peaks to climb include **Ben Loyal,** a Corbett at 2,506 ft. (one down from a Munro, mountains over 3,000 ft.), nicknamed the Queen of Scottish mountains.

West of Tongue, on a promontory, stands the ruin of **Castle Varrich,** said to have been built by the Vikings. Possibly dating from at least the 14th century, this castle was once the stronghold of the MacKays.

For a dramatic hike head from Tongue towards the **Kyle of Tongue,** a shallow sea loch crossed by a narrow causeway. Protected from the wild

The landscape near Tongue.

and raging sea nearby, this is a long, shallow inlet. At low tide, wearing a pair of boots, you can wade out to Rabbit Island. You pass towering cliffs, sandy bays, odd rock formations, and deserted rocky islets.

WHERE TO STAY

Ben Loyal Hotel ★ Good accommodation options are as thin on the ground as people on the far north coast. This small hotel, created from the village's old post office, bakery and stables and known affectionately as The Ben, is not going to win any design awards, but it has great views over the Kyle of Tongue to Ben Loyal and also has its own fishing boats, so the seafood on the menu doesn't come any fresher.

Main St. www.benloyal.co.uk. © **01847/611-216.** 11 units. Doubles £90–£110, includes breakfast. **Amenities:** Restaurant; bar; free Wi-Fi

Tongue Hotel ★ This old hotel dates back to Queen Victoria's day—and feels like it. It has bags of character, period features, tartan carpets, log fires, and a complimentary decanter of sherry for a reviving tipple. Built in 1850 as the hunting lodge for the Duke of Sutherland, the large grey stone building is a mile north of the village center on the road to Durness, with views out over the Kyle of Tongue.

Tongue. www.tonguehotel.co.uk. © **01847/611-206.** 19 units. Doubles £90–£130, suites £260–£360, includes breakfast. **Amenities:** Restaurant; 2 bars; free Wi-Fi.

Durness ★

John Lennon spent his summers in Durness as a teenager and today, there's a memorial garden in his honor. The far north coast of Scotland might not sound like a traditional summer holiday hotspot, but the

Balnakiel Beach, Durness.

beaches here, such as Balnakiel, are drop-dead gorgeous, sheltered coves of honey-hued sand and turquoise water. Sandwood Bay is a mile-long golden sweep, reputed to be haunted and with no road access; you have to hike in. Durness is also the jumping off point for trips to the most northwesterly point in Scotland, Cape Wrath, only accessible by ferry and minibus during the summer, and the Clo Mor cliffs between the Kyle of Durness and Cape Wrath.

Scotland's first Geopark, an austere, rock-hewn landscape covering 772 square miles, stretches from Durness down to Achiltibuie in the south. It's wonderful walking country, bare and rugged. The rocks littering the shoreline are 3 billion years old. In limestone caves under the mountains of Beinn nd Fhuarain, the bones of reindeer, lynx, arctic fox, wolves and bears have been found, some 47,000 years old.

WHERE TO STAY

Mackay's ★ This is a real find: a quirky yet luxurious B&B on the remote north coast. Fiona and Robbie Mackay have a burgeoning portfolio of accommodations including a bunkhouse, cabin, cottage and a couple of stunning five-star eco-retreats. The B&B has seven individually designed rooms featuring a smattering of vintage finds, 500-thread count sheets and goose feather pillows. **Croft 103** ★★ is the eco-retreat featuring Shore Cottage and Hill Cottage. These starkly contemporary state-of-the-art stone and glass buildings hunker into the landscape with vast curved picture windows to make the most of the spectacular views. Highlights include the Caithness stone-clad shower, outside bathtub for two on the terrace, and the huge 7 ft. beds. The cost of these two designer boltholes doesn't come cheap, however, starting at £1,500 per week.

Durine. www.visitdurness.com. ℂ **01971/511-202.** 7 units. £110–£139, includes breakfast. **Amenities:** Free Wi-Fi. Closed Nov–May.

Lochinver ★

This attractive little fishing harbor on the west coast sits in the shadow of the soaring Suilven. It's also home to one of Scotland's best little gourmet hotels which boasts the most northerly Michelin star in Scotland.

WHERE TO STAY & EAT

The Albannach ★★   This tall, white 18th-century house just outside Lochinver is a charmingly eclectic gourmet destination run by chef-proprietors Colin Craig and Lesley Crosfield. Inside walls are daubed rich claret, the wooden floors strewn with Persian rugs. Huge candles give the cozy dining room a mini-baronial air. There are just five bedrooms. One, The Byre, a contemporary space of slate, cream linen and pale grey tweed is in a separate cottage with its own outdoor hot tub. Creaking wooden stairs wind past stained glass windows up to the penthouse suite, with a view out to Lochinver and the mountains beyond. But the highlight is the food: the five-course menus of locally sourced, inventive dishes have won the hotel a Michelin star. Think rich mousseline of wild halibut, lobster sauce langoustine and lobster or garden beetroot soufflé. It is well-worth the schlep to get here and although room rates are high, remember they include Michelin-starred dinner, breakfast, and afternoon tea.

Baddidarroch. www.thealbannach.co.uk. ℂ **01571/844-407.** 5 units Doubles £305, suites £370–£385, includes dinner, breakfast, and afternoon tea. Dinner for non-guests is £70. **Amenities:** Restaurant; conservatory; free Wi-Fi.

CAITHNESS ★

If you're travelling the length of Britain, Land's End (in Cornwall) to John O'Groats is the traditional route: a journey of 876 miles (1,407km). This is the end of the road, the most northerly point on the British mainland—only it isn't, of course. **Dunnet Head** is, in fact, a few miles further north. To the west of Thurso, Dunnet Head is a far more atmospheric spot with a bright, white lighthouse and unspoiled panoramas over the waves to the Orkney Islands. If you're schlepping this far north, however, you probably want to tick off this traditional tourist attraction.

While Caithness doesn't have the grandeur prevalent in much of the Highlands, this northernmost county of mainland Scotland is a rolling, ancient landscape. There are Stone Age relics—most notably the enigmatic **Grey Cairns of Camster,** which date from 4000 B.C. The county is dotted with cairns, mysterious stone rows and circles, and standing stones. The Vikings once occupied the region with its natural harbors, craggy cliffs and quiet coves. Many of the place names derive from Old Norse. Caithness also has churches from the Middle Ages, as well as the odd clifftop castle. The late Queen Mother's home, the **Castle of Mey,** which dates from 1570, is situated between John O' Groats and Thurso and is a must-see. Add rich animal and birdlife, lochs full of trout and rivers brimming with salmon and the reasons to visit soon add up.

This is also, incidentally, where you catch a ferry to the Orkney Islands. The main car-and-passenger services leave from the harbor at Scrabster.

Wick ★

287 miles NW of Edinburgh; 126 miles NW of Inverness

Wick, on the eastern Caithness coastline, was once a famous herring port. Today, a sleepy nostalgia hangs over the town. There's daily **bus** and **rail** service from Inverness and **Wick Airport** (www.hial.co.uk) is served by flights from Aberdeen and Edinburgh.

The **Wick Heritage Museum ★**, 18-27 Bank Row (www.wick heritage.org; ✆ **01955/605-393**), is packed with exhibits relating to Wick's herring-fishing industry. From Easter to October, it's open Monday to Saturday 10am to 5pm; last entrance is at 3:45pm. Admission is £4 for adults and 50p for children 5 to 16.

Wick also produces its own whisky. The **Old Pulteney Distillery ★**, Huddart Street (www.oldpulteney.com; ✆ **01955/602-371**), has been in operation since 1826. Book a distillery tour, which explains the history and art of whisky making. The 45-minute tours take place at 11am and 2pm Monday to Friday and costs £6. For real enthusiasts, there's also the 2-hour Masterclass tour costing £45 and tasting the full range of Old Pulteney whiskies. These tours must be booked in advance.

The most visited sites in the area are the two megalithic **Grey Cairns of Camster ★**, 6¼ miles north of Lybster on the Watten Road off the A9. The ruins of the **Castle of Old Wick ★** are also worth exploring. The castle is located just off the A9, 1½ miles south of Wick. Once known as Castle Olipant, the ruined structure dates back to the 14th century. You can still see three floors of the old castle rising up on a rocky promontory.

WHERE TO STAY & EAT

Ackergill Tower ★★   For a true king of the castle experience check into Ackergill Tower on the coast just north of Wick. This castle dates back to the 15th and is set on 3,000 acres of grounds, with a walled garden, 7-mile beach on the doorstep, a private loch for fishing, a grand wood-paneled Great Hall and its own pub, the Smuggler's Inn. Rooms, of course, come with four-posters draped with tweed. There are also a handful of self-catering properties on the grounds sleeping from 4 to 12 people and ranging from £795 for a 3-night stay.

Ackergill. www.amazingvenues.co.uk. © **01955/603-556.** 28 units. Doubles £165–£450, includes breakfast. **Amenities:** Bar; restaurant; fishing; clay-pigeon shooting; croquet lawn; parking; billiards, free bikes; games room; library; free Wi-Fi.

John O'Groats ★

17 miles N of Wick

For decades John O'Groats was down-at-heel, a tacky tourist spot, its old hotel unloved and boarded up. Visitors would swing by, tick it off and get out of there as fast as possible. Now all that has changed thanks to the vision of Natural Retreats. The company breathed new life into this far-flung spot, revamping the old inn into a stylish hotel and apartments.

John O'Groats was named after Dutch ferryman Jan de Groot, and you can still see his tombstone at Cabisbay Church. From here you can hike along the coast to **Duncansby Head ★**, 1¾ miles east—one of the most dramatic coastlines in Scotland, the jagged cliffs the precarious home of seabirds such as puffins. A road leads out to a lighthouse perched on the cliffs; from where you can gaze out over the churning Pentland Firth to the Orkney Islands. These turbulent waters have claimed the lives of countless mariners, with around 400 wrecks in the past century and a half alone.

John O'Groats has its own **ferry terminal** (www.jogferry.co.uk; © **01955/611-353**), from where a passenger-only ferry service operates

The dramatic coastline at John O'Groats.

to Orkney everyday from May to September. The journey takes 45 minutes, costs £16 one way and the ferry company also offers tour packages that include bus trips around the Orkneys once you're there.

The late Queen Mother's legacy to Scotland is the restored **Castle of Mey ★★**, 6 miles west of John O'Groats on the A836 (www.castleofmey.org.uk; ✆ **01847/851-473**). The Queen Mother first saw the castle in 1952 when she was mourning the death of her husband, King George VI. Hearing that it was to be abandoned, she set out to restore both the castle and its gardens. She returned every summer for the rest of her life, and Prince Charles now follows in her footsteps.

Looking out over the Pentland Firth towards the Orkney Islands, the castle was constructed on a Z-plan between 1566 and 1572, with jutting towers and corbeled turrets. The castle is furnished just as it was when the Queen Mother departed from it. You can even see her gumboots beside the dog bowl and her blue coat hanging on the back of a chair. The guides in each room will regale you with personal anecdotes of her life there. The walled kitchen garden in July is one of the most beautiful private gardens in Scotland. The castle and gardens are open from mid-May to September 30 (closed for a week at the end of July; check the website for exact dates) from 10:20am to last entry at 4pm daily. Admission is £11 for adults, £10 for seniors, and £7 for children 5 to 16, £29 for families. Tickets for the gardens and grounds only cost £7 each, for all adults, £3 for children. Allow at least 1½ hours for a visit.

WHERE TO STAY & EAT

The Inn at John O'Groats ★★   Natural Retreats breezed in to John O'Groats and revamped its derelict, iconic hotel. Revamp is not really the word—rescue is more accurate. The multi-million pound regeneration has transformed this site—and the north coast, which was a wasteland in terms of stylish accommodation. Now there's everything from high-tech (Apple TVs) and high-spec four-bedroom lodges to one-bed studio apartments, a luxury penthouse and simple yet stylishly modern bedrooms in the inn. The design features sleek interiors with a Scandinavian vibe, with antler chandeliers, wood-burning stoves and copper bathtubs along with lights made from lobster pots and rope. There's plenty to keep you occupied while you're here. You can hire bikes, take a day-trip to Orkney or go on a sea safari in the 12-person boat, speeding over the waves towards Duncansby Stacks, keeping an eye out for orca and minke whales, dolphins, grey seals and sea otters. You might also spot seabirds such as puffins, kittiwakes, guillemots, razorbills and shags. Other activities include geocaching, fishing and horseriding. There's a spa and The Storehouse restaurant.

John O'Groats. www.naturalretreats.com. ✆ **01625/839-623.** 37 units. Doubles from £61. **Amenities:** Restaurant; bar; spa; free Wi-Fi.

Scrabster ★

Scrabster is a giant fishing harbor, ferry port, and the location of one of the best seafood restaurants in Scotland.

WHERE TO EAT

The Captain's Galley ★★   Notching up the awards, including the U.K.'s most sustainable chef, Jim Cowie's rustic fish restaurant is housed in a converted 19th-century ice house and salmon bothy on Scrabster harbor. Jim runs the restaurant with his wife, Mary and buys his fish straight off the boats at the fish market across the harbor each morning. Only fish in season features on the menu; he forages for seaweed and winkles on the shore for his homemade sushi and smokes his own fish out back. Starters include mussels and razor clams with vermouth cream, herbs and vegetables and langoustine bisque with skewered prawns and kimchi. For main courses you might tuck into roasted hake fillet with borlotti broth, mussels and chorizo iberico. The restaurant is only open from Easter until October and is the north coast's gourmet highlight. Book ahead.

The Harbor. www.captainsgalley.wordpress.com. 🕐 **01847/894-999.** Set 3-course menu with amuse bouche £49. Easter–Oct, Thurs–Sat from 6:30pm.

WESTER ROSS ★

Ullapool ★

59 miles NW of Inverness; 238 miles N of Glasgow

Ullapool is a tourist hotspot, a bustling harborside village in Wester Ross, built by the British Fishery Society in 1788 as a port for herring

Ullapool Harbour.

A walking trail near Inverpolly.

fishers—chucnks of it still look much the same as it did in the 18th century. Ullapool is the departure point for travelers crossing the Minch, a treacherous stretch of the North Atlantic separating Scotland from the Outer Hebrides. You can catch a ferry from here for Stornoway on the Isle of Lewis.

Ullapool has a picturesque location on the shore of **Loch Broom,** surrounded by rugged mountains. If you fancy bagging a Munro (mountains over 3,000 ft.), the peaks of An Teallach to the south or Beinn Dearg to the east are nearby.

The craggy coastline around here is perfect roadtrip territory, one of the most scenic stretches is from Ullapool to the village of Lochinver (a 40-mile run north along the A835). After the hamlet of Armair on Loch Kanaird, you'll come to **Inverpolly ★**, part of the Assynt Estate. As well as lochs and lochans (many with tiny islands), you can also see the peaks of Cul Mor (849m/2,785 ft.), Cul Beag (769m/2,523 ft.), and Stac Pollaidh (612m/2,008 ft.). It's good country for spotting golden eagles and peregrine falcons during the breeding season.

Knockan Crag ★ (www.nnr-scotland.org.uk), 13 miles north of Ullapool, is a National Nature Reserve where you can explore the landscape that first led geologists in the 19th century to theorize about plate tectonics. Here you can follow signposted nature trail and see "the Moine Thrust," which runs through the crag; geologists observed that the schists at the top of the crag were older than the limestone lower down. The colliding of the great plates of the earth's crust had caused the planes of rock to buckle, creating a fault where older rocks became exposed.

Castle ruins on Loch Assynt.

Much of the countryside north of Knockan has now been designated the North West Highlands Geopark (www.nwhgeopark.com) by UNESCO due to its special scientific interest. To explore farther, continue north on the A835 and at the Ledmore junction, take the A837 to the left, passing along **Loch Awe,** with the mountain peaks of Canisp (847m/2,779 ft.) and Ben More Assynt (984m/3,228 ft.) forming a backdrop. Eventually, you'll reach the spectacular 6¼-mile-long **Loch Assynt ★**.

From Ullapool, you can explore **Corrieshalloch Gorge ★** (www. nts.org.uk) another national nature reserve, 12 miles to the southeast. Corrieshalloch means "ugly hollow" in Gaelic but this spot is anything but. This slot-gorge was carved by glacial meltwater up to 2.6 million years ago. Today the River Droma thunders through it via a series of waterfalls, one of which, the Falls of Measach is 45m (148 ft.) high. The tree-threaded gorge is networked with paths; there's a Victorian suspension bridge over the chasm and a spectacular viewing platform.

Another popular excursion is to **Inverewe Gardens ★** (www.nts. org.uk; ✆ **0844/493-2225**). The garden blooms with over 2,500 species of exotic plants from the South Pacific, the Himalayas, and South America—despite being further north than Moscow, due to the warming effect of the North Atlantic Drift. The gardens are along the A832, 6¼ miles northeast of Gairloch. Opening times are daily, April 10am to 5pm, May 10am to 5:30pm, June to August 9:30am to 6pm, September 10am to 5:30pm, and October 10am to 6pm; £11 for adults, £8 for seniors and children 5 to 15, £25 per family. From November to March, the visitor center is closed, but the gardens can still be visited from 10am to 3pm daily; during this period, admission is by donation.

From either Ullapool or Achiltibuie, you can take excursions in season to the **Summer Isles ★★**, a beautiful group of almost uninhabited islands off the coast. They get their name because sheep are transported here in summer for grazing; the islands are a mecca for bird-watchers. The lovely **Summer Isles Hotel** (www.summerisles hotel.com; ✆ **01854/622-282**) is a perennially popular summer retreat. Boat schedules vary, depending on weather conditions. Information is available from the **Tourist Information Centre** at 6 Argyle St. (✆ **01854/612-486**).

WHERE TO STAY & EAT

The Ceilidh Place ★   This quirky, bohemian little place in a string of pretty whitewashed cottages near the harbor is an Ullapool institution. Downstairs there's a bookshop, bar and buzzing bistro—all exposed brickwork and a bustling vibe. Upstairs the warren of rooms is quaint and shabby chic, with books and radios instead of TVs. The cozy upstairs lounge is a relaxed spot to curl up with a book. You can make yourself a cup of tea in the small kitchen, and there's an honor bar if you fancy a night cap. This cultural hub has a program of live music and events.

12-14 Argyle St. www.theceilidhplace.com. ✆ **01854/612-103.** 13 units. Doubles £100–£168. **Amenities:** Restaurant; bar; lounge; bookshop; free Wi-Fi.

Applecross ★★

On the approach to the Bealach na Ba pass, one of the highest in the U.K., a road sign warns: Road normally impassable in wintry conditions. This is the vertiginous route snaking up, over and down to the remote Applecross peninsula in Wester Ross. (Luckily there is also a coastal road for when severe snowstorms hit). The single-track lane with passing places weaves down to a sprinkling of little cottages and a cozy inn on the waterfront. **The Applecross Inn ★** (www.applecross.uk.com; ✆ **01520/ 744-262**) is famous for its fresh seafood, live music and great atmosphere. The inn also has seven simple rooms if you don't want to move on (£130). **The Potting Shed** (www.applecrossgarden.co.uk; ✆ **01520/ 744-440**), an award-winning farm-to-table restaurant is another good eating place. The vegetables comes from the garden; they raise their own pigs; fish and lobster come from the sea a pebble's throw away and venison is off the estate. They also have a self-catering cottage which sleeps 4 in the village of Camusterrach 3 miles away, from £120 a night.

THE WEST HIGHLANDS ★

Fort William: Gateway to Ben Nevis ★★

133 miles NW of Edinburgh; 68 miles S of Inverness; 104 miles N of Glasgow

There's no escaping it: Fort William is an eyesore. What the town planners were thinking is anyone's guess. Fort William is on most unsuspecting tourists' itineraries of the Highlands because it's the jumping off

Ben Nevis, the highest mountain in the British Isles.

point for **Ben Nevis ★★**, Scotland's highest mountain, at the southern end of the **Great Glen.** The setting is picturesque, on the shores of Loch Linnhe, but as is often the case in Scotland, the natural landscape is spectacular, the manmade, not quite so much.

Historically, Fort William stands on the site of a fort built by General Monk in 1655 in case of rebellion by the Highlanders. The town was later named after Prince William, Duke of Cumberland, who oversaw the crushing of the Jacobite Rebellion at the Battle of Culloden in 1746. After several reconstructions, the fort itself was finally torn down in 1864 to make way for the railroad.

Essentials

GETTING THERE   Fort William is one of the main stops on the scenic West Highland **rail** line from Queen Street Station in Glasgow to Mallaig, on the west coast. You can travel the leg of the West Highland line between Fort William and Mallaig on The Jacobite steam train. This scenic route is popular with Harry Potter fans because of the Glenfinnan Viaduct featured in the films. Services operate between mid-May and the end of October from Monday to Friday, and during the weekends as well in from the end of June until the end of September; visit www.west coastrailways.co.uk.

The **bus** from Glasgow to Fort William, takes approximately 3 hours. Contact **Scottish Citylink** coaches (www.citylink.co.uk; ✆ **0871/266-3333**) for schedules. If you're **driving** from Glasgow, head north along the A82, but this route is often clogged with motor homes in the summer.

VISITOR INFORMATION The **Tourist Information Centre** is at 15 High Street (www.visitscotland.com; ☏ **01397/701-801**). It's open year-round from Monday to Saturday 9am to 5pm and on Sunday 10am to 4pm, except in the summer, when it stays open until 6:30pm from Monday to Saturday, and until 6pm on Sundays.

Exploring the Area

Old Inverlochy Castle ★ You can clamber around the ruins and pick your way through the walled courtyard of this 13th-century castle, 1¾ miles north of Fort William on the A82. The castle looms large in the pages of Scottish history as it was the scene of two famous battles. The first was in 1431, when clansmen of Alexander MacDonald, Lord of the Isles, defeated the larger army of King James I of Scotland. In the second battle, in 1645, the Royalist forces of the Marquess of Montrose won an important victory against the Covenanter army of the Marquess of Argyll. In all, 1,500 men were killed that day.

Neptune's Staircase ★, 3 miles northwest of Fort William, off the A830 at Banavie, is a series of nine locks constructed as part of the Caledonian Canal, which connected the eastern seaboard at Inverness with the west coast at Fort William. This shortened the distance that goods had to be transported from the North Sea to the Atlantic Ocean, avoiding the treacherous storms of Scotland's northern coast. This "staircase" of locks is one of the most prominent engineering triumphs in Scotland in the mid-19th century, raising boats up 19m (62 ft.) in total.

Fort William itself is relatively flat, and therefore a good place for cycling. You can hire bikes at **Alpine Bikes,** 117 High St. (www.alpinebikes.com; ☏ **01397/704-008**). If you feel more adventurous, there are numerous mountain bike trails in the countryside around town (visit www.ridefortwilliam.com). There are routes for all abilities, culminating in the white-knuckle Off Beat Downhill Track (graded Orange Extreme) at the Nevis Range resort, 7 miles north of Fort William on the mountain of Aonach Mor. The gondola takes you and your bike to the top, while gravity does the rest. The downhill track is open only in the summer, from May to September; bikes and protective gear are available for hire. In the winter season

Neptune's Staircase, Fort William.

the resort offers skiing and snowboarding instead. See www.nevisrange. co.uk for details.

Ben Nevis ★★ or The Ben, is the highest mountain in the British Isles, the summit soaring 1,344m (4,408 ft.) above sea level. It's one of the most straightforward Munros to bag, most of the trail up a well-constructed path—although the last part of the climb is a rocky scramble. More than 125,000 people make it to the top each year, another 100,000 part of the way up. But this is not a walk in the park and you need to make sure you are properly equipped. Each year climbers get into trouble, sometimes with tragic consequences, setting off, for instance, in shorts and trainers on a sunny summer's day, unaware of how quickly the weather can change on the slope. Hurricane strength winds, blizzards and fog can all roll in and disorient climbers. For more information swing by the Glen Nevis Visitor Center, open daily from 9am to 3pm in winter and 9am until 5pm in summer (www.ben-nevis. com; ✆ **01397/705-922**).

Glenfinnan Monument ★ MONUMENT A lone Highlander stands on the top of an 18m-high column at the head Loch Shiel, at Glenfinnan. The monument, designed by James Gillespie Graham, a Scottish architect, marks the spot where Bonnie Prince Charlie unfurled his proud red-and-white silk banner on August 19, 1745, in his ill-fated attempt to restore the Stuarts to the British throne. At the visitor center, learn about the prince's campaign, which ended in his defeat at Culloden. About 14 miles west of Fort William, on the A830, toward Mallaig. www.nts.org.uk. ✆ **01397/722-250.** Site free (open year-round). Visitor center £4 adults, £3 children. Apr–June and Sept–Oct daily 10am–5pm; July–Aug daily 9:30am–5pm.

West Highland Museum ★ MUSEUM This quirky little museum in the center of town was founded in 1922 to preserve and showcase artifacts of historical significance from the West Highlands. It's crammed with exhibits from the 1745 Jacobite Rising, items associated with Queen Victoria (including gifts she gave to her beloved personal servant, John Brown), and others that chart the history of mountaineering. Cameron Sq. www.westhighlandmuseum.org.uk. ✆ **01397/702-169.** Free. Mar and Nov–Dec Mon–Sat 10am–4pm; Apr–Oct Mon–Sat 10am–5pm.

Where to Stay
EXPENSIVE

Inverlochy Castle ★★★ Queen Victoria spent a week wandering the grounds of this grand baronial mansion in 1873, sketching and painting against the spectacular backdrop of Ben Nevis. Inverlochy Castle was built in 1863 and was a private home until 1969 when it was converted into a luxury hotel, dripping in antiques and artworks. Past guests include Charlie Chaplin, Robert Redford and Sean Connery. It is now a Relais & Châteaux property, with 17 sumptuous rooms and suites draped in chintz fabrics, frills and flounces and oozing old-world opulence. The

Queen's suite has a four-poster, while some of the rooms have free-standing copper bathtubs.

Torlundy. www.inverlochycastlehotel.com. ✆ **01397/702-177.** 17 units. Doubles £335–£575; suites £550–£695, includes breakfast. **Amenities:** Restaurant; tennis court; snooker room; room service; babysitting; free Wi-Fi.

MODERATE

The Lime Tree ★   This lovely 19th-century manse in the center of town is now a chic boutique-hotel-cum-art-gallery plus award-winning restaurant. Many of the nine characterful rooms (wooden floors, the odd four-poster) come with glorious loch views. There's a lounge with a roaring log fire and the gallery shows the work of contemporary Scottish painters and puts on two exhibitions each year. If you're staying in Fort William this is a no-brainer. Stay here.

The Old Manse, Achintore Rd. www.limetreefortwilliam.co.uk. ✆ **01397/701-806.** 9 units. Doubles £90–£130, includes breakfast. **Amenities:** Restaurant; art gallery; lounge; bike storage; free Wi-Fi.

WHERE TO EAT

Crannog Seafood Restaurant ★ SEAFOOD   From World War II lookout point to fisherman's bait shed, this red-roofed restaurant on the quayside overlooking Loch Linnhe has had a colorful history. Today it serves up seafood straight from the owners' fishing boats or their smokehouse. Check out the "Fishermen's Catch" the daily changing specials board, and the three-course lunch for £19.

Town Pier. www.crannog.net. ✆ **01397/705-589.** Mains £15–£20. Daily noon–2:30pm and 6–9:30pm.

Inverlochy Castle ★★ BRITISH   Curry dusted West Coast scallops with cauliflower, golden raisin and coriander, followed perhaps by Loin of Lochaber red deer with celeriac, pear, beetroot and a green peppercorn jus: The menu of this stately establishment's grand hotel restaurant is gourmet, the experience reassuringly old-school. Gentlemen are requested to wear a jacket and tie and no mobile phones are permitted. The kitchen uses local ingredients, including monkfish from Mallaig, crab from the Isle of Barra, crayfish from Loch Linnhe, and produce from the hotel's gardens. Partridge and grouse are offered in season, while roast filet of Aberdeen Angus beef is a classic. The dining room is decorated with period furniture gifted to Inverlochy Castle from the king of Norway.

Torlundy. www.inverlochycastlehotel.com. ✆ **01397/702-177.** Fixed-price lunch, 2-courses £28, 3 courses £38; fixed-price dinner £67. Daily 12:30–1:30pm and 7–9pm. Closed Jan–Feb.

Glencoe ★★

Bare, brooding grandeur: Glencoe's haunting history stays etched on your memory long after you've left the most famous glen in Scotland.

This is where one of the Highland's most brutal massacres took place in 1692. The drive through Glencoe, which snakes across wild and wind-swept Rannoch Moor to Loch Leven, winding between bleak crags and over boggy moorland, is also one of the most iconic. It's easy to imagine a fierce battle between Highlanders knee-deep in springy heather. It's also easy to understand why this barren place was the perfect film set for blockbusters such as "Harry Potter and the Prisoner of Azkaban."

Known as the "Glen of Weeping," on February 11, 1692, the Campbells massacred the MacDonalds—men, women, and children—who'd been their hosts for 12 days. Mass killings weren't uncommon in those times, but this one shocked even the Highlanders because it was a breach of hospitality. The **Monument to the Massacre of Glencoe,** at Carnoch, was erected by the chief of the MacDonald clan. After the incident, the crime of "murder under trust" was introduced into Scottish law as an aggravated form of murder that carried the same penalty as treason.

The eye-catching state-of-the-art **Glencoe Visitor Centre** ★ (www. nts.org.uk; ℂ **0844/493-2222**) is 1 mile to the south of Glencoe village, just off the A82. There's a moving film of the massacre, plus exhibitions on geology, mountaineering and conservation in the Highlands, as well as information for walkers. The center has a bright cafe and picnic tables outside and is open from April to October daily 9:30am to 5:30pm, and from November to March Thursday to Sunday 10am to 4pm. Admission is £7 for adults and £5 for seniors, students, and children 16 and under.

The village of Glencoe is a pretty backwater where you can stroll around the **Glencoe and North Lorn Folk Museum** ★ (www.glencoe museum.com; ℂ **01855/811-664**) packed with items from Victorian dolls to weapons from the Battle of Culloden. It's open April until the end of October, Monday to Saturday 10am to 4:30pm and costs £3 adults £2 seniors, children under 16 free.

Today, Glencoe is also a vast open-air adventure playground. In the winter it's a skiing and snowboarding hotspot; in the summer, hill-walking, mountain-biking and Munro-bagging take over. Check out **Glencoe Mountain** resort (www.glencoemountain.com; ℂ **01855/851-226**) for more information. There's a cozy cafe serving hearty breakfasts and hot food such as homemade soup and local venison burgers. Swing up to the top of Creag Dhubh for breathtaking views over Glen Etive from the viewpoints. The ride takes 12 minutes and the lift operates all year. It costs £10 for adults, £5 for children and £25 for families.

There are a handful of low-level walks around the valley floor as well as lung-busting climbs. The ramble around picturesque Lochan (a man-made lake surrounded by trees) is just above the village. Follow the red arrows for a 40-minute circuit of the lake weaving through the rhododendrons. To bag a Munro, tick off two in one on a classic Scottish ridge

The Great Glen

The Great Glen is, in fact, a series of glens along a geological fault that slices diagonally through Scotland coast to coast, from Fort William in the southwest to Inverness and the Moray coastline in the northeast. The **Caledonian Canal**, designed by Thomas Telford at the beginning of the 19th century, took advantage of the series of lochs (Dochfour, Ness, Oich, and Lochy) lying along this fault and linked them with a canals to create a watery highway connecting the Atlantic Ocean with the North Sea. The chain of freshwater inland lochs and manmade stretches of canal is 60 miles (96.5km) in length; 22 of those are man-made. There are 29 locks and 10 swing bridges along the way. The **Great Glen Way** is a long distance walking trail which follows the Great Glen. You can hike the route or sail along it. On the **Fingal of Caledonia** (www.caledonian-discovery.co.uk; © **01397/772-167**), an old Belgian barge, you can do both. This floating activity center plies back and forth between Inverness and Fort William once a week in the summer and offers active holidays, including hiking the Great Glen Way, with the boat as a floating hotel.

walk: Meall Dearg and Sgorr nam Fiannaidh are two Munros separated by a narrow, rocky ridge known as the Aonach Eagagh.

WHERE TO STAY & EAT

The Clachaig Inn ★★   This old white inn is a little woodland oasis in the heart of bleak Glencoe. Packed with mountaineering memorabilia, the three bars offer warm Highland hospitality, the best haggis, and around 160 types of whisky and a good selection of real ales. You can also tuck into rich venison casserole or venison pastrami. In the "Boots Bar" at the back (muddy boots allowed) there's a log fire, rustic wooden benches and weekly live folk music. The 23 contemporary rooms are split between the original building (Ossian wing), the newer Bidean Wing and The Lodge. The Clachaig also has self-catering cottages around the glen.

Glencoe. www.clachaig.com. © **01855/811-252.** 23 units. Doubles £94–£104, includes breakfast. **Amenities:** Restaurant; 3 bars; free Wi-Fi.

KYLE OF LOCHALSH ★

204 miles NW of Edinburgh; 82 miles SW of Inverness; 125 miles N of Oban

The Kyle of Lochalsh is the gateway to the Isle of Skye, which is now joined to the mainland by a bridge. You can drive the length of the island in a day, returning to the mainland by night—and you might have to if you don't book somewhere to stay far enough in advance. Kyle itself has a couple of uninspiring hotels. However, head around the coast and you'll find a clutch of cute villages, such as **Plockton** and **Glenelg,** in either direction, with quaint pubs and picture-postcard-pretty waterfronts. Kyle also has a handful of attractions in its own right, such as **Eilean Donan,** the most photographed castle in Scotland.

Essentials

GETTING THERE   You can catch a **train** from Inverness, taking about 2½ hours (www.nationalrail.co.uk; ✆ 08457/484-950). **Scottish City-link buses** (www.citylink.co.uk; ✆ 0871/266-3333) arrive daily from Glasgow at the Kyle of Lochalsh (trip time: 5 hr.) and from Inverness (trip time: 2 hr.). If you're **driving** from Fort William, head north on the A82 to Invergarry, then cut west onto the A87 to the Kyle of Lochalsh.

VISITOR INFORMATION   The **Tourist Information Centre** is in the Kyle of Lochalsh Car Park (www.visitlochalsh.co.uk). It's open Easter to October daily 10am to 4:30pm. It shares space with the award-winning **Seaprobe Atlantis** ★ (www.seaprobeatlantis.com; ✆ 01471/822-716) which offers semi-submersible glass-bottomed boat trips. From the underwater viewing deck you can spot dolphins, seal, otters and even whales.

Eilean Donan Castle ★★ CASTLE   Anyone who remembers Christopher Lambert in the Hollywood blockbuster "Highlander" racing across a causeway, kilt-flapping, to a tiny castle in the middle of a mountain-fringed loch will recognize Eilean Donan. Built in 1214 as a defense against the Danes, it was destroyed by clan fighting and lay in ruins for around 200 years, until it was restored and rebuilt by Colonel MacRae, of Clan MacRae, at the beginning of the 20th century. It is now a clan war memorial and museum. You can clamber around the ramparts and poke around the dimly lit nooks and crannies of this mini-fortress just outside the little village of Dornie. After dousing yourself in Highland history, peruse the shop or grab lunch in the cafe of the contemporary

Eilean Donan Castle, built in 1214.

The bay at Plockton.

visitor center. They also rent out a lovely self-catering cottage sleeping that sleeps four.

Dornie. www.eileandonancastle.com. ℰ **01599/555-202.** £7 adults; £6 seniors, students, and children 5–16; £17 families. Daily Feb–Mar 10am–5pm, Apr–Oct 10am–6pm, Nov–Dec 10am–4pm. Drive 8 miles east of the Kyle of Lochalsh on the A87.

Plockton ★

Palm trees line the waterfront of pretty Plockton. Designated a conservation village by the National Trust for Scotland, the little fishing hamlet dates back to the 19th century. NTS rangers lead regular guided walks of historic Plockton, taking in the old pier and pontoons. Its famously mild climate is thanks to the warming effect of the Gulf Stream and its sheltered position on the east-facing shore of Loch Carron. Tourists flock here to browse the little galleries and tuck into fresh seafood in little pubs, or take a boat trip in the bay. Plockton is one of the best places to learn to kayak because of its calm bay. Alison French (www.seakayak plockton.co.uk; ℰ **01599/544-422**) organises trips and courses for families, beginners and intermediates, paddling out to remote coral beaches or along the coastline, around Strome and Kishorn islands.

WHERE TO STAY & EAT

Plockton Gallery ★   Bed down in an art gallery: Artist Miriam Drysdale runs a vibrant little gallery (a cut above the usual clichéd Highland scenes) in a rambling old manse in the village, and lets out a couple of lovely rooms. The Red Room (four-poster and a bathroom bigger than many bedrooms) and the Blue Room are quirkily decorated, with bags of character along with paintings and etchings on the walls. Miriam holds a summer exhibition each year and also offers lessons and courses. Although there's no Wi-Fi, there's a desk with paper and paints in the eaves where you can sit for inspiration.

The Manse, Innes St. www.plocktongallery.com. ℂ **01599/544-442.** 2 units. Doubles £90–£100, includes breakfast. **Amenities:** Guest kitchen.

Plockton Inn ★ This whitewashed inn, opposite the Plockton Gallery, is also a renowned seafood restaurant. Kenny, the owner, smokes his own fish in the smokehouse at the back of the hotel, while Martin the barman catches Plockton prawns in the bay. This bustling little place has live traditional music every Tuesday and Thursday night, a log fire in the bar and 14 cozy rooms (some with sea views) split between the inn and an old cottage over the street.

Innes St. www.plocktoninn.co.uk. ℂ **01599/544-222.** 14 units. Doubles from £110, includes breakfast. **Amenities:** Restaurant; bar; free Wi-Fi.

Glenelg ★

Veer off the A87 before you reach Dornie and take a left turn for Glenelg. A scenic (read mountainous) drive brings you down to the little hamlet of Glenelg with its picturesque pub on the beachfront and, during the summer, the tiny car ferry over the Kylerhea narrows to Skye.

WHERE TO STAY & EAT

The Glenelg Inn ★ Not only does this traditional whitewashed inn have a stunning location, it is one of those rare finds in the Highlands—a gastropub. Think home-cured gravadlax with horseradish crème fraiche and oatcakes (£8) and loin of rabbit stuffed with Lochalsh black pudding served with carrot and potato rosti and asparagus (£17). The beamed bar has a roaring log fire and great atmosphere. If the weather's good, a gate from the garden leads onto the beach, if it's not there's a bulging bookcase to help you while away the hours. There are seven cozy bedrooms, some with sea views over the Sound of Sleat.

Kirkton. www.glenelg-inn.com. ℂ **01599/522-273.** 7 units Doubles £120–£170, includes breakfast. **Amenities:** Restaurant; bar; free Wi-Fi.

THE ISLE OF SKYE ★★

83 miles W of Inverness; 176 miles NW of Edinburgh; 146 miles NW of Glasgow

The Isle of Skye has a strange, almost mystical, power, pulling tourists towards it like a giant magnet. Its attraction is threefold: a wildly romantic historical claim to fame (Charles Edward Stuart aka Bonnie Prince Charlie fled here, with the help of Flora MacDonald, after his devastating defeat at the Battle of Culloden), it's a mecca for mountain climbers who make the pilgrimage to tackle the mighty Cuillins and, it punches way above its weight class in terms of foodie highlights, home to two of Scotland's most famous restaurants, The Three Chimneys and Kinloch Lodge.

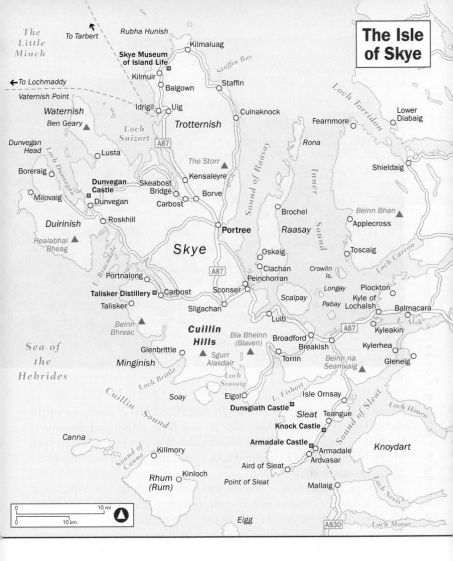

Wreathed in mystery and drama, this giant chunk of rock battered by stormy seas is the largest of the Hebridean islands at 48 miles long and between 3 and 25 miles wide, and separated from the mainland by the Sound of Sleat (pronounced "Slate"). At Kyleakin, on the eastern end, the channel is only ¼ mile wide. Once a choppy boat trip away, it's now connected to the mainland by a more prosaic road bridge.

The bare, brooding landscape, pocked with woodland glens, meandering mountain passes and gushing waterfalls, is dominated by the **Cuillins ★★★**, a monstrous range of jagged black mountains and the Holy Grail for rock climbers. The Sleat Peninsula, the island's southernmost arm, is a lush green pocket known as the "Garden of Skye" and

The Isle of Skye.

home to the High Chief of clan Donald, Lord Macdonald, one of the oldest Highland clans, whose wife is cook book author and doyenne of Scottish cuisine, Lady Claire Macdonald. You can bed down in their luxury hotel, Kinloch Lodge and take a cooking class, or just tuck into a Michelin-starred dinner.

There are numerous stories about the origin of the name *Skye*. Some believe it's from the Norse *ski,* meaning "cloud," and others say it's from the Gaelic word for "winged." There are in fact many Norse names on the island, as the Norsemen held sway here for four centuries until 1263. Overlooking the Kyle is ruined **Castle Maol,** once the home of a Norwegian princess. At the other end of the island is mighty **Dunvegan Castle,** the seat of Clan MacLeod.

The fact that Skye is on most tourists' wish lists does pose one major down side, however. Despite the fact that every other house seems to have a B&B board outside, for the last 2 weeks of July and the whole of August if you don't have a reservation you're unlikely to find anywhere to stay. Many people wind up bunking down around Kyle and hopping across the bridge to Skye each day. It's always worth checking airbnb.com, which has helped the accommodation shortage. Another word on accommodation, there might be a rash of B&Bs but the quality varies. There are a lot of tired and uninspiring hotels, along with a handful of diamonds in the rough. There's also a growing portfolio of modern self-catering properties. Examples of properties with the architectural wow factor include **An Airigh** (www.anairigh.co.uk), **The Shed** in Tokavaig (www.skyeshed.com) and the **Black Shed** in Skinidin (www.blackshed.co.uk).

Essentials

GETTING THERE From the Kyle of Lochalsh, **drive** west along the bridge over the strait to Kyleakin.

VISITOR INFORMATION The **Tourist Information Centre** is at Bayfield House, Bayfield Road in Portree (www.skye.co.uk; ✆ **01478/612-992**). It's open Monday to Saturday 9am to 5pm (6pm in the summer) and Sunday 10am to 4pm.

Exploring Skye

The island is littered with castle ruins, *duns* (hill forts), and *brochs* (prehistoric round stone towers). You can explore on foot, two wheels or by boat. **Island Cycles,** The Green, in Portree (www.islandcycle-skye.co.uk; ✆ **01478/613-121**) is one of the best places to hire a bike and is open Monday through Saturday from 9am to 5pm and charges £9 for half-day, £15 for 1 day and £28 for 2 days.

To take to the seas, **Bella Jane Boat Trips,** The Harbourfront, Elgol (www.bellajane.co.uk; ✆ **01471/866-244**) leaves from the pier in the village of Elgol. The sturdy vessel sails daily (if there's enough business), between Easter and October, into the rock-ringed borders of Loch Coruisk, which are rich in bird life. Most visitors opt for the standard return trip; you're carried to the base of the hills, deposited for 90 minutes of wandering, and then returned over water to Elgol. It lasts 3 hours and costs £24 per person, £13 for children 4 to 14 (children under 4 go free). Alternatively you can book a one-way trip and then hike back, a 14-mile marked trek from the Cuillin Hills across an undulating, rock-strewn landscape to the Sligachan Hotel (see below), the premier hotel for trekkers. You can stay overnight at the hotel or take a bus or taxi the remaining 6¾ miles back to Portree.

Kyleakin ★

Just over the Skye bridge is Kyleakin, where the old ferry used to arrive. Kyleakin sits onto a small bay and is dominated by a ruin, **Castle Maol ★**, on a jagged knoll. For a lovely walk, head up to this ruin, which dates from the 12th century, and was a stronghold of the Mackinnon clan.

Eilean Ban ★ MUSEUM/NATURE RESERVE Author and naturalist Gavin Maxwell's tale about otters "Ring of Bright Water" melted millions and was made into a film. You can visit his home on Eilean Ban, beneath the Skye Bridge. Maxwell bought the old lighthouse keepers' cottages in the 60s and lived here until his death in 1969. The Bright Water Visitor Centre in Kyleakin organizes guided tours of the nature reserve, lighthouse and the cottages which now house the Gavin Maxwell museum. Check out Teko the Otter's memorial stone and the wildlife hide. From here you can spot seals, otters and, in season, minke whales.

Eilean Ban. www.eileanban.org. ℂ **01599/530-040.** £8 adults, £7 seniors and children, £22 families. Access to the island is via a wooden gate on the Skye Bridge. Apr–Oct Mon–Fri 10am–4pm, tours at 2pm

WHERE TO STAY

The White Heather Hotel ★   This friendly little family-run hotel on the harbor has panoramic views of the Torridon mountains across the water. It's a good option if you want to stay near the bridge rather than schlepping to the more remote parts of the island. There are just nine comfortable bedrooms including three family rooms. Dogs are welcome, children are welcome, there are board games and toys, hot water bottles in the rooms, a kitchenette for guests to use and a study.

The Harbour. www.whiteheatherhotel.co.uk. ℂ **01599/534-577.** 9 units. Doubles £52–£95, includes breakfast. **Amenities:** Dining room; 2 lounges; kitchenette; study; free Wi-Fi. Closed Nov–Feb.

Sligachan ★

The village of Sligachan sits at the head of a sea loch, with views of the darkly dramatic Cuillin Hills (pronounced "*Coo*-lin") to the west. It's one of the best bases for exploring Skye because of its central location. Visitors can enjoy sea-trout fishing, and an occasional salmon is caught on the Sligachan River. It's also possible to rent a boat from the Sligachan Hotel (see below) to explore the Storr Lochs, 15 miles from Sligachan, known for good brown-trout fishing from May to September.

WHERE TO STAY & EAT

Sligachan Hotel ★   At the foot of the Cuillins, on the main road between Portree and Kyleakin (you can't miss it) this legendary family-run hotel has been a popular base for walkers and climbers for almost two centuries. It's one of the island's oldest coaching inns, built in the 1830s, and even has its own mountaineering museum. The 21 bedrooms won't win any design awards but they have recently been revamped and modernized. There's a restaurant, two bars and a microbrewery—which is just as well as there's nowhere else to go in Sligachan in the evening. Tuck into starters such as venison pate with red onion marmalade and Highland oatcakes and mains including wild mushroom risotto topped with parmesan shavings and truffle oil in the Sligachan

Steakhouse and Grill before curling up with a dram in Mackenzie's Bar. Next door, the Seumas Bar is a tad livelier with malt whiskies and real ales brewed on site.

Sligachan. www.sligachan.co.uk. © **01478/650-204.** 21 units. Doubles £100–£160, includes breakfast. **Amenities:** Restaurant; 2 bars; room service; free Wi–Fi.

Carbost ★

A 10-minute drive west of Sligachan brings you to the village of Carbost on the shore of Loch Harport, the home of **Talisker Distillery ★** (www.discovering-distilleries.com; © **01478/614-308**). Dating back to 1843, Talisker is the oldest working distillery on the island and was mentioned by Robert Louis Stevenson in his 1880 poem *Scotsman's Return from Abroad.* Today, visitors can choose between three tours of the distillery, ranging from £8 to £35 for adults, based on the comprehensiveness of the tour and the number of tastings included. The distillery is open November to March Monday to Friday, from 10am to 4pm (tours at 10:30am, noon, 2pm, and 3:30pm); and from April to October, Monday to Saturday 9:30am to 5pm (tours throughout the day); from June to September, the distillery is also open Sundays 11am to 5pm.

WHERE TO STAY & EAT

Wilmar Bed & Breakfast ★   This historic whitewashed croft house dating back to the 1920s has just two charming bedrooms: Edinburgh and Glasgow. Edinburgh is ensuite while Glasgow, with its lovely iron bedstead, has a private bathroom next door. There's a cozy guest lounge with wooden floors, comfy sofas, a log fire and a bookcase bulging with maps, guidebooks and board games. Breakfast is a feast—creamy porridge, eggs from their chickens or Achiltibue kippers—all served with sourdough bread and homemade preserves. From the cottage's jetty you can spot dolphins, seals, sea eagles, deer and otters. For dinner, the Old Inn in Carbost, which has regular live music, is within walking distance.

Carbost. www.wilmarbedandbreakfast.com © **01478/640-251.** Doubles £85–£90, includes breakfast; 2-night minimum stay. **Amenities:** Free Wi-Fi.

Portree ★★

Skye's capital is the little town of Portree, set on a picturesque natural harbor. Much of Skye is bare and bleak, dominated by the brooding Cuillins and vast sweeps of brown moorland. However, this little whitewashed town is pretty, fringed by trees and green clifftops, fishing boats and cruising vessels bobbing in the bay. It's bustling during the summer months—during the winter you'll be lucky to find anything open. It can be a bit hit and miss when it comes to good hotels and restaurants, however, but there are a handful of good options.

Sunset at Portree, the Isle of Skye.

WHERE TO STAY

Rowan Tree Cottage ★★ This little B&B is one of the loveliest places to stay on Skye—and with just one room you'll have it virtually to yourself. The low-slung croft house with a jaunty blue trim dates back to 1903. The roomy double is downstairs and is charmingly decorated with owner Alan's antique finds. The walls are tongue and groove, there's an old fireplace and thoughtful touches include a fridge stocked with complimentary sparkling wine and water, fresh milk and shortbread. It's just a 10-minute drive outside Portree in a pretty wooded spot but feels off-the-beaten track. The view of the Red Cuillins in the mornings is spectacular; the breakfast spread just about matches it. Alan bakes his own bread, grinds the coffee beans and makes his own jams and marmalade. Achnahannaid, Portree. www.rowantreecottageskye.com. ℂ **01478/650-278.** 1 unit. £110, includes breakfast. 2-night minimum stay. **Amenities:** Free Wi-Fi.

Viewfield House ★ This wonderful old mansion is tastefully traditional, a real old country house scattered with antiques, wooden floors strewn with Persian rugs, gilt framed oil paintings on the walls along with antlers—and a fair bit of taxidermy hanging around. The original interiors have been preserved, and staying here feels like an old-fashioned Scottish house party. Rooms are big with brass beds, fireplaces and freestanding bathtubs and have views over the 8 hectares (20 acres) of woodland garden or to the sea. It's just a 10-minute walk from the center of Portree. Portree. www.viewfieldhouse.com. ℂ **01478/612-217.** 11 units. Doubles £116–£150, includes breakfast. **Amenities:** Lounge with communal TV; free Wi-Fi.

WHERE TO EAT

The Isle of Skye Baking Company ★★ CAFE/BAKERY   Set up by an enterprising South African couple, Barry and Liza Hawthorne, who fell in love with this corner of Scotland, the bakery and cafe with an artisan gallery upstairs is in an old woolen mill on the edge of Portree. It's a great place to stock up on freshly baked breads, oatcakes and homemade chutneys—their specialty lunchbread (with fillings such as chilli venison chorizo with butternut squash baked inside) is perfect for picnics. Or sit in the funky cafe space with a cup of coffee before heading upstairs to look around the Skyeworks gallery. The artisan blankets, cushions and artworks here are a cut above your usual tourist fare.
The Old Woolen Mill, Dunvegan Rd. www.isleofskyebakingco.co.uk. ✆ **01478/612-669.** Mon–Sat 9am–5pm, Sun 10am–4pm

The Trotternish Peninsula ★

Head north from Portree to the wild and windswept Trotternish Peninsula. An anti-clockwise circular loop takes you past a string of natural landmarks such as the **Old Man of Storr,** the Trottenish ridge, the Quiraing cliffs and a host of mesmerizing seascapes.

A view of the Old Man of Storr, Trotternish Peninsula, Isle of Skye.

On the northern tip swing by the **Skye Museum of Island Life ★** (www.skyemuseum.co.uk; ☎ **01470/552-206**), at Kilmuir, an atmospheric huddle of thatched cottages showcasing the harsh conditions of crofting life in the 19th century. Admission is £3 for adults, £2 for seniors and students, and 50p for children 5 to 16. The museum opens from Easter to October, Monday to Saturday from 9:30am to 5pm. Just up the lane behind the museum is **Kilmuir churchyard** where Flora MacDonald is buried. You can see the grave of this famous Scottish heroine who helped a disguised Bonnie Prince Charlie flee after the Battle of Culloden.

Carrying on, the village of Uig (15 miles north of Portree and 49 miles from the Kyle of Lochalsh) is also the ferry port for Harris and Uist in the Outer Hebrides. Many people anchor themselves here if they have an early departure, however, it also has a stunning location in its own right, opening onto Uig Bay and famous for its sunrises and sunsets.

WHERE TO STAY & EAT

The Glenview ★★ This award-winning restaurant with rooms between Portree and Staffin has reinvented itself as a Pie Cafe, Gallery and B&B. Kirsty Faulds and Simon Wallwork have a young family and the life of a chef isn't always conducive to a healthy work-life balance, so the young couple decided to rejig the business. Australian chef Simon always had a passion for pies, so the Skye Pie Café was born in 2015. They've kept three quirky B&B rooms, two doubles on the first floor and a large twin at the back of the old croft house. Although they no longer offer evening meals, guests who don't want to go out can request an early evening supper—of pies—between 6 to 7pm. Of course, these are no ordinary pies. One of Simon's specialities is lobster and crab caught in Staffin bay and wrapped in a pie crust. And for those who miss his gourmet dishes, on the last Saturday of every month he holds a Supper Club. Culnacnoc. www.glenviewskye.co.uk. ☎ **01470/562-248.** 3 units. £85–£95, includes breakfast. B&B Mon–Sat; cafe Tues–Sat 10:30am–5pm. **Amenities:** Free Wi-Fi.

Woodbine Guesthouse ★ This charming 5-bedroom guesthouse teeters on the hill above the harbour in Uig. The owners, Andi and Vicki Dunkel, met while working as diving instructors on the Great Barrier Reef and, after a stint running sailing holidays on their yacht in the Mediterranean, launched another outdoor activity venture here. They offer a range of activity and accommodation packages including mountain-biking, fishing, sea kayaking and water-skiing. One of the highlights is their wildlife-watching boat trip to see minke whales, puffins, sea eagles and seals. After a day outdoors you can crash out in the cozy and contemporary bedrooms with wooden floors and sea views. Uig. www.skyeactivities.co.uk. ☎ **01470/542-243.** 5 units. £66–£80, includes breakfast. **Amenities:** Lounge; free Wi-Fi.

Skeabost Bridge ★

Skeabost Bridge between Portree and Dunvegan, has an ancient island cemetery where you can see the graves of four Crusaders.

WHERE TO STAY & EAT

The Spoons ★★   This smart, contemporary boutique B&B was built by Marie and Ian Lewis, fresh from running Vanessa Branson's (sister to Richard) private island retreat off the west coast, Eilean Shona. Eclectically decorated with Marie's antique finds, with a wood-burning stove and sofas smothered in Harris tweed, it's a cozy place to hole up after a day's exploring. Situated on their working farm on Loch Snizort, breakfast includes eggs from their hens along with freshly squeezed orange juice, porridge or homemade granola. Bedrooms are sumptuous, featuring a mix of brass beads, monsoon showers, freestanding bathtubs, plantation shutters, sheepskin rugs and lush fabrics. It's light, bright and luxurious.

75 Aird Bernisdale, Skeabost Bridge. www.thespoonsonskye.com. ℂ **01470/532-217.** 3 units. Doubles £145–£165, includes breakfast. **Amenities:** Lounge; free Wi-Fi.

Dunvegan ★

The village of Dunvegan, northwest of Portree, grew up around Skye's main historic sight: **Dunvegan Castle ★** (www.dunvegancastle.com; ℂ **01470/521-206**), the ancestral seat of the chiefs of Clan MacLeod for the past 800 years. Standing on a dramatic rocky promontory and said to be Britain's oldest inhabited castle, it was once accessible only by boat, but now the moat is bridged and the castle is open to the public. You can still hop on a boat, however, as trips to the tiny surrounding islands to see the seal colonies run from the jetty. Inside the castle you can see relics such as a "fairy flag," believed to have been given to the MacLeods by woodland spirits, and reputed to have brought good luck in battle. The castle is open daily: April to mid-October, from 10am to 5:30pm. The castle and gardens cost £11 for adults, £9 for seniors, and £8 for children aged between 5 and 15. A family ticket is £29. Gardens only: £9 for adults, £8 for seniors, and £6 for children.

WHERE TO STAY & EAT

Greshornish House ★   This elegant 18th-century building, surrounded by wooded grounds on the Greshornish peninsula, is an off-the-beaten track retreat, down a long, winding lane between the Trotternish Peninsula and Dunvegan. The name comes from the Norse and means the pig's snout—the shape of the peninsula. Outside there are sweeping lawns, a walled garden and stunning sea views. The house is scattered with antiques, family portraits and photographs. There's a cozy bar, a dining room and wood-panelled drawing room where you can sink into an armchair with a good book and a dram in front of the roaring log fire. The eight bedrooms are all named after Scottish islands. East-facing Jura was once the laird's bedroom with views of Loch Greshornish and a decadent roll-top bath, while grand Rum, once the music room, boasts a four-poster bed and marble fireplace. Islay, originally the Georgian drawing room, also has a four-poster and views over the loch to the Trotternish Ridge.

Edinbane. www.greshornishhouse.com. © **01470/582-266.** 8 units Doubles £140–£160, suites £158–£190, includes breakfast. **Amenities:** Bar; drawing room; billiard room; free Wi-Fi. Closed Nov–Easter.

Three Chimneys Restaurant ★★★ SCOTTISH Foodies have been making a pilgrimage to The Three Chimneys for three decades now, since Shirley and Eddie Spear first put down roots here, turning this far-flung corner of Scotland into a gourmet hotspot. Today, it is the gastronomic highlight of any visit to the island. This Michelin-starred restaurant in an old crofter's house is cozy, rustic chic in design with low-slung ceilings and roaring fires. The seven-course Taste of Skye menu features mouthwatering morsels such as Bracadale brown crab parfait, apple and Mull cheddar followed by scallop with cauliflower, rhubarb, blood orange and ginger. Thankfully there are also six luxury suites within staggering distance of the restaurant in The House Over-By.

Colbost. www.threechimneys.co.uk. © **01470/511-258.** 6 units. Doubles £345, includes breakfast. Fixed-price dinner £60 for 3 courses, £90 for 8 courses; lunch £37 for 3 courses. Dinner daily 6:15–9:45pm (last order); lunch mid-Mar to mid-Nov Mon–Sat 12:15–1:45pm (last order).

Sleat Peninsula ★

When the mist and clouds roll in and the island is drenched in a dark, dreich drizzle, Skye can seem bleak, brown and forbidding. The southeast corner, the **Sleat Peninsula,** in comparison is refreshingly vibrant and green. The shores are washed by the warmer waters of the Gulf Stream and it has long been known as the "Garden of Skye."

Off the A851, about 12 miles south of Broadford, is a ruined stronghold of the MacDonalds, **Knock Castle ★**. Another MacDonald stronghold, **Dunsgiath Castle ★**, also has some well-preserved ruins. It's at Tokavaig on an unclassified road (watch for a sign) 20 miles south and southwest of Broadford. You can visit both these evocative ruins for free, day or night.

Armadale Castle Gardens & Museum of the Isles ★ MUSEUM The ruins of Armadale Castle, the home of Clan Donald, are surrounded by a majestic 20,000-acre estate. Today, you can visit the award-winning Clan Donald Visitor Centre, restored historic gardens and baronial stables which now house a restaurant. In the Museum of the Isles you can travel through 1,500 years of history learning about the MacDonalds, the

Lords of the Isles, while the countryside ranger service offers a summer program of guided walks and talks on the estate. The drive from Kyleakin takes about 30 minutes.

Armadale. www.clandonald.com. (C) **01471/844-305.** £9 adults, £6 seniors and children aged 5–15. Apr–Oct daily 9:30am–5:30pm (last entry at 5pm).

WHERE TO STAY & EAT

Ardvasar Hotel ★ The oldest part of this pretty whitewashed 19th-century coaching inn is a stone-trimmed pub in what was once a stable. On the waterfront of the little village, there are 10 tartan-trimmed rooms to choose from, the ones at the front boasting views over the Sound of Sleet and the mountains of Knoydart in the distance.

Ardvasar. www.ardvasarhotel.com. (C) **01471/844-223.** 10 units. Doubles £90–£145, includes breakfast. **Amenities:** Restaurant; bar; room service; free Wi–Fi.

Toravaig Hotel ★ This graceful whitewashed hotel has nine contemporary rooms, each named after a Hebridean island, a handful with spectacular views over the Skye's rugged coastline and the ruins of Knock Castle. In the lounge downstairs you can sink into a sofa and sip a single malt by the crackling log fire. The **Islay Restaurant** has a daily changing menu with dishes such as line caught sea bass, samphire, braised fennel, cauliflower, crab, surf clams and sauce vierge. The five-course dinner is £48 per person and is open to non-residents. From April and September, the hotel owners offer guests the chance to go sailing for the day on their 42-foot yacht (see listing for the sister hotel, the Duisdale, below) out to the islands of Rhum and Eigg or into Loch Nevis or Loch Hourn.

Sleat. www.skyehotel.co.uk. (C) **01471/820-200.** 9 units. Doubles £232–£270, includes breakfast. **Amenities:** Restaurant; lounge; sailing trips; free Wi–Fi.

Isle Ornsay ★

Adjacent to Sleat Peninsula is the Isle Ornsay, also called Eilean Iarmain in Gaelic. It's a lovely, remote islet in a small, rocky bay with mountains of Knoydart in the background. Its heyday as Skye's main fishing port is long gone. Today you'll find little whitewashed cottages around the small harbor.

WHERE TO STAY

Duisdale Hotel ★ Once a grand hunting lodge, the Duisdale is the larger sister hotel to the Toravaig (see above). Set on 14 hectares (35 acres) of gardens and woodland, it's a contemporary boutique hotel with 18 rooms, many with chunky four posters and one with a free-standing bathtub with a view of the sea. There's a hot tub in the garden and a roaring fire in the lounge where you can tuck into afternoon tea. The restaurant serves the finest Scottish produce while the full Scottish

An interior at Kinloch Lodge, Sleat, Isle Ornsay.

breakfast includes porridge with cream and whisky. A highlight here, as at the Toravaig, are the summer sailing trips on the 42-foot luxury yacht, which is skippered by the hotel's owner, a former sea captain.

Isle Ornsay, Sleat. www.duisdale.com. ℭ **01471/833-202.** 18 units. Doubles £158–£308, suites £288–£338, includes breakfast. **Amenities:** Restaurant; bar; lounge; hot tub; sailing trips; free Wi-Fi.

Hotel Eilean Iarmain ★ Also referred to as the "Isle Ornsay Hotel" inside its crammed with antiques; tartan carpets, antlers on the walls, wood panelling, and chintzy fabrics create a cottagey feel. In winter log fires blaze while musicians perform in the buzzing bar. The suites are housed in a former stable block dating back to the 1870s, while one of the rooms features a huge canopied bed with checked drapes from Armadale Castle.

Isle Ornsay, Sleat. www.eileaniarmain.co.uk. ℭ **01471/833-332.** 16 units. Doubles £120–£190, suites £170–£250, includes breakfast. **Amenities:** Restaurant; bar; room service; babysitting; free Wi-Fi.

Kinloch Lodge ★★★ This is the home of the doyenne of Scottish cuisine and author of countless cookbooks, Lady Claire MacDonald, who is married to the chief of the Donald clan. Built in 1680 as a hunting lodge, it's now their elegant home. Reception rooms are peppered with family portraits, grand fireplaces and antiques. It's also a luxury retreat, with Michelin-starred restaurant and cookery school to boot. After drinks in the drawing room you can savor gourmet dishes conjured up by Head Chef Marcello Tully in the traditional tartan-clad restaurant under the watchful eyes of the MacDonald ancestors on the walls. The seven-course tasting menu costs £80, the daily changing menu £70. The three-course lunch menu costs £33. After dinner you can slope off to bed in the North or South Lodge. Bedrooms have tasteful tartan trim, lambswool blankets, roll-top baths and glorious views towards Kinloch Hill or the sea loch.

Isle Ornsay, Sleat. www.kinloch-lodge.co.uk. ℂ **01471/833-333.** 19 units. Doubles £198–£300, suites £298–£440, includes breakfast and 5-course dinner. **Amenities:** Restaurant; bar, cooking school, free Wi-Fi.

19

PLANNING YOUR TRIP TO ENGLAND & SCOTLAND

by Donald Strachan

GETTING THERE
By Plane

London, England, receives most of Britain's incoming air traffic, and Britain's principal airport is **London Heathrow** (LHR; www.heathrow airport.com), 17 miles west of the city and boasting five hectic, bustling terminals (Terminals 1 to 5). This is the U.K. hub of most major airlines, including British Airways, Virgin Atlantic, and the North American carriers. **London Gatwick** (LGW; www.gatwickairport.com) is the city's second major airport, 31 miles south of central London in the Sussex countryside. As with Heathrow, you can fly direct or with a connection to or from pretty much anywhere. For information on **getting into London** from its various airports, see p. 55.

England also has a number of smaller and regional airports. The only two with a significant number of intercontinental connections are **Manchester** (MAN; www.manchesterairport.co.uk) and **Birmingham** (BHX; www.bhx.co.uk). Scotland's principal airports, **Edinburgh** (EDI; www.edinburghairport.com) and **Glasgow** (GLA; www.glasgowairport. com), also have a few direct connections with North America. For information on getting into city centers from Edinburgh and Glasgow airports, see p. 472 and 539, respectively.

Short-haul passengers are increasingly flying into Britain's smaller airports—particularly as budget airlines have proliferated, and even come to dominate domestic and international routes. **London Stansted** (STN; www.stanstedairport.com), 37 miles northeast of London, is the gateway for a vast array of short-haul destinations in the U.K., continental Europe, and parts of the Middle East. It's also a hub for major budget operator Ryanair. **London Luton** (LTN; www.london-luton.co.uk), anchoring a similarly diverse short-haul network, lies 34 miles northwest of London. Ryanair and easyJet are two of the main users. **London City** (LCY; www.londoncityairport.com), the only commercial airport actually in London itself, is used mainly by business travelers from nearby Docklands and the City, but does have some regular direct flights to New York, Paris, Edinburgh, and Madrid. British Airways and Cityjet are the two major airlines at London City. Outside London, the likes of **Liverpool John Lennon** (LPL; www.liverpoolairport.com), **Leeds Bradford** (LBA; www.leedsbradfordairport.co.uk), and **Newcastle** (NCL; www. newcastleairport.com) are well served by budget airlines offering direct connections to cities and resorts in continental Europe. In Scotland, there are regional airports at **Aberdeen** (ABZ; www.aberdeenairport. com), **Inverness** (INV; www.hial.co.uk), and **Dundee** (DND; www. hial.co.uk).

PREVIOUS PAGE: **King's Cross railway station, London.**

By Train from Mainland Europe

High-speed rail services from Paris and Brussels, via the **Channel Tunnel,** arrive at London's **St Pancras International Station.** You can reach London from Brussels in under 2 hours, and from Paris in 2¼ hours. In the U.K., make reservations for the train by calling **Eurostar** at ✆ **03432/186-186** or book online at **www.eurostar.com**, or contact **Rail Europe** (www.raileurope.com; ✆ **800/622-8600,** or 800/361-7245 in Canada). International visitors arriving from continental Europe should remember that the validity of the Eurail pass ends at the English Channel. You can connect to **Scotland** and northern England from **London King's Cross Station,** linked to St Pancras via an underground concourse. The journey from London to Edinburgh takes around 4¼ hours with some services traveling an additional hour on to Glasgow, and others continuing north to Dundee (an additional 1½ hr.) and Aberdeen (an additional 2½ hr.).

GETTING AROUND
By Train

Train travel in Britain is getting faster and more reliable. It is also a great way to get around, gliding through the countryside in a comfy seat with a coffee in one hand and your iPad in the other. The fastest, best-served routes generally radiate from the capital. There are two main lines north from London, the **East Coast Mainline,** which connects King's Cross with York, Newcastle, and Edinburgh; and the **West Coast Line,** which connects Euston Station with Birmingham, Manchester, Liverpool, the Lake District, and Glasgow. London Waterloo has trains to the south coast and southwestern counties of England. Paddington serves the west and parts of the Midlands. For more information on train connections from London stations see p. 56 in chapter 4. Trains heading north out of the capital are due to get faster still, as work began in 2012 on "HS2," a new high-speed line between London and Birmingham, and eventually onward to Manchester and Leeds. But don't get too excited yet: Opening is scheduled for 2026.

The main train operator in Scotland is **ScotRail** (www.scotrail. co.uk; ✆ **0344/556-5636**), with a network of rail routes around the country. In addition to standard fares, ScotRail offers a number of ticket deals. With the **Kids Go Free** deal (www.scotrail.co.uk/kidsgo free), two children between ages 5 and 15 travel free with an adult as long as you travel during off-peak hours. A number of attractions in Scotland are linked with this deal and allow free entry for children traveling on these tickets.

RAIL PASSES BritRail passes allow unlimited travel in England, Scotland, and Wales on any scheduled train over the whole of the network

RAIL INFO & BAGGING THE
cheapest FARES

Rail travel in Britain can seem baffling, with so many independent, private train companies operating on the same set of (state-owned) tracks. However, getting information about times and routes is simple: **National Rail Enquiries** is a one-stop shop with everything you need to know. Go to the website **www.nationalrail.co.uk** and enter the names of two stations (or towns) and it will give you a list of trains, times, and routes. It also shows fare options, of which there can be many, depending on when you travel and when you book. You can also get the information by phone (℃ **08457/ 48-49-50** in the U.K., or +44 20/7278-5240 from overseas). The site doesn't actually sell tickets but will connect you to one that does in a click. There are also multiple train schedule apps for virtually every smartphone platform.

The key anomaly about rail travel is this: England has some of the most expensive walk-up rail fares in the world, but also the cheapest advance-purchase rail tickets in Europe. For example, a one-way, walk-up fare at peak times (usually before around 9:15am on weekdays) between London and Manchester costs £164. Book ahead, however, and travel away from rush hour or on the weekend and you could bag a round-trip on the same route for little more than £20. Advance fares are only available on long-distance routes and from around

12 weeks ahead of your travel dates. If you are able to book in advance, online agents such as **theTrainline.com** and **RedSpottedHanky.com** can bring huge savings. You can pay with a credit card and collect tickets from your departure station. If you're very fortunate, discount reseller **MegaTrain** (www.megatrain. com) may have a seat on your route at an even bigger saving. Alternatively, take all the hassle and planning out of your rail touring with a BritRail pass (see below).

during the validity of the pass. A pass allows you to dodge lines at ticket machines and travel during peak periods without added expense. Passes are also valid on the expensive rail connections from several key airports. Unless you plan to log lots of miles, they probably aren't the cheapest way to get about—but they are certainly the easiest.

Passes are not available to buy in Britain, nor to residents of the U.K.; they are for international visitors only, and you must purchase one before you arrive. To buy a pass in your local currency, see **www. britrail.com/book-your-britrail-pass**. Passes are also available from **www.visitbritainshop.com**.

A **BritRail Consecutive** allows you to travel for a consecutive number of days. For example, standard adult fare are $220 for 3 days, $273 for 4 days, $397 for 8 days, $589 for 15 days, $737 for 22 days, and $870 for 1 month. **Seniors** (60 and older) qualify for discounts in first-class travel only. Passengers 25 and younger qualify for discounts on first and standard passes. More versatile is the **BritRail Flexi** pass, allowing you to travel for a fixed number of days during a 1-month period. In standard class, it costs $351 for 4 days, $501 for 8 days, and $755 for 15 days. One child aged 5 to 15 can travel free with each adult or senior pass when the **BritRail Family Discount** is requested while buying the adult pass; additional children pay half the regular adult fare for their pass. All children ages 4 and under ride U.K. trains for free. If you plan to stay within the borders of England, the **BritRail England** passes are around 20% cheaper than the all-U.K. passes covered above. Passes are also often 20% cheaper between November and February, and discounts are available for parties of two or more who are traveling together **at all times.**

TRAIN PASSES FOR SCOTLAND ONLY   ScotRail also offers passes covering just Scottish rail networks. The **Freedom of Scotland Travelpass** allows unlimited travel across all routes in Scotland from Carlisle, England (near the western Scotland–England border) and from Berwick-upon-Tweed, England (near the eastern Scotland–England border). This pass also includes rides on ferries operated by Caledonian MacBrayne (www.calmac.co.uk) and travel on a limited selection of bus (coach) routes operated by Scottish Citylink (www.citylink.co.uk), Stagecoach in Fife and the Highlands (www.stagecoachbus.com), and First Edinburgh (www.firstgroup.com). Passes for 4 days of unlimited travel over 8 consecutive days cost £134, and 8 days of unlimited travel over 15 consecutive days cost £180. Children aged 5 to 15 travel for half the cost of an adult ticket and under-5s travel for free.

Direct Train Travel from London to Key Cities

TO	DEPARTURE STATION	DIRECT TRAINS DAILY	MILES	TRAVEL TIME
Bath	Paddington	30	107	1 hr. 30 min.
Birmingham	Euston	45	123	1 hr. 30 min.
Chester	Euston	13	183	2 hr.
Edinburgh	King's Cross	26	396	4 hr. 30 min.
Exeter	Paddington/Waterloo	30	174	2 hr. 15 min./3 hr. 25 min.
Glasgow	Euston	22	392	4 hr. 40 min.
Liverpool	Euston	17	203	2 hr. 15 min.
Manchester	Euston	45	190	2 hr. 10 min.
Newcastle	King's Cross	26	268	3 hr.
Oxford	Paddington	50	60	1 hr. 10 min.
Penzance	Paddington	9	285	5 hr. 30 min.
York	King's Cross	40	198	2 hr.

PLANNING YOUR TRIP TO ENGLAND & SCOTLAND

By Bus

In Britain, a long-distance bus is called a "coach" (a "bus" generally denotes shorter-haul, local transport). Coaches are generally the cheapest way to get around the country, but also the slowest. Most sizable towns have a link with a capital—London, Edinburgh, or both—and several other major English and Scottish cities, either direct or via a connection. Most long-distance services are run by **National Express** (www.nationalexpress.com; ☎ **08717/818181**), which uses coaches equipped with reclining seats and toilets. A good budget alternative on some routes is **Megabus** (www.megabus.com; ☎ **0141/352-4444**), with tickets costing as little as a few pounds. **Scottish Citylink** (www.citylink.co.uk; ☎ **0871/266-3333**) operates frequent and inexpensive coach service for all Scotland's cities and large towns. A Citylink **Explorer Pass** allows unlimited travel on a set number of days within a time period; for example, 5 travel days within 10 days costs £62. In remote Scottish regions, the **Royal Mail Postbus** provides a lifeline of public transportation for locals and visitors. They are one of the most fascinating ways to travel around. For more information, visit **www2.royalmail.com/you-home/your-community/postbus** or call ☎ **08457/740-740.** Local post offices can also provide details of routes.

Most coaches terminate in London at **Victoria Coach Station, 164 Buckingham Palace Rd.** (☎ **0343/222-1234**), although many offer intermediate stops in the capital. **Traveline** (www.traveline.info) is a handy source of integrated service and timetable information.

By Plane

There's rarely any need to take an internal flight within Britain. However, **British Airways** (www.ba.com) flies to several British cities outside London—including Manchester, which is served by connections from London Heathrow and London Gatwick, and Edinburgh, which is served by several daily flights from Heathrow, Gatwick, and London City airports. Flying time to either is around 1 hour. **Flybe** (www.flybe.com) also operates internal flights between London and Newcastle, as well as linking farther-flung airports like Exeter, Norwich, and Newquay—a flight to the latter can dodge the high-season traffic jams on roads to Devon and Cornwall. To reach some of the remotest corners of Scotland's Highlands and Islands, an internal flight is often the quickest (and sometimes the cheapest) option. Flybe links both Aberdeen and Inverness directly with southern England, as does **easyJet** (www.easyjet.com).

By Car

This is the way to see Britain at its best. Motorways, with a maximum speed of 70 mph, allow you to get from area to area swiftly and simply, then lesser roads and eventually country lanes let you meander through villages, reach distant beaches and glorious views, and see everything that's wonderful about England and Scotland.

Visitors from overseas should be aware that in Britain traffic travels on the left side of the road, so steering wheels are on the "wrong" side for most. Rental cars are manual, unless you request otherwise, so the gear shift is on your left. Aside from motorways, other roads outside urban areas have a 60 mph speed limit unless signposted, and 70 mph on a dual carriageway. The limit decreases depending on size of road, conditions, and locality. Built-up areas generally have a 30 mph limit, although a number of towns are introducing a 20 mph limit in local streets. Road signs are clear and use international symbols. The "Highway Code" gives full details of signs and driving requirements. It can be read online at **www.gov.uk/highway-code**.

GETTING THE BEST DEAL ON YOUR RENTAL CAR   The British car-rental market is among the most competitive in Europe. Nevertheless, rentals are expensive, although there are frequent promotional deals, sometimes linked to airlines, and mostly in low season. It's always cheaper to arrange a car in advance; you might also look into a fly/drive deal if you are flying in from overseas.

Car-rental rates vary even more than airline fares. What you pay depends not only on the size of the car, but also where and when you pick it up and drop it off, length of the rental period, where and how far you drive it, whether you get insurance, and a host of other factors. Most companies will rent only to people 23 years and older, and many will not rent to people aged 70 and older.

The big global rental companies all have a presence in England and Scotland: **Avis** (www.avis.com), **Budget** (www.budget.com), and **Hertz** (www.hertz.com). You should also check the prices offered by reputable resellers and agents such as **Kemwel** (www.kemwel.com; © 877/820-0668 in North America) and **AutoEurope** (www.autoeurope.com; © 888/223-5555 in North America). Travel meta-search engines like **Kayak.com** and **Travelsupermarket.com**, as well as price comparison specialists such as **Carrentals.co.uk**, are always worth consulting.

If booking your rental car direct—or comparing prices using various search variables—a few key questions could save you money:

○ Are weekend rates lower than weekday? Find out if the rate is the same for pick-up Friday morning, for instance, as it is for Thursday night.

○ Is a weekly rate cheaper than a daily one? If you need the car for 4 days, it might be cheaper to rent it for 5, even if you don't need it for that long.

○ Is there a drop-off charge if you do not return the car to the pick-up location? Is it cheaper to pick up the car at the airport or a city-center location?

- Are promotional rates available? If you see an advertised price in a newspaper, in a magazine, or online, ask for that specific rate.

- Are discounts available for members of frequent-flier programs, trades unions or organizations such as AARP, AAA, and so on?

- What is the cost of adding an additional driver's name to the contract?

- How many free miles are included in the price? Free mileage may be negotiable, depending on the length of rental.

- How much does the rental company charge to refill your tank if you return it less than full? Rental companies claim their prices are competitive, but fuel is always cheaper if you fill up before returning.

When you reserve a car, or are comparing prices, make sure you find out the total price, including the 20% value-added tax (VAT) and all insurances.

> ### Scenic Scotland by Motor Home
>
> When it comes to exploring Scotland, many visitors prefer to rent a motorhome. **Car Rental Scotland** (www.carrentalscotland.com; ✆ **0141/427-5475**) rents four-, five- and six-berth motorhomes and can arrange transfers from Edinburgh, Glasgow, and Prestwick airports. Fill out an online enquiry for details on rates.

TIPS ON ACCOMMODATIONS

Make reservations as far in advance as possible, even in the quieter months from November to April. Travel to most places in England and Scotland peaks between May and October, and during that period, it's hard to come by a moderate or inexpensive hotel room. In a trendy spot such as Cornwall in southwest England or the East Anglian coast, it's nigh impossible to find a good hotel room, apartment, or cottage to rent on short notice in the summer. And many of the smaller, boutique hotels around England and Scotland can fill up year-round, especially on weekends and in popular city-break or weekend destinations.

You'll find hotels and other accommodations inside every conceivable kind of building, from 21st-century concrete cubes to medieval inns. In older hotels, guest rooms can be smaller than you might expect (if you base your expectation on a modern North American hotel, for example), and each room is usually different, sometimes quirkily

> ### Breakfast Bonus
>
> Most hotels in England and Scotland include breakfast in their rates. You might find that breakfast isn't included in big hotels that have a large business clientele, or very upmarket hotels that have an equally upmarket (and pricey) a la carte breakfast. Even then, there is often a rate offered that includes breakfast.

so. But this is part of the charm. Some rooms may only have a shower, not a bathtub, so if you feel you can't survive without a tub, make that clear when booking. And don't look down on hotel restaurants any more. Several house some of the finest places to eat for miles around. Indeed, the "restaurant with rooms" has become an accommodation category in its own right—and is a particular strong point of rural Britain.

Lodging Classification

British hotels are officially graded by stars, and are judged on standards, quality, services, and hospitality. In a one-star hotel, buildings are required to have hot and cold running water in all rooms. All establishments from two stars upward must have 100% en suite (private bathroom) facilities. To achieve four stars or more, hotels must offer room service. Five stars (deluxe) is the highest rating. Star ratings are posted outside the buildings. However, the system is voluntary, and many hotels do not participate—some of our favorite places have no stars at all.

A parallel star system, operated by the AA (the British equivalent of AAA), awards between one and five stars to guest-house and B&B accommodation. See **www.theaa.com/travel/accommodation_restaurants_grading.html** for a full explanation of their system.

Bed & Breakfasts

An English bed and breakfast (B&B) often used to be a glum place, little more than a house with rooms, and with guests banished from the premises during the day. Nowadays, though, most are reliably comfortable, with rooms that are at worst simple, or decorated to the owners' personal tastes. As in many countries around the world, a new breed has also sprung up, with a boutique-hotel feel. Extravagant or quietly stylish rooms are offered, along with splendid breakfasts, and a decent lounge. Many are run with the care of a small hotel; they simply don't serve lunch or dinner. **Bed & Breakfast Nationwide** (www.bedandbreakfast nationwide.com; ✆ **01255/672377**) is one agency dealing in privately owned bed and breakfasts across the country, from cottages to castles, almost 700 of them. **Sawday's** (www.sawdays.co.uk) is another agency with a carefully chosen selection of 750 or so B&Bs around the country.

Farmhouses

Farms sometimes have rooms set aside for paying guests, occasionally in the main house, but increasingly in converted barns or cottages. You might still find some that simply offer a visitor a simple room for the night, but more and more they are expanding into full B&B or self-catering territory, with breakfasts often sourced from the farm and surrounding producers. The settings are often wonderful, deep in the countryside. Many farms are child-friendly and young guests are often invited to tag along when gathering eggs or at feeding times.

Farm Stay UK (www.farmstay.co.uk; ℂ **02476/696909**) operated by a consortium of farmers, features more than 1,200 rural retreats including farms, B&Bs, and campsites. Most are open year-round.

Historic Properties

National Trust Holiday Cottages (www.nationaltrustcottages.co.uk; ℂ **0344/335-1287**) is part of Britain's leading conservation group. The National Trust is mainly known for the castles, gardens, and historic homes that you can visit, but it also has over 370 houses and cottages for rent in some of the most beautiful parts of England. They sleep from 2 to 12 guests, are self-catering, and mostly available year-round, for weekends, short breaks, and longer. The **National Trust for Scotland** (www.ntsholidays.com; ℂ **866/211-7573** from North America) also rents many incredible historic properties, from flats in old tenements on Edinburgh's Royal Mile to lighthouse cottages and castles.

The **Landmark Trust** (www.landmarktrust.org.uk; ℂ **01628/825925**) is a charity that rescues historic buildings and turns them into places to stay. As well as cottages, you'll find castles, country houses, towers, and other odd buildings. There are around 180, such as the **Gothic Temple,** set in Capability Brown-designed grounds in Buckinghamshire, and **Kingswear Castle,** dating from 1502, on the water's edge near Dartmouth, Devon. Places sleep from 1 to 16 guests, and are ideal for family or group travel.

Cottages & Other Vacation Rentals

Many companies around Britain have cottages for rent, and a cottage makes an ideal base for exploring the rural counties of England and Scotland. **English Country Cottages** (www.english-country-cottages.co.uk; ℂ **0845/268-0785**) focuses on upscale properties. **Cottages 4 You** (www.cottages4you.co.uk; ℂ **0345/268-0760**), deals in more modest options, with more than 10,000 properties in the U.K. **Sheepskin Life** (www.sheepskinlife.com; ℂ **01865/764087**) has a small portfolio of luxury cottages and rural hideaways. Companies specializing in Scotland accommodation include **Embrace Scotland** (www.embracescotland.co.uk; ℂ **01866/822-122**), **Unique Cottages** (www.unique-cottages.co.uk; ℂ **01835/822-277**), and **Wilderness Cottages** (www.wildernesscottages.co.uk; ℂ **01463/719-219**).

Chain Hotels

Many international chains, such as Best Western, Hilton, Sheraton, and Travelodge, are found throughout Britain. In addition, Britain has a number of indigenous brands, including small chains of boutique hotels such as the discreetly stylish, wine-themed **Hotel du Vin** (www.hotelduvin.com) and trendier **Malmaison** (www.malmaison.com; ℂ **0871/943-0350**), whose properties include a former church and prison. At the budget end, **Premier Inn** (www.premierinn.com; ✆ **0871/527-9222**) is the U.K.'s largest hotel chain, offering simple, dependable rooms in convenient locations at fair prices.

House Swapping & Peer-to-Peer Accommodation Networks

HomeLink International (www.homelink.org; ✆ **800/638-3841** in the U.S, or 01962/886882 in the U.K.), which costs $95 for a year's membership, is the oldest, largest, and best home-exchange holiday group in the world. Alternatives include **Intervac** (www.intervac-home exchange.com) and **HomeExchange.com**.

England and Scotland are also well represented in online peer-to-peer accommodation networks. International giants like **AirBnB.com** are well represented, especially in major cities; **9flats.com** is another peer-to-peer site worth checking out for U.K. accommodations. **OneFineStay.com** has a small, but special portfolio of serviced apartments in London.

BIG savings FOR HERITAGE TRAVELERS

Many of the historic homes, estates, museums, and castles of England are owned or managed by one of two national heritage organizations, **English Heritage** (EH; www. english-heritage.org.uk) or the **National Trust** (NT; www.nationaltrust.org.uk). If you plan to visit several heritage sites while you are here—and the list includes the likes of Stonehenge, Chartwell, and Fountains Abbey—short-term visitor passes to one or both of the organizations could save you a lot of money. A **National Trust Touring Pass,** for example, offering unlimited entry to NT properties for seven days, costs £25 for one adult, £45 for two adults, and £50 for a family. The 14-day version costs £30/£54/£62. For instructions on where to buy a pass, see **www.nationaltrust.org.uk/ visit/overseas-visitors/touring-pass**. If you're resident in the U.S., membership of the **Royal Oak Foundation** (www.royal-oak.org; ✆ **800/913-6565**) includes free admission to all England and Scotland's NT sites and properties. Annual membership is $65 (families $115).

An **English Heritage 9-day Overseas Visitor Pass** costs £25 for one adult, £45 for two adults, and £50 for a family. The 16-day pass costs £30/£56/£60. Order it online at **www.english-heritage.org.uk/ daysout/overseas-visitor-pass/over seas-visitor-pass** and collect it from any staffed EH property.

In Scotland you could save by purchasing a **Historic Scotland Explorer Pass** (www.historic-scotland.gov.uk/ explorer). Passes allow entry into all 78 paid-entry Historic Scotland properties.

There are two types of pass: The first is good for 3 days within a 5-day period and costs £29 for adults, £24 for seniors, £17 for children aged 5 to 15, and £58 for families. The second pass is available for 7 days within a 14-day period and costs £38 for adults, £31 for seniors, £22 for children and £76 for families. Explorer Passes can be bought at any staffed Historic Scotland property, at Tourist Information Centres (TICs) across the country, or online at **www.historic-scotland.gov.uk/explorer**.

[FastFACTS] ENGLAND & SCOTLAND

Area Codes The country code for Great Britain is **44.** Cities and towns within the country have their own area codes, all of which begin with **0.** (Omit the 0 when dialing from overseas.) The area code for London is **020;** Manchester is **0161;** Edinburgh is **0131.** A full local telephone number is then usually between 6 and 8 digits long.

Business Hours With many exceptions, business hours are Monday to Friday 9am to 5pm. In general, retail stores are open Monday to Saturday 9am to 6pm, Sunday 11am to 5pm (sometimes noon–6pm). Thursday is often late-night opening in city-center stores; until 8pm or later isn't unusual, sometimes even later in the run-up to Christmas. In rural areas many shops don't open at all on Sundays.

Customs **Non-E.U. nationals aged 17 and over** can bring in, duty-free, 200 cigarettes, or 100 cigarillos, or 50 cigars, or 250 grams of smoking tobacco. You can also bring in 4 liters of wine and 16 liters of beer plus either 1 liter of alcohol more than 22% ("spirits") or 2 liters of "fortified" wine at less than 22%. Visitors may also bring in other goods, including perfume, gifts, and souvenirs, totaling £390 in value. (Customs officials tend to be lenient about these general merchandise regulations, realizing the limits are unrealistically low.) For **arrivals from within the E.U.,** there are no limits as long as goods are for your own personal use, or are gifts.

Disabled Travelers The best U.K. organization to consult for trip-planning advice is **Tourism for All UK** (www.tourismforall.org. uk; © **+44-1539/726-111** from overseas). The organization runs **OpenBritain. net,** the country's largest directory of accessible accommodation and travel services. **Disability Rights UK** (www.disabilityrightsuk. org; © **020/7250-8181**) publishes a number of written resources and, for a small fee, sells the **Radar NKS Key,** which opens over 8,000 locked public disabled toilets countrywide (£10 to mail anywhere in the world).

For public transportation assistance in the capital, **Transport for London** publishes a good deal of accessibility information; visit **www.tfl.gov.uk/ accessguides** for the lowdown on stair-free Underground access, large-print and audio Tube maps, a Tube toilet map, and more. There's also a 24-hour assistance telephone line: © **0343/222-1234.**

London's official "black cab" taxis have interiors adapted to those in wheelchairs. In the "Accessible London" section of the **Visit London** website (**www.visitlondon.com/ access**), you'll find links to details of accessible hotels and information about which parts of the transport network are adapted to your needs. Many London hotels, museums, restaurants, buses, Tube stations, and sightseeing attractions have dedicated wheelchair entry, and persons with disabilities are often granted admission discounts.

Doctors If you need a non-emergency doctor, your hotel can recommend one, or contact your embassy or consulate. Failing that, try the general-practitioner (GP) finder at **www.nhs.uk/ service-search**. North American members of the **International Association for Medical Assistance to Travelers (IAMAT;** www. iamat.org; © **716/754-4883,** or 416/652-0137 in Canada) can consult it for lists of approved local doctors. *Note:* U.S. and Canadian visitors who become ill while they're in England or Scotland are eligible only for free *emergency* care. For other treatment, including follow-up care, you must pay. See also "Insurance," below.

Doctors

In any medical emergency, immediately call ☏ **999** or 112.

Drinking Laws

The legal age for buying alcohol is 18. Those 17 and over may have a glass of beer, wine, or cider with a meal in a pub or restaurant, if it is bought for them by a responsible adult. Children younger than 16 are allowed in pubs only if accompanied by a parent or guardian. Penalties for drunk driving are stiff—not to mention the danger in which you're placing yourself and other road users. Drinking alcohol on **London's public transport network** is forbidden, and on-the-spot fines are issued to transgressors.

Electricity

British electricity operates at 240 volts AC (50 cycles), and most overseas plugs don't fit British wall outlets. Always bring suitable transformers and/or adapters, such as world multiplugs—if you plug some American appliances directly into an electrical outlet without a transformer, for example, you'll destroy your appliance and possibly start a fire. Portable electronic devices such as iPods and mobile phones, however, recharge without problems via USB or using a multiplug. Many long-distance trains have sockets for the charging of laptops or mobile phones.

Embassies & Consulates

The **U.S. Embassy** is at 24 Grosvenor Sq., London (london.usembassy.gov; ☏ **020/7499-9000**). Standard hours are Monday to Friday 8:30am to 5:30pm. However, for passport and visa services relating to U.S. citizens, contact the **Passport Unit** using the online form. There is also a **U.S. Consulate** in Edinburgh, Scotland, at 3 Regent Terrace (edinburgh.usconsulate.gov; ☏ **0131/556-8315**), open Tuesday and Wednesday by appointment only.

The **High Commission of Canada,** Canada House, 1 Trafalgar Sq., London (www.canadainternational.gc.ca/united_kingdom-royaume_uni/index.aspx; ☏ **020/7004-6000**), handles passport and consular services for Canadians. Hours are Monday to Friday 9:30am to 12:30pm.

The **Australian High Commission** is at Australia House, Strand, London (www.uk.embassy.gov.au; ☏ **020/7379-4334**). Hours are Monday to Friday 9am to 5pm.

The **New Zealand High Commission** is at New Zealand House, 80 Haymarket (at Pall Mall), London (www.nzembassy.com/uk; ☏ **020/7930-8422**). Hours are Monday to Friday 9am to 5pm.

The **Irish Embassy** is at 17 Grosvenor Place, London SW1X 7HR (www.embassyofireland.co.uk; ☏ **020/7235-2171**). Hours are Monday to Friday 9:30am to 5pm. Passport services are handled by the **Irish Passport Office,** 114a Cromwell Rd., London (☏ **020/7373-4339**).

Emergencies

Dial ☏ **999** for police, fire, or ambulance. Give your name and state the nature of the emergency. Dialing ☏ **112** also connects you to local emergency services anywhere in the E.U.

Family Travel

Most high-profile museums have quizzes, events, or entertaining resources for youngsters of any age, and many of the venues you will visit are part of the Kids in Museums program; see **www.kidsinmuseums.org.uk**. Most accommodations can provide a crib (or "cot") for a baby on request, and if you're renting a car, children under 12 and under 1.35m (4½ ft.) in height must ride in an appropriate car seat. Consult your car rental company in advance of arrival, but it's the driver's legal responsibility to ensure all child passengers comply (see **www.childcarseats.org.uk/the-law** for details). You'll also find babysitting available at most hotels; enquire ahead of time or at the reception desk when you arrive.

Health

Visiting the U.K. doesn't pose any specific health risks. Common drugs widely available throughout the Western world are generally available over the pharmacy counter and in large supermarkets, although visitors from overseas should note the generic rather than brand names of any medicines they rely on. If you're flying into London, pack **prescription medications** in carry-on luggage and carry prescription medications in their original containers, with pharmacy labels—otherwise they won't make it through airport security. Also bring along copies of your prescriptions, in case you lose your pills or run out. Don't forget an extra pair of contact lenses or prescription glasses. The general-purpose painkiller known in North America as acetaminophen is called **paracetamol** in the U.K.

Hospitals
The **NHS Choices** website (www.nhs.uk) has a search facility that enables you to locate your nearest Accident & Emergency department wherever you are in the U.K. In any emergency requiring an ambulance, you should dial ☏ **999**. Emergency care is free for all visitors, irrespective of country of origin.

Insurance
Visitors from overseas qualify automatically for free **emergency** care in the U.K. **U.S. visitors** should note that most domestic health plans (including Medicare and Medicaid) do not provide coverage, and the ones that do often require you to pay for services upfront and reimburse you only after you return home.

Internet Access
The availability of the Internet across the U.K. is in a constant state of development. How you access it depends on whether you've brought your own computer or smartphone, or if you're searching for a public terminal. Many hotels have computers for guest use. Internet cafes have suffered due to the spread of smartphones and free Wi-Fi (see below), but they are still prevalent close to popular tourist spots frequented by backpackers. Most **hostels** have Internet access, and some **public libraries** allow nonresidents to use terminals.

If you have your own computer or smartphone, **Wi-Fi** makes access much easier. Always check before using your hotel's network—some charge exorbitant rates, and free or cheap Wi-Fi isn't hard to find elsewhere, in urban locations at least. Ask locally, or Google "free Wi-Fi + [town]" before you arrive. You will find Wi-Fi on many long-distance trains; ask whether it's free in standard and first class, and calculate whether it's worth upgrading if you want to surf your journey away. There are also **BT WiFi** hotspots in many cafés, hotels, and public places across the country (see www.btwifi.co.uk/find for a searchable directory and map). If you have a subscription to a global wireless ISP like **Boingo** (www.boingo.com), you can use these hotspots for free, or at a reduced rate depending on your package.

Savvy smartphone users from overseas may find it cheaper and more practical to switch off 3G altogether and call using Wi-Fi in combination with a **Skype** (www.skype.com) or **Roamer** (www.roamerapp.com) account and app.

Legal Aid
If you're visiting from overseas and run into some kind of trouble with law enforcement, contact your consulate or embassy (see "Embassies & Consulates," above). They can advise you of your rights and will usually provide a list of local attorneys (for which you'll have to pay if services are used), but they cannot interfere on your behalf in the English legal process.

For substance-abuse troubles call **Release** (www.release.org.uk; ☏ **020/7324-2989**); the advice line is open Monday to Friday 11am to 1pm and 2 to 4pm. The **Rape Crisis** (www.rapecrisis.org.uk; ☏ **0808/802-9999**) helpline is open daily noon to 2:30pm and 7 to 9:30pm. **Alcoholics Anonymous**(www.alcoholics-anonymous.org.uk; ☏ **0845/769-7555**) answers its helpline daily 10am to 10pm.

LGBT Travelers
Local news about gay and lesbian issues is provided by a number of reliable sources, including **Pink News** (www.pinknews.co.uk). July's annual **Pride in London** march and festival (www.prideinlondon.org) is the highlight of London's LGBT calendar, while **Pride Brighton & Hove** (www.brighton-pride.org) and **Manchester Pride** (www.manchester-pride.com) are the main events outside London, on different weekends in August. In Scotland both

Edinburgh and Glasgow have thriving gay communities. Manchester-based **Gaydio** (www.gaydio.co.uk) was the U.K.'s first dedicated radio station for lesbian, gay, bisexual, and trans listeners.

Mail   An airmail letter from the U.K. to the U.S. costs 97p for up to 100g (3½ oz.) and generally takes 5 to 7 working days to arrive via the **International Standard** service; postcards also require a 97p stamp. Within the U.K, First Class mail ought to arrive the following working day; Second Class mail takes about 3 days. To find your nearest Post Office, consult **www.royalmail.com/branch-finder**.

Mobile Phones   The three letters that define much of the world's wireless capabilities are **GSM** (Global System for Mobiles), a satellite network that makes for easy cross-border mobile phone use throughout most of the planet, including the U.K. If you own an unlocked GSM phone, pack it in your hand luggage and pick up a contract-free **SIM-only plan** when you arrive in the U.K. The SIM card will cost very little, but you will need to load it up with credit to make calls. Tariffs change constantly in response to the market, but in general expect standard charges of around 20p per minute, 10p for a text message, and a deal on data that might allow 500MB in a month for about £5. (And you can

usually get better rates by buying a combined prepaid call/text/data bundle.) Receiving calls on a local number is free. There are phone and SIM card retailers on practically every high-street in the country, but not everywhere will sell SIM-only deals to nonresidents. Larger branches of supermarket Tesco sell **Tesco Mobile** (www.tesco mobile.com) SIMs for 99p that you can top-up in-store with cash or an overseas credit card. Find a convenient branch at **www.tesco.com/storelocator**. **Three** (www.three.co.uk) sells SIMs that you can top-up further at Three stores, supermarkets, and newsagents across England and Scotland. Three SIMs work only in 3G-compatible phones.

There are other options if you're visiting from overseas but don't own an unlocked GSM phone. For a short visit, **renting** a phone may be a good idea. North Americans can rent from **InTouch USA** (www.intouch usa.us; ☏ **800/872-7626** or 703/222-7161). However, handset prices have fallen to a level where you can probably buy a basic U.K. **pay-as-you-go (PAYG) phone** for less than one week's handset rental. Prices at many cellphone retailers start from under £20 for a cheap model, and you can find a basic Android smartphone for around £50. **Carphone Warehouse** (www.car phonewarehouse.com) has retail branches across the country, and a reliable

range of cheap PAYG phones. Buy one, use it while you're here, and recycle it on the way home.

There are several U.K. networks offering a bewildering array of tariffs. **EE** (www.ee.co.uk) has the widest 4G network, while **Three** (www.three.co.uk) usually has the best deals for smartphone users who want data included in their rate. Unfortunately, per-minute charges for international calls can add up whatever network you choose, so if you plan to do a lot of calling home use a VoIP service such as **Skype** (www.skype.com) in conjunction with a Web connection.

If you intend to use your mobile phone *solely* to call overseas, and it's unlocked and GSM-compatible, you may find purchasing a specialist **international SIM card** to be the most convenient option. Calls to the U.S., for example, using a SIM card from **Lyca** (www.lycamobile.co.uk; ☏ **020/7132-0322**) cost 6p per minute to both landlines and cellphones. You can buy one at independent phone retailers, and can top-up with vouchers on sale at branches of Tesco, Sainsbury's, the Post Office, and small retailers around the U.K.

Mobile coverage is very good, although there are still areas where you can't get a signal, and it's as likely to be in a rural area of Suffolk as atop a Scottish mountain.

Money & Costs

Frommer's lists exact prices in the local currency. The currency conversions quoted above were correct at press time. However, rates fluctuate, so before departing consult a currency exchange website such as www.oanda.com/currency/converter to check up-to-the-minute rates. There's also a smartphone app available for pretty much any mobile device; see **www.oanda.com/mobile**.

Britain is among the most expensive countries in Europe, but perceptions of value for overseas visitors are at the mercy of exchange rate fluctuations and large regional variations. As capital cities go, London is not as expensive as Tokyo or Oslo, for example, but even a budget hotel room can cost £100 a night or more. A pint of ale in Yorkshire, though, may well be more than £1 cheaper than one at a London West End bar. While certain items in England might seem extortionate to an experienced European traveler—such as a cup of coffee, a pizza, or a London Tube fare—everyday clothes cost less than in many neighboring countries. Mobile phone charges may seem inexpensive to a visitor from North America, but the same person will shudder at the price of a pair of branded sneakers or an iPod. But with entrance to national state museums costing nothing at all, Britain has more high culture bang for your buck than anywhere in the world.

The chart below lists London prices but keep in mind, London will be the most expensive city you visit on your tour of England and Scotland.

ATMs are everywhere in U.K. cities—at banks, some fuel stations, motorway rest stops, many supermarkets, and post offices. (Watch out for those inside small shops, however, as they charge users for withdrawing money.) These "cash machines" or "cashpoints" are the easiest way to get cash away from home. The **Cirrus**

WHAT THINGS COST IN LONDON	UK£
Taxi from Heathrow to central London	£65–£85
Underground from Heathrow to Piccadilly Circus using Oyster Card, off-peak	£6
Double room at The Langham (expensive)	£312–£444
Double room at The Nadler Soho (moderate)	£135–£255
Double room at Alhambra Hotel (inexpensive)	£80–£111
Lunch for one at J. Sheekey (expensive)	£27
Lunch for one at Gordon's Wine Bar (inexpensive)	£7–£10
Dinner for one, without wine, at Restaurant Story (expensive)	£60
Dinner for one, without wine, at Rochelle Canteen (moderate)	£13–£15
Dinner for one, without wine, at The Fryer's Delight (inexpensive)	£5–£6.20
Pint of beer	£3.50–£4
Cup of coffee	£1.80–£2.50
Admission to national/state museums	Free
Movie ticket	£9–£12
Theatre ticket	£25–£85

(www.mastercard.com) and **PLUS** (www.visa.com) networks span the globe; look at the back of your bank card to see which network you're on, and then check online for ATM locations at your destination if you want to be ultra-organized. Be sure you know your personal identification number (PIN) and daily withdrawal limit before you depart. Note that U.K. machines use **4-digit PINs.** Credit cards are accepted just about everywhere, save street markets and tiny independent retailers or street-food vendors. However, North American visitors should note that American Express is accepted far less widely than at home, and Diners only at the very highest of highflying establishments. To be sure of your credit line, bring a Visa or MasterCard as well.

Britain has been among the world's most aggressive countries in the fight against credit card fraud. As a result, almost everywhere has moved from the magnetic strip credit card to **Chip and PIN** ("smartcards" with chips embedded in them). Most retailers ask for your 4-digit PIN to be entered into a keypad near the cash register. In restaurants, a server usually brings a hand-held device to your table to authorize payment. If you're visiting from a country where Chip and PIN is less prevalent, it's possible that some retailers will be reluctant to accept your

(to Brits, old-fashioned) swipe cards. Be prepared to argue your case: swipe cards are still legal and the same machines that read the smartcard chips can also read your magnetic strip. However, do carry some cash with you, just in case.

Packing British weather is fickle, so although it rains in London much less than in the west of the British Isles or Manchester—and nowhere close to the levels Britain's almost mythical reputation would have you believe—only the foolhardy visitor heads to the U.K. without some rainwear, even in high summer. On the plus side, winter temperatures rarely dip below freezing for long, and while summers can be muggy, they're rarely as hot and humid as southern Europe or the U.S.

Whether you need to find room in your suitcase for formal eveningwear very much depends on where you plan to stay and (especially) dine. Traditional, upscale restaurants in London's West End, for example, still largely expect you to arrive in a collared shirt, non-denim trousers, and "proper" shoes—and the equivalent attire for women. You may feel out of place without similarly formal clothes at a traditional country-house hotel in rural England, too. But anywhere in the country with a contemporary edge, however expensive, will welcome you as you are, even if that means jeans and sneakers.

Police Losses, thefts, and other criminal matters should be reported at the nearest police station immediately. You will be given a crime number, which your travel insurer will request if you make a claim. In a non-emergency, you can contact your local police station from anywhere in Britain by dialing ✆ **101.** Always phone ✆ **999** or 112 if the matter is serious or urgent.

Safety Britain has its share of crime, but in general it is one of the safest countries in the world for visitors. Pickpockets are a concern in London and other major cities, but violent crime is relatively rare everywhere. If you are in any doubt about the neighborhood you're in, ask the bar or restaurant you're leaving to phone you a taxi (or "minicab")—never get into an unlicensed minicab, especially if you are female. Conceal your wallet or else hold on to your purse, and don't flaunt jewelry or cash. Personal electronic devices like smartphones and iPods are another obvious target for opportunist thieves. Never leave valuables on show in an unattended parked car. In short, it's the same advice you'd follow in your hometown.

In general, Brits practice greater **tolerance** than most parts of the world. "Live and let live" is the usual maxim. As a visitor, you're unlikely to experience overt racial, ethnic, or religious discrimination, or that based on sexual preference. However, the country is by no means some cuddly nirvana: You'll know discrimination if you experience it, so take your usual action to deal with it. It is **illegal** for any business offering goods, facilities, or services to discriminate against you because of your race, your religion, or your sexuality.

Senior Travel

Britain offers many discounts to senior visitors. Many of the attractions recommended in this book list a separate, reduced entrance fee for seniors. However, even if discounts aren't posted, ask if they're available. Make sure you carry identification that shows your date of birth. Also, mention you're a senior when you make hotel reservations.

If you're heading to Britain from the U.S., members of **AARP** (www.aarp. org; ✆ **888/687-2277**) can secure discounts on hotels, airfares, and car rentals.

Smoking

Smoking is banned in all indoor public places such as pubs, restaurants, and clubs across England and Scotland. Smoking is allowed in beer gardens and on patios in bars, and the seats outside coffee shops. This generally means that many nice outdoor areas are effectively off-limits to avid nonsmokers.

Student Travelers

Never leave home without your student I.D. card. Visitors from overseas should arm themselves with an **International Student**

Identity Card (ISIC), which offers local savings on rail passes, plane tickets, entrance fees, and more. Each country's card offers slightly different benefits (in the U.S., for example, it provides you with basic travel insurance). Apply before departing in your country of origin. In the U.S. or Canada, at **www.myisic. com**; in Australia, see **www. isiccard.com.au**; in New Zealand, visit **www.isiccard. co.nz**. If you're no longer a student but are still younger than 31, you can get an **International Youth Travel Card (IYTC),** which entitles you to a more limited range of discounts, as does the **International Teacher Identity Card,** aimed at educators.

Taxes

All prices in the U.K. **must** be quoted inclusive of any taxes. Since 2011, the national value-added tax **(VAT)** has been 20%. This is included in all hotel and restaurant bills, and in the price of most items you purchase.

If you are a permanent resident outside the E.U., VAT on goods can be refunded if you shop at stores that participate in the **Retail Export Scheme**— look for the "Tax-Free Shopping" window sticker or ask staff. You need to fill out form VAT 407 in store, which the retailer will supply, and show your passport when you make the purchase. Show your goods, receipt, and form 407 to customs officials when you leave the U.K. (or at your

point of departure from the E.U.) and you then qualify for your refund. Each retailer is allowed to make its own arrangements for processing the refund— some require you to return the countersigned documents to them or an agent, others have an agreement in place with a booth at the airport. Details are posted online at **www.gov.uk/ tax-on-shopping/ taxfree-shopping**.

Time

All Britain follows **Greenwich Mean Time** (GMT) between late October and late March. Daylight-saving **British Summer Time** (BST), 1 hour ahead of GMT, is in operation for the rest of the year. London is generally 5 hours ahead of U.S. Eastern Standard Time (EST), although because of different daylight-saving time practices in the two countries, there's a brief period (about a week) in autumn when Britain is 6 hours ahead of New York or Toronto, and a brief period in spring when it's only 4 hours ahead. Sydney is 10 or 11 hours ahead of U.K. time, Auckland 12 or 13 hours ahead.

Tipping

Whether and how much to tip is not without controversy. Visitors from the U.S., in particular, tend to be more generous than locals—and indeed, some Brits resent a heavy tipping culture being "imported."

Tipping in **restaurants** is standard practice, as long as no automatic service charge is added to your bill.

Leave 10% to 15% if you were happy with your server. However, be aware that a small number of places do not distribute these tips to staff as perks, but use them to pay their wages. This practice is only possible if you pay by credit or debit card, and unfortunately is perfectly legal. Ask who gets the tip, and if you're unhappy about paying the management's wage bill, have any automatic service charge removed and leave cash for your server to pick up. Earnings usually go into a communal pot to be shared among everyone from the kitchen porter to the sommelier, so there is no need to leave more than one tip per meal.

There's absolutely no need to tip the drivers of London's **black taxicabs:** They charge you extra for each item of luggage, and for standing in traffic. However, if the driver is especially helpful, add a pound or so to say thanks. Minicab drivers, on the other hand, generally earn less, and are always grateful if you are able to top up their rates,

provided you're happy with the service.

Tipping in **bars** and **pubs** is practically unheard of, but if you receive table service in an upscale nightclub or wine bar, leave a couple of pounds. In upscale **hotels,** porters expect around £1 per bag. Leave your maid £1 per day if you're happy, but only tip the concierge if they have performed something beyond the call of their regular work. Barbers and **hairdressers** will appreciate an extra pound or two for a good job, but you're not obliged. **Tour guides** may expect £2 for a job well done, although again it's not mandatory. Theater ushers don't expect tips.

Toilets   Also known as "loos" or "public conveniences," these are marked by public toilet signs, and are usually free. You also find well-maintained lavatories in all large public buildings, such as museums and art galleries, large department stores, and railway stations (although the latter generally impose a charge). It's not always acceptable to

use the lavatories in restaurants and pubs if you're not a customer, but we can't say that we always stick to this rule.

Visas   No E.U. nationals require a visa to visit the U.K. Visas are also not required for travelers from Australia, Canada, New Zealand, or the U.S. For nationals of, or visitors from, other countries, check **www.gov.uk/check-uk-visa**.

Websites   The U.K. has made a huge investment in placing comprehensive, up-to-date, and inspirational visitor information online, so the Web is the place to begin your research. Start with the umbrella sites: **www.visitbritain.com**, **www.enjoyengland.com** (or download the Enjoy England iPhone app), **www.visitscotland.com**, and **www.visitlondon.com**. Britain is also active on Facebook; join the conversation at **www.facebook.com/LoveUK**. Almost any city or region also has its own site—see individual chapters for details.

Index

See also Accommodations and Restaurants indexes, below.

General Index

A

Abbey Theatre (St Albans), 176
Abbotsford House (near Melrose), 528–529
Aberfoyle, 572
Aberlour distillery, 615
Abertarff House (Inverness), 604
Academy (Birmingham), 329
Accommodations. See also Accommodations Index
best, 4–5
tips on, 663–666
Achamore House Gardens (Gigha), 586–587
Adam & Eve (Norwich), 376
Adnams Cellar & Kitchen (Southwold), 368
Afflecks (Manchester), 394
Afternoon Tea Tours (Edinburgh), 508
Aintree Racecourse (Liverpool), 406
Aira Force, 419
AirBnB.com, 666
Edinburgh, 493
Air travel, 657, 661
London, 55–57
Alban Arena (St Albans), 176–177
Albert Dock (Liverpool), 406
Albert Memorial (London), 85
Albion Beatnik (Oxford), 169
Aldeburgh, 364, 365
Aldeburgh Festival, 365
Aldeburgh Museum, 366
Alexander Keiller Museum and Barn (Avebury), 233
Alfred Jewel (Oxford), 161
Alfred the Great, 218
Alice's Shop (Oxford), 169
Alloway, 567–568
Alloway Auld Kirk, 568
Alnwick, 464–466
Alnwick Castle, 465
Alnwick Garden, 465–466
Alpine Bikes (Fort William), 635
American Memorial Chapel (London), 92
American Monument (near Port Ellen), 588
Amesbury Hill, 231
An Airigh, 645
The Anchor (Cambridge), 354
The Anchor (Walberswick), 368
Angel of the North, 463

Anne Hathaway's Cottage (Stratford-upon-Avon), 310
"Another Place" (Crosby), 413
Anta (Dornoch), 621
Anta (Edinburgh), 507
Antony Preston Antiques (Stow-on-the-Wold), 296
Applecross, 633
Apsley House (London), 85
ArcelorMittal Orbit (London), 107
The Arches (Glasgow), 564
Architecture, best, 13–14
Ardkinglas Woodland Garden (Inveraray), 574
Ardminish, 586
Arduaine Gardens, 577–578
Area codes, 667
Argyll Arcade (Glasgow), 562
Argyll Forest Park, 576
Armadale Castle Gardens & Museum of the Isles (Skye), 652–653
Arndale Market (Manchester), 394
Arran, Isle of, 578–583
Arran Aromatics, 583
Arran Distillery, 580–581
Arthur's Seat (Edinburgh), 478, 489
Arts and Crafts Movement, 287
Arundel, 211
Arundel Castle, 212
Arundel Cathedral, 213
Ashmolean (Oxford), 160–161
Ashmolean Broadway Museum, 297
Association of Voluntary Guides (York), 440
Athelhampton House & Gardens, 238
ATMs, 671–672
Audley End (Saffron Walden), 358–359
Auld Brig o' Ayr, 567
Auldearn Antiques (Nairn), 617
Auld Kirk of Ayr, 567
Austen, Jane
Festival (Bath), 242
grave (Winchester), 222
House Museum (Chawton), 223
Jane Austen Centre (Bath), 244
Avebury, 233
Aviemore, 611–614
Aynsley China (Stoke-on-Trent), 331
Ayr, 567

B

B. Jannetta (St Andrews), 518
Baggott Church Street Ltd. (Stow-on-the-Wold), 296
Balloch Castle, 571

Balloch Castle Country Park, 571
Balloon Tree Farmshop and Café (York), 445
Balmaha, 572
Balmaha Boatyard, 572
BALTIC Centre for Contemporary Art (Gateshead), 461
Balti Triangle (Birmingham), 327, 328
Bamburgh Castle, 465
Bank Day Boats (Wroxham), 377
Banqueting Hall (near St Albans), 177
The Banqueting House (London), 72–73
Barbara Hepworth Museum & Sculpture Garden (St Ives), 276
Barber Institute of Fine Arts (Birmingham), 323
Barnard Castle, 455–456
Barnes Brinkcraft, 377
Baron's Hall (Penshurst Place), 196
The Barras (Glasgow), 562
Barrowland (Glasgow), 564
Barter Books (Alnwick Station), 466
The Basement (Brighton), 210
Bass Rock, 512
Bateman's (Burwash), 206–207
Bath, 240–252
accommodations, 247–248
entertainment and nightlife, 250
exploring, 242–247
organized tours, 246–247
restaurants, 248–250
shopping, 250
side trips from, 251–252
Bath Abbey, 243
Bath Aqua Glass (Bath), 250
Bath Bus Company, 247
Battle Abbey, 197
Battle Abbey & Battlefield, 199
BBC Broadcasting House Tour (London), 83
BBC Scottish Symphony Orchestra (Glasgow), 563
Beachy Head, 214
Beamish, the Living Museum of the North (near Durham), 456
Beaney House of Art & Knowledge (Canterbury), 182
Bear (Oxford), 170
Bear Steps (Shrewsbury), 333
The Beatles, 408

The Beatles Shop (Liverpool), 413
Beatles Story (Liverpool), 408
Beatrix Potter Gallery (Hawkshead), 429
Beauly, 608
Beauly Priory, 608
Bed & Breakfast Nationwide, 664
Bed & breakfasts (B&Bs), 664
Belfast, HMS (London), 75
Bell (Bath), 250
Bella Jane Boat Trips (Elgol), 645
Bell Harry Tower (Canterbury), 184
Ben Loyal, 623
Ben More, 592, 595
Ben Nevis, 634, 636
Ben's Cookies (Oxford), 168
Bents, 513
Best of Brighton, 205
Best of Suffolk, 367
Bewilderwood (Hoveton), 377–378
Bibury, 284–287
Big Bus Tours (London), 114
Biking
  Cambridge, 355
  Cotswold Way, 293
  Fort William, 635
  Glasgow, 542
  Isle of Skye, 645
  Marlborough to Avebury, 233
  Mull, 593
  Whitstable, 189
Billings & Edmonds (Windsor), 156
Bill Spectre's Oxford Ghost Trails, 158
Birdland (Bourton-on-the-Water), 290
Birmingham, 319–332
  accommodations, 325–326
  canals, 322
  day trips from, 329–332
  entertainment and nightlife, 328–329
  exploring, 323–325
  getting around, 320
  restaurants, 326–328
  shopping, 328
  squares and neighborhoods, 320, 322
  traveling to, 319
  visitor information, 320
Birmingham Hippodrome, 329
Birmingham Museum & Art Gallery, 323
Birmingham Repertory, 329
Birmingham Royal Ballet, 329
Birmingham Symphony Hall, 328–329
Birthplace Pass (Stratford-upon-Avon), 309
Bizarre Bath Walking Tour, 246–247

Black Bottle (Winchester), 225
Black Boy (Winchester), 225
Black Country Living Museum (Birmingham), 324
Black Dog (Whitstable), 191
Black Isle Peninsula, 617–620
Black Isle Show (Beauly), 608–609
Blackpool Illuminations, 398
Blackpool Tower, 398
Black Shed (Skinidin), 645
Black Swan (Stratford-upon-Avon), 319
Blackwell, 422–423
Blackwell's (Oxford), 169
Bladon, 172
Blakeney National Nature Reserve, 379
Blenheim Palace (Woodstock), 171–172
Blickling Estate, 379
Blists Hill Victorian Town (Ironbridge), 340, 341
Boarstone Tartans (Inverness), 607
Boat tours and cruises
  Birmingham, 322
  Canterbury, 185
  Cromarty, 619
  Fort Augustus, 611
  Glasgow, 556
  Gondola (Coniston), 428
  Isle of Skye, 645
  Liverpool, 407
  Loch Lomond, 570, 572
  London, 114
  Mull, 593
  Oxford, 149, 158
  Portsmouth, 225
  River Stour, 360–361
  South Queensferry, 510
  Windsor, 149, 154
  Wroxham, 377
Bodleian Library (Oxford), 161
Bohemia (Brighton), 211
Bolton Abbey, 448
Bon Accord (Glasgow), 564
Bonfire Night, 36
The Boot (St Albans), 177
Boot Inn (Chester), 403
The Borders, 520–521
Borrowdale Valley, 419–420
Botanic Gardens
  Cambridge University, 350
  Glasgow, 552
  Oxford, 163
Bourton Model Railway Exhibition & Toy Shop, 292
Bourton-on-the-Water, 289–293
Bowes Museum (near Durham), 456–457
Bowhill (near Selkirk), 532–533
Bowmore, 588
Bowness, 422–425
Boyz (London), 145
Bramble (Edinburgh), 508

Brantwood (Coniston Water), 428
Bray, 155
Brethren's Kitchen (Warwick), 314
Bridge Cottage (Flatford), 360
Bridge End Garden (Saffron Walden), 359
Bridgewater Hall (Manchester), 394–395
Bridlington, 450
Brighton, 201–211
  accommodations, 205–206
  entertainment and nightlife, 209–211
  exploring, 202–205
  getting around, 202
  restaurants, 206–208
  shopping, 209
  special events, 202
  traveling to, 201
  visitor information, 201–202
Brighton and Hove Pride, 210
Brighton Centre, 209
Brighton Dome, 209
Brighton Festival, 35, 202, 209
Brighton Fishing Museum, 202
Brighton Flea Market, 209
Brighton Holiday Homes, 205
Brighton Museum & Art Gallery, 203–204
Brighton Pier, 202
Brig o' Doon, 568
Britannia Panopticon (Glasgow), 563
British Airways, 661
British Golf Museum (St Andrews), 515
The British Library (London), 63, 66
The British Museum (London), 66–68
British Summer Time (BST), 673
Briton's Protection (Manchester), 395
BritRail passes, 658–660
Britten, Benjamin, 364, 365
Broads National Park, 376–377
Broads Tours (near Wroxham), 377
Broadway, 297–301
Broadway Tower, 297–298
Brodick Castle, 581–582
Brodie Countryfare (Nairn), 617
Broseley Pipeworks (Ironbridge), 341
Brown, Capability, 236
Brown's (Tobermory), 593
Bruce Hamilton (Glasgow), 562
Bruichladdich, 590
Bruntsfield (Edinburgh), 476
Buchanan Castle (Drymen), 572
Buchanan Street Bus Station (Glasgow), 540
Buckingham Palace (London), 73
Buckland Abbey, 263–264

Bullring (Birmingham), 328
Bunnahabhain, 590
Burford, 282–284
Burne-Jones, Edward, 287
Burns, Robert, 566, 570
    Birthplace Museum (Alloway), 567–568
Burns Monument, 568
Burns Night, 35
Burrell Collection (Glasgow), 555
Burwash, 206
Business hours, 667
Bus travel, 661
Buttermere Valley, 419–420
By George Arts and Crafts (St Albans), 176

C

Cadbury World (Birmingham), 324–325
Cadogan Hall (London), 145
Cairngorm Funicular Railway, 612
Cairngorm Reindeer Centre (Glenmore), 612–613
Cairngorms National Park, 611–612
Caithness, 626–630
Caledonian Books (Glasgow), 562–563
Caledonian Canal, 611, 639
Calendar of events, 34–36
Caley Cruisers, 611
Callander, 572–573
Calton Hill (Edinburgh), 487
Calton Old Cemetery (Edinburgh), 487
Cambridge, 344–359
    accommodations, 352–353
    entertainment and nightlife, 354
    exploring Cambridge University, 346–352
    getting around, 345–346
    organized tours, 352
    outdoor activities, 355–356
    restaurants, 353–354
    shopping, 354
    side trips from, 356–359
    traveling to, 344–345
    visitor information, 345
Cambridge Arts Theatre, 354
Cambridge Corn Exchange, 354
Cambridge Tourist Information Centre, 352
Cambridge University Botanic Garden, 350
Cambridge University Press bookshop, 354
Camera Obscura (Edinburgh), 483
Campbell & Co. (Beauly), 608
Campbeltown, 584–585
Campbeltown Cross, 584
Campbeltown Museum, 584

Canterbury, 180–188
    accommodations, 185–186
    entertainment and nightlife, 187
    exploring, 182–185
    restaurants, 186–187
    shopping, 187
    side trip to Dover, 187–188
    traveling to, 182
    visitor information, 182
Canterbury Cathedral, 182–184
Canterbury Historic River Tours, 185
Canterbury Roman Museum, 184
Caol Ila, 590
Captain Cook Memorial Museum (Whitby), 450
Captain James Cook Heritage Trail, 450
Carbost, 647
Carfax Tower (Oxford), 161
Carleton Castle (Turnberry), 569
Carpenters Arms (Windsor), 157
Car Rental Scotland, 663
Carrentals.co.uk, 662
Car travel and rentals, 661–663
    London, 57
Casablanca (Brighton), 209
Cast Court (London), 88–89
Castell & Son (The Varsity Shop; Oxford), 169
Castle Drogo, 264
Castlefield Urban Heritage Park (Manchester), 390
Castle Great Hall (Winchester), 220
Castle Howard, 451
Castle Jail (Jedburgh), 522
Castle Maol (Kyleakin), 644, 645
Castle of Mey, 627, 629
Castle of Old Wick, 627
Castlerigg Stone Circle (near Keswick), 431
Castles and palaces, best, 8–9
Castle Tavern (Inverness), 608
Castle Varrich (near Tongue), 623
Cathedral & Abbey Church of St Alban, 173–174
Cavalier, HMS (Chatham), 192
Cavell, Edith, 372
Cavern City Tours (Liverpool), 408
Cawdor Castle, 615–616
CC Blooms (Edinburgh), 508
Cellphones, 670
Celtic burial cross (Inveraray), 574
Central Station (Glasgow), 540
Cerne Giant, 235
Chagford, 262–263
Chained Library (Hereford), 337

Champagne Bar at the County Hotel (Canterbury), 187
Changing of the Guard
    London, 77
    Windsor, 152
Channel Tunnel, 658
Chanonry Point Lighthouse, 618
Chaos City Comics (St Albans), 176
Chapel of Our Lady Martyrdom (Canterbury), 183
Chapel Street (Penzance), 270
Chapter House
    St Albans, 174
    Salisbury, 228
    Wells, 251
The Charles Dickens Museum (London), 68
Charles Rennie Mackintosh Society (Glasgow), 551
Charles Street Bar & Club (Brighton), 210
Charleston, 206
Charleston Festival, 206
Chartwell (Westerham), 192
Chastleton House, 294
Chatham, 191–192
Chatsworth (Bakewell), 396–397
Chaucer Bookshop (Canterbury), 187
Cheap Street (Sherborne), 235
Chedworth Roman Villa (near Bibury), 285
Cheese Rolling Championships (Chester), 35
Chelsea Flower Show (London), 35
Cherwell Boathouse (Oxford), 165
Chester, 398–404
Chester Cathedral, 401–402
Chester Cross, 400
Chester High Cross, 400
Chester Zoo, 402
Chetham's (Manchester), 388
Chichester, 211–216
Chichester Cathedral, 213
Chichester Festival, 216
Chichester Festival Theatre, 216
Chinese Hillside (Edinburgh), 488
Chinese New Year (London), 34
Chipping Campden, 301–304
Christ Church (Oxford), 161–162
Christ Church Cathedral (Oxford), 162
Christ Church Picture Gallery (Oxford), 162
Churchill, Sir Winston
    Chartwell (Westerham), 192
    grave (Bladon), 172
Churchill Museum (London), 74
Churchill's (Manchester), 395

Churchill War Rooms (London), 73–74
Church Lane (Sherborne), 235
Church of St John the Baptist (Burford), 283
Church of St Martin (Bladon), 172
Church of St Michael (Chagford), 263
Church of St Thomas & St Edmund (Salisbury), 227
Chysauster Ancient Village, 277
Circo Bar and Lounge (Bath), 250
Circus (Bath), 242
Citizens Theatre (Glasgow), 563
The City (London), in brief, 61
City Chambers (Glasgow), 549
City Cruises (London), 114
City Hall, Salisbury, 232
City Halls (Glasgow), 563
City Mill (Winchester), 220–221
City Museum (Winchester), 221
City of Birmingham Symphony Orchestra, 329
City of London Guided Walks, 114
City Sightseeing Glasgow, 556
City Sightseeing Open Top Bus Tours (Windsor), 155
City Sightseeing Oxford, 158
Clans, 18
Clarence House (London), 74–75
Cleveland Way, 451
Climate, 33–34
Clock Tower (Inverness), 604
Clock Tower (St Albans), 173
Cloisters (Lacock), 233
Clo Mor, 623
Cloud 23 (Manchester), 395
Clovelly, 259–260
The Clyde (Glasgow), 553–555
Clyde Auditorium (Glasgow), 553
Clyde Walkway (Glasgow), 553
Coalbrookdale Museum of Iron (Ironbridge), 341
Coalport China Museum (Ironbridge), 341
Coldstream, 527
Coldstream Museum, 527
Coleridge, Samuel Taylor, 432
College Chapel (Eton), 150
Colman's Mustard Shop (Norwich), 376
Colonnade Bar (Brighton), 210
Commonwealth Air Forces Memorial (Runnymede), 151
Concorde 2 (Brighton), 209
Coniston, 427–429
Coniston Boating Centre, 429
Coniston Rambler, 416
Coniston Water, 417–418, 427

Constable Country, 360–361
Coram's Fields (London), 115
Corner on the Square (Beauly), 608
Coronation Chair (London), 82
Corrieshalloch Gorge, 632
Cotswold Motoring Museum & Toy Collection (Bourton-on-the-Water), 290–291
Cotswold Perfumery (Bourton-on-the-Water), 292
Cotswold Pottery (Bourton-on-the-Water), 292
The Cotswolds, 280–304. See also specific towns
  getting around, 280–281
  organized tours, 281–282
  traveling to, 280
  visitor information, 281
Cotswold Way, 293
Cotswold Wildlife Park (near Burford), 284
Cottage rentals, 665
Cottages 4 You, 665
County Museum (Dorchester), 238
The Courtauld Institute of Art Gallery (London), 68
Court Barn Museum (Chipping Campden), 302, 304
Coventry, 329–331
Coventry Cathedral, 329–331
Covered Market (Oxford), 168
Crab and Winkle Way, 189
Craft Beer Co. (Brighton), 210
Craighouse, 592
Craigmillar Castle (Edinburgh), 489–490
Craignure, 593–594
Craignure Golf Course (Mull), 593
Craig Phadrig, 601, 604
Crarae Garden (Inveraray), 574
Cream (Liverpool), 413
The Cricketers (Brighton), 210
Crimson Drawing Room (Windsor), 153
Crinan Canal, 576
Cromarty, 619–620
Cromwell, Oliver, 82
  House (Ely), 357–358
Crosby, 413
Cross Bath (Bath), 246
Cross Lakes Shuttle, 416
Crown Jewels (London), 94
Crypt (London), 93
The Cuillins, 643
Culloden Battlefield (Inverness), 604
Culpepper Garden (Leeds Castle), 196
Culzean Castle & Country Park (near Turnberry), 569–570
Cumberland Pencil Museum (Keswick), 432
Cumberland Stone (Inverness), 604

Curler's Rest (Glasgow), 564
Currency and currency exchange, 63
Custard Factory (Birmingham), 322, 328
Customs regulations, 667
Cuthbert, St, 455
Cutty Sark (Greenwich), 99

D
Dales Way, 448
Daphne du Maurier Festival (Fowey), 267
Darby Houses (Ironbridge), 341
Dartmoor National Park, 261–265
Dawyck Botanic Garden (near Peebles), 535
Deacons (Salisbury), 232
Dean Bridge (Edinburgh), 492
Dean Village (Edinburgh), 492
De Courcy's Arcade (Glasgow), 562
Dedham, 360–361
Dedham Grammar School, 360
Deer Park (Windsor), 154
Delmonicas (Glasgow), 564
Demijohn (Edinburgh), 506–507
Demijohn (York), 445
Dennis Severs' House (London), 96–97
Dentists
  Edinburgh, 477–478
  Glasgow, 543
Dervaig, 594
Derwentwater, 418
Dig! (York), 441
Digbeth (Birmingham), 322, 328
Dirleton, 513
Dirleton Castle, 513
Dirty Duck (Stratford-upon-Avon), 319
Disability Rights UK, 667
Disabled travelers, 667
Discrimination, 672–673
Distilleries, Islay's, 589–590
Dockyard Museum (Bristol), 252
Doctors, 667
  Edinburgh, 478
  Glasgow, 543
  London, 62
Dog Collar Museum (Leeds Castle), 196
Dogpole (Shrewsbury), 333
Dolphin and Seal Centre (North Kessock), 618
Doom painting (Salisbury), 227
Dorchester, 237–240
Dornoch, 620–622
Dornoch Bookshop, 621
Dornoch Cathedral, 621
Dorset County Museum, 238–239
Dove Cottage, the Wordsworth Museum (Grasmere), 425–426

Dover, 187–188
Dover Castle, 188
Down House, 192
Down House (Home of Charles Darwin; Downe), 105, 194
Dragon Hall (Norwich), 370
Drinking laws, 668
Drumnadrochit, 609–610
Dryburgh, 528
Dryburgh Abbey, 531
Dry Dock (Bristol), 251–252
Drygate (Glasgow), 564–565
Drymen, 572
Duart Castle (Craignure), 593–594
Dubliner (Birmingham), 322
Dugald Stewart Monument (Edinburgh), 487
Dukes 92 (Manchester), 395
Dulwich Picture Gallery, 103
Du Maurier, Daphne, 266, 267
Dumbarton Castle, 570
Dunaverty Golf Course (near Campbeltown), 585
Duncansby Head, 628
Dunnet Head, 626
Dunrobin Castle (Golspie), 622–623
Dunsgiath Castle (Skye), 652
Dunvegan, 651–652
Dunvegan Castle, 644, 651
Dunwich, 364
Dunwich Museum, 366
Durham, 453–459
Durham Castle, 454
Durham Cathedral, 454–455
Durness, 624–626
Durrants, 367

E
The Eagle (Cambridge), 354
Eagle and Child (Oxford), 170
Eas-Coul-Aulin waterfall, 623
East Bergholt, 360
East Coast Mainline, 658
Eastgate Shopping Centre (Inverness), 607
East Lothian, 512
Eastside Projects (Birmingham), 322
EasyJet, 661
Eating and drinking, 32
Eating London Tours, 114
Ebor Festival (York), 440
Eclipse (Winchester), 225
Eco Ventures (Cromarty), 619
Eden Court (Inverness), 608
The Eden Project (Fowey), 267
Edinburgh, 472–513
    accommodations, 493–500
    entertainment and nightlife, 507–508
    exploring, 478–508
    festivals, 488–489
    for kids, 489–490
    Leith, 492–493
    organized tours, 486–487
    Royal Mile, 478–485
    underground attractions, 491
    getting around, 473–474
    layout of, 474, 476
    neighborhoods in brief, 476–477
    outdoor activities, 487–488
    restaurants, 500–506
    shopping, 506–507
    side trips from, 508–513
    traveling to, 472–473
    visitor information, 473
Edinburgh Airport, 472
Edinburgh Art Festival, 489
Edinburgh Bus Tours, 486
Edinburgh Castle, 478–479
Edinburgh Comedy Festival, 489
Edinburgh Dungeons, 490
Edinburgh Festival Fringe, 488
Edinburgh Festival Rentals, 493
Edinburgh International Book Festival, 486, 489
Edinburgh International Festival, 36, 488
Edinburgh International Film Festival, 488
Edinburgh International Science Festival, 488
Edinburgh Jazz & Blues Festival, 488
Edinburgh Literary Tours, 486
Edinburgh Principal Hotel Association, 493
Edinburgh's Camera Obscura, 483
Edinburgh World Heritage, 476
Edinburgh Zoo, 490
Eilean Ban (Kyleakin), 645–646
Eilean Donan Castle (Dornie), 639–641
Electricity, 668
Elgin Marbles (The Sculptures of the Parthenon; London), 67
Elizabeth Gaskill's House (Manchester), 386
Elizabeth I, 81, 82, 177, 315, 374
Elm Hill (Norwich), 370
Ely, 356–358
Ely Cathedral, 356–357
Ely Museum, 357
Embassies and consulates, 668
Embo (near Dornoch), 621
Embrace Scotland, 665
Emergencies, 62, 668
Emirates Air Line (London), 107
Emmanuel College (Cambridge), 346
Endecott House (Chagford), 263
Engels, Friedrich, 383, 388
Enginiuty (Ironbridge), 342
English Country Cottages, 665
English Heritage, 666

English National Opera (London), 145
Epping Forest (London), 109
Esk Valley Railway, 450
Eton, 149
Eton College, 150
Eurostar, 658
Evening Star (Brighton), 210
Everyman Theatre (Liverpool), 413
Exeter, 254–261
Exeter Cathedral, 256–257
Exeter Guildhall, 256
Explorer Pass, 661
Eyam, 396
Eye of York, 442

F
15 bus (London), 114
FACT Centre (Foundation for Art and Creative Technology; Liverpool), 413
Fairhaven Woodland & Water Garden (South Walsham), 378
Falcon Inn (Chester), 403
Falkirk Wheel, 508–509
Falls of Leny, 573
Falls of Shin, 623
Families with children, 668
    best experiences for, 6–7
Farmer's Boy (St Albans), 177
Farmers' Market, St Albans, 176
Farmhouses, 664–665
Farm Stay UK, 665
Fashion Museum & Assembly Rooms (Bath), 243
Fat Cat (Norwich), 376
Ferry Cross the Mersey (Liverpool), 407
Festival Flats (Edinburgh), 493
Fiddler's (Drumnadrochit), 609
Fife Coastal Path, 514
Filey, 450
Filmhouse (Edinburgh), 507
Fingal of Caledonia, 639
Fingal's Cave (Staffa), 596
Finlaggan, 588
Finnieston Crane (Glasgow), 554
Fionnphort, 595
Fishbourne Roman Palace & Gardens, 214
Fisher and Donaldson (St Andrews), 518
Fishermen's Museum (Hastings), 199–200
Fisherton Mill (Salisbury), 232
Fish Market (Whitstable), 190
Fish Street (Shrewsbury), 333
Fitzwilliam Museum (Cambridge), 351–352
Five House Pass (Stratford-upon-Avon), 308–309
Flatford Mill & Bridge Cottage (Dedham), 360–361

Flodden Wall (Edinburgh), 478
Floors Castle (near Kelso), 524–525
Flybe, 661
Fort Augustus, 611
Fort George (Inverness), 604–605
Fortnum & Mason (London), 144
Fortrose & Rosemarkie Golf Club, 618
Fortrose Cathedral, 618
Fortune of War (Brighton), 202–203
Fort William, 633–635
The Foundry (Canterbury), 187
Fountains Abbey (Ripon), 447
Fountains Abbey & Studley Royal Park, 447
Fowey, 266–269
Fox Talbot Museum (Lacock), 233
Framlingham Castle, 368–369
Freedom of Scotland Travelpass, 660
Free things to do, best, 11–12
French Brothers (Windsor), 154
Freud Café (Oxford), 170
Friar's Crag, 420–421
Fried Fish Dealers (Ironbridge), 341
Frogmore House (Windsor), 154

G

Gainsborough, Thomas, 29, 84, 361, 363
Gainsborough's House (Sudbury), 363
Gallery of Modern Art (Glasgow), 549–550
Gannet, HMS (Chatham), 192
Garrick Inn (Stratford-upon-Avon), 319
Gateshead, 459
Gateshead Millennium Bridge, 459
G-A-Y (Manchester), 395
Gaydio, 670
Gays and lesbians, 669–670
  Birmingham, 329
  Brighton, 210
  London, 145
  Manchester, 395
Geffrye Museum (London), 97
Gellions Pub (Inverness), 608
George Square (Glasgow), 548
Georgian House (Edinburgh), 485
Get Dressed For Battle (Durham), 459
Gigha, Isle of, 586–587
Gilbert Collection (London), 89
Gingerbeer (London), 145
Gladstone's Land (Edinburgh), 479
Glasgow, 539–573

accommodations, 557–559
arriving in, 539–540
business hours, 543
currency exchange, 543
entertainment and nightlife, 563–565
exploring, 543–556
getting around, 540–542
layout, 542
neighborhoods in brief, 542–543
organized tours, 556
restaurants, 559–561
safety, 543
shopping, 561–563
side trips from, 566–573
visitor information, 542
Glasgow Airport, 539
Glasgow Cathedral, 547
Glasgow City Cruise, 556
Glasgow Cross, 546
Glasgow Green (Glasgow), 546
Glasgow Royal Concert Hall, 563
Glasgow School of Art, 550, 562
Glasgow Science Centre, 554
Glasgow University, 551
Glenashdale, 580
Glencoe, 637–639
Glencoe and North Lorn Folk Museum, 638
Glencoe Mountain, 638
Glencoe Visitor Centre, 638
Glenelg, 639, 642
Glen Finglas, 573
Glenfinnan Monument (near Fort William), 636
Glenlee (Glasgow), 555
The Glenlivet, 615
Glen Rosa, 580
Glen Sannox, 580
Glentress Forest, 535
Gloriette (Leeds Castle), 196
The Goat (St Albans), 177
Goatfell, 580
Godiva, Lady, 330
Golden Gallery (London), 92–93
Golden Tours Open Top Bus Tours (London), 114
Golf
  Dornoch, 620–621
  Fortrose & Rosemarkie Golf Club, 618
  Mull, 593
  Nairn, 615
  Roxburghe Golf Course, 526
  St Andrews, 515–516
  Troon, 568
  Turnberry, 569
Golspie, 622–623
Gondola (Coniston), 428
The Goods Shed (Canterbury), 187
Gordon Russell Design Museum (Broadway), 298

Gothic Temple, 665
Grahams (Inverness), 607
Grainger Market (Newcastle), 460
Grand National (Liverpool), 35
Grand Punch Bowl (London), 95
Grasmere, 425–427
Grasmere Gingerbread Shop, 425
Grassington, 448
Grassington National Park Centre, 448
Graves of the Clans (Inverness), 604
Great Bath (Bath), 244–245
Great Britain, SS (Bristol), 251–252
Great Glen, 600, 634, 639
Great Glen Way, 639
Great Hall (Oxford), 162
Great Hall (Penshurst Place), 196
Great Hospital (Norwich), 370
Great North Museum (Newcastle), 461–462
Great St Mary's Church (Cambridge), 350–351
Great Tower (Dover Castle), 188
Great West Doors (London), 92
Great Western Arcade (Birmingham), 328
Great Yorkshire Show (Harrogate), 446
The Green Man (Cambridge), 356
The Green Park (London), 110
Greenwich, 98–103
Greenwich Guided Walks, 114
Greenwich Mean Time (GMT), 673
Greenwich Park (London), 110
GreetinGlasgow, 556
Gresham Blake (Brighton), 209
Grey Cairns of Camster, 626–627
Greyfriars Bobby (Edinburgh), 485
Grey's Monument (Newcastle), 460
Groam House Museum, 618
Grope Lane (Shrewsbury), 333
Grosvenor Museum (Chester), 402
Grotto (Stourhead), 234
Guildhall (Norwich), 370
Guildhall of Corpus Christi (Lavenham), 361, 363
Gulbenkian Theatre (Canterbury), 187
Gullane, 513

H

Haddon Hall (Bakewell), 396, 397
Hadrian's Wall, 463–464
Hairy Fig (York), 445

Hall's Croft (Stratford-upon-Avon), 311
Hampstead Heath (London), 110
Hampton Court Palace, 103–104
The Handel House Museum (London), 83
The Harbour Inn (Southwold), 368
Harbour Street (Whitstable), 190
Hardwick Hall (Chesterfield), 396, 397
Hardy's Cottage (near Dorchester), 239
Hardy's Original Sweet Shop (Windsor), 157
Hare and Hounds (Birmingham), 329
Harestanes Countryside Visitor Centre (Ancrum), 523
Harrods (London), 144
Harrogate, 446–449
Hart Gold & Silversmiths (Chipping Campden), 304
Hartwells Cycle-Hire (Bourton-on-the-Water), 293
Hastings, 197
Hastings Castle, 199–200
Hastings Stade, 199
Hatfield House (near St Albans), 177
Haunch of Venison (Salisbury), 232–233
Havana House (Windsor), 157
Hawes Inn (South Queensferry), 510
Hawico (Edinburgh), 507
Hawkshead, 429–430
Hawkshead Grammar School, 430
Hay Inclined Plane (Ironbridge), 341, 342
Hay-on-Wye, 337
Hayward Gallery (London), 75
Health concerns, 668–669
Hector Russell (Glasgow), 562
Heddon-on-the-Wall, 464
Heffers (Cambridge), 354
Helmsley, 451
Henderson (Glasgow), 563
Henderson Park (Coldstream), 527
Henshelwoods (York), 445
Hepworth, Barbara, 275–276
Hereford, 336–337
Hereford Cathedral, 337
Hereford Screen (London), 89
Hereford Tourist Information Centre, 332
Heritage Cycle Tours, 233
Hermitage Castle (near Hawick), 523
Hever Castle & Gardens, 194
Hexham, 463
Hidcote (Chipping Campden), 302–303

High Altar (London), 92
Highclere Castle (Newbury), 104–105
Highland Experience (Edinburgh), 508
Highland Games (Inverness), 601
High Moorland Visitor Centre (Dartmoor National Park), 262
Hiking and walking
  Argyll Forest Park, 576
  Cotswold Way, 293
  Kintyre Way, 584
  Mull, 593
  Peebles, 535
  Queen Elizabeth Forest Park, 572
  South Downs Way, 214
  Southern Upland Way, 520
  Thames Path, 149
Hill Top Farm (Hawkshead), 429–430
Hirsel Estate, 527
Historic properties, 665
Historic Scotland Explorer Pass, 666
History of England and Scotland, 17–33
HMS *Belfast* (London), 75
Hogmanay (Edinburgh), 36, 488
Holburne Museum (Bath), 243
Holidays, public, 37
Holkham Hall, 379
Holyroodhouse, Palace of (Edinburgh), 482
Holyrood Park (Edinburgh), 478
Holy Trinity Church (Shakespeare's Tomb; Stratford-upon-Avon), 311
HomeExchange.com, 666
HomeLink International, 666
Home of Charles Darwin (Down House; Downe), 105
Honister Slate Mine, 432
Hootananny (Inverness), 608
Hopetoun House, 510
Hospital of St Cross (Winchester), 221–222
Hospitals, 669
Hotel du Vin, 665
Hotels. *See also* Accommodations Index
  best, 4–5
  tips on, 663–666
Houses of Parliament (London), 76–77
Housesteads Roman Fort & Museum, 463–464
House swapping and peer-to-peer accommodation networks, 666
Hove, 203
The Hub (Edinburgh), 488
The Hub in the Forest (Peebles), 535

Hugh Miller's Cottage (Cromarty), 620
Hunstanton, 378
Hunterian Museum & Art Gallery (Glasgow), 551–552
Huntington's Antiques Ltd. (Stow-on-the-Wold), 296
Hyde Park (London), 110–111
Hypocaust (St Albans), 175

I

Iain Marr Antiques (Beauly), 608
IAMAT (International Association for Medical Assistance to Travelers), 667
Ightham Mote, 194
IJ Mellis
  Edinburgh, 506
  St Andrews, 518
Ikon Gallery (Birmingham), 322
Imperial State Crown (London), 95
Imperial War Museum (Manchester), 390
Imperial War Museum Duxford, 359
Imperial War Museum London, 77
Imperial War Museum North (Manchester), 386–387
Inchcolm Island, 510
Indoor Market (Durham), 459
Insurance, 669
International Association for Medical Assistance to Travelers (IAMAT), 667
International Beatles Week (Liverpool), 406
International Slavery Museum (Liverpool), 409
International Student Identity Card (ISIC), 673
International Teacher Identity Card, 673
International Youth Travel Card (IYTC), 673
Internet and Wi-Fi, 669
Intervac, 666
Inveraray, 573–578
Inveraray Castle, 574
Inveraray Jail, 575–576
Inverewe Gardens, 632
Inverleith House (Edinburgh), 488
Inverness, 600–609
  accommodations, 605–606
  entertainment and nightlife, 608
  exploring, 601, 604–605
  shopping, 607
  side trips from, 608–609
  special events, 601
  traveling to, 600–601
  visitor information, 601

Inverness Museum & Art Gallery, 605
Inverpolly, 631
Iona, 595–596
Iona Abbey, 595–596
Iona Community, 596
Ironbridge, 340–342
Iron Bridge and Tollhouse (Ironbridge), 342
Ironbridge Gorge Museums, 340, 341
Island Cycles (Portree), 645
Islay House Square (Bridgend), 590
Islay Woollen Mill (Bridgend), 590
Isle of Arran, 578–583
Isle of Arran Heritage Museum, 582
Isle of Gigha, 586–587
Isle of Islay, 587–591
Isle of Jura, 591–592
Isle of Skye, 642–655. See also specific villages
Isle Ornsay, 653–655
Italian Centre (Glasgow), 562
Italian Garden (Hever), 194
Itineraries, suggested, 41–53

J
Jackfield Tile Museum (Ironbridge), 341, 342
Jail on Castle Street (Dornoch), 621
Jane Austen Centre (Bath), 244
Jane Austen Festival (Bath), 242
Jedburgh, 521–524
Jedburgh Abbey, 522–523
Jericho Tavern (Oxford), 171
Jermyn Street (London), 144
Jerwood Gallery (Hastings), 200
Jewellery Quarter (Birmingham), 320, 322
The John Buchan Story (Peebles), 534
John F. Kennedy Memorial (Runnymede), 150–151
John Knox House (Edinburgh), 482
John Lennon Airport (Liverpool), 406
John O'Groats, 628–629
John Rylands Library (Manchester), 388
Johnstons of Elgin (Newmill), 617
Jorvik Viking Centre (York), 441, 442
Jubilee Greenway Walk (London), 114
Jubilee Pool (Penzance), 270
Julian of Norwich, 372
Jura, Isle of, 591–592

K
Kailzie Gardens (near Peebles), 535
Kayak.com, 662
Keble College (Oxford), 160
Kelmscott Manor, 285
Kelso, 524–528
Kelso Abbey, 525
Kelvingrove Art Gallery & Museum (Glasgow), 552–553
Kelvingrove Park (Glasgow), 551, 552
Kenilworth Castle, 315
Kensington Gardens (London), 111
Kensington Palace (London), 85–86
Kent, 192–196
Kenwood, 105
Keswick, 431–436
Keswick Ramblers, 416
Kids Go Free, 658
Kilchattan, Church of (Gigha), 586
Kilchoman, 590
Kildalton churchyard (Port Ellen), 588
Kildalton Cross (Port Ellen), 588
Kilmartin Glen, 577
Kilmartin House Museum, 577
Kilmuir churchyard, 650
King's Apartments (London), 86
King's Arms (Oxford), 170
King's College (Cambridge), 346, 348
King's College Chapel (Cambridge), 346
The King's Library (London), 66
King's Theatre (Glasgow), 563
Kingswear Castle, 665
King Tut's Wah-Wah Hut (Glasgow), 565
Kintyre Peninsula, 583–586
Kintyre Way, 584
Knockan Crag, 631
Knock Castle (Skye), 652
Knole, 194–195
Komedia (Brighton), 209
Kyleakin, 645–646
Kyle of Lochalsh, 639–642
Kyle of Tongue, 623–624

L
Lacock, 233–234
Lacock Abbey, 233
Lady Chapel (Wells), 251
Lagavulin, 590
The Lake District, 415–436
  accommodations, 433–434
  brief descriptions of the lakes, 416–419
  geographic terms, 425
  getting around, 415–416
  organized tours, 416
  outdoor activities, 424–425
  restaurants, 435–436
  scenic wonders, 419–421
  traveling to, 415
  visitor information, 416
Lake District National Park, 416
Lake District National Park Visitor Centre (Brockhole), 424
Lakeland Experience, 416
Lakeland Motor Museum (Backbarrow), 423–424
Lake Poets, 432
Lake Windermere, 418–419
Lamb & Flag (Oxford), 170
Lamb House (Rye), 198
Lamlash, 580
Land Gate (Rye), 198
Landmark Trust, 665
Land's End, 271
The Lanes (Brighton), 209
L'Angelier, Pierre Emile, 549
Lantern Lobby (Windsor), 153
Laphroaig, 590
LastMinute.com (London), 145
The Latest Music Bar (Brighton), 209
Latitude (near Southwold), 365
Lavenham, 361–363
Leakey's Bookshop and Café (Inverness), 607
Leeds Castle, 192, 195–196
Legal aid, 669
Legends (Brighton), 210
Leith (Edinburgh), 477, 492–493
  accommodations, 500
  restaurant, 506
Leith Festival, 488
Lennel, 527
Lennox Castle (Inchmurrin), 570
Les Chambres de la Reine (Leeds Castle), 196
LGBT travelers, 669–670
  Birmingham, 329
  Brighton, 210
  London, 145
  Manchester, 395
Liberty (London), 144
Lindisfarne Castle, 467
Lindisfarne Priory, 466–467
Linlithgow, 511
Linlithgow Palace, 511
Little Sparta (near Peebles), 536
The Little Theatre (Nairn), 617
Liverpool, 404–413
  accommodations, 410–411
  exploring, 406–410
  restaurants, 411–412
  shopping, 412–413
  special events, 406
  traveling to, 404, 406
  visitor information, 406
Liverpool Cathedral, 406–407
Liverpool Ferry Terminal, 406

Liverpool One complex, 412
Liverpool Philharmonic Hall, 413
Loch Assynt, 632
Loch Awe, 632
Loch Broom, 631
Loch Fleet, 621
Loch Fyne, 573
Loch Gruinart, 588
Loch Gruinart Nature Reserve, 588
Lochinver, 626
Loch Lomond and the Trossachs National Park, 570–572
Loch Lomond Shores, 571
Loch Ness, 609–611
Loch Ness Centre and Exhibition (Drumnadrochit), 609
Lochranza, 580
The Lodge, Forest Visitor Centre (Aberfoyle), 572
London, 55–146
   accommodations, 115–132
      moderate hotel chains, 130–132
      rates, 125
      Soho, Covent Garden and nearby, 115–125
      Southwark & Westminster, 126–128
      town house hotels, 121
   arriving in, 55–59
   entertainment and nightlife, 145–146
   exploring, 63–115
      The City & South Bank, 90–96
      East London, 96–98
      free attractions, 70
      Greenwich, 98–103
      Kensington, 85–89
      for kids, 115
      late openings, 79
      Marylebone & Mayfair, 83–84
      organized tours and excursions, 114
      outdoor attractions, 109–114
      outside central London, 103–107
      overrated attractions, 107–109
      Soho, Covent Garden & nearby, 63–72
      Westminster and nearby, 72–82
   getting around, 59–60
   layout of, 60–61
   neighborhoods in brief, 61–62
   restaurants, 132–143
      chains, 139
      The City & Southwark, 139–141
      pubs, 143
      Soho, Covent Garden and nearby, 132–138
      Spitalfields & Shoreditch, 142–143
   shopping, 143–144
London City, 657
The London Dungeon, 108
London Eye, 77–78
London Gatwick, 657
London Heathrow, 657
London Luton, 657
London Marathon, 35
London Open House Weekend, 36
London Pass, 63
London Sea Life Aquarium, 108
London Transport Museum, 69
London Walks, 114
The London Zoo, 108
Long Gallery (Penshurst Place), 196
Long Walk (Windsor), 154
The Lord Clifden (Birmingham), 329
Lord Leycester Hospital (Warwick), 314
The Lord Nelson (Southwold), 368
Lost Gardens of Heligan (Fowey), 267–268
Lost World Literary Pub Crawl (Edinburgh), 486
Love-Theatre.com (London), 145
Lower Slaughter, 292–293
Lowry Theatre (Manchester), 390, 395
Low Wood Watersports & Activity Centre (near Windermere), 424–425
Lucy Fisher (Windsor), 154
Ludlow, 334–336
Ludlow Castle, 334
Luss Visitor Centre, 572
Lyke Wake Walk, 451

M

Machrihanish Dunes (near Campbeltown), 585
Machrilhanish Golf Club (near Campbeltown), 585
Mackintosh, Charles Rennie, 551
Mackintosh Interpretation Centre (Glasgow), 551
Madame Tussauds (London), 108
Maddermarket Theatre (Norwich), 376
Magdalen Bridge Boathouse (Oxford), 165
Magdalen College (Oxford), 162–163
Magna Carta, Salisbury, 228
Magna Carta (London), 63, 66
Magna Carta Memorial (Runnymede), 151

Maiden Castle (near Dorchester), 238
Maids Head Bar (Norwich), 376
Mail, 670
Mailbox (Birmingham), 328
The Mainstreet Trading Company (St Boswells), 530–531
Malmaison, 665
Malt Whisky Trail, 615
Manchester, 382–398
   accommodations, 391–392
   entertainment and nightlife, 394–395
   exploring, 386–391
   getting around, 384
   layout of, 384, 386
   restaurants, 392–394
   shopping, 394
   side trips from, 396–398
   traveling to, 384
   visitor information, 384
Manchester Academy and Club Academy, 395
Manchester Arena, 395
Manchester Art Gallery, 387
Manchester Cathedral, 388–389
Manchester Craft Centre, 394
Manchester International Airport, 384
Manchester Irish Festival, 35
Manchester Pride, 669
Manchester Ship Canal Cruises, 407
Manchester Visitor Information Centre, 384
Mappa Mundi (Hereford), 337
Marble Hall (near St Albans), 177
Margate, 189
Margate Main Sands, 189
Maritime Greenwich, 99–100
Market Bar (Inverness), 608
Market Hall (Chipping Campden), 301
Market Hall (Shrewsbury), 333
Market Square (Cambridge), 350, 354
Marlborough (Brighton), 210
Marlborough Maze (Woodstock), 172
Marlowe Theatre (Canterbury), 187
Mary Arden's Farm (Stratford-upon-Avon), 311
Mary Queen of Scots, 81, 397, 482, 511, 520, 522
Mary Queen of Scots' Visitor Centre (Jedburgh), 523
Mary Rose (Portsmouth), 226
The Mash Tun, 615
Maumbury Rings, 237
Maze (Hampton Court Palace), 104

Meantime Brewing Company (Greenwich), 102
Megabus, 56, 661
MegaTrain, 659
Mellerstain (near Kelso), 525–526
Melrose, 528–532
Melrose Abbey, 529
Mendips (Liverpool), 408
Mercat Tours (Edinburgh), 486
Mercer Art Gallery (Harrogate), 446
Merchant's Steeple (Glasgow), 549
Merseyside Maritime Museum (Liverpool), 407–409
Metquarter (Liverpool), 413
Metropolitan Cathedral of Christ the King (Liverpool), 409
Miller, Hugh, 620
Millers of Melrose, 530
Milsom Place (Bath), 250
Minack Theatre (Porthcurno), 272
Minerva Studio Theatre (Chichester), 216
Ministry of Sound (London), 146
Mitchell's (St Andrews), 518
Mobile phones, 670
Model Village at the Old New Inn (Bourton-on-the-Water), 290
Moine Mhor, 576
Moles (Bath), 250
Mompesson House (Salisbury), 228
Money and costs, 671
Monk's House (Rodmell), 206
Monteviot House & Gardens (near Jedburgh), 523–524
The Monument (London), 90
Monument to the Massacre of Glencoe (Carnoch), 638
Moorsbus, 450
Moot Hall (Aldeburgh), 366
Moray Firth, 614
Moreton-in-Marsh, 280–281
Morris, William, 287
Motorhomes, 663
Mountain Goat, 416
Mousehole, 270–271
Mousetrap Cheese Shop (Ludlow), 339
Muggle Tours (London), 114
Muirfield Golf Course (East Lothian), 512
Mull Museum (Tobermory), 594
Mull of Kintyre, 585, 592–598
organized tours, 593
outdoor activities, 593
traveling to, 592–593
visitor information, 593
Museum Gardens (York), 441
Museum of Childhood (London), 97

Museum of Eton Life, 150
Museum of Islay Life (Port Charlotte), 589
Museum of Liverpool, 406, 408, 409–410
Museum of London, 90, 92
Museum of London Docklands, 98
Museum of Natural History (Oxford), 163
Museum of St Albans, 173
Museum of Science and Industry (Manchester), 389, 390
The Museum of the Broads (Stalham), 378
Museum of the Gorge (Ironbridge), 341, 342
Museum of the Jewellery Quarter (Birmingham), 322
Museum of Zoology (Cambridge), 350
Museums, best, 7–8
Music at Oxford, 169

N

9flats.com, 666
Nairn, 614–617
Nairn Book & Arts Festival, 617
Nairn Bookshop, 617
Nairn Dunbar Golf Club, 615
Nairn Golf Club, 615
Nash's House & New Place (Stratford-upon-Avon), 312
Nash's Oxford Bakery, 168
Nation (Liverpool), 413
National Express, 661
National Football Museum (Manchester), 389
National Gallery (London), 69–70
National Gallery Complex (Edinburgh), 485
National Maritime Museum (Greenwich), 100
The National Maritime Museum (Greenwich), 100–101
National Museum of Rural Life (near Glasgow), 566
National Museum of Scotland (Edinburgh), 483
National Museum of the Royal Navy (Portsmouth), 225
National Park Centre (Balmaha), 572
National Park Gateway Centre (Loch Lomond Shores), 571
The National Portrait Gallery (London), 70–71
National Rail Enquiries, 659
National Railway Museum (York), 442
National Trust, 666
National Trust for Scotland, 665
National Trust Holiday Cottages, 665

National Trust Touring Pass, 666
Natural History Museum (London), 86–87
Natural History Museum (Oxford), 163
Neal's Yard Dairy (London), 141
Necropolis (Glasgow), 546
Neidpath Castle (Peebles), 535
Nelson Monument (Edinburgh), 487
Neptune's Staircase (near Fort William), 635
Nether Gallery (Penshurst Place), 196
New Alexandra Theatre (Birmingham), 329
New Bond Street (London), 143
Newcastle, 459–464
Newcastle Castle, 462
New College (Oxford), 164
New Inn (Ironbridge), 340
New Lanark (near Glasgow), 566–567
Newlyn, 270
Newlyn Art Gallery (Penzance), 270
New Street (Painswick), 287
New Theatre (Oxford), 169–170
New Town (Edinburgh), 474, 476
accommodations, 493, 496–498
exploring, 485–486
restaurants, 501–502
New Year, 34
New Year's Day Parade (London), 34
NHS Choices, 669
Nice 'n' Sleazy (Glasgow), 565
Night & Day (Manchester), 395
Nightingale (Birmingham), 329
The Norfolk Broads, 376–377
Norfolk Street Bakery (Cambridge), 353
Norman Gatehouse (Exeter), 256
North Berwick, 511–512
North Kessock, 618
North Laine (Brighton), 209
North Norfolk coast, 378–380
North York Moors National Park, 450, 451
Norwich, 369–380
accommodations, 374–375
entertainment and nightlife, 375–376
exploring, 370–374
getting around, 370
nearby attractions, 376–380
restaurants, 375
shopping, 376
traveling to, 369
visitor information, 370
Norwich Castle, 370–371
Norwich Cathedral, 371–373
Norwich Playhouse, 376

Notting Hill Carnival (London), 36
No. 1 Royal Crescent (Bath), 244

O

Oa Nature Reserve (near Port Ellen), 588
Ocelot, HMS (Chatham), 192
Odyssey (St Albans), 177
Ogham Stone, 586
Ohso Social (Brighton), 203
Oklahoma (Manchester), 394
Old Byre Heritage Centre (Dervaig), 594
Old Byre Showroom (Isle of Arran), 583
The Old Cheese Shop (St Andrews), 518
Old Course (St Andrews), 515
Old Crown (Birmingham), 329
Old Fruitmarket (Glasgow), 564
Old Inverlochy Castle (near Fort William), 635
Old Library (Oxford), 161
Old Man of Storr, 649
Old Mercat Cross (Inverness), 604
Old Mill (Lower Slaughter), 292–293
Old Neptune (Whitstable), 191
Old Pulteney Distillery (Wick), 627
Old Royal Naval College (Greenwich), 100, 101–102
Old Sarum, 229–230
Old Silk Mill (Chipping Campden), 304
Old Town (Edinburgh), 474, 476
  accommodations, 498–500
  restaurants, 502–503
Old Town (Margate), 189
Old Trafford Stadium (Manchester), 389
Oliver Cromwell's House (Ely), 357–358
OneFineStay.com, 666
OpenBritain.net, 667
Oran Mór (Glasgow), 565
Orchard Tea Garden (Cambridge), 356
The Original Tour London Sightseeing, 114
Orwell, George, 592
O2 Academy Oxford, 170–171
O2 Apollo (Manchester), 395
Outdoor activities, best, 9–11
Owlpen Manor (Painswick), 288
Oxford, 157–172
  accommodations, 165–166
  entertainment and nightlife, 169–171
  exploring, 160–165
  getting around, 160
  guided tours, 158
  pubs, 170
  restaurants, 166–169
  shopping, 169
  traveling to, 158
  visitor information, 158, 160
Oxford and Cambridge University Boat Race, 35
Oxford Castle, 164
Oxford Cheese Company, 168
Oxford Playhouse Theatre, 169
Oxford River Cruises, 158
Oxfordshire Museum (Woodstock), 171
Oxford Street (London), 143
Oyster Festival (Whitstable), 189

P

Packing tips, 672
Painswick, 287–289
Painswick Rococo Garden, 288
Palace of Holyroodhouse (Edinburgh), 482
Pallant House Art Gallery (Chichester), 214
Palmer's Farm (Stratford-upon-Avon), 312
Palm House (Kew), 105
P&G Wells (Winchester), 225
Pantheon (Stourhead), 234
Paps of Jura, 592
Pavilion Theatre (Glasgow), 563
Peak District National Park, 396
The Peaks, 421
Peebles, 533–537
Penlee House Gallery and Museum (Penzance), 270
Penshurst Place & Gardens (near Royal Tunbridge Wells), 196
Pentland Hills, 535
Penzance, 269–274
People's History Museum (Manchester), 390
People's Palace (Glasgow), 547–548
Peveril of the Peak (Manchester), 395
Pharmacies, London, 62
Philatelic Exhibition (London), 66
The Pickerel Inn (Cambridge), 354
Pickering, 451
Pier Head (Liverpool), 406
Pink Fringe (Brighton), 210
Pink News, 669
Pitt Rivers Museum (Oxford), 164
Plaiden Ell, 621
Planetarium (Liverpool), 410
Pleasure Beach, 398
Plockton, 639, 641–642
Poet's Corner (London), 81
Poison Garden (Alnwick), 465–466
Police, 672
Pollok House (Glasgow), 555–556
Pool of Life (Liverpool), 408
Port Charlotte, 589
Port Ellen, 587–588
Porter (Bath), 250
Porthcurno, 271
Porthcurno Telegraph Museum, 271
Porthmeor, 276
Porthminster, 276
Portmeiron Factory Shop (Stoke-on-Trent), 331
Portobello (Edinburgh), 489
Portree, 647–649
Portsmouth Historic Dockyard, 225–226
The Pot Still (Glasgow), 565
Potter, Beatrix, 429–430
The Potteries, 331–332
Potteries Museum & Art Gallery (Stoke-on-Trent), 331
Powderham Castle (near Exeter), 257–258
Premier Inn, 666
Prestwick airport (Glasgow), 539–540
Price and Sons (Ludlow), 339
Pride Brighton & Hove, 669
Pride in London, 669
Primrose Hill Park (London), 112
Princetown, 263
The Proms (London), 35–36
Public holidays, 37
Pulteney Bridge (Bath), 243
Pump Room (Bath), 245

Q

Quays (Manchester), 390
Quayside (Newcastle), 460
Queen Elizabeth Forest Park, 572
Queen Elizabeth Oak (near St Albans), 177
Queen Elizabeth Olympic Park (London), 111
Queen Elizabeth's Hunting Lodge (London), 110
Queen Mary's Dolls' House (Windsor), 151–152
Queen Mother's Crown (London), 94
Queens' College (Cambridge), 348
The Queen's Gallery (London), 108–109
The Queen's House (Greenwich), 100, 102
Queen Street Station (Glasgow), 540
Quire (Canterbury), 183–184
QX Magazine (London), 145

R

Rabbie's (Edinburgh), 508
Radar NKS Key, 667

Radcliffe Camera (Oxford), 161
Rai d'Or (Salisbury), 233
Rail Europe, 658
Rail passes, 658–660
Ramshorn Church (Glasgow), 549
Raphael Cartoons (London), 88
Raven of Bath, 250
Real Food Market (Manchester), 394
The Real Mary King's Close (Edinburgh), 491
RedSpottedHanky.com, 659
The Regent (Edinburgh), 508
Regent's Canal (London), 113
Regent's Park (London), 111–112
Regions in brief, 39–41
Restaurants, best, 5–6
Revenge (Brighton), 210
RHS Garden Harlow Carr (Harrogate), 448
Rievaulx Abbey, 451
Ripley's Believe It or Not! (London), 109
Ripon Cathedral, 447
River Cherwell, punting, 165
Riverside Museum (Glasgow), 554–555
River Stour, 360–361
Roamer, 669
Robert Burns Birthplace Museum (Alloway), 567–568
Robert Welch Studio Shop (Chipping Campden), 304
Robin Hood's Bay, 450–451
Rob Roy & Trossachs Visitor Centre (Callander), 572–573
Rocca (St Andrews), 517
Rodmarten Manor (Rodmarton), 289
Rollright Stones (Little Rollright), 294
Roman Amphitheater (Chester), 400–401
Roman Army Museum, 464
Roman Baths & Pump Room (Bath), 244–245
Roman ruins and antiquities
  Bath, 240, 244–245
  Canterbury Roman Museum, 184
  Chedworth Roman Villa (near Bibury), 285
  Chester, 400–401
  Exeter, 254
  Fishbourne Roman Palace & Gardens, 214
  Hadrian's Wall, 463–464
  Roman Townhouse (Dorchester), 239–240
  St Albans, 173
  Segedunum Roman Fort, Baths & Museum (Wallsend), 462
  Winchester, 221

Roman Theatre (St Albans), 174
Roman Townhouse (Dorchester), 237, 239–240
Roman Vindolanda & Roman Army Museum, 464
Roman Walls (Chester), 401
Rose Garden (Hever), 194
Rosemarkie, 618
Rosemarkie cross-slab, 619
Rose Theatre (London), 80
Rosetta Stone (London), 67
Rossetti, Dante Gabriel, 287
Rosslyn Chapel (Roslin), 509
Round Table (Winchester), 220
Round Tower (Windsor), 151
Rows (Chester), 400
Roxburghe Golf Course, 526
Royal Academy of Arts (London), 83–84
Royal Albert Hall (London), 87, 145
Royal Albert Memorial Museum and Art Gallery (Exeter), 258
Royal and Ancient Clubhouse (St Andrews), 515, 516
Royal Ballet (London), 145
Royal Botanic Garden Edinburgh, 488
Royal Botanic Gardens, Kew, 105–106
Royal Dornoch Golf Club, 620–621
Royal Edinburgh, 488–489
Royal Exchange (Manchester), 395
Royal Farms Windsor Farm Shop, 156–157
Royal Liver Building (Liverpool), 406
Royal Lyceum Theatre (Edinburgh), 507
Royal Mail Postbus, 661
Royal Mausoleum (Windsor), 154
The Royal Mews (London), 109
Royal Mile (Edinburgh), 474
  exploring, 478
  shopping, 506
Royal Oak Foundation, 666
Royal Observatory (Greenwich), 100
The Royal Observatory (Greenwich), 102
Royal Opera House (London), 145
Royal Pavilion (Brighton), 201, 204
Royal Pump Room (Harrogate), 446
Royal Scottish National Orchestra (Glasgow), 563
Royal Shakespeare Company (RSC), 308
Royal Shakespeare Theatre (Stratford-upon-Avon), 308
Royal Troon Golf Club, 568

Royal Windsor Information Centre, 150
Royal Yacht Britannia (Edinburgh), 492–493
RSPB Minsmere, 366
Runnymede, 150
Ruskin, John, 428–429
Ruskin Museum (Coniston), 428–429
Rydal Mount (near Ambleside), 426–427
Ryder, Samuel, 173
Rye, 197–201
Rye Castle Museum, 198–199
Rye Pottery, 200–201

S

Saatchi Gallery (London), 87
Safety, 672
Saffron Walden, 358
Sailors' Path, 365
Sailors' Path walk (Aldeburgh), 368
Sailors' Reading Room (Southwold), 366
Sainsbury Centre for Visual Arts (Norwich), 373–374
St Albans, 172–178
St Albans South Signal Box, 173
St Andrews, 514–521
  accommodations, 516–517
  exploring, 514–515
  restaurants, 517–518
  traveling to, 514
  visitor information, 514
St Andrews Castle, 515
St Andrews Cathedral, 515
St Andrew's Cathedral (Inverness), 604
St Andrews Square Bus Station (Edinburgh), 473
St Augustine's Abbey (Canterbury), 184
St Catherine's Castle (Fowey), 266
St Cuthbert's Way, 530
St Enoch Shopping Centre (Glasgow), 562
St Fimbarrus' Church (Fowey), 266
St Gabriel's Chapel (Canterbury), 183
St George's Chapel (Windsor), 153
St George's Hall (Windsor), 152–153
St Giles' Cathedral (Edinburgh), 483–484
St Ives, 274–278
  church of, 275
St James, Church of (Chipping Campden), 301–302
St James's Park (London), 112–113
St Johns' Almshouses (Sherborne), 235

St John's College (Cambridge), 348–349
St John the Baptist (Burford), 283
St Laurence Church (Ludlow), 335
St Margaret's Buildings (Bath), 250
St Margaret's Chapel (London), 82
St Martin-in-the-Fields (London), 145
St Martin's Church (Canterbury), 184–185
St Mary's Church
  Painswick, 287
  Rye, 199
St Mary's Church (Dedham), 360
St Mary's Church (Shrewsbury), 333
St Mary's College (St Andrews), 514
St Mary's Parish Church (Bibury), 285–286
St Mary the Virgin Church (Saffron Walden), 358
St Michael's Mount, 272–273
St Mungo Museum of Religious Life & Art (Glasgow), 548
St Pancras International Station (London), 658
St Patrick's Day, 35
St Paul's Cathedral (London), 92
St Peter and St Paul, Church of (Lavenham), 361–363
St Peter's Church (Buckland-in-the-Moor), 265
St Salvator's College (St Andrews), 514
St Swithun's Day, 222
Salisbury, 227–233
Salisbury Arts Centre, 232
Salisbury Cathedral, 228–229
Salisbury International Arts Festival, 227
Salisbury Museum, 229
Salisbury Playhouse, 232
Salisbury Reds, 230
Sally Lunn's (Bath), 245
Sandringham House & Gardens, 380
Sasi's (Oxford), 168
Savill Garden (Windsor), 154
Sawday's, 664
Scaffold Site (London), 95
Scallop (Aldeburgh), 364
Scarborough, 450
Scarborough Castle, 450
Sceptre with the Cross (London), 94
Science Museum (London), 88
Scissor Arches (Wells), 251
Scotch Whisky Heritage Centre (Edinburgh), 484
The Scotia Bar (Glasgow), 565

ScotRail, 658
Scottish-American Soldiers Monument (Edinburgh), 487
Scottish Ballet (Glasgow), 563
Scottish Chamber Orchestra (Glasgow), 563–564
Scottish Citylink, 661
Scottish Maritime Museum (Irvine), 568–569
Scottish Monument (Edinburgh), 487
Scottish National Gallery of Modern Art (Edinburgh), 485–486
Scottish National Portrait Gallery (Edinburgh), 486
Scottish Opera (Glasgow), 563
The Scottish Parliament (Edinburgh), 484–485
Scottish Seabird Centre (North Berwick), 512
Scott Polar Research Institute (Cambridge), 350
Scott's View, 531
Scrabster, 630
Scudamore's Punting Company (Cambridge), 355
Seacliff, 513
Seafront (Brighton), 202
SeaLife Brighton, 205
Sea Life Surveys, 593
Seasons, 33–34
Second City Boats (Birmingham), 322
Secret Wartime Tunnels (Dover), 188
Sedgwick Museum of Earth Sciences (Cambridge), 350
Segedunum Roman Fort, Baths & Museum (Wallsend), 462
Selfridges (Birmingham), 328
Selfridges (London), 144
Selkirk, 532–533
Semi-State Rooms (Windsor), 152
Senate House Passage (Cambridge), 351
Senior travel, 673
Serpentine Gallery (London), 111
Shakespeare Birthplace Trust, 308
Shakespeare Bookshop (Stratford-upon-Avon), 318
Shakespeare's Birthplace Museum (Stratford-upon-Avon), 312–313
Shakespeare's Globe (London), 78–79
Shakespeare's Tomb (Holy Trinity Church; Stratford-upon-Avon), 311
Shambles (York), 445
The Shard (London), 80
The Shed (Tokavaig), 645
Sheepskin Life, 665

Sheldonian Theatre (Oxford), 164–165
Sherborne, 234–237
Sherborne Abbey, 234, 236
Sherborne Castle, 234, 236
Sherborne Old Castle, 236
The Sherlock Holmes Museum (London), 109
The Ship at Dunwich, 368
Ship Centurion (Whitstable), 191
Shrewsbury, 333–334
Shrewsbury Abbey, 333
Shrewsbury Castle, 334
Shrewsbury Tourist Information Centre, 332
Shrine of St Alban, 174
Silbury Hill, 233
Sir Alfred Munnings Art Museum (Dedham), 361
Sir John Soane's Museum (London), 71–72
Sissinghurst Castle Garden (near Cranbrook), 196
Skeabost Bridge, 651
Skelbo Castle (near Dornoch), 621
Skye, Isle of, 642–655. See also specific villages
Skye Museum of Island Life (Kilmuir), 650
Skype, 669
Sleat Peninsula, 643, 652–653
Sligachan, 646–647
Smith, Madeline, 549
Smoking, 673
Snape Maltings (Aldeburgh), 368
Snowshill Lavender, 300
Snowshill Manor (near Broadway), 299
The Society of London Theatre, 145
Sole Bay Inn (Southwold), 368
Somerset House (London), 69
Souter Johnnie's Cottage (near Turnberry), 570
South Downs, 211, 214
South Downs Way, 214
Southend, 585–586
Southern Upland Way, 520, 528
SouthGate (Bath), 250
South Queensferry, 510
Southwold, 364
Southwold Lettings, 367
Southwold Lighthouse, 366
Spaceport (Liverpool), 407
Spaniards Inn (London), 110
Speakers' Corner (London), 84, 110
Speyside Cooperage, 615
Speyside Way, 615
Spirit of Speyside Whisky Festival, 615
Squeeze Gut Alley (Whitstable), 190
Staffa, 596–597

Stagecoach, 171
The Stand
  Edinburgh, 507
  Glasgow, 564
State Apartments (Windsor), 148, 152
State Rooms (near St Albans), 177
Stockbridge (Edinburgh), 476–477
Stock Ghyll Force, 421
Stoke-on-Trent, 331
Stoke-on-Trent Tourist Information Centre, 331–332
Stokesay Castle (Ludlow), 335–336
Stone Gallery (London), 92
Stonehenge, 227, 230–231
Stonehenge Tour, 230
Stones of Clava, 604
Stourhead, 233, 234
Stow-on-the-Wold, 293–296
Stratford Town Walk, 313
Stratford-upon-Avon, 306–319
  accommodations, 315–317
  entertainment and nightlife, 318–319
  exploring the area, 308–313
  organized tours, 313
  outlying attractions, 313
  restaurants, 317–318
  shopping, 318
  traveling to, 306–307
  visitor information, 307
Strathspey Railway, 612
Student travelers, 673
Studley Royal Park, 447
Sub Club (Glasgow), 565
Sudbury, 361, 363
Sudeley Castle & Gardens (Winchcombe), 294–295
Suffolk coast, 365–367
  side trips from, 368–369
Suffolk Secrets, 367
Summer Isles, 633
Sutherland, 620
Sutton Hoo (Woodbridge), 369
Swanbourne Lake, 212
Swan Theatre (Stratford-upon-Avon), 308
Swinbrook, 283
Sydney Gardens (Bath), 243

T

Talisker Distillery (Carbost), 647
Tantallon Castle, 513
Tarbert, 584
Tarn Hows, 421
Tar Tunnel (Ironbridge), 341, 342
Tate Britain (London), 79
Tate Liverpool, 410
Tate Modern (London), 93
Tate St Ives, 276–277
Taxes, 673

Taynish National Nature Reserve, 576
Temperate House (Kew), 106
The Temple (Manchester), 395
Temple of Flora (Stourhead), 234
Templeton Carpet Factory (Glasgow), 546
Tenement House (Glasgow), 550
Ten Green Bottles (Brighton), 211
Thames Path, 149
Theatre by the Lake (Keswick), 433
Theatre Royal
  Brighton, 209
  Glasgow, 563
  Norwich, 375–376
  Winchester, 225
  Windsor, 157
Theatre Royale (Newcastle), 460
"The Light of the World" (Oxford), 160
Thermae Bath Spa (Bath), 245–246
TheTrainline.com, 659
Thirlestane Castle (near Melrose), 530
Thirst (Oxford), 171
Timbers (Lavenham), 362
Time zones, 673
Tintagel, 260–261
Tintagel Castle, 260–261
Tipping, 63, 673–674
Tippoo's Tiger (London), 89
TKTS (London), 145
Tobermory, 594
Tobermory Golf Club (Mull), 593
Tobermory Malt Whisky Distillery, 594
Toilets, 674
Tolbooth Steeple (Glasgow), 546–547
Tolsey (Burford), 282
Tombland (Norwich), 370
Tombland Antiques Centre (Norwich), 376
Tom Quad (Oxford), 162
Tom Tower (Oxford), 162
Tongue, 623–624
Torrisdale Castle Estate (Campbeltown), 585
Totally Thames (London), 36
Tourism for All UK, 667
Tower (Stratford-upon-Avon), 308
Tower Bridge Exhibition (London), 94
The Tower of London, 94–96
Tower Tour (Salisbury), 228
Town Hall (Manchester), 390
Trafalgar Square (London), 113
Train passes, 658–660
Train travel, 658–660

London, 58–59
Tramway (Glasgow), 563
Transport for London, 667
Traquair House (near Peebles), 536–537
Traveline, 661
Travelsupermarket.com, 662
Traverse Theatre (Edinburgh), 507
Treasurer's House (York), 440
Treasures of the British Library (London), 63
Treehouse Towers (Kew), 106
Trelissick (Feock), 268
Trengwainton Garden, 273–274
Treshnish Isles, 593
Trinity Chapel (Canterbury), 184
Trinity College (Cambridge), 349–350
Trinity College Music Society (Cambridge), 354
Tron Theatre (Glasgow), 563
Troon, 568–569
Trooping the Colour (London), 35
Trotternish Peninsula, 649–650
Turf Tavern (Oxford), 170
Turing, Alan, 234
Turkish Baths (Harrogate), 446–447
Turnberry, 569–570
Turnberry Golf Courses, 569
Turner, J. M. W., 189
Turner Contemporary, 189
Turner Galleries (London), 79
Turner Prize, 36
20 Forthlin Road (Liverpool), 408
21st Century Kilts (Edinburgh), 507
Two Brewers (Windsor), 157
Tynemouth Castle and Priory, 462

U

U-Boat Story (Liverpool), 407
Ullapool, 630–633
Ullswater, 419
Underground (Tube; London), 59–60
Underground Passages (Exeter), 256
UNESCO City of Literature, 486
Unique Cottages, 665
University of St Andrews, 514
Up at the O2 (Greenwich), 103
Upper Slaughter, 292–293
Upper Wharfedale, 448
Urquhart Castle (Drumnadrochit), 609–610
Usher Hall (Edinburgh), 507

V

Valley Gardens (Windsor), 154
V&A (London), 88

Verulam Arms (St Albans), 177
Verulamium Museum (St Albans), 174–175
Victoria Art Gallery (Bath), 246
Victoria Coach Station, 661
Victorian Gallery (Dorchester), 239
Victorian Market (Inverness), 607
Victorian Palm House (Edinburgh), 488
Victorian Tunnels (Newcastle), 463
Victorian Village (Glasgow), 562
Victoria Park (London), 113–114
Victoria Square (Birmingham), 320, 323
Victory, HMS
  Chatham, 192
  Portsmouth, 225–226
View from the Shard (London), 80
Vindolanda, 464
Virginia Water (Windsor), 154
Visas, 674
Voodoo Rooms (Edinburgh), 508

W
Walberswick, 364
Walcot Street (Bath), 250
Walker Art Gallery (Liverpool), 410
Walker Slater (Edinburgh), 507
The Wallace Collection (London), 84
Wallingford Screen (St Albans), 174
Walltown Crags, 464
Warner Bros. Studio Tour London-The Making of Harry Potter (Leavesden), 178
Warriston Cemetery (Edinburgh), 492
Warwick Castle, 313–315
Waterloo Bar (Glasgow), 565
Water of Leith, 490–492
Websites, 674
Wedgwood Museum & Visitor Centre (Stoke-on-Trent), 331
Wee Picture House (Campbeltown), 584–585
Wellington Barracks (London), 77
Well of the Dead (Inverness), 604
Wells Cathedral, 251
Wells Clock, 251
The Welsh Marches, 332–340
  accommodations, 337–339
  exploring, 332–337
  restaurants, 339–340
  traveling to, 332
  visitor information, 332

Wessex Gallery (Salisbury), 229
West (Glasgow), 565
West Coast Line, 658
Wester Ross, 630–633
West Front (Bath), 243
West Highland Museum (Fort William), 636
The West Highlands, 633–639
Westminster Abbey (London), 80–82
West Wittering, 211–212
Wheel of Manchester, 386
Whiski Rooms (Edinburgh), 508
Whispering Gallery (London), 92
Whitby, 449–453
Whitby Abbey, 451
Whitechapel Bell Foundry (London), 98
White Horse (Oxford), 170
White Tower (London), 95
Whitlit (Whitstable), 189
Whitstable, 188–191
Whitstable Harbour Village, 190
Whitstable Shop, 189
Whitworth Art Gallery (Manchester), 390–391
Wick, 627–628
Wick Heritage Museum, 627
Wi-Fi, 669
Wilderness Cottages, 665
Wild Goose (Canterbury), 187
Willow Tea Rooms (Glasgow), 551
Wimbledon, 35
Wimbledon Championships, 107
Wimbledon Lawn Tennis Museum, 106
Winchester, 218–226
  accommodations, 223–224
  entertainment and nightlife, 225
  exploring, 220–223
  organized tours, 223
  restaurants, 224–225
  shopping, 224–225
  side trip to Portsmouth's Historic Dockyard, 225–226
  traveling to, 220
  visitor information, 220
Winchester Cathedral, 222
Winchester College, 223
Windermere, 422–425
Windermere Canoe Kayak, 424
Windsor, 148–157
  accommodations, 155
  entertainment and nightlife, 157
  exploring, 150–155
  organized tours, 154–155
  restaurants, 155–156
  shopping, 156–157
  traveling to, 150
  visitor information, 150
Windsor Castle, 148, 151

Windsor Great Park, 154
Windsor Royal Shopping, 157
Witch's stone (Dornoch), 621
Woods of Windsor (Windsor), 157
Woodstock, 171
Wordsworth, William, 429, 430, 432, 572
  Rydal Mount (near Ambleside), 426
Wordsworth Graves at St Oswald's Church (Grasmere), 427
World Museum Liverpool, 410
World of Beatrix Potter (Bowness-on-Windermere), 424
Worlds Literature Festival (Norwich), 376
Wren, Christopher, 13, 25, 26, 42, 92, 93, 101, 102, 157, 162, 164, 228, 346, 349–351
Writers' Gallery (Dorchester), 239
The Writers' Museum (Edinburgh), 486
Wroxham, 377
Wye Bridge (Hereford), 337
Wyle Coop (Shrewsbury), 333

Y
Yellowcraig, 513
Ye Olde Fighting Cocks (St Albans), 177
Ye Olde King's Head (Chester), 403
Ye Olde Starre Inne (York), 446
Yeoman Warder's Tour (London), 94
York, 438–446
  accommodations, 443–444
  entertainment and nightlife, 445–446
  exploring, 440–442
  restaurants, 444–445
  shopping, 445
  tours and special events, 440
  traveling to, 439–440
  visitor information, 440
York Art Gallery, 442
York Castle Museum & Prison, 441–442
York Minster, 440, 442
York Racecourse, 440
Yorkshire Dales National Park, 448
Yorkshire Museum (York), 441
Ypres Tower (Rye), 198

Accommodations

22 York Street (London), 128
The Abbey (Penzance), 274
Abel Heywood (Manchester), 391

ABode Exeter at the Royal Clarence Hotel, 258
Ace Hotel London Shoreditch, 128–129
Ackergill Tower (Wick), 627–628
Acorn Lodge (Harrogate), 448
Alamo Guest House (Glasgow), 558
The Albannach (Lochinver), 626
Alhambra Hotel (London), 123
Alma House (Windsor), 155
Amba Hotel Charing Cross (London), 122
Amberley Castle, 215
Ancrum Craig, 524
The Anderson (Rosemarkie), 619
An Taigh Osda (Bruichladdich), 591
The Applecross Inn, 633
Apsley House (Bath), 247
The Arden (Stratford-upon-Avon), 315–316
Ardvasar Hotel, 653
Auchrannie House Hotel (Isle of Arran), 582
The Balmoral (Edinburgh), 493, 496
Bannatyne Hotel (Darlington), 457
Bath Place (Oxford), 165–166
B+B Edinburgh, 497–498
Ben Loyal Hotel (Tongue), 624
Black Hole (Winchester), 223–224
Bloc (Birmingham), 325
The Bloomsbury Guest House (York), 443
Blythswood Square (Glasgow), 557
Boath House (Nairn), 616
Bodhi House (Bath), 248
The Bridge Inn (Edinburgh), 493
Bunchrew House Hotel (Inverness), 606
Burlington House (Oxford), 166
Burts Hotel (Melrose), 530
The Caledonian (Edinburgh), 496
Cambo Estate (St Andrews), 517
The Canterbury, 185–186
Canterbury Cathedral Lodge, 185
Captain Bligh House (London), 127
Castlefield Hotel (Manchester), 391
Castle Inn (Hereford), 337
Cathedral Gate (Canterbury), 186
Cawdor Cottages, 616
The Ceilidh Place (Ullapool), 633
Celtic Hotel (London), 123

Citizen M (Glasgow), 557
CitizenM London Bankside, 126–127
The Clachaig Inn (Glencoe), 639
Coach & Horses (Oxford), 166
The Cotswold House Hotel (Chipping Campden), 303–304
Crestfield Hotel (London), 123–124
Crinan Hotel, 578
Cringletie House Hotel (Peebles), 537
Croft 103 (Durness), 625–626
Crofters Bistro (Rosemarkie), 619
The Crown (Southwold), 367
Culloden House (Inverness), 605
De Vere Dunston Hall (Norwich), 374
Dormy House Hotel (Broadway), 299
Dornoch Castle Hotel, 621
DoubleTree by Hilton (Edinburgh), 499–500
Dryburgh Abbey Hotel, 531–532
Duisdale Hotel (Isle Ornsay), 653–654
Durham Castle, 457
The Eastbury (Sherborne), 237
easyHotel (London), 130
Edgar House (Chester), 402
Edinburgh Central, 493
The Feathered Nest Country Inn (Nether Westcote), 295
The Feathers (Ludlow), 338
The Fielding Hotel (London), 122
15 Glasgow, 558
Fowey Hall Hotel, 268–269
The Fox & Anchor (London), 129
G&V Royal Mile Hotel (Edinburgh), 499
Gardens Hotel (Manchester), 391–392
Gigha Hotel, 587
Glamping at Warwick Castle, 316
Glebe House (North Berwick), 513
The Glenelg Inn, 642
Glenforsa Hotel (Mull), 597
Glengorm Castle (Tobermory), 597
Glenmoriston Townhouse Hotel (Inverness), 606
Grand Central Hotel (Glasgow), 557–558
The Grand Hotel & Spa (York), 443
Grasshoppers Hotel (Glasgow), 558
The Grassmarket Hotel (Edinburgh), 500

Gray's Court (York), 443–444
Greshornish House (Edinbane), 651–652
Greywalls Hotel (North Berwick), 512–513
The Halcyon (Bath), 247
Hard Day's Night (Liverpool), 411
Hazlitt's (London), 115, 118
Heywood House (Liverpool), 411
The Highway Inn (Burford), 284
Hilton Coylumbridge Aviemore, 613
Hogs Head Inn (Alnwick), 467–468
Holiday Inn Norwich City, 374
Hope Street (Liverpool), 410–411
Hotel Americana (London), 129
Hotel du Vin (Birmingham), 325
Hotel du Vin (Edinburgh), 499
Hotel du Vin (Glasgow), 559
Hotel du Vin (St Andrews), 517
Hotel Eilean Iarmain (Isle Ornsay), 654
Hotel Felix (Cambridge), 352
Hotel Meridiana (London), 124
House of Agnes (Canterbury), 185
The Howard (Edinburgh), 497
The Hoxton (London), 129
Hub by Premier Inn (London), 131
Ibis (Edinburgh), 493
Ibis Budget (London), 131
Ibis Hotels (London), 130–131
Ibis Styles (London), 131
The Inn at John O'Groats, 629
Inn on the Lake (Glenridding), 433
Inverlochy Castle (Torlundy), 636–637
Islay Hotel, 591
Islay House, 591
Ivy Guest House (Hawkshead), 434
Jesmond Dene House (near Newcastle), 468
Jesmond Hotel (London), 124
Kinloch Lodge (Isle Ornsay), 654–655
Lainston House (Winchester), 224
Lamb Inn (Burford), 284
The Langham (London), 118
La Rosa (Whitby), 452
The Lawrance (Harrogate), 449
Lazy Duck (Nethy Bridge), 613–614
Legacy Rose & Crown (Salisbury), 231
The Lime Tree (Fort William), 637
Links House (Dornoch), 621–622

Linthwaite House Hotel (Bowness-on-Windermere), 433
Lion and Pheasant (Shrewsbury), 338
Littletown Farm Guest House (Keswick), 434
Loch Melfort Hotel (Arduaine), 578
Loch Ness Lodge (Brachla), 610
The London Edition, 118
Lords of the Manor Hotel (Bourton-on-the-Water), 291
Ludlow Castle, 338–339
The Lygon Arms (Broadway), 299
Macdonald Randolph (Oxford), 165
Macdonald Windsor (Windsor), 155
Mackay's (Durness), 625
The Mad Hatter Hotel (London), 127
Maids Head Hotel (Norwich), 374
Malmaison (Edinburgh), 500
The Marine (Whitstable), 190
Matfen Hall Hotel, Golf & Spa, 468–469
Menzies Welcombe Hotel, Spa & Golf Club (near Stratford-upon-Avon), 316
Miller Howe (Windermere), 433
Motel One (Edinburgh), 493
Motel One (London), 130
Mount Royale (York), 444
The Nadler (Liverpool), 411
The Nadler Soho (London), 122
Nineteen (Brighton), 205
Noel Arms Hotel (Chipping Campden), 304
Number 17 (Norwich), 374–375
Oddfellows (Chester), 403
Old Course Hotel (St Andrews), 516–517
Old Parsonage (Oxford), 165
The Old Priory B&B (Kelso), 526
One Aldwych (London), 118–119
One Three Nine (Bath), 247–248
Paskins (Brighton), 205
Peartree Serviced Apartments (Salisbury), 231
Peat Inn (St Andrews), 517
Pedn-Olva Hotel (St Ives), 277
Pelirocco (Brighton), 206
Plockton Gallery, 641–642
Plockton Inn, 642
The Porch House (Stow-on-the-Wold), 296
Premier Inn (Edinburgh), 493
Premier Inn (London), 131
Primrose Valley Hotel (Porthminster Beach), 278

Qbic London City, 129–130
Queensbury (Bath), 248
Radisson Blu Edwardian Mercer Street (London), 123
Regent Hotel (Cambridge), 352
The Ritz London, 120
Rocpool Reserve (Inverness), 605
Rooms at the Apple Pie (Ambleside), 434
Rosewood London (London), 119
Rowan Tree Cottage (Portree), 648
The Roxburghe Hotel & Golf Course, 527–528
Royal Crescent (Bath), 247
St Ann's Forge (Salisbury), 231
St Ann's House (Salisbury), 231
St Michael's Manor (St Albans), 175
St Olaves Hotel (Exeter), 258
Sanctuary House Hotel (London), 127
The Savoy (London), 120–122
Seven Dials Hotel (London), 124
Shangri-La Hotel at the Shard (London), 126
Sheiling Holidays (outside Craigmure), 598
Shepherd's Purse (Whitby), 453
Sheraton Grand Hotel & Spa (Edinburgh), 497
Sherborne Cottages, 236–237
Ship (Chichester), 215
Sligachan Hotel, 646–647
South Place Hotel (London), 128
The Spoons (Skeabost Bridge), 651
Staying Cool at the Rotunda (Birmingham), 325–326
Stratford-upon-Avon Hostel, 317
Summer Isles Hotel, 633
The Sun Inn (Dedham), 361
Swan Hotel (Bibury), 286
Swan Hotel (Lavenham), 363
Tigerlily (Edinburgh), 497
Tilbury Lodge (Oxford), 166
Tongue Hotel, 624
Toravaig Hotel (Sleat), 653
The Townhouse (Durham), 457–458
Townhouse Hotel (Melrose), 530
Travelodge (London), 131
Tune, 469
Tune Hotel Haymarket (Edinburgh), 493
Tune Hotels (London), 131–132
Ugadale Hotel (near Campbeltown), 586
Varsity Hotel and Spa (Cambridge), 353
Velvet Hotel (Manchester), 392

Viewfield House (Portree), 648
The Wardonia Hotel (London), 125
The White Heather Hotel (Kyleakin), 646
White Swan (Stratford-upon-Avon), 317
Wilmar Bed & Breakfast (Carbost), 647
Windlestraw Lodge (near Peebles), 537
The Witchery (Edinburgh), 498–499
Woodbine Guesthouse (Uig), 650
Wordsworth Hotel & Spa (Grasmere), 434
The Z Hotel Soho (London), 125

Restaurants

21212 (Edinburgh), 501
60 Hope Street (Liverpool), 411
Abbey View Café Bookshop (Jedburgh), 524
Abstract (Inverness), 606
Active Cafaidh (Aviemore), 614
Adil (Birmingham), 327
Aizle (Edinburgh), 503
Alba Restaurant (St Ives), 277
Aldeburgh Fish & Chip Shop, 367
Al Faisals (Birmingham), 327
The Almonry Restaurant & Tea Rooms (Ely), 358
Al-Shami (Oxford), 168
Amelie & Friends (Chichester), 215
Andersen & Hill (Birmingham), 326
Anokaa (Salisbury), 232
The Applecross Inn, 633
Apples for Jam (Melrose), 530
Arbutus (London), 132
Ate O Clock (York), 444
Aunties Tea Rooms (Cambridge), 353
Bakerie (Manchester), 392
Balgove Larder (St Andrews), 518
Bar Italia (London), 137
Bay Tree (Arundel), 215
Beigel Bake (London), 140
Bettys Café Tea Rooms (Harrogate), 448
Bill's (London), 133
Bistro 21 (Durham), 458
Bistro du Vin (Birmingham), 326–327
Bistro La Barrique (Bath), 249
The Black Friar (London), 143
Black Rat (Winchester), 224
Blanchette (London), 133, 136
Blue Bicycle (York), 444
Blue Raddle (Dorchester), 240

The Boath House (Auldearn), 616
Borough Market (London), 140
Branca (Oxford), 167
Brewery Tap (Chester), 403
Bridge Tavern (Tyne Bridge), 469
The Britons Arms (Norwich), 375
Broad Chare (Newcastle), 469
Brodick Bar (Isle of Arran), 582
Browns (Cambridge), 353
Browns (London), 136
Brown's (Oxford), 168
Buccleuch Arms (Melrose), 531
Byron Burgers (Manchester), 392–393
Café 1 (Inverness), 607
Café @ All Saints (Hereford), 339
Café Concerto (York), 444
Café in the Crypt (London), 137
Café No8 Bistro (York), 445
The Captain's Galley (Scrabster), 630
Castle Tea Room (Ludlow), 334
Cawdor Tavern, 617
Ceviche (London), 136
The Chef's Dozen (Chipping Campden), 303
Cherwell Boathouse (Oxford), 167
Chesil Rectory (Winchester), 224
Chez Jules (Chester), 403
Chez Roux (Gullane), 513
Chilli Pickle (Brighton), 207–208
Circus Café & Restaurant (Bath), 248
Cley Smokehouse (Cley), 380
Clock Tower Bistro (Jedburgh), 524
The Cobbles (Kelso), 526
The Conservatory (Sherborne), 237
Cornucopia Bistro (Windsor), 155–156
Crannog Seafood Restaurant (Fort William), 637
Creelers Seafood Restaurant (Isle of Arran), 582–583
Cromars (St Andrews), 518
Deeson's (Canterbury), 186
Digby Tap (Sherborne), 237
The Dining Room (Sherborne), 237
Dining Rooms at Cinema City (Norwich), 375
The Dogs (Edinburgh), 502
The Dores Inn (Inverness), 607
The Druie Restaurant Café (Aviemore), 614
The Drunken Duck Inn (near Hawkshead), 435–436
E. Pellicci (London), 142
Earthy (Edinburgh), 504

The Fat Duck (Bray), 155
Ferry Inn (Fowey), 268
Fine Cheese Co. (Bath), 249–250
Fonseca's (Liverpool), 412
Food for Friends (Brighton), 208
Foragers @ the Verulam Arms (St Albans), 175–176
Freddie's (St Albans), 176
The Fryer's Delight (London), 141
The Galleon Inn (Fowey), 269
Gannet's Restaurant (Tobermory), 597
The Gardener's Cottage (Edinburgh), 504–505
Gee's (Oxford), 167
Gelateria 3bis (London), 141
The George Inn (London), 143
George in Rye, 200
Gidleigh Park Hotel (near Chagford), 265
The Glenview (Culnacnoc), 650
The Goods Shed (Canterbury), 186
Gordon's Wine Bar (London), 137–138
The Great House (Lavenham), 363
Great Queen Street (London), 136–137
Grillado (Salisbury), 232
Harbour Inn (Bowmore), 591
Haviland's Tea Room (Stratford-upon-Avon), 317
The Highway Inn (Burford), 284
Hind's Head (Bray), 155
Holbeck Ghyll (Windermere), 435
Hole in t' Wall (Bowness-on-Windermere), 436
The Honours (Edinburgh), 502
The Horseshoe Inn (near Peebles), 537
The Horse with the Red Umbrella (Dorchester), 240
Humble Pie and Mash (Whitby), 452
Inverlochy Castle (Torlundy), 637
The Isle of Skye Baking Company (Portree), 649
J. Sheekey (London), 132
Jack and Linda's Brighton Smokehouse, 208
Joseph Benjamin (Chester), 404
Joseph Pearce (Edinburgh), 505
The Jumble Room (Grasmere), 435
The Kitchin (Edinburgh), 506
The Left Bank (Glasgow), 560
Le Manoir aux Quat' Saisons (Oxford), 166–167
Leo's Fish Bar (Manchester), 393

The Library (Norwich), 375
Lion and Pheasant (Shrewsbury), 339
Livingston's (Linlithgow), 511
Loch Fyne (Cambridge), 353
Loch Fyne (Clachan), 578
Lucy's on a Plate (Ambleside), 436
Lunya (Liverpool), 412
McKechnies (Stratford-upon-Avon), 317
Magpie Café (Whitby), 452–453
Mai Thai (Bath), 249
Manos (Oxford), 168
Marino's (Rye), 200
Mark Greenaway (Edinburgh), 501–502
Mermaid Inn (Rye), 200
Michael Caines (Manchester), 393
Michael Caines Restaurant at ABode Exeter, 258–259
Midland Hotel (Manchester), 393
Monmouth Coffee (London), 141
Mr. Thomas's Chop House (Manchester), 393
Mr. Underhill's (Ludlow), 339–340
Mussel Inn (Glasgow), 559
Nosebag (Oxford), 168
No 9 Church Street (Stratford-upon-Avon), 317–318
Oast House (Manchester), 393–394
Ocean Treasure 235 (Manchester), 394
Old Bridge Inn (near Aviemore), 614
The Old Butchers (Stow-on-the-Wold), 295–296
Olde Ship Inn (Seahouses), 469–470
Oldfield's Noted Eating House (Durham), 458
The Old Sail Loft (Fowey), 269
Oliver's (Sherborne), 237
Olive Tree (Bath), 248
The One Elm (Stratford-upon-Avon), 318
Opus Café (Birmingham), 327
Pancho's Burritos (Manchester), 393
Parford Well (near Chagford), 265
Peckham's (Glasgow), 559
Peel & Stone (Birmingham), 326
Pen Factory (Liverpool), 412
Penny's Tea Rooms (Durham), 458
Peter's Yard (Edinburgh), 504
Pharlanne (Kelso), 526
The Pheasant (Bassenthwaite Lake), 436
Poppies (London), 142–143

Pork & Co. (Canterbury), 186
The Potting Shed (Applecross), 633
The Princess Louise (London), 143
Pump Room (Bath), 249
Punjab Restaurant (London), 138
Purnell's (Birmingham), 327
The Queen's Room at Amberley Castle, 216
Rafael's (Canterbury), 186
Regency (Brighton), 208
Regency Café (London), 138
Regency Tea Rooms (Bath), 249
Restaurant 22 (Cambridge), 353–354
Restaurant Story (London), 139
Richmond Tea Rooms (Manchester), 393
Ring of Bells Inn (North Bovey), 265
Riverhill Coffee Bar (Glasgow), 559
Riverhill Restaurant and Bar (Glasgow), 559–560
Roast (London), 141
Rocca (St Andrews), 518
Rochelle Canteen (London), 139–140
Rocpool (Inverness), 606–607
Roger Hickman's Restaurant (Norwich), 375
Rose and Crown (Durham), 458–459
Royal Crescent Hotel (Bath), 249

Royal Oak (Painswick), 289
RSC Rooftop Restaurant & Bar (Stratford-upon-Avon), 318
Rules (London), 133
St John Bread & Wine (London), 142
Sally Lunn's (Bath), 249
Salt (Canterbury), 186–187
The Scran & Scallie (Edinburgh), 503–504
Seafood Café (St Ives), 278
The Seafood Restaurant (St Andrews), 518
Shakespeare Tavern (Durham), 458
Shellseekers (London), 141
Ship Inn (Exeter), 259
The Ship Inn (Penzance), 274
Slice (Manchester), 392
Sotto Sotto (Bath), 249
The Stockpot (London), 138
Stravaigin (Glasgow), 560–561
The Sun Inn (Dedham), 361
The Table (Cambridge), 353
Tealicious Tearoom (Durham), 458
Three Chimneys Restaurant (Colbost), 652
Timberyard (Edinburgh), 502–503
Tisanes Tea Rooms (Broadway), 299
Treasury Restaurant (Exeter), 259
Treehouse (Alnwick), 470
The Turk's Head (Penzance), 274

Twenty-Four St George's (Brighton), 206–207
Two Brewers (Windsor), 156
Two Fat Ladies West End (Glasgow), 561
Ubiquitous Chip (Glasgow), 561
Urban Angel (Edinburgh), 505
Valvona & Crolla (Edinburgh), 505
Vaults & Garden Café (Oxford), 169
The Vintner (Stratford-upon-Avon), 318
Waltshaw's (Whitstable), 190
The Warehouse Café (Birmingham), 327
Waterside Inn (Bray), 155
The Westleton Crown, 367
Wheeler's Oyster Company (Whitstable), 190–191
Whiddons (Chagford), 265
Wild Garlic Restaurant (Nailsworth), 289
Wild Goose (Canterbury), 186
Willow Tea Rooms (Glasgow), 560
The Wolseley (London), 133
Yak Yeti Yak (Bath), 250
Yalbury Cottage (Dorchester), 240
Ye Olde Cheshire Cheese (London), 143
Ye Olde Mitre (London), 143
Yippee Noodle Bar (Cambridge), 354
Yorke Arms (Harrogate), 449

PHOTO CREDITS